Current trends in international migration in Europe

Evolution actuelle des migrations internationales en Europe

Table of contents

Current trends in international migration in Europe

Evolution actuelle des migrations internationales en

Council of Europe Pu
Editions du Conseil de

Cover: Graphic Design Workshop, Council of Europe

Layout: SAG+/Saverne

Edited by Council of Europe Publishing
F-67075 Strasbourg Cedex
http://book.coe.int

ISBN 92-871-5748-0
© Council of Europe, September 2005
Printed at the Council of Europe

Table des matières

4

1. Introduction

This is the 14th annual report for the Council of Europe describing the main current trends in international migration in Europe. By virtue of their regularity and continuity over the last decade the reports provide an account of how European international migration has evolved since the great political changes of 1989-91.

At their Luxembourg meeting in 1991 the Council of Europe ministers responsible for migration issues were confronted with a new and largely uncharted situation. Suddenly, it seemed, there was likely to be mass migration from the East, towards the lotus lands of western Europe. Growing flows from the countries of the South were creating a new "migration frontier" along the northern shores of the Mediterranean. Italy, Greece, Spain and Portugal, traditionally countries of emigration, faced the fact that they were now ones of net immigration. A new asylum regime came into being as the problems stemming from the break-up of Yugoslavia led to widespread use of temporary protection. In central and eastern Europe, ethnically-based migrations were common, frequently continuations of those that had begun in the aftermath of the Second World War but had ceased with the descent of the Iron Curtain. Other ethnic moves were of co-nationals "returning" to a motherland; some were of populations displaced in communist times. New economic flows developed, between East and West and within central and eastern Europe. Some were permanent, many were short-term and a new lexicon grew up to describe them – labour tourism, "pendular" migration, petty trading and transit migration.

The increasing incorporation of central and eastern Europe into the European migration system as a whole characterised the middle and late 1990s. In political terms attention turned more and more to the management of migration. By the middle 1990s it was possible to say that Europe had largely adapted to a changed migration regime although there was great uncertainty as to how to handle the fall-out from the Yugoslavian crisis. Elements of the picture were still blurred, especially in eastern Europe and the former Soviet Union where data systems remained inadequate. Furthermore, the growing significance of illegal migration, human smuggling and migrant trafficking were already causing concern. As the formerly separate western and eastern

1. Introduction

Cet ouvrage constitue le quatorzième rapport annuel présenté au Conseil de l'Europe sur les principaux aspects de l'évolution actuelle des migrations internationales en Europe. Elaborés à intervalles réguliers et sans interruption au cours de la dernière décennie, ces rapports rendent compte de l'évolution des migrations internationales sur le continent depuis les grands bouleversements politiques des années 1989-1991.

Lors de leur réunion à Luxembourg en 1991, les ministres du Conseil de l'Europe chargés des migrations se sont trouvés face à une situation nouvelle et sans précédent. Voilà que soudain une migration massive venue de l'Est semblait devoir déferler sur les eldorados d'Europe occidentale. Des flux croissants originaires du Sud créaient une nouvelle «frontière migratoire» le long des côtes septentrionales de la Méditerranée. Traditionnels pays d'émigration, l'Italie, la Grèce, l'Espagne et le Portugal devaient dès lors se rendre à l'évidence et réaliser qu'ils étaient devenus des pays d'immigration. Un nouveau régime d'asile s'est instauré lorsque les problèmes générés par le morcellement de la Yougoslavie ont conduit les Etats à rechercher un système de protection temporaire. En Europe centrale et orientale, les migrations à dominante ethnique étaient courantes, faisant souvent suite à celles qui avaient débuté après la seconde guerre mondiale et qui avaient cessé avec l'apparition du rideau de fer. D'autres mouvements ethniques venaient des coressortissants «retournant» dans leur pays; d'autres encore concernaient les populations déplacées sous le régime communiste. De nouveaux flux de nature économique se sont produits entre l'Est et l'Ouest, et également à l'intérieur de l'Europe centrale et orientale. Certains furent permanents, d'autres, nombreux, de courte durée, et une nouvelle terminologie a vu le jour pour les définir: touristes travailleurs, migrations pendulaires, petit commerce et migration de transit.

Les années 1995-2000 ont été marquées par l'intégration accrue de l'Europe centrale et orientale à l'ensemble du système migratoire européen. D'un point de vue politique, la gestion des migrations a pris une importance croissante. Vers le milieu des années 1990, on pouvait affirmer que l'Europe s'était bien adaptée à un régime migratoire nouveau, bien que l'on ne sache pas très bien comment gérer les retombées de la crise yougoslave. Certains éléments du tableau restaient flous, en particulier en Europe orientale et dans l'ex-URSS, où les systèmes de données restaient insuffisants. Par ailleurs, l'ampleur croissante des migrations clandestines, du trafic de main-d'œuvre et de la contrebande humaine commençait à poser problème. Alors que les systèmes migratoires d'Europe orientale et occidentale, autrefois

European migration systems fused into one, some eastern countries had also become ones of immigration.

Today, the burning issues are no longer those of ten years earlier. Recorded migration is now relatively stable, with the exception of the incorporation of large numbers of amnestied former illegal migrants in some countries. Western European countries are growing more concerned with the challenges of their ageing demographies and the role that international migration might be called upon to play. There is also a realisation that the demography of immigrants is an important element in future population developments in Europe (Haug, Compton and Courbage, 2002). The response to some skill shortages at home is increasing openness to those from abroad and there is some evidence of global competition for highly qualified people. Unrecorded and irregular migrations continue to pose challenges, but there is no hard evidence that their scale is increasing. Indeed, some data suggest the numbers might be declining, although this may reflect the diversion of irregular flows into new and less policed routes.

What does seem to be emerging is a more integrated European economic space, characterised by both new and older forms of mobility. There is now widespread circulation of people in informal and short-term movements, but there are also some remarkable parallels with the guest worker phase in the decades after the Second World War.

In the medium term the biggest issue will be the effects of the new round of European Union (EU) enlargement, bringing ten countries and 75 million people into the Union. Past experience and several studies of the prospective enlargement have failed to indicate that further large scale movements from the new to the existing member states will occur, although there is bound to be some redistribution of population as the economies of the Union become more integrated. What may confidently be anticipated is that the attraction of the European theatre as a whole will increase.

indépendants, fusionnaient, certains pays de l'Est devenaient aussi des pays d'immigration.

Aujourd'hui, les questions urgentes ne sont plus les mêmes qu'il y a dix ans. Les migrations répertoriées sont relativement stables, exception faite de l'intégration d'un grand nombre d'anciens immigrés clandestins amnistiés par la suite. Les pays d'Europe occidentale sont de plus en plus préoccupés par les problèmes que pose le vieillissement de leurs populations et par le rôle que les migrations internationales pourraient être appelées à jouer. Ils réalisent en outre que la démographie des populations immigrées sera un élément important de l'évolution future des populations en Europe (Haug, Compton et Courbage, 2002). La réponse à la pénurie de main-d'œuvre qualifiée dans certains domaines réside dans une plus grande ouverture sur l'étranger; il existe déjà des signes d'une concurrence mondiale pour attirer les personnes hautement qualifiées. Les migrations non enregistrées et clandestines demeurent problématiques, mais il n'existe pas de preuves tangibles démontrant que le phénomène s'amplifie. En fait, certaines données suggèrent même que ce phénomène pourrait être en recul; mais elles pourraient aussi bien refléter le fait que les flux irréguliers empruntent de nouvelles voies d'immigration, moins contrôlées.

Ce qui semble se dessiner, c'est l'émergence d'un espace économique européen plus intégré, caractérisé par la coexistence d'anciennes et de nouvelles formes de mobilité. Les mouvements de population informels et de courte durée sont désormais très fréquents, bien qu'il subsiste des parallèles remarquables avec la vague d'arrivées de travailleurs immigrés dans les décennies qui ont suivi la seconde guerre mondiale.

A moyen terme, le plus gros problème sera celui des conséquences du dernier élargissement de l'Union européenne, qui a vu arriver dix nouveaux pays et 75 millions de personnes. L'expérience du passé et de nombreuses études sur cet élargissement ne laissent pas présager d'autres mouvements de grande ampleur en provenance de ces nouveaux pays vers les anciens Etats membres, bien qu'une nouvelle répartition des populations semble inévitable à mesure que les économies de l'Union seront plus intégrées. Mais il ne fait guère de doute que l'attrait de l'ensemble de l'espace européen ira croissant.

2. Migration and population change in Europe

The world's population looks set to continue its rapid growth, rising to around 8919 million by 2050 (Table 1). Europe's share will be increasingly modest, almost halving between 2000 and 2050, while North America's will also fall. Only a small proportion of the world's population migrates in any one year, mostly within their own countries. There are no reliable statistics on the total numbers of people who move to another country during any given period, but United Nations (UN) estimates of numbers of people living outside their own country are around 170 million, although there is no concrete basis for this figure. What is striking about these numbers is not how many people choose (or are able to choose) to live in another country, but how few.

Past Council of Europe reports have indicated that in recent years the importance of migration as an arbiter of population change has fluctuated. Table 2 (also see Figure 1) presents the components of population change averaged for the period 2002-03, indicating that migration was the most important component in 26 (58%) of the 45 countries for which data are available. The migration component is calculated as the difference between the percentage growth rate and the percentage natural increase.

We can classify countries according to the relative importance of migration and natural change in their overall growth rate for the period:

1. *Population loss owing to both natural decrease and net emigration*: Estonia, Georgia, Latvia, Lithuania, Moldova, Poland, Romania, Ukraine.
2. *Population loss owing to natural decrease more than offsetting migration gain*: Belarus, Bulgaria, Croatia, Hungary, Serbia and Montenegro.
3. *Population loss owing to net emigration offsetting natural increase*: Armenia, "the former Yugoslav Republic of Macedonia".
4. *Population gain owing to both natural increase and net immigration*: Andorra, Austria, Belgium, Cyprus, Denmark, Finland, France, Greece, Ireland, Liechtenstein, Luxembourg, Malta, the

9

2. Migrations et évolution démographique en Europe

La population mondiale semble vouloir poursuivre sa croissance rapide, car on devrait passer à quelque 8,919 milliards d'habitants d'ici à 2050 (tableau 1). La part de l'Europe sera de plus en plus modeste, puisqu'elle aura diminué de moitié entre 2000 et 2050; celle de l'Amérique du Nord régressera également. La proportion de la population mondiale qui émigre au cours d'une année est très faible et il semble que la plupart de ces migrations aient lieu à l'intérieur des frontières nationales. Il n'existe pas de statistiques fiables sur le nombre total de personnes qui émigrent en direction d'un autre pays au cours d'une période donnée, mais d'après les estimations de l'Onu, le nombre de personnes vivant à l'extérieur de leur propre pays serait de l'ordre de 170 millions, bien que ce chiffre ne repose sur aucune base certaine. Ce qui est frappant dans ces chiffres, c'est de constater qu'un nombre aussi faible de personnes choisissent de s'établir dans un autre pays, contrairement à ce que l'on aurait pu penser.

Les précédents rapports du Conseil de l'Europe montrent que le rôle des migrations en tant qu'arbitre de l'évolution démographique a été variable au cours des dernières années. Le tableau 2 (voir également la figure 1) présente la moyenne des différentes composantes de l'évolution démographique au cours de la période 2002-2003 et révèle que la migration a été le principal facteur dans vingt-six des quarante-cinq pays (soit 58%) pour lesquels des données sont disponibles. Ce facteur représente la différence entre le pourcentage d'accroissement de la population et le pourcentage de l'évolution naturelle de cette population.

Nous pouvons classer les pays selon l'importance relative de l'immigration et de la croissance démographique naturelle dans leur taux d'accroissement général pour la période donnée:

1. *Diminution de la population due à la fois à une baisse de l'évolution naturelle et à une émigration nette*: Estonie, Géorgie, Lettonie, Lituanie, Moldova, Pologne, Roumanie, Ukraine.

2. *Diminution de la population due à une baisse de l'évolution naturelle non compensée par l'immigration*: Bélarus, Bulgarie, Croatie, Hongrie, Serbie-Monténégro.

3. *Diminution de la population due à une émigration plus importante que l'accroissement naturel*: Arménie, l'«ex-République yougoslave de Macédoine».

4. *Accroissement démographique dû à la fois à l'évolution naturelle et à l'immigration*: Andorre, Autriche, Belgique, Chypre, Danemark, Finlande, France, Grèce, Irlande, Liechtenstein, Luxembourg, Malte,

Netherlands, Norway, Portugal, San Marino, Spain, Sweden, Switzerland, Turkey and the UK.

5. *Population gain owing to natural increase more than offsetting migration loss*: Albania, Azerbaijan, Iceland.

6. *Population gain owing to net immigration more than offsetting natural decrease*: Czech Republic, Germany, Italy, Russian Federation, Slovakia, Slovenia.

Several observations stem from this classification. All of the countries with population loss are in central and eastern Europe or the former Soviet Union. In all but two (Georgia and Poland), natural decrease was the more important component, even when there was net emigration as well. The largest group of countries gained population through a combination of natural increase and net immigration. This was a geographically varied group, encompassing countries of different sizes, all from western and Mediterranean Europe. In sixteen of the twenty-one countries in this group, migration was the main component of change. Only three countries gained population through natural increase while experiencing net emigration and, with the exception of Iceland, they were located in the Balkans and Caucasus. Growing entirely because of migration were six countries, two in western Europe and three in eastern Europe, plus Russia.

The data on components of change illustrate very clearly the demographic diversity of Europe. A salient feature is the geographical division, with countries in the East generally losing population while those to the West are still gaining. However, gains are increasingly being sustained by net immigration. The role of migration in European population change has come under increasing scrutiny in recent years as a result of growing concerns about a cocktail of prospective changes to labour supply and demand. Issues raised include demographic ageing, shortages of working age populations, dependency ratios and payment of pensions, and possible shortages of both skilled and less-skilled labour (see, for example, Punch and Pearce, 2000). The United Nations Population Division has suggested that Europe might need replacement migration to cope with these potential problems ranging from around 1 million to 13 million new migrants per year between 2000 and 2050 (UN Population Division, 2000). Others have contested such a scale of migration as being unnecessary or impractical (Feld, 2000; Coleman, 2000; Coleman and Rowthorn, 2004).

Pays-Bas, Norvège, Portugal, Saint-Marin, Espagne, Suède, Suisse, Turquie et Royaume-Uni.

5. *Accroissement démographique dû à une évolution naturelle supérieur au solde migratoire négatif*: Albanie, Azerbaïdjan, Islande.

6. *Accroissement démographique dû à une immigration plus forte que la baisse de l'évolution naturelle*: République tchèque, Allemagne, Italie, Russie, Slovaquie, Slovénie.

Cette classification appelle plusieurs remarques. Tous les pays ayant enregistré une diminution de leur population sont situés en Europe centrale et orientale et dans l'ex-URSS. A deux exceptions près (Géorgie et Pologne), cette diminution est imputable essentiellement à l'évolution naturelle, même dans les pays affichant un solde migratoire net négatif. Le groupe de pays le plus important a vu sa population augmenter à la fois sous l'effet de l'évolution naturelle et de l'immigration. Ce groupe est constitué de pays dispersés au plan géographique, de superficie variée et appartenant tous à l'Europe septentrionale et méditerranéenne. Dans seize des vingt et un pays de ce groupe, les migrations ont été le principal facteur d'accroissement. Seuls trois pays ont enregistré une augmentation due à la croissance naturelle, alors que leur solde migratoire était négatif; à l'exception de l'Islande, il s'agit de pays des Balkans et du Caucase. Six pays ont vu leur population augmenter exclusivement du fait des migrations; deux sont situés en Europe occidentale et quatre, dont la Russie, en Europe orientale.

Les données sur les facteurs de changement illustrent clairement la diversité démographique de l'Europe. L'un des faits marquants est la division géographique de cette évolution, les pays situés à l'Est du continent voyant généralement leur population diminuer, alors qu'elle continue d'augmenter à l'Ouest. Toutefois, ces augmentations sont de plus en plus imputables aux soldes migratoires nets. Le rôle des migrations dans l'évolution démographique européenne est examiné depuis quelques années avec de plus en plus d'attention en raison des préoccupations croissantes que suscitent les mutations structurelles que pourraient connaître l'offre et la demande de main-d'œuvre. Parmi les problèmes soulevés, on peut citer le vieillissement démographique, l'insuffisance de la population active, le rapport de dépendance, le paiement des pensions et de possibles pénuries de main-d'œuvre qualifiée et moins qualifiée (voir, par exemple, Punch et Pearce, 2000). La Division de la population des Nations Unies a laissé entendre que l'Europe pourrait avoir besoin d'une population complémentaire de 1 à 13 millions de migrants par an entre 2000 et 2050 (Nations Unies, 2000) pour faire face à ces problèmes potentiels. D'autres jugent des mouvements migratoires d'une telle ampleur inutiles ou infaisables (Feld, 2000; Coleman, 2000; Coleman et Rowthorn, 2004).

3. Migration statistics

3.1. Statistical data problems

Although statistical data provision has immeasurably improved in recent years, the situation remains far from ideal. In western Europe, the existing data still pose a wide range of problems for the user, arising largely from incompatibility of sources, conceptual and definitional problems. In central and eastern Europe and the Commonwealth of Independent States (CIS) data availability has improved but methods of collection are still inadequate and there is a lack of well-developed statistical systems. Although considerable strides have been made in some countries in the region, the general picture with regard to data availability is extremely patchy.

A growing problem is the complexity of migration. For the most part the concepts of migration used as the basis for collecting statistics do not reflect many of the realities of today's movements, characterised as they are by new forms and dynamics. Particularly difficult to capture are short-term movements and status changes as well as, most obviously, illegal migrations.

There are two main types of recorded international migration data: stocks of foreigners, defined by nationality or country of birth (either resident or resident and working) and migration flows to and from a country. Stocks are recorded through a system of residence permits, a population register, a census or a survey such as a labour force survey. These figures represent the point in time that they were measured. Stocks of foreign workers are measured using work permits and labour force surveys. Work and residence permits and population registers rely on people to a large extent volunteering to be counted. In some countries registering is linked to the provision of health care and social welfare and this may increase the coverage and efficacy of such recording systems. Censuses also rely on people returning a completed questionnaire and on the whole are only carried out once every five to ten years. Labour force and other surveys tend only to take a comparatively small sample of the population and so the sampling errors are large which inhibits breakdowns according to migrant characteristics.

3. Statistiques relatives aux migrations

3.1. Problèmes de statistiques

Si la disponibilité de données statistiques s'est incommensurablement améliorée ces dernières années, la situation reste loin d'être idéale. En Europe occidentale, les données existantes posent encore à l'utilisateur un grand nombre de problèmes qui découlent dans une large mesure de l'incompatibilité des sources, de problèmes conceptuels et de définition. En Europe centrale et orientale et dans la Communauté d'Etats indépendants (CEI), la disponibilité des données s'est améliorée mais les méthodes de collecte restent inadaptées et il n'y a toujours pas de systèmes statistiques suffisamment développés. Bien que des progrès considérables aient été réalisés dans certains pays de la région, la situation générale en ce qui concerne la disponibilité des données est extrêmement contrastée.

La complexité des migrations est un problème de plus en plus considérable. Les concepts de migration sur lesquels est fondée la collecte des données statistiques reflètent rarement la réalité des flux actuels, caractérisés par des formes et des dynamiques nouvelles. Les flux et les changements de statut à court terme, ainsi que, bien évidemment, les migrations clandestines, sont particulièrement difficiles à saisir.

Il existe deux types principaux de données relatives aux migrations internationales: celles qui recensent les ressortissants étrangers (qui résident dans le pays ou qui résident et travaillent dans ce pays) par nationalité ou pays de naissance, et celles qui analysent les flux migratoires en provenance ou en direction d'un pays donné. Les populations étrangères sont enregistrées par l'attribution de permis de séjour, par les registres de population, les recensements ou des enquêtes telles que les enquêtes sur la main-d'œuvre. Ces chiffres reflètent la situation au moment où ils ont été relevés. Les populations de travailleurs étrangers sont évaluées sur la base du nombre de permis de travail délivrés et des enquêtes sur la main-d'œuvre. Les permis de travail et de résidence ainsi que les registres de population dépendent en grande partie de la bonne volonté des personnes à se faire enregistrer. Dans certains pays, cet enregistrement conditionne l'accès aux soins et à la protection sociale, ce qui peut accroître la portée et l'efficacité des systèmes d'enregistrement. Les recensements dépendent, eux aussi, de la bonne volonté des personnes à compléter et retourner un questionnaire; en général, ils ne sont effectués que tous les cinq ou dix ans. Les enquêtes sur la main-d'œuvre et les autres études de même nature ne prennent souvent en compte qu'un échantillon relativement restreint de la population; il en résulte donc d'importantes erreurs

Flow data are perhaps more difficult to measure accurately as, conceptually, they attempt to measure a movement across a border which only takes a short amount of time and yet to provide a flow figure for a specific year, measurements must be made continuously for that year. Aside from the International Passenger Survey in the United Kingdom that takes a sample of people passing through ports, flow data in the EU member states come from numbers of those joining or leaving a population register or the issue and expiration of residence permits. Again, this demands the compliance of the migrant and so those not wishing to make themselves known are sometimes able to avoid being counted. Emigration figures are notoriously problematic as in most cases they rely on people "unregistering" from a population register before they leave the country, something which many people do not do, especially as there are not the same incentives and potential benefits as registering and very often there is no effective legal or administrative mechanism to enforce deregistration.

3.2. Joint data collection

Since 1995, Eurostat and the United Nations Economic Commission for Europe (UNECE) have used a joint questionnaire to collect statistics from across Europe and from 1999 this collaboration was extended to include the Council of Europe and some of the CIS countries. Thus, the process of harmonisation of statistics that had been going on in western Europe for some time is slowly being extended to the central and east European (CEE) region. What now happens is a single, annual, multinational but still incomplete data harvest.

Despite these developments, considerable gaps exist in data availability. Particular difficulties occur in the CEE countries. The principal reasons are administrative and legal. In some of the countries no collection system exists for some or all of the statistics required. Partly this reflects the inadequacies of the old systems of data collection in the new political environment; but it is also due to conceptual and administrative difficulties in deciding on and implementing new statistical requirements. Only slowly, and haltingly, are the associated metadata and documentation being collected and placed alongside the statistics they describe.

d'échantillonnage, ce qui interdit la ventilation des données en fonction de caractéristiques migratoires.

Les données sur les flux migratoires sont peut-être plus difficiles à évaluer avec exactitude: elles entreprennent en effet de mesurer des mouvements transfrontaliers de courte durée, alors même que la quantification de ces flux sur l'ensemble d'une année suppose qu'ils soient mesurés en continu sur toute l'année concernée. Mis à part l'«*International Passenger Survey*» au Royaume-Uni, qui porte sur un échantillon de personnes transitant par les ports, les données sur les flux migratoires dans les Etats membres de l'Union européenne sont obtenues en comptabilisant le nombre de personnes demandant leur inscription ou leur radiation d'un registre d'immigration ou en prenant en compte la délivrance et l'expiration du permis de séjour. Là aussi la bonne volonté du migrant est en jeu et ceux qui ne souhaitent pas se faire connaître parviennent parfois à éviter d'être comptabilisés dans les statistiques. C'est un fait notoire que les statistiques relatives à l'émigration ne sont pas fiables, car elles dépendent le plus souvent de la bonne volonté des individus à se «faire rayer» des registres de population avant de quitter le pays, ce qu'ils ne font pas, d'autant plus que les motivations et les avantages potentiels ne sont pas les mêmes que lors de l'inscription et que, très souvent, il n'existe aucun dispositif juridique ou administratif pour rendre cette démarche obligatoire.

3.2. Harmonisation de la collecte de données

Depuis 1995, Eurostat et la CEE-Onu collectent les statistiques de toute l'Europe à l'aide de questionnaires similaires et, depuis 1999, cette collaboration s'est étendue au Conseil de l'Europe et à certains pays de la CEI. Ainsi, l'harmonisation des statistiques entreprise depuis quelques temps en Europe occidentale s'étend lentement à la région de la CEE. On a donc désormais une seule collecte annuelle multinationale de données, qui reste toutefois incomplète.

Malgré ces améliorations, des disparités considérables subsistent en ce qui concerne les données disponibles. Des difficultés particulières se posent dans les pays d'Europe centrale et orientale, essentiellement pour des raisons d'ordre administratif et juridique. Cet état de fait révèle en partie l'inadéquation des anciennes méthodes de collecte de données au nouvel environnement politique. Mais le problème réside également dans les difficultés conceptuelles et administratives qui surgissent à l'heure de décider et de mettre en œuvre de nouvelles normes statistiques. Ce n'est que lentement et de façon hésitante que les métadonnées et la documentation nécessaires sont collectées et mises en parallèle avec les statistiques qu'elles décrivent.

The overall lack of harmonisation in definition and data collection across Europe as a whole means there are occasions where countries are unable or unwilling to provide statistics. These are reflected in gaps or omissions in the tables of this report.

3.3. Data for the CIS states

The statistical data available for the CIS countries are of very uneven quantity and quality. A review has recently been produced by the International Organization for Migration (IOM) and the International Centre for Migration Policy Development (ICMPD) (2002). The progress made towards the establishment of new systems of registering the population of the CIS countries and movements among them varies widely. In some countries – especially those that have suffered civil war or major social and ethnic conflict in the recent period – population registration systems have essentially collapsed. In other countries, much attention has been given to institution-building to ensure effective population registration. Therefore, there remain widely differing practices in migration data collection in CIS countries.

Discrepancies between data may also exist within states, as statistics are gathered by a number of different agencies which have often had to set up new procedures for gathering migration data (for example, employing sampling rather than census approaches for the first time) whilst invariably having very poor technical and resource bases. Specific problems are generated by the absence of well-controlled frontiers which makes it difficult to estimate entry and exit figures, especially in those countries that have suffered armed conflict and where terrain makes it difficult to monitor border crossings. In some Transcaucasian countries, the registration of migration has virtually ceased to exist. A further problem, especially in the Russian Federation, is the differing registration policy and practice of regional administrations. In some regions, discrepancies between the reported number of registered migrants and their actual numbers are particularly high. It is estimated that the actual number of refugees and forced migrants in the Russian Federation may be one and a half to three times higher than reflected in official statistical data (ibid.). As a general rule, however, immigration figures are more complete than emigration figures since state benefits are, by and large, directly linked to registration of place of residence. The procedures for registering the entry and registration of foreign citizens, asylum seekers and labour migrants are also extremely disorganised.

Le manque général d'harmonisation dans la définition et la collecte des données dans l'ensemble de l'Europe montre qu'il y a des situations pour lesquelles les pays sont incapables de fournir des statistiques ou qu'ils ne le souhaitent pas. Cet état de fait se reflète dans les lacunes ou les omissions visibles dans les tableaux qui figurent dans le présent rapport.

3.3. Données pour les Etats de la CEI

Les statistiques disponibles pour les pays de la CEI varient beaucoup, tant par la qualité que par la quantité. L'Organisation internationale pour les migrations (OIM) et l'International Centre for Migration Policy Development (ICMPD) viennent de publier une étude à ce sujet (2002). Les progrès réalisés pour mettre en place de nouvelles méthodes d'enregistrement des populations et de leurs mouvements diffèrent énormément d'un pays à l'autre. Dans certains, essentiellement ceux qui ont été confrontés récemment à une guerre civile, à des conflits sociaux ou des affrontements ethniques, les méthodes d'enregistrement des populations ont le plus souvent échoué. D'autres pays se sont efforcés de mettre en place des institutions garantissant un enregistrement efficace de leur population. La collecte de données sur les flux migratoires reste donc soumise à des pratiques très différentes dans les pays de la CEI.

Il peut également exister des disparités dans la collecte de données d'un même Etat. Les statistiques sont en effet collectées par des organismes différents, souvent obligés de concevoir de nouvelles méthodes pour rassembler les données sur les flux migratoires (par exemple le recours à l'échantillonnage plutôt qu'au recensement), avec peu de moyens techniques et de faibles ressources. Des contrôles insuffisants aux frontières créent des problèmes spécifiques et ne permettent guère d'évaluer le nombre d'entrées et de sorties, en particulier dans les pays qui ont été confrontés à des conflits armés et dans lesquels la topographie ne favorise pas ce genre de contrôles. Dans certains pays transcaucasiens, l'enregistrement des migrations n'existe pratiquement plus. Le fait qu'il n'existe aucune coordination entre la politique d'enregistrement et les pratiques des instances régionales en la matière crée un autre problème que l'on rencontre essentiellement dans la Fédération de Russie. Dans certaines régions, les divergences sont grandes entre le nombre officiel des migrants enregistrés et leur nombre réel. En Fédération de Russie, le nombre effectif de réfugiés et de personnes contraintes de migrer serait une fois et demie à trois fois supérieur au chiffre officiel *(ibid.)*. Dans l'ensemble, cependant, les données relatives à l'immigration sont plus complètes que celles concernant l'émigration car les prestations de l'Etat sont généralement conditionnées par l'enregistrement du lieu de résidence. Les procédures d'enregistrement des entrées et celui des

3.4. Data on irregular migration

The biggest potential source of inaccuracy in the data relates to those living and working illegally. Sometimes they are included in official figures, sometimes not. Numbers of illegal migrants published or circulated are often police estimates which may be based on numbers of deportations or of regularisations. They may seriously underestimate total numbers in an illegal situation. For example, numbers of women in irregular, domestic and service-sector jobs are likely to be underestimated because they are "hidden" in private accommodation, and employers do not reveal their presence. Where estimates of the illegal population are made, it is not always possible to discover how they are reached and these figures should be treated with caution (Pinkerton, McLaughlan and Salt, 2004; Jandl, 2004). Even data from regularisation programmes (amnesties) underestimate the total illegal stock because they include only those irregular migrants coming forward.

Irregular migration flow data that are collected by national governments and international organisations include refusals of entry, illegal border crossings, apprehensions, deportations/expulsions and trafficking data. They are flow data that are recorded throughout the year both at the border and in-country. Refusal of entry data reflect numbers of migrants turned away at the border owing to the lack of (genuine) documentation, for failing to meet requirements for entry or for reasons such as a ban on entry. Illegal border crossings indicate numbers of people detected crossing or attempting to cross the border illegally, either entering or leaving the country. Apprehension data record the number of migrants arrested at the border for illegally entering the country or being illegally present in the country. Deportation and expulsion data show the numbers of migrants who have been apprehended and who have had a sufficient case brought against them to be removed from the country. Trafficking and smuggling data can cover any of the above categories but relate specifically to migrants who have been assisted in crossing the border illegally. Such data may give other details pertaining specifically to trafficking or human smuggling such as numbers concealed in vehicles and details of those assisting them.

ressortissants étrangers, des demandeurs d'asile et des travailleurs immigrés manquent également d'organisation.

3.4. Données relatives aux migrations clandestines

Les résidents et travailleurs clandestins constituent le principal facteur susceptible de fausser les statistiques. Certaines données officielles les prennent en compte, d'autres non. Les chiffres publiés ou diffusés sur le nombre d'immigrés clandestins reposent généralement sur des estimations de la police, extrapolées à partir du nombre d'expulsions ou de régularisations. Ces estimations sont probablement très en deçà de la réalité. Par exemple, le nombre de femmes qui travaillent clandestinement comme personnel de maison ou dans les services est sous-estimé, ces personnes étant «cachées» dans des logements privés et leurs employeurs ne déclarant pas leur présence. Il n'est pas toujours possible de savoir comment sont réalisées les estimations de la population clandestine et ces chiffres sont donc à prendre avec circonspection (Pinkerton, McLaughlan et Salt, 2004; Jandl, 2004). Même les chiffres des programmes de régularisation (amnisties) sous-estiment la population clandestine, car ils ne dénombrent que les immigrés en situation irrégulière qui se présentent pour régularisation.

Les données sur les flux d'immigrés clandestins collectées par les gouvernements et les organisations internationales incluent le refoulement, le franchissement clandestin des frontières, les arrestations, les déportations/expulsions et les données relatives au trafic de main-d'œuvre. Ces données sont enregistrées tout au long de l'année à la frontière et à l'intérieur du pays. Les données relatives au refoulement reflètent le nombre de migrants renvoyés à la frontière parce qu'ils ne possèdent pas de papiers (authentiques), parce qu'ils ne remplissent pas les conditions requises pour entrer dans le pays ou parce que l'immigration est interdite. Les données concernant le franchissement clandestin des frontières indiquent le nombre de personnes surprises en train de franchir ou de tenter de franchir la frontière clandestinement, soit pour entrer dans un pays, soit pour en sortir. Les données sur les arrestations font état du nombre de migrants appréhendés à la frontière parce qu'ils cherchent à entrer ou à résider clandestinement dans un pays. Les données sur les reconduites à la frontière et les expulsions indiquent le nombre de migrants appréhendés qui ont fait l'objet de poursuites judiciaires justifiées et ont été expulsés du pays. Enfin, les données relatives au trafic de main-d'œuvre et à la contrebande humaine peuvent ressortir à toutes les catégories ci-dessus, mais se rapportent plus particulièrement aux migrants qui ont bénéficié d'une aide pour passer la frontière clandestinement. Elles peuvent fournir d'autres détails spécifiques au trafic de main-d'œuvre et à la contrebande humaine, tel le nombre de personnes dissimulées dans

The European Commission's Centre for Information, Discussion and Exchange on the Crossing of Frontiers and Immigration (CIREFI) is responsible for the collection of standard datasets covering the different types of data listed above from individual European states. Its aim is to provide a comparable and harmonised set of standard tables which cover the EU15 countries and 15 other non-EU states. These statistics are presented in the form of quarterly reports and are confidential (and thus are not generally available). The national authorities, the border police and ministries such as the Ministry of the Interior or Ministry of Justice (which are usually responsible for the border police) collect data as a result of their operations in border control. These operational data cover the different types of irregular migration but are not necessarily comparable country to country as their collection and presentation is entirely at the discretion of the individual states.

Regularisation programmes are another source of data on irregular migrants. These are amnesties to foreign nationals clandestinely residing or working, allowing them to regularise their status. However, regularisation programmes do not cover all aspects of illegal migration, nor do they attempt to. They may target certain industries or sectors of the workforce and often demand certain requirements (such as having employment or having entered the country before a certain date). Also, they occur infrequently and only in some countries.

3.5. Coverage

There are broad trends in the coverage of the data that are immediately apparent. Firstly, there are, on the whole, more data for western Europe than for central and eastern Europe, not only in that there are fewer gaps in the tables but most of the countries are represented (countries for which there are no data have been omitted from the tables). Secondly, the main indicators (stocks, flows and asylum) have fairly good coverage (at least at the level of annual totals; at a more detailed level, i.e. breakdowns by citizenship and other variables, the data tend to be more uneven). Within the flow data, immigration is generally better represented and less problematic than emigration. This in part reflects the "unregistering" problem mentioned above and emigration data are usually less reliable than those for immigration.

des véhicules, ainsi que des renseignements sur les personnes qui les ont aidées.

Le Centre d'information, de réflexion et d'échanges en matière de franchissement des frontières et d'immigration (Cirefi) est chargé de collecter auprès de tous les pays européens des séries statistiques standardisées couvrant les différents types de données énumérés ci-dessus. Son objectif est de produire une série harmonisée de tableaux standardisés et comparables couvrant les quinze anciens pays de l'Union européenne et quinze autres pays non membres de l'Union. Ces statistiques se présentent sous forme de rapports trimestriels et sont confidentielles (elles ne sont donc pas disponibles). Les instances nationales, la police des frontières et les ministères tels le ministère de l'Intérieur et le ministère de la Justice (généralement responsables de la police des frontières) collectent des données lors de leurs opérations de contrôle aux frontières. Ces données opérationnelles couvrent les différents types de migrations clandestines mais ne sont pas nécessairement identiques d'un pays à l'autre, car la manière dont elles sont collectées et présentées est laissée à l'appréciation des différents Etats.

Les programmes de régularisation constituent une autre source de données sur les immigrés clandestins. Il s'agit de l'amnistie des ressortissants étrangers résidant ou travaillant clandestinement dans un pays afin de leur permettre de régulariser leur situation. Ces programmes de régularisation ne couvrent cependant pas tous les aspects de l'immigration clandestine. Ils peuvent cibler certaines industries ou certains secteurs de la main-d'œuvre, et imposent souvent certaines conditions (obligation d'avoir un emploi ou d'être entré dans le pays avant une certaine date). Ainsi, ces programmes sont rares et n'existent que dans certains pays.

3.5. Champ couvert par les données

Certaines constantes se dégagent de prime abord. Premièrement, on constate que les données sont plus nombreuses pour l'Europe occidentale que pour l'Europe centrale et orientale. Les tableaux sont en effet plus complets et la plupart des pays y sont représentés (les pays pour lesquels il n'existe pas de données ne figurent pas sur ces tableaux). Deuxièmement, les principaux indicateurs (populations, flux et asile) sont assez bien documentés (du moins pour ce qui est des totaux annuels – sur un plan plus détaillé, à savoir la répartition par citoyenneté et autres variables, les données sont plus inégales). S'agissant des données relatives aux flux migratoires, l'immigration est généralement mieux représentée que l'émigration, qui reste plus problématique. Cela reflète en partie le problème de la «déclaration

Several countries (notably France, Greece and Spain) do not provide emigration data. Thirdly, for other indicators, such as stocks and flows of foreign workers, the data are very patchy, even at the level of annual totals. Other data in this report are included on an ad hoc basis, tables being included for other datasets that are available and of interest. Such tables tend to be more complete but are more specialised and focus on more minor and specific indicators.

3.6. Data gathering for this report

Data for this report have been collected predominantly from the major sources mentioned above: the Council of Europe, the Organisation for Economic Co-operation and Development (OECD), the Office of the United Nations High Commissioner for Refugees (UNHCR) and Eurostat. The data were, in the first instance, gathered from reports and statistical volumes published by these organisations (an increasing number of which are now available online), and then supplemented by direct contact with experts and officials in various countries. The data in this report, therefore, represent as reasonably complete a picture of international migration in Europe as it is currently possible to produce from available data, although gaps and errors may still exist.

de sortie» mentionné plus haut et les données relatives à l'émigration sont généralement moins fiables que celles de l'immigration. Plusieurs pays (notamment la France, la Grèce et l'Espagne) ne fournissent pas de statistiques sur l'émigration. Troisièmement, pour les indicateurs comme les populations et les flux de travailleurs immigrés, les données sont très inégales, même pour les totaux annuels. D'autres données sont incluses dans ce rapport de manière empirique, dont des tableaux regroupant d'autres données disponibles et présentant un certain intérêt. Ces tableaux sont souvent plus complets mais plus spécialisés et concernent des indicateurs moins importants et plus spécifiques.

3.6. Collecte de données pour ce rapport

Ces données ont été puisées auprès des sources principales mentionnées ci-dessus: Conseil de l'Europe, OCDE, HCR et Eurostat. Elles ont été rassemblées à partir de rapports et de statistiques publiées par ces organisations (dont un nombre croissant est aujourd'hui accessible sur Internet) et complétées ensuite lors de contacts directs avec des experts et des responsables de différents pays. Elles présentent donc le tableau le plus complet des migrations internationales en Europe qu'il est actuellement possible de produire à partir des données disponibles, bien qu'il puisse y subsister des lacunes et des erreurs.

4. Stocks of foreign population

4.1. Stocks of foreign population

The total recorded stock of foreign national population living in European countries in 2003 or the latest year available (listed in Table 3) stood at around 24.56 million people. Foreign citizens thus appear to constitute some 4.5% of the aggregate population of Europe. The greater part of this foreign stock was resident in western Europe. Table 3 and Figures 2.*a-f* set out data on 30 European states, from which the estimate of total numbers is derived.

Past reports have demonstrated that in western Europe as a whole, stocks of foreign population have been rising. Table 3 suggests that in 2003 or thereabouts (using the latest date for which statistics are available) there were around 23.49 million foreign nationals resident in western Europe, representing over 5.5% of the total population of that area. In 1995 the figure for foreign nationals was 19.05 million. Hence, in the period since then, the total foreign national stocks in western Europe increased by 23.3%. However, a major difficulty in estimating the size and trend in the number of foreigners is that data for France are available only for 1999 (census year). In the trend calculation above, the same number for France was included in the estimate for both 1995 and 2003. If France is excluded, the percentage change for western Europe is 27.6%.

By contrast, although most countries in central and eastern Europe have also experienced some permanent immigration, some of it return migration, flows have been modest and stocks of foreign population remain relatively small. Table 3 indicates that in 2003, or the latest year, there were some 932 000 foreigners recorded as resident in the countries of that region listed (excluding Russia), representing about 0.4% of a total population of over 242 million. However, information on stocks of foreign population is only slowly becoming available for east European countries and the data in Table 3 are less than comprehensive, derived from a variety of sources, concepts and definitions. In so far as they are based on official sources, they almost certainly underestimate the real total of foreign population currently living in the countries listed. Transit and other temporary migrants, for example, are excluded.

The foreign population of western Europe is spread unevenly. Germany has about 31% of the total, France about 14%, the United

4. Populations étrangères

4.1. Populations étrangères

Le nombre total d'étrangers vivant dans les pays d'Europe enregistré en 2002-2003, ou au cours de la dernière année pour laquelle des données sont disponibles (qui est indiquée dans le tableau 3), s'élevait à quelque 24,56 millions de personnes. Ils représentent donc environ 4,5 % de la population totale du continent. La majeure partie d'entre eux résidait en Europe occidentale. Le tableau 3 (figures 2.*a-f*) présente les données de trente Etats européens, à partir desquelles le total a été estimé.

Les rapports antérieurs ont montré que la population étrangère a augmenté dans l'ensemble de l'Europe occidentale. Le tableau 3 indique qu'il y avait, vers 2003 (les données utilisées sont celles de la dernière année disponible), environ 23,49 millions de résidents étrangers en Europe occidentale, soit plus de 5,5 % de la population totale de cette région. En 1995, ce chiffre était de 19,05 millions. Ainsi, depuis cette date, la population étrangère totale en Europe occidentale s'est accrue de 23,3 %. Cependant, les estimations du nombre total et de l'évolution de la population étrangère se heurtent à un obstacle majeur, puisque les dernières données en date concernant la France remontent à 1999 (année du dernier recensement). L'évolution indiquée ci-dessus a été calculée en utilisant les mêmes chiffres pour la France en 1995 et en 2003. Si l'on exclut la France, le pourcentage d'augmentation pour l'Europe occidentale est de 27,6 %.

En revanche, si la plupart des pays d'Europe centrale et orientale ont également enregistré, dans une certaine mesure, une immigration définitive, dont une bonne part de migrations de retour, les mouvements ont été modestes et les populations étrangères restent relativement réduites. Le tableau 3 indique qu'en 2003, ou au cours de la dernière année disponible, environ 932 000 résidents étrangers étaient inscrits dans les pays de cette région (Russie non comprise), soit environ 0,4 % d'une population totale de plus de 242 millions d'habitants. Toutefois, les statistiques relatives aux populations d'étrangers ne font que lentement leur apparition dans les pays d'Europe orientale et les données du tableau 3 sont très incomplètes; elles proviennent de multiples sources et reposent sur des concepts et définitions variables. Il est presque certain que celles qui reposent sur des sources officielles sous-estiment le chiffre total d'étrangers vivant réellement dans ces pays. Elles ne comptabilisent pas, par exemple, les personnes en transit et les immigrants temporaires.

En Europe occidentale, les populations étrangères sont réparties de façon inégale, avec environ 31 % du total en Allemagne, près de 14 %

Kingdom 12% and Italy has risen to 9%. Several other countries have significant numbers. Switzerland and Spain both have around a million and a half, Austria and Belgium over three quarters of a million. In central and eastern Europe numbers of recorded migrants are much smaller. Estonia is the leader in the field with 270 000 followed by the Czech Republic with nearly a quarter of a million, and then Hungary with around 130 000.

4.2. Rate and direction of change in stocks

Previous reports have taken a longer view, looking at change from the early 1980s onwards. In those countries of western Europe for which data were available at or around 1981, 1988 and 1999 (the major omissions being France and the UK), rates of increase of foreign national stocks showed that during the period 1981-88 the annual increase averaged 122 700 (1.4%), but rose to 789 400 (8.3%) per annum in 1988-93, then fell to 210 650 (1.5%) per annum in 1993-99.

After 1995 the foreign national stock in Europe as a whole rose by 5.51 million from 19.05 to 24.56 million, an increase of about 3.6% per annum, somewhere between the rates of the early and later 1990s. Since 2000 the annual increase has been about 3.7% per annum. Most of the increase was in western Europe and most was accounted for by the four Mediterranean countries of Greece, Italy, Portugal and Spain. Their share of the western European total almost doubled, from 9.5 to 18% of the total, an absolute increase of 2.7 million. However, the bald statistics are misleading. Much of this rise can be attributed to regularisation programmes, which have had the effect of converting unrecorded migrant stocks into recorded ones. As such, they do not reflect such a large rise in new stocks as might otherwise be surmised.

What are the trends in stock numbers? Western European countries have experienced varied trends during the second half of the 1990s. For some of them it was the earlier years that saw the largest annual increases, 1995-96 in the cases of Denmark and Germany, 1996-97 for Finland and Turkey, 1998-99 and 2002-03 for Austria, 1996-97 and 2001-03 for Italy, and 1998-99 and 2000-01 for Portugal.

en France, 12 % au Royaume-Uni et une proportion qui est passée à 9 % en Italie. Leur nombre est important dans plusieurs autres pays: environ 1,5 million en Suisse et en Espagne et plus de 750 000 en Autriche et en Belgique. En Europe centrale et orientale, le nombre d'immigrés en situation régulière est beaucoup plus faible. L'Estonie vient néanmoins en tête avec quelque 270 000 étrangers, suivie par la République tchèque avec près de 250 000 étrangers, et la Hongrie qui en compte environ 130 000.

4.2. Ampleur et tendances de l'évolution des populations étrangères

Les rapports précédents se sont intéressés à une période plus longue et ont étudié cette évolution depuis le début des années 1980. Dans les pays d'Europe occidentale pour lesquels des données relatives aux années 1981, 1988 et 1989 sont disponibles (les principales omissions étant la France et le Royaume-Uni), le taux d'accroissement annuel de la population étrangère a été d'environ 122 700 personnes (1,4 %) pour la période 1981-1988. Cette augmentation est passée à 789 000 personnes (8,3 %) par an pour la période 1988-1993, puis elle est tombée à 210 650 (1,5 %) par an de 1993 à 1999.

Après 1995, la population étrangère en Europe a augmenté de 5,51 millions, passant de 19,05 millions à 24,56 millions, ce qui représente une hausse d'environ 3,6 % par an, soit un taux compris entre celui du début des années 1990 et celui enregistré à la fin de la décennie. Depuis l'an 2000, la progression annuelle a été d'environ 3,7 % par an. Cette augmentation a concerné essentiellement l'Europe occidentale et plus particulièrement les quatre pays méditerranéens (Grèce, Italie, Portugal et Espagne). Leur part dans le total enregistré en Europe occidentale a pratiquement doublé, passant de 9,5 à 18 % du total, soit une augmentation en valeur absolue de 2,7 millions de personnes. Il faut toutefois se garder de tirer des conclusions hâtives. Cette augmentation est en grande partie le résultat des programmes de régularisation qui ont permis aux immigrés clandestins d'être régulièrement enregistrés. Elle ne reflète donc pas une augmentation aussi importante du nombre de nouveaux immigrés qu'on pourrait le penser.

Quelle est l'évolution de ces populations étrangères? En Europe occidentale, les rythmes d'évolution ont varié d'un pays à l'autre entre 1995 et 2000. Dans certains pays, les plus fortes augmentations annuelles du nombre de résidents étrangers ont été enregistrées au début de cette période: en 1995-1996 pour le Danemark et l'Allemagne, en 1996-1997 pour la Finlande et la Turquie, en 1998-1999 et 2002-2003 pour l'Autriche, en 1996-1997 et 2001-2003 pour l'Italie, et en 1998-1999 et 2000-2001 pour le Portugal.

For most western European countries the current picture is one of relative stability, with either little change or small rises in the most recent statistics. Only Germany and Ireland show falls and they are modest. Italy and Spain particularly, with Austria and the UK, had substantial increases. In some countries, long-standing upward trends appear to have halted, examples being Ireland and Luxembourg. In contrast the slow decline in numbers in Belgium, the Netherlands and Sweden has levelled off. There are different reasons for these trends, some more general, others specific to individual countries. Regularisation has been the most important factor in continuing the rise in Italy and Spain. In the case of the UK a combination of increased labour flows and asylum seeking has raised numbers, while in Austria family reunion has been important as well as labour migration. Ireland's rapid economic growth sucked in foreign workers after 2000 but the process has now slowed. Changes in foreign national stocks do not only reflect the balance of flows and changes of status that result in their incorporation in the statistics. Important also are rates of naturalisation which have greater or lesser effects, depending on destination country policies.

The situation in central and eastern Europe is more varied and more difficult to assess because of the inadequacy of the data sources in many cases. Over the period as a whole, Romania recorded a fall, but more recently a modest rise, although the overall numbers recorded are small anyway. In the case of the Czech Republic, both 1999-2000 and 2000-01 saw substantial falls after several years of gain but since 2001 there has been a recovery. Hungarian numbers have fluctuated, falling at the beginning of the period then again after 1999, but rising in 2003.

It is difficult to generalise from the above but several observations may be made. First, it is probably true to say that foreign national stocks are continuing to rise: in most countries the trend in the most recent year is upward, but for the most part gains are modest. Except for the amnesty countries, there is no evidence of large and sustained increases. Second, there are temporal variations between countries in their growth peaks. Third, there are distinctive geographical variations at work. Countries differ in the rate, direction and timing of change in their foreign populations.

Dans la plupart des pays d'Europe occidentale, la tendance actuelle est à une stabilité relative, les statistiques les plus récentes indiquant une quasi-stagnation ou de modestes augmentations. Seules l'Allemagne et l'Irlande ont enregistré une diminution, cependant limitée. En revanche, l'Italie et l'Espagne ont affiché une augmentation sensible du nombre d'étrangers, suivies par l'Autriche et le Royaume-Uni. Dans certains pays, l'évolution à la hausse qui se poursuivait depuis de nombreuses années semble s'être arrêtée, notamment en Irlande et au Luxembourg. Parallèlement, la lente diminution des populations immigrées en Belgique, aux Pays-Bas et en Suède s'est stabilisée. Ces évolutions s'expliquent par différentes raisons, certaines générales, d'autres propres à chaque pays. La régularisation a été le facteur principal de l'augmentation continue observée en Italie et en Espagne. Dans le cas du Royaume-Uni, l'augmentation est due à des flux croissants de main-d'œuvre et de demandeurs d'asile, tandis qu'en Autriche le regroupement familial a été le facteur le plus important avec les migrations de main-d'œuvre. En Irlande, la croissance économique rapide a attiré la main-d'œuvre étrangère après 2000, mais le phénomène s'est ralenti depuis. Les variations du nombre d'étrangers dans chaque pays ne reflètent pas seulement le solde des flux migratoires et les changements de statut, qui se traduisent par leur prise en compte dans les statistiques. Les naturalisations, dont l'impact est plus ou moins important selon les politiques des pays de destination, jouent aussi un rôle important.

La situation est plus diversifiée et plus difficile à cerner en Europe centrale et orientale en raison de l'inadéquation fréquente des sources de données. Sur l'ensemble de la période, la Roumanie a enregistré une baisse puis, tout récemment, une légère hausse, bien que les chiffres relevés restent globalement modestes. La République tchèque a connu une baisse importante en 1999-2000 et en 2000-2001, après plusieurs années d'augmentation, mais une reprise s'est amorcée en 2001. En Hongrie, les chiffres ont fluctué avec une baisse au début de la période et une autre en 1999, avant de remonter en 2003.

Il est difficile de tirer des conclusions générales de ces chiffres, mais plusieurs remarques peuvent être faites. Tout d'abord, il est probablement justifié d'affirmer que le nombre d'étrangers dans les différents pays continue d'augmenter: dans la plupart des pays, la tendance des dernières années est à la hausse, mêmes si les gains sont, pour l'essentiel, limités. Mis à part les pays dans lesquels une amnistie a été accordée, il n'y a pas d'augmentations importantes et durables des populations étrangères. Deuxièmement, les pics d'augmentation enregistrés ne se produisent pas en même temps dans tous les pays. Troisièmement, on observe des différences liées à la géographie: l'ampleur, la direction et la chronologie des flux migratoires varient selon les pays.

4.3. Foreign stocks as proportion of total population

The importance of foreigners in the total population varies considerably from country to country (Table 4 and Figures 3.*a-f*). In 2003 (or the latest available date) the largest proportions of foreigners, relative to the total population, were in Luxembourg (38.9% of the total population) and Switzerland (20%). In two countries – Austria and Germany – the proportion was around 9%, with Belgium slightly behind, then Ireland and Sweden. In another group of countries – Denmark, France, the Netherlands, Norway and the United Kingdom – it was around 4-5%. In all other countries of western Europe listed in Table 4, foreign citizens constituted fewer than 4%. With the major exception of Estonia, all countries in central and eastern Europe recorded around 2% or less.

During the period since 1995, the foreign population has grown as a proportion of the total in most of western Europe, thirteen countries recording rising percentages with only Belgium and Sweden moving in the opposite direction. In two cases (Germany and the Netherlands) there was no discernible trend. The situation in central and eastern Europe is harder to summarise. In five countries (Bulgaria, Hungary, Poland, Slovakia and Slovenia) there was little change in proportion, while that in the Czech Republic has fluctuated, rising since 2000. Only Latvia, with small numbers, seems to have a continuously rising proportion of foreigners recorded.

Explanations for the trends identified are complex and reflect a number of forces. The ratio between the domestic and foreign population is influenced by the rate of naturalisation, which affects both components in the calculation. As alluded to in the previous section, regularisation is also important in bringing into the recorded population those who hitherto were uncounted. Ultimately, the statistics reflect what individual countries choose to measure, define and collect: this is a particular problem when making calculations with respect to central and eastern Europe.

4.4. Nationalities of the foreign population in Europe

There are broad differences between the foreign populations of western Europe and of central and eastern Europe, as well as individual differences between countries. The following analysis therefore looks first at the situation in western Europe and then separately at that in

4.3. Part des populations étrangères dans la population totale

La proportion d'étrangers dans la population totale varie considérablement d'un pays à l'autre (tableau 4 et figures 3.*a-f*). En 2003 (dernière année pour laquelle on dispose de chiffres), les pays dans lesquels on a enregistré les plus forts pourcentages d'étrangers par rapport à la population nationale sont le Luxembourg (38,9 % de la population totale) et la Suisse (20 %). Cette proportion se situe autour de 9 % dans deux autres pays, l'Autriche et l'Allemagne, la Belgique étant légèrement en dessous, suivie de l'Irlande et de la Suède. Dans un autre groupe de pays (Danemark, France, Pays-Bas, Norvège et Royaume-Uni), elle est comprise entre 4 et 5 %. Dans tous les autres pays d'Europe occidentale figurant dans le tableau 4, les ressortissants étrangers représentent moins de 4 % de la population. Dans tous les pays d'Europe centrale et orientale, à l'exception notable de l'Estonie, ce chiffre est d'environ 2 % ou moins.

A partir de 1995, la population étrangère a augmenté par rapport à la population totale dans la plupart des pays d'Europe occidentale. Pour treize pays, ce pourcentage a été plus élevé, seules la Belgique et la Suède ayant connu une baisse. Dans deux pays, l'Allemagne et les Pays-Bas, aucune tendance n'est décelable. Il est plus difficile de résumer la situation en Europe centrale et orientale. Dans cinq pays (Bulgarie, Hongrie, Pologne, Slovaquie et Slovénie), la part de la population étrangère n'a guère varié, tandis qu'elle a fluctué en République tchèque où elle est en hausse depuis 2000. Seule la Lettonie semble avoir enregistré une augmentation continue de la part des étrangers dans sa population, les chiffres restant néanmoins modestes.

L'explication de ces tendances est complexe et reflète plusieurs influences. Le nombre de naturalisations a une incidence sur le rapport entre la population autochtone et les étrangers, et affecte les deux composantes du calcul. Comme nous l'avons évoqué dans la section précédente, les régularisations ont leur importance car elles viennent ajouter à la population déjà enregistrée les personnes qui n'avaient pas été comptabilisées auparavant. Enfin, les statistiques reflètent ce que les différents pays choisissent de mesurer, de définir et de collecter, et cela pose un problème, en particulier pour le calcul des données concernant l'Europe centrale et orientale.

4.4. Nationalités des populations étrangères en Europe

Il existe, d'une part, des différences générales entre les populations étrangères de l'Europe occidentale et celles d'Europe centrale et orientale, et, d'autre part, des différences entre les divers pays. C'est pourquoi notre analyse s'intéresse d'abord à la situation en Europe occidentale, avant d'aborder séparément celle de l'Europe centrale et

central and eastern Europe. It is based on the most recent data published by Eurostat.

The composition of the foreign population in western Europe is a reflection of successive waves of post-war migration associated first with labour shortages and more recently (especially since the mid-1970s) with family reunion and formation, as well as the flight of refugees from war-torn areas both within and outside Europe. The dominant foreign groups within each country reflect the sources from which labour has been recruited since the war; particular historical links and bilateral relations with former colonies; and ease of access (in terms of geography or policy) for refugees and asylum seekers from different places. Despite their recent status as immigration countries, the largest foreign national groups continue to be from the traditional labour recruitment countries of southern Europe (Italy, Portugal, Spain and Greece), plus Turkey and the former Yugoslavia, and more recently North Africa.

Comparative statistics on the national composition of the foreign population are available for 2000 for some but not all countries (dates indicated on Table 5), but the pace of change of composition is slow enough for them to give a reasonable picture of the current situation. Of particular significance is the number of fellow European Economic Area (EEA) nationals in member states, since these groups have rights of free movement and are not subject to the same immigration and residence controls as non-EEA citizens.

Within the EEA as a whole, there were 20.29 million foreigners of whom 13.04 million (64%) were Europeans. Africans numbered 3.15 million (15.6%) and Asians 2 million (11.1%). There were 18.69 million foreign nationals resident in EU states at the beginning of 2000 (Table 5). About 5.7 million of these (30.5%) were nationals of other member states. It would appear that the relative importance of other EU foreigners in EU states is fairly static, the comparative numbers for the two previous years being 5.6 and 5.7 million (31.9% and 31.7%). The inclusion of the EEA states plus Switzerland (i.e. the EU and the European Free Trade Association (EFTA)) brings this total to 5.67 million, 30.5% of all foreigners in the EU.

The data in Table 5 illustrate the considerable diversity of foreign migrant origins that exists in western Europe. In Luxembourg, Ireland, and Belgium, over half of the foreign population is from other EU

orientale. Elle se fonde sur les données les plus récentes publiées par Eurostat.

La répartition par nationalité de la population étrangère dans les pays d'Europe occidentale reflète les vagues successives de migration enregistrées depuis la dernière guerre mondiale, dues dans un premier temps à une pénurie de main-d'œuvre et, plus récemment (surtout depuis le milieu des années 1970), au phénomène de regroupement et de formation des familles. Les principales communautés d'étrangers au sein de chaque pays sont le reflet des politiques de recrutement de main-d'œuvre et, en particulier, de liens historiques et de relations bilatérales avec les anciennes colonies. Même si leurs pays sont eux-mêmes devenus récemment des terres d'immigration, les groupes d'étrangers les plus nombreux proviennent de régions d'Europe méridionale, où l'on a traditionnellement recruté beaucoup de main-d'œuvre (Italie, Portugal, Espagne et Grèce, ainsi que la Turquie et la Yougoslavie, auxquels il faut ajouter, plus récemment, l'Afrique du Nord).

Des statistiques comparatives sur la répartition par nationalité sont disponibles pour l'année 2000, mais pas pour tous les pays (les dates sont indiquées dans le tableau 5). Cependant, le rythme d'évolution de cette répartition est suffisamment lent pour que ces chiffres nous donnent tout de même une idée relativement exacte de la situation actuelle. Il est à noter en particulier la part importante des ressortissants d'Etats de l'Espace économique européen (EEE) dans les différents pays membres, un phénomène qui s'explique par le droit de libre circulation dont jouissent ces personnes, non soumises aux mêmes réglementations en matière d'immigration et de résidence que les personnes non membres de l'EEE.

L'ensemble des pays de l'EEE comptait 20,29 millions d'étrangers, dont 13,04 millions (64 %) d'Européens. Les Africains étaient au nombre de 3,15 millions (15,6 %) et les Asiatiques de 2 millions (11,1 %). Au début de 2000, 18,69 millions de résidents étrangers vivaient dans les Etats membres de l'Union européenne (tableau 5), dont près de 5,7 millions (30,5 %) étaient des ressortissants d'autres Etats membres de l'Union européenne. Il semble que l'importance relative de ces derniers soit assez stable, le nombre correspondant pour les deux années précédentes étant de 5,6 et 5,7 millions (31,9 et 31,7 %). Si l'on ajoute les pays de l'EEE et la Suisse (c'est-à-dire l'Union et l'Association européenne de libre-échange (AELE)), on arrive à un peu plus de 5,67 millions, soit 30,5 % du total des étrangers dans l'Union.

Les données contenues dans le tableau 5 illustrent la diversité d'origine considérable des migrants étrangers en Europe occidentale. Au Luxembourg, en Irlande et en Belgique en particulier, plus de la moitié

countries; for Spain, UK, France and Sweden between a third and a half. Around 60% of Switzerland's (not an EEA country) foreign nationals are EU citizens. For most countries, however, the bulk of their foreign national population comes from outside the EEA.

The statistics in Table 5 reflect a complex set of geographical locations and migration histories. In the case of the UK, Ireland and Spain, proximity to a fellow EU member, together with a long history of population interchange, is clearly important (although this is not the case for Portugal as a destination). The situation in Belgium and Luxembourg reflects their geographical location, surrounded as they are by larger EU neighbours with open borders.

The significance of other regions as sources of foreign migrants varies depending on the destination country. Africa is a particularly important source for France and Portugal reflecting earlier colonial ventures, and for Italy and Belgium to a lesser extent. America is important for Portugal and Spain (mainly South America), and also for Greece and Italy. Asia is a major source for the UK, Greece and Italy, though for different reasons and with emphases on different parts of that large and diverse continent. The UK receives Asian immigrants mainly from the Indian sub-continent, largely for settlement purposes; Italy's Asian contingent is mainly from Southeast Asia (particularly Filipinos); Greece's comes from proximate countries in the Middle East region.

The dominance of Germany as a destination for foreign nationals from non-EU European countries is also clear: it received over a quarter of EEA foreigners, over half of those from central and eastern Europe and three-quarters from "other" Europe (which includes Turkey). Germany's Asian numbers are enhanced by Vietnamese recruited to the former German Democratic Republic (GDR). However, African nationals in Germany are comparatively few. Despite the links between Spain and Portugal and the Americas, the UK receives the largest proportion of foreign nationals from that continent (mainly the United States) and, not surprisingly, about three-quarters of those from Australasia and Oceania.

de la population étrangère vient d'autres pays de l'Union; pour l'Espagne, le Royaume-Uni, la France et la Suède, la proportion se situe entre un tiers et la moitié. En Suisse (pays qui ne fait pas partie de l'EEE), 60 % des étrangers sont des citoyens de l'Union. Dans la plupart des pays, cependant, l'essentiel de la population étrangère vient de pays qui ne font pas partie de l'EEE.

Les statistiques du tableau 5 reflètent un ensemble complexe de situations géographiques et d'histoires migratoires. Dans le cas du Royaume-Uni, de l'Irlande et de l'Espagne, la proximité d'un autre pays de l'Union ainsi qu'une longue tradition d'échanges de populations jouent de toute évidence un rôle important (bien que cela ne soit pas le cas pour le Portugal en tant que destination). La situation en Belgique et au Luxembourg reflète leur position géographique, enserrée par de plus grands pays, membres de l'Union et aux frontières ouvertes.

L'importance d'autres régions en tant que sources de migrants étrangers varie selon le pays de destination. L'Afrique est une région source particulièrement importante pour la France et le Portugal, une situation qui est le reflet de l'histoire coloniale de ces deux pays, ainsi que pour l'Italie et la Belgique dans une moindre mesure. L'Amérique est importante pour le Portugal et l'Espagne (principalement l'Amérique du Sud), ainsi que pour la Grèce et l'Italie. L'Asie est une source importante pour le Royaume-Uni, la Grèce et l'Italie, pour des raisons différentes dans chaque cas et à des degrés divers selon les régions de ce grand continent composite. Le Royaume-Uni accueille des immigrants asiatiques qui viennent en majorité du sous-continent indien, le plus souvent pour s'installer. Les immigrants qui arrivent en Italie sont principalement originaires d'Asie du Sud-Est (en particulier des Philippines), tandis que les nouveaux arrivants en Grèce viennent des pays voisins du Proche-Orient.

La prédominance de l'Allemagne parmi les pays où les non-ressortissants de l'Union européenne choisissent de s'installer est évidente: en effet, l'Allemagne a reçu plus du quart des étrangers de l'EEE, plus de la moitié de ceux originaires d'Europe centrale et orientale, et les trois quarts de ceux venant du reste de l'Europe (qui comprend la Turquie). Le nombre d'Asiatiques en Allemagne est d'autant plus important que s'y ajoutent les Vietnamiens recrutés par l'ex-RDA. En revanche, on trouve relativement peu de ressortissants africains en Allemagne. Malgré les liens qui unissent l'Espagne et le Portugal au continent américain, c'est le Royaume-Uni qui reçoit la plus forte proportion d'étrangers en provenance de ce continent (principalement des Etats-Unis) et, fait peu surprenant, environ les trois quarts de ceux originaires d'Australasie et d'Océanie.

Analysis of the data in Table 5 with earlier years demonstrates, not unexpectedly, a stable distribution pattern that changes only slowly, as a result of net migration flows. It serves to emphasise that western European countries may well have sharply divergent perspectives on migration, derived from their different foreign stocks.

Data availability on the nationalities of the foreign population in central and eastern Europe varies from country to country. The major part appears to comprise nationals from other CEE states, though the picture is clearly not static and is complicated by changes in numbers which result from changes in citizenship.

In Hungary in 2004, the foreign population of 130 109 was dominated by those from central and eastern Europe and the former Soviet Union. Romanians comprised the largest foreign group, 42.8% of the total, Ukrainians were 10.1%, those from former Yugoslavia 9.5%. EU nationals totalled 9.3%. The eastern dominance is also to be seen in Czech data for the year 2003 on foreign residents. CEE countries, plus Russia and Ukraine, accounted for 168 600 people, 70% of the total. Slovakia and Ukraine were the largest origins, with 27% and 26% respectively. Of around 40 000 permanent residents of foreign origin in Bulgaria in 2000, a third were from the former Soviet Union, 8% from the EU and 12% from the rest of Europe. Romanian data for 2002 list 66 535 temporarily resident foreigners. The main national groups were Moldovans (12.2%), Chinese (11.4%), Turks (8%), Italians (6.9%), and Greeks (5.5%).

4.5. The foreign-born population of Europe

The foreign-born population in European countries exceeds that of foreign nationals, the extent of the difference varying between countries. In addition to those with foreign citizenship, the foreign-born include citizens of the country who may have been born abroad, together with former foreign nationals who have naturalised.

Table 6 is derived from the 2000-01 round of national censuses, the data brought together by the OECD for the first time (Dumont and Lemaitre, 2004). For the European countries listed there were 82.6 million born outside the country in which they were living. The largest group was in Germany, a reflection of both post-Second World War foreign immigration and the inflow of ethnic Germans, especially in the

Une comparaison des données du tableau 5 avec les chiffres d'années antérieures révèle un schéma de répartition qui évolue lentement, ce qui n'a rien d'étonnant, en fonction des flux migratoires nets. Cet élément permet de souligner que les pays d'Europe occidentale ont peut-être des points de vue très différents sur les migrations, qui s'expliquent par les différences entre leurs populations étrangères.

En Europe centrale et orientale, les statistiques disponibles sur les populations étrangères varient d'un pays à l'autre. Les étrangers y sont pour la plupart des ressortissants d'autres pays d'Europe centrale et orientale, mais la situation est loin d'être figée et l'analyse des statistiques est compliquée par les modifications induites par les changements de nationalité.

En 2004 la Hongrie comptait 130 109 ressortissants étrangers, venus pour la plupart d'Europe centrale et orientale ainsi que de l'ex-URSS. Le groupe le plus important venait de Roumanie (42,8 % du total), les Ukrainiens représentaient 10,1 % et les immigrés venus de l'ex-Yougoslavie 9,5 %. Les ressortissants de l'Union constituaient 9,3 % du total. Les données tchèques pour l'année 2003 reflètent la même prédominance de l'Est dans la population étrangère. Les pays d'Europe centrale et orientale, plus la Russie et l'Ukraine, représentaient 70 % du total, soit 168 600 personnes. La Slovaquie et l'Ukraine étaient les principaux pays d'origine, avec respectivement 27 % et 26 % des immigrés. Sur les quelque 40 000 résidents étrangers permanents en Bulgarie pour l'année 2000, le tiers était originaire de l'ex-URSS, 8 % de l'Union européenne et 12 % du reste de l'Europe. Pour 2002, les données relevées en Roumanie recensent 66 535 résidents étrangers temporaires. Les groupes les plus importants étaient originaires de Moldova (12,2 %), de Chine (11,4 %), de Turquie (8 %), d'Italie (6,9 %) et de Grèce (5,5 %).

4.5. Population européenne de naissance étrangère

La population des pays européens de naissance étrangère est supérieure à celle des ressortissants étrangers, l'écart entre les deux variant d'un pays à l'autre. Outre les personnes ayant la nationalité d'un autre pays, la population de naissance étrangère inclut les ressortissants nationaux nés à l'étranger ainsi que les anciens ressortissants étrangers qui ont été naturalisés.

Le tableau 6 est tiré des recensements nationaux effectués en 2000-2001, dont les données ont été pour la première fois réunies par l'OCDE (Dumont et Lemaitre, 2004). Les pays européens figurant dans ce tableau comptaient 82,6 millions de personnes nées hors du pays dans lequel elles vivent. Le nombre le plus important était relevé en Allemagne, ce qui s'explique à la fois par l'immigration étrangère à la

late 1940s and early 1950s and again in the early 1990s. France, with nearly six million, and the UK, with nearly five million, occupied the next two positions. Eight other countries had over a million foreign-born citizens.

Across Europe as a whole, 7.8% of the population was born outside the country in which they are now residing, compared with about 4.5% who are foreign nationals. Proportionately, the smaller countries had the largest proportions of foreign-born, especially Luxembourg and Switzerland. Overall, in ten countries the foreign-born constituted over 10% of the population.

The composition of the foreign-born is a reflection of immigration and colonial history. For example, of 5.9 million foreign-born in France, about 1.6 million were born with French nationality in colonial locations. Geographically, 2.8 million of France's foreign-born are from Africa, 80% from the Maghreb. Portugal tells a similar story: 350 000 of its 650 000 foreign-born originated in Africa.

fin de la seconde guerre mondiale et par l'arrivée d'Allemands de souche, en particulier à la fin des années 1940 et au début des années 1950, puis, plus tard, au début des années 1990. Viennent ensuite la France, avec près de 6 millions de personnes concernées, et le Royaume-Uni, avec 5 millions. Huit autres pays comptaient plus d'un million de personnes de naissance étrangère.

Dans l'ensemble de l'Europe, 7,8 % de la population est née hors du pays dans lequel elle réside, alors que la part des résidents étrangers est d'environ 4,5 %. Proportionnellement, ce sont les petits pays qui comptent le plus de personnes de naissance étrangère, notamment le Luxembourg et la Suisse. On dénombre en tout dix pays dans lesquels les personnes de naissance étrangère représentent plus de 10 % de la population nationale.

La composition de cette catégorie de population reflète l'histoire migratoire et coloniale des pays concernés. Ainsi, sur les 5,9 millions de personnes de naissance étrangère en France, environ 1,6 million sont nées dans les territoires coloniaux et avaient la nationalité française à leur naissance. Sur le plan géographique, 2,8 millions des personnes de naissance étrangère en France sont originaires d'Afrique, 80 % venant du Maghreb. Le cas du Portugal est similaire, puisque 350 000 des 650 000 personnes de naissance étrangère résidant dans ce pays sont originaires d'Afrique.

5. Flows of foreign population

The data problems discussed above apply *a fortiori* to migration flows. Statistics on emigration are particularly problematical; many countries do not collect them, and those that do tend towards underestimation (Salt, Singleton and Hogarth, 1994; Salt and Hogarth, 2000). Even in countries with well-developed data collection systems, more often than not there are substantial differences between the estimates of a particular flow made by its origin and destination countries respectively. It is still surprisingly difficult to monitor migration flows involving the countries of central and eastern Europe. The recording systems developed during Communist times were designed to record only certain types of flows, mainly those regarded as "permanent", and have proved grossly inadequate for assessing most of the flows that have occurred in the region since 1989. Indeed, many of the categories of movement seen there defy most collection systems regarded as "normal".

It is clear that the lifting of the Iron Curtain heralded increases in migration flows both within and from the region. One estimate is that in the early 1990s the annual average number of officially recorded net migrations from CEE countries to western countries was around 850 000 (Garson, Redor and Lemaitre, 1997), compared with less than half this in the three preceding decades (Frejka, 1996; Okolski, 1998). Most emigration during the Communist period was ethnically based, mainly Jews and Germans.

5.1. Flows of migrants into and within Europe

Migration flow data for European countries are now more comprehensive than they have ever been, though significant gaps remain. As discussed in Chapter 3, there are still incompatibilities of measurement and definition between countries and this is a particular problem in the former Communist countries. Most illegal flows may be assumed to escape the statistical record, although in some individual cases in-movement may occur legally after which the migrant adopts an illegal status.

Because statistics for all countries are not available for every year it is impossible to produce an accurate set of annual inflows of foreign population for the whole of Europe. Some countries have no usable data;

5. Flux de populations étrangères

Les problèmes statistiques évoqués ci-dessus valent *a fortiori* pour les flux migratoires. Les statistiques sur l'émigration sont particulièrement problématiques; de nombreux pays n'en recueillent pas et ceux qui le font ont une tendance à la sous-estimation (Salt, Singleton et Hogarth, 1994; Salt et Hogarth, 2000). Même dans les pays dont le système de collecte de données est bien développé, on observe régulièrement des différences notables entre les estimations relatives à un flux donné, selon qu'elles sont fournies par le pays d'origine ou par celui de destination. Il reste étonnamment difficile d'étudier les flux migratoires impliquant les pays d'Europe centrale et orientale. Les systèmes de collecte conçus à l'époque communiste visaient à enregistrer exclusivement certains types de mouvements, principalement ceux qui étaient considérés comme «permanents»; ils se sont révélés largement inadaptés à l'évaluation de la plupart des flux intervenus dans la région depuis 1989. En fait, nombre des catégories de déplacements qu'ils répertorient échappent à la plupart des systèmes de collecte de statistiques réputés «normaux».

Il est clair que la disparition du rideau de fer a entraîné une intensification, d'une part, des flux migratoires au sein de la région, d'autre part, de l'émigration à partir de celle-ci. Au début des années 1990, le nombre moyen annuel des émigrations nettes enregistrées de l'Europe centrale et orientale vers les pays d'Europe occidentale était estimé à environ 850 000 (Garson, Redor et Lemaitre, 1997), soit deux fois plus qu'au cours des trois décennies précédentes (Frejka, 1996; Okolski, 1998). Sous le communisme, l'essentiel des migrations était de nature ethnique et concernait principalement les Juifs et les Allemands.

5.1. Flux de migrants vers l'Europe et à l'intérieur de ses frontières

Les données relatives aux flux migratoires en Europe sont aujourd'hui bien plus complètes qu'elles ne l'ont jamais été, même s'il reste encore des zones d'ombre. Comme il a été souligné dans la section 3, des incompatibilités subsistent entre les pays pour ce qui est des mesures et des définitions, ce problème étant particulièrement crucial dans les ex-pays communistes. On peut estimer que la plupart des flux clandestins échappent aux statistiques car, si dans certains cas particuliers l'immigration se fait légalement, par la suite l'immigré se place dans une situation irrégulière.

Faute de statistiques annuelles pour tous les pays, il est impossible de donner une image précise pour l'ensemble de l'Europe des flux de populations étrangères entrant chaque année. Certains pays disposent de données utilisables, d'autres n'ont qu'un état partiel. Le tableau 7

others have only a partial record. Table 7 and Figures 4.*a-h* show big differences between countries in available data and in the scale of inflow. By aggregating the flows for the latest year for the countries in Table 7, a best estimate of the current annual recorded flow may be produced. On this basis, the annual flow into western Europe is about 2.46 million, that into the CEE area 285 500, giving an overall total of around 2.75 million.

The largest inflow is still to Germany, 601 800 in 2003. Spain is in second place, followed by the UK. Of the other countries, only Italy (2002) and France (2001) had an inflow in excess of 100 000. Switzerland's inflow in 2003 fell below 100 000 for the first time since 2000. Inflows in central and eastern Europe were much lower, Russia being the main recipient. The Czech Republic's inflow has recently risen rapidly, reaching 60 000 in 2003. However, there is little doubt that inflows in CEE countries are significantly under-recorded.

There are fewer data on outflows than inflows. In western Europe in 2003 or thereabouts, Germany lost around half a million to emigration; the UK was in second place with 170 600. No other country came near to matching this absolute scale of outflow (Table 8 and Figures 5.*a-g*). Data for central and eastern Europe mostly record permanent emigration. Russia was the main source of emigration, 105 500 in 2002, followed by Ukraine with 88 800 (in 2001). Losses elsewhere were relatively low.

The combination of these in- and outflows resulted in a net gain in western Europe in 2003 (or nearest year) of around 953 400 and a further 102 900 in CEE countries, giving a net overall gain of 1.05 million (Table 9 and Figures 6.*a-g*). Italy had the largest net gain of 380 400 (2002), largely as a result of regularisation. The UK was in second place, with almost a quarter of a million. Of the other countries listed, only Germany had a substantial net gain. Perhaps most significantly, however, all the western European countries listed had net migration gains in the most recent year for which data are available.

et les figures 4.*a-h* révèlent de grandes différences entre les pays en ce qui concerne les données disponibles et l'ampleur des flux entrants. Le total des entrées recensées la dernière année dans les pays figurant dans le tableau 7 donne la meilleure estimation possible des flux annuels actuellement enregistrés. Sur cette base, le flux annuel entrant en Europe occidentale est d'environ 2,46 millions de personnes et de 285 500 personnes pour les Peco (pays d'Europe centrale et orientale), soit un total général d'environ 2,75 millions de personnes.

C'est l'Allemagne qui a enregistré, une fois de plus, le plus grand nombre d'arrivants en 2003, avec 601 800 personnes. L'Espagne venait en deuxième position, suivie par le Royaume-Uni. Parmi les autres pays, seules l'Italie (2002), la France (2001) et la Suisse ont enregistré plus de 100 000 arrivées. En 2003, le nombre d'entrées enregistré en Suisse est tombé sous la barre des 100 000 pour la première fois depuis 2000. L'immigration a été bien moindre en Europe centrale et orientale, la Russie étant la principale destination. En République tchèque, elle a connu récemment une augmentation rapide, pour arriver à 60 000 personnes en 2003. Il ne fait toutefois guère de doute que l'immigration dans les Peco est fortement sous-estimée.

On possède moins de données sur l'émigration que sur l'immigration. En Europe occidentale, aux environs de 2003, l'Allemagne a perdu quelque 500 000 habitants qui ont émigré à l'étranger, suivie par le Royaume-Uni avec 170 600 départs. Aucun autre pays n'a connu une telle émigration (tableau 8 et figures 5.*a-g*). Les données relatives à l'Europe centrale et orientale recensent essentiellement l'émigration permanente. La Russie est la principale source d'émigration, avec 105 500 départs en 2002, suivie par l'Ukraine, avec 88 800 départs (en 2001). Ailleurs, leur nombre a été relativement faible.

La différence entre ces entrées et sorties se traduit par un gain net de quelque 953 400 personnes en Europe occidentale en 2003 (ou l'année la plus récente pour laquelle des données sont disponibles) et de 102 900 personnes dans les Peco (tableau 9 et figures 6.*a-g*), soit un solde général de 1,05 million de personnes (tableau 9 et figures 6.*a-g*). L'Italie a enregistré le gain le plus important avec 380 400 personnes (2002), ce qui s'explique en grande partie par sa politique de régularisation. Le Royaume-Uni venait en deuxième place, avec un solde positif de presque 250 000 personnes. Parmi les autres pays étudiés, seule l'Allemagne a connu un gain net important. Le fait que tous les pays d'Europe occidentale ont enregistré un gain net d'immigrés au cours de la dernière année pour laquelle des données sont disponibles est peut-être plus significatif.

The situation is different in CEE countries. Although, with the exception of the Czech Republic and, especially, Russia, net gains were modest, three countries recorded net losses in their emigration data in 2003.

5.2. Recent trends in migration flows

Past reports have shown that in the countries for which data were available, during the period 1980-99 there was a net aggregate gain of 8.48 million by migration.

In the first half of the 1980s, inflows of foreign population to western Europe declined, then from the mid-1980s there were net gains for most countries. Since 1994 net gains have, on the whole, tended to fall. In the period 1995-2003 most countries experienced fluctuations in the annual rate of change of inflows and for most of them, rates of increase were higher in the early part of the period, especially 1998-99. Those countries with data for 2003 show universal declines from numbers entering the year before. In several cases, notably Denmark, Germany and the Netherlands, the most recent fall follows a longer-term trend. In other cases the downturn in 2003 follows a period of steady increase, cases in point being Ireland, Spain, Switzerland and the UK. In a few cases the trend from the mid-1990s has been fairly flat, the latest year being one of minor fluctuation, examples being Finland and Luxembourg.

Central and eastern Europe presents a more varied picture. There is evidence of increase in 2003 in the Czech and Slovak Republics, Poland and Slovenia, falls in Lithuania and Romania, while Croatia and Latvia show no discernible trend.

In western Europe since the mid-1990s there seems to have been an increasing trend in emigration from Denmark, Luxembourg, Norway and the UK, with the reverse in Ireland, Sweden and Switzerland. The other countries listed displayed no particular trend in either direction, though all had some annual fluctuation. Where available, the statistics for 2003 show little difference from those a year earlier. Falls are more likely than rises although the actual numbers are small. "Flatlining" is probably the best description of the current trend.

La situation est différente dans les Peco. A l'exception de la République tchèque et, plus particulièrement, de la Russie, les gains nets étaient modestes; trois pays ont même enregistré un solde migratoire négatif en 2003.

5.2. Evolution récente des flux migratoires

Les rapports précédents ont montré que dans les pays pour lesquels on dispose de données, la période 1980-1999 a été marquée par un gain net total de 8,48 millions d'immigrés.

Dans la première moitié des années 1980, la migration de populations étrangères vers l'Europe occidentale s'est ralentie, mais la plupart des pays ont enregistré un gain net à partir de 1985. Depuis 1994, ces gains nets ont eu tendance à diminuer. Au cours de la période 1995-2003, la plupart des pays ont noté des fluctuations du rythme annuel des mouvements migratoires et, pour la plupart d'entre eux, l'augmentation a été plus élevée au début de la période, en particulier en 1998-1999. Les pays disposant de données pour 2003 ont tous enregistré une diminution des flux entrants par rapport à l'année précédente. Dans plusieurs cas, notamment le Danemark, l'Allemagne et les Pays-Bas, cette diminution toute récente s'inscrit dans une tendance à plus long terme. Dans d'autres cas (Irlande, Espagne, Suisse et Royaume-Uni), le retournement de tendance observé en 2003 a suivi une période d'augmentation régulière. Dans de rares cas, comme en Finlande ou au Luxembourg, la tendance a été relativement stable depuis le milieu des années 1990, la dernière année s'étant caractérisée par des fluctuations mineures.

En Europe centrale et orientale, la situation est plus contrastée. Il y a eu, en 2003, une augmentation en République tchèque, en Slovaquie, en Pologne et en Slovénie, alors que la Lituanie et la Roumanie enregistraient une baisse et qu'aucune tendance n'était décelable en Croatie et en Lettonie.

En Europe occidentale, depuis le milieu des années 1990, l'émigration s'est accrue au Danemark, au Luxembourg, en Norvège et au Royaume-Uni, alors qu'elle diminuait en Irlande, en Suède et en Suisse. Dans les autres pays étudiés, aucune tendance claire ne se dégageait, bien qu'ils aient tous enregistré quelques fluctuations annuelles. Les statistiques disponibles pour l'année 2003 diffèrent peu de celles de l'année précédente. Les diminutions sont plus probables que les augmentations, bien que les valeurs absolues soient faibles. Parler de stagnation est sans doute le meilleur moyen de décrire la tendance actuelle.

The outflow data for central and eastern Europe are difficult to interpret because of the small numbers of permanent emigrants. In general,
outflows fluctuated after the mid-1990s, Poland, for example, increasing its outflows between 1995 and 1998, then experiencing falls. In
most cases, however, changes have occurred in quite small recorded
annual flows. This situation broadly applies to the change between
2002 and 2003. Outflows from Lithuania and the Czech Republic have
risen slightly; those from Poland and Slovenia have done the reverse.

Net migration trends show a clear West-East distinction. In western
Europe, eight countries (Austria, Iceland, Ireland, Italy, Norway,
Sweden and the UK) had a general upward trend over the period, with
only Denmark clearly moving in the opposite direction. Five other
countries (Belgium, Finland, Germany, Luxembourg and Switzerland)
showed marked fluctuations from year to year. Four CEE countries
(Estonia, Hungary, Latvia and Romania) showed a relative net gain by
virtue of a declining net loss; the Czech and Slovak Republics and
Russia all had a declining positive trend.

New migrations have appeared. Some of these reflect the emergence
of new areas of origin. There were an estimated 63 000 Chinese
migrants in Germany in 2001, double the figure in 1993 and ten times
that of 1988 (Giese, 2003). In Italy, 68 000 residence permits were
granted to Chinese citizens in 2001, more than five times that in 1993
(Ceccagno, 2003). Albanians have also been on the move, remittances
from them representing the country's main source of external income
after aid in the mid-1990s. By 2000, 133 000 of them had permits to
stay in Italy (Mai and Schwander-Sievers, 2003).

There is also evidence of new types of flow. Peraldi (2004) describes
how over the last ten years Algerian migratory routes have undergone radical change. The traditional labour migration into France has
been replaced by forms of circulation in which many Algerians have
become suitcase traders throughout the Mediterranean region. Often
serving tourist markets, their moves take place within family networks which allow them to seize trading opportunities in whichever
city they are presented. Romanians have also been observed to cir-
culate within informal transnational networks which they use to
exploit whatever "work niches" are opened to illegal workers (Potot,
2004). There is some evidence, too, that ethnic migrations have been
metamorphosed into ones of circulation. Michalon (2004) demonstrates that the migration of ethnic Germans from Transylvania to

Il n'est pas facile d'interpréter les données relatives à l'émigration pour l'Europe centrale et orientale en raison du faible nombre d'émigrés définitifs. De manière générale, les flux sortants ont connu des fluctuations dans la deuxième moitié des années 1990; ainsi, en Pologne, l'émigration a augmenté entre 1995 et 1998, mais elle a diminué par la suite. Le plus souvent, cependant, cette évolution s'est traduite par des flux annuels relativement faibles. Globalement, il en a été de même en 2002 et 2003. En Lituanie et en République tchèque, l'émigration a légèrement augmenté, alors que la tendance était inverse en Pologne et en Slovénie.

L'évolution des flux migratoires a été très différente entre l'Est et l'Ouest. En Europe occidentale, ces flux ont eu tendance à augmenter dans huit pays (Autriche, Islande, Irlande, Italie, Norvège, Suède, Royaume-Uni), le Danemark seul laissant percevoir une tendance contraire. Cinq autres pays (Belgique, Finlande, Allemagne, Luxembourg et Suisse) ont connu d'importantes fluctuations d'une année sur l'autre. Quatre pays d'Europe centrale et orientale (Estonie, Hongrie, Lettonie et Roumanie) ont enregistré un certain gain net dû à une émigration nette moins importante, tandis qu'en République tchèque, en Slovaquie et en Russie les gains nets ont diminué.

De nouvelles migrations apparaissent. Dans certains cas, elles reflètent l'émergence de nouvelles régions d'origine. L'Allemagne a compté 63 000 immigrants chinois en 2001, soit deux fois plus qu'en 1993 et dix fois plus qu'en 1988 (Giese, 2003). En Italie, 68 000 permis de résidence ont été délivrés à des citoyens chinois en 2001, soit cinq fois plus qu'en 1993 (Ceccagno, 2003). Les Albanais se déplacent aussi de plus en plus: dans le milieu des années 1990, leurs transferts de fonds représentaient la principale source de revenus extérieure du pays, après l'aide internationale. En 2000, ils étaient 133 000 à bénéficier d'un permis de séjour en Italie (Mai et Schwander-Sievers, 2003).

Certains éléments montrent en outre l'apparition de nouveaux types de flux. Peraldi (2004) décrit la modification radicale des voies migratoires suivies par les Algériens au cours des dix dernières années. Les traditionnelles migrations de main-d'œuvre vers la France ont laissé place à d'autres formes de déplacements: de nombreux Algériens sillonnent tout le Bassin méditerranéen en marchands ambulants. Officiant souvent sur les marchés touristiques, ils se déplacent en fonction de réseaux familiaux qui leur permettent de saisir les occasions commerciales dans les villes où ils se trouvent. On a également constaté que les Roumains empruntent aussi pour leurs déplacements des réseaux transnationaux informels, qu'ils utilisent pour exploiter les «niches de travail» ouvertes aux travailleurs clandestins (Potot, 2004). Certains éléments amènent aussi à conclure que les migrations

Germany in the early 1990s has become a circulatory movement with periods of work in Germany interspersed with living back in Romania.

The trends described here are complex and indicate considerable variations from country to country and at different time periods. In the circumstances, explanations will also be complex, related to general economic conditions, stage of economic development reached in the CEE countries, the effects of the Balkan wars, individual national policy initiatives, regularisation programmes, levels of asylum-seeking and the efforts of smugglers and traffickers, as well as other factors. Even so, it should nevertheless be noted that the trends identified underestimate total flows, since for the most part they exclude asylum seekers and some categories of temporary immigrants, many of whom it is known stay illegally.

5.3. The migration of the former Soviet Union

5.3.1. The situation in 2000

Migration in the former Soviet Union is currently characterised by internal circulation, with some international spill-over. The causes of this movement are multiple, and include falling living standards, socio-political instability and a series of armed conflicts. The result is a complex typology of movement, some elements of which may be characterised as "normal" (such as labour migrations), others as the products of a series of emergencies.

Table 10 shows recorded migration flows for the countries of the CIS in 2000. The information comes from a study compiled by the International Organisation for Migration (IOM and ICMPD, 2002). The data are of uneven quantity and quality and in some cases should be regarded at best as indicative, as was pointed out in Chapter 3. Flows are divided into those within the CIS region and between it and other countries. What the data in Table 9 show is that most of the CIS countries are hardly engaging with those outside the region, indicating a potential for considerable growth as development proceeds. This is likely to be uneven because of the different social, economic and political paths taken by the countries and the dismantling of the previous unified economic system (ibid.).

ethniques se sont transformées en migrations circulaires. Michalon (2004) démontre que la migration des Allemands de souche de Transylvanie vers l'Allemagne du début des années 1990 a adopté un mouvement circulaire, avec des périodes de travail en Allemagne, entrecoupées de séjours en Roumanie.

Les tendances évolutives décrites ci-dessus sont complexes et laissent percevoir des variations considérables d'un pays à l'autre et à différentes périodes. Les explications seront donc complexes, elles aussi liées à la situation économique générale, au stade de développement économique des Peco, aux conséquences des guerres dans les Balkans, aux initiatives prises par les différents pays en matière de politique migratoire, aux programmes de régularisation, au nombre de demandeurs d'asile et aux efforts des trafiquants, ainsi qu'à d'autres facteurs encore. Il convient cependant de noter que les tendances qui se sont révélées sous-estiment l'ampleur de l'immigration, car elles excluent généralement les demandeurs d'asile et certaines catégories d'immigrés temporaires dont il est notoire que beaucoup séjournent clandestinement dans le pays.

5.3. Migrations de l'ex-Union soviétique

5.3.1. La situation en 2000

Dans l'ex-Union soviétique, les migrations sont actuellement caractérisées par une circulation interne, avec quelques débordements internationaux. Les causes de ce mouvement sont multiples et comprennent la chute du niveau de vie, l'instabilité sociopolitique et une série de conflits armés. Il en résulte une typologie de mouvement complexe, dont certains éléments peuvent être considérés comme «normaux» (les migrations de main-d'œuvre, par exemple) et d'autres comme résultant d'une série de situations d'urgence.

Le tableau 10 présente les flux migratoires enregistrés pour les pays de la CEI en 2000. Les données proviennent d'une étude réalisée par l'Organisation internationale des migrations (OIM et ICMPD, 2002). Elles sont de qualité et de quantité inégales et, dans certains cas, il ne faut y voir que de simples indications, ce qui a été souligné dans la section 3. Ces flux migratoires sont subdivisés entre flux internes à la CEI et flux entre la CEI et d'autres pays. Les données du tableau 9 indiquent que la plupart des pays de la CEI n'ont guère de contacts avec les pays extérieurs à la région, ce qui laisse percevoir un potentiel d'accroissement considérable à mesure que la région se développera. Celui-ci sera vraisemblablement inégal étant donné les orientations sociales, économiques et politiques prises par les différents pays et le

In the Communist past the movements would have been regarded as internal migration and it is not surprising that the bulk of movement is within the region, frequently more than 90%. With the notable exception of Tajikistan, inflows are largely within the region. Outflows are more likely to go outside the region, particularly in the cases of the western republics of Russia, Belarus and Ukraine.

Predictably, easily the largest flows involve Russia, which saw a net increase of 213 600 in 2000. Russia had a positive migration balance with all other CIS states, except for Belarus. The bulk of the flow consisted of Russian repatriates. Only Belarus of the other states recorded a net gain. Kazakhstan recorded the biggest net loss, most of its emigrants going to Russia, though with significant numbers of ethnic Germans and Jews continuing to move out. However, its net losses have been falling in the last couple of years as its own economy has improved while Russia has experienced economic downturn.

5.3.2. Trends in the region

Recent trends have been dominated by a mixture of politico-military crises and economic fluctuations (ibid.). In general, officially recorded migration flows have been decreasing: in 2000 they were 40% down within the region and around 30% down to and from outside. Russia continues to be the main migration partner of all the other countries in the region. Russian, Ukrainian and Belarusian repatriates have continued to be the main actors in the recorded migration flows, although the number of ethnic Slavs involved has decreased as their pool elsewhere has diminished.

Permanent migration outside the region is small and has continued to decrease, the main groups being Jews and Germans, although Russians and Ukrainians are now more in evidence among long-term emigrants. Short-term movement for work purposes is high and rising, much of which is irregular (ibid.). In some countries, remittances have become a major element in household survival strategies, mainly from emigrants to Russia but increasingly outside. It is recognised that official statistics underestimate the real numbers. In Russia, the trend in the last few years has been a reorientation from regular to irregular flows of labour migrants in response to the worsening financial situation and a tightening of regulations for the employment of foreign workers (Ivakhniouk, 2003).

démantèlement du précédent système économique centralisé (OIM et ICMPD, 2002).

Sous le régime communiste, ces mouvements auraient été considérés comme des migrations internes et il n'est guère surprenant qu'ils s'opèrent principalement à l'intérieur de la région, souvent pour plus de 90 %. A l'exception notable du Tadjikistan, l'immigration se fait essentiellement d'un Etat à l'autre de la région, l'émigration s'orientant plutôt vers l'extérieur, en particulier dans le cas des républiques occidentales de Russie, du Bélarus et de l'Ukraine.

De manière prévisible, les flux les plus importants concernent, de loin, la Russie, qui a enregistré un excédent migratoire net de 213 600 personnes en 2000. Elle affichait un solde migratoire positif avec tous les autres pays de la CEI, à l'exception du Bélarus. Parmi ces migrants figuraient essentiellement des rapatriés russes. Le Bélarus a été le seul de tous les autres Etats à noter un gain net. La perte nette la plus importante a été relevée au Kazakhstan dont la plupart des émigrants vont en Russie, alors qu'un grand nombre d'Allemands et de Juifs de souche continuent à quitter ce pays. Ses pertes nettes ont néanmoins diminué ces deux dernières années avec la reprise de son économie au moment où la Russie connaît une récession.

5.3.2. Evolution dans la région

L'évolution récente a été dominée par un mélange de crises politico-militaires et de fluctuations économiques (OIM et ICMPD, 2002). Dans l'ensemble, on note une baisse des flux migratoires enregistrés: baisse de 40 % à l'intérieur de la région en 2000 et de 30 % environ pour les migrations vers l'extérieur et venant de l'extérieur. La Russie reste le partenaire principal de tous les autres pays de la région. Les rapatriés russes, ukrainiens et bélarusses restent les principaux acteurs des flux migratoires enregistrés, bien que le nombre de Slaves de souche ait diminué à mesure que leurs effectifs diminuaient dans les autres régions.

L'émigration permanente est faible à l'extérieur de la région et en baisse constante, elle concerne essentiellement les Juifs et les Allemands, bien que les Russes et les Ukrainiens soient maintenant plus nombreux parmi les émigrants de longue durée. L'émigration de main-d'œuvre temporaire est importante et en hausse, en grande partie clandestine *(ibid.)*. Dans certains pays, les envois de fonds sont devenus un élément essentiel pour la survie de certaines familles et proviennent de personnes ayant émigré en Russie, mais de plus en plus dans d'autres pays. Il est reconnu que les statistiques officielles sous-estiment les chiffres réels. En Russie, depuis quelques années, en réponse à la dégradation de la situation financière

Over the last couple of years, the number of asylum seekers and internally displaced persons from within the region remained largely stable, while those from outside fell (ibid.).

5.4. Europe's migration fields

What has been the outcome for the European migration system as a whole of the trends in migration flows and the processes creating them indicated above? Table 11 is an attempt to measure the degree of self-containment within Europe of the migration fields of individual countries, based on the proportion of immigration and emigration flows to and from the regions listed, and using the latest available data for those countries for which appropriate statistics exist. For both flow directions there are considerable differences between countries.

With regard to immigration, countries fall into several groups. For those in central and eastern Europe for which we have data (notably "the former Yugoslav Republic of Macedonia", Romania, Estonia and Croatia) the vast majority of immigrants come from elsewhere in Europe, mainly from other CEE countries, and with only small proportions from EU and EFTA states. Slovenia appears to be the exception with 88.9% of immigrants coming from outside Europe. Scandinavian countries also display a relatively high degree of "Euro self-containment", mainly from EU and EFTA states, and from "other Europe" (largely Turkey and the former Yugoslavia) with only small proportions of flows from central and eastern Europe. Germany's immigration field is quite strongly European, and along with Austria, Finland and Liechtenstein receives a high proportion of its immigrants from central and eastern Europe. In contrast, almost three quarters of the UK's immigrants come from outside Europe. The Mediterranean countries also tend to look beyond Europe, as does the Netherlands.

Emigration data project a stronger picture of regional self-containment (the data for Spain are anomalous, including only Spaniards known to be moving abroad). Most of those leaving the CEE countries go elsewhere in the region or to the EU and EFTA. Only Germany, Austria and Liechtenstein in the west send a substantial proportion eastwards. Polish, Romanian and Czech data suggest a strong tendency for movement to EU and EFTA states.

et au renforcement de la réglementation sur l'embauche de travailleurs étrangers, les flux de travailleurs sont de plus en plus largement clandestins (Ivakhniouk, 2003).

Ces deux dernières années, le nombre de demandeurs d'asile et de personnes déplacées à l'intérieur de la région est resté relativement stable, alors que le nombre de ces personnes venant de l'extérieur a baissé *(ibid.)*.

5.4. Champs migratoires de l'Europe

Quel effet l'évolution des flux migratoires et leurs causes décrites cidessus ont-elles eu sur le régime migratoire de l'Europe dans son ensemble? Le tableau 11 s'efforce de mesurer le degré de confinement en Europe des champs migratoires de chacun des pays, en se fondant sur les parts respectives d'immigration et d'émigration vers les régions répertoriées et à partir de celles-ci, à l'aide des données les plus récentes concernant les pays pour lesquels des statistiques appropriées existent. Des différences considérables apparaissent, d'un pays à l'autre, pour l'immigration comme pour l'émigration.

S'agissant de l'immigration, les pays peuvent être ventilés en plusieurs groupes. Dans les pays d'Europe centrale et orientale pour lesquels des données existent (notamment l'«ex-République yougoslave de Macédoine», la Roumanie, l'Estonie et la Croatie), la grande majorité des immigrés viennent d'autres régions d'Europe, principalement d'autres Peco et, dans une moindre mesure, de pays membres de l'Union et de l'AELE. La Slovénie constitue une exception, avec 88,9 % d'immigrés en provenance de pays extérieurs à l'Europe. Les pays scandinaves présentent également un degré relativement élevé «d'euroconfinement», leurs immigrés venant principalement des pays de l'Union, de l'AELE et de «l'autre Europe» (surtout la Turquie et l'ex-Yougoslavie), et pour une faible part d'Europe centrale et orientale. Le champ migratoire allemand est très européen; comme l'Autriche, la Finlande et le Liechtenstein, l'Allemagne se caractérise par une forte proportion d'immigrés d'Europe centrale et orientale. En revanche, presque trois quarts des immigrés au Royaume-Uni viennent de pays extérieurs à l'Europe. Les pays méditerranéens accueillent également des non-Européens en plus grand nombre, tout comme les Pays-Bas.

Les données de l'émigration accentuent encore cette impression de confinement dans la région (les données pour l'Espagne sont atypiques en ce qu'elles concernent exclusivement les Espagnols qui partent s'installer à l'étranger). La plupart des personnes qui quittent les pays d'Europe centrale et orientale s'installent ailleurs dans la région ou dans l'Union et l'AELE. A l'Ouest, seuls l'Allemagne, l'Autriche et le Liechtenstein se caractérisent par des mouvements substantiels vers

It is difficult to generalise from Table 11 because of data interpretation problems for some countries, and the absence of statistics for many others. Nevertheless, three major conclusions may be drawn. First, there is some evidence of regional self-containment, especially for CEE countries, in that the majority of exchanges are with elsewhere in Europe as a whole or its constituent parts. Second, there are marked differences in the migration fields of individual countries, reflecting a range of historical (such as post-colonial links) and geographical (especially proximity) processes. Finally, the patterns depicted reinforce the diversity of migration experience across Europe.

l'Est. Les données relatives à la Pologne, à la Roumanie et à la République tchèque font apparaître une nette prédilection pour les pays de l'Union et de l'AELE.

Il est difficile de généraliser à partir des chiffres du tableau 11 en raison de problèmes d'interprétation des données pour certains pays et de l'absence de statistiques pour de nombreux autres. Nous pouvons cependant tirer trois grandes conclusions. Premièrement, on observe un certain degré de confinement dans la région, surtout dans le cas des pays d'Europe centrale et orientale, en ce sens que la plupart des échanges se font avec d'autres parties de l'Europe. Deuxièmement, des différences marquées apparaissent entre les champs migratoires des divers pays. Elles sont le reflet de tout un éventail de processus historiques (liens postcoloniaux) et de facteurs géographiques (principalement la proximité). Enfin, les schémas décrits confirment la diversité des expériences de la migration qu'ont les différents pays d'Europe.

6. Labour migration

6.1. Stocks of foreign labour

6.1.1. Western Europe

It is more difficult to obtain accurate and comparable data across Europe for stocks of labour than for the foreign population as a whole. There are problems of knowing who is included, and which sources might be used. In addition, unrecorded workers are almost certainly proportionately more important in the labour market than are unrecorded residents in the total population.

The evidence from Table 12 (and Figures 7.a-f) suggests that in western Europe around 2002/03 (using the latest data for each country) there were about 10.07 million recorded foreign workers, an increase of 38 % on the 1995 figure of about 7.29 million. However, this increase does not represent such a large increment to the foreign workforce as it appears. In some countries, notably Ireland, Switzerland and the UK, there have been significant rises in stocks owing to the entry of new foreign workers. The bulk of the increase tabulated is the result of amnesties for illegal workers in some countries, notably Italy, Spain, Portugal and Greece. Indeed, it would appear that if these groups are omitted, over the last few years stocks of recorded foreign labour have changed little. Elsewhere, stocks of recorded foreign labour have gone down (Germany) or remained relatively static (for example, France). Germany, France, Italy and the UK between them contained 6.32 million, 62.8 % of the western European total. Among those countries with 2003 data, Austria, Greece, Luxembourg, Spain and the UK recorded increases on the year before, Germany was more or less unchanged while foreign labour stocks in Switzerland fell.

6.1.2. Central and eastern Europe

Data for central and eastern Europe are limited. Recording of foreign labour is much more patchy and the relative incidence of irregular or informal working probably higher than in western Europe. For the countries listed in Table 12, but excluding Russia, the total was around 372 000. Both the Czech Republic and Hungary increased their

6. Migration de main-d'œuvre

6.1. Main-d'œuvre étrangère

6.1.1. Europe occidentale

Il est plus difficile d'obtenir des données précises et comparables pour la main-d'œuvre étrangère en Europe que pour la population étrangère dans son ensemble. Il faut savoir en particulier quelles sont les personnes qui ont été incluses dans les chiffres et connaître également les sources que l'on peut utiliser. En outre, les travailleurs non enregistrés sont presque certainement plus nombreux, proportionnellement, sur le marché du travail que les résidents non enregistrés dans la population totale.

Il ressort du tableau 12 (et des figures 7.a-f) qu'il y avait en Europe occidentale, aux alentours de 2001-2003 (sur la base des dernières données disponibles pour chaque pays) environ 10,07 millions de travailleurs étrangers enregistrés, soit une augmentation de 38% par rapport aux chiffres de 1995 (environ 7,29 millions). Pourtant cette augmentation de la main-d'œuvre n'est pas si importante qu'il y paraît à première vue. Dans certains pays, notamment l'Irlande, la Suisse et le Royaume-Uni, la main-d'œuvre étrangère a augmenté de façon importante en raison de l'arrivée de nouveaux travailleurs étrangers. L'augmentation présentée dans le tableau 11 résulte en grande partie de l'amnistie accordée par certains pays aux travailleurs clandestins, en particulier en Italie, en Espagne, au Portugal et en Grèce. En effet, si l'on ne tient pas compte de ces groupes, la main-d'œuvre enregistrée au cours des dernières années semblerait relativement stable. Ailleurs, le nombre de travailleurs étrangers enregistrés a diminué (Allemagne) ou est resté relativement stable (en France, notamment). L'Allemagne, la France, l'Italie et le Royaume-Uni ont accueilli 6,32 millions de travailleurs étrangers, soit 62,8 % du total de l'Europe occidentale. Parmi les pays dans lesquels des données sont disponibles pour 2003, l'Autriche, la Grèce, le Luxembourg, l'Espagne et le Royaume-Uni ont enregistré une augmentation par rapport à l'année précédente; la situation est restée à peu près inchangée en Allemagne, tandis que la Suisse a vu diminuer le nombre de travailleurs étrangers.

6.1.2. Europe centrale et orientale

On ne dispose que de données limitées sur les populations de travailleurs étrangers en Europe centrale et orientale. L'enregistrement de la main-d'œuvre étrangère est beaucoup plus inégal et la fréquence relative du travail clandestin ou illégal est probablement plus élevée qu'en Europe occidentale. Pour les pays figurant dans le tableau 12,

recorded foreign labour stocks over the period. The figure for Estonia includes Russians and others with former Soviet Union passports.

6.2. Flows of labour

There are major difficulties in estimating inflows of foreign labour to individual countries and in aggregate. Across Europe as a whole there is a multiplicity of (usually) administrative sources which are frequently partial in coverage. For example, work permits are a common source but they exclude EEA nationals for member states, for which other sources have to be used. Only non-Nordic citizens are included in the figures in Nordic states. There are also severe problems in relation to the recording of seasonal, frontier and other short-term workers: they are included in the data for some countries but not for others. In the UK, for example, in 2002 the figure from the Labour Force Survey (used here) was 99 000 but when all types of foreign workers are included (such as short-term entrants under a range of special schemes as well as EEA nationals) the figure is almost a quarter of a million. Flows of irregular migrants are an added source of uncertainty. The statistics presented here are thus at best indicative.

Recorded inflows of foreign labour have been modest in most countries in recent years, the biggest recipient being Germany (Table 13 and Figures 8.*a-d*). In a majority of the countries of western Europe for which data are available the numbers moving per year are less than 20 000. More countries had higher numbers at the end of the period than at the beginning, but only Germany and the UK showed large numerical increases.

The countries of central and eastern Europe have had variable experiences. Recorded inflows increased in Hungary and fell in the Czech Republic, Poland and Slovakia and were static at a low level in Bulgaria and Romania.

Around 3 000 contract workers and 40 000 temporary workers from CEE countries go to Germany each year under bilateral agreements. As workers from most CEE countries often no longer need a visa to travel to western Europe for three months, movement there is rela-

moins la Russie, le total était d'environ 372 000 travailleurs étrangers. La République tchèque et la Hongrie ont vu augmenter leur nombre de travailleurs étrangers durant la période étudiée. Les données concernant l'Estonie englobent les Russes et les autres personnes titulaires de passeports de l'ex-Union soviétique.

6.2. Flux de main-d'œuvre

L'estimation des entrées de main-d'œuvre étrangère dans chaque pays considéré individuellement et dans l'ensemble se heurte à des difficultés majeures. On constate dans l'ensemble de l'Europe une multiplicité de sources (généralement) administratives, qui ne couvrent souvent que partiellement le phénomène. Ainsi, les permis de travail sont une source fréquemment utilisée, mais elle ne concerne pas les ressortissants de l'EEE travaillant dans d'autres Etats membres de cet espace, pour lesquels d'autres sources doivent donc être utilisées. Dans les pays nordiques, seuls les ressortissants de pays non nordiques sont comptabilisés dans les statistiques. L'enregistrement des travailleurs saisonniers, frontaliers ou de courte durée pose aussi de graves problèmes: certains pays les incluent dans leurs données, alors que d'autres les ignorent. Au Royaume-Uni, par exemple, les chiffres tirés de l'«Etude de la population active» en 2002 *(Labour Force Survey)*, utilisés ici, font état de 99 000 travailleurs étrangers, mais si l'on inclut toutes les catégories (comme les immigrants de courte durée au titre de toute une série de régimes spéciaux, ainsi que les ressortissants de l'EEE) on arrive pratiquement à 250 000 personnes. L'immigration clandestine constitue une source supplémentaire d'incertitude. Les chiffres présentés ici sont donc, au mieux, indicatifs.

Ces dernières années, l'afflux de main-d'œuvre étrangère enregistrée a été modeste dans la plupart des pays, l'Allemagne étant le premier pays de destination (tableau 13 et figures 8.*a-d*). Dans la plupart des pays d'Europe occidentale pour lesquels on dispose de données, le nombre annuel de migrants est inférieur à 20 000. Ce chiffre est plus élevé à la fin qu'au début de la période pour un plus grand nombre de pays, mais seuls l'Allemagne et le Royaume-Uni ont connu une forte augmentation.

Dans les pays d'Europe centrale et orientale, la situation a été variable. Les flux de travailleurs immigrés ont augmenté en Hongrie et baissé en République tchèque, en Pologne et en Slovaquie; ils stagnent à un faible niveau en Bulgarie et en Roumanie.

Quelque 3 000 travailleurs sous contrat et 40 000 intérimaires des Peco se rendent en Allemagne chaque année dans le cadre d'accords bilatéraux. Le visa n'étant plus exigé des travailleurs de la plupart des pays d'Europe centrale et orientale lors de leurs déplacements en Europe

tively easy, followed by overstay and undocumented work. It seems that much of this migration is to the newer immigration countries of the EU, notably southern Europe and Ireland, and both Spain and Portugal entered into negotiations with selected CEE states to establish bilateral labour agreements to regulate the arrival of CEE workers (Laczko, 2002). However, most forms of labour migration from the CEE countries, including "pendular migration" and petty trading, are to other CEE countries rather than to western Europe (Kraler and Iglicka, 2002). Management of labour migration in some of these countries is taking a new turn; for example, the Czech Republic introduced a points system where migrants are selected according to their skills and qualifications (ibid.).

6.3. Labour migration in an enlarged Europe

One of the major political developments in 2004 has been the expansion of the EU eastwards. In anticipation of this event, in the last few years several studies have attempted to estimate the likely migration consequences. Although usually edged with caveats, numbers suggested are not large (Dustmann, 2003). The general consensus is that between a quarter and a third of a million people from CEE countries would move westwards per annum, the period for which this persisted depending upon the speed and success of economic transformation in the origin countries. Overall, these figures suggest that perhaps 3% of the population of the candidate countries would move. Further movement is unlikely, regardless of economic development, because the migration potential of CEE countries is likely to decrease for demographic reasons (Fassmann and Münz, 2002).

Since accession to the EU of eight CEE countries (A8) in May 2004, most existing western European states have instituted a transition period before allowing free movement of A8 nationals into their labour markets, the exceptions being the UK, Ireland and Denmark. The UK Government decided to introduce a new Worker Registration Scheme (WRS) for A8 workers which came into operation in the spring of 2004. During the period May to September there were 87 220 applications from individual workers, the vast majority of which (92.6%) were approved. Poles were the largest national group with over half the total, followed by Lithuanians and Slovaks.

occidentale pour une durée n'excédant pas trois mois, il est relativement simple de s'y rendre, de dépasser la durée légale du séjour et de
trouver un travail au noir. Il semble que ces migrations se font le plus
souvent vers les nouveaux pays d'immigration de l'Union, notamment
l'Europe septentrionale et l'Irlande. L'Espagne et le Portugal ont engagé
des négociations avec certains Etats déterminés des Peco afin de
conclure des accords bilatéraux destinés à endiguer l'arrivée de travailleurs de ces régions (Laczko, 2002). Les migrations des Peco, quelle
que soit leur forme, y compris les «migrations pendulaires» et le petit
commerce, se font en grande partie en direction d'autres pays d'Europe
centrale et orientale plutôt que vers l'Europe occidentale (Kraler et
Iglicka, 2002). Dans certains de ces pays, la gestion des migrations de
main-d'œuvre prend une nouvelle tournure: la République tchèque,
par exemple, a mis en place un système de points par lequel les
migrants sont sélectionnés en fonction de leurs compétences et de
leurs qualifications *(ibid.)*.

6.3. Migration de main-d'œuvre dans une Europe élargie

L'un des événements politiques majeurs de l'année 2004 a été l'élargissement de l'Union européenne à l'Est. En prévision de cette évolution, plusieurs études ont été entreprises ces dernières années pour
tenter d'en évaluer les conséquences probables sur les flux migratoires. Bien qu'ils soient généralement assortis de mises en garde
quant à leur fiabilité, les chiffres avancés ne sont pas élevés
(Dustmann, 2003). De l'avis général, quelque 250 000 à 300 000 personnes des Peco partiront chaque année vers l'Ouest, et la durée de ce
mouvement dépendra de la rapidité et du succès de la transformation
économique des pays d'origine. Globalement, ces chiffres indiquent
que 3 % peut-être de la population des nouveaux Etats membres de
l'Union se déplaceront. D'autres mouvements sont peu probables, quel
que soit le développement économique, car le potentiel migratoire des
Peco va vraisemblablement décroître pour des raisons démographiques (Fassmann et Münz, 2002).

Depuis l'entrée de huit Peco dans l'Union, en mai 2004, la plupart des
pays d'Europe occidentale ont décrété une période de transition avant
d'autoriser la libre circulation des ressortissants de ces huit pays sur
leur marché du travail, le Royaume-Uni, l'Irlande et le Danemark
constituant des exceptions de ce point de vue. Le Gouvernement britannique a décidé de mettre en place un nouveau programme d'enregistrement des travailleurs *(Worker Registration Scheme)* pour les ressortissants de ces huit pays, système qui est entré en vigueur au
printemps 2004. De mai à septembre, 87 220 demandes ont été dépo-
sées par des particuliers au titre de ce système, dont la grande majorité (92,6 %) a été approuvée. Les Polonais représentaient le groupe le

Across Europe, patterns of foreign labour recruitment and use provide echoes of the 1960s. Several examples demonstrate this, including the UK Worker Registration Scheme. Almost all registrations were for low-skilled work. The largest group (16.3%) were process operatives in factories, followed by kitchen and catering assistants (7.2%), waiters/waitresses (6.5%), packers (5.4%) and cleaners/domestic staff and farm workers (each 5.1%). Thus the WRS is very much a route of entry for low-skilled workers – at least for those working for an employer, since self-employed workers do not have to register. Not all of those registering were newly entering workers. Only 55.3% arrived in the country after 1 May. Thus, most were already in the UK, some of them for quite a long time. It is not known how many of these were working illegally but it is likely that many/most of them were. It would appear then that the WRS has had the effect of legalising several thousand people.

The UK is not alone in western Europe in importing foreign workers to work in low-skilled occupations. Germany's bilateral agreement with Poland brings in over a quarter of a million seasonal workers a year, mostly in agriculture (Dietz and Kaczmarczyk, 2004). In Ireland the most rapid increases in work permit issues were in agriculture, hotels and catering (Hughes, 2004). The Netherlands tells a similar story. In recent years the number of temporary work permits issued has risen, especially for agriculture, horticulture and a range of low-skilled service jobs such as drivers and hotel and catering workers (Snel, de Boom and Engbersen, 2004). In Austria, agriculture and forestry and parts of the tourist sector have been increasing their foreign labour intake (Biffl, 2004).

In the years following the collapse of Communism, the CEE countries developed their own migration novelties, characterised by a wide range of circulatory and informal flows and sometimes referred to by the epithet "pendular". By the turn of the millennium, labour migration within and to the CEE countries was highly differentiated according

plus important, avec plus de la moitié du total des demandes, suivis par les Lituaniens et les Slovaques.

Dans toute l'Europe, la typologie de l'embauche de main-d'œuvre étrangère rappelle celle des années 1960. Plusieurs exemples le montrent, dont le programme britannique d'enregistrement des travailleurs *(Worker Registration Scheme)*. Presque tous les enregistrements concernent des travailleurs peu qualifiés. Le groupe le plus important (16,3 %) est constitué d'ouvriers de l'industrie manufacturière, suivi par les commis d'hôtellerie et de restauration (7,2 %), les serveurs et serveuses (6,5 %), les personnes travaillant dans l'emballage (5,4 %), les agents d'entretien et le personnel de maison (5,1 %) et les ouvriers agricoles (5,1 %). Le programme d'enregistrement des travailleurs est donc très largement une porte d'entrée pour les travailleurs peu qualifiés, tout au moins pour ceux qui travaillent pour un employeur, car les personnes travaillant à leur compte n'ont pas à s'enregistrer. Toutes les personnes qui se sont enregistrées n'étaient pas des travailleurs nouvellement arrivés. Seuls 55,3 % sont arrivés dans le pays après le 1ᵉʳ mai. La plupart était donc déjà au Royaume-Uni, certains depuis assez longtemps. On ne sait pas combien d'entre eux travaillaient clandestinement auparavant, mais il est probable que cela fût le cas de beaucoup d'entre eux, sinon de la majorité. Il semblerait que le programme d'enregistrement a eu pour effet de légaliser la situation de plusieurs milliers de personnes.

Le Royaume-Uni n'est pas le seul pays d'Europe occidentale à importer de la main-d'œuvre étrangère pour occuper des emplois peu qualifiés. L'accord bilatéral conclut entre l'Allemagne et la Pologne permet d'importer chaque année plus de 250 000 travailleurs saisonniers, essentiellement dans l'agriculture (Dietz et Kaczmarczyk, 2004). En Irlande, les secteurs dans lesquels la délivrance de permis de travail a augmenté le plus rapidement sont l'agriculture, l'hôtellerie et la restauration (Hughes, 2004). La situation est identique aux Pays-Bas. Le nombre de permis de travail temporaires délivrés ces dernières années a augmenté, en particulier dans l'agriculture, l'horticulture et pour toute une série d'emplois dans les services peu qualifiés tels que chauffeurs et employés de l'hôtellerie et de la restauration (Snel, de Boom et Engbersen, 2004). En Autriche, l'agriculture et la sylviculture ainsi que certaines parties du secteur touristique ont fait appel de manière accrue à la main-d'œuvre étrangère (Biffl, 2004).

Dans les années qui ont suivi l'effondrement du communisme, des phénomènes migratoires propres aux Peco sont apparus, caractérisés par toute une série de flux informels, parfois qualifiés de «pendulaires». A la fin des années 1990, les migrations de main-d'œuvre au sein et à destination des Peco étaient très différenciées pour ce qui est

to the duration, skills and origins of migrants (Wallace, 1999; Kraler and Iglicka, 2002). Migrants were more likely than indigenous workers to be in the private sector and working in small firms, generally in more insecure jobs. Among migrants of different nationalities some segmentation occurred. Examples include Romanian and Ukrainian casual, seasonal and construction workers. In contrast to those from elsewhere in eastern Europe and the former Soviet Union, Chinese and Vietnamese are frequently to be found as entrepreneurs, especially in restaurants and trading companies (ibid.).

The current situation in the CEE region shows some similarities with western Europe during its guest worker phase. In the A8 states, foreign workers from further east are to be found (often working illegally) in the agriculture and construction industries and in the low-skilled and low-paid service sector. Often they are replacing the nationals of these countries who have moved to work in western Europe. Turkish employers in agriculture and construction employ foreign men from an arc of countries to the north and east, and foreign women to work, usually illegally, in domestic service and entertainment (Içduygu, 2004).

de la durée, des qualifications et de l'origine des migrants (Wallace, 1999; Kraler et Iglicka, 2002). Ils étaient plus fréquemment employés que les autochtones dans le secteur privé et les petites entreprises, et occupaient généralement des emplois plus précaires. Parmi les migrants, des différences se dessinaient en fonction de la nationalité. Ainsi, les Roumains et Ukrainiens se retrouvaient par exemple travailleurs occasionnels, saisonniers ou dans le bâtiment et les travaux publics (BTP). Contrairement aux immigrés venus d'autres pays de l'Europe de l'Est et de l'ex-URSS, les Chinois et les Vietnamiens avaient souvent leur propre entreprise, en particulier dans la restauration et l'import-export *(ibid.)*.

Actuellement, la situation des Peco présentent plusieurs similitudes avec celle qu'a connue l'Europe occidentale lors de l'arrivée massive de travailleurs immigrés. Dans les huit Peco entrés dans l'Union, on assiste à l'immigration de travailleurs (souvent clandestins) venus de pays situés plus à l'Est et travaillant dans l'agriculture, les BTP et les services peu qualifiés et peu payés. Ils remplacent souvent les ressortissants de ces pays, partis travailler en Europe occidentale. En Turquie, les entreprises du secteur agricole et du BTP embauchent des hommes originaires des pays situés plus au nord et à l'est, tandis que les femmes travaillent, souvent clandestinement, comme employées de maison et dans le secteur des loisirs (Içduygu, 2004).

7. Asylum

7.1. Trends in numbers of asylum applications

Much of the discussion about the scale of migration into and within Europe separates out asylum seekers from "normal" (predominantly labour and family reunion) migration flows. There are sound reasons for this. Not only are the motivations of the two sets of moves different, but the data are also collected and presented differently. However, the distinction between the two has become increasingly blurred. Many asylum seekers are not in need of protection and are attempting to migrate for economic and/or family reasons, while the statistical distinction is no longer clear.

Most of the literature on asylum has focused on policy, legislation and procedures. Analyses of how and why asylum seekers choose particular destinations are scarce, though increasingly the role of smugglers and traffickers is emphasised. In the majority of cases the choice of country for asylum is not a conscious, rational choice by the asylum seeker and certainly not based on a comparison of the advantages and disadvantages of various options. Four interconnected factors appear to be very important for explaining the patterns of destination for asylum seekers: existing communities of compatriots, colonial bonds, knowledge of the language and, increasingly important, the smugglers and traffickers. Chain migration effects seem important, especially in terms of friendship and kinship networks. One study, mainly carried out in the Netherlands, Belgium and the UK, but with reference to the North American literature as well, found that most asylum seekers are not well informed with regard to possible destination countries: indeed, the influence of rumour is strong (Böcker and Havinga, 1997). A recent study in the UK found that facilitators/smugglers were primarily responsible for the choice of destination (Gilbert and Koser, 2004). Asylum policy and reception vary in importance between countries and this information is used by facilitators as well as by individual asylum seekers.

7.2. The destination perspective in western Europe, 1995-2003

Inflows of asylum seekers to western Europe have fluctuated in total and between destination countries since the mid-1980s. In 1985 the region received 169 710 asylum seekers and reached a peak of 695 580 in 1992. By 1995 the number had fallen to 293 500 but rose

7. Asile

7.1. Evolution du nombre de demandeurs d'asile

Une grande partie du débat sur l'ampleur des migrations vers l'Europe et en son sein repose sur une distinction entre les demandeurs d'asile et les flux migratoires normaux (essentiellement pour l'emploi et le regroupement familial). Il y a de bonnes raisons à cela. Non seulement les motivations des deux types de mouvements sont distinctes mais les données sont aussi collectées et présentées de manière différente. Cependant, la distinction entre les deux est devenue de plus en plus floue. De nombreux demandeurs d'asile n'ont pas besoin de protection et tentent de migrer pour des raisons économiques et/ou familiales alors que la distinction statistique n'est pas plus claire.

La plupart des ouvrages traitant de l'asile s'attachent aux politiques, aux lois et aux procédures. Peu d'analyses tentent de découvrir pourquoi et comment les demandeurs d'asile optent pour certaines destinations, bien que des études récentes soulignent l'importance des passeurs dans ce domaine. Dans la plupart des cas, le choix du pays d'asile n'est pas le fruit d'un choix conscient et rationnel de la part du demandeur et ne résulte certainement pas d'une comparaison des avantages et des inconvénients des diverses options. L'étude a dégagé quatre facteurs interdépendants qui déterminent largement le choix d'une destination par les demandeurs d'asile: l'existence de communautés de compatriotes, des liens coloniaux, la connaissance de la langue et, de plus en plus importants, les filières de passeurs et trafiquants. Les effets de migration en chaîne semblent importants, surtout par le biais de réseaux d'amitié et de parenté. Une étude, réalisée en grande partie aux Pays-Bas, en Belgique et au Royaume-Uni, et avec quelques références tirées d'ouvrages nord-américains, révèle que la plupart des demandeurs d'asile sont mal informés des pays de destination possibles: en effet, les rumeurs jouent un rôle important (Böcker et Havinga, 1997). Une étude réalisée récemment au Royaume-Uni a montré que les passeurs/trafiquants jouent un rôle primordial dans le choix de la destination (Gilbert et Koser, 2004). Les politiques d'asile et l'accueil de demandeurs varient d'un pays à l'autre et ces informations sont exploitées par les passeurs aussi bien que par les demandeurs individuels.

7.2. Tendances quant aux pays de destination en Europe occidentale, 1995-2003

Depuis le milieu des années 1980, le nombre des demandeurs d'asile en Europe occidentale varie, de même que leur pays de destination. En 1985, cette région a accueilli au total 169 710 demandeurs d'asile; elle

again in 1998-99, mainly because of trouble in the Balkans, before falling back to around 420 000 in the three years 2000-02. However, the number rose slightly to 420 000 in 2001 and then to 425 400 in 2002 (Table 14 and Figures 9.*a-f*). Overall, western Europe experienced an increase in asylum seeker numbers of 42% between 1995 and 2002. In 2003 the trend changed, total numbers being down by 22% on the year before (Italy is excluded from this calculation because there are no data for 2003) to reach the lowest total since 1997. Some countries had particularly large falls, notably Germany (-29%), Ireland (-32%) and the UK (-41%). Thirteen of the eighteen countries listed in Table 14 with data for 2003 had fewer asylum seekers than the year before, three showed little change and only two had more. Explanation of these patterns is complex and the falls reflect a changing situation within Europe and globally. The perturbations in the Balkans had largely subsided, ceasefires had occurred in some troubled parts of the world (for example, Sri Lanka) and other countries were deemed now to be safe (Afghanistan, Iraq). Several destination countries have also put into operation asylum reduction models designed to interdict flows, curtail administrative processes and reduce benefits to asylum seekers.

A more even spread of asylum requests across western Europe appears to be happening (Tables 14 and 15). A major feature is the changing situation in Germany. In 1985 it accounted for 43.5% of requests, almost two thirds in 1992 but fell to 15.2% in 2003. Its asylum seeker numbers fell every year between 1995 and 2003, with the exception of 2001. In contrast, France experienced a sharp rise in numbers of requests for asylum after 1998, and in 2003 its share of the western European total had risen to 15.2%, almost on a par with Germany. The UK's situation has changed radically, from only 3.7% of the total in 1985 to 24.5% in 2002. Despite a fall in 2003 to 18.4% of the total it has taken from Germany its traditional role of leading destination. Other countries with major increases in their numbers in the last few years are Austria, Belgium and Denmark. During the period since 1995 the major proportionate changes (sometimes, as with Greece, from a low base) are Ireland, Norway, Austria, Greece, Sweden and Denmark.

a enregistré un pic en 1992, avec 695 580 demandes. En 1995, ce chiffre était retombé à 293 500 pour remonter en 1998-1999, surtout à cause de la situation dans les Balkans, avant de chuter à nouveau aux environs de 420 000 au cours des années 2000-2002. La tendance est cependant légèrement repartie à la hausse, avec 420 000 demandes en 2001 et 425 400 en 2002 (tableau 14 et figures 9.*a-f*). Dans l'ensemble, l'Europe occidentale a connu une augmentation de 42 % du nombre de demandeurs d'asile entre 1995 et 2002. En 2003, la tendance s'est inversée, avec une baisse de 22 % par rapport à l'année précédente (sans l'Italie, pour laquelle aucune donnée n'est disponible pour 2003) et le total le plus bas enregistré depuis 1997. Cette diminution a été particulièrement importante en Allemagne (– 29 %), en Irlande (– 32 %) et au Royaume-Uni (– 41 %). Treize des dix-huit pays figurant dans le tableau 14 et disposant de données pour 2003 comptaient moins de demandeurs d'asile que l'année précédente, alors qu'aucun changement notable n'était recensé dans trois autres pays et que seuls deux faisaient état de chiffres à la hausse. L'explication est complexe; ces diminutions reflètent toutefois un changement de situation en Europe et à l'échelle planétaire. Les troubles dans les Balkans se sont largement apaisés, des cessez-le-feu sont intervenus dans certaines régions du monde en proie à des conflits (comme au Sri Lanka) et, dans d'autres pays, la sécurité semblait rétablie (Afghanistan, Irak). Parallèlement, plusieurs pays de destination ont mis en place des procédures de restriction de l'asile de manière à empêcher les arrivées, à limiter les procédures administratives et à réduire les avantages accordés aux demandeurs d'asile.

Les demandes d'asile semble se répartir plus équitablement entre les différents pays d'Europe occidentale (tableaux 14 et 15). L'une des évolutions les plus marquantes est le changement de situation en Allemagne. Ce pays accueillait 43,5 % des demandeurs d'asile en 1985, près des deux tiers en 1992, mais seulement 15,2 % en 2003. Le nombre de demandes d'asile n'a cessé de chuter entre 1995 et 2003, avec toutefois une augmentation en 2001. La France, au contraire, a enregistré une forte augmentation du nombre de demandeurs d'asile après 1998; en 2003, sa part dans le total des demandes enregistrées en Europe occidentale atteignait 15,2 %, soit presque autant que l'Allemagne. La situation du Royaume-Uni a changé radicalement, puisqu'il est passé de seulement 3,7 % du total en 1985 à 24,5 % en 2002. Malgré une diminution en 2003, avec 18,4 %, il a détrôné l'Allemagne de sa position traditionnelle de première destination. Les autres pays ayant connu une augmentation importante du nombre de demandeurs d'asile au cours des dernières années sont l'Autriche, la Belgique et le Danemark. Depuis 1995, les principales augmentations, en proportions (parfois, comme en Grèce, à partir

There have also been significant changes in asylum pressure, measured in terms of number of asylum requests per 10 000 population (Table 15). For the EU and EFTA states as a whole, pressure increased from 4.6 in 1985 to a peak of 18.4 in 1992 caused mainly by conflict in former Yugoslavia. There was then a fall to just under 11 in the years 2000-02, then down further to 8.5 in 2003. The countries experiencing the greatest pressure in 2003 are small in population, Austria, Luxembourg, Sweden and Norway. In the case of Ireland, asylum requests have risen from very small numbers since the early 1990s, partly in response to the strength of its economy, partly to its citizenship law. At the other end of the scale, Portugal, Iceland, and Spain have low asylum pressure, reflecting their geographical position, their relative popularity as destinations and their asylum laws. The countries with the largest numbers of applications, Germany and the UK, have relatively modest levels of pressure. What is not clear from Table 15, however, is how far these numbers are affected by registration of asylum flows.

7.3. Asylum applications in central and eastern Europe, 1995-2003

For most countries in the region, the 1990s was a period of evolution for migration and asylum legislation and for statistical recording. In most cases, countries of the region were senders rather than receivers of asylum seekers. Even when they started to receive applications, most were a device for staying in the country prior to an attempt to get to western Europe rather than being genuine requests. There is some recent evidence that asylum seekers are now targeting CEE countries for settlement because of their political freedom and economic growth. In effect, they too have become attractive destinations.

Data on asylum seeking in central and eastern Europe are still very partial, and for the most part the numbers recorded are low (Table 14). In 2003 there were a total of 35 000 applications for asylum in the ten countries listed, a significant fall from the peak of 47 000 in 2001 but a substantial increase on 1995 when the aggregate was only 3 200. The trend in 2002-03 varied. In some countries the numbers were too small to identify a trend; among the rest, three experienced falling numbers, three rising. The Czech and Slovak Republics were the most

d'un faible seuil), sont observées en Irlande, en Autriche, en Grèce, en Suède et au Danemark.

Sont à noter aussi des variations importantes dans la pression exercée par les demandeurs d'asile, mesurée par le nombre de demandes pour 10 000 personnes (tableau 15). Pour l'ensemble de l'Union européenne et de l'AELE, le chiffre est passé de 4,6 en 1985 à 18,4 en 1992, ce pic s'expliquant principalement par les conflits dans l'ex-Yougoslavie. Le niveau est ensuite retombé juste en dessous de 11 en 2000-2002, puis à 8,5 en 2003. Les pays ayant connu la plus forte pression en 2003 sont des pays à faible population, comme l'Autriche, la Norvège, la Suisse et l'Irlande. En Irlande, les demandes d'asile, très peu nombreuses au départ, augmentent depuis le début des années 1990, cela étant dû à la prospérité économique du pays et à la loi sur la citoyenneté. A l'autre extrémité, le Portugal, l'Islande et l'Espagne ont peu de demandes d'asile, par suite de leur position géographique, de leur popularité toute relative en tant que destinations pour les demandeurs d'asile et de leur législation en matière de droit d'asile. Dans les pays qui enregistrent le plus grand nombre de demandes, à savoir l'Allemagne et le Royaume-Uni, la pression est relativement modeste. Le tableau 15 ne permet toutefois pas de dire clairement dans quelle mesure ces chiffres reflètent l'enregistrement des flux de demandeurs d'asile.

7.3. Demandes d'asile en Europe centrale et orientale, 1995-2003

Pour la plupart des pays de la région, les années 1990 ont marqué une évolution dans la législation sur l'immigration et le droit d'asile ainsi que dans les données statistiques. Ces pays étaient le plus souvent amenés à envoyer plutôt qu'à recevoir des demandeurs d'asile. Même lorsqu'ils ont commencé à recevoir des demandes d'asile, celles-ci étaient, dans la plupart des cas, plutôt un moyen de rester dans le pays pour tenter ensuite de gagner l'Europe occidentale que de réelles demandes d'asile. Certains indices récents montrent que les demandeurs d'asile cherchent maintenant à s'établir dans les pays d'Europe centrale et orientale en raison de leur liberté politique et de leur croissance économique. Ces pays sont, à leur tour, devenus des destinations attrayantes.

Les données concernant les demandes d'asile en Europe centrale et orientale restent très incomplètes et, dans la majorité des cas, les chiffres recueillis sont peu élevés (tableau 14). En 2003, 35 000 demandes ont été enregistrées dans les dix pays observés, ce qui représente une baisse importante par rapport au pic de 47 000 demandes enregistrées en 2001, mais une augmentation substantielle par rapport à l'année 1995 pour laquelle le total n'était que de 3 200 demandes. En 2002-2003, la tendance a été variable. Dans certains pays, les chiffres

attractive destinations, between them accounting for nearly two thirds of the region's applications, their numbers now exceeding those in several western European countries.

7.4. Trends in asylum decisions, 1995-2003

Statistics on asylum decisions are difficult to interpret because of the time lag between an application being made and a decision being reached. A further complication is the appeals procedure, which may mean several "decisions" on a single case. How these are recorded in the statistics affects the recognition rate. Table 16, based on UNHCR data, shows the number of initial asylum decisions for selected countries, together with the numbers and proportions granted refugee status under the 1951 UN Convention on the Status of Refugees (Refugee Convention) or other humanitarian status, and those refused.

During the period 2000-03 there were 1.47 million decisions. Numbers rose in 2001 and 2002 but fell by 10% in 2002 to 346 000. In 2003 western European countries made the bulk of decisions (87.9%); the proportions for southern and central and eastern Europe were 7.4% and 4.7% respectively, indicating clearly where the main asylum pressure falls. France, Germany and the UK were the leading countries, each making about the same number of decisions.

Recognition rates vary considerably, across countries and over time for both full Refugee Convention and other humanitarian status. In the four years 2000-03 the proportion granted Refugee Convention status fell from 15.7% to 8.5%. Recognition on other humanitarian grounds also went down, from 14.7% to 7.9%. In contrast, refusal rates rose from 69.6% to 83.5%, the proportion being highest in the CEE region (87.7%) and lowest in southern Europe (75.9%).

There were considerable variations in full Refugee Convention recognition rates between countries, with Turkey, Austria and Belgium having the highest rates. In most countries, fewer than one in ten was recognised as deserving full asylum status. In the most recent year, 2003, Turkey had the highest recognition rate. The three countries

relevés étaient trop faibles pour parler de tendance; pour les autres, trois ont enregistré une diminution et trois une augmentation. Les Républiques tchèque et slovaque étaient les destinations les plus attractives, puisqu'elles réunissaient environ deux tiers des demandes enregistrées dans toute la région, dépassant désormais les niveaux enregistrés dans plusieurs pays d'Europe occidentale.

7.4. Evolution des décisions relatives aux demandes d'asile, 1995-2003

Il est difficile d'interpréter les statistiques sur les demandes d'asile en raison du délai qui s'écoule entre le dépôt de la demande et la décision qui est prise à son sujet. Une autre complication tient à la procédure de recours qui peut générer plusieurs «décisions» concernant une même demande. La manière dont elles sont comptabilisées dans les statistiques affecte le taux de reconnaissance. Le tableau 16, établi d'après les données du HCR, indique le nombre de décisions en matière d'asile concernant des pays déterminés, ainsi que le nombre et la proportion de demandeurs qui ont obtenu le statut de réfugié prévu par la Convention des Nations Unies de 1951 ou un autre statut humanitaire et de ceux qui ont été déboutés.

Au cours de la période 2000-2003, 1,47 million de décisions ont été prises. Ces chiffres ont augmenté en 2001 et 2002, puis ont diminué de 10 % en 2003, avec 346 000 décisions. En 2003, les pays d'Europe occidentale ont représenté l'essentiel des décisions rendues (87,9 %), contre 7,4 % pour l'Europe méridionale et 4,7 % pour l'Europe centrale et orientale, ce qui montre clairement les pays où s'exerce principalement la pression de l'asile. La France, l'Allemagne et le Royaume-Uni étaient en tête, chacun de ces pays rendant à peu près le même nombre de décisions.

Le pourcentage de demandes acceptées varie considérablement selon les pays et les périodes, aussi bien pour le statut complet prévu par la convention sur les réfugiés que pour d'autres statuts humanitaires. Au cours des quatre années de 2000 à 2003, la proportion des demandeurs qui ont obtenu le statut de la convention sur les réfugiés est tombée de 15,7 % à 8,5 %. L'octroi du statut pour d'autres raisons humanitaires est également tombé de 14,7 % à 7,9 % des demandes. Inversement, le taux de refus est passé de 69,6 % à 83,5 %, la proportion étant plus élevée dans les Peco (87,7 %) et plus faible en Europe méridionale (75,9 %).

Pour ce qui est de la pleine reconnaissance du statut de réfugié accordé par la convention, les variations ont été considérables d'un pays à l'autre, la Turquie, l'Autriche et la Belgique ayant les taux d'acceptation les plus élevés. Dans la plupart des pays, moins d'un demandeur sur dix s'est vu octroyer le droit d'asile à part entière. En 2003, la Turquie a

making the most decisions – UK, France and Germany – had only modest recognition rates, 14.1%, 8.0% and 4.3% respectively.

Full asylum is not the only protection status, although appropriate statistics are less systematically available. Most countries have some form of humanitarian ("B") status, granting asylum on humanitarian grounds but without full refugee rights. In those that do, the proportions are generally higher than of those granted full Refugee Convention status; this seems to be the case across Europe as a whole. In a few countries in 2003, including some making only a small number of decisions, humanitarian status was given in approaching half of all decisions.

Refusal rates of over 90% were not uncommon, especially in the CEE region. Countries with such high refusal rates were Germany, Ireland, Greece, the Czech and Slovak Republics, Poland and Romania. It should be pointed out, however, that these figures are for initial decisions only and in some countries the final refusal rate is lower as individual applications are granted after appeal.

Various forms of temporary protection have been offered by European governments in recent years, mainly to citizens of the former Yugoslavia. Such schemes are beyond the UNHCR convention system and other formal humanitarian statuses and assume that once conflict ends those given protection will return home.

7.5. Asylum applications by unaccompanied minors

A subject of concern to a number of governments, intergovernmental organisations (IGOs) and humanitarian organisations in recent years has been the growing number of unaccompanied minors applying for asylum. Many of these would seem to have been smuggled or trafficked and they present particular problems for the authorities who have to deal with them, including the need for special housing and educational arrangements. In 2001 and 2002 in Europe as a whole the numbers of unaccompanied minors and separated children claiming asylum rose to over 20 000 but in 2003 they fell steeply to 12 781 (Table 17). This fall in absolute numbers was echoed in their importance as a proportion of all asylum applications, down from 5.4% in 2002 to 4.2% in 2003. The fall between 2002 and 2003 (-37%) was greater than that in total asylum applications at the same time.

dominé les statistiques quant au pourcentage de décisions accordant le droit d'asile. Dans les trois pays qui ont pris le plus de décisions – le Royaume-Uni, la France et l'Allemagne –, le taux de demandes acceptées était faible, avec respectivement 14,1 %, 8,0 % et 4,3 %.

Le droit d'asile au sens plein du terme n'est pas le seul statut de protection, bien qu'il soit plus difficile d'obtenir des statistiques fiables sur les autres formes. La plupart des pays ont une forme ou une autre de statut humanitaire («B»), accordant le droit d'asile pour des motifs humanitaires mais sans y associer l'intégralité des droits reconnus aux réfugiés. Pour les pays dans lesquels de tels statuts existent, ils sont plus fréquemment accordés que la pleine protection prévue par la convention sur les réfugiés, ce qui semble être le cas dans toute l'Europe. En 2003, dans quelques pays, y compris les pays qui ne rendent qu'un petit nombre de décisions, un statut humanitaire a été accordé dans pratiquement la moitié des cas examinés.

Des taux de refus dépassant les 90 % n'étaient pas rares, en particulier dans les Peco. Ce niveau de refus était constaté en Allemagne, en Irlande, en Grèce, en République tchèque, en Slovaquie, en Pologne et en Roumanie. Il faut toutefois signaler que ces chiffres ne concernent que les décisions initiales et que, dans certains pays, le taux de refus définitif est plus faible, certaines demandes étant acceptées en appel.

Diverses formes de protection temporaire ont été proposées par les gouvernements européens ces dernières années, essentiellement aux citoyens de l'ex-Yougoslavie. De telles formules dépassent la convention du HCR et d'autres statuts humanitaires formels partent du principe qu'à la fin du conflit les personnes bénéficiant d'une protection retourneront dans leur pays.

7.5. Demandes d'asile présentées par des mineurs non accompagnés

Depuis quelques années, beaucoup de gouvernement, d'organisations internationales gouvernementales et d'organisations humanitaires s'inquiètent du nombre croissant de mineurs non accompagnés qui demandent l'asile. Dans de nombreux cas, ils sont arrivés clandestinement ou sont victimes de trafics et posent des problèmes particuliers aux autorités qui doivent les prendre en charge, notamment pour ce qui est des questions d'hébergement et d'éducation. En 2001 et 2002, plus de 20 000 mineurs non accompagnés et enfants séparés de leurs familles ont demandé l'asile dans toute l'Europe; en 2003, ce nombre a fortement chuté, pour s'établir à 12 781 (tableau 17). Cette baisse en valeur absolue reflète aussi la diminution proportionnelle de ces demandes par rapport au total des demandes d'asile, dont elles représentaient 4,2 % en 2003, contre 5,4 % en 2002. Cette baisse entre 2002

The data record some marked imbalances between destination countries as well as in trends over the period. Three main destinations stand out: Austria, the Netherlands and the UK. In 2000 the Netherlands received the largest number (6 705), where they accounted for 15.3% of all applications. In succeeding years the number and proportion fell significantly to 1 216 in 2003, 9.1% of all applications. In contrast, applications to Austria rose after 2000, falling back in 2003 but with still over 2 000. Applications to the UK, already high in number in 2000, rose in the two succeeding years to peak in 2002 before falling to under 3 000 in 2003 when they accounted for 5.7% of all asylum applications. Other countries experienced marked fluctuations, notably Hungary where in 2001 they accounted for over a fifth of all asylum applications. In Germany, numbers increased in 2001, fell in 2002 but rose again in the most recent year; however, they formed only a very small proportion of all applications. Although the totals for 2003 are modest for most countries compared with earlier years, it was common for these applications to be between 5% and 10% of the national total.

et 2003 (– 37 %) était plus importante que celle de l'ensemble des demandes d'asile pour la même période.

Les données révèlent des déséquilibres marqués entre les pays de destination, de même qu'en ce qui concerne les tendances observées sur la période. Trois principaux pays de destination se détachent nettement: l'Autriche, les Pays-Bas et le Royaume-Uni. En 2000, ce sont les Pays-Bas qui ont accueilli le plus de mineurs non accompagnés (6 705), qui ont représenté, cette année-là, 15,3 % des demandes enregistrées dans le pays. Les années suivantes, leur nombre ainsi que leur part du total ont diminué de manière significative, pour atteindre 1 216 en 2003, soit 9,1 % des demandes. En revanche, en Autriche, le nombre de ces demandes enregistrées en 2000 a augmenté, avant de retomber en 2003, en restant toutefois supérieur à 2 000. Au Royaume-Uni, le nombre des demandes, déjà élevé en 2000, a continué d'augmenter les deux années suivantes, pour retomber au-dessous des 3 000 en 2003, ce qui représentait 5,7 % du total des demandes d'asile. D'autres pays ont observé des fluctuations importantes, notamment la Hongrie, où ces demandes représentaient plus de 20 % des demandes d'asile en 2001. En Allemagne, le nombre de demandes a augmenté en 2001, diminué en 2002, puis augmenté à nouveau au cours de la dernière année étudiée; elles ne représentent cependant qu'une très faible proportion des demandes totales. Si, dans la plupart des pays, le total de ces demandes enregistrée en 2003 est modeste comparé aux années précédentes, elles représentent néanmoins souvent de 5 % à 10 % du nombre total de demandes.

8. Migration of expertise

8.1. Introduction: the global migration market for skills

The last two decades have seen the emergence of a global migration market for skills. It affects all levels of skill but the real competition is for those with high levels of human expertise and there is now a complex pattern of movement by professional, managerial and technical staff. Since these movements are multi-directional, involving most states to a greater or lesser degree, we may call them "international brain exchanges". Some countries are now more active than others in seeking to make net gains from these exchanges.

The main stimuli for competition in the global migration market has come from governments and multinational employers. Some national health systems are also competing for medical staff. Competition was led in the 1980s by Australia and Canada, followed in the 1990s by the United States. Europe held itself largely aloof until late in the 1990s with little action and almost no debate about competition in the migration skills market. The shortage of information technology (IT) workers in particular prompted European governments to adopt more proactive policies to compete. Employers worldwide are now facing the problem of integrating new processes and technologies which require specific skills but are finding they must compete internationally, where their main competitors are OECD states but with India and China increasingly visible in this regard.

8.2. The main market forces

The migration market for expertise has two main drivers. The first is the attempt to increase the national bank of expertise through the acquisition of high-level human resources; the other is the development of policies to counter specific skill shortages. Both of these are designed to increase the competitiveness of individual businesses and national economies in general.

8.2.1. Gathering expertise

Underlying the first of these is evidence that highly skilled migrants bring economic benefits to the host economy. Although some of the

8. Migration de compétences

8.1. Introduction: le marché migratoire international pour les compétences

Les deux dernières décennies ont vu émerger un marché migratoire mondial des compétences. Ce marché affecte tous les niveaux de connaissances, mais surtout les personnes hautement qualifiées, pour lesquelles les pays sont en concurrence, et il existe actuellement un schéma complexe de mobilité de professionnels, de cadres et de techniciens. Parce que ces mouvements sont multidirectionnels et concernent la plupart des Etats à un degré plus ou moins important, nous pouvons les qualifier d'«échanges internationaux de cerveaux». Certains pays sont aujourd'hui plus actifs que d'autres dans leurs efforts pour tirer un bénéfice net de tels échanges.

La concurrence sur le marché migratoire international est encouragée par les gouvernements et les multinationales. Certains systèmes de santé nationaux font aussi la course au personnel médical. La concurrence a été inaugurée dans les années 1980 par l'Australie et le Canada, suivis dans les années 1990 par les Etats-Unis. Jusqu'à la fin des années 1990, l'Europe s'est largement tenue à l'écart de ce mouvement, n'intervenant que très rarement et évitant de débattre de la concurrence sur le marché migratoire des compétences. C'est la pénurie de spécialistes des technologies de l'information qui a, en particulier, incité les gouvernements à adopter des politiques de concurrence davantage proactives. Les employeurs du monde entier se trouvent aujourd'hui confrontés à la nécessité d'utiliser de nouveaux procédés et de nouvelles technologies qui réclament des compétences spécifiques et ils se rendent compte qu'ils doivent être compétitifs au plan international, où leurs principaux concurrents sont les pays de l'OCDE, l'Inde et la Chine devenant cependant de plus en plus visibles dans ce domaine.

8.2. Les principales forces du marché

Le marché migratoire international pour les compétences est mû par deux facteurs principaux: une tentative pour augmenter le réservoir national de compétences par l'acquisition de ressources humaines de haut niveau et l'élaboration de politiques visant à résoudre le manque de compétences spécifiques. Ces deux approches ont pour objectif d'accroître la compétitivité des entreprises et des économies nationales en général.

8.2.1. Accumulation de compétences

Le premier facteur repose sur la prémisse selon laquelle des migrants très qualifiés sont sources de bénéfices financiers pour l'économie du

results are ambiguous or contradictory (see, for example, Coleman and Rowthorn, 2004), studies from as far afield as the UK, Denmark, Germany, Australia, Singapore and the United States have shown that the higher the skill level of immigrants, the greater the likelihood of net fiscal gains to the economy (Gott and Johnston, 2002). Put bluntly, the more skilled the immigrants, the greater the economic benefit on the whole.

Studies also show that the fiscal effects vary by national origin of the migrants, with higher benefits flowing from those coming from high GDP countries. Thus, it is not surprising that those countries which still seek to attract permanent immigrants, notably Australia, Canada, New Zealand and the United States, have been putting increasing emphasis on the skilled entry route. Among the main drivers are opportunities for high-tech entrepreneurship: by 1998, for example, Chinese and Indian engineers were running a quarter of Silicon Valley's high technology businesses, their companies providing 58 000 jobs. Others include the globalisation of corporate activities and the development by multinationals of global conditions of service to go with global career paths.

Other countries are following suit. The UK's new Highly Skilled Migrant Programme, which began in January 2002, is designed to allow people of high human capital to migrate to the UK in order to seek and take up work. In effect, it encourages highly skilled foreigners to nominate themselves for immigration. It uses a points system based on educational qualifications, work experience, past earnings, achievements in chosen fields and whether the skill is a priority area (the last is mainly for qualified overseas doctors). Four main groups dominate those entering under the scheme: finance (including accountancy, banking, investment, etc.); business management (including consultants, directors and executives); information and communication technology (ICT) (including software engineers, computer specialists and telecommunications specialists); and medical occupations.

8.2.2. Specific skill shortages

Work permit systems have long existed to bring in skills from abroad that are in short supply. Mostly they have been seen as short-term measures to deal with temporary shortages, or to bring in specialists and corporate assignees. Nowadays, many developed countries have shortage lists for specific skills and have adopted new government

pays d'accueil. Bien que certaines de leurs conclusions soient ambiguës ou contradictoires (voir, par exemple, Coleman et Rowthorn, 2004), des études menées dans des pays aussi divers que le Royaume-Uni, le Danemark, l'Allemagne, l'Australie, Singapour et les Etats-Unis ont prouvé que plus le niveau de compétences des immigrés est élevé, plus la probabilité de bénéfices financiers nets pour l'économie est élevée (Gott et Johnston, 2002). Autrement dit, plus les immigrés sont qualifiés, plus le bénéfice économique est important.

Les études montrent également que les retombées financières varient selon l'origine des migrants, les plus grands bénéfices étant apportés par les migrants des pays dont le PIB est élevé. Il n'est donc pas surprenant que les pays qui cherchent encore à attirer des immigrés permanents, notamment l'Australie, le Canada, la Nouvelle-Zélande et les Etats-Unis, mettent de plus en plus l'accent sur les possibilités d'accès réservées aux personnes très qualifiées. Parmi les principales motivations figurent les opportunités offertes aux entrepreneurs de secteurs de pointe: en 1998, par exemple, les ingénieurs chinois et indiens dirigeaient le quart des entreprises de haute technologie de la Silicon Valley, leurs entreprises fournissaient 58 000 emplois. D'autres incluent la mondialisation des activités des sociétés et la création par les multinationales d'emplois internationaux associés à des perspectives de carrières internationales.

D'autres pays ont suivi. Le nouveau *Highly Skilled Migrant Programme* du Royaume-Uni, qui a débuté en janvier 2002, vise à permettre à des personnes représentant un capital humain élevé d'immigrer au Royaume-Uni afin d'y chercher et d'y exercer un emploi; il encourage en fait les étrangers très qualifiés à se déclarer eux-mêmes candidats à l'immigration. Il repose sur un système de points prenant en compte les diplômes universitaires, l'expérience professionnelle, les gains précédents, les réalisations dans des domaines déterminés et également des compétences prioritaires (celles-ci concernant essentiellement les médecins étrangers diplômés). Les personnes immigrant au titre de ce programme se répartissent en quatre groupes principaux: finance (comptabilité, banque, investissements, etc.), dirigeants d'entreprises (consultants, directeurs et cadres supérieurs), TCI (ingénieurs *software*, spécialistes de l'informatique et des télécommunications) et secteur médical.

8.2.2. Pénurie de compétences spécifiques

Les permis de travail existent depuis longtemps et sont un moyen pour les pays de s'assurer des compétences de l'étranger quand celles-ci sont déficitaires chez eux. Ils ont été le plus souvent perçus comme des mesures à court terme pour résoudre des carences temporaires ou faire venir des spécialistes et des cessionnaires de sociétés. Aujourd'hui, de nombreux pays industrialisés répertorient les compétences spécifiques

schemes or programmes to deal with them. Skill shortages can occur because of the inefficiencies of the international labour market and because of mismatches caused by growth in demand outstripping local training capability or by an inadequacy of supply at the prevailing wage rate. In many countries in recent years, substantial skill shortages have occurred among two groups in particular: the ICT sector (including those working as practitioners and as users); and the more skilled end of public services, especially health (particularly nurses) and education. Developing strategies and procedures to recruit specific skills in shortage occupations has been predominantly employer led, with governments acting as facilitators.

One of the best known examples of a scheme designed to attract specific skills has been put into operation in Germany. Foreigners with an ICT related degree or who have graduated from German universities with an ICT degree can apply for a "Green Card". Those without an ICT degree can apply if their ability in the field is confirmed by an agreement of an annual salary of over 100 000 DM (€51 130). The permit is valid for a maximum of five years and applications will be accepted until January 2005. Up to the beginning of 2004 around 16 000 permits had been granted. Permit holders can switch employers in Germany without a labour market test to check whether a German or EU specialist is available to fill the vacancy. Recent changes to German immigration law have facilitated the entry of highly-skilled workers, such as computer and senior business staff, engineers and researchers.

The idea that in a tight job market the demand for staff can be met by rising inflows of foreign workers has attracted attention in the media and among market analysts and consultants. How successful this might be as a solution is unclear. For ICT skills the market downturn since 2001 has demonstrated that the migration solution may not be a permanent requirement and has focused attention on how best countries might manage temporary migration programmes.

8.3. Expatriate numbers and education levels

Comprehensive information on the skill levels of migrants remains elusive. Work permit systems provide some idea but they exclude the

qui leur font défaut et adoptent de nouveaux systèmes ou programmes gouvernementaux pour les trouver. Il peut y avoir une pénurie de compétences par suite du manque d'efficacité du marché du travail international et des disparités dues à une plus forte demande, supérieure aux possibilités de formation locale, ou encore à l'inadéquation de l'offre au taux de salaire en vigueur. Ces dernières années, de nombreux pays ont connu une forte pénurie de compétences dans deux secteurs en particulier: l'informatique (aussi bien pour ce qui est des praticiens que des utilisateurs) et les domaines les plus qualifiés des services publics, en particulier la santé (essentiellement les infirmiers) et l'éducation. Les stratégies et les méthodes pour recruter des personnes possédant des qualifications spécifiques dans les professions en déficit ont été élaborées essentiellement par les employeurs, les gouvernements jouant le rôle de médiateurs.

L'une des mesures les plus connues pour attirer des compétences spécifiques a été mise en œuvre en Allemagne. Des étrangers possédant un diplôme en informatique ou qui ont fait des études d'informatique dans une université allemande peuvent demander une «carte verte». Ceux qui ne possèdent pas de diplôme d'informatique peuvent la demander si leurs compétences dans ce domaine sont confirmées par un contrat pour un salaire annuel de plus de 100 000 deutsche marks (51 130 euros). Ce permis est valable cinq ans au maximum et les demandes seront reçues jusqu'en janvier 2005. Début 2004, environ 16 000 permis avaient ainsi été accordés. Les détenteurs de cette carte peuvent changer d'employeur en Allemagne sans qu'il soit nécessaire de vérifier auprès du marché de l'emploi si un spécialiste allemand ou de l'Union européenne est disponible pour occuper le poste vacant. De récentes modifications de la législation allemande sur l'immigration ont facilité l'entrée de travailleurs très qualifiés, comme les informaticiens, les cadres dirigeants d'entreprise, les ingénieurs et les chercheurs.

L'idée qui veut que dans un marché du travail étroit il soit possible de répondre à la demande de personnel par des flux croissants de travailleurs étrangers a retenu l'attention des médias ainsi que des analystes et consultants du marché. La solution est-elle efficace? C'est toute la question. S'agissant des compétences en informatique, le recul du marché depuis 2001 a prouvé que le recours à l'immigration peut ne pas être une nécessité permanente et a attiré l'attention sur la meilleure façon pour les pays de gérer les programmes de migrations temporaires.

8.3. Nombres d'expatriés et niveaux d'éducation

Il est toujours difficile d'obtenir des informations complètes sur les niveaux de qualification des immigrés. Les systèmes de permis de tra-

nationals of common labour market areas such as the EEA. Using census information on birthplace, the OECD has created a database for its member states on educational levels as a proxy for skill level, with tertiary education being regarded as a proxy measurement of the highly skilled (Dumont and Lemaitre, 2004). Table 18, derived from this database, shows the proportions of expatriates from the European countries listed resident in other OECD states. For western Europe as a whole there were almost 15.8 million expatriates, 26.2% of whom had a tertiary education and might thus be described as highly skilled. The proportions were lower for the central and "other" European regions, but still around a fifth.

In western Europe it was common for a third or more of expatriates from the countries listed to have a tertiary education and for more than a quarter of those from central Europe. Russian expatriates, modest in number compared with some other countries, were particularly likely to have a tertiary education. Comparison of these figures on expatriates with those on immigrants from other OECD states (Table 19) shows that most European members are net losers but that the picture changes significantly when movement from all countries to the OECD are included. For example, France and Germany send more highly skilled people to other OECD states than they receive, but when all source countries are considered they become net gainers.

8.4. Foreign students

One of the major migration growth industries in recent years has been that of international students. An increasing number of students are taking the opportunity to study abroad in a growing variety of courses and curricula. Improving language skills (especially English) is seen by many young people as a key to promotion to positions of responsibility. In addition, the cultural experience acquired while studying abroad is an additional advantage for young people wanting to get on in the job market. Studying abroad has become much easier as host countries have competed to attract foreign students and "education for trade" rather than "education for aid" is now commonplace in higher education systems. The internationalisation of education systems has resulted in more complex and varied degree and other programmes and a much more cosmopolitan student population (OECD,

vail permettent de se faire une idée, mais ils excluent les ressortissants des zones de libre circulation des travailleurs comme l'AELE. A partir des informations sur le lieu de naissance contenues dans les recensements, l'OCDE a créé une base de données pour ses Etats membres sur les niveaux d'éducation, lesquels sont un indicateur approximatif du niveau de qualification, le niveau d'étude supérieur permettant de supposer qu'une personne est hautement qualifiée (Dumont et Lemaitre, 2004). Le tableau 18, tiré de cette base de données, montre la proportion d'expatriés des pays européens inscrits comme résidents dans d'autres pays de l'OCDE. Pour l'ensemble de l'Europe occidentale, il y a, en tout, presque 15,8 millions d'expatriés, dont 26,2 % diplômés de l'enseignement supérieur, qui peuvent donc être décrits comme hautement qualifiés. La proportion est plus faible pour les pays d'Europe centrale et orientale, mais se situe tout de même aux environs de 20 %.

En Europe occidentale, au moins un tiers des expatriés venant des pays étudiés ont généralement un niveau d'études supérieures; cette proportion est de plus d'un quart pour les expatriés d'Europe centrale. Les expatriés russes, dont les contingents sont modestes comparés à ceux d'autres pays, ont très fréquemment un niveau d'études supérieures. La comparaison des données relatives aux expatriés avec celles concernant les immigrés venus d'autres pays de l'OCDE (tableau 19) montre que la plupart des pays européens accusent des pertes nettes; mais le tableau est très différent lorsque les mouvements en provenance de tous les pays à destination de l'OCDE sont pris en compte. Ainsi, la France et l'Allemagne envoient plus de personnes hautement qualifiées dans d'autres pays de l'OCDE qu'elles n'en reçoivent, mais lorsque tous les pays d'origine sont pris en compte, elles affichent un excédent net.

8.4. Etudiants étrangers

L'un des secteurs migratoires qui a connu la plus forte croissance ces dernières années est celui des étudiants internationaux. De plus en plus d'étudiants saisissent l'occasion d'aller étudier à l'étranger, pour suivre des formations et des cursus de plus en plus diversifiés. L'amélioration des connaissances linguistiques (essentiellement l'anglais) est considérée par de nombreux jeunes comme l'une des clés de l'accès à des postes à responsabilité. De plus, l'expérience culturelle acquise lors d'études à l'étranger est un avantage supplémentaire pour les jeunes qui veulent entrer sur le marché de l'emploi. Il est aujourd'hui beaucoup plus facile de faire des études dans un autre pays car les pays hôtes se concurrent pour attirer les étudiants étrangers; dans la plupart des systèmes d'enseignement supérieur, «l'éducation pour les affaires» a désormais fréquemment pris le dessus sur «l'éducation pour l'aide». L'internationalisation des systèmes éducatifs a

2001). There is a case for arguing that student mobility is another form of mobility by the highly skilled, given the potential for foreign students to enter the host country workforce upon graduation. Entry into the labour market is facilitated by their (usually) foreign language skills, their ability to adjust, their research and analytical capabilities and their familiarity with the customs and culture of the host country in which they have studied.

One area to which attention is increasingly being paid is that of "student switching", that is, allowing foreign graduates to switch status from education to workforce directly instead of having to return home at the conclusion of their studies. Australia, France, Germany, Norway and the UK have already done this. The German "Green Card" scheme has successfully sought to attract foreign graduates from German universities graduating with ICT-related degrees: 1 500 of the first 10 400 "Green Card" permits were granted to them. The French Government is keen to encourage student switching by foreign ICT graduates at French universities although there is little evidence of how successful this has been.

8.4.1. Trends in student migration

Numbers of students vary by country of origin and destination (Table 20). Country size and geographical proximity once again show the efficacy of the gravity model, but numerous other factors play a role, including EU policies on freedom of movement, recognition of degrees (currently under discussion in the Bologna process) and exchange and network programmes such as Erasmus/Socrates. OECD calculations (2001) indicate that certain countries, notably the UK, Austria, Denmark, France and Germany host large numbers of foreign students relative to their size. The existence of former student networks through institutional channels encourages chain movements.

There are several problems in compiling statistics on stocks of foreign students. They are a very heterogeneous group, with courses of varying content, length and different qualification requirements. Students come under a range of bilateral and multilateral agreements as well as under their own steam. Their statuses on arrival carry different

généré des diplômes et autres programmes plus complexes et variés, ainsi qu'une population étudiante beaucoup plus cosmopolite (OCDE, 2001). Il est sans doute justifié d'affirmer que la mobilité étudiante est une autre forme de mobilité des personnes hautement qualifiées, étant donné les possibilités d'intégration du marché du travail national ouvertes aux étudiants étrangers après l'obtention de leur diplôme. Leur entrée sur le marché du travail est facilitée par leurs connaissances (généralement bonnes) de langues étrangères, leur capacité d'adaptation, leurs aptitudes à la recherche et à l'analyse, et leur connaissance des coutumes et de la culture du pays dans lequel ils ont étudié.

Un domaine qui retient de plus en plus l'attention est celui du passage du statut d'étudiant à celui de travailleur, qui permet à des diplômés étrangers de passer directement de l'enseignement au travail sans avoir à retourner dans leur pays à la fin de leurs études. Ce système existe déjà en Australie, en France, en Allemagne, en Norvège et au Royaume-Uni. La formule allemande de la «carte verte» a cherché, avec succès, à attirer des étudiants étrangers des universités allemandes diplômés en informatique: ils se sont vu accorder 1 500 des 10 400 premières «cartes vertes». Le Gouvernement français encourage beaucoup les étudiants étrangers diplômés de ses universités en informatique à travailler en France, mais l'on connaît mal le résultat de cette démarche.

8.4.1. Tendances des migrations estudiantines

Les contingents d'étudiants migrateurs varient selon le pays d'origine et le pays de destination (tableau 20). La taille du pays et la proximité géographique montrent une fois de plus l'efficacité du modèle gravitationnel, mais de nombreux autres facteurs jouent un rôle, notamment les politiques de l'Union européenne pour la libre circulation, la reconnaissance des diplômes (actuellement à l'étude dans le cadre du Processus de Bologne), les programmes d'échanges et de coopération comme Erasmus ou Socrates. Les calculs de l'OCDE (2001) montrent que certains pays, en particulier le Royaume-Uni, l'Autriche, le Danemark, la France et l'Allemagne, accueillent un nombre important d'étudiants étrangers par rapport à leur taille. L'existence de réseaux d'anciens étudiants relayés par des canaux institutionnels encourage les mouvements en chaîne.

La compilation de statistiques sur les contingents d'étudiants étrangers pose plusieurs problèmes. Ceux-ci constituent en effet un groupe très hétérogène, avec des cursus de durée et de contenu variables et des conditions d'admission différentes. Ils arrivent au titre de toute une série d'accords bilatéraux ou multilatéraux ou de leur propre chef.

entitlements from country to country. Responsibility for counting their numbers falls to a range of administrative institutions, frequently using different definitions. In these circumstances, comparative data are indicative rather than absolute.

Despite these caveats, Table 20 is instructive. Overall, the total in 2001-02 for the countries listed was 1.06 million. The UK is the clear market leader but Germany and France are other major destinations. Outside western Europe, Russia has the largest number. There has been a clear upward trend in numbers, with only a few countries, mainly in central and "other" Europe, experiencing declines. For Europe as a whole the number rose by 19.5% over the period, a rate of increase exceeded by many countries, albeit in some case on small absolute numbers.

Data on annual flows of foreign students are patchy mainly because most countries do not collect them in a systematic way. Those that do exist are from a range of sources and provide only a partial picture of numbers and trends.

A leur arrivée, leur statut est assorti de droits variables d'un pays à l'autre. Leur dénombrement est de la responsabilité de diverses administrations, qui utilisent souvent des définitions différentes. Dans ces circonstances, les données comparatives ont, au mieux, une valeur indicative.

Malgré ces limites, le tableau 20 est riche d'enseignements. Au total, pour les pays figurant dans le tableau, le nombre d'étudiants étrangers recensés en 2001-2002 s'élevait à 1,06 million. Le Royaume-Uni domine nettement, mais l'Allemagne et la France sont d'autres grandes destinations. En dehors de l'Europe occidentale, c'est la Russie qui enregistre le plus grand nombre d'étudiants étrangers. La tendance est clairement à l'amplification du phénomène, sauf quelques pays, essentiellement en Europe centrale et orientale, enregistrant une diminution du nombre d'étudiants venus de l'étranger. Pour l'ensemble de l'Europe, l'augmentation a été de 19,5 % au cours de la période étudiée, taux qui a été dépassé dans de nombreux pays, même si, dans certains cas, les chiffres réels sont faibles.

Les données sur les flux annuels d'étudiants étrangers sont parcellaires, ce qui est surtout dû au fait que la plupart des pays ne les collectent pas de manière systématique. De plus, elles proviennent de diverses sources et ne donnent qu'une image partielle des effectifs et des tendances.

9. Irregular migration

The subject of illegal migration and particularly international trafficking and smuggling in human beings has captured a lot of attention in the last decade from many different interest groups. There are few parts of the world untouched by what may now be regarded as an expanding and usually criminal business always seeking out new markets. Many of the migrations under its auspices take place over extremely long distances; others are relatively local affairs.

It is clear that illegal migration, trafficking and human smuggling have the capacity to excite attention and divide opinion. The role of criminal organisations has been highlighted in a human trade on a par with drugs and arms smuggling, in both its profitability and perniciousness. Governments are increasingly co-operating to introduce measures to control what they deem to be an assault on their borders. Some politicians and media regard all illegal migrants as criminals, to be returned across borders as soon as possible. In contrast, human rights organisations argue that for many seeking asylum, traffickers and smugglers represent the best hope for safety and that the real victims are those migrants who have lost control of their own lives.

As the issues raised by irregular migration, especially migrant trafficking and human smuggling, have risen on the political agenda, so the enormous complexities inherent in them have become more apparent. In a very real sense, however, the rhetoric has run ahead of the research. There is a fundamental lack of hard evidence relating to most aspects of the problem. Methodologies for studying both traffickers/smugglers and their clientele are barely developed, the theoretical basis for analysis is weak and, most importantly, substantial empirical surveys are few and far between. Slowly, these deficiencies are being met. For example, two recent IOM studies have thrown light on the geographically pivotal role of Turkey with respect to irregular migration (İçduygu, 2003) and trafficking in women (Erder and Kaska, 2003). The ICMPD now carries out an annual survey and analysis of border management and apprehension data (ICMPD, 2004).

Previous reports have examined irregular migration, migrant trafficking and human smuggling at some length. After an initial review of

9. Immigration clandestine

Ces dix dernières années, l'immigration clandestine et en particulier le trafic international de main-d'œuvre et la contrebande humaine ont fortement retenu l'attention de très nombreux groupes d'intérêts. Peu de régions du monde sont à l'abri de ce que l'on peut aujourd'hui considérer comme une entreprise généralement criminelle et en forte expansion, sans cesse à la recherche de nouveaux marchés. Un grand nombre de migrations de ce type se font sur de très grandes distances, d'autres sont des activités relativement locales.

Il est clair que l'immigration clandestine, le trafic et la contrebande d'êtres humains ont le pouvoir d'attirer l'attention et de diviser l'opinion. On a souligné le rôle des organisations criminelles dans ce commerce humain, aussi rentable et aussi malfaisant que le trafic de drogue ou d'armes. Les gouvernements renforcent leur coopération pour introduire des mesures de lutte contre ce qu'ils estiment être une menace pour leurs frontières. Certains politiciens et certains médias considèrent tous les immigrés clandestins comme des délinquants qu'il convient de renvoyer chez eux le plus rapidement possible. En revanche, les organisations de défense des droits de l'homme estiment que, pour beaucoup de demandeurs d'asile, les trafiquants et les passeurs représentent le meilleur espoir de sécurité et que les véritables victimes sont ces migrants qui ont perdu tout contrôle sur leur propre vie.

A mesure que les problèmes soulevés par l'immigration clandestine, en particulier le trafic de migrants et la contrebande humaine, ont pris une importance croissante dans les programmes politiques, leur grande complexité est devenue plus apparente. Mais au sens réel du terme, la rhétorique a devancé la recherche. La plupart des aspects du problème ne sont corroborés par aucune preuve sérieuse. La méthodologie pour étudier les trafiquants/passeurs et leur clientèle est pratiquement inexistante, le fondement théorique nécessaire à l'analyse est insuffisant et, surtout, les quelques études empiriques sérieuses qui existent sont très espacées dans le temps. Ces lacunes sont comblées progressivement. Ainsi, deux études récentes de l'OIM ont mis en lumière le rôle de plaque tournante de la Turquie dans les migrations clandestines (Içduygu, 2003) et la traite des femmes (Erder et Kaska, 2003). L'ICMPD réalise maintenant une étude et une analyse annuelles des données relatives à la surveillance et aux arrestations aux frontières (ICMPD, 2004).

Les rapports précédents ont étudié assez longuement l'immigration clandestine, le trafic des migrants et la contrebande humaine. Après un bilan des tentatives pour évaluer l'ampleur du phénomène, on

attempts to assess the scale of the phenomena, the rest of the section looks at the findings of some recent studies.

9.1. The scale of the irregular population

Any attempt to measure this complex population is based on the simple principle that those people who are resident illegally will at some point manifest their identity in a researchable form. Due to the clandestine nature of the illegally resident population, all data types are substantially uncertain.

Futo and Tass (2002) identified four root causes for the lack of data on illegal immigration. Firstly, data collection on illegal migrants faces the problem of identifying and counting those people who have intentionally made themselves unobservable. Even apprehended illegal migrants will hide important personal data on their status to avoid removal. Secondly, information and data that may establish a person's illegal status are frequently dispersed between different agencies such as government departments, the police, employment offices etc., making access to data difficult. Thirdly, legal problems may also prohibit the counting of cases; for example, in some countries irregular entry itself is not a criminal offence, therefore criminal statistics may not sufficiently cover the phenomenon. Fourthly, country-specific legislation and definitions on legality and illegality result in a lack of internationally comparable data on illegal immigration.

The first thing that must be said is that no one knows the size of the illegal population stock across Europe or in individual countries. Attempts have been made in some countries to estimate the size of the irregular population, using a variety of methods and assumptions, and they should be regarded as indicative at best. Among recent ones are a figure of 569 000 illegal foreign workers in Italy (Baldassarini, 2001), 90 000 in Belgium (Poulain, 1998) and a range of 70 000 to 180 000 illegal workers in Switzerland (Piguet and Losa, 2002). It was estimated that 40 000 worked illegally in the four cities of Amsterdam, Rotterdam, The Hague and Utrecht (van der Leun, Engbersen and van der Heijden, 1998).

One of the main sources used as an indicator of numbers of migrants living or working in an irregular situation is the number who apply to regularise their status when an amnesty programme is introduced. One by-product of an amnesty is that it usually provides information on the illegal population. By implementing such a programme, the government

trouvera dans le reste de la section une analyse des conclusions auxquelles sont parvenues certaines études récentes.

9.1. Taille de la population clandestine

Toute tentative pour mesurer le nombre de cette population complexe repose sur le principe simple selon lequel les gens qui résident clandestinement dans un pays manifesteront tôt ou tard leur identité sous forme identifiable. Par suite du caractère clandestin de la population en situation irrégulière, aucun type de données n'est vraiment fiable.

Futo et Tass (2002) distinguent quatre causes principales du manque de données sur l'immigration clandestine. Premièrement, la collecte de données relatives aux immigrés clandestins se heurte au problème de l'identification et du comptage des personnes qui ont décidé de passer volontairement inaperçues. Les immigrés clandestins dissimulent même des renseignements personnels importants sur leur statut lorsqu'ils sont appréhendés afin d'éviter le renvoi. Deuxièmement, l'information et les données pouvant établir la clandestinité d'une personne sont souvent éparpillées entre différentes instances, tels les ministères, la police, les agences pour l'emploi, etc., rendant ainsi leur accès difficile. Troisièmement, des problèmes juridiques peuvent également aller à l'encontre de ces calculs; ainsi, dans certains pays, l'entrée clandestine n'est pas un délit en soi et les statistiques sur les infractions peuvent ne pas prendre suffisamment en compte le phénomène. Enfin, les différentes législations spécifiques à chaque pays et leur définition de la légalité et de l'illégalité conduisent à l'absence de données comparables au plan international en matière d'immigration clandestine.

Il nous faut commencer par admettre que personne ne connaît le nombre de clandestins en Europe ou dans les différents pays. Certains de ces pays ont cherché à évaluer l'ampleur de leur population clandestine par diverses méthodes et hypothèses, mais ces tentatives fournissent tout au plus des indications. Parmi ces indications, on retiendra le chiffre de 569 000 travailleurs étrangers clandestins en Italie (Baldassarini, 2001), 90 000 en Belgique (Poulain, 1998) et quelque 70 000 à 180 000 clandestins en Suisse (Piguet et Losa, 2002). On estime que 40 000 travailleurs sont employés clandestinement dans les quatre villes d'Amsterdam, Rotterdam, La Haye et Utrecht (Van der Leun, Engbersen et van der Heijden, 1998).

On peut estimer la taille de la population clandestine d'un pays à partir du nombre de régularisations effectuées à l'occasion de programmes d'amnistie. Par ailleurs, l'amnistie apporte généralement des informations sur les populations en situation irrégulière. Par la mise en œuvre d'un tel programme, le gouvernement peut déterminer le nombre et

is able to ascertain the number and whereabouts of irregular migrants, who they are, how they live and work and at what. In effect, the programme provides a means to estimate a minimum number for the stock of the illegal population until they are actually regularised.

Amnesty programmes have been a fairly common feature in Mediterranean countries during the last two decades and have occurred in some other countries. Analysis of regularisations up to the beginning of 2000 (Apap et al., 2000) suggests that the total number regularised in the programmes of Greece, France, Spain and Italy was 1.75 million. Since then further amnesties in southern Europe have resulted in approaching several hundred thousand more applications. Thus, in total, the numbers are considerable and, in the absence of better estimates, numbers regularised provide the most solid baseline for estimating the scale of irregular populations.

9.2. Trends in flows of irregular migrants

Most statistics on flows of irregular migrants come from border crossing data. The problems in using border crossing statistics to analyse the scale of illegal migration have attracted relatively little detailed comment, mainly because until recently so few studies have attempted to use them. Quite frequently there are differences of opinion between border guards and officials about the proportions of those trying to cross borders illegally who are apprehended (for Hungary, see Juhasz, 2000, and for Ukraine, Klinchenko, 2000). A further problem is what is actually to be measured. Juhasz's study (2000) used an "illegal crossing event" as the unit of measurement in creating a database of illegal migration to and from Hungary. Such an event occurs each time an individual is arrested. Creating a statistical record to fit the variety of potential situations soon makes the complexity apparent. Multiple events can occur for a single person who is arrested, sent back, tries again and is again caught.

In 2003 about 164 400 apprehensions were recorded at the borders of 17 CEE countries surveyed by the ICMPD (Table 21) (ICMPD, 2004). This represents a considerable reduction on the figures for 2001 and 2002. Between 2001 and 2002 total numbers recorded fell by 22.7%, then by a further 18.4% the following year. Relatively high numbers

les endroits où se trouvent les migrants en situation irrégulière, qui ils sont, comment ils vivent et travaillent, et quel genre de travail ils font. Ce programme est en fait un moyen d'évaluer la taille minimale de la population clandestine jusqu'à ce que la situation de ces personnes soit réellement régularisée.

Les programmes d'amnistie ont été relativement courants dans les pays méditerranéens au cours des deux dernières décennies et se sont développés dans certains autres pays. L'analyse des régularisations jusqu'au début de l'an 2000 (Apap *et al.*, 2000) indique que les programmes d'amnistie de la Grèce, de la France, de l'Espagne et de l'Italie ont permis à un total de 1,75 million de personnes de régulariser leur situation. Depuis, de nouvelles amnisties en Europe méridionale se sont traduites par le dépôt de plusieurs centaines de milliers de demandes. Au total, ces chiffres sont donc considérables et, en l'absence de meilleures estimations, le nombre des personnes dont la situation a été régularisée constitue la meilleure base d'évaluation du nombre de personnes en situation irrégulière.

9.2. Tendances des flux d'immigrants clandestins

La plupart des statistiques sur l'entrée d'immigrants clandestins provient des données relatives au franchissement des frontières. Les problèmes que pose l'utilisation de ces statistiques pour analyser l'ampleur du nombre de migrants clandestins n'ont guère fait l'objet de commentaires détaillés, surtout parce que, jusqu'à une date récente, très peu d'études ont tenté de les mettre à profit. Les avis des gardes-frontières et des responsables politiques sur le nombre de personnes arrêtées en tentant de franchir illégalement les frontières divergent très fréquemment (pour la Hongrie, voir Juhasz, 2000, et pour l'Ukraine, Klinchenko, 2000). Quant à savoir ce qu'il convient de mesurer, c'est un autre problème. L'étude de Juhasz (2000) a pris la «tentative de franchissement clandestin de la frontière» comme unité de mesure pour créer une banque de données sur la migration clandestine vers et en provenance de Hongrie. Un tel cas se produit chaque fois qu'une personne est arrêtée. La complexité ne tarde pas à apparaître lorsqu'on s'attache à concevoir des statistiques capables de répondre à la variété de situations possibles. De multiples situations peuvent se présenter pour la même personne qui est arrêtée, renvoyée, tente à nouveau sa chance et est arrêtée une deuxième fois.

En 2003, environ 164 400 arrestations ont été enregistrées aux frontières de dix-sept Peco étudiés par l'ICMPD (tableau 21) (ICMPD, 2004). Ce chiffre est en diminution considérable par rapport à 2001 et 2002. Le nombre total d'arrestations a diminué de 22,7 % entre 2001 et 2002, puis de 18,4 % l'année suivante. En 2003, un nombre relati-

of apprehensions in 2003 occurred at the borders of Turkey, Armenia, Hungary, the Czech and Slovak Republics and Ukraine. In most cases the trend for both years was downward, although a few countries did show increases.

Similar systematic data are available in published form for only some western European countries. Those in Table 22 have been compiled from several sources rather than one survey and they record different sorts of border action against irregular migration. The numbers vary from country to country. They fluctuate from one year to another but the most recent data generally show declines from the peaks of earlier years.

The trends in Tables 21 and 22 may be explained in a number of ways. The fall in numbers of apprehensions may be because there are fewer irregular migrants attempting to cross borders. This may be the result of better border management which has deterred attempted crossings. It may in some cases be a consequence of a slackening in visa regimes as was the case for Romanian travellers after 2002 (ICMPD, 2004). There may also have been diversion of flows into other routes and channels: this might explain the big increase in apprehensions in Cyprus in 2003 and frequent press reports of a surge in apprehensions in the Canary Islands in 2004-05.

On the face of it, however, the data here do not support the view that irregular migration flows are on the increase; indeed, they suggest the reverse.

9.3. Characteristics of irregular migrants

The ICMPD survey shows that most illegal migrants are still single males aged 20 to 45 and that cases of complete families with young children are fewer than five years ago. About a fifth are female and a twelfth are minors, both proportions having been increasing.

The geographical distribution of flows has become more complex as irregular migrants and their facilitators develop new routes in response to governmental measures against them. In consequence, although the main direction of movement is still towards western Europe, there are no longer such clear-cut migration routes. It also seems that a substantial number of apprehensions are of return migrants who travelled legally but then overstayed their visas. There

vement élevé d'arrestations a été enregistré aux frontières de la Turquie, de l'Arménie, de la Hongrie, de la République tchèque, de la Slovaquie et de l'Ukraine. Dans la plupart des cas, la tendance pour les deux années était à la baisse, bien que quelques pays aient connu une augmentation.

En Europe occidentale, seuls quelques pays publient des données systématiques similaires. Celles qui figurent dans le tableau 22 ont été compilées à partir de plusieurs sources plutôt que d'une seule étude et recensent différentes sortes d'interventions aux frontières contre l'immigration clandestine. Les chiffres varient d'un pays à l'autre et d'une année sur l'autre, mais les données les plus récentes montrent en général une diminution par rapport aux pics des années précédentes.

Les tendances qui se dégagent des tableaux 21 et 22 peuvent s'expliquer de plusieurs manières. La baisse du nombre d'arrestations peut être due au fait que moins de clandestins tentent de franchir les frontières ou que la surveillance de ces dernières s'est améliorée, dissuadant ainsi les tentatives de franchissement illégal. Dans certains cas, elle peut être la conséquence d'un assouplissement du régime des visas, comme ce fut le cas pour les voyageurs roumains après 2002 (ICMPD, 2004). Elle peut aussi être due à la réorientation des flux vers d'autres itinéraires et canaux, ce qui pourrait expliquer la forte augmentation du nombre d'arrestations à Chypre, en 2003, et la multiplication des dépêches signalant des arrestations aux Canaries en 2004-2005.

Toutefois, de prime abord, les données ne semblent pas étayer les affirmations selon lesquelles les flux de migrants clandestins seraient en augmentation; elles indiqueraient même plutôt l'inverse.

9.3. Caractéristiques des migrants clandestins

L'étude de l'ICMPD montre que la plupart des migrants clandestins sont des hommes, célibataires, âgés de 20 à 45 ans, et que le nombre de familles complètes avec des jeunes enfants est inférieur à ce qu'il était il y a cinq ans. Environ un cinquième des clandestins sont des femmes et un douzième des mineurs, ces deux catégories ayant vu leur part relative augmenter.

La distribution géographique des flux est devenue plus complexe: les migrants clandestins et ceux qui facilitent leur entreprise inaugurent de nouveaux itinéraires en réaction aux mesures de lutte prises par les gouvernements. En conséquence, bien que le mouvement général se fasse toujours à destination de l'Europe occidentale, il n'y a plus d'itinéraires de migration clairement établis. Il semble en outre qu'un nombre non négligeable d'arrestations concernent des migrants sur le

are three main origin regions. The largest is the former Soviet Union, the main groups being those with Russian citizenship (especially Chechens). The second largest group is from the Middle East, Central Asia, China and the Indian sub-continent. A declining proportion of this group comes from places of armed conflict. The smallest group is from the CEE region itself. Formerly the largest groups were from Romania and the former Yugoslavia, but numbers of these have fallen.

9.4. The scale of migrant trafficking and human smuggling

There is a paucity of data on how many irregular migrants are smuggled or trafficked and those that exist come from a wide range of sources (Laczko and Gramegna, 2003). Even when numbers trafficked are presented, they tend to be low, usually measured in hundreds, and a far cry from the tens and hundreds of thousands often quoted (ibid.).

Table 23 is an attempt to bring together the various estimates made of the scale of smuggling and trafficking at the global and European level. Globally, numbers are put at 4 million annually, including up to 2 million women and children. Estimates for the EU as far apart as 1993 and 1999 give the same range of 50000 to 400000 for both sexes. Numbers of women smuggled and trafficked annually into the EU and central and eastern Europe have been put at 300000. Still regarded as the most authoritative annual estimate – because the assumptions upon which it was based are available – is Widgren's 100000 to 220000 in 1994.

Rarely is it clear how the estimates have been derived, though in general they rely on assumptions about the ratio between those apprehended at borders and those who succeed in getting through undetected. Thus, Heckmann and Wunderlich (2000) derive their estimate of the number trafficked and smuggled into the EU (400 000 in 1999) from apprehension statistics. For every one person caught entering the EU illegally (260 000), it is assumed two pass unhindered.

Estimating how many illegal crossings are trafficked or smuggled presents further difficulties. Incidences of trafficking are probably

retour, qui sont venus légalement mais qui ont dépassé la durée de validité de leur visa. Il y a trois grandes régions d'origine: la principale est l'ex-Union soviétique, les principaux groupes étant constitués par des personnes ayant la nationalité russe (particulièrement des Tchétchènes). La deuxième région est constituée par le Moyen-Orient, l'Asie centrale, la Chine et le sous-continent indien. La part des personnes de cette région venant de zones en proie à des conflits armés est en diminution. Les flux les moins importants proviennent des Peco eux-mêmes. Auparavant, les groupes les plus nombreux venaient de Roumanie et de l'ancienne Yougoslavie, mais leur nombre a chuté.

9.4. Ampleur du trafic de main-d'œuvre et de la contrebande humaine

Les données sur le nombre de migrants clandestins qui font l'objet d'une contrebande ou d'un trafic sont rares et celles qui sont disponibles proviennent d'une grande variété de sources (Laczko et Gramegna, 2003). Même lorsque des chiffres sont donnés sur le nombre de personnes introduites clandestinement, ils sont souvent faibles, en général présentés en centaines, bien loin des dizaines et centaines de milliers souvent annoncés *(ibid.)*.

Le tableau 23 constitue une tentative pour rassembler les différentes estimations de l'ampleur du trafic et de la contrebande aux niveaux mondial et européen. Au niveau mondial, les chiffres avancés sont de 4 millions de personnes concernées chaque année, dont quelque 2 millions de femmes et d'enfants. Pour l'Union européenne, les estimations pour des années aussi éloignées que 1993 et 1999 sont dans la fourchette de 50 000 à 400 000 personnes pour les deux sexes. Le nombre de femmes introduites dans l'Union et l'Europe centrale et orientale dans le cadre d'un trafic ou en contrebande a été évalué à 300 000. L'estimation annuelle toujours considérée comme la plus fiable, parce que l'on connaît les hypothèses sur lesquelles elle est fondée, reste celle faite par Widgren pour l'année 1994, avec un chiffre de 100 000 à 200 000 personnes.

On ignore souvent comment les estimations ont été calculées, bien qu'elles reposent en général sur des hypothèses concernant le rapport entre les personnes appréhendées aux frontières et celles qui réussissent à passer sans se faire repérer. Ainsi, Heckmann et Wunderlich (2000) basent leur estimation du nombre de personnes introduites clandestinement par trafic ou contrebande dans l'Union (400 000 en 1999) sur les statistiques relatives aux interpellations. Ils supposent que pour chaque personne prise à entrer clandestinement dans l'Union (260 000 au total), deux passent sans encombre.

L'estimation du nombre de passages clandestins dus au trafic ou à la contrebande présente d'autres difficultés. La fréquence du trafic est

severely underestimated in data of illegal border crossings since the involvement of a smuggler is registered only if he or she is caught, or if an immigrant admits to having been assisted by a smuggler. Several countries in the CEE region report recent increases in smuggling through official road border crossings, with migrants hidden in the back of lorries or using forged documents.

9.5. Payments to smugglers and traffickers

Payments are very variable, depending on such factors as distance travelled, scale of the facilitating organisation, destination and conditions of travel. Table 24 was compiled by the Migration Research Unit at University College London (UCL) from nearly 600 reported cases in the literature/media worldwide since the mid-1990s (Petros, 2004). On average, the most costly moves are from Asia to the Americas, followed by Asia to Europe. In comparison, moves within Africa are cheap. The aggregate figures in the table are consistent with those reported by ICMPD for flows into the Schengen space: examples, include US$10 000 to US$15 000 from China and US$4 000 to US$6 000 from Afghanistan; €5 000 to €10 000 from Ukraine and €1 500 to €2 000 from Moldova.

There is little evidence from the UCL data that smuggling and trafficking costs are increasing or falling. However, it appears from the ICMPD survey that although the overall number of border apprehensions has been falling, detection rates for smuggling and trafficking have remained high and may have risen and that a greater proportion of irregular migrants transiting the area use the services of facilitators than hitherto.

9.6. Trafficking in women

Much energy has been expended by governments, NGOs, IGOs and academics in writing about trafficking in women and children, one study pointing out that something like 40% of the literature on trafficking and smuggling in Europe was addressed to this subject (Salt and Hogarth, 2000). However, both statistical data and empirical research are still lacking. Thus, although the European Commission reported estimates of up to 120 000 women and children trafficked into western Europe each year, no clear basis for the calculation exists.

Because of the paucity of good data, it is by no means clear if the scale of trafficking is increasing. German statistics show a fall in the number

probablement grandement sous-estimée, dans les statistiques relatives au franchissement illicite de la frontière, du fait que la participation du passeur n'est enregistrée que s'il est pris ou si un immigré reconnaît que ce dernier l'a aidé. Plusieurs pays d'Europe centrale et orientale signalent une augmentation récente de la contrebande empruntant les postes frontières routiers classiques, les migrants étant cachés à l'arrière de camions ou munis de faux papiers.

9.5. Sommes versées aux contrebandiers et trafiquants

Les montants versés sont très variables; ils dépendent de facteurs tels que la distance parcourue, de l'ampleur de l'organisation nécessaire, de la destination et des conditions de voyage. Le tableau 24 a été compilé par l'Unité de recherche sur les migrations de l'UCL (University College London) à partir de pratiquement 600 cas relevés dans la documentation et les médias de par le monde depuis le milieu des années 1990 (Petros, 2004). En moyenne, les trajets les plus chers sont ceux qui vont d'Asie vers le continent américain, suivis par les trajets d'Asie en Europe. En comparaison, les déplacements internes à l'Afrique sont peu coûteux. Les chiffres fournis dans ce tableau correspondent à ceux communiqués par l'ICMPD pour les flux à destination de l'espace Schengen: à titre d'exemple, le voyage depuis la Chine va de US$10 000 à US$15 000, de US$4 000 à US$6 000 depuis l'Afghanistan, de €5 000 à €10 000 depuis l'Ukraine et de €1 500 à €2 000 depuis la Moldova.

Il est difficile de savoir, à partir des données de l'UCL, si le coût de la contrebande et du trafic augmente ou baisse. Il ressort cependant de l'étude de l'ICMPD que, en dépit de la diminution du nombre total d'interceptions aux frontières, le taux de détection de la contrebande et du trafic reste élevé, qu'il a peut-être même augmenté et que la proportion des migrants clandestins qui recourent aux services de passeurs est plus importante qu'auparavant.

9.6. Le trafic de femmes

Les gouvernements, les ONG, les OIG et les universitaires ont dépensé beaucoup d'énergie pour dénoncer le trafic de femmes et d'enfants dans leurs publications. Une étude a souligné que quelque 40 % des écrits sur le trafic et la contrebande en Europe sont consacrés à ce sujet (Salt et Hogarth, 2000). Mais les statistiques et la recherche empirique font toujours défaut. Aussi, bien que la Commission européenne ait estimé que le trafic de femmes et d'enfants en Europe concernait 120 000 personnes par an, ce chiffre ne repose sur aucun fondement précis.

Parce les données fiables sont rares, il n'est pas possible de savoir si le trafic se développe. Les statistiques allemandes indiquent une baisse

of trafficked women registered between 1995 and 1999, but the trend may reflect a lower number of police investigations rather than a real fall in numbers trafficked (Laczko, Klekowski von Koppenfels and Barthel, 2002). What does seem to be happening is a change in the origin countries of the women coming to western Europe, with more from central and eastern Europe replacing those from Asia, Latin America and Africa. In 2000, 56% of trafficking victims in Germany were from CEE countries, 28% from the CIS. Data from German NGOs confirm this trend (ibid.)). UK data also support the view that CEE countries are the main suppliers (Kelly and Regan, 2000). However, Polish police intelligence reports suggest that cases of trafficking in Polish women are decreasing each year (Laczko, Klekowski von Koppenfels and Barthel, 2002).

A new trend is that the CEE countries are not only sending trafficked women but have become important receiving and transit countries as trafficking from further east, notably from Belarus, Russia, Lithuania, Ukraine and Moldova, has increased (ibid.). Trafficking in women to parts of the Balkans has also grown, including flows from Moldova, Romania and Ukraine.

Similar sources account for most deportations for prostitution from Turkey, 93% of the 3 500 in 2001 coming from the six countries of Azerbaijan, Georgia, Moldova, Romania, Russia and the Ukraine (Erder and Kaska, 2003).

du nombre de femmes victimes de ce trafic entre 1995 et 1999, mais cette tendance pourrait refléter une diminution des enquêtes de police plutôt qu'une baisse réelle du nombre de victimes (Laczko, Klekowski von Koppenfels et Barthel, 2002). Ce qui semble se produire, c'est un changement dans les pays dont sont originaires les femmes venant en Europe occidentale, un plus grand nombre d'entre elles étant originaires d'Europe centrale et orientale en remplacement de leurs sœurs d'Asie, d'Amérique latine et d'Afrique. En 2000, 56 % des victimes du trafic en Allemagne étaient originaires des Peco, 28 % de la CEI. Les données des ONG allemandes confirment cette tendance *(ibid.)*. Les données du Royaume-Uni confirment également le fait que les Peco sont les principaux pourvoyeurs (Kelly et Regan, 2000). Cependant, les rapports des services de renseignements de la police polonaise laissent entendre que le trafic de Polonaises diminue chaque année (Laczko, Klekowski von Koppenfels et Barthel, 2002).

Ce qui est nouveau, c'est que les Peco ne sont pas seulement des pourvoyeurs de femmes victimes de ce trafic mais deviennent également des pays de transit et d'accueil en raison de l'augmentation du trafic de femmes originaires de pays situés plus à l'Est, notamment du Bélarus, de Russie, de Lituanie, d'Ukraine et de Moldova *(ibid.)*. Le trafic de femmes vers les Balkans a également augmenté, notamment les flux en provenance de Moldova, de Roumanie et d'Ukraine.

La plupart des expulsions de Turquie pour cause de prostitution concernent des personnes des mêmes origines: sur les 3 500 personnes concernées en 2001, 93 % venaient de six pays, à savoir l'Azerbaïdjan, la Géorgie, la Moldova, la Roumanie, la Russie et l'Ukraine (Erder et Kaska, 2003).

10. Recent initiatives in international co-operation

Over the last few years governments and intergovernmental organisations have begun to match the rhetoric of the need to "manage" rather than "control" international migration with firm proposals for action. The first systematic attempt was that of the Council of Europe in 1998, followed by a series of Communications by the European Commission to the European Council and Parliament. These are briefly described below.

10.1. The Council of Europe's Migration Management Strategy

The strategy was designed to apply at the pan-European scale and based on four integrated principles:

• *Orderliness*

to develop a set of measures able to manage migration in an orderly manner, so as to maximise opportunities and benefits to individual migrants and to host societies and to minimise trafficking and illegal movement;

• *Protection*

to provide an appropriate capability for protection and for dealing with disorderly or sudden movements;

• *Integration*

to provide an environment conducive to integration;

• *Co-operation*

to engage in dialogue and co-operation with sending countries in order to link foreign policy and migration policy objectives.

The strategy accepted the reality that Europe is a region of immigration, the management of which has to be organised on a comprehensive basis. It emphasised that the protection of individual human rights is the basis of management. At the heart of the strategy was the conviction that many of the migration problems now confronting governments have resulted from a piecemeal approach to specific problems, such as the economy, asylum, illegality or return. A management strategy should be regarded as a comprehensive whole, to be applied over the long term.

10. Récentes initiatives de coopération internationale

Au cours des dernières années, les gouvernements et les organisations intergouvernementales ont commencé à assortir leur discours rhétorique sur la nécessité de «gérer» plutôt que de «contrôler» les migrations internationales de solides propositions d'action. La première tentative méthodique fut celle du Conseil de l'Europe, en 1998, suivie par une série de communications de la Commission européenne au Conseil et au Parlement européens. On en trouvera une brève description ci-dessous.

10.1. Stratégie de gestion des migrations du Conseil de l'Europe

Cette stratégie était destinée à être appliquée à un niveau paneuropéen et reposait sur quatre principes cohérents:

• *L'ordre*

Définir un ensemble de mesures permettant de gérer l'immigration de façon ordonnée, de telle manière que les migrants comme les sociétés d'accueil en tirent le meilleur profit et que le trafic et les mouvements illégaux soient réduits.

• *La protection*

Offrir une capacité suffisante de protection et de traitement des afflux désordonnés ou soudains.

• *L'intégration*

Créer un environnement favorisant l'intégration.

• *La coopération*

Nouer le dialogue et des liens de coopération avec les pays émetteurs afin d'établir une cohérence entre la politique étrangère et les objectifs en matière d'immigration.

Cette stratégie accepte le fait que l'Europe est une région d'immigration, laquelle doit être gérée dans une perspective globale. Elle souligne que la protection des droits fondamentaux de la personne humaine constitue l'élément de base de cette gestion. Cette stratégie repose sur la conviction que nombre des difficultés que rencontrent aujourd'hui les gouvernements en matière de politique migratoire résultent du fait que des problèmes spécifiques tels que l'économie, l'asile, la clandestinité ou les retours font l'objet d'une approche morcelée. La stratégie de gestion proposée dans le présent rapport est une stratégie globale, applicable sur le long terme.

10.2. The European Commission's Community immigration policy

Support for such a management approach has come also from the European Commission in its proposals for a common EU immigration policy over the next 20 to 30 years. It identifies four essentials for such a policy (European Commission, 2000a):

1. the need to control migration movements through measures which promote legal immigration and combat illegal entry;
2. co-operation with the countries of origin of immigrants within the framework of policies of development aid designed to minimise migration push factors;
3. definition of a policy of integration which establishes the rights and obligations of immigrants;
4. the elaboration of a legislative framework common to all member states aimed at imposing penal sanctions on traffickers and smugglers, as well as providing support for the victims of trafficking.

The basis of the policy is the recognition that the "zero" immigration policies of the past 30 years are no longer appropriate, that immigration will continue and should be properly regulated in order to maximise its positive effects on the Union, on the migrants themselves and on the countries of origin. Migration of all types should be taken into account – humanitarian, family reunion and economic – to deal with the impact on sending and receiving countries as a whole.

The success of such a policy depends on effective co-ordination by all those concerned and on the adoption and implementation of new measures, as appropriate at both Community and member state levels. A further Communication (COM(2001)387 final) set out proposals for the adaptation of an open method of co-ordination in the implementation of immigration policy. It proposed that member states would prepare national action plans in order to develop and evaluate the Community Immigration Policy.

10.3. The European Commission's Communication on immigration, integration and employment

This Communication, produced in June 2003, aimed to provide a single document setting out what had been done towards immigration policy as detailed in documents from the Amsterdam Treaty in May 1999, the European Council in Tampere later that year and the November 2000 Communication on Community immigration policy.

10.2. Politique communautaire d'immigration de la Commission européenne

Cette approche a également reçu l'appui de la Commission euro-péenne à travers ses propositions relatives à une politique commu-nautaire d'immigration pour les vingt ou trente prochaines années, comportant quatre grands axes (Commission européenne, 2000 *b*.):

1. la nécessité de contrôler les mouvements migratoires par des mesures propres à encourager l'immigration légale et à lutter contre l'immigration clandestine;
2. la coopération avec les pays d'origine des migrants dans le cadre des politiques d'aide au développement conçues pour réduire les facteurs de répulsion;
3. la définition d'une politique d'intégration qui établisse les droits et les devoirs des immigrés;
4. l'élaboration d'un cadre législatif commun à tous les Etats membres visant à sanctionner au pénal les trafiquants et à venir en aide aux victimes de ces trafics.

Cette politique repose sur l'idée que les politiques d'immigration «zéro» des trente dernières années ne sont plus de mise, que l'immi-gration se poursuivra et doit être soigneusement réglementée afin que l'Union, les immigrés eux-mêmes et les pays d'origine en tirent le plus grand profit. Il convient de prendre en compte tous les types de migra-tions – pour des motifs humanitaires, familiaux ou économiques – afin d'en gérer l'impact sur l'ensemble des pays d'origine et des pays d'accueil.

Le succès d'une telle politique dépend de la coordination effective de tous les acteurs œuvrant dans ce domaine, de l'adoption et de la mise en œuvre de nouvelles mesures appropriées au niveau de la Communauté et des Etats membres. Une autre communication (COM(2001)387 final) définit des propositions en vue de l'adoption d'une méthode transparente de coordination dans la mise en œuvre de la politique d'immigration. Elle propose que chacun des Etats membres prépare un plan d'action national destiné à développer et évaluer la politique communautaire d'immigration.

10.3. Communication de la Commission européenne concernant l'immigration, l'intégration et l'emploi

Cette communication, publiée en juin 2003, avait pour objectif d'ex-poser en un seul document ce qui avait été fait en matière de politique d'immigration et se trouvait détaillé dans les documents du Traité d'Amsterdam de mai 1999, du Conseil européen de Tampere, à la fin de la même année, et dans la communication de novembre 2000

It also takes account of important relevant developments since Tampere:

- it responds to the Tampere conclusions by reviewing current practice and experience with integration policy at national and EU level;

- it examines the role of immigration in relation to the Lisbon objectives in the context of demographic ageing; and

- it outlines, on this basis, policy orientations and priorities, including action at EU level, to promote the integration of immigrants.

10.4. The European Commission's Communications on a common asylum procedure

These Communications in late 2000 and March 2003 propose a directive on minimum standards of procedures in member states for granting and withdrawing refugee status in order to establish a minimum level of harmonisation of the rules applicable. In effect, there is to be a move towards a "one-stop shop" type of procedure in order to centralise the examination of all protection needs at a single place so as to assure the applicant that no form of persecution or risk is ignored and also to reduce the time taken to examine the request for protection.

Initially states retain their national systems, subject to respect for certain norms and conditions regarding competent authorities and the applicable procedures. At a second stage there is to be a move towards laying down a common procedure, with less scope for national flexibility and achievement of some convergence in national interpretation of procedures. Ultimately the objective is the adoption of a common asylum procedure and a uniform status for those given asylum.

10.5. The European Commission's Communication towards more accessible, equitable and managed asylum systems

This Communication, produced in June 2003, results from an invitation by the Council to explore the issues raised in a white paper sent in March 2003 to the Presidency detailing the need for a "better management of the asylum process". The UK paper outlined problems common to the current asylum system of the EU and proposed a new approach of regional protection areas in origin countries and "transit processing centres" in third countries along transit routes to the EU.

concernant l'immigration. Elle prend aussi en compte les développements importants intervenus depuis Tampere et:

- répond aux conclusions de Tampere en passant en revue les pratiques actuelles et l'expérience en matière de politique d'intégration au niveau national et à celui de l'Union européenne;

- examine le rôle de l'immigration en relation avec les objectifs de Lisbonne, dans le contexte du vieillissement des populations; et

- esquisse, sur cette base, les orientations et priorités politiques afin de promouvoir l'intégration des immigrés, y compris au niveau de l'Union.

10.4. Communications de la Commission européenne concernant une politique commune d'asile

Ces communications, publiées à la fin de l'année 2000 et en mars 2004, proposent une directive sur des normes minimales de procédure d'octroi et de retrait du statut de réfugié dans les Etats membres afin de parvenir à un minimum d'harmonisation des règles applicables. Il faut en effet tendre vers un type de procédure «unique» afin que toutes les demandes de protection soient examinées en un seul et même lieu, de manière à garantir au demandeur que toutes les formes de persécution ou de risque sont prises en compte et de réduire le temps passé à examiner chaque demande.

Au début, les Etats conservent leur système national, mais sont tenus de respecter certaines normes et conditions relatives aux autorités compétentes et aux procédures applicables. Dans un deuxième temps, on s'oriente vers une procédure commune, ce qui laisse moins de latitude aux Etats et conduit à une certaine convergence dans leur interprétation des procédures. L'objectif final est l'adoption d'une procédure d'asile commune et d'un statut uniforme pour les personnes qui se voient accorder l'asile.

10.5. Communication de la Commission européenne «Vers des régimes d'asile plus accessibles, équitables et organisés»

Cette communication, émise en juin 2003, résulte d'une invitation du Conseil à explorer les problèmes soulevés dans un libre blanc envoyé à la présidence en mars 2003 et détaillant la nécessité d'une «meilleure gestion du processus d'asile». Le document présenté par le Royaume-Uni expose les problèmes du système actuel d'asile de l'Union et propose une nouvelle approche des centres de protection régionaux dans les pays d'origine et des «centres de transit pour le traitement des demandes d'asile» dans des pays tiers, sur les axes de transit vers l'Union.

The Communication suggests that such a new approach would need to build upon the ongoing harmonisation of existing asylum systems in the European Union. While Community legislation lays down a minimum level playing field for in-country asylum processes in the EU, the new approach intends to move beyond the realm of such processes and to address the phenomenon of mixed flows and the external dimension of these flows. Embracing the new approach, it asserts, would not render the ongoing harmonisation obsolete: spontaneous arrivals will continue to occur in the future and should remain subject to common standards. However, the new approach would reinforce the credibility, integrity and efficiency of the standards underpinning the systems for spontaneous arrivals by offering a number of well-defined alternatives.

10.6. The European Commission's Communications on a common policy on illegal migration, smuggling and trafficking of human beings, external borders and the return of illegal residents

In these Communications, produced at the end of 2001 and June 2003 (after the European Council of Thessaloniki), the Commission proposed the adoption of a comprehensive approach to tackling the issues of illegal migration, trafficking and smuggling. It identified six areas of action: visa policy; infrastructure for information exchange, co-operation and co-ordination; border management; police co-operation; aliens law and criminal law; and return and admission policy.

Visa policy covers country lists, uniform standards, the creation of common administrative structures and the development of a European visa identification system. Information needs include better statistics, information gathering, intelligence and analysis and the development of an early warning system. Pre-frontier measures are important, including liaison and financial support in third countries and awareness-raising campaigns. Better border management includes the setting up of a European Border Guard, with surveillance by joint teams and an advanced role for Europol. Better legal instruments were proposed to deal with trafficking, smuggling and employment exploitation. Finally, it argued that a Community return policy should be based on common principles, standards and measures.

Cette communication suggère qu'une telle approche devrait s'inscrire dans la lignée de l'harmonisation en cours des systèmes d'asile de l'Union européenne. Tandis que la législation communautaire fixe un cadre minimal pour les procédures d'asile dans les Etats membres de l'Union, cette nouvelle approche entend aller au-delà en traitant le phénomène des flux mixtes et la dimension extérieure de ces flux. Elle affirme que l'adoption de cette nouvelle approche ne rendra pas le processus d'harmonisation actuel caduc: il y aura toujours à l'avenir des arrivées spontanées qui devront rester soumises aux normes communes. Cependant, la nouvelle approche renforcera la crédibilité, l'intégrité et l'efficacité des normes applicables aux arrivées spontanées en proposant un certain nombre de solutions bien définies.

10.6. Communications de la Commission européenne sur le développement d'une politique commune en matière d'immigration clandestine, de trafic illicite et de traite des êtres humains, de frontières extérieures et de retour des personnes en séjour irrégulier

Par ces communications datant de la fin de 2001 et de juin 2003 (après le Conseil européen de Thessalonique), la Commission propose d'adopter une approche globale de l'immigration clandestine, du trafic et de la contrebande d'êtres humains. Elle définit six domaines d'action: la politique en matière de visas, une infrastructure pour les échanges d'informations, pour la coopération et la coordination, la gestion des frontières, une coopération de la police, la législation concernant les étrangers et les délinquants, et une politique concernant les admissions et les retours.

La politique en matière de visas englobe les listes par pays, des normes uniformes, la création de structures administratives communes et la mise en place d'un système européen de reconnaissance des visas. Les besoins d'information incluent de meilleures statistiques, la collecte d'informations, le renseignement et l'analyse ainsi que la mise en place d'un «système d'alerte anticipée». Les mesures avant le passage de la frontière sont importantes et comprennent la coopération et l'aide financière dans les pays tiers ainsi que des campagnes de sensibilisation. Une meilleure gestion des frontières implique la création d'un corps de gardes-frontières européen et la surveillance des frontières par des équipes communes, ainsi qu'un rôle accru pour Europol. De meilleurs instruments juridiques sont proposés pour combattre le trafic et la contrebande ainsi que l'exploitation des travailleurs. Enfin, la Commission a souligné qu'une politique communautaire de retour doit reposer sur des principes, des normes et des mesures communs.

10.7. The European Commission's Communication on a Community return policy on illegal residents

This Communication at the end of 2002 followed that on combating illegal migration. Four items were highlighted: first, the need to step up operational co-operation; second, the development of a suitable legal framework; third, the need for the programme to be an integrated one; and finally, that close co-operation with third countries is essential.

Among the detailed proposals made was that a return policy is best developed gradually by short-term measures that can be implemented immediately, that states should offer and provide mutual assistance in facilitating returns and that better co-ordination of an enhanced operational co-operation on return should be achieved with the development of the information and co-ordination network proposed in the Communication on illegal migration. Furthermore, common minimum standards on removal are required to ensure efficient return policies. Overall, it argued that the EU should develop its own approach for integrated return programmes, covering all phases of the return process and tailored to specific countries.

10.8 Other proposals to combat illegal migration

Outside the Commission, other organisations were active in combating trafficking. In May 2000, the UNHCR issued "Recommended Principles and Guidelines on Human Rights and Human Trafficking" as part of a report to the UN Economic and Social Council. In November 2000 the United Nations General Assembly adopted a "New Protocol to Prevent, Suppress and Punish Trafficking in Persons, especially Women and Children". The protocol was in response to the general dissatisfaction felt with regard to the inadequacy of the 1949 protocol and pledged support for trafficking victims and the intent to promote co-operation between states to meet objectives to combat trafficking. The Parliamentary Assembly of the OSCE urged in Chapter 3 of its Bucharest Declaration another resolution to criminalise trafficking while ensuring the victims' immunity from prosecution.

10.9. Migration management: summary

Some generalisations can be made from these brief descriptions of the various migration management strategies proposed.

10.7. Communication de la Commission européenne concernant une politique commune de retour des résidents clandestins

Cette communication de la fin de 2002 fait suite à la communication concernant la lutte contre l'immigration clandestine. Elle souligne quatre points: tout d'abord, la nécessité d'accroître la coopération opérationnelle, l'élaboration d'un cadre juridique approprié, un programme cohérent et enfin l'importance d'une coopération étroite avec les Etats tiers.

Parmi d'autres propositions circonstanciées, cette communication précise qu'il est préférable de mettre en place une politique de retour progressive par des mesures à court terme applicables de suite, que les Etats doivent s'entraider afin de faciliter les retours et qu'il convient de mieux coordonner une plus grande coopération des opérations en développant le réseau d'information et de coordination proposé dans la communication concernant l'immigration clandestine. En outre, des normes minimales communes en matière de renvoi sont nécessaires pour garantir l'efficacité de telles politiques. Dans l'ensemble, la communication souligne que l'Union doit développer ses programmes de retour intégrés, couvrant toutes les étapes du processus de retour et en les adaptant à chaque pays.

10.8. Autres propositions pour lutter contre l'immigration clandestine

D'autres organisations extérieures à la Commission ont lutté activement contre la contrebande d'êtres humains. En mai 2000, le HCR a publié ses «Recommandations concernant les droits de l'homme et le trafic de main-d'œuvre» dans le cadre d'un rapport au Conseil économique et social des Nations Unies. En novembre 2000, l'Assemblée générale des Nations Unies a adopté un «Nouveau protocole pour la prévention, la suppression et la répression du trafic d'êtres humains, en particulier de femmes et d'enfants». Ce protocole répondait au mécontentement général devant les insuffisances du Protocole de 1949 et s'engageait à aider les victimes d'un tel trafic et à promouvoir la coopération entre les Etats afin de mener à bien les objectifs visant à le combattre. Au chapitre 3 de sa «Déclaration de Bucarest», l'Assemblée parlementaire de l'OSCE insistait sur une nouvelle résolution qui irait jusqu'à faire de ce trafic un crime tout en garantissant l'immunité de poursuites pour les victimes.

10.9. Gestion des migrations: résumé

Cette brève description des différentes stratégies de gestion des migrations proposées appelle certaines généralisations.

First, management rather than control is now the name of the game. There is a recognition by individual states and by intergovernmental organisations that international migration cannot be controlled, in the sense that countries can turn the taps of movement on or off at their borders. In reality they were never able to do that anyway.

Second, there is an acceptance that migration is generally a positive phenomenon and that the prime purpose of management is to ensure an all-round positive outcome.

Third, migration management strategies require a comprehensive approach that takes in the complete spectrum of movement and deals with both legal and illegal moves. Tackling one issue invariably leads to unintended consequences elsewhere, frequently observed in the exploitation of loopholes which allow the diversion of migration streams from one channel to another.

Fourth, countries can no longer act alone. Co-operation is vital, both with European neighbours and with countries further afield. The consequence is the move towards greater commonality of policy within the EU. Such is the momentum that even non-EU states are now having to harmonise their policies to fit a single model.

Tout d'abord, l'enjeu consiste aujourd'hui à gérer les migrations et non à les endiguer. Les Etats et les organisations internationales reconnaissent qu'il n'est pas possible d'endiguer les migrations internationales, en ce sens que les pays ne peuvent ouvrir et fermer le robinet de ces flux aux frontières. Ils n'ont d'ailleurs jamais pu le faire.

Deuxièmement, on admet généralement que les migrations sont un phénomène positif et que la gestion des migrations doit avant tout veiller à ce que ces mouvements se traduisent par un bilan positif sur toute la ligne.

Troisièmement, les stratégies de gestion des migrations réclament une approche globale de l'ensemble du phénomène traitant des mouvements réguliers comme des mouvements clandestins. La recherche de solutions pour un aspect du problème entraîne invariablement des conséquences involontaires ailleurs, ce que l'on observe fréquemment dans le recours à des échappatoires qui permettent de détourner les flux migratoires d'une filière à une autre.

Enfin, les pays ne peuvent plus se permettre d'agir isolément. La coopération est vitale, à la fois avec les voisins européens et les pays plus éloignés. Il s'ensuit un mouvement vers une plus grande standardisation de la politique migratoire dans l'Union européenne. La dynamique est telle que même les Etats ne faisant pas partie de l'Union se voient aujourd'hui contraints d'harmoniser leurs politiques pour s'inscrire dans un modèle unique.

Bibliography

Apap, J. et al., 2000, "Rapport de synthèse sur la comparaison des régularisations d'étrangers illégaux dans l'Union européenne", in De Bruycker, P., (ed.), *Regularisations of illegal immigrants in the European Union*, Bruylant, Brussels, pp. 23-82.

Baldassarini, A., 2001, "Non regular foreign input of labour in the new national accounts estimates", OECD Meeting of National Accounts Experts, Paris, STD/NA(2001)30.

Biffl, G., 2004, "International migration and Austria", the report of the Austrian SOPEMI correspondent to the OECD, Paris.

Böcker, A. and Havinga, T., 1997, *Asylum migration to the European Union: patterns of origin and destination*, European Commission, Luxembourg.

Ceccagno, A., 2003, "New Chinese migrants in Italy" in *International Migration*, 41(3), pp. 187-214.

Coleman, D. A., 2000, "Who's afraid of low support ratios? A UK response to the UN Population Division's report on replacement migration", in *UN Expert Group Meeting on Policy Responses to Population Ageing and Population Decline*, UN, New York, pp. 15-51.

Coleman, D. and Rowthorn, R., 2004, "The economic effect of immigration into the United Kingdom", *Population and Development Review*, 30, No. 4, pp. 579-624.

Dietz, B. and Kaczmarczyk, P., 2004, "On the demand side of international labour mobility: the structure of the German labour market as a causal factor of Polish seasonal migration" in *International migration in Europe: new trends, new methods of analysis*, papers from the 2nd Conference of the EAPS Working Group on International Migration in Europe, Rome, Italy, 25-27 November 2004.

Dumont, J-C. and Lemaitre, G., 2004, *Counting immigrants and expatriates in OECD countries: a new perspective*, OECD, Paris.

Dustmann, C., 2003, *The impact of EU enlargement on migration flows*, Home Office Online Report, 25/03, Home Office, London.

Erder, S. and Kaska, S., 2003, *Irregular migration and trafficking in women: the case of Turkey*, IOM, Geneva.

Bibliographie

Apap, J. *et al.*, «Rapport de synthèse sur la comparaison des régularisations d'étrangers illégaux dans l'Union européenne», in De Bruycker, P., *Regularisations of Illegal Immigrants in the European Union*, Bruylant, Bruxelles, 2000, pp. 23-82.

Baldassarini, A., *Non Regular Foreign Input of Labour in the New National Accounts Estimates*, OECD Meeting of National Accounts Experts, STD/NA, 30, Paris, 2001.

Biffl, G., *International Migration and Austria*, rapport des correspondants autrichiens du Sopemi à l'OCDE, OCDE, Paris, 2004.

Böcker, A. et Havinga, T., *Asylum Migration to the European Union: Patterns of Origin and Destination*, Commission européenne, Luxembourg, 1997.

Ceccagno, A.,«New Chinese Migrants in Italy», in *International Migration*, 41, 3, 2003, pp. 187-214.

Coleman, D. A., «Who's Afraid of Low Support Ratios? A UK Response to the UN Population Division's Report on Replacement Migration», in *UN Expert Group Meeting on Policy Responses to Population Ageing and Population Decline*, Nations Unies, New York, 2000, pp. 15-51.

Coleman, D. et Rowthorn, R., «The economic effect of immigration into the United Kingdom», in *Population and Development Review*, 30, 4, 2004, pp. 579-624.

Commission européenne, *Communication de la Commission sur la politique commune d'asile et l'agenda pour la protection (2ᵉ rapport de la Commission sur la mise en œuvre de la communication COM(2000) 755 final du 22 novembre 2000)*, Bruxelles, 2003.

Commission européenne, *Communication sur le développement d'une politique commune en matière d'immigration clandestine, de trafic illicite et de traite des êtres humains, de frontières extérieures et de retour des personnes en séjour irrégulier*, COM (2003) 323/F, Bruxelles, 2003.

Commission européenne, *Communication sur l'immigration, l'intégration et l'emploi*, COM (2003) 336/F, Bruxelles, 2003.

Commission européenne, *Communication «Vers des régimes d'asile plus accessibles, équitables et organisés»*, COM (2003) 315/F, Bruxelles, 2003.

European Commission, 2000a, *Communication on a Community immigration policy*, Brussels, COM(2000)757/F.

European Commission, 2000b, *Communication: towards a common asylum procedure and a uniform status, valid throughout the Union, for persons granted asylum*, Brussels, COM(2000)755/F.

European Commission, 2001, *Communication on a common policy on illegal migration*, Brussels, COM(2001)672/F.

European Commission, 2002, *Communication on a Community return policy on illegal residents*, Brussels, COM(2002)175/F.

European Commission, 2003, *Communication on immigration, integration and employment*, Brussels, COM(2003)336/F.

European Commission, 2003, *Communication on the common asylum policy and the Agenda for protection (Second Commission report on the implementation of Communication COM(2000)755 final of 22 November 2000)*, Brussels, COM(2003)152/F.

European Commission, 2003, *Communication on the development of a common policy on illegal immigration, smuggling and trafficking of human beings, external borders and the return of illegal residents*, Brussels, COM(2003)323/F.

European Commission, 2003, *Communication: towards more accessible, equitable and managed asylum systems*, Brussels, COM(2003)315/F.

Fassmann, H. and Münz, R., 2002, "EU enlargement and future East-West migration", in Laczko, F., Stacher, I. and Klekowski von Koppenfels, A., 2002, *New challenges for migration policy in central and eastern Europe*, TMC Asser Press, The Hague, pp. 57-84.

Feld, S., 2000, "Active population growth and immigration hypotheses in western Europe", *European Journal of Population*, 16, pp. 3-40.

Frejka, T. (ed.), 1996, *International migration in central and eastern Europe and the Commonwealth of Independent States*, United Nations, Geneva and New York.

Futo, P. and Tass, T., 2002, "Border apprehension statistics of central and eastern Europe. A resource for measuring illegal migration?" in Laczko, F., Stacher, I. and Klekowski von Koppenfels, A., 2002, *New*

Commission européenne, *Une politique communautaire en matière d'asile*, COM (2000) 755/F, Bruxelles, 2000*a*.

Commission européenne, *Une politique communautaire en matière de retour forcé en cas de résidence illégale*, COM (2002) 175/F, Bruxelles, 2002.

Commission européenne, *Une politique communautaire en matière d'immigration*, COM (2000) 757/F, Bruxelles, 2000*b*.

Commission européenne, *Une politique communautaire en matière d'immigration clandestine*, COM (2001) 672/F, Bruxelles, 2001.

Dietz, B. et Kaczmarczyk, P., «On the demand side of international labour mobility: the structure of the German labour market as a causal factor of Polish seasonal migration», in *International migration in Europe: new trends, new methods of analysis*, actes de la 2ᵉ Conférence du Groupe de travail de l'EAPS sur les migrations internationales en Europe, Rome, 25-27 novembre 2004.

Dumont, J.-C. et Lemaitre, G., *Counting Immigrants and Expatriates in OECD Countries : a New Perspective*, OCDE, Paris, 2004.

Dustmann, C., *The Impact of EU Enlargement on Migration Flows*, Home Office Online Report, 25/03, Home Office, Londres, 2003.

Erder, S. et Kaska, S., *Irregular Migration and Trafficking in Women: the Case of Turkey*, OIM, Genève, 2003.

Fassmann, H. et Münz, R., «EU Enlargement and Future East-West Migration», *in* Laczko, F., Stacher, I. et Klekowski von Koppenfels, A., *New Challenges for Migration Policy in Central and Eastern Europe*, TMC Asser Press, La Haye, 2002.

Feld, S., «Active population growth and immigration hypotheses in Western Europe», in *European Journal of Population*, 16, 2000, pp. 3-40.

Frejka, T., *International Migration in Central and Eastern Europe and the Commonwealth of Independent States,* Nations Unies, Genève, New York, 1996.

Futo, P. et Tass, T., «Border Apprehension Statistics of Central and Eastern Europe. A Resource for Measuring Illegal Migration?», *in* Laczko, F., Stacher, I. et Klekowski von Koppenfels, A., *New Challenges for Migration Policy in Central and Eastern Europe*, TMC Asser Press, La Haye, 2002.

challenges for migration policy in central and eastern Europe, TMC Asser Press, The Hague, pp. 85-116.

Garson J-P., Redor, D. and Lemaitre, G., 1997, "Regional integration and the outlook for temporary and permanent migration in central and eastern Europe", in Biffl, G. (ed.), *Migration, free trade and regional integration in central and eastern Europe*, Verlag Österreich, Vienna.

Giese, K., 2003, "New Chinese migration to Germany: historical consistencies and new patterns of diversification within a globalised migration regime", in *International Migration*, 41(3), pp. 155-186.

Gilbert, A. and Koser, K., 2004, *Information dissemination to potential asylum seekers in countries of origin and/or transit*, Research findings 220, Home Office, London.

Gott, C. and Johnston, K., 2002, *The migrant population in the UK: fiscal effects*, RDS Occasional Paper No. 77, Home Office, London.

Haug, W., Compton, P. and Courbage, Y. (eds), 2002, *The demographic characteristics of immigrant populations*, Council of Europe, Strasbourg.

Heckmann, F. and Wunderlich, T., 2000, "Transatlantic workshop on human smuggling: a conference report", *Georgetown Immigration Law Journal*, 15, pp. 167-182.

Hughes, G., 2004, *International migration and Ireland*, the report of the Irish SOPEMI correspondent to the OECD, Paris.

Içduygu, A., 2003, *Irregular migration in Turkey*, IOM Migration Research Series, No. 12, IOM, Geneva.

Içduygu, A., 2004, *International migration and Turkey*, the report of the Turkish SOPEMI correspondent to the OECD, Paris.

ICMPD, 2004, *2003 Year Book on illegal migration, human smuggling and trafficking in central and eastern Europe*, ICMPD, Vienna.

IOM and ICMPD, 2002, *Migration trends in eastern Europe and central Asia: 2001-02 Review*, IOM, Geneva.

Ivakhniouk, I., 2003, *Eastern Europe: current and future migration trends*, 4th Regional Conference of the Council of Europe, Kiev, October 2003, Council of Europe, Strasbourg.

Garson J.-P., Redor, D. et Lemaitre, G., «Regional Integration and the Outlook for Temporary and Permanent Migration in Central and Eastern Europe», *in* Biffl, G., *Migration, Free Trade and Regional Integration in Central and Eastern Europe*, Verlag Österreich, Vienne, 1997.

Giese, K., «New Chinese Migration to Germany: Historical Consistencies and New Patterns of Diversification within a Globalised Migration Regime», in *International Migration*, 41, 3, 2003, pp. 155-186.

Gilbert, A. et Koser, K., «Information dissemination to potential asylum seekers in countries of origin and/or transit», in *Research findings*, 220, Home Office, Londres, 2004.

Gott, C. et Johnston, K., *The Migrant Population in the UK: Fiscal Effects*, RDS Occasional Paper No. 77, Home Office, Londres, 2002.

Haug, W., Compton, P. et Courbage, Y., *Les caractéristiques démographiques des populations immigrées*, Conseil de l'Europe, Strasbourg, 2002.

Heckmann, F. et Wunderlich, T., «Transatlantic workshop on human smuggling: a conference report», in *Georgetown Immigration Law Journal*, 15, 2000, pp. 167-182.

Hughes, G., *International Migration and Ireland*, rapport du correspondant irlandais du Sopemi à l'OCDE, OCDE, Paris, 2004.

Içduygu, A., *International Migration and Turkey*, rapport du correspondant turc du Sopemi à l'OCDE, OCDE, Paris, 2004.

Içduygu, A., *Irregular Migration in Turkey*, IOM Migration Research Series, 12, OIM, Genève, 2003.

ICMPD, *2003 Year Book on illegal migration, human smuggling and trafficking in Central and Eastern Europe*, ICMPD, Vienne, 2004.

Ivakhniouk, I., *Eastern Europe: current and future migration trends*, 4ᵉ Conférence régionale du Conseil de l'Europe, Kyiv, octobre 2003, Conseil de l'Europe, Strasbourg, 2003.

Jandl, M., «The estimation of illegal migration in Europe», in *Studi Emigrazione*, 41, 2004, pp. 141-155.

Juhasz, J., «Migrant Trafficking and Human Smuggling in Hungary», *in* OIM, *Migrant Trafficking and Human Smuggling in Europe*, OIM, Genève, 2000, pp.167-232.

Jandl, M., 2004, "The estimation of illegal migration in Europe", *Studi Emigrazione*, 41, pp. 141-155.

Juhasz, J., 2000, "Migrant trafficking and human smuggling in Hungary", in IOM, *Migrant trafficking and human smuggling in Europe*, IOM, Geneva, pp. 167-232.

Kelly, L. and Regan, L., 2000, *Stopping traffic: an exploratory study of trafficking in women for sexual exploitation in the UK*, Report to the Home Office, University of North London.

Klinchenko, T., 2000, "Migrant trafficking and human smuggling in Ukraine", in IOM, *Migrant trafficking and human smuggling in Europe*, IOM, Geneva, pp. 329-416.

Kraler, A. and Iglicka, K., 2002, "Labour migration in central European countries" in Laczko, F., Stacher, I. and Klekowski von Koppenfels, A., 2002, *New challenges for migration policy in central and eastern Europe*, TMC Asser Press, The Hague, pp. 27-56.

Laczko, F., Stacher, I. and Klekowski von Koppenfels, A. (eds), 2002, *New challenges for migration policy in central and eastern Europe*, TMC Asser Press, The Hague.

Laczko, F., 2002, "Introduction", in Laczko, F., Stacher, I. and Klekowski von Koppenfels, A., 2002, *New challenges for migration policy in central and eastern Europe*, TMC Asser Press, The Hague, pp. 1-10.

Laczko, F., Klekowski von Koppenfels, A. and Barthel, J., 2002, "Trafficking in women from central and eastern Europe: a review of statistical data", in Laczko, F., Stacher, I. and Klekowski von Koppenfels, A., 2002, *New challenges for migration policy in central and eastern Europe*, TMC Asser Press, The Hague, pp. 151-172.

Laczko, F. and Gramegna, M., 2003, "Developing better indicators of human trafficking", in *Brown Journal of World Affairs*, Summer/Fall 2003, Volume X, Issue 1.

Van der Leun, J.P., Engbersen, G., van der Heijden, P., 1998, *Illegaliteit en criminaliteit. Schattingen, aanhoudingen en uitzettingen*, Erasmus University Rotterdam.

Mai, N. and Schwander-Sievers, S., 2003, "Albanian migration and new transnationalisms", in *Journal of Ethnic and Migration Studies*, 29(6), pp. 939-948.

Kelly, L. et Regan, L., *Stopping traffic: an exploratory study of trafficking in women for sexual exploitation in the UK*, Report to the Home Office, University of North, Londres, 2000.

Klinchenko, T., «Migrant Trafficking and Human Smuggling in Ukraine», *in* OIM, *Migrant Trafficking and Human Smuggling in Europe*, OIM, Genève, 2000, pp. 167-232 et 329-416.

Kraler, A. et Iglicka, K., «Labour Migration in Central European Countries», in Laczko, F., Stacher, I. et Klekowski von Koppenfels, A., *New Challenges for Migration Policy in Central and Eastern Europe*, TMC Asser Press, La Haye, 2002, pp. 27-56.

Laczko, F., Stacher, I. et Klekowski von Koppenfels, A., *New Challenges for Migration Policy in Central and Eastern Europe*, TMC Asser Press, La Haye, 2002.

Laczko, F., «Introduction», *in* Laczko, F., Stacher, I. et Klekowski von Koppenfels, A., *New Challenges for Migration Policy in Central and Eastern Europe*, TMC Asser Press, La Haye, 2002, pp. 1-10.

Laczko, F., Klekowski von Koppenfels, A. et Barthel, J., «Trafficking in Women from Central and eastern Europe : a review of statistical data», *in* Laczko, F., Stacher, I. et Klekowski von Koppenfels, A., *New Challenges for Migration Policy in Central and Eastern Europe*, TMC Asser Press, La Haye, 2002, pp. 151- 172.

Laczko, F. et Gramegna, M., «Developing Better Indicators of Human Trafficking», in *the Brown Journal of World Affairs*, X, 1, été 2003.

Mai, N. et Schwander-Sievers, S., «Albanian migration and new trans-nationalisms», in *Journal of Ethnic and Migration Studies*, 29, 6, 2003, pp. 939-948.

Michalon, B., «Playing on ethnicity to be there and here: The three paradoxes of "ethnic migrations"», in *International migration in Europe: new trends, new methods of analysis*, actes de la 2ᵉ Conférence du Groupe de travail de l'EAPS sur les migrations internationales en Europe, Rome, 25-27 novembre 2004.

Nations Unies, Division de la population, *Replacement Migration. Is it a Solution to Declining and Ageing Populations?*, Nations Unies, New York, 2000.

Michalon, B., 2004, "Playing on ethnicity to be there and here: the three paradoxes of 'ethnic migrations'", in *International migration in Europe: new trends, new methods of analysis*, papers from the 2nd Conference of the EAPS Working Group on International Migration in Europe, Rome, Italy, 25-27 November 2004.

OECD, 2001, "Student mobility between and towards OECD countries: a comparative analysis", in OECD, *Trends in International Migration: Annual Report 2001*, OECD, Paris, pp. 93-117.

Okolski, M., 1998, "Regional dimension of international migration in central and eastern Europe", *GENUS* 54, pp. 1-26.

Peraldi, M., 2004, "Algerian routes: a new perspective on migrant and social mobilities", in *International migration in Europe: new trends, new methods of analysis*, papers from the 2nd Conference of the EAPS Working Group on International Migration in Europe, Rome, Italy, 25-27 November 2004.

Petros, M., 2004, *The cost of human smuggling and trafficking*, Migration Research Unit, University College London, London.

Piguet, E. and Losa, S., 2002, *Travailleurs de l'ombre? Demande de main-d'œuvre du domaine de l'asile et ampleur de l'emploi d'étrangers non déclarés en Suisse*, Seisomo, Zurich.

Pinkerton, C., McLaughlan, G. and Salt, J., 2004, *Sizing the illegally resident population in the UK*, Home Office Online Report 58/04, Home Office, London.

Potot, S., 2004, "The Romanian circulatory migration: a case study", in *International migration in Europe: new trends, new methods of analysis*, papers from the 2nd Conference of the EAPS Working Group on International Migration in Europe, Rome, Italy, 25-27 November 2004.

Poulain, M., 1998, "Belgium", in Delauney, D. and Tapinos, G. *La mesure de la migration clandestine en Europe*, Population and Social Conditions Working Paper 3/1998/E/No. 7, Eurostat, Luxembourg.

Punch, A. and Pearce, D., 2000, *Europe's population and labour market beyond 2000*, Council of Europe, Strasbourg.

Salt, J. and Hogarth, J., 2000, "Migrant trafficking and human smuggling in Europe: a review of the evidence", in IOM, *Migrant trafficking and human smuggling in Europe*, IOM, Geneva, pp. 13-163.

OCDE, «Student mobility between and towards OECD countries: a comparative analysis» *in* OECD, *Trends in International Migration: Annual Report 2001*, OCDE, Paris, 2001, pp. 93-117.

OIM et ICMPD, *Migration Trends in Eastern Europe and Central Asia: 2001-02 Review*, OIM, Genève, 2002.

Okolski, M., «Regional Dimension of International Migration in Central and Eastern Europe», in *Genus*, 54, 1998, pp. 1-26.

Peraldi, M., «Algerian routes: a new perspective on migrant and social mobilities», in *International migration in Europe: new trends, new methods of analysis*, actes de la 2ᵉ Conférence du Groupe de travail de l'EAPS sur les migrations internationales en Europe, Rome, 25-27 novembre 2004.

Petros, M., *The Cost of Human Smuggling and Trafficking*, Migration Research Unit, University College London, Londres, 2004.

Piguet, E. et Losa, S., *Travailleurs de l'ombre? Demande de main-d'œuvre du domaine de l'asile et ampleur de l'emploi d'étrangers non déclarés en Suisse*, Seisomo, Zurich, 2002.

Pinkerton, C., McLaughlan, G. et Salt, J., *Sizing the illegally resident population in the UK*, Home Office Online Report, 58/04, Home Office, Londres, 2004.

Potot, S., *The Romanian circulatory migration: a case study'* in *International migration in Europe: new trends, new methods of analysis*, actes de la 2ᵉ Conférence du Groupe de travail de l'EAPS sur les migrations internationales en Europe, Rome, 25-27 novembre 2004.

Poulain, M., «Belgium», *in* Delauney, D. et Tapinos, G., *La mesure de la migration clandestine en Europe*, Population and Social Conditions Working Paper 3/1998/E/n° 7, Eurostat, Luxembourg, 1998.

Punch, A. et Pearce, D., *Europe's Population and Labour Market Beyond 2000*, Conseil de l'Europe, Strasbourg, 2000.

Salt, J. et Hogarth, J., «Migrant trafficking and human smuggling in Europe: a review of the evidence», *in* OIM, *Migrant Trafficking and Human Smuggling in Europe*, OIM, Genève, pp. 13-163.

Salt, J., Singleton A. et Hogarth, J., *Europe's international migrants: data sources, patterns and trends*, HMSO, Londres, 1994.

Salt, J., Singleton A., and Hogarth, J., 1994, *Europe's international migrants: data sources, patterns and trends*, HMSO, London.

Snel, E., de Boom, J. and Engbersen, G., 2004, *International migration and the Netherlands*, the report of the Dutch SOPEMI correspondent to the OECD, Paris.

UN Population Division, 2000, *Replacement migration. Is it a solution to declining and ageing populations?* UN, New York.

Wallace, C., 1999, *Economic hardship, migration and survival strategies in east-central Europe*, HIS, Vienna.

Widgren, J., 1994, "Multilateral co-operation to combat trafficking in migrants and the role of international organisations", 11th IOM Seminar on Migration, October, Geneva.

Snel, E., de Boom, J. et Engbersen, G., *International Migration and the Netherlands*, rapport du correspondant néerlandais du Sopemi à l'OCDE, OCDE, Paris, 2004.

Van der Leun, J. P., Engbersen, G., van der Heijden, P., *Illegaliteit en criminaliteit. Schattingen, aanhoudingen en uitzettingen*, Erasmus University, Rotterdam, 1998.

Wallace, C., *Economic Hardship, Migration and Survival Strategies in East-Central Europe*, HIS, Vienne, 1999.

Widgren, J., *Multilateral co-operation to combat trafficking in migrants and the role of international organisations*, 11ᵉ séminaire de l'OIM sur les migrations, Genève, octobre 1994.

Appendices/Annexes

Figure 1

Net migration as a component of average annual population growth in European countries, 2002-2003

Proportion de la migration nette dans la moyenne annuelle de l'évolution démographique dans les pays européens, 2002-2003

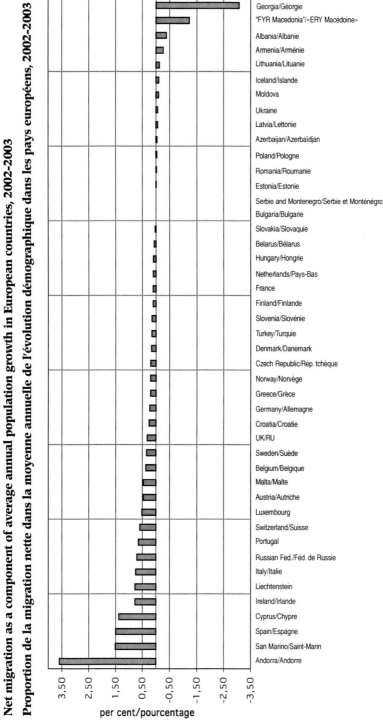

For sources and explanatory notes, please refer to corresponding table./Pour les sources et les notes explicatives, se reporter au tableau correspondant.

Figure 2.*a*

Stock of foreign population in selected western European countries, 1995–2003

Population étrangère dans les pays d'Europe occidentale étudiés, 1995–2003

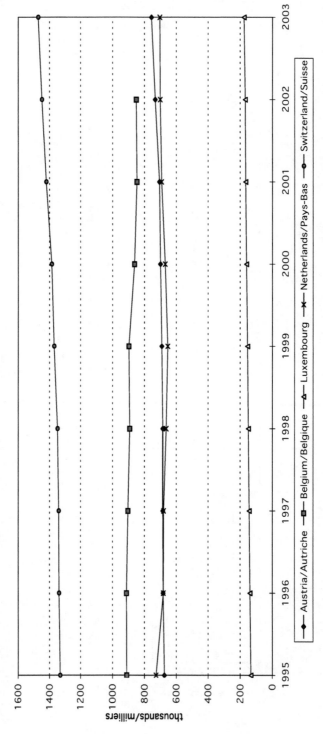

For sources and explanatory notes, please refer to corresponding table./Pour les sources et les notes explicatives, se reporter au tableau correspondant.

Figure 2.b

Stocks of foreign population in Germany and the United Kingdom, 1995-2003

Population étrangère en Allemagne et au Royaume-Uni, 1995-2003

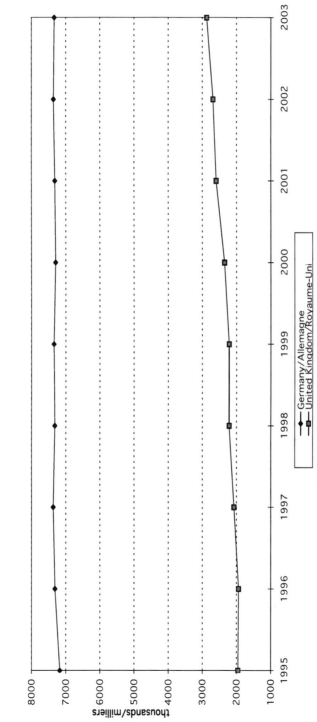

For sources and explanatory notes, please refer to corresponding table./Pour les sources et les notes explicatives, se reporter au tableau correspondant.

Figure 2.c

Stocks of foreign population in selected Scandinavian countries, 1995-2003

Population étrangère dans les pays scandinaves étudiés, 1995-2003

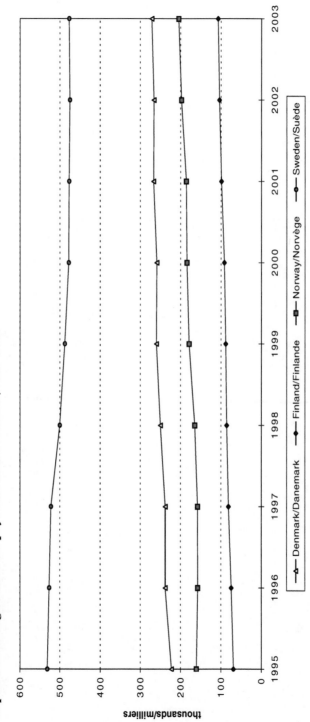

For sources and explanatory notes, please refer to corresponding table./Pour les sources et les notes explicatives, se reporter au tableau correspondant.

Figure 2.d

Stocks of foreign population in selected Mediterranean countries, 1995-2003
Population étrangère dans les pays méditerranéens étudiés, 1995-2003

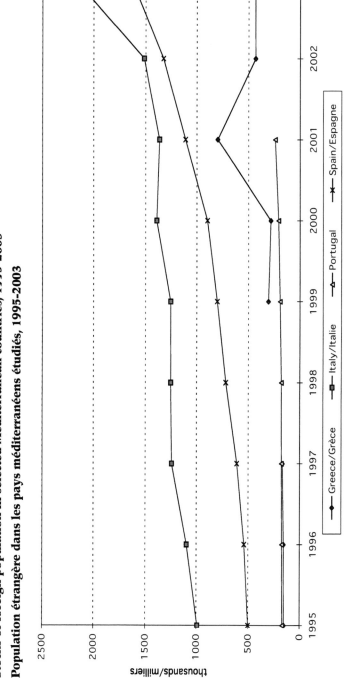

For sources and explanatory notes, please refer to corresponding table./Pour les sources et les notes explicatives, se reporter au tableau correspondant.

Figure 2.e

Stocks of foreign population in selected central and east European countries, 1995-2003
Population étrangère dans les pays d'Europe centrale et orientale étudiés, 1995-2003

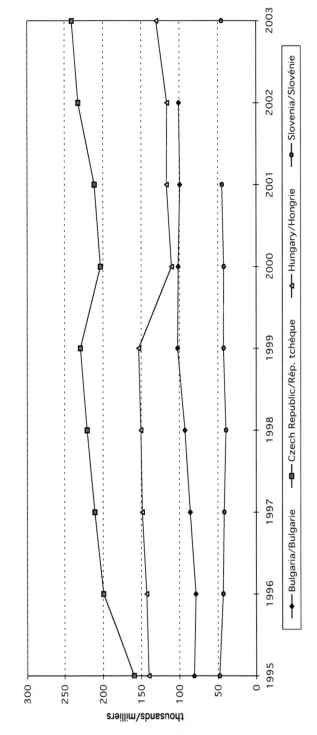

For sources and explanatory notes, please refer to corresponding table./Pour les sources et les notes explicatives, se reporter au tableau correspondant.

Figure 2.*f*

Stocks of foreign population in selected central and east European countries, 1995-2003
Population étrangère dans les pays d'Europe centrale et orientale étudiés, 1995-2003

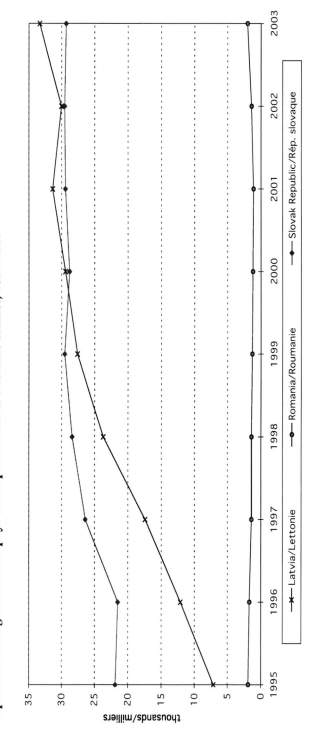

For sources and explanatory notes, please refer to corresponding table./Pour les sources et les notes explicatives, se reporter au tableau correspondant.

Figure 3.a

Stocks of foreign population as a percentage of the total population in selected western European countries, 1995-2003
Part de la population étrangère dans la population totale des pays d'Europe occidentale étudiés, 1995-2003

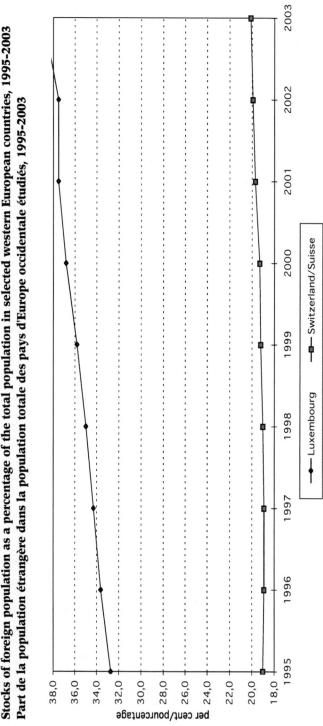

For sources and explanatory notes, please refer to corresponding table./Pour les sources et les notes explicatives, se reporter au tableau correspondant.

Figure 3.*b*

Stocks of foreign population as a percentage of the total population in selected western European countries, 1995-2003
Part de la population étrangère dans la population totale des pays d'Europe occidentale étudiés, 1995-2003

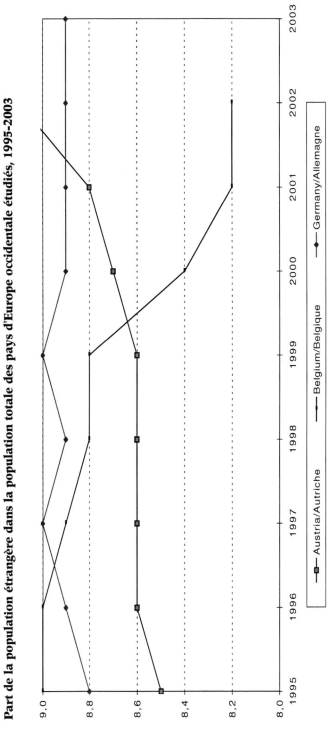

For sources and explanatory notes, please refer to corresponding table./Pour les sources et les notes explicatives, se reporter au tableau correspondant.

79

Figure 3.c

Stocks of foreign population as a percentage of the total population in selected western European countries, 1995-2003

Part de la population étrangère dans la population totale des pays d'Europe occidentale étudiés, 1995-2003

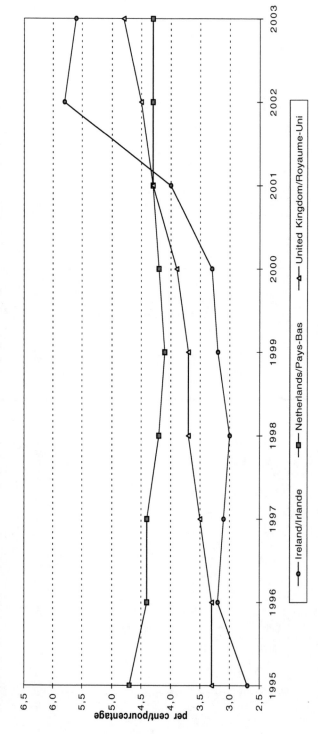

For sources and explanatory notes, please refer to corresponding table./Pour les sources et les notes explicatives, se reporter au tableau correspondant.

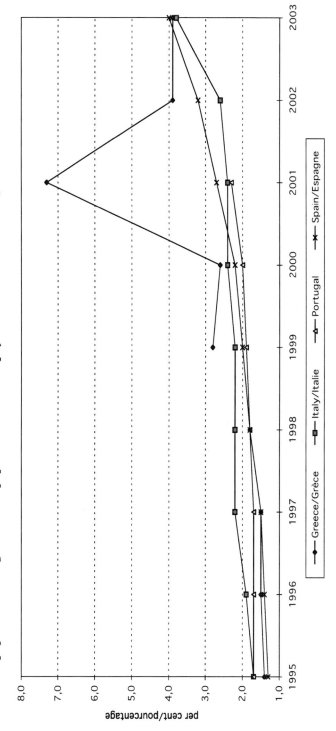

Figure 3.*d*

Stocks of foreign population as a percentage of the total population in selected Mediterranean countries, 1995-2003
Part de la population étrangère dans la population totale des pays méditerranéens étudiés, 1995-2003

For sources and explanatory notes, please refer to corresponding table./Pour les sources et les notes explicatives, se reporter au tableau correspondant.

81

Figure 3.e

Stocks of foreign population as a percentage of the total population in selected Scandinavian countries, 1995-2003
Part de la population étrangère dans la population totale des pays scandinaves étudiés, 1995-2003

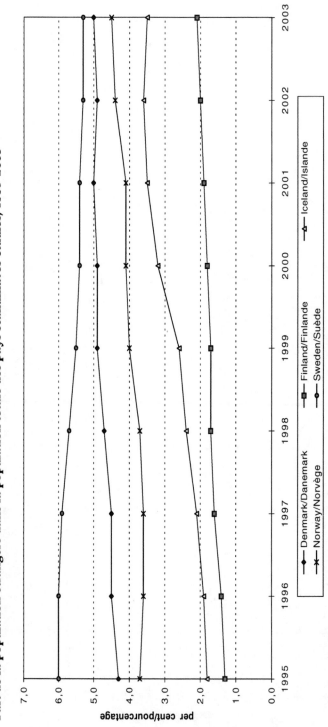

For sources and explanatory notes, please refer to corresponding table./Pour les sources et les notes explicatives, se reporter au tableau correspondant.

Figure 3.f

Stocks of foreign population as a percentage of the total population in selected central and east European countries, 1995-2003

Part de la population étrangère dans la population totale des pays d'Europe centrale et orientale étudiés, 1995-2003

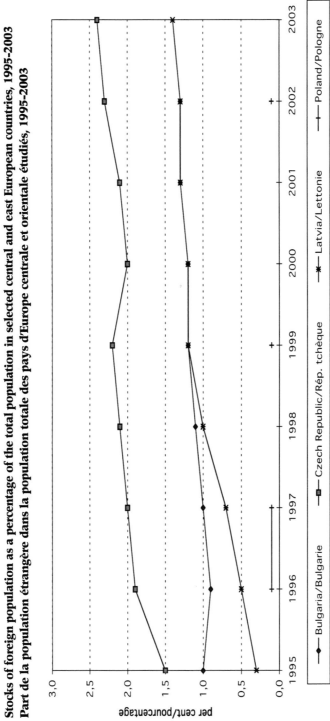

For sources and explanatory notes, please refer to corresponding table./Pour les sources et les notes explicatives, se reporter au tableau correspondant.

Figure 4.a

Inflows of foreign population to selected western European countries, 1995-2003

Arrivées de population étrangère dans les pays d'Europe occidentale étudiés, 1995-2003

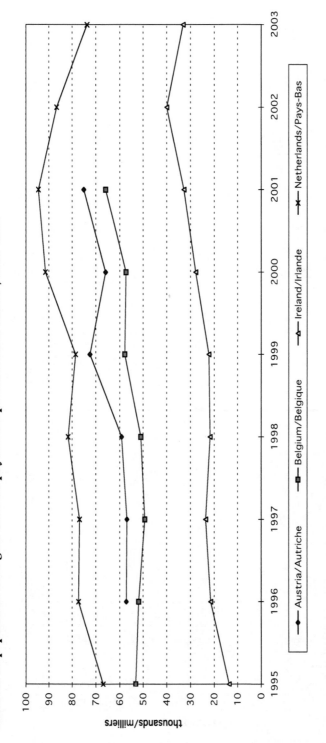

For sources and explanatory notes, please refer to corresponding table./Pour les sources et les notes explicatives, se reporter au tableau correspondant.

Figure 4.b

Inflows of foreign population to selected western European countries, 1995-2003

Arrivées de population étrangère dans les pays d'Europe occidentale étudiés, 1995-2003

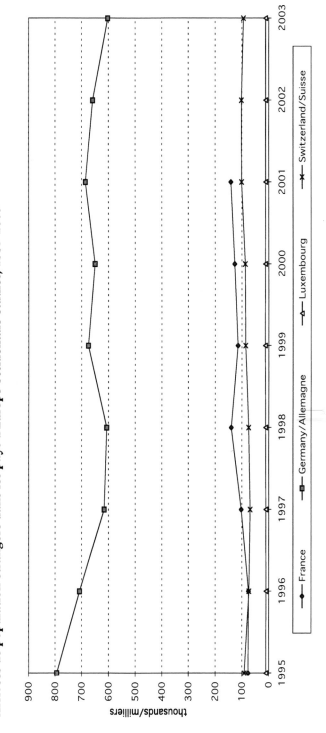

For sources and explanatory notes, please refer to corresponding table./Pour les sources et les notes explicatives, se reporter au tableau correspondant.

Figure 4.c

Inflows of foreign population to selected Scandinavian countries, 1995-2003
Arrivées de population étrangère dans les pays scandinaves étudiés, 1995-2003

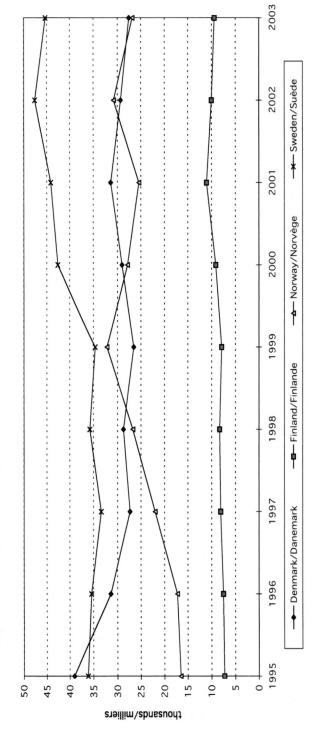

For sources and explanatory notes, please refer to corresponding table./Pour les sources et les notes explicatives, se reporter au tableau correspondant.

Figure 4.d

Inflows of foreign population to selected Mediterranean countries, 1995-2003

Arrivées de population étrangère dans les pays méditerranéens étudiés, 1995-2003

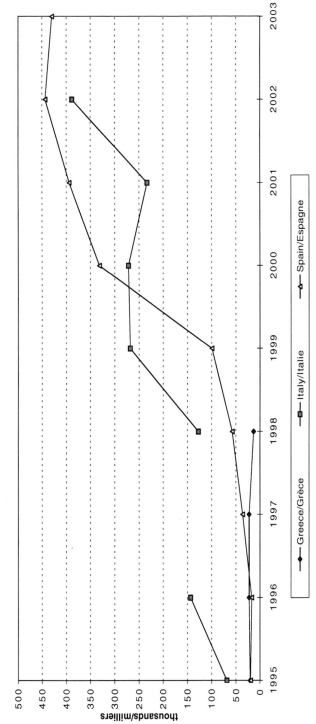

For sources and explanatory notes, please refer to corresponding table./Pour les sources et les notes explicatives, se reporter au tableau correspondant.

Figure 4.e

Inflows of foreign population to selected central and east European countries, 1995-2003

Arrivées de population étrangère dans les pays d'Europe centrale et orientale étudiés, 1995-2003

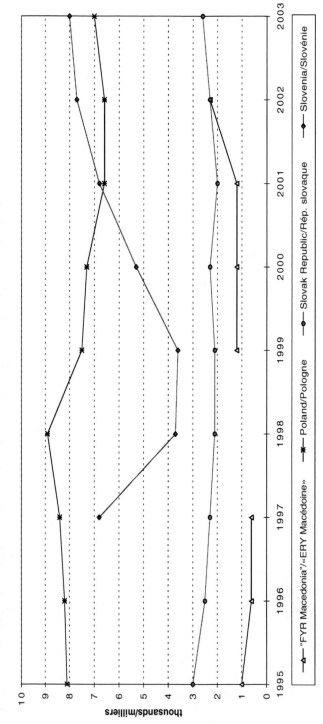

For sources and explanatory notes, please refer to corresponding table./Pour les sources et les notes explicatives, se reporter au tableau correspondant.

Figure 4.f

Inflows of foreign population to selected central and east European countries, 1995-2003
Arrivées de population étrangère dans les pays d'Europe centrale et orientale étudiés, 1995-2003

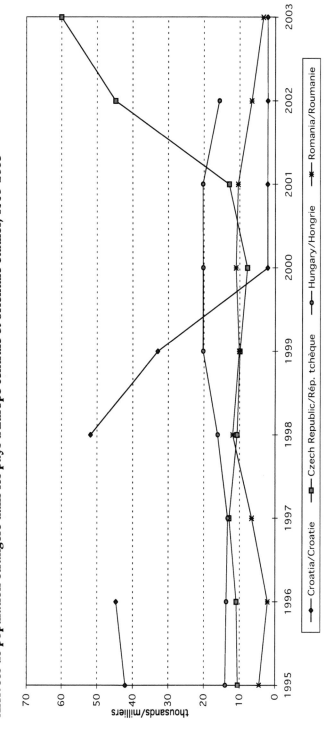

For sources and explanatory notes, please refer to corresponding table./Pour les sources et les notes explicatives, se reporter au tableau correspondant.

Figure 4.g

Inflows of foreign population to the Baltic states, 1995-2003
Arrivées de population étrangère dans les Etats baltes, 1995-2003

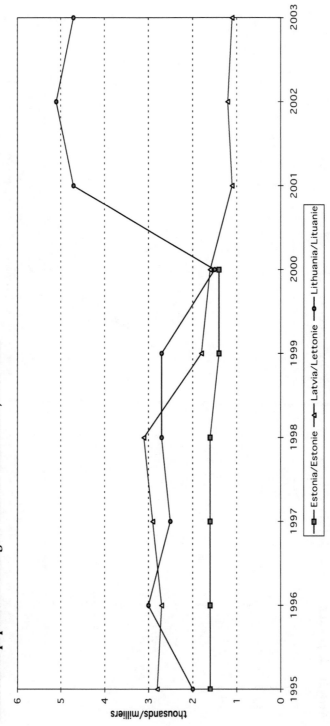

For sources and explanatory notes, please refer to corresponding table./Pour les sources et les notes explicatives, se reporter au tableau correspondant.

Figure 4.h

Inflows of foreign population to Russian Federation, 1995-2003

Arrivées de population étrangère en Fédération de Russie, 1995-2003

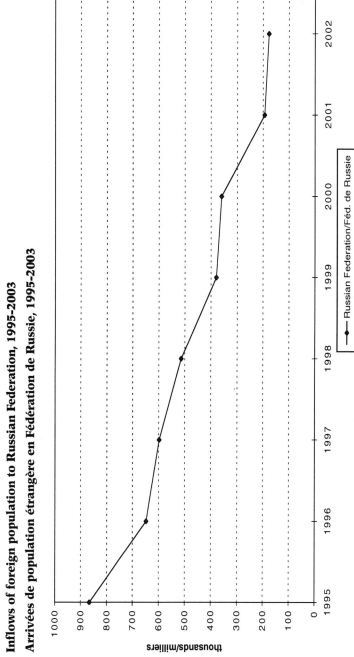

For sources and explanatory notes, please refer to corresponding table./Pour les sources et les notes explicatives, se reporter au tableau correspondant.

Figure 5.a

Outflows of foreign population from the Benelux countries, 1995-2003

Départs de population étrangère du Benelux, 1995-2003

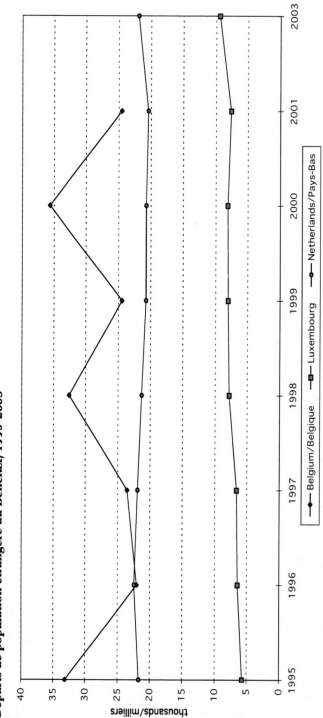

For sources and explanatory notes, please refer to corresponding table./Pour les sources et les notes explicatives, se reporter au tableau correspondant.

Figure 5.*b*

Outflows of foreign population from selected western European countries, 1995–2003

Départs de population étrangère des pays d'Europe occidentale étudiés, 1995–2003

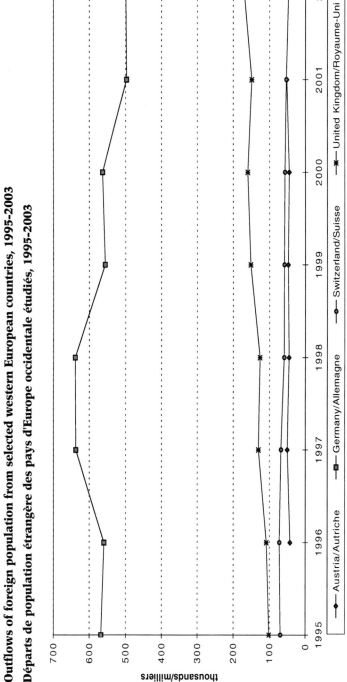

For sources and explanatory notes, please refer to corresponding table./Pour les sources et les notes explicatives, se reporter au tableau correspondant.

Figure 5.c

Outflows of foreign population from selected Scandinavian countries, 1995-2003
Départs de population étrangère des pays scandinaves étudiés, 1995-2003

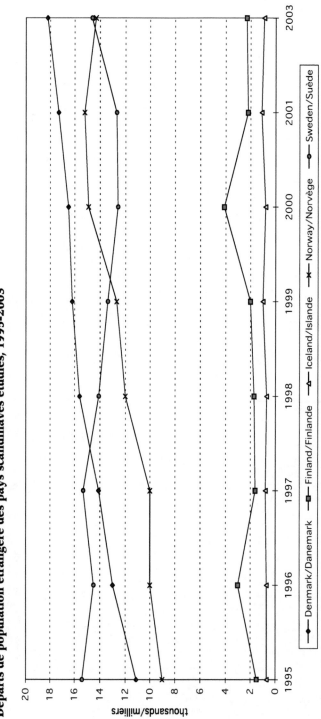

For sources and explanatory notes, please refer to corresponding table./Pour les sources et les notes explicatives, se reporter au tableau correspondant.

Figure 5.*d*

Permanent emigration from Russian Federation, 1995-2003

Emigration permanente de Fédération de Russie, 1995-2003

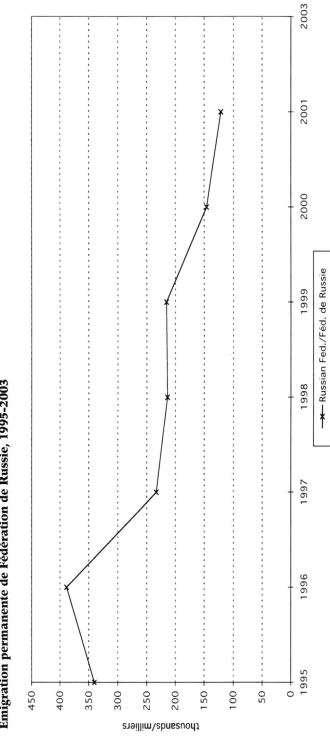

For sources and explanatory notes, please refer to corresponding table./Pour les sources et les notes explicatives, se reporter au tableau correspondant.

Figure 5.e

Permanent emigration from the Baltic states, 1995-2003

Émigration permanente des Etats baltes, 1995-2003

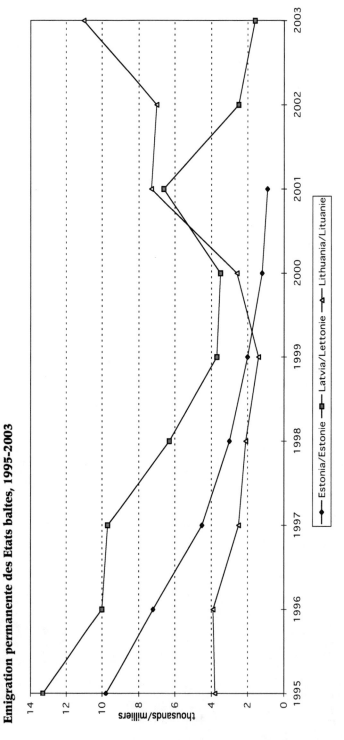

For sources and explanatory notes, please refer to corresponding table./Pour les sources et les notes explicatives, se reporter au tableau correspondant.

Figure 5.*f*

Permanent emigration from selected central and east European countries, 1995–2003

Emigration permanente des pays d'Europe centrale et orientale étudiés, 1995–2003

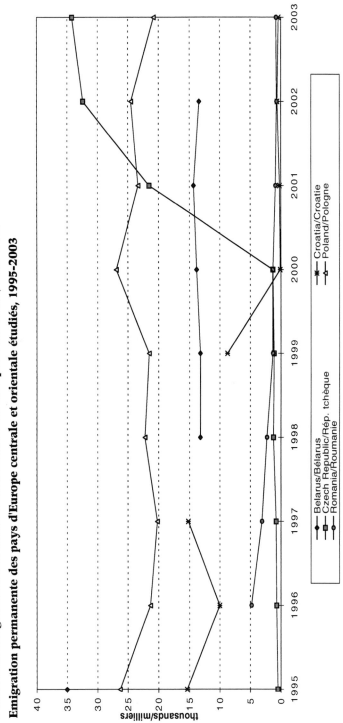

For sources and explanatory notes, please refer to corresponding table./Pour les sources et les notes explicatives, se reporter au tableau correspondant.

Figure 5.*g*

Permanent emigration from selected central and east European countries, 1995-2003

Emigration permanente des pays d'Europe centrale et orientale étudiés, 1995-2003

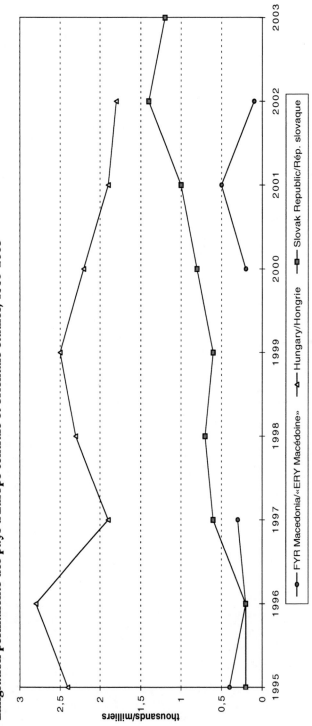

●── FYR Macedonia/«ERY Macédoine»   △── Hungary/Hongrie   ■── Slovak Republic/Rép. slovaque

For sources and explanatory notes, please refer to corresponding table./Pour les sources et les notes explicatives, se reporter au tableau correspondant.

Figure 6.a

Net flows of foreign population to/from selected western European countries, 1995-2003

Flux nets de population étrangère vers/en provenance des pays d'Europe occidentale étudiés, 1995-2003

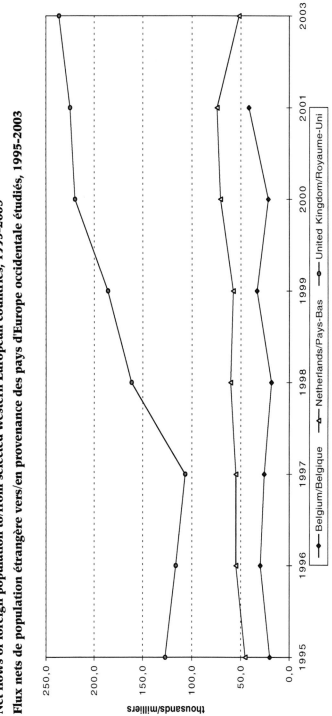

For sources and explanatory notes, please refer to corresponding table./Pour les sources et les notes explicatives, se reporter au tableau correspondant.

Figure 6.b

Net flows of foreign population to/from selected western European countries, 1995-2003

Flux nets de population étrangère vers/en provenance des pays d'Europe occidentale étudiés, 1995-2003

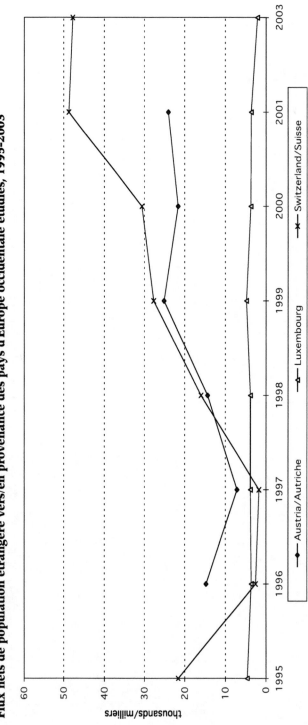

For sources and explanatory notes, please refer to corresponding table./Pour les sources et les notes explicatives, se reporter au tableau correspondant.

Figure 6.c

Net flows of foreign population to/from Germany, 1995-2003

Flux nets de population étrangère vers/en provenance de l'Allemagne, 1995-2003

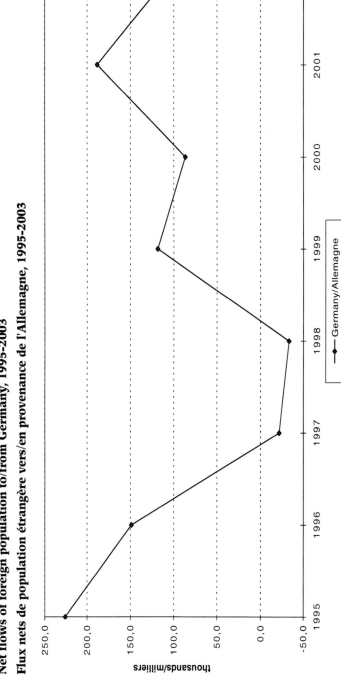

For sources and explanatory notes, please refer to corresponding table./Pour les sources et les notes explicatives, se reporter au tableau correspondant.

Figure 6.*d*

Net flows of foreign population to/from selected Scandinavian countries, 1995-2003
Flux nets de population étrangère vers/en provenance des pays scandinaves étudiés, 1995-2003

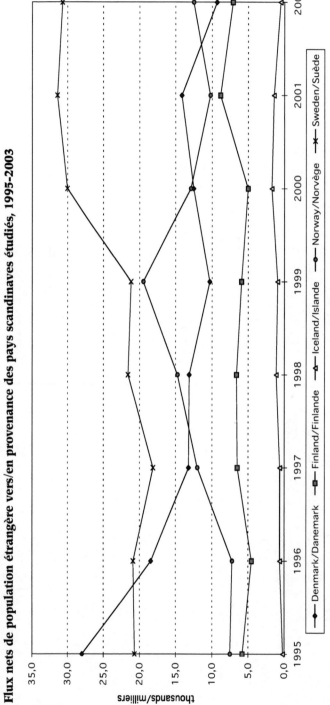

For sources and explanatory notes, please refer to corresponding table./Pour les sources et les notes explicatives, se reporter au tableau correspondant.

Figure 6.e

Net flows of foreign population to/from selected central and east European countries, 1995-2003

Flux nets de population étrangère vers/en provenance des pays d'Europe centrale et orientale étudiés, 1995-2003

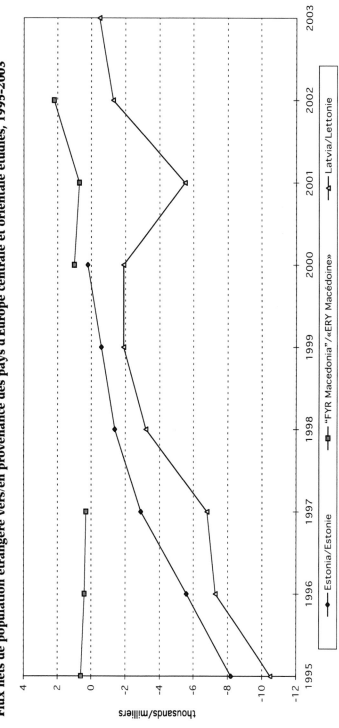

For sources and explanatory notes, please refer to corresponding table./Pour les sources et les notes explicatives, se reporter au tableau correspondant.

Figure 6.f

Net flows of foreign population to/from selected central and east European countries, 1995-2003

Flux nets de population étrangère vers/en provenance des pays d'Europe centrale et orientale étudiés, 1995-2003

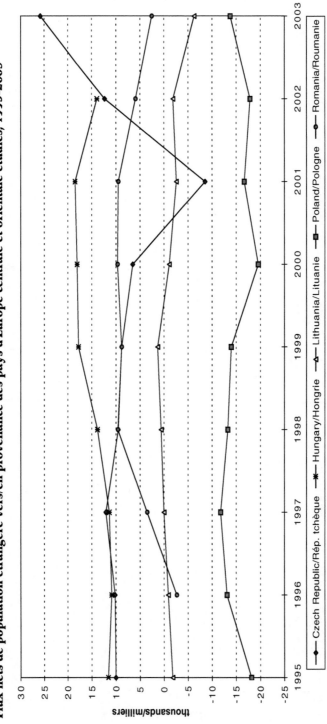

For sources and explanatory notes, please refer to corresponding table./Pour les sources et les notes explicatives, se reporter au tableau correspondant.

Figure 6.*g*

Net flows of foreign population to/from selected central and east European countries, 1995-2003

Flux nets de population étrangère vers/en provenance des pays d'Europe centrale et orientale étudiés, 1995-2003

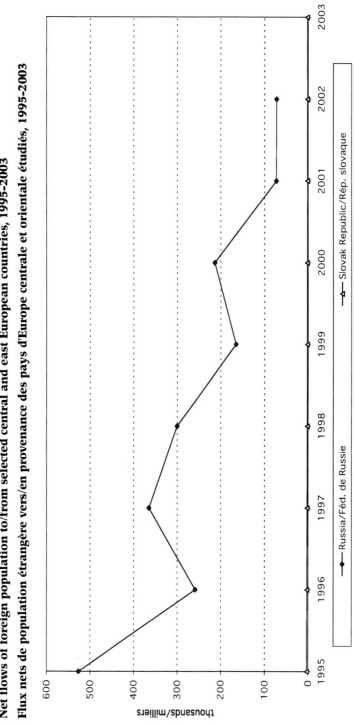

For sources and explanatory notes, please refer to corresponding table./Pour les sources et les notes explicatives, se reporter au tableau correspondant.

Figure 7.a

Stock of foreign labour in selected western European countries, 1995-2003

Réserve de main-d'œuvre étrangère dans les pays d'Europe occidentale étudiés, 1995-2003

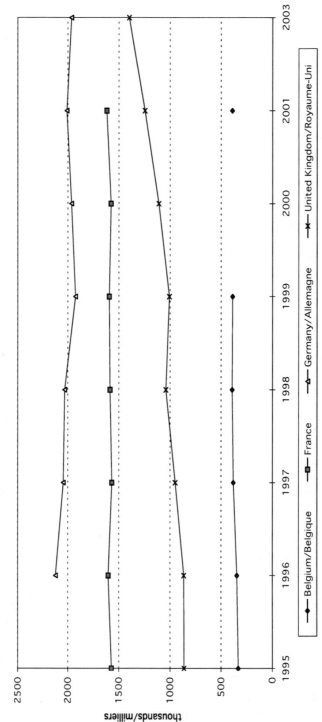

For sources and explanatory notes, please refer to corresponding table./Pour les sources et les notes explicatives, se reporter au tableau correspondant.

Figure 7.b

Stock of foreign labour in selected western European countries, 1995-2003

Réserve de main-d'œuvre étrangère dans les pays d'Europe occidentale étudiés, 1995-2003

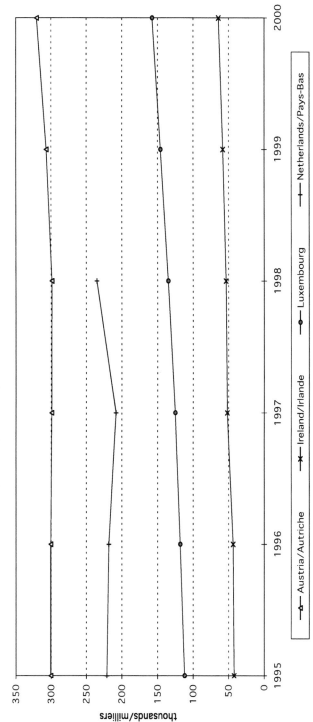

For sources and explanatory notes, please refer to corresponding table./Pour les sources et les notes explicatives, se reporter au tableau correspondant.

Figure 7.c

Stock of foreign labour in selected Scandinavian countries, 1995-2003

Réserve de main-d'œuvre étrangère dans les pays scandinaves étudiés, 1995-2003

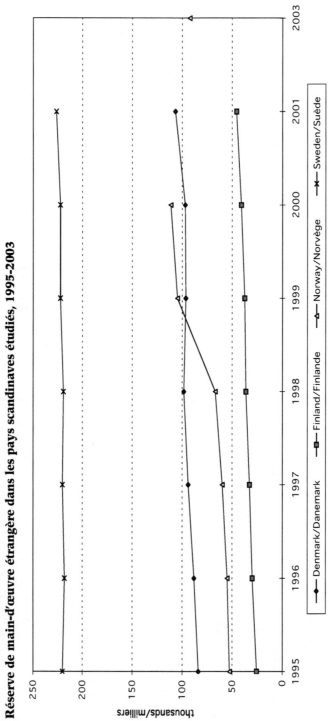

For sources and explanatory notes, please refer to corresponding table./Pour les sources et les notes explicatives, se reporter au tableau correspondant.

Figure 7.d

Stock of foreign labour in selected Mediterranean countries, 1995-2003

Réserve de main-d'œuvre étrangère dans les pays méditerranéens étudiés, 1995-2003

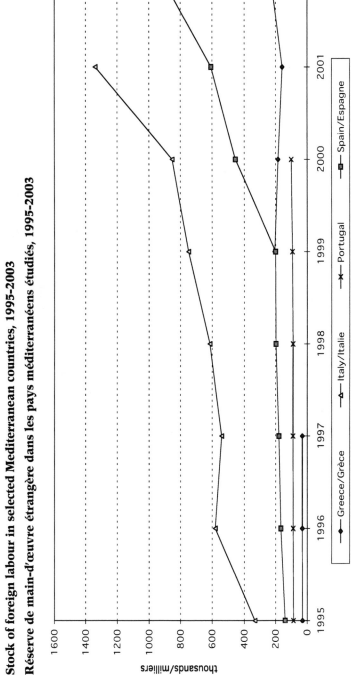

For sources and explanatory notes, please refer to corresponding table./Pour les sources et les notes explicatives, se reporter au tableau correspondant.

Figure 7.e

Stock of foreign labour in selected central and east European countries, 1995–2003

Réserve de main-d'œuvre étrangère dans les pays d'Europe centrale et orientale étudiés, 1995–2003

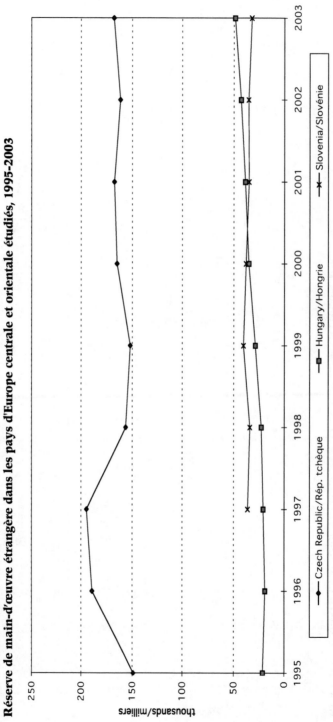

For sources and explanatory notes, please refer to corresponding table./Pour les sources et les notes explicatives, se reporter au tableau correspondant.

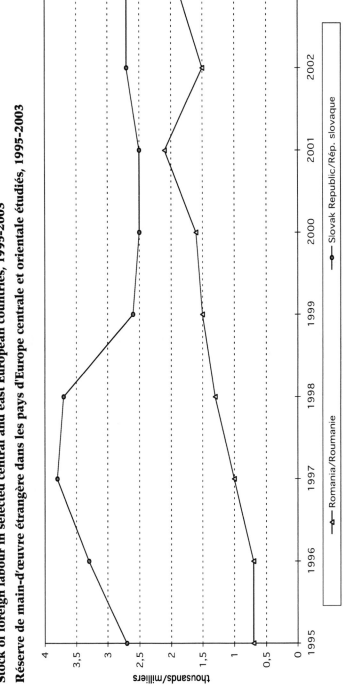

Figure 7.f

Stock of foreign labour in selected central and east European countries, 1995-2003

Réserve de main-d'œuvre étrangère dans les pays d'Europe centrale et orientale étudiés, 1995-2003

For sources and explanatory notes, please refer to corresponding table./Pour les sources et les notes explicatives, se reporter au tableau correspondant.

111

Figure 8.a

Inflows of foreign labour to selected western European countries, 1995-2003

Arrivées de main-d'œuvre étrangère dans les pays d'Europe occidentale étudiés, 1995-2003

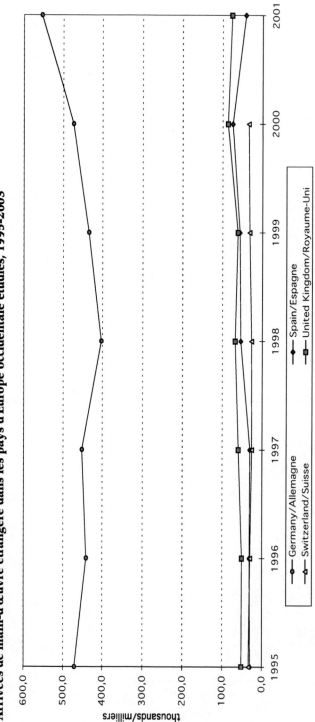

For sources and explanatory notes, please refer to corresponding table./Pour les sources et les notes explicatives, se reporter au tableau correspondant.

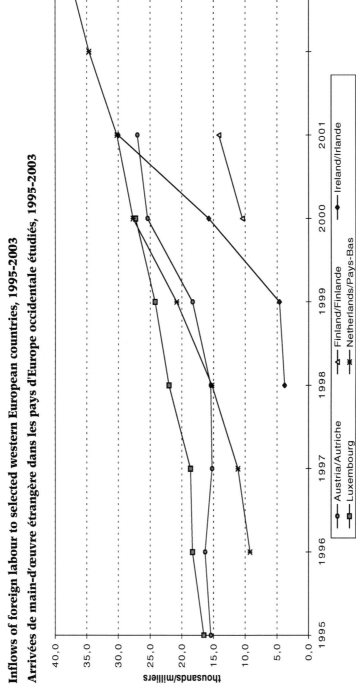

Figure 8.b

Inflows of foreign labour to selected western European countries, 1995-2003

Arrivées de main-d'œuvre étrangère dans les pays d'Europe occidentale étudiés, 1995-2003

For sources and explanatory notes, please refer to corresponding table./Pour les sources et les notes explicatives, se reporter au tableau correspondant.

Figure 8.c

Inflows of foreign labour to selected western European countries, 1995-2003

Arrivées de main-d'œuvre étrangère dans les pays d'Europe occidentale étudiés, 1995-2003

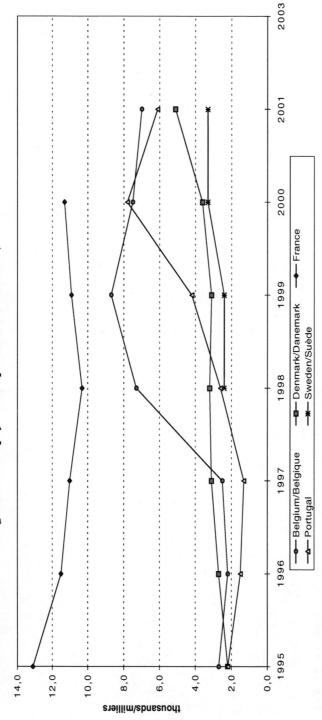

For sources and explanatory notes, please refer to corresponding table./Pour les sources et les notes explicatives, se reporter au tableau correspondant.

Figure 8.*d*

Inflows of foreign labour to selected central and east European countries, 1995-2003
Arrivées de main-d'œuvre étrangère dans les pays d'Europe centrale et orientale étudiés, 1995-2003

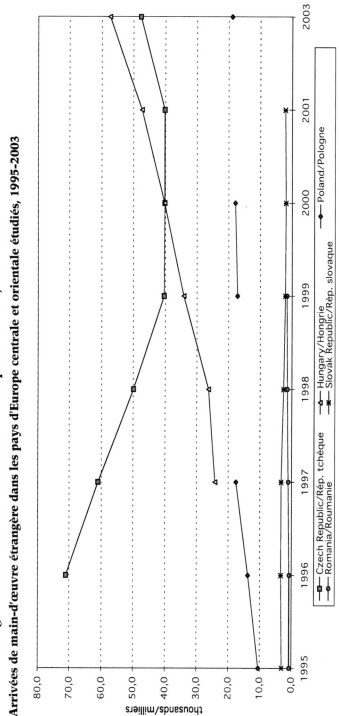

For sources and explanatory notes, please refer to corresponding table./Pour les sources et les notes explicatives, se reporter au tableau correspondant.

115

Figure 9.a

Asylum applications in selected European countries, 1995-2003

Demandes d'asile dans les pays européens étudiés, 1995-2003

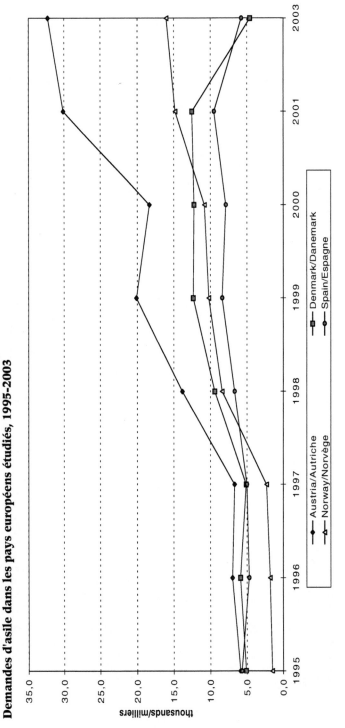

For sources and explanatory notes, please refer to corresponding table./Pour les sources et les notes explicatives, se reporter au tableau correspondant.

Figure 9.b

Asylum applications in selected European countries, 1995–2003
Demandes d'asile dans les pays européens étudiés, 1995–2003

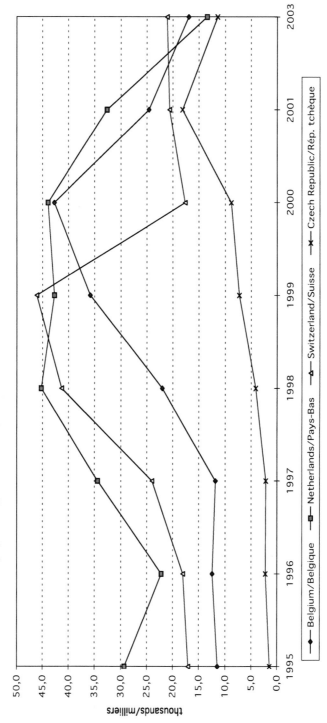

For sources and explanatory notes, please refer to corresponding table./Pour les sources et les notes explicatives, se reporter au tableau correspondant.

Figure 9.c

Asylum applications in selected European countries, 1995-2003
Demandes d'asile dans les pays européens étudiés, 1995-2003

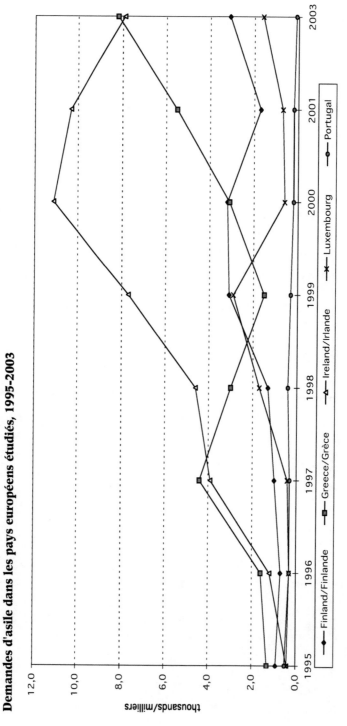

For sources and explanatory notes, please refer to corresponding table./Pour les sources et les notes explicatives, se reporter au tableau correspondant.

Figure 9.d

Asylum applications in selected European countries, 1995-2003

Demandes d'asile dans les pays européens étudiés, 1995-2003

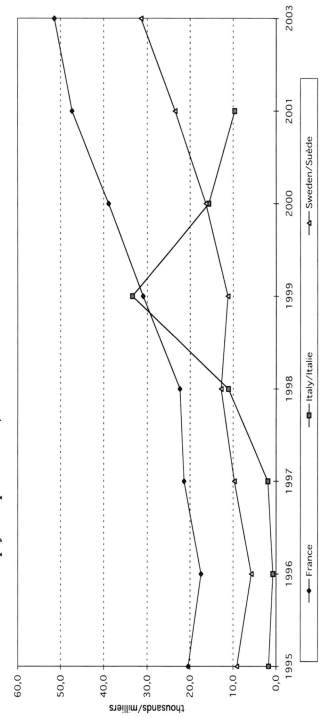

For sources and explanatory notes, please refer to corresponding table./Pour les sources et les notes explicatives, se reporter au tableau correspondant.

Figure 9.e

Asylum applications in Germany and the United Kingdom, 1995-2003

Demandes d'asile en Allemagne et au Royaume-Uni, 1995-2003

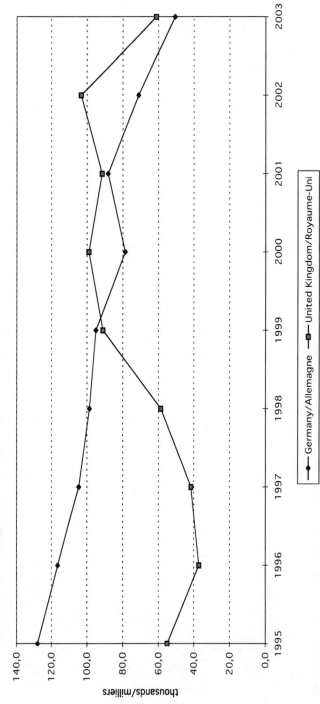

For sources and explanatory notes, please refer to corresponding table./Pour les sources et les notes explicatives, se reporter au tableau correspondant.

Figure 9.f

Asylum applications in selected European countries, 1995-2003

Demandes d'asile dans les pays européens étudiés, 1995-2003

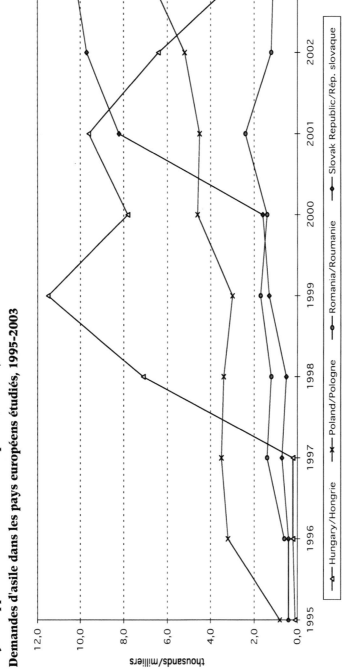

For sources and explanatory notes, please refer to corresponding table./Pour les sources et les notes explicatives, se reporter au tableau correspondant.

Table 1/Tableau 1

Estimated and projected population of the world and major areas, 1950, 2000 and 2050

Nombre estimé et projeté de la population dans le monde et dans les principales régions, 1950, 2000 et 2050

Region/Région	Millions and per cent/En millions et pourcentage					
	1950		2000		2050	
	Nos./N°	%	Nos./N°	%	Nos./N°	%
Total	2519	100,0	6057	100,0	8919	100,0
Africa/Afrique	221	8,8	794	13,1	1803	20,2
Asia/Asie	1399	55,5	3672	60,6	5222	58,5
Europe	548	21,8	727	12,0	632	7,1
Latin America and the Caribbean/ Amérique latine et Caraïbes	167	6,6	519	8,6	768	8,6
North America/ Amérique du Nord	172	6,8	314	5,2	448	5,0
Oceania/Océanie	13	0,5	31	0,5	46	0,5

Source: United Nations Population Division, World Population Prospects: the 2002 Revision.

Notes:
The 2050 data are based upon medium fertility variants.
Les données de 2050 sont basées sur des variants de fertilité moyenne.

Table 2/Tableau 2

**Components of population change in Europe,
2002-03 average (unless stated)**

**Composantes de l'évolution démographique en Europe,
moyenne 2002-2003 (ou donnée établie)**

Country/Pays	Annual average per cent/ Pourcentage moyen annuel			
	Growth Rate/ Taux de croissance	Natural Increase/ Augmentation naturelle	Net Migration/ Migration nette	
Albania/Albanie	0,82	1,20	-0,38	(1)
Andorra/Andorre	4,35	0,76	3,59	
Armenia/Arménie	-0,01	0,26	-0,27	
Austria/Autriche	0,47	0,02	0,46	p
Azerbaijan/Azerbaïdjan	0,75	0,79	-0,04	(2)
Belarus/Bélarus	-0,52	-0,57	0,06	
Belgium/Belgique	0,42	0,05	0,37	p
Bulgaria/Bulgarie	-0,58	-0,58	0,00	
Croatia/Croatie	-0,04	-0,24	0,19	(2)
Cyprus/Chypre	1,76	0,37	1,38	p
Czech Republic/Rép. tchèque	0,03	-0,16	0,19	
Denmark/Danemark	0,27	0,12	0,16	
Estonia/Estonie	-0,39	-0,38	-0,01	p
Finland/Finlande	0,24	0,14	0,11	
France	0,47	0,37	0,10	p
Georgia/Géorgie	-3,08	-0,02	-3,07	(3)
Germany/Allemagne	0,06	-0,16	0,23	*
Greece/Grèce	0,24	0,00	0,25	p
Hungary/Hongrie	-0,29	-0,38	0,09	p
Iceland/Islande	0,69	0,79	-0,10	
Ireland/Irlande	1,58	0,81	0,77	e
Italy/Italie	0,71	-0,04	0,75	*
Latvia/Lettonie	-0,57	-0,51	-0,06	
Liechtenstein	1,23	0,46	0,77	p
Lithuania/Lituanie	-0,43	-0,31	-0,12	p
Luxembourg	0,84	0,32	0,52	

Country/Pays	Annual average per cent/ Pourcentage moyen annuel			
	Growth Rate/ Taux de croissance	Natural Increase/ Augmentation naturelle	Net Migration/ Migration nette	
Malta/Malte	0,67	0,21	0,46	
Moldova	-0,26	-0,17	-0,09	(2)
Netherlands/Pays-Bas	0,46	0,37	0,10	p
Norway/Norvège	0,59	0,28	0,32	
Poland/Pologne	-0,06	-0,03	-0,04	
Portugal	0,70	0,06	0,65	
Romania/Roumanie	-0,28	-0,26	-0,02	
Russian Federation/ Féd. de Russie	0,08	-0,63	0,71	
San Marino/Saint-Marin	1,81	0,31	1,51	
Serbia and Montenegro/ Serbie-Monténégro	-0,27	-0,27	0,00	(4) p
Slovakia/Slovaquie	0,01	-0,01	0,03	
Slovenia/Slovénie	0,06	-0,08	0,14	
Spain/Espagne	1,63	0,13	1,50	p
Sweden/Suède	0,38	0,04	0,34	
Switzerland/Suisse	0,73	0,14	0,60	p
"FYR Macedonia"/ «ERY Macédoine»	-0,74	0,48	-1,22	(2)
Turkey/Turquie	1,55	1,41	0,15	
Ukraine	-0,82	-0,76	-0,06	
United Kingdom/ Royaume-Uni	0,32	0,13	0,19	

Source: Eurostat.

Notes:

1. 1999 data only./Données de 1999 seulement.
2. 2002 data only./Données de 2002 seulement.
3. 2000 data only./Données de 2000 seulement.
4. Does not include Kosovo./Kosovo non compris.
* - national estimate/estimation nationale.
p - provisional data/donnée provisoire.
e - Eurostat estimate/estimation d'Eurostat.

Table 3/Tableau 3

Stock of foreign population in selected European countries, 1995-2003 (thousands)
Population étrangère dans les pays européens étudiés, 1995-2003 (milliers)

(a) Western Europe/Europe occidentale

	1995	1996	1997	1998	1999
Austria/Autriche	673,8	680,3	683,1	683,7	689,3
Belgium/Belgique	909,8	911,9	903,1	892,0	897,1
Denmark/Danemark	222,7	237,7	237,7	249,6	259,4
Finland/Finlande	68,6	73,8	81,0	85,1	87,7
France	–	–	–	–	3263,2
Germany/Allemagne	7173,9	7314,0	7365,8	7319,6	7343,6
Greece/Grèce (1)	153,0	155,0	165,4	–	305,3
Iceland/Islande	4,8	5,1	5,6	6,5	7,3
Ireland/Irlande	96,1	117,5	113,9	110,9	118,0
Italy/Italie (2)	991,4	1095,6	1240,7	1250,2	1252,0
Luxembourg	132,5	138,1	142,8	147,7	152,9
Netherlands/Pays-Bas	725,4	679,9	678,1	662,4	651,5
Norway/Norvège	160,8	157,5	158,0	165,1	178,7
Portugal	168,3	172,9	175,3	178,1	190,9
Spain/Espagne	499,8	539,0	609,8	719,6	801,3
Sweden/Suède (3)	531,8	526,6	522,0	499,9	487,1
Switzerland/Suisse (4)	1330,6	1337,6	1340,8	1347,9	1368,7
Turkey/Turquie (5)	–	68,1	135,9	162,2	–
United Kingdom/Royaume-Uni	1948,0	1934,0	2066,0	2207,0	2208,0

(b) Central and Eastern Europe/Europe centrale et orientale

	1995	1996	1997	1998	1999
Bulgaria/Bulgarie (6)	81,0	78,7	86,0	92,8	102,2
Czech Republic/Rép. tchèque (7)	159,2	199,2	210,3	220,2	228,9
Estonia/Estonie	–	–	–	323,0	291,7
Hungary/Hongrie (8)	140,0	142,5	148,3	150,2	153,1
Latvia/Lettonie	7,1	12,1	17,4	23,7	27,6
Lithuania/Lituanie	–	–	–	–	–
Poland/Pologne (9)	–	29,9	32,5	–	42,8
Romania/Roumanie (10)	1,9	1,7	1,4	1,4	1,3
Russian Fed./Féd. de Russie (11)	171,6	158,5	138,3	–	–
Slovak Republic/Rép. slovaque (12)	21,9	21,5	26,4	28,4	29,5
Slovenia/Slovénie	48,0	43,0	41,7	39,4	42,5

Sources: Council of Europe, National Statistical Offices, OECD Sopemi Correspondents.
Conseil de l'Europe, Offices de statistique nationale, correspondants OCDE Sopemi.

Notes:
1. 1999 and 2000 do not include 0-14 year olds./1999 et 2000 n'incluent pas les 0-14 ans.
2. Figures refer to residence permits./Les chiffres se réfèrent aux permis de séjour.
3. Some foreigners permits of short duration are not counted (mainly citizens of other Nordic countries)./Certains permis de séjour de courte durée ne sont pas comptabilisés (principalement les citoyens d'autres pays nordiques).
4. Numbers of foreigners with annual residence permits (including, up to 31 December 1982, holders of permits of durations below 12 months) and holders of settlement permits (permanent permits). Seasonal and frontier workers are excluded./Nombre d'étrangers possédant un permis de séjour annuel (y compris, jusqu'au 31 décembre 1982, les détenteurs de permis de durée inférieure à douze mois) et de détenteurs de permis de séjour permanents. Les travailleurs saisonniers et frontaliers ne sont pas compris.
5. 2000 figure from the 2000 Census./Chiffres pour 2000 provenant du recensement de 2000.

	2000	2001	2002	2003
Austria/Autriche	698,6	704,9	731,6	755,1
Belgium/Belgique	861,7	846,7	850,1	–
Denmark/Danemark	258,6	266,7	265,4	271,2
Finland/Finlande	91,1	98,6	103,7	107,0
France	–	–	–	–
Germany/Allemagne	7296,8	7318,6	7355,6	7334,8
Greece/Grèce (1)	281,5	797,1	431,0	433,1
Iceland/Islande	8,8	9,9	10,2	10,2
Ireland/Irlande	126,5	152,2	227,7	223,1
Italy/Italie (2)	1388,2	1362,6	1512,3	2194,0
Luxembourg	159,4	164,7	166,7	174,2
Netherlands/Pays-Bas	667,8	690,4	700,0	702,2
Norway/Norvège	184,3	185,9	197,7	204,7
Portugal	207,6	238,7	–	–
Spain/Espagne	895,7	1109,1	1324,0	1647,0
Sweden/Suède (3)	477,3	476,0	474,1	476,1
Switzerland/Suisse (4)	1384,4	1419,1	1447,3	1471,0
Turkey/Turquie (5)	272,9	–	–	–
United Kingdom/Royaume-Uni	2342,0	2587,0	2681,0	2865,0

	2000	2001	2002	2003
Bulgaria/Bulgarie (6)	101,3	99,2	100,5	–
Czech Republic/Rép. tchèque (7)	203,0	210,8	231,6	240,4
Estonia/Estonie	287,1	273,8	269,5	–
Hungary/Hongrie (8)	110,0	116,4	115,9	130,1
Latvia/Lettonie	29,4	31,3	30,0	33,3
Lithuania/Lituanie	–	31,2	30,5	32,7
Poland/Pologne (9)	–	–	49,2	–
Romania/Roumanie (10)	1,2	1,1	1,4	2,0
Russian Fed./Féd. de Russie (11)	–	–	–	–
Slovak Republic/Rép. slovaque (12)	28,8	29,4	29,5	29,3
Slovenia/Slovénie	42,3	44,7	–	45,3

6. Stock of long-term resident foreigners, Ministry of Interior. 2001 figure is provisional./Population étrangère résidente de longue durée, ministère de l'Intérieur. Les chiffres pour 2001 sont provisoires.
7. Data derived from Ministries of Labour and Interior, and include only those holding permanent and long-term residence permits./ Données provenant des ministères du Travail et de l'Intérieur, incluant les détenteurs de permis de séjour permanents et de longue durée.
8. Temporary residence permit holders only./Détenteurs de permis de séjour temporaires.
9. 2002 figure from the Census/Chiffres de 2002 issus du recensement.
10. Foreign nationals with permanent residence visas./Nationaux étrangers possédant des visas de résidence permanente.
11. Only permanent resident foreigners, Ministry of Interior, 1998./Les étrangers résidents uniquement, ministère de l'Intérieur, 1998.
12. Number of residence permits. Source Presidium of Police Corps, in Slovak Correspondent's SOPEMI Report, 2001./Nombre de permis de séjour. Source: Presidium of Police Corps, Rapport des correspondants slovaques du Sopemi, 2001.

Table 4/Tableau 4

Stock of foreign population as a percentage of total population in selected European countries, 1995-2003 (per cent)

Part de la population étrangère dans la population totale dans les pays européens étudiés, 1995-2003 (pourcentage)

(a) Western Europe/Europe occidentale

	1995	1996	1997	1998	1999
Austria/Autriche	8,5	8,6	8,6	8,6	8,6
Belgium/Belgique	9,0	9,0	8,9	8,8	8,8
Denmark/Danemark	4,3	4,5	4,5	4,7	4,9
Finland/Finlande	1,3	1,4	1,6	1,7	1,7
France	–	–	–	–	5,6
Germany/Allemagne	8,8	8,9	9,0	8,9	9,0
Greece/Grèce	1,4	1,5	1,5	–	2,8
Iceland/Islande	1,8	1,9	2,1	2,4	2,6
Ireland/Irlande	2,7	3,2	3,1	3,0	3,2
Italy/Italie	1,7	1,9	2,2	2,2	2,2
Luxembourg	32,7	33,6	34,3	35,0	35,8
Netherlands/Pays-Bas	4,7	4,4	4,4	4,2	4,1
Norway/Norvège	3,7	3,6	3,6	3,7	4,0
Portugal	1,7	1,7	1,7	1,8	1,9
Spain/Espagne	1,3	1,4	1,5	1,8	2,0
Sweden/Suède	6,0	6,0	5,9	5,7	5,5
Switzerland/Suisse	19,0	18,9	18,9	19,0	19,2
Turkey/Turquie	–	0,1	0,2	0,2	–
United Kingdom/Royaume-Uni	3,3	3,3	3,5	3,7	3,7

(b) Central and Eastern Europe/Europe centrale et orientale

	1995	1996	1997	1998	1999
Bulgaria/Bulgarie	1,0	0,9	1,0	1,1	1,2
Czech Republic/Rép. tchèque	1,5	1,9	2,0	2,1	2,2
Estonia/Estonie	–	–	–	23,2	21,1
Hungary/Hongrie	1,4	1,4	1,4	1,5	1,5
Latvia/Lettonie	0,3	0,5	0,7	1,0	1,2
Lithuania/Lituanie	–	–	–	–	–
Poland/Pologne	–	0,1	0,1	–	0,1
Romania/Roumanie	0,0	0,0	0,0	0,0	0,0
Russian Fed./Féd. de Russie	–	–	–	–	–
Slovak Republic/Rép. slovaque	0,4	0,4	0,5	0,5	0,5
Slovenia/Slovénie	2,4	2,2	2,1	2,0	2,1

Sources: Council of Europe, National Statistical Offices, OECD SOPEMI Correspondents.
Conseil de l'Europe, Offices de statistique nationale, correspondants OCDE Sopemi.

Note:
See Table 3/Voir tableau 3.

	2000	2001	2002	2003
Austria/Autriche	8,7	8,8	9,1	9,4
Belgium/Belgique	8,4	8,2	8,2	–
Denmark/Danemark	4,9	5,0	4,9	5,0
Finland/Finlande	1,8	1,9	2,0	2,1
France	–	–	–	–
Germany/Allemagne	8,9	8,9	8,9	8,9
Greece/Grèce	2,6	7,3	3,9	3,9
Iceland/Islande	3,2	3,5	3,6	3,5
Ireland/Irlande	3,3	4,0	5,8	5,6
Italy/Italie	2,4	2,4	2,6	3,8
Luxembourg	36,8	37,5	37,5	38,9
Netherlands/Pays-Bas	4,2	4,3	4,3	4,3
Norway/Norvège	4,1	4,1	4,4	4,5
Portugal	2,0	2,3	–	–
Spain/Espagne	2,2	2,7	3,2	4,0
Sweden/Suède	5,4	5,4	5,3	5,3
Switzerland/Suisse	19,3	19,7	19,9	20,1
Turkey/Turquie	0,4	–	–	–
United Kingdom/Royaume-Uni	3,9	4,3	4,5	4,8

	2000	2001	2002	2003
Bulgaria/Bulgarie	1,2	1,3	1,3	–
Czech Republic/Rép. tchèque	2,0	2,1	2,3	2,4
Estonia/Estonie	20,9	20,0	19,8	–
Hungary/Hongrie	1,1	1,1	1,1	1,3
Latvia/Lettonie	1,2	1,3	1,3	1,4
Lithuania/Lituanie	–	0,9	0,9	0,9
Poland/Pologne	–	–	0,1	–
Romania/Roumanie	0,0	0,0	0,0	0,0
Russian Fed./Féd. de Russie	–	–	–	–
Slovak Republic/Rép. slovaque	0,5	0,5	0,5	0,5
Slovenia/Slovénie	2,1	2,2	–	2,3

Table 5.a/Tableau 5.a

Foreign population in EU and EFTA countries, as of 1 January 2000 (or latest year available)
Population étrangère dans les pays de l'UE et de l'AELE, au 1er janvier 2000 (ou dernière année disponible)

Absolute figures/Chiffres absolus

Year/Année	B	DK	D	EL	E	F	IRL	I	L	NL	A	P
	2000	1999	2000	1997	2000	1999	2000	2000	1998	2000	2000	2000
Total	853369	256276	7343591	161148	801329	3263186	126533	1270553	147700	651532	753528	190898
Europe	661258	157203	5930311	97432	352974	1555679	92209	498170	–(1)	333380	474728	56712
EU 15 & EFTA/UE 15 et AELE	570531	72473	1905432	46789	326388	1225755	–	161024	–	200087	–	54253
EU 15/UE 15	563556	53195	1858672	45020	312203	1195498	92209	148506	131410	195886	–	52429
EFTA/AELE	6975	19278	46760	1769	14185	30257	–	12518	–	4201	–	1824
Central and east Europe/ Europe centrale et orientale	21544	46626	1969760	47264	25733	119849	–	328144	–	32468	340499	2361
Other Europe/Autres Europe	69183	38104	2055119	3379	853	210075	–	9002	–	100825	–	98
Africa/Afrique	153356	23871	300611	13237	213012	1419758	8044	411492	–	149764	–	89518
Americas/Amérique	18744	9808	205373	19996	166709	81293	–	120898	–	36484	–	35987
Asia/Asie	19047	55524	823092	27884	66922	203432	–	236369	–	62368	–	7890
Oceania/Océanie	648	1110	10033	1242	1013	3024	–	3154	–	3168	–	516
Other/Autres (3)	316	8760	74171	–	699	–	–	470	–	66368	278800	275

Absolute figures/Chiffres absolus

Year/Année	FIN 2000	S 2000	UK 1999	IS 2000	LI 1997	N 2000	CH 2000	EU 15 (2)	EFTA (2)	EEA (2)	EU & EFTA (2)
Total	87680	487175	2297947	7271	11714	178686	1406630	1892445	1592587	18878402	20285032
Europe	60171	330763	1057261	5094	11414	118354	1254001	11658251	1377449	11781699	13035700
EU 15 & EFTA/UE 15 et AELE	17333	214757	874272	2941	9629	83355	810512	5669094	896808	5755390	6565902
EU 15/UE 15	16328	177430	859138	2617	5012	78482	807332	5701480	888431	5782579	6589911
EFTA/AELE	1005	37327	15134	324	4617	4873	3180	191233	8377	196430	199610
Central and east Europe/ Europe centrale et orientale	41066	99424	118395	2142	985	31467	362624	3193133	396233	3226742	3589366
Other Europe/Autres Europe	1772	16582	64594	11	800	3532	80865	2569586	84408	2573129	2653994
Africa/Afrique	7791	27726	291388	184	18	11567	35446	3101524	47197	3113275	3148721
Americas/Amérique	3649	31814	249669	828	178	14318	46955	988468	62101	1003614	1050569
Asia/Asie	13813	84140	559042	1104	99	33274	67386	2159523	101764	2193901	2261287
Oceania/Océanie	495	2171	98669	56	5	761	2568	125243	3385	126060	128628
Other/Autres (3)	1761	10561	23846	5	34	412	274	466027	691	466444	466718

Sources: Eurostat.

Table 5.b/Tableau 5.b

Foreign population in EU and EFTA countries, as of 1 January 2000 (or latest year available)
Population étrangère dans les pays de l'UE et de l'AELE, au 1er janvier 2000 (ou dernière année disponible)

Proportion of total foreign population of reporting country (per cent)
Part de la population étrangère totale dans les pays étudiés (pourcentage)

Year/Année	B 2000	DK 1999	D 2000	EL 1997	E 2000	F 1999	IRL 2000	I 2000	L 1998	NL 2000	A 2000	P 2000
Total	100,0	100,0	100,0	100,0	100,0	100,0	100,0	100,0	100,0	100,0	100,0	100,0
Europe	77,5	61,3	80,8	60,5	44,0	47,7	72,9	39,2	–	51,2	63,0	29,7
EU 15 & EFTA/UE 15 et AELE	66,9	28,3	25,9	29,0	40,7	37,6	–	12,7	–	30,7	–	28,4
EU 15/UE 15	66,0	20,8	25,3	27,9	39,0	36,6	72,9	11,7	89,0	30,1	–	27,5
EFTA/AELE	0,8	7,5	0,6	1,1	1,8	0,9	–	1,0	–	0,6	–	1,0
Central and east Europe/ Europe centrale et orientale	2,5	18,2	26,8	29,3	3,2	3,7	–	25,8	–	5,0	45,2	1,2
Other Europe/Autres Europe	8,1	14,9	28,0	2,1	0,1	6,4	–	0,7	–	15,5	–	0,1
Africa/Afrique	18,0	9,3	4,1	8,2	26,6	43,5	–	32,4	–	23,0	–	46,9
Americas/Amérique	2,2	3,8	2,8	12,4	20,8	2,5	6,4	9,5	–	5,6	–	18,9
Asia/Asie	2,2	21,7	11,2	17,3	8,4	6,2	–	18,6	–	9,6	–	4,1
Oceania/Océanie	0,1	0,4	0,1	0,8	0,1	0,1	–	0,2	–	0,5	–	0,3
Other/Autres (3)	0,0	3,4	1,0	–	0,1	–	–	0,0	–	10,2	37,0	0,1

Proportion of total foreign population of reporting country (per cent)
Part de la population étrangère totale dans les pays étudiés (pourcentage)

Year/Année	FIN 2000	S 2000	UK 1999	IS 2000	LI 1997	N 2000	CH 2000	EU 15 (2)	EFTA (2)	EEA (2)	EU & EFTA (2)
Total	100,0	100,0	100,0	100,0	100,0	100,0	100,0	100,0	100,0	100,0	100,0
Europe	68,6	67,9	46,0	70,1	97,4	66,2	89,1	62,4	86,5	62,4	64,3
EU 15 & EFTA/UE 15 et AELE	19,8	44,1	38,0	40,4	82,2	46,6	57,6	30,3	56,3	30,5	32,4
EU 15/UE 15	18,6	36,4	37,4	36,0	42,8	43,9	57,4	30,5	55,8	30,6	32,5
EFTA/AELE	1,1	7,7	0,7	4,5	39,4	2,7	0,2	1,0	0,5	1,0	1,0
Central and east Europe/ Europe centrale et orientale	46,8	20,4	5,2	29,5	8,4	17,6	25,8	17,1	24,9	17,1	17,7
Other Europe/Autres Europe	2,0	3,4	2,8	0,2	6,8	2,0	5,7	13,7	5,3	13,6	13,1
Africa/Afrique	8,9	5,7	12,7	2,5	0,2	6,5	2,5	16,6	3,0	16,5	15,5
Americas/Amérique	4,2	6,5	10,9	11,4	1,5	8,0	3,3	5,3	3,9	5,3	5,2
Asia/Asie	15,8	17,3	24,3	15,2	0,8	18,6	4,8	11,6	6,4	11,6	11,1
Oceania/Océanie	0,6	0,4	4,3	0,8	0,0	0,4	0,2	0,7	0,2	0,7	0,6
Other/Autres (3)	2,0	2,2	1,0	0,1	0,3	0,2	0,0	2,5	0,0	2,5	2,3

Sources: Eurostat.

Table 5.c/Tableau 5.c

Foreign population in EU and EFTA countries, as of 1 January 2000 (or latest year available)
Population étrangère dans les pays de l'UE et de l'AELE, au 1er janvier 2000 (ou dernière année disponible)

Proportion of total foreign citizenship in EU and EFTA countries (per cent)
Part de citoyens étrangers dans les pays de l'UE et de l'AELE (pourcentage)

Year/Année	B 2000	DK 1999	D 2000	EL 1997	E 2000	F 1999	IRL 2000	I 2000	L 1998	NL 2000	A 2000	P 2000
Total	4,2	1,3	36,2	0,8	4,0	16,1	0,6	6,3	0,7	3,2	3,7	0,9
Europe	5,1	1,2	45,5	0,7	2,7	11,9	0,7	3,8	–	2,6	3,6	0,4
EU 15 & EFTA/UE 15 et AELE	8,7	1,1	29,0	0,7	5,0	18,7	–	2,5	–	3,0	–	0,8
EU 15/UE 15	8,6	0,8	28,2	0,7	4,7	18,1	1,4	2,3	2,0	3,0	–	0,8
EFTA/ELE	3,5	9,7	23,4	0,9	7,1	15,2	–	6,3	–	2,1	–	0,9
Central and Eastern Europe/ Europe centrale et orientale	0,6	1,3	54,9	1,3	0,7	3,3	–	9,1	–	0,9	9,5	0,1
Other Europe/Autres Europe	2,6	1,4	77,4	0,1	0,0	7,9	–	0,3	–	3,8	–	0,0
Africa/Afrique	4,9	0,8	9,5	0,4	6,8	45,1	–	13,1	–	4,8	–	2,8
Americas/Amérique	1,8	0,9	19,5	1,9	15,9	7,7	0,8	11,5	–	3,5	–	3,4
Asia/Asie	0,8	2,5	36,4	1,2	3,0	9,0	–	10,5	–	2,8	–	0,3
Oceania/Océanie	0,5	0,9	7,8	1,0	0,8	2,4	–	2,5	–	2,5	–	0,4
Other/Autres (3)	0,1	1,9	15,9	–	0,1	–	–	0,1	–	14,2	59,7	0,1

Proportion of total foreign citizenship in EU and EFTA countries (per cent)
Part de citoyens étrangers dans les pays de l'UE et de l'AELE (pourcentage)

Year/Année	FIN 2000	S 2000	UK 1999	IS 2000	LI 1997	N 2000	CH 2000	EU 15 (2)	EFTA (2)	EEA (2)	EU & EFTA (2)
Total	0,4	2,4	11,3	0,0	0,1	0,9	6,9	92,1	7,9	93,1	100,0
Europe	0,5	2,5	8,1	0,0	0,1	0,9	9,6	89,4	10,6	90,4	100,0
EU 15 & EFTA/UE 15 et AELE	0,3	3,3	13,3	0,0	0,1	1,3	12,3	86,3	13,7	87,7	100,0
EU 15/UE 15	0,2	2,7	13,0	0,0	0,1	1,2	12,3	86,5	13,5	87,7	100,0
EFTA/ELE	0,5	18,7	7,6	0,2	2,3	2,4	1,6	95,8	4,2	98,4	100,0
Central and Eastern Europe/ Europe centrale et orientale	1,1	2,8	3,3	0,1	0,0	0,9	10,1	89,0	11,0	89,9	100,0
Other Europe/Autres Europe	0,1	0,6	2,4	0,0	0,0	0,1	3,0	96,8	3,2	97,0	100,0
Africa/Afrique	0,2	0,9	9,3	0,0	0,0	0,4	1,1	98,5	1,5	98,9	100,0
Americas/Amérique	0,3	3,0	23,8	0,1	0,0	1,4	4,5	94,1	5,9	95,5	100,0
Asia/Asie	0,6	3,7	24,7	0,0	0,0	1,5	3,0	95,5	4,5	97,0	100,0
Oceania/Océanie	0,4	1,7	76,7	0,0	0,0	0,6	2,0	97,4	2,6	98,0	100,0
Other/Autres (3)	0,4	2,3	5,1	0,0	0,0	0,1	0,1	99,9	0,1	99,9	100,0

Sources: Eurostat.

Notes:

1. "¦" refers to data which are unavailable./«–» signifie que les données sont indisponibles.
2. These sub-totals have been calculated by summing relevant figures where available in the preceeding columns. Therefore, owing to unavailable figures and data from different years, some of these figures are (under-)estimates./Ces sous-totaux ont été obtenus en additionnant les chiffres appropriés disponibles dans les colonnes précédentes. Ainsi, en raison de chiffres non disponibles et de données concernant des années différentes, certains de ces résultats sont sous-estimés.
3. Includes those not included in other categories, stateless and unknown./Comprend ceux non inclus dans d'autres catégories, non déterminés et inconnus.

Table 6/Tableau 6

Size of the foreign-born and foreign-national populations in selected European countries, according to the 2001 (or latest) national census

Population née à l'étranger et population nationale dans les pays européens étudiés, selon le recensement national de 2001 (ou dernier en date)

	Foreign-born/Nés à l'étranger	
	thousands/ en milliers	proportion of total population/ part de la population totale
Total	82627,1	7,8
Austria/Autriche	1002,5	12,5
Belgium/Belgique	1099,2	10,7
Czech Republic/Rép. tchèque	448,5	4,5
Denmark/Danemark	361,1	6,8
Finland/Finlande	131,4	2,5
France	5868,2	10,0
Germany/Allemagne	10256,1	12,5
Greece/Grèce	1122,6	10,3
Hungary/Hongrie	292,9	2,9
Ireland/Irlande	400	10,4
Luxembourg	142,7	32,6
Netherlands/Pays-Bas	1615,4	10,1
Norway/Norvège	333,8	7,3
Poland/Pologne	775,3	2,1
Portugal	651,5	6,3
Slovak Republic/Rép. slovaque	119,1	2,5
Spain/Espagne	2172,2	5,3
Sweden/Suède	1077,6	12,0
Switzerland/Suisse	1570,8	22,4
Turkey/Turquie	1259,4	1,9
United Kingdom/Royaume-Uni	4865,6	8,3

Source: National censuses, compiled and calculated by the OECD.
    Recensements nationaux, rassemblés et calculés par l'OCDE.

Table 7/Tableau 7

Inflows of foreign population to selected European countries, 1995-2003 (thousands)

Arrivées de population étrangère dans les pays européens étudiés, 1995-2003 (en milliers) (1)

(a) Western Europe/Europe occidentale

	1995	1996	1997	1998	1999
Austria/Autriche	–	57,1	56,9	59,2	72,4
Belgium/Belgique	53,1	51,9	49,2	50,9	57,8
Denmark/Danemark	39,0	31,4	27,3	28,7	26,5
Finland/Finlande	7,3	7,5	8,1	8,3	7,9
France	77,0	75,5	102,4	139,5	114,9
Germany/Allemagne	792,7	707,9	615,3	605,5	673,9
Greece/Grèce	20,2	22,2	22,1	12,6	–
Iceland/Islande	0,9	1,3	1,4	1,8	1,9
Ireland/Irlande (2)	13,6	21,5	23,6	21,7	22,2
Italy/Italie	68,2	143,2	–	127,1	268,0
Liechtenstein	–	–	–	–	2,7
Luxembourg	10,3	10,0	10,4	11,6	12,8
Netherlands/Pays-Bas	67,0	77,2	76,7	81,7	78,4
Norway/Norvège (3)	16,5	17,2	22,0	26,7	32,2
Portugal	5,0	3,6	3,3	6,5	14,5
Spain/Espagne	19,5	16,7	35,6	57,2	99,1
Sweden/Suède (4)	36,1	35,4	33,4	35,7	34,6
Switzerland/Suisse (5)	91,0	74,4	69,6	74,9	85,8
United Kingdom/Royaume-Uni (6)	228,0	224,2	237,2	287,3	337,4

(b) Central and eastern Europe/Europe centrale et orientale

	1995	1996	1997	1998	1999
Croatia/Croatie	42,0	44,6	–	51,8	32,9
Czech Republic/Rép. tchèque (7)	10,5	10,9	12,9	10,7	9,9
Estonia/Estonie (10)	1,6	1,6	1,6	1,6	1,4
"FYR Macedonia"/«ERY Macédoine»	1,0	0,6	0,6	–	1,2
Hungary/Hongrie (8)	14,0	13,7	13,3	16,1	20,2
Latvia/Lettonie (10)	2,8	2,7	2,9	3,1	1,8
Lithuania/Lituanie (10)	2,0	3,0	2,5	2,7	2,7
Poland/Pologne (9)	8,1	8,2	8,4	8,9	7,5
Romania/Roumanie (11)	4,5	2,1	6,6	11,9	10,1
Russian Fed./Féd. de Russie	866,3	647,0	597,7	513,6	379,7
Slovak Republic/Rép. slovaque	3,0	2,5	2,3	2,1	2,1
Slovenia/Slovénie	–	–	6,8	3,7	3,6

Sources: Council of Europe, National Statistical Offices, OECD SOPEMI Correspondents.
Conseil de l'Europe, Offices de statistique nationale, correspondants OCDE Sopemi.

Notes:

1. Asylum seekers are excluded./Les demandeurs d'asile ne sont pas inclus.
2. CSO immigration estimates./Estimations CSO immigration.
3. Entries of foreigners intending to stay longer than six months in Norway./Entrées d'étrangers ayant l'intention de rester plus de six mois en Norvège.
4. Some short duration entries are not counted (mainly citizens of other Nordic countries)./Certaines entrées de courte durée ne sont pas comptabilisées (principalement des citoyens d'autres pays nordiques).
5. Entries of foreigners with annual residence permits, and those with settlement permits (permanent permits) who return to Switzerland after a temporary stay abroad. Seasonal and frontier workers, and transformations are excluded./Entrées des étrangers avec un permis de séjour annuel et de ceux disposant de permis de séjour permanents qui retournent en Suisse après un

	2000	2001	2002	2003
Austria/Autriche	66,0	75,0	–	–
Belgium/Belgique	57,3	66,0	–	–
Denmark/Danemark	29,0	31,4	29,3	27,5
Finland/Finlande	9,1	11,0	10,0	9,4
France	126,8	141,0	–	–
Germany/Allemagne	649,2	685,3	658,3	601,8
Greece/Grèce	–	–	–	–
Iceland/Islande	2,5	2,5	1,9	1,4
Ireland/Irlande (2)	27,8	32,7	39,9	33,0
Italy/Italie	271,5	232,8	388,1	–
Liechtenstein	–	–	–	–
Luxembourg	11,8	11,2	11,0	11,5
Netherlands/Pays-Bas	91,4	94,5	86,6	73,6
Norway/Norvège (3)	27,8	25,4	30,8	26,8
Portugal	18,4	19,0	17,0	13,8
Spain/Espagne	330,9	394,0	443,1	429,5
Sweden/Suède (4)	42,6	44,1	47,6	45,3
Switzerland/Suisse (5)	87,4	101,4	101,9	94,0
United Kingdom/Royaume-Uni (6)	379,3	373,3	418,2	406,8

	2000	2001	2002	2003
Croatia/Croatie	2,1	2,1	2,0	2,1
Czech Republic/Rép. tchèque (7)	7,8	12,9	44,7	60,0
Estonia/Estonie (10)	1,4	–	–	–
"FYR Macedonia"/«ERY Macédoine»	1,2	1,2	2,3	–
Hungary/Hongrie (8)	20,2	20,3	15,7	–
Latvia/Lettonie (10)	1,6	1,1	1,2	1,1
Lithuania/Lituanie (10)	1,5	4,7	5,1	4,7
Poland/Pologne (9)	7,3	6,6	6,6	7,0
Romania/Roumanie (11)	11,0	10,4	6,6	3,3
Russian Fed./Féd. de Russie	359,3	193,4	177,3	–
Slovak Republic/Rép. slovaque	2,3	2,0	2,3	2,6
Slovenia/Slovénie	5,3	6,8	7,7	8,0

séjour temporaire à l'étranger. Les travailleurs saisonniers et frontaliers, les changements de statut ne sont pas inclus.

6. Source: International Passenger Survey, ONS.

7. Immigrants are persons who have been granted a permanent residence permit./Les immigrés sont des personnes dotées d'un permis de séjour permanent.

8. Data refer to foreigners with long-term resident permits or immigration permits, except for foreigners with labour permits./Les données se réfèrent aux étrangers possédant un permis de séjour de longue durée ou un permis d'immigration, à l'exception des étrangers dotés d'un permis de travail.

9. Immigrants are persons granted a permanent residence permit. Numbers may be underestimates since not all children accompanying immigrants are registered./Les immigrés sont des personnes dotées d'un permis de séjour permanent. Les chiffres peuvent être sous-estimés puisque les enfants accompagnant les immigrés ne sont pas tous enregistrés.

10. Recorded as "external" migration flows referring to non-Baltic countries./Enregistré en tant que flux migratoire «externe» pour les pays non Baltes.

11. Persons granted a permanent residence permit./Personnes dotées d'un permis de séjour permanent.

Table 8/Tableau 8

Outflows of population from selected European countries, 1995-2003 (thousands)
Départs de populations des pays européens étudiés, 1995-2003 (en milliers)

(a) Outflows of foreign nationals from western Europe
   Départs de nationaux étrangers de l'Europe occidentale

	1995	1996	1997	1998	1999
Austria/Autriche	–	42,4	49,8	44,9	47,3
Belgium/Belgique	33,1	22,0	23,5	32,5	24,4
Denmark/Danemark	11,1	13,0	14,1	15,6	16,2
Finland/Finlande	1,5	3,0	1,6	1,7	2,0
Germany/Allemagne (1)	567,4	559,1	637,1	639,0	555,6
Iceland/Islande	0,7	0,7	0,8	0,7	1,0
Italy/Italie	8,4	8,5	–	7,9	8,6
Luxembourg	5,7	6,4	6,6	7,8	8,0
Netherlands/Pays-Bas	21,7	22,4	21,9	21,3	20,7
Norway/Norvège	9,0	10,0	10,0	12,0	12,7
Portugal	–	0,2	–	–	0,4
Sweden/Suède (2)	15,4	14,5	15,3	14,1	13,4
Switzerland/Suisse (3)	69,4	71,9	67,9	59,0	58,1
United Kingdom/Royaume-Uni	101,0	108,0	130,6	125,7	151,6

(b) Permanent emigration from central and eastern Europe
   Emigration permanente d'Europe centrale et orientale

	1995	1996	1997	1998	1999
Belarus/Bélarus	35,0	–	–	13,2	13,2
Bulgaria/Bulgarie	55,0	62,0	–	–	–
Croatia/Croatie (8)	15,4	10,0	15,2	–	8,7
Czech Republic/Rép. tchèque (4)	0,5	0,7	0,8	1,2	1,1
Estonia/Estonie	9,8	7,2	4,5	3,0	2,0
"FYR Macedonia"/«ERY Macédoine»	0,4	0,2	0,3	–	–
Hungary/Hongrie (7)	2,4	2,8	1,9	2,3	2,5
Latvia/Lettonie	13,3	10,0	9,7	6,3	3,7
Lithuania/Lituanie	3,8	3,9	2,5	2,1	1,4
Poland/Pologne (5)	26,3	21,3	20,2	22,2	21,5
Romania/Roumanie (6)	–	4,8	3,1	2,3	1,3
Russian Fed./Féd. de Russie	340,0	388,0	233,0	213,4	215,0
Slovak Republic/Rép. slovaque	0,2	0,2	0,6	0,7	0,6
Slovenia/Slovénie	–	–	–	–	–
Ukraine	2,6	–	4,6	–	110,6

Sources: Council of Europe, National Statistical Offices, OECD SOPEMI Correspondents.
   Conseil de l'Europe, Offices de statistique nationale, correspondants OCDE Sopemi.

Notes:

1. Data includes registered exits of asylum seekers./Les données incluent les sorties enregistrées de demandeurs d'asile.
2. Some foreign citizens (in particular from other Nordic countries) are not included./Certains citoyens étrangers (en particulier d'autres pays nordiques) ne sont pas inclus.
3. Exits of foreigners with annual residence permits and holders of settlement permits (permanent permits)./Sorties d'étrangers disposant de permis de séjour annuels et des détenteurs de permis de séjour permanents.
4. Includes only emigrants who report their departure./Inclus seulement les émigrés qui ont signalé leur départ.
5. Only persons who register their intention to establish a permanent residence abroad with the authorities are included in statistics./Seules les personnes ayant enregistré auprès des autorités leur intention de s'établir de façon permanente à l'étranger sont incluses dans les statistiques.

	2000	2001	2002	2003
Austria/Autriche	44,4	51,0	–	–
Belgium/Belgique	35,6	24,5	–	–
Denmark/Danemark	16,5	17,3	17,8	18,2
Finland/Finlande	4,1	2,2	2,8	2,3
Germany/Allemagne (1)	562,8	497,0	505,6	499,1
Iceland/Islande	0,8	1,1	1,1	0,9
Italy/Italie	12,4	–	7,7	–
Luxembourg	8,1	7,6	8,3	9,4
Netherlands/Pays-Bas	20,7	20,4	21,2	21,9
Norway/Norvège	14,9	15,2	12,3	14,3
Portugal	–	–	10,0	–
Sweden/Suède (2)	12,6	12,7	14,2	14,6
Switzerland/Suisse (3)	56,8	52,7	49,7	46,3
United Kingdom/Royaume-Uni	159,6	148,5	173,7	170,6

	2000	2001	2002	2003
Belarus/Bélarus	13,8	14,3	13,4	–
Bulgaria/Bulgarie	–	–	–	–
Croatia/Croatie (8)	0,1	0,2	0,6	0,4
Czech Republic/Rép. tchèque (4)	1,3	21,5	32,4	34,2
Estonia/Estonie	1,2	0,9	–	–
"FYR Macedonia"/«ERY Macédoine»	0,2	0,5	0,1	–
Hungary/Hongrie (7)	2,2	1,9	1,8	–
Latvia/Lettonie	3,5	6,6	2,5	1,6
Lithuania/Lituanie	2,6	7,3	7,0	11,0
Poland/Pologne (5)	26,9	23,3	24,5	20,8
Romania/Roumanie (6)	1,3	0,9	0,7	0,8
Russian Fed./Féd. de Russie	145,7	121,2	105,5	–
Slovak Republic/Rép. slovaque	0,8	1,0	1,4	1,2
Slovenia/Slovénie	–	–	4,6	4,0
Ukraine	110,3	88,8	–	–

6. Foreign nationals emigrating./Nationaux étrangers émigrant.
7. 1997 figure – Source: HCSO. Data refer to foreigners with long-term resident permits or immigration permits, except for foreigners with labour permits./Chiffres de 1997 – Source: HCSO. Les données se réfèrent aux étrangers dotés de permis de séjour de longue durée ou de permis d'immigration, à l'exception des étrangers dotés d'un permis de travail.
8. Includes only emigrants who report their departure./Inclus seulement les émigrés ayant enregistré leur départ.

Table 9/Tableau 9

Net population flows of selected European countries, 1995-2003 (thousands)
Flux nets de populations de pays européens étudiés, 1995-2003 (en milliers)

(a) Western Europe/Europe occidentale

	1995	1996	1997	1998	1999
Austria/Autriche	–	14,7	7,1	14,3	25,1
Belgium/Belgique	20,0	29,9	25,7	18,4	33,4
Denmark/Danemark	27,9	18,4	13,2	13,1	10,3
Finland/Finlande	5,8	4,5	6,5	6,6	5,9
Germany/Allemagne	225,3	148,8	-21,8	-33,5	118,3
Iceland/Islande	0,2	0,6	0,6	1,1	0,9
Italy/Italie	59,8	134,7	–	119,2	259,4
Luxembourg	4,6	3,6	3,8	3,8	4,8
Netherlands/Pays-Bas	45,3	54,8	54,8	60,4	57,7
Norway/Norvège	7,5	7,2	12,0	14,7	19,5
Portugal	–	3,4	–	–	14,1
Sweden/Suède	20,7	20,9	18,1	21,6	21,2
Switzerland/Suisse	21,6	2,5	1,7	15,9	27,7
United Kingdom/Royaume-Uni	127,0	116,2	106,6	161,6	185,8

(b) Central and eastern Europe/Europe centrale et orientale

	1995	1996	1997	1998	1999
Croatia/Croatie	26,6	34,6	–	–	24,2
Czech Republic/Rép. tchèque	10,0	10,2	12,1	9,5	8,8
Estonia/Estonie	-8,2	-5,6	-2,9	-1,4	-0,6
"FYR Macedonia"/«ERY Macédoine»	0,6	0,4	0,3	–	–
Hungary/Hongrie	11,6	10,9	11,4	13,8	17,7
Latvia/Lettonie	-10,5	-7,3	-6,8	-3,2	-1,9
Lithuania/Lituanie	-1,8	-0,9	0,0	0,6	1,3
Poland/Pologne	-18,2	-13,1	-11,8	-13,3	-14,0
Romania/Roumanie	–	-2,7	3,5	9,6	8,8
Russian Fed./Féd. de Russie	526,3	259,0	364,7	300,2	164,7
Slovak Republic/Rép. slovaque	2,8	2,3	1,7	1,4	1,5
Slovenia/Slovénie	–	–	–	–	–

Sources: Council of Europe, National Statistical Offices, OECD SOPEMI Correspondents.
Conseil de l'Europe, Offices de statistique nationale, correspondants OCDE Sopemi.

Note:
See Tables 6 and 7./Voir tableaux 6 et 7.

	2000	2001	2002	2003	2003 or latest year/ ou année la plus récente
Austria/Autriche	21,6	24,0	–	–	24,0
Belgium/Belgique	21,7	41,5	–	–	41,5
Denmark/Danemark	12,5	14,1	11,5	9,3	9,3
Finland/Finlande	5,0	8,8	7,2	7,1	7,1
Germany/Allemagne	86,4	188,3	152,7	102,7	102,7
Iceland/Islande	1,7	1,4	0,8	0,5	0,5
Italy/Italie	259,1	–	380,4	–	380,4
Luxembourg	3,7	3,6	2,7	2,1	2,1
Netherlands/Pays-Bas	70,7	74,1	65,4	51,7	51,7
Norway/Norvège	12,9	10,2	18,5	12,5	12,5
Portugal	–	–	7,0	–	7,0
Sweden/Suède	30,0	31,4	33,4	30,7	30,7
Switzerland/Suisse	30,6	48,7	52,2	47,7	47,7
United Kingdom/Royaume-Uni	219,7	224,8	244,5	236,2	236,2
				Total	953,4

	2000	2001	2002	2003	2003 or latest year/ ou année la plus récente
Croatia/Croatie	2,0	1,9	1,4	1,7	1,7
Czech Republic/Rép. tchèque	6,5	-8,6	12,3	25,8	25,8
Estonia/Estonie	0,2	–	–	–	0,2
"FYR Macedonia"/«ERY Macédoine»	1,0	0,7	2,2	–	2,2
Hungary/Hongrie	18,0	18,4	13,9	–	13,9
Latvia/Lettonie	-1,9	-5,5	-1,3	-0,5	-0,5
Lithuania/Lituanie	-1,1	-2,6	-1,9	-6,3	-6,3
Poland/Pologne	-19,6	-16,7	-17,9	-13,8	-13,8
Romania/Roumanie	9,7	9,5	5,9	2,5	2,5
Russian Fed./Féd. de Russie	213,6	72,2	71,8	–	71,8
Slovak Republic/Rép. slovaque	1,5	1,0	0,9	1,4	1,4
Slovenia/Slovénie	–	–	3,1	4,0	4,0
				Total	102,9

143

Table 10/Tableau 10

Migration flows for east European and central Asian countries, 2000

Flux migratoires pour les pays d'Europe orientale et d'Asie centrale, 2000

	Absolute figures (thousands)/ Chiffres absolus (en milliers)			Proportions (per cent)/ Part (pourcentage)		
	Inflow/ Entrées	Outflow/ Départs	Net Flow/ Flux nets	Inflow/ Entrées	Outflow/ Départs	Gross Flow/ Flux bruts
Armenia/Arménie	1,6	12,5	-10,9	100,0	100,0	100,0
Total Within region/ A l'intérieur de la région	1,6	12,0	-10,4	99,6	96,4	96,5
Outside region/ A l'extérieur de la région	0,0	0,5	-0,4	0,4	3,6	3,5
Azerbaijan/Azerbaïdjan	4,4	9,9	-5,6	100,0	100,0	100,0
Total Within region/ A l'intérieur de la région	4,3	9,5	-5,3	97,5	95,7	96,5
Outside region/ A l'extérieur de la région	0,1	0,4	-0,3	2,5	4,3	3,5
Belarus/Bélarus	25,9	13,8	12,1	100,0	100,0	100,0
Total Within region/ A l'intérieur de la région	24,2	7,4	16,8	93,4	53,7	79,6
Outside region/ A l'extérieur de la région	1,7	6,4	-4,7	6,6	46,3	20,4
Georgia/Géorgie	2,3	21,5	-19,2	100,0	100,0	100,0
Total Within region/ A l'intérieur de la région	2,3	21,5	-19,2	100,0	100,0	100,0
Outside region/ A l'extérieur de la région	–	–	–	–	–	–
Kazakhstan	33,6	156,8	-123,2	100,0	100,0	100,0
Total Within region/ A l'intérieur de la région	31,6	117,5	-85,9	94,0	74,9	78,3
Outside region/ A l'extérieur de la région	2,0	39,4	-37,3	6,0	25,1	21,7
Kyrgyzstan/Kirghizistan	5,3	27,9	-22,5	100,0	100,0	100,0
Total Within region/ A l'intérieur de la région	5,3	24,7	-19,4	99,1	88,7	90,4
Outside region/ A l'extérieur de la région	0,0	3,2	-3,1	0,9	11,3	9,6
Moldova	5,0	20,5	-15,5	100,0	100,0	100,0
Total Within region/ A l'intérieur de la région	4,0	16,6	-12,6	80,0	81,0	80,8
Outside region/ A l'extérieur de la région	1,0	3,9	-2,9	20,0	19,0	19,2

	Absolute figures (thousands)/ Chiffres absolus (en milliers)			Proportions (per cent)/ Part (pourcentage)		
	Inflow/ Entrées	Outflow/ Départs	Net Flow/ Flux nets	Inflow/ Entrées	Outflow/ Départs	Gross Flow/ Flux bruts
Russian Fed./Féd. de Russie	359,3	145,7	213,6	100,0	100,0	100,0
Total Within region/ A l'intérieur de la région	350,3	83,4	266,9	97,5	57,3	85,9
Outside region/ A l'extérieur de la région	9,0	62,3	-53,2	2,5	42,7	14,1
Tajikistan/Tadjikistan	8,7	13,2	-4,5	100,0	100,0	100,0
Total Within region/ A l'intérieur de la région	2,0	13,1	-11,1	22,9	99,3	68,9
Outside region/ A l'extérieur de la région	6,7	0,1	6,6	77,1	0,7	31,1
Turkmenistan/Turkménistan	1,2	10,7	-9,5	100,0	100,0	100,0
Total Within region/ A l'intérieur de la région	1,2	10,2	-9,0	96,3	95,5	95,8
Outside region/ A l'extérieur de la région	0,0	0,5	-0,4	3,7	4,5	4,2
Ukraine	53,7	100,3	-46,6	100,0	100,0	100,0
Total Within region/ A l'intérieur de la région	49,7	55,4	-5,7	92,6	55,2	68,2
Outside region/ A l'extérieur de la région	4,0	44,9	-40,9	7,4	44,8	31,8
Uzbekistan/Ouzbékistan	5,4	62,5	-57,1	100,0	100,0	100,0
Total Within region/ A l'intérieur de la région	5,0	57,8	-52,8	92,4	92,4	92,5
Outside region/ A l'extérieur de la région	0,4	4,7	-4,3	7,6	7,6	7,5

Source: IOM/OIM, 2002.

Notes:
"Region" refers to the EECA and Baltic States (former Soviet Union).
«Région» se réfère à l'EECA et aux Etats baltes (ex-Union soviétique).

Table 11/Tableau 11

Percentage of total immigration/emigration by previous/next residence, 2001 or latest year available

Pourcentage de l'émigration/immigration totale par résidence antérieure/prochaine, 2001 ou dernière année disponible

	Immigration				
	EU & EFTA/UE et AELE	C&E Europe	Other Europe/Autres Europe	Europe	Rest of world/Reste du monde
Austria/Autriche	29,3	41,8	9,2	80,3	19,7
Croatia/Croatie (1)	12,5	74,1	0,0	86,6	13,4
Czech Republic/ Rép. tchèque (2)	11,8	66,7	0,2	78,7	21,3
Denmark/Danemark	40,7	10,2	4,1	55,0	45,0
Estonia/Estonie (2)	15,3	75,3	0,0	90,6	9,4
Finland/Finlande	44,1	28,4	1,9	74,4	25,6
"FYR Macedonia"/ «ERY Macédoine»	1,5	97,4	0,2	99,1	0,9
Germany/Allemagne	19,1	41,0	6,5	66,6	33,4
Iceland/Islande (3)	63,6	16,1	0,3	80,0	20,0
Italy/Italie (3)	14,0	34,9	0,6	49,5	50,5
Latvia/Lettonie (4)	12,3	64,5	0,1	76,9	23,1
Liechtenstein (2)	3,4	81,4	0,0	84,8	15,2
Lithuania/Lituanie (4)	13,0	66,0	0,4	79,4	20,6
Netherlands/Pays-Bas	27,6	8,8	4,9	41,3	58,7
Norway/Norvège	44,9	10,9	2,1	57,9	42,1
Poland/Pologne	53,2	14,6	0,3	68,1	31,9
Portugal (4)	44,0	2,3	0,1	46,4	53,6
Romania/Roumanie (5)	5,5	89,2	0,3	95,0	5,0
Slovakia/Slovaquie	13,9	67,9	0,8	82,6	17,4
Slovenia/Slovénie (4)	5,4	5,6	0,1	11,1	88,9
Spain/Espagne (4)	14,1	14,6	0,2	28,9	71,1
Sweden/Suède	42,2	12,3	2,2	56,7	43,3
United Kingdom/ Royaume-Uni (4)	22,8	2,3	2,1	27,2	72,8

Source: Eurostat.

Notes:
1. Emigration figure refers to 1999./Les chiffres de l'émigration se réfèrent à 1999.
2. Figures refer to 1999./Les chiffres se réfèrent à 1999.
3. Figures refer to 2000./Les chiffres se réfèrent à l'année 2000.
4. Emigration figure refers to 2000./Les chiffres de l'émigration se réfèrent à l'année 2000.
5. Emigration figure refers to 1997./Les chiffres de l'émigration se réfèrent à 1997.

	Emigration				
	EU & EFTA/UE et AELE	C&E Europe	Other Europe/Autres Europe	Europe	Rest of world/Reste du monde
Austria/Autriche	36,4	39,6	5,4	81,4	18,6
Croatia/Croatie (1)	3,9	20,9	0,0	24,8	75,2
Czech Republic/ Rép. tchèque (2)	56,8	31,3	0,3	88,4	11,6
Denmark/Danemark	52,6	6,6	3,8	63,0	37,0
Estonia/Estonie (2)	40,8	47,6	-0,1	88,3	11,7
Finland/Finlande	76,0	6,0	0,4	82,4	17,6
"FYR Macedonia"/ «ERY Macédoine»	1,3	80,1	18,3	99,7	0,3
Germany/Allemagne	29,1	38,0	6,3	73,4	26,6
Iceland/Islande (3)	82,2	4,0	0,2	86,4	13,6
Italy/Italie (3)	56,6	7,0	1,3	64,9	35,1
Latvia/Lettonie (4)	16,6	63,3	0,0	79,9	20,1
Liechtenstein (2)	12,2	57,9	0,0	70,1	29,9
Lithuania/Lituanie (4)	20,9	57,0	0,1	78,0	22,0
Netherlands/Pays-Bas	57,9	3,6	1,7	63,2	36,8
Norway/Norvège	63,3	8,4	0,6	72,3	27,7
Poland/Pologne	82,7	0,6	0,0	83,3	16,7
Portugal (4)	82,2	0,0	0,0	82,2	17,8
Romania/Roumanie (5)	60,5	7,9	0,8	69,2	30,8
Slovakia/Slovaquie	42,6	43,2	0,2	86,0	14,0
Slovenia/Slovénie (4)	29,3	59,0	0,6	88,9	11,1
Spain/Espagne (4)	0,6	0,0	14,5	15,0	85,0
Sweden/Suède	64,0	3,8	0,7	68,5	31,5
United Kingdom/ Royaume-Uni (4)	33,6	2,3	0,8	36,7	63,3

Table 12/Tableau 12

Stocks of foreign labour in selected European countries, 1995-2003 (thousands)
Réserves de main-d'œuvre dans les pays européens étudiés, 1995-2003 (en milliers)

(a) Western Europe/Europe occidentale (1)

	1995	1996	1997	1998	1999
Austria/Autriche (2)	300,3	300,4	298,8	298,6	306,4
Belgium/Belgique (3)	328,8	343,8	377,4	390,7	386,2
Denmark/Danemark (4)	83,8	88,0	93,9	98,3	96,3
Finland/Finlande	25,5	29,7	32,5	36,0	37,2
France (5)	1573,3	1604,7	1569,8	1586,7	1593,9
Germany/Allemagne (6)	–	2119,6	2044,2	2030,3	1924,8
Greece/Grèce (7)	27,4	28,7	29,4	–	204,6
Ireland/Irlande	42,1	43,4	51,7	53,3	57,7
Italy/Italie (8)	332,2	580,6	539,8	614,0	747,6
Luxembourg (9)	111,8	117,8	124,8	134,6	145,7
Netherlands/Pays-Bas (10)	221,0	218,0	208,0	235,0	–
Norway/Norvège (11)	52,6	54,8	59,9	66,9	104,6
Portugal (12)	84,3	86,8	87,9	88,6	91,6
Spain/Espagne (13)	139,0	166,5	178,7	197,1	199,8
Sweden/Suède	220,0	218,0	220,0	219,0	222,0
Switzerland/Suisse (14)	729,0	709,1	692,8	691,1	701,2
Turkey/Turquie	–	16,3	21,0	23,4	–
United Kingdom/Royaume-Uni (15)	862,0	865,0	949,0	1039,0	1005,0

(b) Central and eastern Europe/Europe centrale et orientale

	1995	1996	1997	1998	1999
Albania/Albanie	–	0,4	0,7	–	–
Czech Republic/Rép. tchèque (16)	148,9	188,7	194,3	156,5	151,9
Estonia/Estonie	–	–	–	–	–
Hungary/Hongrie (17)	21,0	18,8	20,4	22,4	28,5
Latvia/Lettonie	–	–	–	–	–
Lithuania/Lituanie	0,4	0,5	1,0	–	1,2
Romania/Roumanie (18)	0,7	0,7	1,0	1,3	1,5
Russian Fed./Féd. de Russie (19)	–	292,2	241,5	–	–
Slovenia/Slovénie (20)	–	–	36,1	33,9	40,3
Slovak Republic/Rép. slovaque (21)	2,7	3,3	3,8	3,7	2,6

Sources: Council of Europe, National Statistical Offices, OECD SOPEMI Correspondents.
Conseil de l'Europe, Offices de statistique nationale, correspondants OCDE Sopemi.

Notes:

1. Includes the unemployed, except in Benelux and the U.K. Frontier and seasonal workers are excluded unless otherwise stated./Inclut le chômage, sauf au Benelux et au Royaume-Uni. Les travailleurs frontaliers et saisonniers ne sont pas compris sauf indication contraire.
2. Annual average. Work permits delivered plus permits still valid. Figures may be over-estimated because some persons hold more than one permit. Self-employed are excluded./Moyenne annuelle. Permis de travail délivrés ainsi que permis en cours de validité. Les chiffres peuvent être surestimés car certaines personnes détiennent plus d'un permis. Les travailleurs indépendants ne sont pas compris.
3. Excludes the unemployed and self-employed./A l'exclusion des chômeurs et travailleurs indépendants.
4. Data from population registers and give the count as of the end of November each year except December (end of December)./Données tirées de registres de population arrêtés à la fin novembre de chaque année, à l'exception de décembre (fin décembre).
6. Data refer to employed foreigners who are liable for compulsory social insurance contributions./Les données se réfèrent aux travailleurs étrangers assu- jettis aux cotisations obligatoires de l'assurance sociale.
7. Excludes the unemployed. From 2001 constitutes foreign nationals, over the age of 15 years old, in employment./Chômeurs non inclus. Constitue depuis 2001 les nationaux étrangers possédant un emploi, âgés de plus de 15 ans.
8. Work permit holders./Détenteurs de permis de travail.
9. Data as of 1 October each year. Foreigners in employment, including apprentices, trainees and frontier workers. Excludes the unemployed./Données au

	2000	2001	2002	2003
Austria/Autriche (2)	319,9	329,3	334,4	350,4
Belgium/Belgique (3)	–	388,6	–	–
Denmark/Danemark (4)	96,8	106,6	–	–
Finland/Finlande	40,7	45,4	46,1	–
France (5)	1577,6	1617,6	–	–
Germany/Allemagne (6)	1963,6	2008,1	1960,0	1964,1
Greece/Grèce (7)	184,0	157,4	203,6	233,5
Ireland/Irlande	63,9	82,1	–	–
Italy/Italie (8)	850,7	1338,2	–	–
Luxembourg (9)	157,5	170,7	177,6	182,8
Netherlands/Pays-Bas (10)	–	–	–	–
Norway/Norvège (11)	111,2	–	–	92,3
Portugal (12)	99,8	–	–	–
Spain/Espagne (13)	454,6	607,1	831,7	925,3
Sweden/Suède	222,0	226,0	–	–
Switzerland/Suisse (14)	717,3	738,8	830,0	809,0
Turkey/Turquie	82,8	–	–	–
United Kingdom/Royaume-Uni (15)	1107,5	1243,0	1303,0	1396,0

	2000	2001	2002	2003
Albania/Albanie	–	–	–	–
Czech Republic/Rép. tchèque (16)	165,0	167,7	161,7	168,0
Estonia/Estonie	–	–	–	111,0
Hungary/Hongrie (17)	35,0	38,6	42,7	48,7
Latvia/Lettonie	–	–	–	7,0
Lithuania/Lituanie	0,7	0,6	0,5	0,6
Romania/Roumanie (18)	1,6	2,1	1,5	1,9
Russian Fed./Féd. de Russie (19)	–	–	–	–
Slovenia/Slovénie (20)	37,8	34,8	35,3	32,1
Slovak Republic/Rép. slovaque (21)	2,5	2,5	2,7	2,7

1ᵉʳ octobre de chaque année. Les étrangers possédant un emploi, y compris les apprentis, les stagiaires et les travailleurs frontaliers.

10. Estimates as of 31 March, including frontier workers, but excluding the self-employed and their family members as well as the unemployed./Estimations au 31 mars, y compris les travailleurs frontaliers, non compris les travailleurs indépendants et les membres de leur famille, ainsi que les chômeurs.

11. Excludes unemployed./Chômeurs non compris.

12. *Idem.*

13. Data derived from the annual labour force survey. There is a break in the series between 1999 and 2000. Figures from 2000 onwards include regularised foreign workers./Données tirées d'une étude annuelle sur la main-d'œuvre. Il y a une interruption dans la série entre 1999 et 2000. Les chiffres à partir de 2000 incluent les travailleurs étrangers régularisés.

14. Data as of 31 December each year. Numbers of foreigners with annual residence permits and holders of settlement permits (permanent permits) who engage in gainful activity./Données au 31 décembre de chaque année. Nombres d'étrangers dotés d'un permis de séjour annuel et détenteurs de permis de séjour permanents engagés dans une activité rémunératrice.

15. Excludes the unemployed./Chômeurs non compris.

16. Source: Ministry of Labour and Social Affairs./Ministère du Travail et des Questions sociales.

17. 1996 figure for first half of year. Valid work permits./Chiffre de 1997 pour la première moitié de l'année. Permis de travail valables.

18. Total work permit holders./Total des détenteurs de permis de travail.

19. Source: Federal Migration Service, 1998./Service fédéral des migrations.

20. Total work permit holders. Source: Slovenian Employment Service./Total des détenteurs de permis de travail. Source: Service slovène de l'emploi.

21. Total work permit holders./Total des détenteurs de permis de travail.

Table 13/Tableau 13

Inflows of foreign labour into selected European countries, 1995-2003 (thousands)
Entrées de main-d'œuvre étrangère dans les pays européens étudiés, 1995-2003 (en milliers)

(a) Western Europe/Europe occidentale

	1995	1996	1997	1998	1999
Austria/Autriche (1)	15,4	16,3	15,2	15,4	18,3
Belgium/Belgique	2,7	2,2	2,5	7,3	8,7
Denmark/Danemark (2)	2,2	2,7	3,1	3,2	3,1
Finland/Finlande	–	–	–	–	–
France (3)	13,1	11,5	11,0	10,3	10,9
Germany/Allemagne (4)	470,0	439,7	451,0	402,6	433,7
Ireland/Irlande (5)	–	–	–	3,8	4,6
Luxembourg (6)	16,5	18,3	18,6	22,0	24,2
Netherlands/Pays-Bas (7)	–	9,2	11,1	15,2	20,8
Portugal	2,2	1,5	1,3	2,6	4,2
Spain/Espagne (8)	29,6	31,0	30,1	53,7	56,1
Sweden/Suède	–	–	–	2,4	2,4
Switzerland/Suisse (9)	32,9	29,8	25,4	26,8	31,5
United Kingdom/Royaume-Uni (10)	51,0	50,0	59,0	68,0	61,2

(b) Central and eastern Europe/Europe centrale et orientale

	1995	1996	1997	1998	1999
Bulgaria/Bulgarie (11)	0,3	0,3	0,2	0,2	0,2
Czech Republic/Rép. tchèque (12)	–	71,0	61,0	49,9	40,3
Hungary/Hongrie	–	–	24,2	26,3	34,1
Poland/Pologne (13)	10,5	13,7	17,5	–	17,1
Romania/Roumanie (14)	0,7	0,7	1,0	1,3	1,5
Slovak Republic/Rép. slovaque (15)	3,0	3,3	3,2	2,5	2,0

Sources: Council of Europe, National Statistical Offices, OECD SOPEMI Correspondents.
Conseil de l'Europe, Offices de statistique nationale, correspondants OCDE Sopemi.

Notes:

1. Data for all years covers initial work permits for both direct inflow from abroad and for first participation in the Austrian labour market of foreigners already in the country./Pour toutes les années, les données se réfèrent aux premiers permis de travail à la fois pour les flux directs en provenance de l'étranger et pour une première participation au marché du travail autrichien des étrangers déjà installés dans le pays.
2. Residence permits issued for employment. Nordic citizens are not included./Permis de séjour à des fins d'emploi. Les citoyens nordiques ne sont pas compris.
3. Issue of initial work permits for non-EU-residents./Question des premiers permis de travail pour les résidents non ressortissants de l'UE.
4. Break in series 1998-1999./Interruption dans la série 1998-1999.
5. Work permits issued for non-EU nationals./Permis de travail délivrés pour les nationaux non ressortissants de l'UE.
6. Data cover both arrivals of foreign workers and residents admitted for the first time to the labour market./Les données couvrent à la fois les arrivées de travailleurs étrangers et les résidents admis pour la première fois sur le marché du travail.

	2000	2001	2002	2003
Austria/Autriche (1)	25,4	27,0	24,6	24,1
Belgium/Belgique	7,5	7,0	–	–
Denmark/Danemark (2)	3,6	5,1	5,3	–
Finland/Finlande	10,4	14,1	20,1	24,2
France (3)	11,3	–	–	–
Germany/Allemagne (4)	473,0	553,7	529,6	502,7
Ireland/Irlande (5)	15,7	30,0	23,8	22,5
Luxembourg (6)	27,3	–	22,4	22,6
Netherlands/Pays-Bas (7)	27,7	30,2	34,6	38,0
Portugal	7,8	6,1	–	–
Spain/Espagne (8)	74,1	41,6	–	–
Sweden/Suède	3,3	3,3	–	–
Switzerland/Suisse (9)	34,0	–	–	–
United Kingdom/Royaume-Uni (10)	86,5	76,2	99,0	80,0

	2000	2001	2002	2003
Bulgaria/Bulgarie (11)	0,3	0,3	–	–
Czech Republic/Rép. tchèque (12)	40,1	40,1	44,6	47,7
Hungary/Hongrie	40,2	47,3	49,8	57,4
Poland/Pologne (13)	17,8	–	22,8	18,8
Romania/Roumanie (14)	–	–	–	–
Slovak Republic/Rép. slovaque (15)	1,8	2,0	–	–

7. Number of temporary work permits (WAV). 2002 data refer to January-September./Nombre de permis de travail temporaires. Les données de 2002 se réfèrent à la période de janvier à septembre. Source: CWI.
8. Work permits granted./Permis de travail accordés.
9. Seasonal and frontier workers are not taken included./Travailleurs saisonniers et frontaliers ne sont pas inclus.
10. Data from the Labour Force Survey./Données tirées de l'Etude sur la main-d'œuvre.
11. Work permits, new and extensions./Nouveaux permis de travail et prolongations.
12. Work permits issued for foreigners./Permis de travail délivrés aux étrangers.
13. Numbers of Individual work permits./Nombre de permis de travail individuels.
14. New work permits issued to foreign citizens./Nouveaux permis de travail délivrés aux citoyens étrangers.
15. Work permits granted. Czech nationals do not need work permits in Slovakia./Permis de travail accordés. Les nationaux tchèques n'ont pas besoin de permis de travail en Slovaquie.

Table 14/Tableau 14

Asylum applications in selected European countries, 1995-2003 (thousands)
Demandes d'asile dans les pays européens étudiés, 1995-2003 (en milliers)

(a) Western Europe/Europe occidentale

	1995	1996	1997	1998	1999
Austria/Autriche	5,9	7,0	6,7	13,8	20,1
Belgium/Belgique	11,4	12,4	11,8	22,0	35,8
Denmark/Danemark	5,1	5,9	5,1	9,4	12,3
Finland/Finlande	0,9	0,7	1,0	1,3	3,1
France	20,4	17,4	21,4	22,4	30,9
Germany/Allemagne	127,9	116,4	104,4	98,6	95,1
Greece/Grèce	1,3	1,6	4,4	3,0	1,5
Iceland/Islande	0,0	–	0,0	0,0	0,0
Ireland/Irlande	0,4	1,2	3,9	4,6	7,7
Italy/Italie	1,7	0,7	1,9	11,1	33,4
Liechtenstein	–	–	–	0,2	0,5
Luxembourg	0,4	0,3	0,4	1,7	2,9
Netherlands/Pays-Bas	29,3	22,2	34,4	45,2	42,7
Norway/Norvège	1,5	1,8	2,3	8,4	10,2
Portugal	0,5	0,3	0,3	0,4	0,3
Spain/Espagne	5,7	4,7	5,0	6,7	8,4
Sweden/Suède	9,1	5,8	9,7	12,8	11,2
Switzerland/Suisse	17,0	18,0	24,0	41,3	46,1
United Kingdom/Royaume-Uni	55,0	37,0	41,5	58,5	91,2
Totals (western Europe)/ Totaux (Europe occidentale)	293,5	253,4	278,2	361,4	453,4

(b) Central and eastern Europe/Europe centrale et orientale

	1995	1996	1997	1998	1999
Bulgaria/Bulgarie	0,5	0,3	0,4	0,8	1,3
Czech Republic/Rép. tchèque	1,4	2,2	2,1	4,1	7,3
Estonia/Estonie	–	–	–	0,0	0,0
Hungary/Hongrie	0,1	0,2	0,2	7,1	11,5
Latvia/Lettonie	–	–	–	0,1	0,0
Lithuania/Lituanie	–	–	0,3	0,2	0,1
Poland/Pologne	0,8	3,2	3,5	3,4	3,0
Romania/Roumanie	–	0,6	1,4	1,2	1,7
Slovakia/Slovaquie	0,4	0,4	0,7	0,5	1,3
Slovenia/Slovénie	–	0,0	0,1	0,5	0,9
Totals (central and eastern Europe)/ Totaux (Europe centrale et orientale)	3,2	6,9	8,7	17,9	27,1

Source: Governments, UNHCR. Compiled by UNHCR (Population Data Unit).
Gouvernements, HCR. Réalisé par le HCR (Unité de données sur la population).

	2000	2001	2002	2003
Austria/Autriche	18,3	30,1	39,4	32,3
Belgium/Belgique	42,7	24,6	18,8	16,9
Denmark/Danemark	12,2	12,5	6,1	4,6
Finland/Finlande	3,2	1,7	3,4	3,1
France	38,8	47,3	51,1	51,4
Germany/Allemagne	78,6	88,3	71,1	50,6
Greece/Grèce	3,1	5,5	5,7	8,2
Iceland/Islande	0,0	0,1	0,1	0,1
Ireland/Irlande	11,1	10,3	11,6	7,9
Italy/Italie	15,6	9,6	7,3	–
Liechtenstein	0,0	0,1	0,1	0,1
Luxembourg	0,6	0,7	1,0	1,6
Netherlands/Pays-Bas	43,9	32,6	18,7	13,4
Norway/Norvège	10,8	14,8	17,5	16,0
Portugal	0,2	0,2	0,3	0,1
Spain/Espagne	7,9	9,5	6,3	5,8
Sweden/Suède	16,3	23,5	33,0	31,4
Switzerland/Suisse	17,6	20,6	26,1	21,1
United Kingdom/Royaume-Uni	98,9	91,6	103,1	61,1
Totals (western Europe)/ Totaux (Europe occidentale)	419,8	423,6	420,7	325,6

	2000	2001	2002	2003
Bulgaria/Bulgarie	1,8	2,4	2,9	1,6
Czech Republic/Rép. tchèque	8,8	18,1	8,5	11,4
Estonia/Estonie	–	0,0	0,0	0,0
Hungary/Hongrie	7,8	9,6	6,4	2,4
Latvia/Lettonie	–	0,0	0,0	0,0
Lithuania/Lituanie	0,2	0,3	0,3	0,2
Poland/Pologne	4,6	4,5	5,2	6,9
Romania/Roumanie	1,4	2,4	1,2	1,1
Slovakia/Slovaquie	1,6	8,2	9,7	10,3
Slovenia/Slovénie	9,2	1,5	0,7	1,1
Totals (central and eastern Europe)/ Totaux (Europe centrale et orientale)	35,4	47,0	34,9	35,0

Table 15/Tableau 15

Asylum applications in selected European countries, 1995-2003 (thousands)/
Demandes d'asile dans les pays européens étudiés, 1995-2003 (en milliers)

	1985			1992		
	absolute figures/ chiffres absolus	proportion of EU & EFTA total (per cent)/part du total UE et AELE (pourcentage)	per 10 000 population/ pour 10 000 personnes	absolute figures/ chiffres absolus	proportion of EU & EFTA total (per cent)/part du total UE et AELE (pourcentage)	per 10 000 population/ pour 10 000 personnes
EU 15/UE 15	159,2	93,8	4,4	672,4	96,7	18,3
Austria/Autriche	6,7	4,0	8,9	16,2	2,3	20,6
Belgium/Belgique	5,4	3,2	5,5	17,7	2,5	17,6
Denmark/Danemark	8,7	5,1	17,0	13,9	2,0	26,9
Finland/Finlande	0	0,0	0,0	3,6	0,5	7,2
France	28,9	17,0	5,2	28,9	4,2	5,0
Germany/Allemagne	73,8	43,5	9,5	438,2	63,0	54,6
Greece/Grèce	1,4	0,8	1,4	2,1	0,3	2,0
Ireland/Irlande	–	–	–	0	0,0	0,1
Italy/Italie	5,4	3,2	1,0	2,6	0,4	0,5
Luxembourg	0,1	0,0	2,1	0,1	0,0	3,1
Netherlands/Pays-Bas	5,6	3,3	3,9	20,3	2,9	13,4
Portugal	0,1	0,0	0,1	0,7	0,1	0,7
Spain/Espagne	2,3	1,4	0,6	11,7	1,7	3,0
Sweden/Suède	14,5	8,5	17,4	84	12,1	97,2
United Kingdom/ Royaume-Uni	6,2 0	3,7	1,1	32,3 0	4,6	5,6
EFTA 4/AELE 4	10,5	6,2	9,7	23,2	3,3	20,3
Iceland/Islande	–	–	–	0	0,0	0,6
Liechtenstein	–	–	–	–	–	–
Norway/Norvège	0,8	0,5	2,0	5,2	0,8	12,3
Switzerland/Suisse	9,7 0	5,7	15,0	18 0	2,6	26,2
EU 15 + EFTA 4/ UE 15 + AELE 4	169,7	100,0	4,6	695,6	100,0	18,4

Source: UNHCR/HCR, Eurostat.

Notes:

EFTA: 1985, 1999 estimated./AELE: estimations 1985, 1999.
EU15: 1985, 2003 estimated./UE 15: estimations 1985, 2003.

	1999			2000		
	absolute figures/ chiffres absolus	proportion of EU & EFTA total (per cent)/part du total UE et AELE (pourcentage)	per 10 000 population/ pour 10 000 personnes	absolute figures/ chiffres absolus	proportion of EU & EFTA total (per cent)/part du total UE et AELE (pourcentage)	per 10 000 population/ pour 10 000 personnes
EU 15/UE 15	396,6	87,5	10,6	391,4	93,2	10,4
Austria/Autriche	20,1	4,4	25,2	18,3	4,4	22,9
Belgium/Belgique	35,8	7,9	35,0	42,7	10,2	41,7
Denmark/Danemark	12,3	2,7	23,1	12,2	2,9	22,9
Finland/Finlande	3,1	0,7	6,0	3,2	0,8	6,2
France	30,9	6,8	5,3	38,8	9,2	6,6
Germany/Allemagne	95,1	21,0	11,6	78,6	18,7	9,6
Greece/Grèce	1,5	0,3	1,4	3,1	0,7	2,8
Ireland/Irlande	7,7	1,7	20,6	11,1	2,6	29,4
Italy/Italie	33,4	7,4	5,8	15,6	3,7	2,7
Luxembourg	2,9	0,6	67,9	0,6	0,1	13,8
Netherlands/Pays-Bas	42,7	9,4	27,1	43,9	10,5	27,7
Portugal	0,3	0,1	0,3	0,2	0,0	0,2
Spain/Espagne	8,4	1,9	2,1	7,9	1,9	2,0
Sweden/Suède	11,2	2,5	12,6	16,3	3,9	18,4
United Kingdom/ Royaume-Uni	91,2	20,1	15,6	98,9	23,6	16,9
EFTA 4/AELE 4	56,8	12,5	47,8	28,4	6,8	23,8
Iceland/Islande	0,0	0,0	0,0	0,0	0,0	0,0
Liechtenstein	0,5	0,1	156,3	0,0	0,0	0,0
Norway/Norvège	10,2	2,2	22,9	10,8	2,6	24,1
Switzerland/Suisse	46,1	10,2	64,7	17,6	4,2	24,6
EU 15 + EFTA 4/ UE 15 + AELE 4	453,4	100,0	11,7	419,8	100,0	10,8

155

Table 15 (continued)/Tableau 15 (suite)

Asylum applications in selected European countries, 1995-2003 (thousands)
Demandes d'asile dans les pays européens étudiés, 1995-2003 (en milliers)

	2001			2002		
	absolute figures/ chiffres absolus	proportion of EU & EFTA total (per cent)/part du total UE et AELE (pourcentage)	per 10 000 population/ pour 10 000 personnes	absolute figures/ chiffres absolus	proportion of EU & EFTA total (per cent)/part du total UE et AELE (pourcentage)	per 10 000 population/ pour 10 000 personnes
EU 15/UE 15	388,0	91,6	10,3	376,9	89,6	9,9
Austria/Autriche	30,1	7,1	37,5	39,4	9,4	49,0
Belgium/Belgique	24,6	5,8	24,0	18,8	4,5	18,2
Denmark/Danemark	12,5	3,0	23,4	6,1	1,4	11,4
Finland/Finlande	1,7	0,4	3,3	3,4	0,8	6,5
France	47,3	11,2	8,0	51,1	12,1	8,6
Germany/Allemagne	88,3	20,8	10,7	71,1	16,9	8,6
Greece/Grèce	5,5	1,3	5,0	5,7	1,4	5,2
Ireland/Irlande	10,3	2,4	26,9	11,6	2,8	29,7
Italy/Italie	9,6	2,3	1,7	7,3	1,7	1,3
Luxembourg	0,7	0,2	15,9	1,0	0,2	22,5
Netherlands/Pays-Bas	32,6	7,7	20,4	18,7	4,4	11,6
Portugal	0,2	0,0	0,2	0,3	0,1	0,3
Spain/Espagne	9,5	2,2	2,4	6,3	1,5	1,5
Sweden/Suède	23,5	5,5	26,5	33,0	7,8	37,0
United Kingdom/ Royaume-Uni	91,6	21,6	15,6	103,1	24,5	17,5
EFTA 4/AELE 4	35,6	8,4	29,6	43,8	10,4	36,2
Iceland/Islande	0,1	0,0	3,5	0,1	0,0	3,5
Liechtenstein	0,1	0,0	30,3	0,1	0,0	29,4
Norway/Norvège	14,8	3,5	32,9	17,5	4,2	38,7
Switzerland/Suisse	20,6	4,9	28,6	26,1	6,2	35,9
EU 15 + EFTA 4/ UE 15 + AELE 4	423,6	100,0	10,9	420,7	100,0	10,8

	2003		
	absolute figures/ chiffres absolus	proportion of EU & EFTA total (per cent)/part du total UE et AELE (pourcentage)	per 10 000 population/ pour 10 000 personnes
EU 15/UE 15	295,6	88,8	7,8
Austria/Autriche	32,3	9,7	40,0
Belgium/Belgique	16,9	5,1	16,3
Denmark/Danemark	4,6	1,4	8,5
Finland/Finlande	3,1	0,9	6,0
France	51,4	15,4	8,6
Germany/Allemagne	50,5	15,2	6,1
Greece/Grèce	8,2	2,5	7,5
Ireland/Irlande	7,9	2,4	19,9
Italy/Italie	–	–	–
Luxembourg	1,6	0,5	35,7
Netherlands/Pays-Bas	13,4	4,0	8,3
Portugal	0,1	0,0	0,1
Spain/Espagne	5,8	1,7	1,4
Sweden/Suède	31,4	9,4	35,1
United Kingdom/ Royaume-Uni	61,1	18,4	10,3
EFTA 4/AELE 4	37,3	11,2	30,6
Iceland/Islande	0,1	0,0	3,5
Liechtenstein	0,1	0,0	29,4
Norway/Norvège	16,0	4,8	35,1
Switzerland/Suisse	21,1	6,3	28,8
EU 15 + EFTA 4/ UE 15 + AELE 4	332,9	100,0	8,5

Table 16/Tableau 16

Number of initial decisions made on asylum applications and corresponding recognition rates for selected European countries, 2000-03

Nombre de décisions initiales prises sur des demandes d'asile et taux de reconnaissance correspondants pour les pays européens étudiés, 2000-2003

	2000						
	Convention number/ Nombre statuts de la convention	%	Humanitarian number/ Nombre statuts humanitaires	%	Refusals number/ Nombre de refus	%	Total (1) number/ Nombre total
Total	55057	15,7	51764	14,7	244732	69,6	351553
Western Europe/ Europe occidentale	49299	16,1	49962	16,3	206738	67,6	305999
Austria/Autriche	1002	17,3	0	0,0	4787	82,7	5789
Belgium/Belgique	1192	23,5	750	14,8	3133	61,7	5075
Denmark/Danemark	1202	17,1	2265	32,1	3579	50,8	7046
Finland/Finlande	9	0,7	458	35,3	832	64,0	1299
France	5185	17,1	0	0,0	25093	82,9	30278
Germany/Allemagne	10894	15,0	1363	1,9	60274	83,1	72531
Iceland/Íslande	1	3,6	2	7,1	25	89,3	28
Ireland/Irlande	211	4,2	0	0,0	4767	95,8	4978
Liechtenstein	–	–	–	–	–	–	–
Luxembourg	17	0,9	42	2,3	1782	96,8	1841
Netherlands/Pays-Bas	896	11,6	5968	77,2	869	11,2	7733
Norway/Norvège	97	1,2	2856	36,4	4899	62,4	7852
Sweden/Suède	343	2,1	6647	41,6	8983	56,2	15973
Switzerland/Suisse	2061	4,7	16966	38,7	24759	56,5	43786
United Kingdom/Royaume-Uni	26189	25,7	12645	12,4	62956	61,8	101790
Southern Europe/Europe du Sud	5051	14,7	604	1,8	28646	83,5	34301
Cyprus/Chypre	39	14,9	0	0,0	223	85,1	262
Greece/Grèce	222	11,3	175	8,9	1573	79,8	1970
Italy/Italie	1649	6,6	0	0,0	23255	93,4	24904
Malta/Malte	28	38,4	1	1,4	44	60,3	73
Portugal	16	17,0	46	48,9	32	34,0	94
Spain/Espagne	381	14,7	382	14,8	1821	70,5	2584
Turkey/Turquie	2716	61,5	0	0,0	1698	38,5	4414
Central and eastern Europe/ Europe centrale et orientale	707	6,3	1198	10,6	9348	83,1	11253
Bulgaria/Bulgarie	267	22,3	421	35,2	509	42,5	1197
Czech Rep./Rép. tchèque	88	4,8	0	0,0	1736	95,2	1824
Estonia/Estonie	4	57,1	0	0,0	3	42,9	7
Hungary/Hongrie	197	5,1	680	17,6	2978	77,3	3855
Latvia/Lettonie	1	25,0	0	0,0	3	75,0	4
Lithuania/Lituanie	3	3,7	0	0,0	79	96,3	82
Poland/Pologne	52	2,0	0	0,0	2519	98,0	2571
Romania/Roumanie	85	5,9	86	6,0	1271	88,1	1442
Slovakia/Slovaquie	10	7,5	0	0,0	123	92,5	133
Slovenia/Slovénie	0	0,0	11	8,0	127	92,0	138

Source: UNHCR/HCR. Notes: 1."Total" refers to the sum of the substantive decisions: Convention recognition, humanitarian leave to remain and refusals. Other closures of cases, such as withdrawals, are not included./«Total» se réfère à la somme des décisions importantes: reconnaissance par la convention, autorisation humanitaire de rester dans le pays de destination et refus.

	2001						
	Convention number/ Nombre statuts de la convention	%	Humanitarian number/ Nombre statuts humanitaires	%	Refusals number/ Nombre de refus	%	Total (1) number/ Nombre total
Total	53557	13,9	57425	14,9	273623	71,1	384605
Western Europe/							
Europe occidentale	47035	13,7	54849	15,9	242494	70,4	344378
Austria/Autriche	1152	23,1	0	0,0	3840	76,9	4992
Belgium/Belgique	898	26,5	0	0,0	2486	73,5	3384
Denmark/Danemark	1857	21,2	2740	31,4	4142	47,4	8739
Finland/Finlande	4	0,3	809	55,4	646	44,3	1459
France	7323	17,0	0	0,0	35730	83,0	43053
Germany/Allemagne	17547	23,6	2395	3,2	54279	73,1	74221
Iceland/Íslande	0	0,0	1	7,1	13	92,9	14
Ireland/Irlande	456	9,0	69	1,4	4532	89,6	5057
Liechtenstein	0	0,0	8	18,2	36	81,8	44
Luxembourg	89	4,5	353	17,9	1531	77,6	1973
Netherlands/Pays-Bas	244	1,1	5161	23,4	16647	75,5	22052
Norway/Norvège	292	2,2	4036	30,3	8976	67,5	13304
Sweden/Suède	165	1,1	4330	28,6	10644	70,3	15139
Switzerland/Suisse	2253	9,5	8922	37,7	12470	52,7	23645
United Kingdom/Royaume-Uni	14755	11,6	26025	20,4	86522	68,0	127302
Southern Europe/Europe du Sud	5514	24,5	1036	4,6	16002	71,0	22552
Cyprus/Chypre	36	11,0	0	0,0	291	89,0	327
Greece/Grèce	147	11,2	148	11,3	1017	77,5	1312
Italy/Italie	2102	15,9	564	4,3	10553	79,8	13219
Malta/Malte	39	41,5	24	25,5	31	33,0	94
Portugal	7	14,6	34	70,8	7	14,6	48
Spain/Espagne	314	12,2	266	10,4	1989	77,4	2569
Turkey/Turquie	2869	57,6	0	0,0	2114	42,4	4983
Central and eastern Europe/							
Europe centrale et orientale	1008	5,7	1540	8,7	15127	85,6	17675
Bulgaria/Bulgarie	385	17,5	1185	53,8	633	28,7	2203
Czech Rep./Rép. tchèque	75	1,2	0	0,0	6032	98,8	6107
Estonia/Estonie	0	0,0	3	50,0	3	50,0	6
Hungary/Hongrie	174	5,0	290	8,4	2995	86,6	3459
Latvia/Lettonie	1	6,7	0	0,0	14	93,3	15
Lithuania/Lituanie	0	0,0	0	0,0	145	100,0	145
Poland/Pologne	271	8,7	0	0,0	2846	91,3	3117
Romania/Roumanie	83	3,5	38	1,6	2232	94,9	2353
Slovakia/Slovaquie	18	12,2	0	0,0	130	87,8	148
Slovenia/Slovénie	1	0,8	24	19,7	97	79,5	122

Table 16 (continued)/Tableau 16 (suite)

Number of initial decisions made on asylum applications and corresponding recognition rates for selected European countries, 2000-03

Nombre de décisions initiales prises sur des demandes d'asile et taux de reconnaissance correspondants pour les pays européens étudiés, 2000-2003

	2002						
	Convention number/ Nombre statuts de la convention	%	Humanitarian number/Nombre statuts humanitaires	%	Refusals number/ Nombre de refus	%	Total (1) number/ Nombre total
Total	37243	9,7	43946	11,4	304009	78,9	385198
Western Europe/							
Europe occidentale	32322	9,6	40938	12,1	263942	78,3	337202
Austria/Autriche	1073	20,0	0	0,0	4285	80,0	5358
Belgium/Belgique	1166	25,4	0	0,0	3427	74,6	4593
Denmark/Danemark	1134	12,7	1389	15,5	6428	71,8	8951
Finland/Finlande	14	0,8	577	34,6	1078	64,6	1669
France	8495	16,2	0	0,0	43880	83,8	52375
Germany/Allemagne	6034	7,2	1016	1,2	77124	91,6	84174
Iceland/Islande	0	0,0	1	1,9	51	98,1	52
Ireland/Irlande	893	12,8	111	1,6	5966	85,6	6970
Liechtenstein	0	0,0	25	55,6	20	44,4	45
Luxembourg	–	–	–	–	–	–	–
Netherlands/Pays-Bas	198	0,7	3359	11,2	26471	88,2	30028
Norway/Norvège	332	2,7	2958	23,9	9066	73,4	12356
Sweden/Suède	264	1,1	4860	20,6	18496	78,3	23620
Switzerland/Suisse	1729	8,9	4172	21,5	13500	69,6	19401
United Kingdom/Royaume-Uni	10990	12,5	22470	25,6	54150	61,8	87610
Southern Europe/Europe du Sud	4333	13,6	958	3,0	26675	83,4	31966
Cyprus/Chypre	92	10,8	0	0,0	762	89,2	854
Greece/Grèce	36	0,4	64	0,7	9278	98,9	9378
Italy/Italie	1121	7,6	704	4,8	12888	87,6	14713
Malta/Malte	20	4,8	101	24,1	298	71,1	419
Portugal	14	8,8	16	10,1	129	81,1	159
Spain/Espagne	165	10,4	73	4,6	1352	85,0	1590
Turkey/Turquie	2885	59,4	0	0,0	1968	40,6	4853
Central and eastern Europe/							
Europe centrale et orientale	588	3,7	2050	12,8	13392	83,5	16030
Bulgaria/Bulgarie	75	5,0	646	43,3	770	51,6	1491
Czech Rep./Rép. tchèque	101	1,9	0	0,0	5154	98,1	5255
Estonia/Estonie	0	0,0	0	0,0	20	100,0	20
Hungary/Hongrie	104	3,9	1304	48,6	1274	47,5	2682
Latvia/Lettonie	0	0,0	3	15,8	16	84,2	19
Lithuania/Lituanie	1	1,0	80	76,2	24	22,9	105
Poland/Pologne	250	5,1	0	0,0	4677	94,9	4927
Romania/Roumanie	36	3,6	15	1,5	952	94,9	1003
Slovakia/Slovaquie	20	6,2	0	0,0	303	93,8	323
Slovenia/Slovénie	1	0,5	2	1,0	202	98,5	205

	2003						
	Convention number/ Nombre statuts de la convention	%	Humanitarian number/ Nombre statuts humanitaires	%	Refusals number/ Nombre de refus	%	Total (1) number/ Nombre total
Total	29485	8,5	27441	7,9	289078	83,5	346004
Western Europe/ Europe occidentale	25266	8,3	23496	7,7	255474	84,0	304236
Austria/Autriche	2084	29,6	0	0,0	4951	70,4	7035
Belgium/Belgique	1201	23,1	0	0,0	3988	76,9	5189
Denmark/Danemark	500	14,5	270	7,8	2683	77,7	3453
Finland/Finlande	8	0,5	486	29,5	1152	70,0	1646
France	9790	14,1	0	0,0	59818	85,9	69608
Germany/Allemagne	2854	4,3	1174	1,8	61721	93,9	65749
Iceland/Islande	0	0,0	7	10,6	59	89,4	66
Ireland/Irlande	345	5,9	0	0,0	5460	94,1	5805
Liechtenstein	0	0,0	12	12,0	88	88,0	100
Luxembourg	62	6,9	149	16,5	690	76,6	901
Netherlands/Pays-Bas	393	2,0	4228	22,0	14560	75,9	19181
Norway/Norvège	577	4,7	2962	24,3	8640	70,9	12179
Sweden/Suède	435	1,7	3090	11,8	22560	86,5	26085
Switzerland/Suisse	1638	8,3	3314	16,8	14739	74,9	19691
United Kingdom/Royaume-Uni	5379	8,0	7804	11,6	54365	80,5	67548
Southern Europe/Europe du Sud	3541	13,7	2653	10,3	19559	75,9	25753
Cyprus/Chypre	180	11,1	1	0,1	1445	88,9	1626
Greece/Grèce	3	0,1	25	0,5	4523	99,4	4551
Italy/Italie	726	5,4	2181	16,3	10501	78,3	13408
Malta/Malte	49	9,1	268	49,7	222	41,2	539
Portugal	2	9,1	11	50,0	9	40,9	22
Spain/Espagne	238	8,6	167	6,1	2350	85,3	2755
Turkey/Turquie	2343	82,2	0	0,0	509	17,8	2852
Central and eastern Europe/ Europe centrale et orientale	678	4,2	1292	8,1	14045	87,7	16015
Bulgaria/Bulgarie	19	1,3	411	28,0	1036	70,7	1466
Czech Rep./Rép. tchèque	187	2,3	0	0,0	7838	97,7	8025
Estonia/Estonie	0	0,0	0	0,0	14	100,0	14
Hungary/Hongrie	178	10,3	772	44,8	773	44,9	1723
Latvia/Lettonie	0	0,0	6	54,5	5	45,5	11
Lithuania/Lituanie	3	4,1	32	43,2	39	52,7	74
Poland/Pologne	221	6,6	24	0,7	3099	92,7	3344
Romania/Roumanie	42	5,8	27	3,7	655	90,5	724
Slovakia/Slovaquie	11	2,5	0	0,0	421	97,5	432
Slovenia/Slovénie	17	8,4	20	9,9	165	81,7	202

Table 17/Tableau 17

Asylum applications made by unaccompanied and separated children in selected European countries, 2000-03

Demandes d'asile d'enfants non accompagnés et séparés de leur famille dans les pays européens étudiés, 2000-2003

	2000		2001	
	number/ nombre	% of total apps/% des demandes totales	number/ nombre	% of total apps/% des demandes totales
Total	15858	4,2	20127	5,1
Austria/Autriche	553	3	3484	11,6
Belgium/Belgique	848	2	747	3
Bulgaria/Bulgarie	44	2,5	–	–
Croatia/Croatie	0	–	2	2,4
Cyprus/Chypre	1	0,2	0	–
Czech Rep./Rép. tchèque	298	3,4	280	1,5
Denmark/Danemark	219	1,8	239	1,9
Finland/Finlande	94	3	35	2,1
"FYR Macedonia"/ «ERY Macédoine»	0	–	0	–
Germany/Allemagne	946	1,2	1068	1,2
Greece/Grèce	–	–	206	3,7
Hungary/Hongrie	1170	15	2018	21,1
Ireland/Irlande	300	2,7	600	5,8
Latvia/Lettonie	0	–	0	–
Liechtenstein	–	–	2	1,8
Malta/Malte	–	–	1	0,9
Netherlands/Pays-Bas	6705	15,3	5951	18,3
Norway/Norvège	566	5,2	–	–
Poland/Pologne	69	1,5	80	1,8
Portugal	10	4,5	9	3,8
Romania/Roumanie	34	2,5	121	5
Slovakia/Slovaquie	145	9,3	–	–
Slovenia/Slovénie	45	0,5	113	7,5
Spain/Espagne	4	0,1	2	0
Sweden/Suède	350	2,1	461	2
Switzerland/Suisse	727	4,1	1238	6
United Kingdom/ Royaume-Uni	2730	3,4	3470	4,9

Source: UNHCR/HCR.

	2002		2003	
	number/ nombre	% of total apps/% des demandes totales	number/ nombre	% of total apps/% des demandes totales
Total	20241	5,4	12781	4,2
Austria/Autriche	3163	8	2049	6,3
Belgium/Belgique	603	3,2	589	3,5
Bulgaria/Bulgarie	205	7,1	152	9,8
Croatia/Croatie	4	4	6	9,5
Cyprus/Chypre	0	–	2	0
Czech Rep./Rép. tchèque	216	2,5	129	1,1
Denmark/Danemark	137	2,3	159	3,5
Finland/Finlande	68	2	108	3,4
"FYR Macedonia"/ «ERY Macédoine»	1	0,8	10	0,4
Germany/Allemagne	873	1,2	977	1,9
Greece/Grèce	247	4,4	314	3,8
Hungary/Hongrie	658	10,3	190	7,9
Ireland/Irlande	288	2,5	277	3,5
Latvia/Lettonie	0	–	0	–
Liechtenstein	3	3,1	3	3
Malta/Malte	14	4	16	2,8
Netherlands/Pays-Bas	3232	17,3	1216	9,1
Norway/Norvège	894	5,1	916	5,9
Poland/Pologne	213	4,1	217	3,1
Portugal	18	7,3	6	5,6
Romania/Roumanie	53	4,6	21	1,9
Slovakia/Slovaquie	1058	10,9	704	6,8
Slovenia/Slovénie	24	3,4	34	3,1
Spain/Espagne	1	0	1	0
Sweden/Suède	550	1,7	561	1,8
Switzerland/Suisse	1518	5,8	1324	6,3
United Kingdom/ Royaume-Uni	6200	7,4	2800	5,7

Table 18/Tableau 18

Expatriates of selected European countries of birth in OECD countries (1) and the proportion who have tertiary education, 2000 (or nearest census date) (thousands and per cent)

Expatriés de pays européens étudiés dans d'autres pays de l'OCDE (1) et part d'expatriés diplômés de l'enseignement supérieur, 2000 (ou date du dernier recensement) (en milliers et pourcentage)

	Expatriates/Expatriés	% with tertiary education/ % de diplômés de l'enseignement supérieur
Western Europe/Europe occidentale	15790,0	26,2
Austria/Autriche	366,0	28,7
Belgium/Belgique	321,5	33,8
Cyprus/Chypre	138,7	25,2
Denmark/Danemark	173,0	34,6
Finland/Finlande	265,2	25,4
France	1013,6	34,4
Germany/Allemagne	2933,8	29,5
Greece/Grèce	735,4	16,1
Iceland/Islande	23,1	33,8
Ireland/Irlande	792,3	23,5
Italy/Italie	2430,3	12,4
Liechtenstein	3,5	19,3
Luxembourg	27,2	26,2
Malta/Malte	96,8	19,5
Netherlands/Pays-Bas	616,9	34,0
Norway/Norvège	122,1	32,1
Portugal	1268,7	6,5
Spain/Espagne	763,0	18,0
Sweden/Suède	206,6	37,8
Switzerland/Suisse	262,5	35,8
United Kingdom/Royaume-Uni	3229,7	39,2
Central Europe/Europe centrale	4044,2	22,0
Albania/Albanie	389,3	9,1
Bulgaria/Bulgarie	527,8	14,5
Czech Republic/Rép. tchèque	215,9	24,6
Estonia/Estonie	35,1	32,0
Former Czechoslovakia/ Ex-Tchécoslovaquie	110,0	29,8
Hungary/Hongrie	314,9	28,7
Latvia/Lettonie	54,2	37,4
Lithuania/Lituanie	132,8	22,1

	Expatriates/Expatriés	% with tertiary education/ % de diplômés de l'enseignement supérieur
Poland/Pologne	1276,5	25,7
Romania/Roumanie	613,2	26,3
Slovak Republic/Rép. slovaque	374,6	13,8
Other Europe/Autres Europe	8180,7	19,0
Belarus/Bélarus	149,9	25,0
Bosnia and Herzegovina/ Bosnie-Herzégovine	536,3	11,5
Croatia/Croatie	422,3	14,0
Federal Rep. of Yugoslavia/ Rép. féd. de Yougoslavie	1064,6	11,9
Former USSR/Ex-URSS	2222,3	29,0
Former Yugoslavia/ Ex-Yougoslavie	54,8	11,8
"FYR Macedonia"/«ERY Macédoine»	149,0	11,8
Russian Fed./Féd. de Russie	580,6	43,0
Slovenia/Slovénie	52,3	17,5
Turkey/Turquie	2195,6	6,3
Ukraine	753,1	27,2

Source: National censuses in OECD countries, collated by the OECD in Dumont and Lemaitre, 2004.
Recensements nationaux dans des pays de l'OCDE, *in* Dumont et Lemaitre, 2004.

Note:
All OECD countries, excluding Italy and Japan./Tous les pays de l'OCDE sauf Italie et Japon.

Table 19/Tableau 19

Stock of foreign-born with tertiary education for selected European countries, 2001 or latest year available

Immigrés diplômés de l'enseignement supérieur dans les pays étudiés, 2001 ou dernière année disponible

	thousands/milliers	per cent/pourcentage
Austria/Autriche	104,7	11,3
Belgium/Belgique	176,9	21,6
Czech Republic/Rép. tchèque	54,8	12,8
Denmark/Danemark	62,2	19,5
Finland/Finlande	21,3	18,9
France	1011,4	18,1
Germany/Allemagne	1372,3	15,5
Greece/Grèce	153,1	15,3
Hungary/Hongrie	54,5	19,8
Ireland/Irlande	128,8	41
Luxembourg	23,9	21,7
Netherlands/Pays-Bas	208,9	17,6
Norway/Norvège	65,5	31,1
Poland/Pologne	86,4	11,9
Portugal	113,3	19,3
Slovak Republic/Rép. slovaque	16,4	14,6
Spain/Espagne	404,4	21,8
Sweden/Suède	207,6	24,2
Switzerland/Suisse	276,8	23,7
Turkey/Turquie	161,6	16,6
United Kingdom/Royaume-Uni	1374,4	34,8

Source: OECD/OCDE.

Table 20/Tableau 20

Stock of foreign students in selected European countries, academic years 1998-99 to 2001-02 (thousands)

Etudiants étrangers dans les pays européens étudiés, années scolaires 1998-1999 et 2001-2002 (en milliers)

	1998-99	1999-00	2000-01	2001-02	% change 1998-99 to 2001-02/ % de variation entre 1998-1999 et 2001-2002
Western Europe/ Europe occidentale	762,6	795,1	820,2	898,2	17,8
Austria/Autriche	29,8	30,4	31,7	28,5	-4,4
Belgium/Belgique	36,1	38,8	38,2	40,4	11,9
Cyprus/Chypre	1,9	2,0	2,5	3,1	63,2
Denmark/Danemark	12,3	12,9	12,5	14,5	17,9
Finland/Finlande	4,8	5,6	6,3	6,8	41,7
France (1)	131,0	137,1	147,4	165,4	26,3
Germany/ Allemagne	178,2	187,0	199,1	219,0	22,9
Greece/Grèce	–	–	–	8,6	–
Ireland/Irlande (2)	7,2	7,4	8,2	9,2	27,8
Italy/Italie	23,5	24,9	29,2	28,4	20,9
Netherlands/ Pays-Bas (3)	13,6	14,0	16,6	18,9	39,0
Norway/Norvège	9,0	8,7	8,8	9,5	5,6
Portugal	–	11,2	–	15,7	–
Spain/Espagne	33,0	40,7	39,9	44,9	36,1
Sweden/Suède	24,4	25,5	26,3	28,7	17,6
Switzerland/Suisse	25,3	26,0	27,8	29,3	15,8
United Kingdom/ Royaume-Uni (4)	232,5	222,9	225,7	227,3	-2,2
Central Europe/ Europe centrale	42,7	39,9	55,1	52,5	23,0
Bulgaria/Bulgarie	8,4	8,1	8,1	8,0	-4,8
Czech Republic/ Rép. tchèque (5)	4,6	5,5	7,8	9,8	113,0
Hungary/Hongrie (6)	8,9	–	11,2	11,8	32,6
Latvia/Lettonie (7)	1,8	6,0	7,9	3,3	83,3
Poland/Pologne (8)	5,7	6,1	6,7	7,4	29,8
Romania/Roumanie	13,3	12,6	11,7	10,6	-20,3
Slovak Republic/ Rép. slovaque	–	1,6	1,7	1,6	–

	1998-99	1999-00	2000-01	2001-02	% change 1998-99 to 2001-02/ % de variation entre 1998-1999 et 2001-2002
Other Europe/ Autres Europe	82,3	21,3	101,6	110,4	34,1
Belarus/Bélarus	2,7	2,7	1,8	2,6	-3,7
Croatia/Croatie	0,5	–	2,7	0,7	40,0
Moldova	–	–	2,6	2,9	–
Russian Federation/ Féd. de Russie	41,2	–	64,1	70,7	71,6
Serbia and Montenegro/ Serbie-Monténégro	1,3	0,9	0,8	–	–
Turkey/Turquie (9)	18,3	17,7	16,7	16,3	-10,9
Ukraine	18,3	–	12,9	17,2	-6,0

Source: UNESCO.

Notes:
1. 1998-99, 1999-00 and 2000-01 figures are partial data./Les chiffres de 1998-1999 et 2000-2001 sont des données partielles.
2. 1998-99, 1999-00 and 2000-01 data refer to full time students only./Les données de 1998-1999, 1999-2000 et 2000-2001 concernent seulement des étudiants à plein temps.
3. 1998-99, 1999-00 and 2000-01 data do not include ISCED 6./Les données de 1998-1999, 1999-2000 et 2000-2001 n'incluent pas ISCED 6.
4. 1999-00 and 2000-01 figures are an estimate./Les chiffres de 1998-1999 et 2000-2001 sont des estimations.
5. 1999-00 data refer to ISCED 5A and 6 only./Les données de 1999-2000 se réfèrent seulement à ISCED 5A et 6.
6. 1998-99, 2000-01 and 2001-02 data refer to ISCED 5A and 6 only./ Les données de 1998-1999, 2000-2001 et 2001-2002 se réfèrent seulement à ISCED 5A et 6.
7. 1998-99 data refer to ISCED 5A and 6 only./ Les données de 1998-1999 se réfèrent seulement à ISCED 5A et 6.
8. Data refer to ISCED 5A and 6 only, except for 2000-01 where data refer to ISCED level 5A only./ Les données se réfèrent seulement à ISCED 5A et 6, sauf pour 2000-2001 où les données renvoient seulement au niveau ISCED 5A.
9. 1998-99 data do not include ISCED 6./Les données 1998-1999 n'incluent pas ISCED 6.

Table 21/Tableau 21

Number of border violation related apprehensions in selected central and east European countries, 2001-03

Nombre de violations de frontières lié au nombre d'arrestations dans les pays d'Europe centrale et orientale étudiés, 2001-2003

	2001	2002	2003	% change 2001-02/ % de variation 2001-2002	% change 2002-03/ % de variation 2002-2003
Armenia/Arménie	–	15,8	19,0	–	20,5
Azerbaijan/Azerbaïdjan	7,6	8,3	3,8	8,6	-53,7
Bosnia and Herzegovina/ Bosnie-Herzégovine	–	0,4	1,0	–	145,4
Bulgaria/Bulgarie	6,0	6,5	5,1	8,2	-20,4
Croatia/Croatie	17,4	5,9	4,2	-66,3	-28,1
Cyprus/Chypre	0,2	0,7	3,7	298,4	413,9
Czech Republic/ Rép. tchèque	23,8	14,7	13,2	-38,2	-10,4
Hungary/Hongrie	16,6	16,0	13,5	-4	-15,3
Latvia/Lettonie	7,8	9,7	8,6	24,2	-12
Lithuania/Lituanie	1,4	0,8	0,8	-41,2	0,8
Poland/Pologne	5,2	4,3	5,1	-18,2	18,6
Romania/Roumanie	32,0	3,1	2,1	-90,4	-30,8
Yugoslavia/Yougoslavie	1,3	0,8	0,9	-35,6	3,9
Slovak Republic/ Rép. slovaque	15,5	15,2	12,5	-2	-18
Slovenia/Slovénie	20,9	6,9	5,0	-67	-27,2
Turkey/Turquie	92,4	82,8	56,2	-10,3	-32,1
Ukraine	12,6	9,6	9,6	-23,6	0
Total	260,7	201,5	164,4	-22,7	-18,4

Source: ICMPD.

Table 22/Tableau 22

Enforcement action against irregular migration in selected western European countries, 1995-2003 (thousands)

Interventions contre les migrations irrégulières dans les pays d'Europe occidentale étudiés, 1995-2003 (en milliers)

	1995	1996	1997	1998	1999	2000	2001	2002	2003
Apprehensions at border/ *Arrestations aux frontières* Germany/Allemagne	29,6	27,0	35,2	40,2	37,8	31,5	28,6	22,6	–
Refusals of entry/ *Refus d'entrée* Austria/Autriche	134,7	134,0	80,7	25,5	24,7	19,1	17,6	–	–
Italy/Italie (1)	–	–	–	31,7	37,7	27,2	34,0	31,8	25,7
Switzerland/Suisse	10,4	9,9	9,8	9,8	9,1	10,1	8,8	8,7	8,4
Enforcement actions against *illegal entry/Interventions* *contre des entrées illégales* United Kingdom/ Royaume-Uni	10,8	14,6	14,4	16,5	21,2	47,3	69,9	48,1	–

Sources: National ministries of the interior and border police, in SOPEMI national correspondents' reports.
  Ministères nationaux de l'Intérieur et de la Police des frontières, dans les rapports des correspondants nationaux du Sopemi.

Notes:
1. Figures are for July to June – i.e. 1998 figures refer to July 1998 to June 1999./Les chiffres concernent la période de juillet à juin – par exemple les chiffres de 1998 concernent juillet 1998 à juin 1999.

Table 23/Tableau 23

Estimates of human trafficking and smuggling, by region, 1994-2001

Estimations du trafic et de la contrebande humains, par région, 1994-2001

Number/Nombre	Time period/Période	Region/Région
100 000 to 200 000/ 100 000 à 200 000	1993	to western European states/ vers des Etats d'Europe occidentale
100 000 to 220 000/ 100 000 à 200 000	1993	to western European states/ vers des Etats d'Europe occidentale
300 000	Annually/Annuelle	to EU and central Europe/ vers UE et Europe centrale
400 000	Last Decade/Dernière décennie	out of Ukraine/hors d'Ukraine
4000	Annually/Annuelle	into US from NIS & eastern Europe/Aux Etats-Unis de CEI et Europe orientale
2 000 - 6 000/2 000 à 6 000	Annually/Annuelle	into Italy/En Italie
400 000+/+ de 400 000	1999	into European Union/ dans l'Union européenne
50 000-/ – de 50 000	1993	into European Union/ dans l'Union européenne
1 million+	Annually/Annuelle	Globally/Globalement
1 million+	Annually/Annuelle	Globally/Globalement
1 to 2 million/ 1 à 2 millions	Annually/Annuelle	Globally/Globalement

Based on (assumptions)/Fondé sur (suppositions)	Source
All, (smuggled) calculated by 15 to 30% of immigrants entering illegally/Tout (contrebande), calculé sur 15 à 30% des immigrés entrés illégalement	ICMPD (in *Transcrime*, 8, 1996)
All (traff) 15-30% of illegal migrants, 20-40% of a-s without founded claims, make use of traffickers (at some point in journey)/Tout (trafic): 15 à 30 % de migrants illégaux, 20 à 40 % de demandeurs d'asile sans fondement, utilisant des passeurs (à certains points du voyage)	Widgren, 1994, pp. 9-10 (prepared for IOM/préparé pour OIM)
Women (Smug.)/Femmes (contrebande)	Economist.com, 2000
Women, estimate from Ukranian Ministry of Interior/Femmes, estimations du ministère de l'Intérieur ukrainien	*Trafficking in Migrants*, 23, IOM/OIM, 2001, p. 5
Women & Children/Femmes et enfants	CIA briefing, «Global Trafficking in Women and Children» (*in* O'Neill, Richard 1999)
Women, into sex industry (estimated from per cent of irregular female migrants who enter the sex industry p.a.)/Femmes, industrie du sexe (estimé à partir du pourcentage de migrantes irrégulières qui entrent dans l'industrie du sexe)	*Trafficking in Migrants*, 23, IOM/OIM, 2001, p. 6
All (smuggled into) on EU apprehension data (equation = 1 is caught, 2 pass)/Tout (parmi les contrebandiers), d'après des données de l'UE sur les arrestations (équation = 1 arrêté, 2 passés)	Heckmann *et al.*, 2000, p. 5
All (smuggled into) on EU apprehension data (equation = 1 is caught, 2 pass)/Tout (parmi les contrebandiers) d'après les données de l'UE sur les arrestations (équation = 1 arrêté, 2 passés)	Heckmann *et al.*, 2000, p. 5
Women & Girls (Smug.) (most ending up in US)/Femmes et jeunes filles (contrebande) (la plupart finissant aux Etats-Unis)	UN and FBI statistics, (Tehran Times, March 18, 2001)/ Statistiques Onu et FBI, *Tehran Times*, 18 mars 2001
Women & Girls, for sexual exploitation in sex industries/ Femmes et jeunes filles, pour exploitation dans l'industrie du sexe	Hughes, 2001 (from international agencies and governmental estimates)/ (d'après des estimations des agences internationales et des gouvernements)
Women & Children, for forced labour, domestic servitude or sexual exploitation/Femmes et enfants, pour travail forcé, esclavage domestique ou exploitation sexuelle	US Department of State, 1998 (in Miko and/et Park, 2000)

Table 23 (continued)/Tableau 23 (suite)

Estimates of human trafficking and smuggling, by region, 1994-2001

Estimations du trafic et de la contrebande humains, par région, 1994-2001

Number/Nombre	Time period/Période	Region/Région
1-2 million(s)	Annually/Annuelle	Globally/Globalement
4 million(s)	Annually/Annuelle	Globally/Globalement
4 million(s)	Annually/Annuelle	Globally/Globalement
4 million(s)	Annually/Annuelle	Globally/Globalement
4 million(s)	Annually/Annuelle	Globally/Globalement
700 000 to 2 million/ 700 000 à 2 millions	Annually/Annuelle	Globally/Globalement
700 000 to 2 million/ 700 000 à 2 millions	Annually/Annuelle	Globally/Globalement
100 000+/+ de 100 000	Annually/Annuelle	from Soviet Union/ depuis l'Union soviétique
150 000+/+ de 150 000	Annually/Annuelle	from South Asia/ Depuis l'Asie du Sud
75 000+/+ de 75 000	Annually/Annuelle	from eastern Europe/ depuis l'Europe orientale
400 000	1999	European Union/ Union européenne
50 000	1993	European Union/ Union européenne

Compiled by the Migration Research Unit, 2001./Réalisé par l'Unité de recherche sur les migrations, 2001.

Based on (assumptions)/Fondé sur (suppositions)	Source
Women & Children/Femmes et enfants	US Government (cited in/cité dans ECRE, 2001)
All (Smug. or Traff.)/Tout (contrebande et trafic)	IOM/OIM (in Graycar, 1999, p. 1)
All (Smug. or Traff.) /Tout (contrebande et trafic)	IOM News – North American Supplement, 6, 1998
All (Smug. or Traff.) /Tout (contrebande et trafic)	IOM, 1996 (in McInerny, 2000)
All (Smug. or Traff.) /Tout (contrebande et trafic)	IOM/OIM, 1996 (in Tailby, 2000)
Women & Children, across International borders/Femmes et enfants, à travers les frontières internationales	Trafficking in Migrants, 23, IOM/OIM, 2001, p. 1, based on US Government figures (1998)/ d'après les chiffres du Gouvernement des Etats-Unis (1998)
Women & Children, excl. internal trafficking within countries such as India and Thailand/Femmes et enfants, sauf trafic interne dans des pays comme l'Inde ou la Thaïlande	IOM/OIM (in O'Neill Richard, 1999)
Women & Children/Femmes et enfants	Miko and/et Park, 2000
Women & Children/Femmes et enfants	US Department of State, (in Miko and/et Park, 2000)
Women & Children/Femmes et enfants	Miko and/et Park, 2000
All (smug.) based on apprehension data/ Tout (contrebande), d'après les données sur les arrestations	Heckmann, Wunderlich, Martin and/et McGrath, 2001, p. 5
All (smug.) based on apprehension data/ Tout (contrebande), d'après les données sur les arrestations	Heckmann, Wunderlich, Martin and/et McGrath, 2001, p. 5

Table 24/Tableau 24

Global costs for human smuggling and trafficking
Coûts globaux de la contrebande et du trafic humains

Regional movement/ Mouvement régional	USD Mean cost/ Coût principal	Median cost/ Coût moyen
Africa-Africa/Afrique-Afrique	203	158
Africa-Americas/Afrique-Amérique	2 200	2 200
Africa-Australasia/Afrique-Australasie	1 951	1 951
Africa-Europe/Afrique-Europe	6 533	2 675
Africa -Other/Afrique-autres	4 000	4 000
Americas-Americas/Amérique-Amérique	2 984	1 625
Americas-Europe/Amérique-Europe	4 528	5 000
Asia-Americas/ Asie-Amérique	26 041	27 745
Asia-Asia/Asie-Asie	12 240	3 500
Asia-Australasia/Asie-Australasie	14 011	14 011
Asia-Europe/Asie-Europe	9 374	5 000
Asia-Other/Asie-autres	6 350	4 000
Europe-Americas/Europe-Amérique	6 389	4 000
Europe-Asia/Europe-Asie	16 462	15 000
Europe-Australasia/Europe-Australasie	7 400	7 400
Europe-Europe	2 708	2 000
Europe-Other/Europe-autres	4 000	4 000

Source: Various documentary sources, compiled by the Migration Research Unit, 2004.
Sources de documentation variées, rassemblées par l'Unité de recherche sur les migrations, 2004.

Sales agents for publications of the Council of Europe
Agents de vente des publications du Conseil de l'Europe

BELGIUM/BELGIQUE
La Librairie européenne SA
50, avenue A. Jonnart
B-1200 BRUXELLES 20
Tel.: (32) 2 734 0281
Fax: (32) 2 735 0860
E-mail: info@libeurop.be
http://www.libeurop.be

Jean de Lannoy
202, avenue du Roi
B-1190 BRUXELLES
Tel.: (32) 2 538 4308
Fax: (32) 2 538 0841
E-mail: jean.de.lannoy@euronet.be
http://www.jean-de-lannoy.be

CANADA
Renouf Publishing Company Limited
5369 Chemin Canotek Road
CDN-OTTAWA, Ontario, K1J 9J3
Tel.: (1) 613 745 2665
Fax: (1) 613 745 7660
E-mail: order.dept@renoufbooks.com
http://www.renoufbooks.com

CZECH REP./ RÉP. TCHÈQUE
Suweco Cz Dovoz Tisku Praha
Ceskomoravska 21
CZ-18021 PRAHA 9
Tel.: (420) 2 660 35 364
Fax: (420) 2 683 30 42
E-mail: import@suweco.cz

DENMARK/DANEMARK
GAD Direct
Fiolstaede 31-33
DK-1171 COPENHAGEN K
Tel.: (45) 33 13 72 33
Fax: (45) 33 12 54 94
E-mail: info@gaddirect.dk

FINLAND/FINLANDE
Akateeminen Kirjakauppa
Keskuskatu 1, PO Box 218
FIN-00381 HELSINKI
Tel.: (358) 9 121 41
Fax: (358) 9 121 4450
E-mail: akatilaus@stockmann.fi
http://www.akatilaus.akateeminen.com

GERMANY/ALLEMAGNE
AUSTRIA/AUTRICHE
UNO Verlag
August-Bebel-Allee 6
D-53175 BONN
Tel.: (49) 2 28 94 90 20
Fax : (49) 2 28 94 90 222
E-mail: bestellung@uno-verlag.de
http://www.uno-verlag.de

GREECE/GRÈCE
Librairie Kauffmann
Mavrokordatou 9
GR-ATHINAI 106 78
Tel.: (30) 1 38 29 283
Fax: (30) 1 38 33 967
E-mail: ord@otenet.gr

HUNGARY/HONGRIE
Euro Info Service
Hungexpo Europa Kozpont ter 1
H-1101 BUDAPEST
Tel.: (361) 264 8270
Fax: (361) 264 8271
E-mail: euroinfo@euroinfo.hu
http://www.euroinfo.hu

ITALY/ITALIE
Libreria Commissionaria Sansoni
Via Duca di Calabria 1/1, CP 552
I-50125 FIRENZE
Tel.: (39) 556 4831
Fax: (39) 556 41257
E-mail: licosa@licosa.com
http://www.licosa.com

NETHERLANDS/PAYS-BAS
De Lindeboom Internationale
Publikaties
PO Box 202, MA de Ruyterstraat 20 A
NL-7480 AE HAAKSBERGEN
Tel.: (31) 53 574 0004
Fax: (31) 53 572 9296
E-mail: lindeboo@worldonline.nl
http://home-1-worldonline.nl/
~lindeboo/

NORWAY/NORVÈGE
Akademika, A/S
Universitetsbokhandel
PO Box 84, Blindern
N-0314 OSLO
Tel.: (47) 22 85 30 30
Fax: (47) 23 12 24 20

POLAND/POLOGNE
Głowna Księgarnia Naukowa
im. B. Prusa
Krakowskie Przedmiescie 7
PL-00-068 WARSZAWA
Tel.: (48) 29 22 66
Fax: (48) 22 26 64 49
E-mail: inter@internews.com.pl
http://www.internews.com.pl

PORTUGAL
Livraria Portugal
Rua do Carmo, 70
P-1200 LISBOA
Tel.: (351) 13 47 49 82
Fax: (351) 13 47 02 64
E-mail: liv.portugal@mail.telepac.pt

SPAIN/ESPAGNE
Mundi-Prensa Libros SA
Castelló 37
E-28001 MADRID
Tel.: (34) 914 36 37 00
Fax : (34) 915 75 39 98
E-mail: libreria@mundiprensa.es
http://www.mundiprensa.com

SWITZERLAND/SUISSE
Adeco – Van Diermen
Chemin du Lacuez 41
CH-1807 BLONAY
Tel.: (41) 21 943 26 73
Fax: (41) 21 943 36 05
E-mail: info@adeco.org

UNITED KINGDOM/
ROYAUME-UNI
TSO (formerly HMSO)
51 Nine Elms Lane
GB-LONDON SW8 5DR
Tel.: (44) 207 873 8372
Fax: (44) 207 873 8200
E-mail:
customer.services@theso.co.uk
http://www.the-stationery-office.co.uk
http://www.itsofficial.net

UNITED STATES and CANADA/
ÉTATS-UNIS et CANADA
Manhattan Publishing Company
468 Albany Post Road, PO Box 850
CROTON-ON-HUDSON,
NY 10520, USA
Tel.: (1) 914 271 5194
Fax: (1) 914 271 5856
E-mail:
Info@manhattanpublishing.com
http://www.manhattanpublishing.com

FRANCE
La Documentation française
(Diffusion/Vente France entière)
124, rue H. Barbusse
F-93308 AUBERVILLIERS Cedex
Tel.: (33) 01 40 15 70 00
Fax: (33) 01 40 15 68 00
E-mail: commandes.vel@
ladocfrancaise.gouv.fr
http://www.ladocfrancaise.gouv.fr

Librairie Kléber (Vente Strasbourg)
Palais de l'Europe
F-67075 Strasbourg Cedex
Fax: (33) 03 88 52 91 21
E-mail: librairie.kleber@coe.int

Council of Europe Publishing/Editions du Conseil de l'Europe
F-67075 Strasbourg Cedex
Tel.: (33) 03 88 41 25 81 – Fax: (33) 03 88 41 39 10 – E-mail: publishing@coe.int – Website: http://book.coe.int

177

RETHINKING THE SOURCES OF INTERNATIONAL LAW

by

G.J.H. van Hoof

Kluwer Law and Taxation Publishers
Deventer/Netherlands
Antwerp - Boston - Frankfurt - London

Distribution in USA and Canada:
Kluwer Academic Publishers
190 Old Derby Street
Hingham MA 02043   U.S.A.

JX 3091

ISBN 90 6544 085 2

RETHINKING THE SOURCES OF
INTERNATIONAL LAW

TO MARION

IN GRATITUDE TO MY PARENTS

PREFACE

The title of this book may strike the reader as rather immodest. Its author can come up with no better justification for the selection of the subject matter than the fundamental character of the doctrine of sources to any study of international law. Particularly in today's world, the many questions involved leave hardly any field of international law unaffected, and no international lawyer can hope to escape them completely. I felt that in my case this early stage of my legal writing was as good a time as any to face some of these questions. However, I am perfectly aware that the contribution of this book to the doctrine of sources of international law can only be a modest one.

The completion of this book would have been impossible without the advice, assistance and support of many persons and institutions. First of all, I am grateful to all those whose scholarly work I have been able to use in writing this book, including those whom I have criticized. Often one learns best from those with whom one disagrees.

More specifically I am indebted to the scholars under whose guidance this study was conducted. Professor P. van Dijk, over the years that I had the privilege of working with him, taught me the craft of scholarship by patiently correcting my many mistakes. As my supervisor he meticulously read consecutive versions of the manuscript and in each stage stimulated me by offering ideas, suggestions and comments which have improved this book to no small extent. Professor M. Bos provided very valuable advice and comments on the manuscript. Moreover, he was my main teacher of the theory of international law, both during the time I was a student and afterwards, as is witnessed by the numerous references to his scholarly work throughout this book. I have also benefited greatly from discussing the manuscript with Professor J. de Vree. His advice and comments as a political scientist have prevented me from losing sight of the many other than legal aspects involved in the subject-matter.

I thank all my (former) colleagues of the Department of International and Social and Economic Law of the University of Utrecht for their inspiring interest in my work. Among them particularly Professor A. Koers and Professor L. Bouchez provided me with encouraging comments on my research. In addition, Professor Koers has been extremely helpful with respect to the technical aspects of this publication. Mr. J. Rood offered to read parts of the manuscript and made useful suggestions.

During the academic year 1979/1980 I was given the opportunity to conduct research at the Harvard Law School in Cambridge (Mass.), U.S.A.. The inspiring atmosphere and the excellent facilities of that place have contributed considerably to the completion of this book. I am indebted to Professor L. Sohn who supervised my work at Harvard. Dean D. Smith and his staff, as well as the staff of the library of International Legal Studies, in particular Mr. F. Chapman, in various ways helped to make may visit rewarding.

My stay in the U.S.A. was made possible through generous financial support of the Netherlands Organization for the Advancement of Pure Research (ZWO). The University of Utrecht kindly granted me leave of absence. I also received funding from the Foundation Hugo Grotius. I am sincerely thankful to these institutions for thus enabling me to conduct the research for this book.

The Netherlands Organization for the Advancement of Pure Research (ZWO) in addition enabled me to finalize my research in U.S.A. during October and November of 1982. At that time I had the opportunity to profit from the expert-advice of Professor L. Henkin of Columbia University in New York, who had kindly offered to read major parts of the manuscript.

A number of friends have been extremely helpful. Mr. J. de Jong has rendered invaluable services by checking all the footnotes and reading the entire manuscript. I asked Professor H. Hovenkamp to correct the English and Mr. K. de Vey Mestdagh to assist in proof-reading. Both readily agreed and did an excellent and speedy job. In the process each of them managed to critically read the manuscript and suggested me a number of important improvements. Messrs. M. Sikking and G. Knol encouraged me at times when this book seemed never to be completed.

Last but not least, Mrs. M. Kiel has earned my gratitude for the vital role she played in the publication of this book. She patiently typed and retyped the various versions and studiously prepared the manuscript for printing. In the final stage she was efficiently assisted by Mrs. M. Smith. The attention paid to the publication of this book by Mr. W. Siegers of Meyers and Siegers Printers, and by Messrs. M. Nieuwenhuis and A. Vonk of Kluwer Law and Taxation Publishers is gratefully acknowledged.

It goes without saying that the errors, which this book contains despite all this help, are mine.

The contribution of my parents is beyond description. The role of my family has been pivotal. Marion's support has been indispensable *inter alia* by her ability to create a balance between an atmosphere conducive to writing and the requirements of family-life. Joost, Esther and Gijs contributed in their own particular way by their tireless efforts to upset that balance, thereby enabling me to put my work in a proper perspective.

IJsselstein, May 1983.

TABLE OF CONTENTS

LIST OF ABBREVIATIONS

AdV	Archiv des Völkerrechts
AFDI	Annuaire Français de Droit International
AJIL	American Journal of International Law
ASDI	Annuaire Suisse de Droit International
BJIL	Brooklyn Journal of International Law
BYIL	British Yearbook of International Law
CLR	Columbia Law Review
CWILJ	California Western International Law Journal
CWRJIL	Case Western Reserve Journal of International Law
CYIL	Canadian Yearbook of International Law
DA	Deutsche Aussenpolitik
DJILP	Denver Journal of International Law and Policy
FW	Die Friedens-Warte
GJICL	Georgia Journal of International and Comparative Law
GYIL	German Yearbook of International Law
IA	International Affairs
ICJ Communiqué	Communiqué of the International Court of Justice
ICJ Reports	International Court of Justice, Reports of Judgments, Advisory Opinions and Orders
ICLQ	International and Comparative Law Quarterly
IJIL	Indian Journal of International Law
ILC Yearbook	Yearbook of the International Law Commission
ILM	International Legal Materials
ILR	Israel Law Review
IO	International Organization
JICJ	Journal of the International Commission of Jurists
JöRG	Jahrbuch des öffentlichen Rechts der Gegenwart
JZ	Juristenzeitung
NILR	Netherlands International Law Review
NYIL	Netherlands Yearbook of International Law
ÖZöR	Österreichische Zeitschrift für öffentliches Recht
PASIL	Proceedings of the American Society of International Law
PCIJ Series B	Permanent Court of International Justice, Collection of Advisory Opinions
Ph	Philosophica
PYIL	Polish Yearbook of International Law
RBDI	Revue Belge de Droit International
RCADI	Recueil des Cours de l'Académie de Droit International de La Haye
RDISDP	Revue de Droit International de Sciences Diplomatiques et Politiques

CHAPTER I

GENERAL INTRODUCTION: STATE-MENT OF THE PROBLEM AND METHOD OF STUDY

As law is primarily a device for regulating and ordering relations in society, any system of law should be able to answer clearly the question of what the law is or where it can be found.[1] The question of sources is therefore fundamental in any system of law. Particularly in the present time in which so large a number of most important fields of international relations require so quick and effective a regulation, it is a matter of great anxiety to international lawyers and, more generally, to all those concerned with the destiny of the international community that in international law this vital issue of the sources so controversial and confusing. In a nutshell the foregoing represents both the focus of the present study as well as the main justification for undertaking it.

The era following World War II and particularly the most recent decades have been witnessing a kind of revival of attention for the theory of international law. The space devoted to the theoretical aspects in books and leading journals on international law is considerable. Furthermore, if this author is not mistaken, the theoretical renaissance in international law is still gaining momentum. At least from hindsight this is not surprising. The post-war history of international relations up to the present moment has seen far-reaching changes. The ensuing new situations have raised new questions and posed new problems to States in the conduct of their international relations. As international law is a major instrument for keeping these relations viable, the new situations referred to have also put (new) strains on that body of law. It is therefore not surprising that this state of affairs has prompted renewed reflection on the theoretical underpinnings of international law. The wide-ranging and multifarious questions and problems arising in practice can be adequately coped with only on the basis of a consistent and appropriate concept of what international law is and how it actually works. The theories inherited from past centuries and preceding generations of international lawyers may still provide powerful insights, but they cannot meet, in all respects, the challenges posed by modern developments. Consequently, the need is felt to review, reconsider and, if necessary, reformulate the traditional views in the light of the changed circumstances.

The question of the sources of international law is an important aspect of the theoretical revival just mentioned. Indeed, as one of the fundamental issues of international law, the doctrine of the sources has always attracted considerable

---

1. Similarly R. Jennings, "What Is International Law And How Do We Tell It When We See It?", XXXVII *ASDI* (1981), pp. 59-88 (59): "although lawyers know that the quality of certainty of law is one on which there must be much compromise, not least in the interest of Justice, it is a *desideratum* of any strong law that there is reasonable certainty about where one should look to find it".

attention. Similarly, because of the peculiar features of the international society, the sources of international law have at all times been, to a greater or lesser extent, controversial. However, one may wonder whether or not the recent changes have affected the sources of international law and if so to what extent. On the one hand, it would seem that they have resulted in a situation where an increasing need is felt for rapid and often detailed regulation in many fields of international relations. On the other hand, the process of creating international law would seem to grow more cumbersome, in that it becomes more time-consuming and its outcome less satisfactory measured against what is needed in practice. These two contradictory tendencies no doubt help to explain the greater attention for the sources and probably also contribute to the fact that the issue has taken on a more confusing and controversial character.

Every international lawyer is of course familiar with the problems surrounding the sources, because their impact is felt, at least to some extent, in nearly every field of international law. However, the magnitude and the ramifications of the problematical nature of the sources become clear above all in the newer fields of international law. It is particularly in these fields that the impact of the uncertainties and ambiguities which at present characterize the doctrine of the sources of international law are felt. The present author was first confronted with these issues as a student of the international law of human rights. In that comparatively young area of international law the question quite frequently arises of what the precise legal status of a certain document is. Well-known, for instance, is the long-standing debate on whether or not the Universal Declaration on Human Rights, adopted by the General Assembly of the United Nations in 1948, constitutes binding international law.

Comparable difficulties may be encountered when one tries to pinpoint the legal or non-legal character of instruments belonging to other fields of international law, such as that of peace and security or that of the international economic relations, including the documents relating to a "new international economic order". Because it is the main task of the doctrine of sources to answer questions like how rules of international law come into being and whether or not (and if so, to what extent exactly) a given rule is a rule of international law, it is here that the heart of the problem concerning the sources lies. For, to the extent that the doctrine of sources is incapable of answering these questions, the ability of international law to serve effectively as an instrument for ordering and regulating international relations diminishes.

Because of the fundamental character of the issue of the sources, moreover, the scope of the problem is not confined to the just-mentioned questions. The uncertainties and ambiguities surrounding the sources also permeate other important issues in international law. A notable example can be found in a matter which has equally dominated and troubled the theory of international law, i.e. the question of enforcement of international law, or, to put it more broadly, of the supervision of international obligations on the part of States. With respect, for instance, to the supervision of implementation of international obligations on the part of States in the field of human rights, which the present author's research has to a large extent been concentrated upon thus far, it frequently appears that the (effectiveness of the) supervision is not only dependent upon the particular features of the supervisory mechanism concerned, notably the functions and powers of the organs entrusted with supervision, but also on

the precise legal status of the obligations to be supervised.[2] To put it differently, supervision as a rule appears to be more effective in the case of rules of a clear normative status than in the case of rules whose precise legal character is more ambiguous.

This suggested relation between supervision and the exact normative status of a rule was made one of the objects of study, although not a primary one, in a research project on supervision within international economic organizations initiated by the Department of the Law of International Organizations of Utrecht University, in which the present author participated. This research project purported to analyze the supervisory mechanisms of various international economic organizations and other arrangements of an economic character in search of their effectiveness. From the outset it was taken into account that the activities of supervisory organs or law-determining agencies in general are seldom confined to the application of existing law strictly speaking. Judgments and other assessments, of course, never evolve mechanically from the mere application of existing rules to a given set of facts. Some measure of interpretation is always involved. Furthermore, existing rules frequently require concretization, adaptation, elaboration and even sometimes the creation of new (additional) rules by law-determining agencies before they can be successfully applied in practice. From the beginning, therefore, a so-called "creative-function" was introduced in the model according to which the activities of supervisory mechanisms were to be analyzed.

It turned out *inter alia* that the amount of "creative" aspects involved in the work of supervisory organs of various international organizations was considerably more important than was expected. These organs proved to perform a good deal of law-making, although this is usually disguised as determination, interpretation or application of the law.[3] One of the main explanations for the fact that supervisory organs on the international plane usually resort to "creative" activities on a larger scale than at the national level would seem to be found in the international law-making process itself. In a number of important respects the latter is inferior to the legislative mechanisms usually found in municipal legal systems; mainly because of its decentralized or horizontal character the international law-making process not infrequently produces quite ambiguous rules of law and, more importantly, it is not very well equipped to adapt international law to changing circumstances. As a result it was found that the defects of the international law-making process came to the fore very clearly in the phase of supervision and, therefore, quite often had to be remedied in that phase.

The present author initially intended to further elaborate this relation between law-making and supervision. For a number of reasons the Final Act of Helsinki of 1975 was chosen as the principle object of study for that purpose. The Final Act constitutes the concluding document of the Conference on Security and Cooperation in Europe which assembled in three phases between

2. For a detailed study on the supervision of international obligations in the field of human rights, with reference also to the just-mentioned link between supervision and the legal status of the rules concerned, see A. Khol, *Zwischen Staat und Weltstaat* (Wien 1969).
3. The results of the researchproject will be published in 1983 by Kluwer, Deventer, under the title: P. van Dijk (ed.), *Supervision within International Economic Organizations: The NIEO Perspective* .

3

3 July 1973 and 1 August 1975 in Helsinki, Geneva and Helsinki again.[4] It was solemnly signed by the heads of state and the heads of government of the United States, Canada and all European States with the exception of Albania. This very elaborate document comprising more than sixty pages in print deals with a great variety of highly important issues in the political, military, economic, humanitarian, cultural and educational field.[5] Furthermore, the Final Act established a highly interesting kind of supervisory or, in its own terminology, follow-up mechanism in the form of subsequent meetings of representatives of participating States at intervals of approximately two years.

This summary description of the Final Act's general features is sufficient to show that there were a number of reasons for studying the document. Generally speaking, the Helsinki Final Act was widely considered to be a very important instrument. More important, however, from the perspective of the object of study which the present author had in mind was the fact that the Final Act, although it did not result in an institutional set-up belonging to the class of international organizations, does provide for some form of international organization consisting of regular follow-up meetings. Furthermore, the Helsinki Final Act shows a number of characteristics which are interesting in view of the link between law-making and supervision just mentioned. In the part devoted to the follow-up of the Conference the participating States first declare their resolve to continue the multilateral process initiated by the Conference. Subsequently, they map out a two-tier system to this end. Their aim is to be attained "by proceeding to a thorough exchange of views on the implementation of the provisions of the Final Act and of the tasks defined by the Conference, as well as, in the context of the questions dealt with by the latter, on the deepening of their mutual relations, the improvement of security and the development of cooperation in Europe, and the development of the process of détente in the future;". In other words, the Final Act in fact charges the follow-up meetings with a twofold task: firstly, review of implementation; and, secondly, a more "law-making" task of deepening, improving and developing what has already been achieved.

In addition to this special arrangement on follow-up, another feature making the Helsinki Final Act a most interesting object of study is that its precise legal nature or status was left vague and consequently uncertain by the participating States.[6] Apart from the exact reasons of this state of affairs, the combination of

---

4. For an elaborate report on the *travaux préparatoires* and the course of the Conference, see L. Ferraris (ed.), *Report on a Negotiation, Helsinki-Geneva-Helsinki 1972-1975*, Institut Universitaire de Hautes Etudes Internationales (Alphen aan den Rijn/Genève 1979); see also the commentary on the text of the Final Act contained in Publication No. 115 of the Netherlands Ministry of Foreign Affairs, *Conferentie over Veiligheid en Samenwerking in Europa, Helsinki-Genève-Helsinki 1973-1975* [Conference on Security and Cooperation in Europe, Helsinki-Geneva-Helsinki 1973-1975] ('s Gravenhage 1976). The most important documents relevant to the Conference are collected in H. Jacobsen e.a. (eds.), *Sicherheit und Zusammenarbeit in Europa; Analyse und Dokumentation 1973-1978* (Köln 1978).
5. For a fairly recent survey of the various aspects of the Helsinki Final Act with a great number of further references, see P. van Dijk, "The Final Act of Helsinki - Basis for a Pan-European System?", XI *NYIL* (1980), pp. 97-124.
6. See in this respect the analysis of the declarations by the representatives of the participating States at the occasion of the signing of the Final Act by A. Klafkowski, "CSCE Final Act - The Bases for Legal Interpretation", 8 *SIR* (Warsaw 1977), pp. 76-87 (79-84). The classifications

4

its uncertain legal nature coupled with a follow-up mechanism designed *inter alia* to perform a kind of "law-making" function seemed to make the Helsinki Final Act a perfect case to study the relation between law-making and supervision. It was decided to undertake first an effort to pinpoint the precise legal nature of the Helsinki Final Act and subsequently, on that basis, to expand the analysis into the relation between the legal status thus established and the Final Act's follow-up system. More specifically, the latter task was designed to answer the question as to what extent and in what ways the legally binding or non-binding (or the intermediate) status of the Final Act has an impact on its follow-up and *vice versa*, that is whether and how the follow-up mechanism can add to that status of the Final Act.

It was estimated that the pinpointing of the legally binding or non-binding character of the Final Act would be comparatively easy. There was already, at that time, a great deal of writing on the legal nature of the Helsinki Final Act analyzing the peculiar features which that document shows in this respect. It was therefore thought that the classification of the Helsinki Final Act in terms of its legal nature was to consist in the relatively simple task of testing these peculiar features against the criteria which the doctrine of sources provides for deciding whether or not a given instrument or rule constitutes binding international law. However, all this turned out to be more complicated than was contemplated.

First of all, most of the existing literature on the legal status of the Final Act proved to be only partially helpful and in some respects even unsatisfactory. With few exceptions, authors tackling the issue are inclined to deny to the Helsinki Final Act the status of full-fledged international law. They usually reach this conclusion after drawing attention to a number of provisions contained in the Helsinki Final Act and certain circumstances accompanying its coming into existence, which indeed seem to point in that direction. The result is, as Kimminich has concluded on the basis of a survey of relevant literature, that: "Bezuglich der Rechtsnatur der KSZE-Schlussakte bleibt festzuhalten, dass ... ihrer Einordnung in die herkommlichen Kategorien der internationale Instrumente bisher nicht gelungen ist".[7] Conversely, however, there are other provisions in and circumstances surrounding the Final Act which make the picture less unequivocal and which make it difficult to rank the Final Act as an entirely non-legal document. These latter aspects are taken into consideration in doctrine, but their effects in terms of the legal nature of the Helsinki Final Act remain largely unexplained. The upshot is that the latter question still remains more or less unanswered; it is made clear what the document is not, but it remains unclear what it is.

The (alleged) impossibility of precisely classifying the Helsinki Final Act in terms of its legal or non-legal status is fairly generally attributed to the hybrid character of the document itself. In itself that argument is correct. No doubt the Final Act contains conflicting indications as to its legal nature reflecting the diverging aims with which the participating States conducted the negotiating

of the Final Act ranged from "Magna Charta of Peace in Europe" via "insight into the future" and "declaration of intent" to "an act of unilateral commitment". Similarly, other statements on the part of the participating States earlier during the Conference contain very divergent descriptions as to its precise legal nature.
7. O. Kimminich, "Konferenz über Sicherheit und Zusammenarbeit in Europa und Menschenrechte", 17 *AdV* (1977/78), pp. 274-294 (281).

process. However, in the present author's view this is only part of the story. The other part is that not only is the Final Act quite ambiguous, but also that the criteria on the basis of which its legal status would have to be tested are far from unequivocal. In the course of the study it became more and more apparent that the doctrine of sources too entails ambiguities and uncertainties which on their part cause difficulties in classifying certain instruments in terms of their legal nature. So it became clear that elaborating on these latter questions would constitute a far more ambitious approach to the sources of international law than was originally contemplated.

Consequently, in order to avoid undertaking a work of too great a scope and magnitude, the choice had to be faced between two alternative courses on which to proceed: either to concentrate on the questions involved concerning the sources, or to take as a point of departure or as a hypothesis a given concept of the sources and apply this to the Helsinki Final Act. It was decided to take the former course and postpone the application of the ensuing results to the Helsinki Final Act for a later study. The main reason for this choice was that taking the latter course would have constituted, to a considerable degree, a duplication of existing literature, as this is the approach usually taken to deal with the question of the Final Act's legal nature. Furthermore, as the exploration of the doctrine of sources of international law progressed the present author became more and more fascinated by the puzzling questions involved.

After it had been decided to focus on the sources of international law, the precise object of study was still to be narrowed down. For, what is often loosely referred to as the doctrine of sources of international law in fact covers a rather vast area of the theory of international law, comprising a considerable number of quite diverging questions, such as "How are rules of international law created, that is, what factors contribute to or determine the substantive content of a particular rule?", "How can one tell whether or not a given rule is a rule of international law?", and "How effective is a certain rule of international law in practice?".These questions are usually all discussed as parts of the doctrine of sources of international law. Nevertheless, it is clear that these questions address highly different, although related issues. Furthermore, questions like these may of course be approached from different angles. Attempts at answering such questions can be made, for instance, from a legal, a philosophical and, an empirical or political science point of view. As is clearly indicated throughout this study, the present author tries to take a strictly legal approach.[8]

Even confined to a strictly legal approach, the sources of international law raise very wide-ranging problems as is exemplified by the questions just posed. They will not all be dealt with here. As was explained, the present study was in fact prompted by the difficulties encountered in trying to solve the quite practical question as to the legal or non-legal nature of the Helsinki Final Act. Consequently, although any re-examination of the sources of international law obviously entails entering into the theory of international law, it was attempted to maintain a practice-oriented outlook throughout the present study. In other words, the statement of the problem to be dealt with in the present study is in

8. For a political scientist's approach see J. de Vree, "On the Origins and Growth of Law and Morals", 23 Ph(1979), pp. 129-176; as to examples of the philosophical approach the reader may be referred to chapter IV and the various studies cited there.

fact summarized by the second of the three questions just posed, that is, "How can one tell whether or not a rule is indeed a rule of international law?". Clearly, therefore, the present study does not purport to address all the issues which may be involved in the doctrine of sources, let alone to set forth an all-embracing comprehensive theory of sources of international law.

This focus may be clarified a little further by briefly relating the subject of the present study to a scheme designed to be of such all-embracing or comprehensive character, as it has been put forward in a number of consecutive studies by Bos.[9] According to that author his scheme is intended to provide a fresh look at "the origin, nature, and process of law generally, and at the points at which international law branches off into its own direction, acquiring thereby its own specific and very distinct appearance".[10] Put summarily, the scheme is made up of three basic elements. First, there is the *General Concept of Law* which "is above all supposed to delimit the phenomenon of law as such, *i.e.*, to enable one to distinguish law from non-law."[11] Secondly, Bos distinguishes the *Normative Concept of Law* which "arose as an answer to explain the presence, side by side of so many national legal orders".[12] The explanation is according to the author, "in the fact that inside the GCL over the centuries a great number of NCL were developed all of which led to the creation of a corresponding number of legal orders".[13] Finally, the *Legal Process* is mentioned which "as a whole is the combined projection of GCL and NCL".[14] It is said to consist of three phases. In phase I "the genesis of the abstract rule takes place, stretching from inception to provisional crystallyzation in the shape of a RML" (*Recognized Manifestation of Law*, which term Bos proposes to substitute for the term "source" - vH).[15] In phase II "all the manifestations of law recognized in a certain legal order are to be found ... In this phase, the abstract rule is 'at rest'"[16], while phase III "is the stage in which the abstract rule normally valid for all the subjects of a particular legal order evolves into a concrete rule determining a specific legal relationship between a limited number of these subjects".[17]

This brief survey suffices for our purpose here. It offers a framework within which the object of the present study can be outlined. The main focus of the present study is on what Bos labels the *Legal Process*, particularly phase II thereof, because it is there where the sources of law, in this case of international law, are to be found. Nevertheless, in Part III of this book, excursions will have to be made into phase I and phase III, because, as will be argued, law-making in the present-day international society has become a more or less continuing process, and, consequently, the legal status of a given rule can very often be adequately determined only if all consecutive stages of the law-making cycle are taken into account. As far as the *General Concept of Law* and the *Normative*

9. See the author's most recent study entitled: "Will and Order in the Nation-State System, Observations on Positivism and Positive International Law", XXIX - 1 *NILR* (1982), pp. 3-31, and the references to earlier work provided there.
10. *Ibidem*, p. 4.
11. *Ibidem*.
12. *Ibidem*, p. 7.
13. *Ibidem*; for more details on this Normative Concept of Law, see *infra*, pp. 14-15.
14. *Ibidem*, p. 8.
15. *Ibidem*.
16. *Ibidem*.
17. *Ibidem*, pp. 8-9.

Concept of Law are concerned, they will be dealt with only to the extent that they influence or have a bearing upon the question as to the legal status or character of a certain rule. For the remainder these complex and multi-facetted phenomena will not be considered.

In order to be able to stick as strictly as possible to the object of the present study it was found useful to introduce two types of distinctions which together constitute the point of departure of the present author's approach to the sources of international law. These two distinctions, which to some extent overlap, will be elaborated below,[18] but for the sake of clarity they should be summarily set forth from the outset.

First, we will discern between *material* and *procedural* aspects of the sources of international law by means of a comparison with the prototype of a national constitution. It goes without saying that in international law there is no constitution in the sense of that term as used in municipal legal systems. Nevertheless, as will be argued, international law does encompass constitution-like provisions and just like in the case of a national legal system they can be generally speaking divided into two types. The material type of provisions lays down the fundamental political orientation of a given society in the form of basic values and ideas which it wants to uphold or attain. The procedural provisions on the other hand outline the legal and/or organizational structure of the society in question. These latter include provisions laying down the way in which rules belonging to the legal system concerned are to be created. It is upon these procedural provisions that the present study on the sources is focused.

Secondly, with respect to the term "source" or "sources" of international law itself it was found necessary to make a threefold distinction. This distinction was prompted by the awareness that the confusion and controversy over the sources of international law, which was already hinted at, is to no small extent caused by different concepts of sources. In order to avoid this pitfall it was decided to discern between three meanings of sources or rather to analyze the sources on three different levels. At the first level, "source" is used to indicate *the basis of the binding force of international law*. Secondly, we will discern source in the sense of *constitutive element for rules of international law*, being a criterion by which one can decide whether or not a rule is indeed a rule of international law. The third level refers to sources as meaning the *relevant manifestations on the basis of which the presence or absence of the constitutive element can be established.* In line with the above-mentioned practice-oriented outlook of the present study emphasis will be on the sources in the second and third sense. The three levels set forth, however, are closely intertwined and an analysis of the second and third level might be somewhat in the air if not preceded by a discussion of at least the most relevant aspects of the first level. Consequently, some observations on the basis of the binding force of international law will have to be made, although this issue strictly speaking falls outside the scope of the present study.

After having thus put forward the main points of departure, the set-up of the present study may be summed up as follows. It became clear rather quickly that in order to be able to make even a very modest contribution to the doctrine of the sources of international law it was necessary to retrace the questions involved to their very roots. Issues concerning the sources are linked up very

18. See *infra* pp. 57-60.

closely to other fundamental questions of the theory of international law which go in fact to the heart of what was called the normative concept of international law. The implicit or explicit disagreements on these latter questions to some extent cause the controversy and confusion over the sources. It was therefore considered necessary to deal first with these matters. Consequently, Part I, in its first chapters, sets forth the present author's own views on those aspects of the normative concept of international law which to him seem most relevant to problems concerning the sources. These views will be compared to a number of well-known theories or, more generally speaking, basic approaches to international law which have for a long time dominated and in certain respects still dominate thinking about international law. By contrasting these theories with the author's own views the latter may be clarified a little further. More importantly, the survey of the so-called basic approaches is designed to identify the elements contained in them which might contribute to answering the questions concerning the sources.

Subsequently, the concept of sources itself is analyzed. At first glance this concept of sources is usually taken to have a fairly clear connotation. However, as was already observed, closer inspection reveals that the term "source" or "sources" is not altogether free from ambiguity and for this reason the threefold distinction just outlined was introduced. After settling some matters of terminology an analysis of the different meanings of the term "sources" will be conducted, particularly in the light of the changes which have taken place in international relations. For, it is the main theme of the present study to find out whether or not and, if so, in what ways and to what extent the changes which have taken place in international society have affected the sources of international law.

From this perspective and on the basis of the theoretical frame outlined in Part I, the so-called "traditional" sources of international law (the items listed in Article 38 of the Statute of the International Court of Justice) are dealt with in Part II. Although there is growing scepticism as to the adequacy of Article 38, the provision still constitutes the point of departure for any discussion of the sources of international law. Consequently, successive chapters will critically re-examine treaties, customary international law and the general principles as well as judicial decisions and doctrine, the latter being subsidiary means for the determination of rules of international law. In each case the analysis focuses on the impact of societal changes on the traditional sources of international law and is aimed at answering the question of whether or not these sources are still capable of performing the main task required of them within the framework of international law, that is, answering the question of whether or not a given rule is to be considered a rule of international law. The final chapter of this part then sums up the results, and purports to draw some conclusions.

Finally, in Part III the issue will first be addressed whether or not and, if so, how the sources of international law may be changed. Subsequently, it will be attempted, on the basis of the results gathered from Part II, to provide an outline of an approach as to how the doctrine of sources might cope with such changes, if and to the extent that such is necessary.

PART I

THE APPROACH TO THE PROBLEM OF THE SOURCES OF INTERNATIONAL LAW

CHAPTER II

THE CONFUSION OVER THE SOURCES AND THE NORMATIVE CONCEPT OF LAW

There are probably few fields of international law where confusion and unclarity reign more supreme than that of the sources.[19] First, there is a terminological debate. As has been said above, no agreement exists on the meaning of the term "source" or "sources". We will get back to this point later.[20] Furthermore, each writer dealing with the sources of international law seems to have his or her own personal opinion, deviating in at least some respects from that of others, both on what the sources are and the number thereof, as well as on the exact meaning of each of the sources, which he or she lists. Recently, one commentator has pointedly summarized the state of affairs as follows: "One of the aspects of international law that best exemplifies the tenuous nature of its claim to legitimacy and efficacy is the continuing debate over the nature of its sources. In municipal legal systems the sources of legal rules - be they constitutions, statutes, precedents, or judicially filled 'interstitial gaps' - are widely accepted. In the international legal system, the legitimacy of such sources remains the subject of scholarly dispute. Although bilateral and multilateral treaties are generally accepted as sources of international law, other purported sources, such as 'international custom' and 'general principles' remain controversial".[21]

This disagreement is apparent at all levels, irrespective of the particular meaning of the term "source" one is talking about. It is visible, for instance, both in the discussions of "sources" as meaning "places where the law can be found" (in order to find out what the law is)[22] as in the quest for a "source" or "sources" in the sense of "the basis of the binding force of international law".[23] Against this background it is not surprising that the effort to determine the international legal character of a particular document or rule is often a hazardous undertaking. Not only is the character of international documents and rules often

---

19. As was aptly put by R. Jennings, *loc.cit.* (note 1), p. 60: "I doubt whether anybody is going to dissent from the proposition that there has never been a time when there has been so much confusion and doubt about the tests of validity - or sources - of international law, than the present. This is natural enough at a time when the tide of development, change and elaboration in international law is flowing stronger than ever before. So the present confusion is far from being of itself a reason for pessimism. All the same, there is no denying that it is a major problem calling for, if not necessary a speedy solution, at least a sound one".
20. See *infra* pp. 57-60.
21. H. Schrader, "Custom and General Principles as Sources of International Law in American Federal Courts", 82 *CLR* (1982), pp. 751- 783 (751).
22. See in this respect C. Parry, *The Sources and Evidences of International Law* (Manchester 1965), pp. 1-27, who considers the problem of sources of international law of such a nature that "what the sources of international law are cannot be stated; it can only be discussed" (p. 27).
23. According to O. Schachter, "Towards a Theory of International Obligation", 8 *VJIL* (1967), pp. 300-322, one can list "at least a baker's dozen of 'candidates' which have been put forward as the basis (or as one of the bases) of obligation in international law" (p. 301).

obscure, but so are the standards on the basis of which such a determination has to be made.

The chaotic and confusing state of affairs which was said to prevail with respect to the sources of international law has a broad practical impact. Schachter has enumerated six types of developments which are a main cause of and, at the same time, particularly affected by the indeterminacy of international obligation: (1) the "quasi-legislative" activities of United Nations bodies, (2) the so-called "rules of the game" concerning, above all, Great Power behaviour in regard to their use of armed force, (3) social revolutions challenging fundamental assumptions about traditional international law, (4) the growing interdependence of States which has partly outdated the traditional modes of law-making, (5) the increased "permeability" of States resulting in the expansion of matters of international concern and the shrinking of those of domestic jurisdiction, and (6) the benefits and problems deriving from scientific and technological advances giving rise to informal means of setting standards and exercising supervision.[24] This list could be expanded. Schachter's examples, however, suffice to show that the problem of the sources has a far-reaching impact in various fields of international law, in that it may affect the effective operation of the law in those fields.[25] The foregoing prompts the question as to the reason of the great "division of minds" on the issue of the sources of international law. Why do writers hold often radically divergent views on this point, and is it impossible to discover a larger amount of common ground between them?

Bos has elaborated an answer to the first-mentioned question on the basis of what he has termed the *Normative Concept of Law*. This is to be understood in this context as somebody's opinion of what law is as contained in his definition or description of the various elements of which the phenomenon "law" consists. The author himself describes the *Normative Concept of Law* as "the concept we accept as normative for ourselves in our daily lives. A Dutchman, for example, would designate the present Dutch concept of law as his choice for a *Normative Concept,* an Englishman the English concept of law, and so on. But doing so, they will not mean to say that at no time anything not consonant with these concepts could be called 'law'. Law it was, and law it still may be, but in a general, not in a normative sense: they simply would not accept it for their personal use".[26] In a subsequent study Bos has elaborated his explanation of the *Normative Concept of Law* as follows: "This NCL, evidently, is a highly schematic notion. How indeed is one to devise any notion at all responsible for the elaboration, ..., of an entire legal order? The notion, even if understood as an immensely complex one, can but be a schematic representation of reality. Nor should one think of it as of something leaving no doubt as to its 'interpretation': the oppo-

---

24. *Ibidem*, pp. 302-303.
25. See also R. Kearney, "International Legislation: The Negotiating Process", 9 *CWILJ* (1979), pp. 504-513 (505).
26. M. Bos, "Legal Archetypes and the Normative Concept of Law as Main Factors in the Defining and Development of International Law", XXIII-1 *NILR* (1976), pp. 71-87 (82). This Normative Concept is set against the so-called General Concept which "should be wide enough to accommodate anything which throughout history was held to be 'law', ... ; even if we would not for a moment contemplate its practibility *hic et nunc*" (*ibidem*). See *supra* p. 7.

14

site seems to be true.... Finally, the NCL must be deemed to be perpetually subject to change."[27]

In a study on the sources the same author has pointed to "the apparent link between the question *which are* the 'sources' of law, on the one hand, and the normative concept of law, on the other hand. Strangely enough, writers hardly ever make the link, yet, how self-evident it is! Any enquiry into the 'sources' of law should not only define the notion of 'sources', but that of 'law' as well".[28] The connection established here between what was called the *Normative Concept of Law* and the concept of sources is indeed obvious. In the final analysis, it is somebody's *Normative Concept of Law* which determines the number and the content of the sources of law which he thinks necessary and/or desirable in a given legal system.

At the same time the link mentioned may help to explain the "division of minds" which was said to exist with respect to the sources of international law. This division is rooted in the fact that the problem of the sources is approached or dealt with by different writers from a great variety of different perceptions of what international law is, *i.e.* from different normative concepts of international law. As a result of the afore-mentioned link these diverging points of departure are bound to lead to more or less equally diverging "concepts of sources".

All this makes the present doctrine of sources intricate enough already, but the situation is further complicated by the fact that many writers operate from a normative concept of law, the scope and content of which are more or less kept a secret or are, at any rate, not made explicit. Consciously or unconsciously, they outline their view on the sources while leaving obscure their notion or conception of international law on which the former is necessarily based. Consequently, their concept of sources remains unverifiable to a large extent. The division of minds referred to above becomes a confusion of tongues in addition.

The foregoing makes it abundantly clear that any discussion of the sources of international law must be preceded by an explanation of the notion or conception of international law which is accepted as its basis. We will undertake such an explanation in the following sections.

A preliminary question which would seem to arise in this respect is whether or not the choice of one's normative concept is entirely free or, at least, to a large extent so. In other words, will almost any concept of international law do and, therefore, do writers indeed enjoy a great latitude in this respect? An affirmative answer to this question would entail far-reaching consequences. It would imply that the multiplicity of, and the wide divergence between existing opinions concerning the sources of international law is inevitable and, consequently, that the search for at least some common ground in this matter, on which a more coherent or even more generally accepted view could be built, would be largely in vain. If the question concerning the freedom of choice is given an unconditionally affirmative answer, doubts may be raised about the usefulness of just

---

27. M. Bos, *loc.cit.* (note 9), p. 8.
28. M. Bos, "The Recognized Manifestations of International Law; A New Theory of 'Sources'", 20 *GYIL* (1977), pp. 9-76 (13); see also M. Bos, *loc.cit.* (note 9), p. 9. In the same vein, G. Fitzmaurice, "Some Problems Regarding the Formal Sources of International Law", in: *Symbolae Verzijl* (The Hague 1958), pp. 153-176 (156).

another analysis of the sources of international law, because it would amount to no more than an intellectual voyage in search of the sources.[29] From the perspective of complete freedom or even anarchy the problem of the sources indeed becomes, to use Parry's words, a matter which cannot be stated but only discussed.[30] Moreover, it should be realized that ultimately the recognition of such a complete freedom calls into question the very relevance of international law itself. For, how could a body of rules, even if it is called international law, adequately play an ordering and regulating role in international relations, if one of its most vital constituent elements is subject to such great controversy?

The mere existence of the above-mentioned multiplicity of diverging opinions on the sources would seem to indicate that the question as to the freedom of choice of one's normative concept must, as far as international law is concerned, be answered positively. Both Bos and Parry, who explicitly deal with the question and whose thoughts were used as a point of departure in the foregoing, reach the same conclusion. As far as the latter is concerned, this would seem to be implied in his contention that the sources of international law cannot be stated, but only be discussed. The former, in asking himself the said question, explicitly holds: "The answer is yes. In an integrated community like the State, however, any normative concept too far remote from the one underlying the national legal system runs the risk of irrelevancy. In the non-integrated international community, on the contrary, almost anything goes. Nevertheless, here too one should never lose sight of reality."[31]

To the present writer this latter qualification appears to be of the utmost importance. As will be argued in the following, the realities of present international relations indeed pose considerable limitations on one's choice of a normative concept of international law. Particularly as far as the sources are concerned, the structure of the international society and the nature of the relations it comprises leave far less room for discretion in the choice of a normative concept than usually seems to be taken for granted in doctrine. With respect to the sources we will even endeavour to defend the thesis that the present state of affairs brings to the fore one, more or less, exclusive concept of international law. In short, we will try to argue against freedom of choice of the normative concept of international law.

The foregoing already shows that the question concerning freedom of choice cannot be treated as a preliminary one, which at first sight it seemed to be. On closer inspection it becomes clear that the answer to that question is itself a product of the normative concept. That answer, in other words, is implied in the normative concept a person adheres to, and can therefore be given only after having set forth the relevant elements of that concept.

---

29. M. Bos, *loc.cit.* (note 28), p. 10.
30. See *supra*, note 22.
31. *Loc.cit.* (note 26), p. 83; similarly, the same author in a subsequent study warns that "those who have spent their lives in international relations will have learnt to be sober in their expectations and to refrain from a NCL contradicted by reality", M. Bos, *loc.cit.* (note 9), p. 17.

CHAPTER III

CONCEPT OF INTERNATIONAL LAW

3.1. Introduction: doctrine and the sources of international law

Many different tasks may be contemplated for the doctrine of international law. The particular orientation of a scholar will depend upon the goal he sets himself. A rough distinction is often made between research which is practice-related and research by scholars who prefer a more theoretical approach. The distinction is not very clear and the consequences sometimes drawn from it seem at times to be exaggerated. The one approach cannot do without the other and *vice versa*. At any rate, in the final analysis theory itself is, or at least should be, practice-orientated. Indeed, what is theory other than a device or an instrument aimed at enhancing our understanding of one or more elements of reality in order to be better able to cope with present and future situations and problems?

As far as international law is concerned, the realization of this goal is hampered by the fact that international legal doctrine is characterized by a divergence of views and approaches. A reason for this could be the essentially national outlook of international lawyers which leads them to reflect their national legal viewpoints in their work on international law.[32] Some even suspect that the reason is sometimes to be found in downright political bias.[33]

Obviously, nobody can or is expected to be completely detached from or

---

32. See C. Parry, *op.cit.* (note 22), p. 105, who considers it exceedingly strange "that, in the long history of literature on international law, that literature has remained so essentially national".
33. See in this respect E. McWhinney, *The World Court and the Contemporary International Law-Making Process* (Alphen aan den Rijn 1979), p. 15, who wonders whether there still is a place for the independent legal scholar and jurist of yesteryear. According to him "the 'publicists' - the law professors and the legal text-writers - as a legal skill group, have been too generally touched by that *dédoublement fonctionnel* involved in accepting legal briefs or acting as special legal adviser to their own national government in pursuit of national political interests: the legal publicists may therefore run the risk of being seen a *parti pris* and of losing in consequence that reputation for intellectual detachment and political neutrality that characterised the writings of great text-writers in the classical, 19th century and early 20th century, ... ". Put in such an unqualified fashion the statement certainly is an exaggeration. Obviously, not all publicists are engaged in advising governments, and even those who are cannot be assumed, simply on the basis of their advisory capacity, to be lacking sufficient intellectual detachment and political neutrality in their scholarly publications.

uninfluenced by some kind of basic philosophical or political ideas.[34] Many legal issues can probably be approached only on the basis of one or another express or tacit view on ultimate values. This, however, does not free theory from the duty to strive for the highest attainable objectivity. In particular, international legal doctrine should overcome any alleged national outlook or bias and look for common elements in the various schools of thought prevailing at the moment rather than emphasizing those which keep them apart.

Friedmann has pointed to still another, yet closely related, characteristic of legal theory in general. It may be called the excessively "uncooperative" or "individualistic" attitude to be found in a great part of legal writing. In the preface of his excellent survey of principal movements in legal theory he professes an "increased scepticism about the novelty of the many legal theories that appear under ambitious and high-sounding names. I do not think we have to pretend, to ourselves and to others, that we have discovered or can discover basic new philosophies. More than enough remains to be done to see basic philosophic ideas in their relation to the constantly changing tasks and techniques of law as an instrument of social order".[35] In discussing the universality and cleavage in contemporary theories he reiterates: "If legal philosophers were less wrapped up in their own nomenclatures, less easily convinced that their own systems offer a radically new solution, instead of a modest addition to the formulation of age-old problems, the links between the various modern legal theories would become far more apparant".[36] It is certainly correct that many legal theories have often much more in common than their respective proponents would want us to believe. Indeed, most of these theories can be fitted into one or more of a fairly limited number of schools of legal thinking.

Because of reasons of efficiency and simplicity to be explained later [37] we will try to relate the analysis of the most relevant aspects of the concept of international law in the following section to a number of important schools of legal thinking. For that purpose it suffices to discern three basic schools of legal thought, or rather three basic approaches to the phenomenon of law. The first approach, which may be called "legal idealism", comprises those theories which search for and try to formulate the ideals and values constituting the basis of, or are underlying, a legal system. Secondly, there is the "analytical approach" which does not preoccupy itself with values and ideals. It is concerned rather with the legal technique in that it tries to order and clarify the structure of a legal system. Thirdly, there exists a "sociological approach" which, generally speaking, focuses on the relations between law and society.

Admittedly, this is a very general classification. It would be very hard to fit each and every theory neatly into one of the categories or prototypes men-

---

34. According to J. Watson, "Legal Theory, Efficacy and Validity in the Development of Human Rights Norms in International Law", 3 *UILF* (1979), pp. 609-641 (637), there is an "inevitable mixture of the scientist and the propagandist in the scholar's role" which "is made even more problematic in international law because of the lack of institutional finality. At all stages the process is very subjective, and the eventual outcome cannot help but be affected by an unconscious predisposition of the writer, either towards a particular conclusion, or else towards the genteel pastime of reaffirming one's own beliefs at a universal level".
35. W. Friedmann, *Legal Theory*, 4th edition (London 1960), p. XIII.
36. *Ibidem*, p. 322.
37. See *infra* p. 29.

18

tioned. Indeed, most theories, although leaning probably more towards one of the three approaches, contain elements of two or even all three of these approaches. Nevertheless, it seems useful to make the distinction between these approaches in order to be able to select the elements contained in each of them which may be relevant to the problem of the sources. In fact, none of these approaches would seem to be the only "right" one, nor are they mutually exclusive in most respects. To a large extent their relevancy or irrelevancy depends on the focus of the study one is undertaking. In this respect it is worthwhile to recall the following statement by Falk: "There is a tendency to discuss which approach to international legal studies is the correct one. This produces rather sterile arguments by advocates of one approach against those of another. Such polemics overlook the important fact that the main established approaches all serve a useful function, and this usefulness normally accounts for their existence ... . One way to avoid this necessity for choice is to recognize that each particular approach has its own set of intellectual objectives".[38]

Consequently, after setting out the most relevant aspects of the normative concept of international law in the following section we will get back to the basic approaches just mentioned in order to see to what extent each of them might contribute to answering one of the main questions involved in the sources of international law: "How can one tell whether or not a given rule is a rule of international law?"

3.2. Some aspects of the normative concept of international law: its function and functioning

The normative concept [39] of international law is bound to be rather comprehensive and complicated. Law in general is a multi-faceted and complex phenomenon and this holds true for international law also. The normative concept of international law comprises many elements of a wide-ranging diversity. Within the framework of the present study it is impossible to deal with them all. The focus of this study constitutes the problem of the sources of international law and, consequently, the subsequent account of the normative concept of international law will have to be confined to those aspects which are most relevant with respect to the sources. No attempt will be made to provide a more or less all-embracing definition or description of the phenomenon of international law.

In this section, moreover, the most relevant aspects of the normative concept will be discussed in a rather general fashion in terms of the function and functioning of international law. For as was explained above, one of the purposes of the preliminary outline of the most relevant aspects of the normative concept of international law is to relate it to the basic approaches in legal thinking, in order to be able to draw from those various approaches those elements most useful for tackling the problem of the sources of international law. Consequently, when we will come to deal with the sources of international law in more depth in sub-

---

38. R. Falk, "International Legal Order: Alwyn V. Freeman vs. Myres S. McDougal", 59 *AJIL* (1965), pp. 66-71 (66).
39. See *supra* pp. 14-15.

sequent sections, some of the aspects of the normative concept will be elaborated in more detail.

The function of international law does not need to detain us very long. Few people will object to the notion that, like of all law, it is international law's primary function to regulate and order relations in society, in this instance the international society. As man is not solitary, he is bound to live together with his fellow-men. The ensuing relations between man and his fellow-men have to be regulated and ordered so as to make their living together possible and, therefore, society viable. This explains the need for law: *ubi societas, ibi jus.* The same applies *mutatis mutandis* to the international society and the function of international law to regulate and order the relations between states.[40]

Admittedly, the description of the function of international law as that of regulating and ordering relations in the international society is a very abstract one which needs further explanation in several respects. Still, for our purposes here, it is specific enough to be able to deduce from it a number of important characteristics of international law.

Firstly, but quite obviously, international law's function, like that of all law, implies that it is accepted as binding. For, how else than through rules which are binding upon the members of society could the necessary regulation and order the law is to attain be achieved. Nobody probably questions the binding character of law and, indeed, the words "law" and "binding" are most often considered to be synonyms. "Binding" has to be understood here as to mean that by law human behaviour is made non-optional in some sense. Where there is law, the number of behavioural options for its subjects is narrowed down. People can have very different reasons for considering law binding, for holding that rules of law should be obeyed. We will get back to the variety of motives for acknowledging international law as binding when discussing the basis of its binding force.[41] Whatever these various motives and whatever one may think of them, what counts is the fact that people think of the law as binding. When they speak of law, they mean binding rules. When they mean non-binding rules, or at least legally non-binding rules, they refer to them as political rules, rules of morality, usage or some other kind of rules of conduct.

There is a second, most notable, feature of law which immediately flows from, or is indeed inherent in the law's function of regulating and ordering relations in society. It is the very close and insoluble link existing between law on the one hand and the society in which it is to operate on the other. The nature of society and the structure of the relations in it are truly the alpha and omega of law. In the present author's view, society stands at the beginning of law in that

40. It is true that relations between States and private persons have come within the purview of modern international law, but inter-state relations can still be said to constitute its primary aim.
41. See *infra* pp. 71-76 and 259-261; in reference to law in general H. Hart, *The Concept of Law*, 10th impression (Oxford 1979), p. 198, rejects the view that the reason for obeying the law is exclusively to be found in a sense of moral obligation: "Not only may vast numbers be coerced by laws which they do not regard as morally binding, but it is not even true that those who do accept the system voluntarily, must conceive of themselves as morally bound to do so, though the system will be most stable when they do so. In fact, their allegiance to the system may be based on many different considerations: calculations of long-term interest; disinterested interest in others; an unreflecting inherited or traditional attitude; or the mere wish to do as others do".

law is a derivation, a function of society, and it also stands at the end, because society is the law's ultimate purpose.[42] Therefore, if the law is effectively to fulfil its task, it has, first of all, closely to reflect or even to mirror the underlying nature and structure of society. While the link between law and society is not a one-way street, in that law also has a "steering" function,[43] it cannot be doubted that the impact of society on its law is greater than the other way around. Revolutions or great upheavals in society are bound to have dramatic repercussions on the law; dramatic changes in the law seldom precede significant alterations in societal relations. If the law removes itself too far from reality, *i.e.* from what is happening in society, it runs the risk of becoming irrelevant.[44]

It is important to stress this mirror-image of law in relation to society, because it has far-reaching consequences for the normative concept of law, in particular international law. Most writers probably can subscribe to the general and abstract formula of the function of law as regulating and ordering relations in society. Things get different, however, once the abstract level is left and more concrete questions are asked. There is, of course, a tremendous difference between establishing or maintaining order *in general* and establishing or maintaining a *particular* order. Some might be inclined to deny the character of law to a set of rules laying down a particular kind of order - for instance, an oppressive "legal" regime imposed upon the subjects by a dictatorship -, because it runs counter to their idea of justice or because it does not reflect the wishes of the majority of the population or because they use some other criterion based on certain values to decide whether or not a certain rule is indeed a rule of law. Others, on the contrary, still hold such rules to be rules of law, even if they too dislike the rules concerned because they are oppressive or incompatible with their idea of justice for some other reason. They regard such rules as law, although they might consider them to be "bad" law.[45] In a nutshell we have here the fundamental distinction between the law as it is and the law as it ought to be, which has been elaborated by scholars belonging to the positivistic approach to legal thinking.[46]

As was observed already the "is" and the "ought" cannot always be separated completely. At any rate it proves difficult to keep the two strictly apart. And, in the final analysis, probably every approach to law in general and every tackling of a certain legal problem is ultimately based upon some underlying philosophy or fundamental values. It is submitted, however, that for the purpose of analysis, specifically in analyzing the sources, a quite rigid separation should, and indeed can be attained between what is on the one hand and what ought to be on the other. This holds true for international law in particular. It is possible that law in a national society, which may have reached a relatively high degree of integra-

---

42. Others, of course, deny this contention; see for instance the legal idealistic approaches mentioned *infra* pp. 30-34.
43. See *infra* pp. 27-28.
44. See *supra* p. 16.
45. If it is taken as a point of departure that oppression is bound to lead to some kind of forceful reaction in one way or another, such oppressive rules are particularly "bad" law. For, they breed social unrest and upheaval and, therefore, do not achieve regulation and order in the long run, but on the contrary prepare for disorder and chaos.
46. In particular H. Kelsen. See, for instance, *The Pure Theory of Law*, translation by M. Knight (Berkeley 1970), pp. 70-107.

tion and homogenity, is based on one or more fundamental philosophies or values as embodied for instance in the national constitution. In such a case the analysis will have to take into account such philosophies or values, although here too one has to be careful not to substitute one's own interpretation of it for the one which is in fact contained in, or underlying, the constitution and the national system of law in general.[47]

As far as international law is concerned, the situation in international society poses far stricter limitations upon the normative concept and, in the present author's view, leaves hardly any room for choice in this respect. For, one of the most eye-catching characteristics of present international society is undoubtedly that it is made up of a number of independent sovereign States which are neither subjected to some kind of higher authority nor otherwise integrated to the extent that some kind of fundamental philosophy or set of values can be assumed as the basis of relations in international society.[48] In other words, States function as autonomous centres of decision in international society and hold widely diverging "world outlooks" or views on the various aspects of international relations. Consequently, the State finds itself in international society in the position of a *homo liber*[49] and the result is a kind of "anarchy" of "world outlooks" and values competing for supremacy.

Although it is almost a commonplace, it would seem important to emphasize this fundamental feature of present international society once again, because it cannot fail to make its impact felt on international law, while at the same time international legal doctrine does not always fully adhere to this basic point of departure. If the foregoing characterization of the present state of affairs in international society is essentially a correct one, it follows that no single "world outlook" or set of values with a substantive content can *a priori* be considered as the only guiding principle for or, the ultimate foundation of, all rules of international law. As far as international law is concerned, no State can proclaim its own outlook or idea of justice to be the sole or overriding fundament precisely because it is not completely, or even not at all, acceptable to all States. What goes for States, goes *a fortiori* for scholars, because the latter's impact on international law is obviously in no way comparable to the former's.

Surprisingly enough, the opposite attitude is not seldom taken. More than a few writers start from one single value or idea to explain all of international law or to approach the problems with which international society is confronted. Such an attitude may take various forms. It can be found very openly, for instance, in the many ideal blueprints for a better world which have been set forth from biblical days to the present. To be sure, such schemes may be very useful in that they may create a sharper awareness of the shortcomings of present international society and stimulate legal thinking into finding solutions. They do not, however, themselves contribute directly to overcome or solve

47. H. Hart, *op.cit.* (note 41), p. 200, very pointedly observes in this respect: "Judicial decision, especially on matters of high constitutional import, often involves a choice between moral values, and not merely the application of some single outstanding moral principle; for it is folly to believe that where the meaning of the law is in doubt, morality always has a clear answer to offer".
48. See for more details *infra* pp. 62 and 71-76.
49. See M. Bos, "Old Germanic Law Analogies in International Law, or the State as *Homo Liber*", XV-1 *NILR* (1978), pp. 51-62.

present theoretical and practical problems. As was observed by Fitzmaurice: "The truth is that the intellectual distaste, which, as a jurist, we feel for the idea of Utopia, and many other of the kind, is that it solves too much. It disposes of difficulties not by dealing with them on their merits, but by creating conditions in which they must automatically disappear - in short be transcended .... . Our task as international jurists is not to imagine conditions in which the Gordian knot would be cut by the fading out of the independent nation-State, but to make the international system work in the world of the nation-State".[50]

The same attitude is sometimes more concealed. Some writers approach issues of international law from one single or, at least, a limited outlook which does not sufficiently reflect the variety of outlooks in fact held by States themselves and without making this explicit. Implicitly, international law is approached from a limited angle which does not take into account other philosophies, ideas, values and conceptions which also underly that law. Such a confusion between what is and what, in view of the author or authors concerned, ought to be can be extremely dangerous. To read a certain outlook into a set of rules, which is not shared by all the parties to it, creates unrealistic expectations with respect to compliance and, therefore, regarding the effectiveness of such rules. Such an approach usually will leave room for one "correct" interpretation only. Deviating interpretations resulting from the fact that a different outlook is considered to underly the rules, are likely to be regarded as "violations". In other words, an approach which treats one outlook as exclusive tends to overlook other views which may also be reflected in the rules concerned and, consequently, relevant for their interpretation. In the worst possible case, the result may be that the law is used, not as a mechanism to regulate and order relations in society by trying to harmonize the interests of all its members which underly these divergent views, but, consciously or not, as a tool only to promote certain interests or the interests of certain members of society at the expense of others.

In national as well as in international law such an approach can be dangerous. Given the nature and structure of present international society it is likely to sharpen existing and to promote potential conflicts between States rather than to accommodate them and, therefore, diminishes rather than enhances the viability of international society.

Now, all this does not imply that world outlooks do not have any impact at all on the content of rules of international law. Obviously they do. In the process of making international law each State operates from its own outlook. It will try to have the implications of that outlook laid down in the rules of international law. To the extent that it succeeds and gets its view accepted by other States, its outlook influences the content of international law.[51] Needless to say that such an

---

50. G. Fitzmaurice, "The Future of Public International Law and of the International Legal System in the Circumstances of Today", in: *Livre du Centenaire de l'Institut de Droit International 1873-1973: Evolution et perspective du droit international* (Bâle 1973), pp. 196-363 (258). A somewhat comparable view is held by G. Tunkin, *Theory of International Law*, translation by W. Butler (Cambridge, Mass. 1974), p. 375, with respect to the various schemes to create a world state: "Attempts to implement them even partially would bring great harm to the cause of developing and strengthening the United Nations and other international organizations as instruments of peace, since they are directed against the very bases of contemporary international organizations, defined by the laws of societal development".

51. For reasons of convenience the world outlook of a State is presented here as a coherent unity. In practice, of course, it is not. The policy which a State pursues in the process of making inter-

23

acceptance by other States will almost never be complete, because those other States in their turn will try to have their own position reflected as much as possible in the rules of international law. The result inevitably is a compromise in which various outlooks are embodied to a smaller or larger extent. But this resulting compromise in itself again shows that no outlook can be considered the only relevant one.

As far as doctrine is concerned, one has to be even more careful. Unlike States, writers do not have any direct impact on the making of international law. At the very best their ideas or proposals might be adopted by one or more States which can inject them into the process of law-creation. With respect to doctrine, therefore, one should be cautioned particularly against proclaiming a certain outlook, philosophy or set of values as the main or only conception underlying international law. It is, of course, perfectly legitimate for somebody to advocate a specific conception as the right one, in the sense that in his opinion it should be the point of departure by which the content of rules of international law should be inspired. However, for the purpose of analyzing what is the content of rules of international law and where they can be found, it is of the utmost importance simultaneously to point out that the conception advocated does not necessarily or even likely serve as the only or even the main basic philosophy underlying international law, simply because the States, as the international legislators, do not unequivocally accept it as such.[52] Consequently, the rules of international law are in most cases at best only partly derived from it, while other, possibly conflicting philosophies or conceptions may also have an impact and maybe even a greater one. In other words, in conducting such an analysis one has to stick to the "is" of international law as much as possible.

On the other hand, the "is" of international law should not be equated to the "is" of international relations. The effort to stick to the "is" of international relations as much as possible should not be taken to the extreme. Law cannot and should not reflect relations in society completely: it cannot and should not mirror social realities in all its details. This would not only be impossible because realities in society are too fluid to be caught into one single picture. It would also not be desirable because the effort to have the law provide such an all-embracing picture would deprive it of its regulating and ordering capabilities. Law, therefore, cannot and should not be equated fully with political processes or with politics in general.

Put in a black-and-white fashion, those who approach law as that what ought

national law is most often the product of diverging and/or conflicting views and interests within that State. It may be very relevant, also from the perspective of international law, to know what particular views or interests contributed to what extent to the position a State is taking on a certain issue. For our purposes it is not necessary to analyze this process of the formulation of a State's foreign policy, because we are not trying to assess what the impact is of a specific outlook of a particular State on the content of rules of international law.

52. J. Watson, *loc.cit.* (note 34), p. 638, warns for the confusion between "is" and "ought" in doctrine. In reference to McDougal who, he says, "advocates the worldwide expansion of Western values with the United States playing the primary rule" he upholds: "This complete confusion of the roles of the academic and the advocate, of *lex ferenda* with *lex lata*, results in a system of very limited utility, contrasting starkly with Kelsen's statement that 'the task of the science of law is not to approve or to disapprove its subject, but to know and to describe it'. Even those who take issue with Kelsen on other grounds must acknowledge the increased utility of any theory that results from such a commitment to objectivity".

to be often make a sharp distinction between law and politics. Law and politics are viewed as more or less mutually exclusive. On the international level "politics" in this perception stands for the unbridled striving by States for the realization of some kind of narrowly conceived national interest. International politics, therefore, is made almost the opposite of international law, which is held to express the goals and values of the international community and is regarded to be geared to serve the general interest. Clearly, views like these are based on a very narrow conception of politics. Those, on the other hand, who take the "is" approach to international law are often tempted to overstate the relation between international law and international politics. In their extreme, these views sometimes make law and politics almost coincide. Obviously, in these cases too, the conclusion, at least partly, results from the particular definition of politics which is used as a point of departure.

"Politics" is not a very unequivocal concept. As far as the relation between law and politics is concerned, a distinction can be made between politics in the sense of conduct and politics in the sense of policy. Generally speaking, policy, in the present author's view, can be described as encompassing all action directed at the structuring and functioning of society.[53] Conduct, as this very broad term implies, comprises those activities on the part of the States which are not specifically aimed at some general community goal. Although conduct may be compatible with or even enhance policy goals, it is not primarily designed to do so and politics in the sense of conduct, therefore, also includes behaviour which runs counter to policy-objectives.

On the basis of this distinction between conduct and policy some aspects between law and politics may be clarified.[54] As far as politics in the sense of policy is concerned, it cannot be denied that it has a great deal in common, or at least shares a number of characteristics with the law. A very important common characteristic within the framework of the present study is to be found in their respective functions. The description of policy as consisting of activities aimed at the structuring and functioning of society, and of law as a mechanism for ordering and regulating societal relations, make it clear that their ultimate tasks are not very divergent. Both law and policy result from the agreement (or the recognition of the necessity) to live together in society. Both, therefore, are principally aimed at ordering, regulating, steering, coordinating, influencing and adjusting human behaviour in order to make life in society possible.

However, acknowledging similarity of aim is not the same thing as saying that law and policy are identical. Where they differ is in the methods they employ in fulfilling their ordering and regulating functions. It is particularly in its functioning that law distinguishes itself from policy. In its own specific manner law performs the task of establishing and maintaining social order, which policy is intended to perform in a more general way. Law furthers social order by making the behaviour of members of society more regular and predictable. To that end it poses binding rules for the subjects of the law requiring a certain behaviour in a given situation or set of circumstances. Most of the time law formalizes policy decisions and makes them binding. At the same time this way of functioning of the law shows its relation with politics in the sense of conduct. Law performs its

---

53. See in this respect also J. de Vree, *loc.cit.* (note 8), pp. 136-140.
54. For more details on the relations between conduct, law and policy, see *infra* pp. 126-128.

ordering and regulating task by classifying and categorizing types of behaviour. Law makes a classification of types of possible behaviour of the members of society. It divides this whole range of possible types of behaviour into different categories, declares some permissible and others non-permissible under certain specified conditions, and attaches consequences to them, if only by declaring them legal or illegal. Law, so to say, distils clearly arranged pictures from an otherwise almost infinitely variable number of behavioural patterns. Put differently, law makes a condensation of reality. In that way law permits generalizing about relations in society by making them more clear and transparent.

International law in this manner enables States to get a clear picture of their own position in international society. It provides them with a criterion to choose for themselves a particular line of conduct out of the numerous types of possible behaviour. Similarly, it constitutes a standard for judging the behaviour of other States. Apart from being a device for making behaviour non-optional, *i.e.* binding, international law at the same time often serves as a kind of means of communication. Through international law States can convey to each other the intentions, ideas and interests which are reflected in it and, conversely, are able to develop expectations with regard to each other's future conduct. In this way too, international law contributes to regulating and ordering international relations. It is important to note that such a "communication" function also exists on a somewhat different level. Properly speaking, there we are not confronted with legal rules anymore but with legal claims. For what is envisaged here is not a situation where States are in agreement with regard to the content of a certain rule, but, on the contrary, where there occurs a dispute between States. In such a situation States very often clarify their position by putting forward legal claims, *i.e.* they state their position in legal terms which functions as a language understandable to all.[55]

It is clear that in order to fulfil its regulating and ordering function international law cannot fully reflect social reality, because this would deprive it of its capacity to provide the required certainty and predictability. In other words, it is essential that international law, like all law, to a certain extent simplifies social reality through the classification and categorization of the various types of behaviour. In order to make relations in society transparent and, therefore, manageable law has to be a reduction, a condensation of reality thereby transforming the complicated network of relations in society into a more or less clearly arranged picture.

The foregoing suffices to show that, while it is a mistake to confuse international law with what ought to be in international society, it is equally incorrect to fully equate international law with what is in international relations. International law cannot and should not be a complete reflection of everything that actually happens in relations between States. It would loose the main characteristic distinguishing it from conduct in international relations and thereby loose much, if not all, of its usefulness. All this holds true particularly with respect to

55. See in this respect R. Falk, *The Status of Law in International Society* (Princeton 1970), who has described the functioning of international law in such circumstances as "to establish an agreed system of communication of claims and counterclaims between international actors and thereby to structure argument in diplomatic settings" (p. 178) and as "an assured medicum of diplomatic communication, allowing for interactions of claim and counterclaim to delimit the area of dispute and clarify the stakes of a particular conflict" (p. 452).

the process designed for creating rules of international law. As has been pointedly observed by Levi, "The 'legislative' process ... encompasses a large number of participants, many arenas of action, and the homogenization of many interests and values. They are all relevant to discovering the meaning of what eventually becomes the law. They can all assist in explaining the efficacy or inefficacy of the law. *But for a rule to become a legal rule, there is in all societies a narrowing and formalization of this process towards a more technical procedure. This procedure and its outcome must be the focus in a study of international law*".[56]

In other words, for international law to properly meet its task the certainty, stability and predictability it is to ensure has to start with the criteria governing the process of making international law. If international law is to play its regulating and ordering role it has, on the basis of such certainty, stability and predictability with respect to the international law-making process, at the very least to provide an answer to the question whether or not a given rule is a rule of international law. Therefore, this requirement of certainty and clarity has to be duly taken into account when studying the problem of sources of international law. As will be pointed out below, one of the consequences of the nature and structure of international society is, that there does not exist in international law a clear-cut narrowing and formalizing technical procedure in the sense of a pre-established process consisting of a number of (more or less formal) consecutive phases which, after being exhausted, can be said to have given birth to a rule of international law.[57] Consequently, the peculiar characteristics of international society make the quest for certainty and clarity with respect to the sources of international law even more pertinent.

Finally, one feature of the functioning of international law has to be emphasized in this survey of the normative concept. The preceding observations on the relation between law and politics might have given rise to the impression that international law is utterly conservative in that it serves solely to uphold the *status quo*. With respect to this it was said that international law most of the time formalizes policy decisions. Some might be tempted to conclude from this that the functioning of international law is confined to registering or petrifying policy decisions into formally binding rules. It is true that, generally speaking, policy precedes the law in that the former is more a vehicle for change than the latter. More often than not, law is a "follower" instead of a "leader" in respect of social changes brought about by processes of policy-making. The most important decisions in society, *i.e.* those regarding the structure, the functioning and the goals of society, are policy decisions. Law, so to say, registers and executes these decisions and in this sense can be considered an instrument of policy.

In addition, with respect to politics in the sense of conduct it was observed that law has to reflect or mirror relations in society to the extent necessary. How-

---

56. W. Levi, *Law and Politics in the International Society* (Beverly Hills/London 1976), pp. 28-29 (emphasis added). At another place the same writer upholds: "While it is inevitable that the sources - material or formal - of international law are related to all aspects of that society, some limits upon the consideration of other aspects are imperative if the study of the sources is to be productive", *ibidem*, p. 86.
57. See *infra* pp. 76 and 199-203.

ever, law is not solely a derivation of politics in the sense of conduct. The interaction between law and politics in this sense should not be conceived of as a one-way street, where traffic flows only from conduct to law and not in the opposite direction. Apart from its registering function, law sometimes plays a particularly strong steering role too. To be sure, steering effects are inherent in the ordinary functioning of law. Once a rule of law comes into existence it starts influencing conduct, and for that matter policy too, by putting limits to political activities thereby providing the regularity and predictability which is indispensable to social order. But the law's steering function can go further. It is not solely an instrument to maintain the *status quo*. As Friedmann has pointed out, it is one of the major antinomies in law and in legal theory to reconcile the conflicting demands of the need of stability and the need of change.[58] Stability in society cannot always be achieved by simply trying to preserve "das Nützliche von Gestern". Sometimes stability requires opening up avenues of change. Law has to adapt to changing circumstances, to changes in relations in society. This kind of adaptation can still be regarded to belong to the law's registering function.

Sometimes, however, maintaining or establishing stability requires the law to be ahead of politics in the sense of conduct. This occurs when the law reflects policy in that the perceptions on how social relations in a given field should develop, on what the goal in a particular field is, are laid down in rules of law. Such rules of law truly have a steering function with regard to politics in the sense of conduct, because they purport to direct the behaviour of (some of) the members of society away from its actual course towards the (new) policy aim, which is now held to be more conducive to the viability of society. In this manner policy is effected through rules of law; the law in this form serves as an instrument of changes which are, although at first sight paradoxically, necessary to keep relations in society stable and orderly. In integrated national societies with a full-fledged legal system this close relationship between policy decisions and legal rules is not uncommon, although it goes often unnoticed. Perceptions of the proper functioning of society and the goals it is to attain, and, more generally, of the course society has to go, while stemming from political ideas and ensuing decisions, very often are subsequently embodied in legal rules. It should be remembered in this respect that in national societies the constitution is not only the supreme law, but usually constitutes at the same time the most important political document. Moreover, minor modifications in policy are sometimes effected through a (different) interpretation of the legal rules concerned.

Traditional international law almost completely lacked rules of the character just described. It was more a "registration office" than a "steering instrument". The character of modern international law in many fields is changing in this respect. As will be elaborated in more detail below, developments in the structure of international relations have affected international law in that it now (of necessity) has become geared to serve as a vehicle for change too. Modern international law, far more than its traditional counterpart, has to be a steering mechanism to be able to continue its regulating and ordering role. This relatively new role, as we shall try to argue, has affected the sources of international law, the nature of the rules stemming from these sources, and the implementation of these rules in practice.[59]

58. W. Friedmann, *op.cit.* (note 35), pp. 32-33.
59. See *infra* pp. 65-71, 126-128 and 261-265.

28

CHAPTER IV

THE NORMATIVE CONCEPT AND SOME BASIC APPROACHES TO INTERNATIONAL LAW

4.1. Introduction

As was announced earlier,[60] we will now try to relate the normative concept as set forth in the preceding section to some basic approaches to international law, which in our opinion are most relevant to the problem of the sources of international law.

The purpose of this enterprise is twofold. First of all, it is aimed at identifying those elements contained in existing approaches, which in our view are most instrumental in analyzing the sources of international law. By identifying these aspects we can build upon an already existing basis and avoid having to map out ourselves in great detail the theoretical framework within which such an analysis has to be conducted. The latter undertaking is not only unnecessary, but would also greatly complicate things. The search for a link with existing approaches or theories is therefore prompted by reasons of both efficiency and simplicity.

A second purpose of the following survey is to create an additional opportunity for elaborating a little further the views expressed earlier. By briefly discussing the basic approaches referred to above, we may help to clarify the most relevant aspects of our own normative concept.

It is clear that the twofold purpose of the present section puts far-reaching limits on the scope of the survey which is to follow. Writing on legal theory is voluminous. No single person could hope to give an account doing justice to the numerous theories and contributions to theories which have been developed over time. Even a survey of a much more modest ambition already would require work of tremendous magnitude and scope. Nothing of the kind will be undertaken here. The following sections will only discuss three categories or prototypes which, in the present writer's view, can be considered as representing the main distinguishable approaches from which the problem of the sources of international law is explicitly or implicitly approached.

In the foregoing it was proposed to term these categories: legal idealism, the analytical approach, and the sociological approach.[61] These names were chosen because they provide at least some indication as to the most fundamental feature of the respective approaches as far as the sources of international law are

---

60. See *supra* p. 18.
61. This classification is based on the different trends of legal thinking discerned by W. Fried-

concerned. On the other hand, this terminology might be confusing because it places under a certain heading theories which, apart from their approach to the sources, do not fit that description or do not in other respects resemble theories of the same category. It should be kept in mind, however, that the focus of enquiry is on the sources here, and that it is not intended or attempted to provide a more general classification which would be valid also with respect to issues other than the sources.

Furthermore, the present writer is well aware that the classification proposed here is extremely broad and general. For our purpose it is believed to be sufficient, because it sets forth and distinguishes the three main approaches to questions concerning the sources of international law. Nevertheless, it is clearly not elaborated enough to bear out the many and multifarious differences of opinion on details which exist between proponents of various theories belonging to one of the major categories. Conversely, because the classification focuses on the sources only, not all theories or views can be fitted into one single category. Some theories consist of elements belonging to two or even all categories, or mainly to one while also possessing some flavour of the others.[62]

Finally, there is a last restriction inherent in the following account. Obviously, we cannot examine all the writers representative of the three basic approaches. Instead, the following paragraphs will discuss only a few representatives who, in the present author's view, may be considered most typical and have been and/or continue to be influential in the field of international law.

4.2. Legal idealism

The first category, that of legal idealism, was defined in the foregoing as comprising those theories that search for, and try to formulate, the ideals and values constituting the basis of a legal system.[63] As was observed above, the categories used here are very broad. The approach called legal idealism, however, is extremely wide-ranging. Indeed, one could probably classify most theories under this heading, because there are few which, in the final analysis, do not build on, or at least strive for or draw upon, some ultimate ideal(s) or value(s).[64]

---

mann, *Legal Theory*, 5th edition (London 1967), p. 72.
62. A good example is the Historical School of Savigny who, although he takes as his point of departure the social origin of law, introduces strong ideological or mystical features into his theory by requiring conformity of all law to the "consciousness of the people" (*Volksgeist*); see F.C. von Savigny, *On the Vocation of Our Age for Legislation and Jurisprudence*, translation by A. Hayward (London 1831), p. 24: "In the earliest times to which history extends, the law will be found to have already attained a fixed character, peculiar to the people like their language, manners and constitution. Nay, these phenomena have no separate existence, they are but the particular faculties and tendencies of an individual people, inseparably united in nature, and only wearing the semblance of distinct attributes to our view. That which binds them into one whole is the common conviction of the people, the kindred consciousness of an inward necessity, excluding all notion of an accidental and arbitrary origin;". See also W. Friedmann, *op.cit.* (note 61), pp. 209-213; and M. McDougal, H. Lasswell and W. Reisman, "Theories about International Law: Prologue to a Configurative Jurisprudence", 8 *VJIL* (1967), pp. 188-299 (227-243).
63. See *supra* p. 18.
64. It is noteworthy in this respect that even theories which are particularly known for their focus

Even if the analysis is confined to what is usually called the Natural Law approach, the circle of authors to be counted is very wide. Obviously, the number depends upon one's definition or description of the Natural Law frame.[65] But also taken in a strict sense as comprising those theories which make ideals and values the core of their analyses, the approach has had and still has many adherents.

This probably is both a reason for and a result of the fact that Natural Law thinking has exerted a tremendous influence, albeit varying from time to time, over at least the last 2,500 years. It has particularly played a pre-eminent role in the West and has sometimes even been equated with Western legal thinking.[66] As traditional international law is primarily a Western product, it is not surprising that the Natural Law approach has also had a sizable impact on the law regulating relations in the international society. Not only were the so-called fathers of international law, like Grotius and Vattel, mostly Natural Law thinkers, also more modern parts of international law, such as, for instance, the international law of human rights,[67] are to a large extent inspired by Natural Law ideals.

No doubt its considerable influence on the international plane is partly also due to the fact, that the Natural Law frame seems particularly apt to be applied to the international setting. Natural Law protagonists start from a more or less comprehensive natural order and, consequently, from a very broad conception of community. Usually, its proponents use as their frame of reference the world as a whole. Needless to say, such an outlook puts no impediments on, but rather promotes studying (legal) relations between States.

As was already observed, even if narrowly defined, the Natural Law approach comprises a great number of writers sometimes holding diverging points of view with respect to many issues. Nevertheless, viewed from the issue of the sources of international law it would seem possible to discern some important similarities. The essence of this approach has aptly been typified by Chroust as follows: "From its very inception Natural Law has been primarily the quest for the ultimate and absolute meaning of law and justice. ... For in its own right it contains one essential element ... *viz.* that it seeks certain comprehensive

upon the practice of international relations, like the Policy-Oriented school headed by McDougal, show this characteristic; see M. McDougal, H. Lasswell and W. Reisman, *loc.cit.* (note 62), pp. 199-200, where the authors describe the role of scholarly observers as "that of identifying and clarifying for the different participants in community process the common interests *which they themselves may not have been able to perceive"* (emphasis added), and p. 206, where they recommend for clarification and implementation those goals and values "which are today commonly characterized as the basic values of human dignity, or of a free society".

65. W. Friedmann's notion of Natural Law, *op.cit.* (note 61), p. 154, seems to be very wide: "Natural law terminology thus adopted by some modern legal philosophers, but not by others, may disguise the fundamental affinity between all those modern legal theories which, in opposition to positivism, stress the need for legal ideals. Spencer's principle of evolution, Duguit's social solidarity, Kohler's evolution of '*Kultur*', Pound's 'social engineering', Ripert's '*règle morale*', these and a host others are natural law ideals in the modern relativist and evolutionary sense, whether they choose to adopt the term or not".

66. As has been pointed out, however, Natural Law ideas in no way have been an exclusively Western affair, but have its precursors in ancient India and China: see M. McDougal, H. Lasswell and W. Reisman, *loc.cit.* (note 62), pp. 215-216 and the studies cited there.

67. See in this respect J. Watson, *loc.cit.* (note 34), p. 613: "Since natural law is the only legal system with any clear claim to authority over the state it is not at all surprising that those concerned with human rights should find themselves attracted to the natural law philosophy".

ideas or values transcending the multifariousness of merely 'given' empirical data and facts; that it never ceases to search for a unifying higher point of view which would endow the notion of law with something above its naive 'given-ness'; and that it is intended to discover on a higher plane the 'law' among the 'laws'."[68] In other words, the constant factor in Natural Law has been the appeal to something superior to positive law, whether this superior factor was seen as a directive or as a guide to positive law.

Many different ideals and values have been adduced to serve as ultimate superior factor. Roughly speaking, they can be divided into two classes.[69] On the one hand, there are those which could be called "theocratic" or "religious", which are ultimately based on some kind of divine source.[70] The "metaphysical" or "secular" school in Natural Law, on the other hand, bases itself on the presumed structure and/or some major characteristic(s) of the human nature or the physical environment.[71] Whatever the differences between the various Natural Law proponents concerning the ultimate "source" of their theory, in this respect too they show a common element. In the final analysis, every Natural Law protagonist can be characterized as mystic or ideological, because the basic tenets of his theory ultimately prove scientifically unverifiable by others.[72] From the point of view of "non-believers" all Natural Law theories start from presumptions and, therefore, are a kind of "faith".

Given this feature it is not surprising that Natural Law has been invoked to defend all and sundry positions. It has been relied upon both to justify and to reject a particular legal order, and also in more specific controversies each side has pleaded Natural Law to state its case.[73] This "elasticity" of Natural Law theories has been very lucidly exposed by Hart Ely: "All theories of Natural Law have a singular vagueness which is both an advantage and a disadvantage in the application of the theories. The advantage, one gathers, is that you can invoke Natural Law to support anything you want. The disadvantage is that everybody understands that."[74]

68. A. Chroust, "On the Nature of Natural Law", in: P. Sayre (ed.), *Interpretations of Modern Legal Philosophies; Essays in Honor of Roscoe Pound* (New York 1947), pp. 70-84 (72).
69. W. Friedmann, *op.cit.* (note 61), pp. 345-346, uses a fourfold division to clarify the foundations of what he has called "absolute ideals of justice": (1) theories resting on a theological basis; (2) Hegel's deduction of specific legal principles from an absolute idea of justice which is both metaphysical and rational; (3) legal theories basing the knowledge of justice on inspiration and intuition; and (4) attempts to deduce principles of justice from a universal rational basis.
70. A well-known example is Th. Aquinas, *Summa Theologiae*, Latin text and English translation, T. Gilby (general editor), (London/New York 1964-1981), Volume XXVIII (1966), p. 23. See also J. Finnis, *Natural Law and Natural Rights* (Oxford 1980), pp. 398-403.
71. A famous representative of this type of view is H. Grotius; see his *De Jure Belli ac Pacis Libri Tres*, translation in: J. Brown Scott (ed.), *The Classics of International Law*, Volume II (New York/London 1964), pp. 11-12.
72. M. McDougal, H. Lasswell and W. Reisman, *loc.cit.* (note 62), p. 226, describe this as trans-empiricalism which is defined as "a statement presented as a scientific verity, which, because of its formulation or its content, is not susceptible to scientific investigation".
73. The issues concerning slavery and racial equality in the U.S. are just two of the most eye-catching examples; see J. Hart Ely, *Democracy and Distrust; A Theory of Judicial Review* (Cambridge, Mass. 1980), p. 51, and studies cited there.
74. *Ibidem*, p. 50.

From the point of view of the sources of international law this vague and unverifiable character of Natural Law is problematical. If Natural Law cannot provide a common frame of reference for national systems of law which function in a centralized and usually more or less integrated society, then it should *a fortiori* be discredited for the international society with its low degree of organization and with members which not infrequently hold radically different world outlooks. It is difficult to see how international law with respect to its sources could draw upon a doctrine which may be embraced by some, but is either rejected or interpreted in a totally different way by others.[75] This conclusion holds particularly true now that the international society in the course of this century has developed from a small and relatively homogeneous "club" of Western or at least Western-minded States to a far larger grouping of States characterized by deep ideological cleavages in many fields.[76]

Nevertheless, recent years have witnessed a kind of revival of Natural Law thinking, also in international law.[77] In itself this development is not at all surprising. Friedmann has pointed to a kind of undulatory motion of Natural Law thinking. In setting forth one of his principal antinomies of legal theory, *viz.* intellect and intuition, he says: "When a disappointed generation, dissatisfied with the self-complacency of Positivism, becomes doubtful about the power of reason, instinct and intuition come again to the fore."[78]

The revival is particularly understandable as far as international law is concerned. It was prompted, of course, by the horrors of two world wars, but also, more generally, the changes in international society prepared the ground for a renewed turn towards Natural Law ideals and values. As will be explained in more detail below, the changes in international society have resulted in both a horizontal and vertical expansion of international law. Today it must cover more fields and it must do this in a more penetrating manner.[79] In such a situation, where completely new areas have to be entered into, it is quite understandable that there is a tendency in international law, which lacks a constitution or some other type of basic framework, to start from general and often vague notions or principles from which more concrete rules of law are contemplated to be deduced. Below we will get back to this development when arguing that emphasis in international law has shifted from conduct to policy.[80]

With respect to the alleged revival of Natural Law, however, a distinction has to be made between two shools of thought. On the one hand there is the traditional, absolutist point of view holding that Natural Law is a higher kind of law

75. See, for instance, the repudiation by socialist doctrine as set forth by G. Tunkin, *op.cit.* (note 50), pp. 225-231. The latter doctrine itself, however, would seem to suffer from comparable shortcomings as far as verifiability is concerned; see *infra* p. 74 note 268.
76. See *infra* pp. 69-71.
77. See W. Friedmann, *op.cit.* (note 61), pp. 152-156; in particular with respect to international law, see W. O'Brien, "Natural Law and International Law in the American Tradition", 141 *WA* (1978), pp. 104-117; and with respect to international law of human rights, see J. Watson, *loc.cit.* (note 34). For some very concrete examples, see H. Schrader, *loc.cit.* (note 21), p. 752, who, on the basis of an analysis of a number of important recent international law cases in American federal courts, concludes "that some courts seem to have begun to see the hitherto narrowly restricted category of 'general principles' as synonymous with internationally accepted notions of equity and of natural law".
78. *Op.cit.* (note 61), p. 85.
79. See *infra* pp. 67-69.
80. See *infra* pp. 126-128.

from which no derogation is permitted. Positive law has to conform to this superior law and, if it does not, it must be considered invalid. In the more modern, relativist view, on the other hand, Natural Law is a standard to which rules of positive law should conform without necessarily being invalidated, if this proves not to be the case.[81] The former school, therefore, takes Natural Law as a command, the latter treats it rather as a guide. The absolutist point of view, it was argued in the foregoing, cannot serve as a point of departure with respect to the question of the sources of international law, because its basic tenets are subject to sharp controversies. The situation with respect to the relativist school, which is adhered to by most modern proponents of the Natural Law frame, is different. Even within the framework of the divided world of to-day such an approach is not only justified but can indeed, because of its guiding character, have a stimulating effect on the progressive development of international law.

However, there is always a danger of the two schools being confused. Because of the fundamental character of the ideals and values usually constituting the basis of Natural Law theories, the line between a guide which ought to be followed and a command which must be followed is easily crossed. Obviously, if the relativist position is not strictly adhered to and mixing takes place with absolutist points of view, the risks involved in the latter are being revived.

A final shortcoming of the Natural Law frame which concerns both the absolutist and relativist bent has been described as follows: "Either the allegedly universal ends are too few and abstract to give content to the idea of the good, or they are too numerous and concrete to be truly universal. One has to choose between triviality and implausibility."[82] To put it a little differently in terms of international law, most of the time States are prepared to accept vague and abstract notions which in their view are to be taken as the point of departure, or constitute the guiding principle with respect to a certain field of international law. Well-known examples are the common heritage of mankind with respect to the law of the sea, (the spirit of) détente in East-West relations and the principle of solidarity underlying proposals on a new law of international economic relations. It is equally true, however, that afterwards it proves extremely difficult to reach agreement on the elaboration of such vague and abstract notions into concrete rules of law. Developments in the fields just mentioned make this point abundantly clear.

4.3. The analytical approach

The analytical approach to international law was described in the foregoing as essentially concerned with the legal technique and primarily aimed at ordering and clarifying the structure of the legal system.[83] Usually, it is equated with Positivism. This analytical or Positivistic frame, too, is very broad and, just as in the case of legal idealism, it is rather difficult to pinpoint the common features of those theories which are taken to belong to the analytical or Positivistic approach.

81. See for this distinction also M. McDougal, H. Lasswell and W. Reisman, *loc.cit.* (note 62), p. 217 and W. Friedmann, *op.cit.* (note 61), p. 96.
82. See R. Unger, *Knowledge and Politics* (New York/London 1975), p. 241.
83. See *supra* p. 18.

From the outset we can exclude a bent of Positivism which is sometimes called pragmatic Positivism or Legal Realism.[84] Legal Realism originated in the United States where John Chipman Gray and Oliver Wendell Holmes, Jr., were its early proponents. It distinguishes itself from analytical Positivism in that more emphasis is placed on the social effect of law, on its consequences for the relevant part of the community, while the role of logic is greatly depreciated. Particularly from the point of view of the sources, Legal Realism has more in common with the sociological than with the analytical approach.[85]

Even if we leave the pragmatic approach out of consideration the field covered by the term Positivism is extremely vast, due to the fact that the concept of Positivism usually is very loosely defined. The very elastic character of "Positivism" may be illustrated by five different meanings of Positivism which, according to Hart, "are bandied about in contemporary jurisprudence: (1) the contention that laws are commands of human beings; (2) the contention that there is no necessary connection between law and morals or law as it is and ought to be; (3) the contention that the analysis (or study of meaning) of legal concepts is (a) worth pursuing and (b) to be distinguished from historical inquiries into the causes or origins of laws, from sociological inquiries into the relation of law and other social phenomena, and from the criticism or appraisal of law whether in terms of morals, social aims, 'functions', or otherwise; (4) the contention that a legal system is a 'closed logical system' in which correct legal decisions can be deduced by logical means from predetermined legal rules without reference to social aims, policies, moral standards; and (5) the contention that moral judgment cannot be established or defended as statements of fact, by rational argument, evidence or proof (non-cognitivism in ethics)".[86]

This enumeration shows that Positivism can be taken to encompass theories dealing with very different aspects of the law. Nevertheless, it would seem possible to discover some common ground among them. The first and foremost feature which characterizes all, or at least all traditional, Positivistic theories is that these are not concerned with values and ideals. To the Positivist values and ideals, whether they are politically, ethically, sociologically or historically based, do not belong to the province of law. Indeed, strict separation between the law as it is and the law as it ought to be, is the most fundamental assumption of legal Positivism. Positivism, therefore, is first of all a reaction against legal idealism. It wants to replace the mysticism and unverifiability of legal idealism by rationality and scientific methods of investigation. Most of the time Positivists are strongly concerned with legal stability and certainty; they show an extraordinary preoccupation with the efficacy of the legal system in general and with sanctions in particular. The result is that, unlike legal idealism with its flavour of intuition and "faith", the Positivist's view on the law is usually well-

---

84. See W. Friedmann, *op.cit.* (note 61), pp. 292-311; see also M. McDougal, H. Lasswell and W. Reismann, *loc.cit.* (note 62), pp. 87-90.
85. See in this respect Wendell Holmes' definition of law: "The prophecies of what the courts will do in fact and nothing more pretentious are what I mean by the law", quoted by W. Friedmann, *op.cit.* (note 61), p. 293.
86. H. Hart, "Positivism and the Separation of Law and Morals", in: R. Dworkin (ed.), *The Philosophy of Law* (Oxford 1979), pp. 17-37 (18); see for the impact of Positivism on international law the excellent analysis by R. Ago, "Positive Law and International Law", 51 *AJIL* (1957), pp. 691-733.

structured and transparant.

This holds true in particular also with respect to the way in which the sources of law are dealt with by Positivists. The Positivistic approach to the sources may best be explained on the basis of what Dworkin has labeled the skeleton of Positivism. According to Dworkin Positivism has a few central and organizing propositions. Within the framework of the present study the most important of these key tenets is the so-called test of *pedigree*: "(a) The law of a community is a set of special rules used by the community directly or indirectly for the purpose of determining which behaviour will be punished or coerced by the public power. These special rules can be identified and distinguished by specific criteria, by tests having to do not with their content but with their *pedigree*, *i.e.* the manner in which they were adopted or developed. These tests of *pedigree* can be used to distinguish valid legal rules from spurious legal rules (rules which lawyers and litigants wrongly argue are rules of law) and also from other sorts of social rules (generally lumped together as 'moral rules') that the community follows but does not enforce through public power."[87]

This so-called test of *pedigree* is indeed characteristic of the notion of law as usually adhered to by Positivists. The theory of Austin, for instance, who can be considered the founding father of legal Positivism, perfectly fits this model. To Austin: "Every positive law, or every law simply and strictly so-called, is set by a sovereign individual or a sovereign body of individuals, to a person or persons in a state of subjection to its authority".[88] In other words, Austin conceives of law as commands emanating from a sovereign who enjoys habitual obedience from the bulk of a given society.

The criticism which has been voiced with respect to Austin's quite simple model from various quarters can be left out of consideration here.[89] Austin's theory has not been able to exert a dramatic influence on international law. This is hardly surprising, if it is remembered that this theory entails entirely negative consequences with respect to international law. In fact the key tenets of Austin's theory lead him to deny the character of law to international law.[90]

Kelsen, another leading Positivist and "founder" of the Vienna School, has had a more far-reaching impact on international law. Kelsen's Pure Theory of Law is built upon the fundamental assumption that law consists of a hierarchy of normative relations. The strong hierarchical or even pyramidical structure of the Pure Theory of Law makes it an attractive model to serve as a tool for trying

87. R. Dworkin, *Taking Rights Seriously*, 6th print (Cambridge, Mass. 1979), p. 17. Dworkin adds two more key tenets to his skeleton of Positivism: "(b) The set of these valid legal rules is exhaustive of 'the law', so that if someone's case is not clearly covered by such a rule ... then that case cannot be decided by 'applying the law'. It must be decided by some official, like a judge 'exercising discretion' ...; (c) To say that someone has a 'legal obligation' is to say that his case falls under a valid legal rule that requires him to do or to forbear from doing something" (*ibidem*).

88. J. Austin, *Lectures on Jurisprudence or the Philosophy of Positive Law*, Vol. I, reprint of the 5th edition, revised and edited by R. Campbell, London 1885 (Glashütten im Taunus 1972), p. 34. According to Austin, sovereignty or supremacy exists "if a determinate human superior, not in habit of obedience to a like superior, receive habitual obedience from the bulk of a given society, that determinate superior is sovereign in that society, and the society (including the superior) is a society political and independent", *ibidem*, p. 221.

89. For a critical appraisal of Austin's theory, see H. Hart, *op.cit.* (note 41), chapters II, III and IV; Hart has summarized his criticism on pp. 77-78.

90. See J. Austin, *op.cit.* (note 88), pp. 173 and 182-184.

to bring some order into international law, which is generally considered to be very poorly structured. It is indeed one of Kelsen's primary aims to replace chaos by order and to transform multiplicity into unity. This result is achieved by Kelsen's requirement that ultimately each and every norm in a particular legal system derives its binding force from a superior norm, the so-called *Grundnorm* or the highest fundamental norm.

Kelsen uses different terms to describe this highest fundamental norm. Interchangeably it is called "postulated ultimate norm",[91] "rule existing in the juristic consciousness",[92] "hypothetical norm",[93] and "assumption".[94] More concretely, the fundamental norm in the case of national legal systems would, according to Kelsen, seem to be contained in the rule that the constitution or those who laid down the first constitution ought to be obeyed.[95] Applied to international law the fundamental norm would seem to read that States ought to behave as they have customarily behaved.[96]

These "concretizations" of the fundamental norm are still rather vague.[97] It should be borne in mind, however, what Kelsen's aim is when postulating his fundamental norm. The Pure Theory of Law itself is not really interested in the particular content of the fundamental norm. To Kelsen and his followers it is not for legal theory or for lawyers to decide whether a specific fundamental norm is the "correct" one or not, or whether it is good or bad. This question, it is argued, does not belong to the realm of law but to that of politics, ethics, or religion. Consequently, from the point of view of law as conceived by the Pure Theory several "candidates" for the function of fundamental norm would seem to be acceptable.[98] To put it bluntly, the Positivism of the Vienna School would seem to be quite indifferent towards the content of the fundamental norm, or at least, it takes a kind of neutral position. From the point of view of law this content does not really matter, as long as there is some fundamental norm constituting the foundation of the entire legal system.

This "neutralism", however, would seem to constitute a major weakness of Kelsen's brand of Positivism. As was already observed, Positivism arose mainly as a reaction against legal idealism or, more particularly, against the Natural Law frame.[99] Kelsen himself is one of the most ardent opponents of the mysticism and unscientific attitude contained in Natural Law thinking. Paradoxically enough, however, his own scheme shows a flaw the effect of which is comparable to those involved in the shortcomings of the Natural Law frame. To be sure, the Pure Theory of Law cannot be put on the same line as Natural Law theories; it cannot be said to have the same mystical characteristics. But what is a key trait

91. H. Kelsen, *General Theory of Law and State*, translated by A. Wedberg (Cambridge, Mass. 1949), p. 113.
92. *Ibidem*, p. 116.
93. *Ibidem*, p. 396.
94. *Ibidem*.
95. *Ibidem*, pp. 115-116.
96. H. Kelsen, *Principles of International Law*, second printing (New York 1956), p. 418.
97. H. Hart, for instance, characterizes the proclaimed basic norm of international law that States should behave as they have customarily behaved as "a mere useless reduplication of the fact that a set of rules are accepted by states as binding rules", *op.cit.* (note 41), p. 230.
98. A. Verdross, a follower of Kelsen, for instance, recognizes the maxim *pacta sunt servanda* as the fundamental norm for international law; see *Die Quellen des universellen Völkerrechts* (Freiburg 1973), p. 24.
99. See *supra* p. 35.

of legal idealism would appear to be a defect of Kelsen's Positivism too, albeit to a lesser degree: the *Grundnorm* thesis is to a large extent divorced from reality in the society concerned. According to the Pure Theory of Law the fundamental norm does not necessarily exist or operate in actual fact, but is rather presented as a postulate or an assumption. In his own words Kelsen has described the *Grundnorm* "as a constitution in the transcendental-logical sense, as distinct from the constitution in the positive legal sense. The latter is the constitution posited by human acts of will, the validity of which is based on the assumed (*vorausgesetzte*) basic norm".[100] As a result the fundamental norm becomes highly fictitious.

In this way Kelsen has opened up his theory to attacks of inconsistency. Particularly striking in this respect is the suspicion that Kelsen's theory itself is implicitly based on Natural Law principles.[101] If substantiated this of course would constitute a very serious charge to make to a theory which starts, as one of its basic tenets, from the strict separation between law as it is and law as it ought to be. We do not need to investigate any further here whether these alleged inconsistencies or even Natural Law flaws do indeed exist in Kelsen's theory. For the purpose of the present study it suffices to note the following consequences which would seem to flow from the pure science type of Positivism. Even if one takes for granted that the Pure Theory takes as its point of departure a conception of law as it is and not of law as it ought to be, it is hard to escape the impression that it proceeds from a peculiar kind of "is".Kelsen's theory appears to be built not on the structure of the relations, as they actually exist in society, but on a set of presumed fictions, or on a hypothetical fundamental norm, which to some looks more like a postulate of what law ought to be than a description of the law as it actually works. This "large distance" from reality in society is a major disadvantage of Kelsen's theory. If it comes to answering the question how and where the law in a given society is to be found, it might even prove an insurmountable obstacle. Because the theory hardly takes account of societal developments it might come up with answers which are as fictitious as its own *a priori* postulate or assumption.

On the other hand, important lessons can be learned from Positivism as described here. Legal Positivists in general, and Kelsen in particular, are extremely concerned with order, stability and certainty. The well-structured pyramidical set-up of the "Grundnorm" lays stress on, or to some even heavily overemphasizes, this point. Even if the Pure Theory of Law is regarded one-sidedly biased in this respect, it still has the merit of making abundantly clear that for any order to be correctly called a legal order some kind of ultimate authority, rule or standard, whatever its particular form or content, is required to judge the legal nature of the rules of the order or system concerned. This salient point Kelsen has made impossible to ignore.

---

100. Quoted by W. Friedmann, *op.cit.* (note 61), p. 277, note 3.
101. See H. Lauterpacht, *International Law; Collected Papers*, Vol. I: The General Works, edited by E. Lauterpacht (Cambridge 1970), pp. 54-55.

4.4. The sociological approach

Just as the analytical or Positivistic approach constitutes a reaction against Natural Law thinking or, more generally, legal idealism, so the sociological approach can be considered the counterpart of the analytical or Positivistic frame. In the same way as Positivists denounce the mysticism and unverifiability of Natural Law theories, those who are inclined to a sociological approach unmistakenly show a disdain for Positivism.[102] Sociological jurists denounce Positivism's formalism and rigidity or, more generally, its "distance" to societal relations.

In contrast the sociological approach itself focuses on the link between law and the society in which it is operating. It is difficult to go beyond this very general formula in characterizing the sociological approach. Very different theories of law are considered, or call themselves, sociological. Pound once described the common element in sociological jurisprudence as to look more for the working of law than its abstract content.[103] Formulas like these, of course, are not very helpful to arrive at a somewhat sharper delimitation of the sociological approach to law, and indeed a good deal of the work of sociological jurists up until now has been devoted precisely to mapping out and delimiting the field to be covered.

It is hardly surprising that no general consensus has yet been reached on the exact program of work. To no small extent this is probably due to the fact that the rise of the sociological school of jurisprudence, dating from the late nineteenth and twentieth century, is young compared to other approaches. Secondly, objectives like the relation between law and society and the search for the actual functioning of the law rather than its formal content clearly point to an extremely vast field of action.

Some authors claim that there is as yet no sociological school but rather a sociologistic fashion or style of communication. It is contended that "The general conceptions and operational techniques of the contemporary sociologist have not as yet been applied with any degree of rigor by any 'sociological' jurist".[104] Whatever there may be of this alleged non-existence of the sociological school of jurisprudence, it cannot be denied that a fairly great and, it would seem, growing number of jurists are approaching law in a way which is distinctive enough from the other basic approaches to justify separate discussion and can, on the basis of their primary objectives and methods of investigation, legitimately be labeled sociological jurists.

The foundations of this approach have mainly been laid by Durkheim,[105]

---

102. M. McDougal, H. Lasswell and W. Reismann, loc.cit. (note 62), pp. 259-260, for instance, note in discussing theories about international law that "the most disappointing feature of analyticalism is the enormous amount of intellectual effort which its devotees have expended with so little relevance to effective and ameliorative transnational decision". They conclude their appraisal of the analytical frame by stating that it "has been at best irrelevant and at worst a guide to the magnification of semi-relevant dimensions of law in the world community".

103. Quoted by W. Friedmann, op.cit. (note 61), p. 243.

104. M. McDougal, H. Lasswell and W. Reisman, loc.cit. (note 62), p. 260.

105. E. Durkheim, De la Divison du Travail Social, 5th edition (Paris 1926).

Weber,[106] and Ehrlich.[107] From the point of view of international law, Huber has played an important role when in the beginning of this century he drew attention to the fact that of all law international law is most closely linked to the underlying societal structure, because it lacks institutions capable of implementing the legal order independently from the consent of its subjects. In other words, international law, designed mainly to pose rules for the behaviour of States, at the same time depends heavily on those same States.[108] Other eminent international jurists, such as De Visscher[109] and Schwarzenberger,[110] also have a strong sociological inclination. This "European branch" of the sociological approach, however, would seem to be both more loosely organized and less vigorous about its gospel than its American sister movement. In the United States the sociological inclination has found fertile ground, because it has to a considerable extent dominated modern legal thinking in that country. This is exemplified mainly by the American Legal Realism.[111] Its influence has not been confined to the American legal system, but has also spread to international law. McWhinney observes that "The emphasis on a Law-as-Fact approach, with corresponding de-emphasis of juridical formalism and of the quest for an *a priori* category of legal sources into which a claimed legal rule can, somehow or other, be consigned, is part of the new Legal Realist conception of the international law-making process".[112]

As far as international law is concerned, the so-called Policy Oriented approach championed by Myres McDougal in particular has made its impact felt. It can be considered an offspring of, or is at any rate closely akin to, the Legal Realist movement.[113] As was already observed,[114] the Legal Realist movement can be regarded to belong to the sociological frame. Similarly, the Policy Oriented approach has strong sociological traits as will be pointed out in the following. Moreover, adherents to the Policy Oriented approach are clearly sympathetic towards the sociological frame and sometimes even give the impression that they themselves have no objections to be regarded as part of it, if certain present shortcomings of the sociological approach are remedied. McDougal, Lasswell and Reisman, for instance, conclude their appraisal of the sociological frame as follows: "The division and sovereigntization of the many

106. M. Weber, *Law in Economy and Society*, edited with introduction and annotations by M. Rheinstein; translation by E. Shills and M. Rheinstein, 2nd print (New York 1954).
107. E. Ehrlich, *Grundlegung der Soziologie des Rechts* (München/Leipzig 1929); see also Th. Geiger, *Vorstudien zu einer Soziologie des Rechts* (København 1947).
108. M. Huber, "Beiträge zur Kenntnis der Soziologischen Grundlagen des Völkerrechts und der Staatengesellschaft", in: IV JörG (1910), pp. 56-134 (62); see also the same author's, *Die Soziologischen Grundlagen des Volkerrechts* (Berlin 1928).
109. Ch. de Visscher, *Theory and Reality in Public International Law*, revised edition, translated by P. Corbett (Princeton 1968).
110. See in particular G. Schwarzenberger, *The Frontiers of International Law* (London 1962).
111. See *supra* p. 35.
112. E. McWhinney, *op.cit.* (note 33), p. 3.
113. Dworkin, *op.cit.* (note 87), pp. 4-5, is clearly of the same opinion, when he upholds that Legal Realism's emphasis on designing tactics for social change has had a lasting effect within American law schools. As a result: "Scholars like Myres McDougal and Harold Lasswell at Yale, and Lon L. Fuller, Henry Hart and Albert Sacks at Harvard, though different from one another, all insisted on the importance of regarding the law as an instrument for moving society toward certain large goals, and tried to settle questions about the legal process instrumentally, by asking which solutions best advanced these goals".
114. See *supra* p. 35.

foci within the social sciences have encouraged specialization; however, a cumulative cost of specialization is an aggregate of disjointed perspectives upon social process. We shall sugggest that the optimum approach, and the probable trend of future development, is an inclusive social scientific approach, that incorporates the several foci of specialization upon the environmental habitat, and variable psycho-cultural characteristics of man. The challenge to sociological jurisprudence then, is to become genuinely 'sociological' by providing a comprehensive map and a repertory of techniques for the continuing study of authoritative decision".[115] Given its affiliation with the sociological bent of jurisprudence and particularly because of its impact on international law, it would seem justified to focus on the Policy Oriented approach. Nevertheless, it has to be readily admitted that the peculiar features of the Policy Oriented school of thought are not always representative of the sociological approach in general.

The writings of scholars belonging to the Policy Oriented approach are extensive and the theory, in fact, concerns the legal process in its entirety. Obviously, all the aspects involved are not to be dealt with here. With respect to the focus of the present study two characteristics of the Policy Oriented approach are particularly relevant.

The first one was suggested when we pointed at the Legal Realist movement's emphasis on designing tactics for social change. The Policy Oriented approach clearly wants to use law as a means to an end, that is as an instrument to move society towards certain predetermined goals. We have already mentioned that this "missionizing" aspect of the Policy Oriented approach brings it quite closelegal idealism in this respect.[116] That to the Policy Oriented approach law is indeed purposive, is witnessed throughout the work of its principal proponent McDougal. In one of his major works he describes the contemporary challenge to legal scholars *inter alia* as follows: "In this perilous epoch of threatened catastrophe legal scholars have an opportunity of unparalleled urgency to assist in performing at least two indispensable functions: the functions of providing intelligence and of making recommendations to all who have the will and capability of decision. As old orders crumble and dissolve under the ever-accelerating impact of scientific, technological, and other changes, the future becomes increasingly plastic in our hands, holding out the possibility of molding a world order nearer to the aspirations of human dignity, or of losing out to the most ruthless and comprehensive tyranny that man has ever known".[117] According to McDougal and his school this recommending and molding has to lead to the clarification and aiding in the implementation of a universal order of human dignity, which is proclaimed to be the overriding aim.[118]

Now this of course is a lofty aim and, formulated in this general fashion, few are likely to object to it. Things change, however, when other (sub)values are

---

115. M. McDougal, H. Lasswell and W. Reisman, *loc.cit.* (note 62), p. 275.
116. See *supra* p. 30 note 64.
117. M. McDougal and Associates, *Studies in World Public Order* (New Haven 1960), p. 39.
118. *Ibidem*, p. 16. The essential meaning of human dignity is said to refer "to a social process in which values are widely and not narrowly shared, and in which private choice, rather than coercion, is emphasized as the predominant modality of power" (*ibidem*).

introduced and the method for their enquiry is outlined.[119] It is not indicated how these values fit into international law, whether and to what extent they form part of international law, and whether they are generally accepted by States. Clearly, they are not generally accepted in the way they are interpreted and dealt with by McDougal and his school. In other words, they mainly constitute the subjectivities of the Policy Oriented approach. The enumeration of these values is not a statement of what is contained in international law, but rather represents what some would like to see contained in international law. In short, this characteristic of the Policy Oriented approach embodies the "ought" rather than the "is" of international law.

As was repeatedly observed in the foregoing this is a perfectly legitimate and even useful task of doctrine.[120] It was also stressed, however, that there is a danger involved if the "is" and the "ought" are not kept strictly apart. It takes only a little step to cross the often thin line between the two, thereby confusing a recommendation of what the law should be for a statement of what the law actually stipulates. The Policy Oriented approach has not remained free from this error. One of its adherents, for instance, in defending the lawfulness of the U.S. involvement in Vietnam has written: "Lawfulness of assistance to either faction [that is the rival factions of North and South Vietnam; v.H.] must be determined in reference to genuine self-determination and the requirement of minimum public order, not in blind reliance on black-letter rules as to which side, if any, can be aided in a civil war and sometimes suggesting an Alice-in-Wonderland search for neutral principles".[121]

This passage and, more generally, the study from which it is quoted quite openly and unambiguously reveal how easily the Policy Oriented approach is led to substitute its subjective aspirations for the black-letter rules of international law. At the same time it indicates that its purposive character is not confined to doctrine. Not only scholars may use international law as a means to a (self-proclaimed) end, it would seem that decision-makers and therefore States may do the same. This is implied in the foregoing statement and set forth even more clearly in the description of the role of international law given by McDougal and Feliciano. In their view, the realistic function of rules of international law considered as a whole is "not mechanically to dictate specific decision but to guide the attention of decision-makers to significant variable factors in typical recurring contexts of decision to serve as summary indices to relevant crystallized community expectations and, hence, to permit creative and adaptive, instead of arbitrary and irrational decisions".[122]

119. Certain important values are: security; wealth-economic growth and trade; respect - the articulation and implementation of human rights; enlightenment and top skills; well-being; rectitude; affection (including loyalties), see *ibidem*, pp. 32-36.
120. See *supra* pp. 22 and 24.
121. J. Moore, "The Lawfulness of Military Assistance to the Republic of Vietnam", 61 *AJIL* (1967), pp. 1-34 (31). See the devastating comment by W. Friedmann, "Law and Politics in the Vietnamese War: A Comment", 61 *AJIL* (1967), pp. 776-785 (783) according to whom "The reference to 'neutral principles', if it means anything, means that policy objectives decide what is right and wrong. And in the absence of third party determination, 'minimum world public order' means Humpty-Dumpty-like what the policy-maker wants it to mean, a catch-all phrase to justify whatever action the writer wishes to justify".
122. M. McDougal and F. Feliciano, *Law and Minimum World Public Order: The Legal Regulations of International Coercion* (New Haven 1961), p. 57.

Nobody probably would want to uphold that international law spells out in detail the specific decisions national authorities often have to make. And even the description of law as a guide of summary indices to relevant crystallized community expectations does not give rise to major objections. It was already observed that law, or more generally legal arguments, may be used as "a means of communication".[123] But even if this latter function is considered a feature of the law properly so-called, it is neither its only function nor even the most important one. The first and foremost function of international law is, of course, to regulate state behaviour by providing a standard to which States have to conform their own behaviour and on the basis of which they can judge that of others. It does this by posing binding rules which States have to obey. These rules do not specify each and every decision States have to make, but rather put limits to the decision-making process.

The Policy Oriented approach does not recognize this as the core-function of international law. The definition just quoted makes it clear that, in the view of adherents to the Policy Oriented approach, international law is a guide for States when deciding on their way of behaviour rather than a command which they have to follow.[124] In the worst possible case, this view can lead to international law being used by States as a device for *post facto* justifying decisions which they made without really taking international law into account. This is more than just another way of looking at international law. In its extreme the view amounts to a virtual denial of the existence of international law. For, in this way international law is deprived of almost all normative character and cannot any longer be considered as law properly so-called.

This brings us to the second characteristic of the Policy Oriented approach which is most relevant with respect to the question of the sources of international law. The downplaying of the normative character of international law and its near identification with policy leads to, or if one wants, results from, a second characteristic position of the Policy Oriented approach: its emphasis on the process-character of international law. Again this point may best be explained in the words of its major protagonist. In discussing the impact of international law on national law, McDougal projects a conception of international law on the basis of the world social and power processes and from the perspectives of human dignity and the efficiency of inquiry into varying patterns of authority and control. He recommends "that international law be regarded not as mere rules but as a whole *process* of authoritative decisions in the world arena, a process in which authority and control are appropriately conjoined and which includes, along with an inherited body of flexible prescriptions explicitly related to community policies, both a structure of established decision-makers and a whole arsenal of methods and techniques by which policy is projected and implemented".[125]

In reaction one observer has pointedly characterized the Policy Oriented approach as a kind of "panta-rhei-view".[126] Indeed, in the policy oriented per-

123. See *supra* p. 26.
124. This point was made clear in an earlier study by McDougal, "International Law, Power and Policy; A Contemporary Conception", 82 *RCADI* (1953-I), pp. 137-258, in particular pp. 143-157.
125. M. McDougal and Associates, *op.cit.* (note 117), pp. 169-170.
126. See M. Schweitzer, "Synopsis des Völkerrechtlers", in: B. Simma and E. Blenk-Knocke (eds.), *Zwischen Intervention und Zusammenarbeit* (Berlin 1979), pp. 505-517 (509).

spective the focus is on a great many, sometimes very detailed, aspects of almost the entire international process, which are, moreover, in more or less constant motion. It is not surprising, therefore, that this frame does not provide one or more "sources" in the sense of rules or even devices which serve as an aid in answering the question what the law requires in a given situation. Faithful to its basic orientation the Policy Oriented approach rather distinguishes seven functional phases of decision-making and execution "in order to identify and compare the role of law in the process of power".[127]

Now, this focus of the Policy Oriented approach may certainly serve useful purposes. Particularly for scholars it is advisable to take cognizance of its methods, because they provide powerful tools for analyzing the many multifarious factors which in some way or another have an impact on the creation and implementation of international law. At the same time, however, the Policy Oriented approach is bad counsel when one wants to solve the question where the law can be found and what its exact content is. In this respect it suffers from a shortcoming which is the opposite of that of Positivism. Where Positivism does not go far enough in taking account of what is happening in society and therefore is too rigid, the Policy Oriented approach goes too far and ends up almost equating international law with the entire world social and political process. The die-hard Positivist is like a photographer who once makes a picture with a defective camera which does not even register the most relevant aspects of reality. In addition, he refuses to update his picture at regular intervals. The Policy Oriented jurist, on the other hand, tries to make a continuing three-dimensional movie of society. The former was said to be likely to come up with fictitious answers. The latter cannot provide that minimum of certainty and stability which is required for the law to be able to perform its ordering and regulating function.

4.5. The middle path of Structural Positivism

4.5.1. Introduction

The foregoing analysis of the possible contribution of the three basic approaches to law to the questions concerning the sources of international law may be briefly summarized as follows. We found that legal idealism, at least as far as international law is concerned, has little contribution to make to solving the problem of the sources. As was observed, the absolutist point of view cannot serve as a point of departure because, whatever the "ultimate source" propagated, it is neither scientifically verifiable nor generally accepted in the present heterogenuous international society. The relativist position on the other hand treats its "ultimate source" as a guide to which positive international law should preferably conform, rather than as a standard to which international law has to

---

127. These phases are: prescription, recommendation, intelligence, invocation, application, appraisal and termination; McDougal and Associates, *op.cit.* (note 117), pp. 14-15 juncto pp. 24-25. See also the very complicated multifactor analysis under the heading "process of agreement" in: M. McDougal, H. Lasswell and J. Miller, *The Interpretation of Agreements and World Public Order, Principles of Content and Procedure* (New Haven 1967), pp. 13-21.

conform and does, as such, not directly relate to the question whether a rule or provision or principle is indeed one of international law.

The other two approaches each stress, or at least overemphasize, one of the two requirements which in our view must be satisfied by a viable theory of, or approach to, the sources of international law. We said that for the law to be able to play its ordering and regulating role in society, it needs to mirror relations in the society concerned to the extent necessary. On the other hand, however, there are limits to this mirror-image of law. For, the same ordering and regulating function requires the law to provide certainty and clarity. This can be achieved only if the law at the same time constitutes a narrowing and formalizing process, or rather if it provides a condensation of social reality.[128]

As we have seen, the sociological approach is inclined to overemphasize the link of law with society, thereby sacrificing the element of certainty and clarity, while analyticalism, particularly the traditional Positivist branch of it, lays one-sided stress on stability and certainty to the point where it becomes fictitious because it is removed too far from actual practice. In short, each of these two frames takes adequately into account only one of the conditions which in our view must be fulfilled by a successful approach to the sources of international law. What is needed, therefore, is an approach or a model which satisfies both requirements mentioned to the largest possible extent.

From what has been observed in the foregoing it is clear that such an approach will have to take a kind of middle-of-the-road-position somewhere halfway between the certainty and clarity of traditional Positivism and the extreme flexibility which characterizes the Policy Oriented school of sociological jurisprudence. In our view the outlines of such a model for approaching the questions concerning the sources of international law are provided for by Hart in his major jurisprudential statement, *The Concept of Law*.[129] The model of a union of primary and secondary rules, which according to Hart is at the centre of a legal system,[130] can successfully be applied to explain the question of the sources of international law. As will be shown in more detail below, the model goes a long way in meeting the conditions mentioned. On the one hand it is relatively simple and consequently produces a large degree of certainty and clarity. On the other hand, it takes due account of the law's link with social relations in that, in the final analysis, it seeks the foundations of law in existing practice in society. Hart in short goes the middle path which we meant in the foregoing.[131]

Hart's approach has been labeled the New Positivism.[132] Indeed his theory is generally classified as a modern version of the analytical or Positivist approach to jurisprudence.[133] Generally speaking, the name New Positivism does not raise any mayor objections. But, although it indicates the general orientation of Hart's theory, it obscures the fact that Hart distinguishes his theory from tradi-

128. See *supra* pp. 25-27.
129. H. Hart, *op.cit.* (note 41).
130. *Ibidem*, p. 96.
131. He makes more or less explicit references to this middle path; see, for instance, *ibidem*, p. 127.
132. See M. Rogoff, "International Law in Legal Theory: The New Positivism", 1 *UTLR* (1970), pp. 1-30 (particularly also note 6); see also A. D'Amato, "The Neo-Positivist Concept of International Law", 59 *AJIL* (1965), pp. 321-324.
133. See W. Friedmann, *op.cit.* (note 61), pp. 287-289; M. McDougal, H. Lasswell and W. Reisman, *loc.cit.* (note 62), pp. 243-260; and R. Dworkin, *op.cit.* (note 87), pp. 20-22.

tional Positivism in important respects. One of the differences is to be found precisely in the approach to the sources of law. As will be pointed out in the following section, Hart, unlike traditional Positivism, seeks the key to answering the question of the sources of law in the final analysis in the practice of the relations between the members of the society, *i.e.* in the structure of society. For this reason it is preferred not to retain the name New Positivism in the present context, but to refer to Hart's theory as Structural Positivism.

In the following section we will briefly outline Hart's model of the union between primary and secondary rules of law, as far as it is relevant to the problem of the sources of international law. Subsequently, we will test its applicability to questions concerning the sources of international law.

4.5.2. The union of primary and secondary rules

To Hart the union of primary and secondary rules constitutes the foundation of a legal system. The term "legal system" is used on several occasions in his book,[134] but it is nowhere defined. Consequently, what Hart means by "legal system" remains unclear, though generally speaking of course the term "system" connotes something which is unified. It is probable that this is how the term has to be understood, when Hart tells us that a "legal system" results from the combined existence of primary and secondary rules of law.

The central place which Hart accords to the existence of a union of primary and secondary rules is more clearly set forth in the description of the consequences resulting from it. Such a union, according to Hart, marks the transition from a primitive set of legal rules to a developed "system" of law. Primitive communities or societies are said to have only primary rules of law. These primary rules are concerned with the actions that individuals must or must not do. They lay down rights and obligations for members of the community or society and could therefore also be called material rules. Secondary rules are different: "They specify the ways in which the primary rules may be conclusively ascertained, introduced, eliminated, varied, and the fact of their violation conclusively determined."[135] Consequently, they are of a more procedural character.

The primary rules in primitive societies have, according to Hart, the status of law simply because they are *accepted* as such. But this simplicity of the social structure carries with it some serious defects. The first, and within the framework of the present study the most important of these defects Hart calls the *uncertainty* of primary rules: "if doubts arise as to what the rules are or as to the precise scope of some given rule, there will be no procedure for settling this doubt, either by reference to an authoritative text or to an official whose declarations on this point are authoritative".[136] The two other closely related defects are the *static* character of the primary rules and the *inefficiency* of the diffuse social pressure by which these rules are to be maintained in simple forms of social life. The former means that the rules can be changed only through "the slow process of growth, whereby courses of conduct once thought optional

134. See, for instance, H. Hart, *op.cit.* (note 41), pp. 97-107, 113, 114 and 208.
135. *Ibidem*, p. 92.
136. *Ibidem*, p. 90.

become first habitual or usual, and then obligatory, and the converse process of decay, when deviations, once severely dealt with, are first tolerated and then pass unnoticed".[137] The latter amounts to a situation where "Disputes as to whether an admitted rule has or has not been violated will always occur and will, in any but the smallest societies, continue interminably, if there is no agency specially empowered to ascertain finally, and authoritatively, the fact of violation".[138]

These defects, which hamper the functioning of the law in primitive societies, are remedied, Hart argues, in societies with a more full-fledged legal system through the operation of secondary rules. The defect of uncertainty, which interests us most at this moment, [139] is removed by the introduction of what Hart calls a "rule of recognition". A rule of recognition, it is said, "will specify some feature or features possession of which by a suggested rule is taken as a conclusive affirmative indication that it is a rule of the group to be supported by the social pressure it exerts".[140] In other words, the rule of recognition provides a test for deciding whether or not a rule is a legal rule. It does this by prescribing a procedure for the creation or enactment of legal rules. If a rule has come about in conformity with the way stipulated by the rule of recognition, it is a binding rule of law. Its *validity* can be established beyond doubt. A rule of recognition, therefore, furnishes the certainty and clarity which the law needs in order to play its ordering and regulating role.[141]

Hart discusses the rule of recognition at great length. Here it suffices to highlight some of its most relevant features. First of all, it is important to note that a rule of recognition may take any of a huge variety of forms. It may be quite simple or very complex, depending on the society concerned. The form of the rule of recognition, however, is not decisive: "It may, as in the early law of many societies, be no more than that an authoritative list or text of the rules is to be found in a written document or carved on some public monument. No doubt as a matter of history this step from the pre-legal to the legal may be accomplished in distinguishable stages, of which the first is the mere reduction to writing of hitherto unwritten rules. This is not itself the crucial step, though it is a very important one: what is crucial is the acknowledgement of reference to the writing or inscription as *authoritative, i.e.* as the *proper* way of disposing of doubts as to the

---

137. *Ibidem.*
138. *Ibidem*, p. 91.
139. See also *supra* pp. 1-2.
140. *Ibidem*, p. 92.
141. H. Hart, *op.cit.* (note 41); the static and inefficient character of primary rules are remedied in developed societies possessing a "legal system" by "rules of change" and "rules of adjudication" respectively. The simplest form of the former is said to consist of a rule "which empowers an individual or body of persons to introduce new primary rules for the conduct of the life of the group, or of some class within it, and to eliminate old rules", *ibidem*, p. 93. Rules of adjudication "empower individuals to make authoritative determinations of the question whether, on a particular occasion, a primary rule has been broken", *ibidem*, p. 94. Hart is aware that the application of his model in practice might also entail disadvantages: "the step from a simple form of society, where primary rules of obligation are the only means of social control, into the legal world with its centrally organized legislature, courts, officials and sanctions brings its solid gains at a certain cost. The gains are those of adaptability to change, certainty, and efficiency, and these are immense; the cost is the risk that the centrally organized power may well be used for the oppression of numbers with whose support it can dispense, in a way that the simpler regime of primary rules could not", *ibidem*, pp. 197-198.

existence of the rule".[142] Similarly, the rule of recognition may in fact be not just one rule but a whole pyramidical structure of several rules of recognition in a hierarchical order: "In a modern legal system ... the criteria for identifying the law are multiple and commonly include a written constitution, enactment by a legislature, and judicial precedents. In most cases, provision is made for possible conflict by ranking these criteria in an order of relative subordination and primacy".[143] Furthermore, rules of recognition very often are not visible in the daily operating of a system of law. Most of the time rules of recognition are not expressly stated but simply taken for granted. Their existence is concealed, or at least implied, in the way in which primary rules of obligation are, more or less, mechanically, identified in a given legal system. Usually they are expressly referred to only in extreme cases.[144]

A very fundamental question concerns the basis of the rule of recognition. For, the foregoing description of the character of a rule of recognition as conceived by Hart shows that it is an ultimate rule.[145] It is an ultimate rule in the sense that it provides the criteria of validity for all the other rules of the system laying down rights and obligations. There is of course no rule determining the validity of the ultimate rule of recognition, because in that case the former rule would itself be the ultimate rule and the same question would arise as to the basis or the "source" from which that ultimate rule derives its binding force.

The question of the binding force of the ultimate rule of recognition is not a matter of validity, which would have to be conferred by another rule. There is a similarity in this respect between the (ultimate) rule of recognition in a developed legal system and the primary rules in a primitive society. In Hart's model the former's just like the latter's binding force results from their *acceptance* in practice. Therefore, unlike the traditional Positivist view, the Structural Positivism does not conceive of the ultimate rule (of recognition) as a "postulate", as "existing in the juristic consciousness", as a "hypothetical norm" or as an "assumption", but simply as a matter of fact. In Hart's own words: "In this respect ... a rule of recognition is unlike other rules of the system. ... For whereas a subordinate rule of a system may be valid and in that sense 'exist' even if it is generally disregarded, the rule of recognition exists only as a complex, but normally concordant, practice of the courts, officials, and private persons in identifying the law by reference to certain criteria. Its existence is a matter of fact".[146] Hart's model is designed and explained with a view to municipal legal systems,[147] and the phrase "practice of the courts, officials, and private persons" should not be taken too literally. Generally speaking and put in terms of international law, it could be substituted by the "practice of the main law-determining agencies in a given society". What is important is that, in the final analysis, the acceptance in practice constitutes the decisive criterion for the binding force of the rule of

142. *Ibidem*, p. 92.
143. *Ibidem*, p. 98.
144. *Ibidem*, pp. 98-99.
145. In the case of a complex structure of several rules of recognition the question as to the basis arises only with respect to the supreme rule of recognition, which is at the top of the pyramidical structure. In Hart's model "a criterion of legal validity or source of law is supreme if rules identified by reference to it are still recognized as rules of the system, even if they conflict with rules identified by reference to the other criteria ...", *ibidem*, p. 103.
146. *Ibidem*, p. 107.
147. *Ibidem*, p. 17.

48

recognition; from a theoretical point of view, it is only of subsidiary interest in what direction practice actually points. The actual content of practice with respect to the rule of recognition will have to be established from case to case. Different societies may of course use different ultimate tests of law.

Hart's model may be summed up as follows. There are two ways for a rule to acquire the status of law. Firstly, in developed legal systems rules may become binding because they have come about, are created or enacted, in conformity with another rule, a secondary rule of recognition stipulating the criteria for binding force. A primary rule which satisfies the conditions of this secondary rule of recognition is a *valid* legal rule. Secondly, in primitive societies rules may become binding because they are *accepted* as a standard for conduct. In primitive societies acceptance of primary rules has to take place by a large majority of the group concerned. In more developed societies the rule of recognition or the structure of several rules of recognition are, theoretically at least, the only rules whose binding force depends upon acceptance. They need to be accepted in the practice of the main law-determining agencies in the society concerned.[148]

The foregoing shows that Structural Positivism goes a long way in satisfying both the conditions which in our view a sound theory of the sources of international law has to fulfil. It was already noted that Hart's approach produces a relatively large degree of certainty and clarity by introducing the concept of the rule of recognition as a test to establish whether a given rule is a rule of law.[149] On the other hand, as was just pointed out, it leaves at the same time ample room to take account of the law's link with the actual situation as it exists in society by insisting that the binding force of a legal system's ultimate rules (of recognition) depends upon practice.

This, to be sure, does not imply that Hart's model of a union between primary and secondary rules has gone unchallenged. On the contrary, it has met with a considerable flow of criticism and comment.[150] We shall briefly touch on one or two objections raised which offer an opportunity to elucidate a little further the Structural Positivism's stand on questions concerning the sources of law.

A more or less predictable attack has come from sociological or Policy Oriented jurists. Their main charge would seem to be that Hart's approach constitutes an oversimplification: "Hart's notion of authority conceals the complexity of the concept and the multiplicity of its empirical manifestations under the disarmingly simple rubric of '*rules* of recognition'. It should be clear that his rules of recognition, if given empirical reference, must extend to the entire constitutive process of authoritative decision in any community, and hence, that

---

148. "Acceptance" means in this respect that those who follow the practice regard the rule as binding. Hart makes a distinction between the internal and the external point of view: "The natural expression of this external point of view is not 'It is the law that ...' but 'In England they recognize as law ... whatever the Queen in Parliament enacts'. The first of these forms of expression we shall call an internal statement, because it manifests the internal point of view and is naturally used by one who, accepting the rule of recognition and without stating the fact that it is accepted, applies the rule in recognizing some particular rule of the system as valid. The second form of expression we shall call an external statement, because it is the natural language of an external observer of the system who, without himself accepting its rule of recognition, states the fact that others accept it", *ibidem*, p. 99; see also pp. 86-88.
149. See *supra* p. 45.
150. See the select bibliography of critical writings, H. Hart, *op.cit.* (note 41), pp. 257-258.

one barely begins to grasp the notion by reference only to rules".[151]

On the one hand, the argument would seem to misconceive Hart's model. For, as was pointed out, according to that model the basis of rules of recognition is, in the final analysis, to be found in the practice of the society concerned. On the other hand, it is beyond doubt that Structural Positivism takes a different view of that practice than the Policy Oriented approach. The former refuses, and in our opinion rightly so, to adhere to the latter's all-embracing conception of practice which was characterized as a "panta-rhei-view".[152] It does so on the basis of the awareness that the law's function requires it to be a "condensation" of social reality.[153] The Policy Oriented approach itself has to concede that "the public functions of prescription and application are necessarily restricted, in terms of direct participation to a very small, though hopefully, representative group, ...".[154]

A different kind of criticism has been launched by Dworkin. Dworkin, of course, is not a Policy Oriented kind of jurist. Nor can he be said to belong to the Positivist school; on the contrary, his intricate and ambitious theory in fact constitutes a frontal attack on Positivism, in particular Hart's version thereof.[155] It is therefore surprising to learn that some consider Dworkin an adherent of, what is called, New Positivism.[156] Dworkin's theory would seem to contain some important characteristics of the legal idealist approach. It shows some of the rigidity usually involved in theories of the legal idealist bent, in that it reduces everything to one right that is said to be fundamental and even axiomatic: the right to equal concern and respect.[157]

It is precisely the lack of rigidity in Hart's theory, the fact that it does not provide answers to all questions, which may arise in practice, that seems to bother Dworkin most. His attack focuses on the concept of the rule of recognition which Dworkin calls the test of *pedigree*. Dworkin argues that even the existence of a rule of recognition may leave open grey areas, in that it does not provide clear-cut answers in all situations where the question arises whether a given rule is indeed a legal rule. According to him, Hart's treatment of custom amounts to a confession that the test of *pedigree* does not fit all cases: "This chips at the neat pyramidical architecture we admired in Hart's theory."[158] More important, according to Dworkin, is the fact that a number of crucial principles and policies cannot be identified as legal rules on the basis of a test of *pedigree*.[159] He con-

---

151. M. McDougal, H. Lasswell and W. Reisman, *loc.cit.* (note 62), p. 253.
152. See *supra* p. 43; see also M. Rogoff's denunciation of Hart's theory, *loc.cit.* (note 132), p. 18, where he advocates, after qualifying Hart's conception of authority as unnecessarily restricted, that "It is far better to conceive authority as referrable to the patterns of subjectivities of all the participants in the community ...".
153. See *supra* p. 45.
154. M. McDougal, H. Lasswell and W. Reisman, *loc.cit.* (note 62), pp. 192-193.
155. See R. Dworkin, *op.cit.* (note 87), p. IX.
156. M. Rogoff, *loc.cit.* (note 132), p. 3, note 6.
157. See R. Dworkin, *op.cit.* (note 87), particularly chapters 6 and 9. Dworkin is careful to point out, that "it is no part of this theory that any mechanical procedure exists for demonstrating what the rights of parties are in hard cases", *ibidem*, p. 81. Nevertheless, in arguing for a fusion of constitutional law and moral theory, *ibidem*, p. 149, he succeeds to the error, as J. Hart Ely, *op.cit.* (note 73), p. 58, has rightly observed, of confusing a method of moral philosophy for the method of moral philosophy and asks judges and lawyers to abide by it.
158. R. Dworkin, *op.cit.* (note 87), p.43.
159. *Ibidem.*

cludes, therefore, that the tenet "that the law of a community is distinguished from other social standards by some test in the form of a master rule" must be rejected.[160]

It is true that Hart's position is not rigid in that it represents an absolutist point of view. In view of the actual operation of the law he has realistically relaxed his theory and introduced the necessary flexibility into it by recognizing that a rule of recognition may be uncertain.[161] Just like any other rule, a rule of recognition too may suffer from what Hart calls 'open texture' which is used to describe summarily the well-known fact that "Whichever device, precedent or legislation, is chosen for the communication of standards of behaviour, these, however smoothly they work over the great mass of ordinary cases, will at some point where their application is in question, prove indeterminate".[162] In other words, with regard to a legal system's ultimate criteria of legal validity, too, questions may arise "to which there is no answer - only answers".[163] Dworkin of course is well aware of Hart's qualification. To him, however, it does not add flexibility and sophistication to the theory, but on the contrary undermines it.[164] He is not very interested in discussing the degree or the extent of the uncertainty that would still be acceptable for a rule of recognition in order to perform its task of test of *pedigree* or master rule.[165] His rejection of Hart's view is not based upon practical objections but rather constitutes a matter of principle. Hart's view on how "problems of the penumbra", that is problems which arise outside the hard core of standard instances or settled meanings, are handled or dealt with in practice, is unacceptable to Dworkin. Speaking of national legal systems Hart suggests: "The truth may be that, when courts settle previously unenvisaged questions concerning the most fundamental rules, they *get* their authority to decide them accepted after the questions have arisen and the decision has been given. Here all that succeeds is success. It is conceivable that the constitutional question at issue may divide society too fundamentally to permit of its disposition by a judicial decision. ... But where less vital social issues are concerned, a very surprising piece of judicial law-making concerning the very sources of law may be calmly 'swallowed'".[166] In other words, in cases of doubt concerning the ultimate criteria of legal validity law-implementing agencies by some kind of "usurpation of power" sometimes take over from the legislative agencies *stricto sensu*

160. *Ibidem*, p. 44.
161. H. Hart, *op.cit.* (note 41), pp. 144-150.
162. *Ibidem*, p. 124.
163. *Ibidem*, p. 147.
164. R. Dworkin, *op.cit.* (note 87), p. 62.
165. This would seem to be an important question, though, because a rule of recognition leaving vast areas of uncertainty would obviously be of little practical value. Hart, *op.cit.* (note 41), pp. 148-149, reminds us in this respect "that though every rule may be doubtful at some points, it is indeed a necessary condition of a legal system existing that not every rule is open to doubt on all points. The possibility of courts having authority at any given time to decide these limiting questions concerning the ultimate criteria of validity, depends merely on the fact that, at that time, the application of those criteria to a vast area of law, including the rules which confer that authority raises no doubts, though their precise scope and ambit do".
166. *Ibidem*, pp. 149-150. It is interesting to note in this respect that in these cases of the penumbra, where there is not really a law "as it is", the conception of law "as it ought to be" may come to play the more direct role to which we made reference above, see *supra* pp. 21-22 and note 47. With respect to these problematical cases of the penumbra Hart observes: "it seems true to say that the criterion which makes a decision sound in such cases is some concept of what the law ought to be", H. Hart, *loc.cit.* (note 86), p. 23.

and exercise a law-creative function. Such a law-creative capacity necessarily entails the recognition of some form of discretion.[167]

It is at this point of attributing discretion to judges or law-implementing agencies where the heart of Dworkin's criticism of the Structural Positivistic approach would seem to be. In his reply to critics appended to his book he writes that according to the Positivistic theory "law provides a settled, public and dependable set of standards for private and official conduct, standards whose force cannot be called into question by some individual's perception of policy or morality. This theory of law's function acknowledges, as it must, that no set of public rules can be complete or precise. But it therefore insists on a distinction between occasions on which the law, so conceived, does dictate a decision and occasions on which, in the language of Positivists, the judge must exercise his discretion to make new law just because the law is silent. The distinction is vital, on this view of the law's function, because it is important to acknowledge that *when reasonable men can disagree about what the law requires, a judicial decision cannot be a neutral decision of the sort promised in the idea of law. It is more honest to concede that the decision is not, in this case, a decision of law at all"*.[168]

In reply to Dworkin's statement it may first of all be submitted that the distinction which is implicit in the phenomenon of open texture is not as black-and-white as Dworkin seems to suggest. There are few occasions where rules literally dictate decisions, where decisions mechanically result from legal rules without any judgment being necessary. On the other hand, judges or other law-implementing agencies are very seldom confronted with situations where the law is absolutely silent in the sense that no legal guidance whatsoever for a decision can be found. Secondly, it was already observed, that open texture is a matter of the penumbra which occurs in a comparatively small number of borderline cases.[169] In the bulk of the cases no doubts requiring absolute discretion (in what Dworkin calls the strong sense) arise. In those comparatively few borderline cases the law-implementing agencies' "usurpation of power" may succeed or not. If their decisions concern vital social issues and run counter to a powerful enough opposition, they will be somehow reversed, remain a dead letter, or otherwise be denied the status of law. If the authors of these decisions succeed in getting them accepted - sometimes by reiterating them -, they acquire the status of law or rather are *ex post facto* considered as "legal" from the start. This latter situation shows in a nutshell how the law-making process sometimes works in practice which the thesis of open texture/discretion wants to describe. It is difficult to see why the ensuing rules, provisions or principles should be denied the status of law. Because these are borderline cases this status of law is not confirmed by the rule of recognition, but not denied by it either. Moreover, the rules concerned have been accepted as binding in practice.

Dworkin is not satisfied by this explanation and would, therefore, seem forced to come up with some alternative criterion or principle which is all-embracing and would cover all questions that could possibly arise. He claims that such an all-embracing criterion or principle can be found in the fundamental and axiomatic right to equal concern and respect. However, this right to

---

167. See Dworkin's distinction between various senses of discretion, *op.cit.* (note 87), pp. 31-39.
168. *Ibidem*, p. 347 (emphasis added).
169. See *supra* p. 51 and note 166.

equal concern and respect is comparable to other ideas or values claimed to constitute the ultimate source by legal idealist protagonists. Consequently, it is open to the objection which was already stressed in the foregoing: it is not generally accepted as a fundamental or axiomatic right or, at least, is interpreted differently by different people. Or to put it in Dworkin's own words, reasonable men are most likely to disagree on what the criterion or pinciple requires in concrete hard cases.

4.5.3. Structural Positivism and international law

As was argued in the preceding sections, the model of a union between primary and secondary rules as it is advocated by Hart's Structural Positivism goes a long way in satisfying the requirements which a sound approach to the sources of international law in our view must fulfil. It stresses the highest possible extent of certainty and clarity with respect to the sources and, at the same time, takes due account of the law's connection with social relations. The question, therefore, arises what the result is of the application of this model to international law. Within the framework of the present study the main question of course is: does international law possess a rule of recognition? Does it have a criterion or criteria satisfying the requirements just mentioned to identify rules as rules of international law?

Although Hart's book is aimed mainly at providing an analysis of the distinctive structure of municipal legal systems,[170] an entire (final) chapter is devoted to international law. The view expressed therein is simple: international law does not have a rule of recognition. To be sure, Hart does not deny the character of law to international law. He concludes that rules of international law are binding. They are binding rules of law, however, not because they derive legal validity from a rule of recognition, but simply because "they are accepted and function as such".[171]

On what grounds does Hart conclude that international law does not possess a rule of recognition? In fact no grounds are adduced and Hart's view in this respect cannot really be called a conclusion; it is rather a presumption. He simply asserts that international law has no rule of recognition. In referring to international law he observes: "in this simple form of social structure, we have not something which we do have in municipal law: namely a way of demonstrating the validity of individual rules by reference to some ultimate rule of the system".[172] Hart's *a priori* approach to international law is evidenced by the fact that in the final chapter he changes his focus of enquiry. While all the chapters dealing with municipal law are concerned with the search for the existence of a union of primary and secondary rules, in the beginning of the final chapter he announces that the focus will be on the question "whether the common wider usage that speaks of 'international law' is likely to obstruct any practical or the-

---

170. See *supra* p. 48.
171. H. Hart, *op.cit.* (note 41) pp. 225-226 jo. 230.
172. *Ibidem*, p. 229. At the same page it is submitted: "In the simpler case we cannot ask: 'From what ultimate provision of the system do the separate rules derive their validity or binding force?', for there is no such provision ...".

oretical aim".[173] This sudden shift remains unexplained. Instead of sticking to his point of departure, and trying to find out whether international law possesses a rule of recognition, Hart in fact sets out in the final chapter to prove his point that "it is a mistake to suppose that a basic rule of recognition is a generally necessary condition of the existence of rules of obligation or 'binding' rules".[174] This, we are told now, is not a necessity but simply a luxury found in advanced societies, but not in primitive social systems like the international system.[175]

It may be true that rules of law can derive their binding force from acceptance and do not need an ultimate rule of recognition. However, this is small comfort, if it is remembered that rules of recognition serve to alleviate uncertainty concerning the legal character of primary rules. They, therefore, play an essential role in the functioning of the law and cannot be portrayed simply as a luxury, thereby suggesting that it is not really worthwhile to make a serious effort to pinpoint the existence of a rule of recognition in international law. Hart does not make this effort, but instead has himself drawn into discussing, what he calls, two sources of doubt concerning the legal character of international law. The first source of doubt is provided by the absence of sanctions in international law, the second by the (absolute) concept of sovereignty. Both these questions are important as well as familiar to international jurists. From a theoretical point of view they are, however, only ancillary to the main problem: can a criterion or criteria be found to identify rules as rules of international law?[176]

The reason which leads Hart to this surprising treatment of international law is remarkable. In fact, he falls victim to a trap for which he cautions others: an adverse comparison of international law with municipal law.[177] He starts from the premise that the absence of an international legislature, courts with compulsory jurisdiction, and centrally organized sanctions means "that the rules for states resemble that simple form of social structure, consisting only of primary rules of obligation, which, when we find it among societies of individuals, we are accustomed to contrast with a developed legal system".[178] Hart's downright equation of the international community with primitive (national) societies gets him into trouble; it forces him to the remarkable contradiction that "In form, international law resembles such a regime of primary rules, even though the content of its often elaborate rules are very unlike those of a primitive society, *and many of its concepts, methods, and techniques, are the same as those of mod-*

173. *Ibidem*, p. 209.
174. *Ibidem*, p. 229.
175. *Ibidem*.
176. In the process Hart dismisses both consent and the principle *pacta sunt servanda* as the basic norm of international law. The former is repudiated on the ground that "It has never been doubted that when a new, independent state emerges into existence ... it is bound by the general obligations of international law ...", *ibidem*, p. 221. The latter is said to have been abandoned "since it seems incompatible with the fact that not all obligations under international law arise from 'pacta', however widely that term is construed", *ibidem*, p. 228. As we will try to make clear in the following both arguments would seem to be untenable, see *infra* pp. 75-81.
177. *Ibidem*, p. 210.
178. *Ibidem*, p. 209.

ern municipal law".[179]

It is equally difficult to understand how Hart can conclude that "in this analogy of content, no other social rules are so close to municipal law as those of international law"[180] after having asserted in his explanation of rules of recognition that "It is plain that only a small community closely knit by ties of kinship, common sentiment, and belief, and placed in a stable environment, could live successfully by such a regime of unofficial rules [that is a legal regime characterized *inter alia* by the absence of rules of recognition; v.H.]."[181] Many different views are conceivable and are in fact held concerning the structure of the international society, but the present author has never seen it described as a small community closely knit by ties of kinship, common sentiment, and belief, and placed in a stable environment.

Undoubtedly, the special characteristics of the international society, which can be summarily described as its low degree of organization, are of the utmost importance to, and even should permeate, any analysis of international law. But it in no way necessitates the foregone conclusion that no rule of recognition can be found in international law. As soon as it comes to international law, Hart's approach would seem to become much more restrictive. He then implies that a rule of recognition requires the existence of a legislature. His own general theory, on the other hand, is framed more broadly. As will be remembered, a rule of recognition was said to be a rule specifying some feature or features possession of which by a suggested rule is taken as conclusive affirmative indication that it is a rule of the group to be supported by the social pressure it exerts. Moreover, Hart repeatedly stresses that a rule of recognition can take various forms ranging from very simple to extremely complex and, most importantly, that it may be concealed, and, therefore, sometimes cannot be detected at the first glance. All this would seem to be sufficient reason to justify a thorough search for rules of recognition, rather than jumping to conclusions on the basis of a cursory look at

179. *Ibidem*, p. 222 (emphasis added); see in this respect C. Parry who, after observing that because of the lack of legislative institutions international law is often patronizingly described as a primitive system, adds "But it is not to be assumed without enquiry that this verdict is correct, or that the international community requires legislative institutions", *op.cit.* (note 22), p. 8.
180. H. Hart, *op.cit.* (note 41), p. 231.
181. *Ibidem*, pp. 89-90.

one characteristic of a certain social structure.[182] As Hart makes abundantly clear in his discussion of the English constitutional formula "Whatever the Queen in Parliament enacts is law",[183] such a search has to consist of an analysis of the relevant practice.[184]

We will undertake such an analysis in the subsequent sections. Before embarking upon it, a preliminary question has to be dealt with. It concerns the terminological confusion which surrounds the "sources" of international law. It was already indicated that the discussion of the sources is hampered by the different meanings which are attached to that word. An analysis of the sources of international law, therefore, has to be preceded by a clarification of the terms used.

182. A. D'Amato, *The Concept of Custom in International Law* (Ithaca/London 1971), avowedly bases himself upon Hart's distinction between primary and secondary rules. D'Amato, however, adds a special flavour to it by starting from the premise "that the content of the rules of international law depends upon the consensus of nation-state officials", as understood in his own specific manner, *ibidem*, p. 33; and see also A. D'Amato, "On Consensus", VII *CYIL* (1970), pp. 104-122. Subsequently, he maintains that "international consensus as to secondary rules ... can be found in the method of argumentation in international claim conflict situations", *ibidem*, p. 42. On this basis he concludes that custom is "perhaps the most important secondary rule in international law", *ibidem*, p. 44. For the remainder, however, D'Amato's application of Hart's model to international law remains rather vague: "One example of a secondary rule has just been mentioned: a rule found in the majority opinion of a World Court Judgment. ... Another example ... is the possibility that a 'general principle of law' ... is also a universal international rule. Another possibility is that the 'teachings of the most highly qualified publicists of the various nations', ... can be a way of determining primary rules of international law. In some respects, General Assembly resolutions may be acquiring the status of secondary rules in current international practice", *ibidem*, pp. 43-44. R. Walden, "Customary International Law: A Jurisprudential Analysis", XIII *ILR* (1978), pp. 86-102, too, takes Hart's theory as a point of departure, but emphasizes rather what Hart calls "the internal aspect of rules".
183. H. Hart, *op.cit.* (note 41), pp. 144-150.
184. In discussing the question whether international law is a consensual system Hart advocates that "Only a dispassionate survey of the actual practice of states can show whether this view is correct or not", *ibidem*, p. 220.

CHAPTER V

CONCEPT OF SOURCES

5.1. The preliminary question of terminology

In the foregoing the term "source" or "sources" was quite indiscriminately used to designate a number of different, albeit closely related, phenomena. In discussing the *Normative Concept of Law* and the various basic approaches in legal theory it was not felt necessary to probe deeper into the phrase "source or sources of international law", because, in general, its connotations are sufficiently clear. An analysis of the sources of international law themselves, however, requires that the various meanings of the term "source" are more thoroughly grasped.

Reference was made already to the confusion surrounding the concept of sources.[185] This confusion is by no means new. Writing in 1925 Corbett already noticed a "fluctuation in terms" in this respect.[186] According to Corbett, "the word 'source' had such a history of confusion behind it that it might well be abandoned".[187] In the meantime, little improvement has been achieved in this respect. More recently, D'Amato has proposed that "because of the confusions resulting from its use, the term 'evidence', along with the term 'sources' is best relegated to the domain of counterproductive terminology",[188] and Bos, too, has concluded to the inadequacy of the term "source".[189] Consequently, the writers cited and others, who have addressed these terminological matters, have forwarded proposals to replace the word "sources" by some other term or terms.[190] It would seem doubtful, however, whether this is a very fruitful course to take. It is probably quite difficult to erase the term "source" from legal language, where it has made its way for a long time. Generations of lawyers have

---

185. See *supra* pp. 13-16.
186. P. Corbett, "The Consent of States and the Sources of the Law of Nations", VI *BYIL* (1925), pp. 20-30 (20). The caution he expressed for the dangers involved in this "fluctuation in terms" are still noteworthy today: "Agreement upon fixed and uniform terms in the statement of the general principles with which the science of international law begins is eminently desirable as being a condition of didactic clearness. ... The movement towards general codification is gathering force, and is it not quite conceivable that the wide-spread confusion in relation to the various ideas connoted by the word 'source' may manifest itself in an equal uncertainty as to what are the substantive rules to be codified?", *ibidem*, p. 21.
187. *Ibidem*, p. 30.
188. A. D'Amato, *op.cit.* (note 182), p. 268.
189. M. Bos, *loc.cit.* (note 28), p. 15.
190. See Corbett, who introduced the terms "cause", "basis", "source" (in the sense of "origin") and "evidence" to designate the various meanings of "source", *loc.cit.* (note 186), pp. 29-30. Bos discerns five different meanings of "source" and suggests to replace the term by "recognized manifestations", *loc.cit.* (note 28), pp. 15-20.

been accustomed to it and apparently experienced no insurmountable difficulties in employing it as a term of art. Nevertheless, it is important to be aware of the various meanings the term can have.

The classic distinction with respect to the sources is that between formal and material sources. But even with respect to this fundamental distinction terminology is far from uniform. According to Parry, who relies on Salmond, formal sources are those imparting to a given rule the force of law, while material sources consist of those from which the substance of the law is drawn.[191] In Brownlie's treatise on international law, on the other hand, the material sources are described as those which provide evidence of the existence of rules which, when proved, have the status of legally binding rules of general application.[192] In particular the term material sources, therefore, causes difficulties. In Parry's view this type of sources clearly has a link with, or refers to, the substantive content of a rule, whereas Brownlie, despite the use of the adjective "material", has a different kind of sources in mind. To him material sources provide evidence of the existence of a rule, irrespective of its substantive content.

The distinction may be clarified on the basis of the notion of the "Völkerrechtsverfassung" (constitution of the international society) introduced by Verdross.[193] It is true that the use of the term "constitution" with respect to international law carries the danger of creating confusion by putting international law at par with national legal systems. It was already pointed out that, generally speaking, this is an adverse comparison.[194] It is clear that the international society does not possess a constitution in the sense most national societies do.[195] Nevertheless, constitutional traits or elements can be discerned in international law too. At any rate, the notion of an "international constitution" might serve to explain the distinction between formal and material sources.

A prototype of constitution, as may be encountered in most national legal systems, contains broadly speaking two types of provisions. On the one hand there are provisions outlining the legal/organizational structure of the society in question. The other type of provisions lay down the fundamental political orientation in the form of basic values or ideas which the society wants to uphold or attain. The term "material" could more properly be reserved for this latter type of provisions, while the former could be called "formal" or "procedural".[196] The same distinction between "material" and "procedural" provisions can be made with respect to the "constitutional" traits or elements of international law. It is with the procedural provisions that the following analysis is primarily con-

191. C. Parry, op.cit.(note 22), p. 1. See also the terminology used by G. Fitzmaurice, loc.cit.(note 28), pp. 153-154.
192. I. Brownlie, Principles of Public International Law, 3rd edition (Oxford 1979), p. 1.
193. See A. Verdross, Die Einheit des rechtlichen Weltbildes auf der Grundlage der Völkerrechtsverfassung (Tübingen 1923); and Die Verfassung der Völkerrechtsgemeinschaft (Wien/Berlin 1926).
194. One can, therefore, subscribe to Brownlie's warning that "In the context of international relations the use of the term 'formal source' is awkward and misleading since the reader is put in mind of the constitutional machinery of law-making which exists within states" (emphasis added), op.cit. (note 192), p. 1.
195. See also G. Arangio-Ruiz, The UN Declaration on Friendly Relations and the System of Sources of International Law (Alphen aan den Rijn 1979), pp. 279-280.
196. In the same vein H. Mosler, "Völkerrecht als Rechtsordnung", 36 ZaörV (1976), pp. 6-49 (31); for a comparable distinction between "procedural" and "substantive" rules from a political scientist's point of view see J. de Vree, loc.cit. (note 8), pp. 16-18.

cerned.[197] As was made clear in the foregoing, we will focus particularly on those procedural provisions which Verdross has characterized as follows: "Zu den *notwendigen* Normen des Verfassungsrechts gehören vor allem ... jene, die bestimmen, in welchem Verfahren diese Normen [*i.e.* norms of international law; v.H.] gebildet werden können .....".[198] In other words, the "procedural" provisions include, first of all, those which relate to the question of the sources of international law.[199]

With respect to these so-called procedural provisions relating to the sources of international law we will discern three levels of analysis, thereby closely following the lines mapped out in Corbett's above-mentioned study.[200] At the first level the term "source", used in the singular, is designed to indicate *the basis of the binding force of international law*. It is the "source" in the sense of Kelsen's basic norm or *Grundnorm*, which, in the case of international law he claimed to be the rule that States ought to behave as they have customarily behaved.[201] When Corbett has in mind the basis of the binding force of international law, he speaks of the *cause* defined as "the desire of states to have the mutual relations which their social nature renders indispensable regulated with the greatest possible rationality and uniformity".[202] This first level or meaning of the term "source" is the most abstract and probably also the most controversial.[203]

At the second level we mean source in the sense of *constitutive element for rules of international law*.[204] By this we mean source in the form of a criterion by which one can decide whether or not a rule is in fact a rule of international law.[205] In Corbett's fourfold division this second level is described as "The basis of international law as a system and of the rules of which it is composed" which according to him is "the consent of states".[206]

Finally, at the third level there are the sources as meaning *the relevant manifestations on the basis of which the presence or absence of the constitutive element can be established*. As was noted, in Brownlie's conception these would be called material sources,[207] while Corbett refers to "The records or evidence of

197. We will get back to the "material" aspects of international "constitutional" law when the issue of *jus cogens* is discussed; see *infra* pp. 148-151.
198. A. Verdross, *op.cit.* (note 98), p. 21.
199. According to Verdross, *ibidem*, p. 11, the basis of the confusion over the sources of international law is to be found above all in the fact "dass die alte Unterscheidung zwischen formellen und materiellen Rechtsquellen vergessen wurde".
200. See *supra* (note 186); Parry has characterized Corbett's scheme as "golden rules", *op.cit.* (note 22), p. 2.
201. See *supra* p. 37.
202. P. Corbett, *loc.cit.* (note 186), pp. 29-30.
203. The controversy is quite ardent between protagonists and antagonists of legal idealist theories, see *supra* pp. 30-34. It is important to note that the first level or meaning of "source" is classified here as a "procedural" provision. Particularly from the perspective of a legal idealist approach this might seem paradoxical; for the latter deduces the binding force of international law from ideas or values with a substantive content, or in the terminology employed here, from "material" provisions. As will be argued below, the binding force of international law, in the present author's view, cannot be based upon some substantive material idea or value and, therefore, has to be confined to a "procedural" provision.
204. Compare in this respect the term "constitutive requirements for the making of treaty law and customary law" used by H. Meijers, "How is international law made? - The stages of growth of international law and the use of its customary rules", IX *NYIL* (1978), pp. 3-26 (3).
205. See *supra* pp. 47-49.
206. P. Corbett, *loc.cit.* (note 186), p. 30.
207. See *supra* p. 58.

international law are documents or acts proving the consent of states to its rules".[208] This third level, which is closely related to the second, is typical for international law. In developed national legal systems the third level of sources is constituted by formalized legislative procedures. In international law, where the subjects themselves act as the "legislator", there do not always exist similar procedures.[209] Consequently, the question whether a rule is indeed a rule of international law has to be answered on the basis of less formal and structured phenomena, which are termed here *manifestations of the constitutive element.*

As was just observed, it is the notion of sources in the second sense of "constitutive element" which comes closest to Hart's idea of a rule of recognition. His definition of that concept and, in fact, the way in which he deals with it throughout his book leave little room for doubt as to this question. On the other hand, Hart does not make a subdivision with respect to what we have termed "procedural constitutional provisions", but discusses the latter as a whole, and there are no indications that he intended the first and third meaning to be excluded. Occasionally, one finds references to the first level.[210] Hart does not mention the third level separately. This should be no surprise, if it is remembered that developed systems of municipal law possess formalized legislative procedures. Consequently, the phenomena making up the third level can so easily be traced, that it is hardly worthwhile to deal with them as a separate category. Obviously, there are many references to the legislative mechanisms of municipal legal systems in Hart's book.

At any rate the three levels which we have discerned are obviously closely intertwined. Moreover, all three are subject to the requirements which in our view must be satisfied by a viable theory of the sources of international law.[211] While the following sections will focus, as a result of the point of departure of the present study,[212] on the sources in the second and third sense, something will have to be said about the basis of the binding force of international law as well.

208. P. Corbett, *loc.cit.* (note 186), p. 19; Bos starts from a more elastic conception when he defines his recognized manifestations as "the phenomena which in a given legal order one is allowed to invoke in order to legitimize a reasoning alleged to be a legal one", *loc.cit.* (note 28), p. 19. It will not be gone unnoticed that in discerning three levels for analyzing the sources we have passed over one of Corbett's four distinctions, that is the third one: "The origins of the rules of international law ... are the opinions, decisions or acts constituting the starting-point from which their more or less gradual establishment can be traced", *loc.cit.* (note 186), p. 30. In our view, however, the origins as defined here relate to the substantive content of rules of international law rather than to their procedural or formal aspects. They seem to belong to the material sources as defined by Parry, see *supra* p. 58.

209. See also G. Arangio-Ruiz, *op.cit.* (note 195), p. 290, according to whom there is in international law no legislation in the proper sense of that term which designates "the creation of norms of a binding character enacted by an organ deliberately in order to regulate mainly, although not exclusively, the conduct of persons other than those concurring, as members of the organ, in the making of the norm". Particularly, the latter aspect of legislation makes it clear that the term is confusing with respect to international law and that, therefore, terms like "law-making" or "law-creation" are to be preferred. Compare H. Thirlway, *International Customary Law and Codification* (Leiden 1972), p. 78.

210. A clear reference to source in the first sense is contained in Hart's words that "Kelsen and many modern theorists insist that, like municipal law, international law possesses and indeed must possess a 'basic norm', *or what we have termed a rule of recognition ...*" (emphasis added), *op.cit.* (note 41), p. 228.

211. See *supra* pp. 44-45.

212. See *supra* pp. 7-8.

5.2. Introduction

In chapter III we concluded that a sound approach to the sources of international law has to fulfil two requirements, *viz.* the highest possible degree of certainty and clarity and sufficient attention for the link between law and relations in society.[213] The three levels or meanings of sources which were discerned in the preceding section are all subject to these two requirements, although not each of them to exactly the same extent. Depending on the particular level under discussion, emphasis may be more on one or the other requirement.

The link between law and societal relations is particularly relevant for the sources in the sense of the basis of the binding force of international law and the constitutive element of rules of international law. From the concept of law as the mirror of society in which it has to function, as set forth above,[214] it follows that sources in the first and second sense have to reflect closely relations in society. In fact, as far as these first two levels are concerned, the sources are particularly determined by the fundamental characteristics of the society concerned. Therefore, the following section will provide an outline of the fundamental characteristics of the international society in the form of a description of its basic features. As will be shown, these basic features of international society prove to be quite immanent, or have, at least, remained largely unaltered for a long time up to the present moment.

At the same time attention will have to be paid to the changes that have taken place in international relations and some of the ensuing consequences for international law. For, it cannot be denied that international society has changed quite considerably, particularly in this century. These changes have had a far-reaching impact, despite the fact that they have, in our view, occurred on the "surface" and have approximately left unaffected the basic features of international society. They concern rather, what will be called, the structure of international relations. This structure has a strong influence upon the sources in the third sense of manifestations of the constitutive element of rules of international law. As will be argued in detail below, this influence is evidenced by the relation between the changes in the structure of international society and the changes in custom, treaty and general principles, which are sources in the third sense and, therefore, manifestations. The manifestations or sources in the third sense in fact constitute what was described above as the narrowing and formalization of the broad and diffuse process of international law-making into a more technical procedure.[215] Consequently, it is particularly at this third level that the requirements of certainty and clarity of the sources come into play.

5.3. Basic features of the international society

The major characteristics of the international society, which will be briefly outlined here, are on the whole well-known and sometimes even considered plain. Hardly any scholar in international law fails to point to the fact that the interna-

213. See *supra* pp. 44-45.
214. See *supra* pp. 20-21.
215. See *supra* pp. 26-27.

tional society lacks a legislature, courts with compulsory jurisdiction, and centrally organized sanctions.[216] Nevertheless, a short recapitulation seems justified particularly because no agreement exists on the consequences resulting from these basic features of international society for the sources of international law.

Basically speaking, three main characteristics of international society condition international law. First of all, the fact that a number of States are bound to co-exist. The most important characteristic of States, as entities for human co-existence organized on a territorial basis, is that they are independent, that is they are not subject to any higher authority. Secondly, there is the fact that interaction takes place between the various States belonging to the international system. As soon as this interaction, or simply the relations between the States, transcends a certain level of both frequency and intensity, a necessity arises to regulate these relations on a more or less permanent basis. Closely linked to this second factor is the third factor which consists of the recognition or perception on the part of the States of the necessity to regulate their mutual relations. It is in particular this third, psychological, factor which makes it possible to conceive of international law.[217]

As to the first feature, it was already observed that the position of States in the international society is first of all characterized by independence: no higher authority is superimposed upon the States. This idea has since long found expression in the form of the fundamental principle of "state sovereignty", which in modern international law has more fittingly been renamed the principle of "sovereign equality". In this context, sovereignty is looked at, not as a principle of international law, but rather as a basic feature of the international society in the sense that it is a precondition for the existence of international law in its present form.

In the latter sense sovereignty has a number of consequences. First, when viewed from the perspective of the States as a group, it implies that the States are for all practical purposes the decisive factors in international law. Because of the low degree of organization of the international society they face no competition from any other kind of entity. Consequently, States find themselves in a position which differs markedly from that of the subjects of most national legal systems. The latter are confronted with some kind of legislature empowered to enact binding rules without the consent of individual subjects being required. Moreover, in the case of a dispute with a fellow citizen or with the organized community in the form of the State itself, they are subject to the compulsory jurisdiction of courts of law. Finally, the binding rules are applied to them and, if necessary, enforced against the subject's will by the executive branch of the government. On the international plane the situation is more or less the opposite. The States

216. For a lucid description, see M. Bos, *loc.cit.* (note 49); see also P. Weil, "Vers une normativité relative en droit international?", 86 *RGDIP* (1982), pp. 6-47 (13-17).
217. A somewhat similar opinion is expressed by H. Mosler, when he says that an international legal order presupposes: "Die Tatsache, dass eine gewisse Anzahl von selbständigen, organisierten Verbänden auf territorialer Basis nebeneinander besteht, und ein psychologisches Element, nämlich die allgemeine Überzeugung, dass diese Einheiten untereinander durch gleicherweise geltende, auf alle anwendbaren Regeln gebunden sind, welche Rechten gewähren, Verpflichtungen auferlegen und Kompetenzen zuweisen", *loc.cit.* (note 196), p. 16; see in the same vein H. Strebel, "Quellen des Völkerrechts als Rechtsordnung", 36 *Zaörv* (1976), pp. 301-346 (335).

act as their own "legislator"; if it comes to the peaceful settlement of disputes, they more often than not are *"iudex in sua causa"*; the application of rules of international law lies in the States' own hands and because of the lack of organized international sanctions they as a rule also have to enforce international law themselves.

Undoubtedly, the state of affairs just pictured is too black and white and needs some corrective shading in a number of respects. Particularly recent decades have witnessed important changes in the structure of international relations, which will be discussed in some detail below.[218] At this place it is not necessary to go further than noting that other entities have come within the purview of international law. It is true that international organizations and even private persons and organizations have come to play a more important role, not only as subjects of international law, but also in its creation and implementation. In any case, however, this has not basically altered the primary position of States. For, it should be remembered that, in the final analysis, international organizations as well as private entities depend for their position under international law on the States. Individuals and private organizations are subjects of international law to the extent only provided for by States in rules of international law. Their contribution to the creation and implementation of international law, moreover, is always indirect in the sense it needs to be "finalized" in one way or another by state-action. Therefore, the often heard criticism, particularly from adherents to the Policy Oriented approach, that focusing on the States in investigating international law leads to a distortion of reality,[219] would seem to miss the point. As was already observed, it is very relevant for a proper understanding of international law to take cognizance of the multifarious actions, interests and values of the many participants in the international arena.[220] But if one wants to know whether a rule is a rule of international law, it is what States say and do that really matters.[221]

More or less the same goes for international organizations. It cannot be denied that international organizations have added a new dimension to international law.[222] The most eye-catching novelty is the (supranational) power, exceptionally granted to international organizations, to make decisions which are binding upon member States even if they do not consent to them. Nevertheless, most organizations are inter-governmental instead of supranational and, consequently, do not represent radical innovations.[223] When all is said and

---

218. See *infra* pp. 65-71.
219. See for instance M. Rogoff, *loc.cit.* (note 132), pp. 8-10.
220. See *supra* pp. 43-44.
221. C. Parry expresses the same opinion in the following words: "Not only are states the normal members of the international community but the whole theory of the law of that community, and of modern innovations in it no less, is constructed upon the basis of that fact. States are thus not only subjects of the law but they are objects as well: their territory is themselves. Equally, while it is to them the law is given, they are the lawgivers", *op.cit.* (note 22), p. 8.
222. See *infra* pp. 210-212.
223. The two best known examples of supranational developments are the powers of the United Nations' Security Council to take binding decisions in peace and security matters and the powers of EEC organs *vis-à-vis* Member States. Due to the particular political constellation in the Security Council its supranational powers have largely remained a dead letter. As far as the EEC is concerned, the practice of its organs shows, at least in comparison to their formal powers granted, a return to inter-governmentalism rather than progress on the road towards supranationalism.

done, international organizations today still constitute mainly a continuation of the traditional system, albeit it by different means. They are frameworks for cooperation *between* States and not some kind of an order *above* States. As a rule their organs are composed of representatives of national governments and cannot make decisions which are binding upon a State against its will. Moreover, States are free in most cases to withdraw from the organizations at will. In most important respects, therefore, the independence of States has remained largely unaltered.[224] And although a change in this situation is conceivable from the point of view of theory, there are no indications to make such a change likely to occur in the near future.[225]

A second consequence of the independence of States as a basic feature of the international society concerns the relations between the States *inter se*. With respect to this aspect, sovereignty implies that, at least formally, a State is neither superior nor inferior *vis-à-vis* another State. As far as international law is concerned, all States are considered equal. Obviously, there are between the various States considerable differences of fact, such as for instance regarding the size of their territory and their population, their military and economic power, and their cultural and historical background. These and other dissimilarities result of course in an unequal influence of States in the various fields of international relations. Similarly, they do not fail to make their impact felt in international law, too, including the process of making international law, as we will try to point out later.[226] The equality of States set forth by international law is, therefore, highly formal.

All this does not detract from the fact that in the final analysis, particularly with respect to the creation of international law, the independence of States *vis-à-vis* each other or the sovereign equality among States constitutes the point of departure.[227] Moreover, as will be pointed out in the following section, the changes in the structure of international relations have strengthened this equality in the direction of substantive equality in that they have enhanced the position of the smaller States.[228]

The second basic feature of international society was said to consist of the interaction taking place between the States. It might seem superfluous to mention this as a separate feature or element. It is true that state-interaction has to transcend a certain level before a need arises for the regulation of mutual rel-

224. See also H. Mosler, who holds that "Solange die selbständigen Staaten das Rückgrat dieser Rechtsordnung bilden und solange die Organisationen, die sie selbst geschaffen haben, sie nicht derart überwuchern, dass sie in wesentlichen Fragen ihrer Existenz von ihnen abhängen, solange wird Völkerrecht bestehen", *loc.cit.* (note 196), p. 21.
225. H. Hart, however, upholds that the lack of a legislature in international law "is just a lack which many think of as a defect one day to be repaired", *op.cit.* (note 41), p. 225; see on the other hand the words of G. Fitzmaurice quoted above p. 23.
226. See *infra* pp. 160 and 162.
227. See conform R. Bernhardt, "Ungeschriebenes Völkerrecht", 30 *Zaörv* (1976), pp. 50-76 (55): "In der Tat ist die rechtliche Gleichheit der Staaten trotz aller tatsächlichen Unterschied für die gegenwärtige Völkerrechtsordnung grundlegend".
228. See L. Henkin's observation that "In our day, 'power' (*i.e.* influence both in law-making and elsewhere in international relations) belongs also to small developing states, joined in blocs, adroit at exploiting the competition of the powerful, and armed with ideas claiming their time has come", *How Nations Behave; Law and Foreign Policy*, 2nd edition (New York 1979), p. 34.

ations on a permanent basis, *i.e.* for a system of law. Nobody doubts, however, that international society has long since passed this stage.[229] The reason for introducing the interaction between States as a separate element is that it reminds us of the fact, that the frequency and intensity of this interaction remains relevant even after the level where law becomes a necessity for the first time has been passed. For, variations in the frequency and intensity of relations in society find their reflection in the law. If relations in society increase and get more penetrating, the law requires adaptation.

Thirdly, we have discerned the recognition of the necessity contained in the second basic feature. This psychological factor of recognizing the need to regulate relations in society is a key element in the notion of law. As will be argued later, rules of law are indeed those rules which are recognized as being necessary for the maintenance of society or an important aspect of the life in society, and consequently are to be obeyed. It is important to keep the third feature apart from the second. For law to come into existence, it does not suffice that there is an "objective" need to systematically regulate relations. What is required in addition, is the "subjective" recognition of this factor on the part of the members of society. At the same time this makes clear that there can be a gap between the "objective" need on the one hand, and the "subjective" recognition of it on the other. There might be a gap, in other words, between what would seem to be exigent in view of the facts and what is feasible given the political will in society.[230]

Theoretically, in the worst possible case the continuation of such a gap can have fatal results for life in society or might even lead to its disruption. In the practice of international relations the divergence between the "objective" necessity and the extent to which this is "subjectively" recognized often manifests itself in that rules of international law turn out to be inadequate to provide satisfactory solutions for the problems States encounter in their mutual relations. This is, at least partly, due to the fact that the political will of the States does not go so far as to coincide with the "objective" requirements of the factual situation.

5.4. The changes in the structure of international relations

Although, as was pointed out, the basic features of the international society have largely remained the same, it is equally true that a cursory look at present-day international relations reveals that these have undergone far-reaching changes in the present century. These changes have had and still have a substantial impact on international law in general, and on its sources in the sense of

229. At best there is arguing as to what was the period in history when states literally existed next to each other, that is when they were more or less self-sufficient in the sense that mutual relations could be dealt with on an *ad hoc* basis instead of the more structural form of rules of law. See, for instance, M. Steinert and H. Kapur, "New Configurations of Power in International Relations", in: *Les relations internationales dans un monde en mutation,* Institut universitaire de hautes études internationales (Genève/Leiden 1977), pp. 123-161 (124).
230. At another place we have described this distinction as that between factual and psychological interdependence. See G. van Hoof and K. de Vey Mestdagh, "Mechanisms of International Supervision", in: P. van Dijk (ed.), *Supervision within International Economic Organizations: The NIEO Perspective,* to be published in 1983 by Kluwer, Deventer.

manifestations in particular. Like in the case of the basic features described above, the developments which are meant here are very well documented in international legal writing. It suffices, therefore, to confine this description to sketching some brief outlines.[231]

Basically, the changes which have occurred in international relations can be divided into two main developments: the first one can be summarily described by the key-word interdependence, the second one by heterogeneity. Although both of them have occurred more or less simultaneously and are to some extent even intertwined, their distinctive features nevertheless warrant separate discussion.

The first trend, which has resulted in what is nowadays usually labeled as interdependence, is caused by scientific and technological developments which have been the main vehicles of change in the present century. Science and technology have been going through revolutionary stages and very few fields of human activity have been left untouched. It is far beyond the scope of the present study to provide even a summary indication of the fields concerned. However, all that is needed to become aware of the real proportions of the transformations that have taken place is a superficial comparison between the situation prevailing before the First World War and the present-day situation in such fields as for instance armament, energy, transport, telecommunication, trade and economic activities in general. From our perspective, one of the most eye-catching aspects of these changes is the "internationalization" or "globalization" of human activities and relations.

As a result the intercourse between States has also dramatically changed. In the traditional system they were comparatively limited, incidental, and of a quite simple nature. Today, international relations have first of all become much more all-embracing. The scope of state-intercourse has grown considerably. Due to the scientific and technological revolution a far greater number of issues and problems has become the subject of international relations; the number of issues and problems with which States can cope all by themselves is shrinking constantly. All this, therefore, can be called the "horizontal" expansion of international relations.

In addition, a "vertical" expansion has taken place. Not only has the scope of international relations been broadened, at the same time they have gained speed and intensity. Interaction between States has become both more frequent and more penetrating. Dealing with or solving the issues and problems which States nowadays encounter requires them to meet more often and to take a more in depth approach towards the aspects involved.

The developments just referred to are very often described by the words "increased and increasing interdependence". Increased and increasing interdependence should be taken to mean here simply the fact that States, and for that matter private persons too,[232] have become and still are becoming more

---

231. Of the voluminous literature on the subject the following pioneering studies were taken as a point of departure: B. Röling, *International Law in an Expanded World* (Amsterdam 1960); W. Friedmann, *The Changing Structure of International Law* (London 1964), and "General Course in Public International Law", 127 *RCADI* (1969-II), pp. 41-246; and W. Jenks, *The Common Law of Mankind* (London 1958), and *A New World of Law* (London 1969).
232. For an analysis of international interdependence in terms of international transactions and their political and theoretical implications, with a great number of references to other studies on interdependence, see P. Katzenstein, "International interdependence: some long-term

dependent upon each other in an increasing number of respects. Dependence and interdependence should not be construed as antitheses, but are indeed closely intertwined.[233] Interdependence, therefore, does not at all imply some kind of equilibrium in the relationships between the various partners. Some may be stronger than others and, consequently, less dependent upon those others than *vice versa*. It needs no explaining that the latter situation prevails in cases of interaction between States or groups of States. This, however, does not detract from the fact that as a result of the increased and increasing interdependence even for the strongest States the capability to manage their affairs on their own has greatly diminished.

It goes without saying that this growing interdependence has not failed to make its impact felt on international law. International law too can be said to have expanded in both horizontal and vertical directions. Present-day international law encompasses far more aspects of inter-state relations than the traditional system. Its scope has been broadened and it covers considerably more ground than used to be the case. Scientific and technological advances not only added new fields, like for instance air and space law, they also brought more features of traditional areas like security and economic relations within the purview of international law.[234]

This latter aspect may be referred to as the "globalization" of international law.[235] At the same time, it has to be admitted, certain areas like security and economic relations tend to show a kind of "regionalization" in that specific matters pertaining to these areas are tackled within certain regions, or at least within a limited group of States. However, "globalization" and "regionalization" are parallel developments rather than mutually exclusive. In the present author's view it can, therefore, be maintained that the ambit of general international law has expanded and is still expanding.[236]

Now, "general international law" is an unfortunate term causing a great deal of confusion. Usually it is employed to refer to those rules of international law, which are (considered) binding for all States or at least an overwhelming majority of the States. As such it is contrasted with regional or local international law.

trends and recent changes", 29 *IO* (1975), pp. 1021-1034; and by the same author, "International relations and domestic structures: foreign economic policies of advanced industrial states", 30 *IO* (1976), pp. 1-45. See also The World Bank, *World Development Report 1981* (Washington D.C. 1981), pp. 18-19. See also M. McDougal, H. Lasswell and W. Reisman, *loc.cit.* (note 62), p. 190.

233. B. Cohen, *The Question of Imperialism: The Political Economy of Dominance and Dependence* (London 1974), p. 201, has very aptly described the link between the two concepts as "Dependence is simply the price for the benefit of a division of labour. Independence is possible only in isolation. Dependence follows automatically from participation in any system of interrelationships. It is the logical corollary of interdependence. This is true of the individual family as it is for the family of nations. All participants are dependent to a greater or lesser extent".

234. For a more detailed description of the horizontal expansion of international law, see *inter alia* W. Friedmann, *op.cit.* (note 231), pp. 152-187; W. Jenks, "The New Science and the Law of Nations", 17 *ICLQ* (1968), pp. 327-345; and W. Jenks, *op.cit.* (note 231), pp. 27-119.

235. In the same vein W. Levi, *op.cit.* (note 56), pp. 88-91.

236. Similarly, B. Buzan, "Negotiating by Consensus: Developments in Technique at the United Nations Conference on the Law of the Sea", 75 *AJIL* 1981), pp. 324-348 (327), opines: "Interdependence does not appear to be on the wane, and the burgeoning, scope, variety, speed and intensity of human activity on and off the planet can scarcely fail to generate new and pressing problems of a global nature".

The designation of a rule as belonging to "general international law" often carries the danger of taking for granted its binding character with respect to all States, without this being justified in all cases.[237] "General international law" will be used here in a different sense. It does not refer to the circle of States bound by a certain rule, but rather to the subject-matter the rule is designed to regulate.[238] Consequently, a rule of general international law is here used in the sense of a rule concerning a subject-matter in which the interests of all States or nearly all States are involved, without the implication being that all these States are actually bound by those rules. Rules, on the other hand, dealing with issues affecting the interests of a limited number of States, can be called rules of specific or special international law.[239] What is meant by the "globalization" of international law, therefore, is that many issues which used to be regulated by rules applicable to a restricted number of States are increasingly becoming the concern of the international community as a whole. This trend obviously has consequences for the international law-making process.[240]

In addition to this horizontal-quantitative expansion or change, a vertical-qualitative development has taken place. The function of traditional international law consisted mainly of the delimitation of powers between the various sovereign States. It was, therefore, a relatively simple body of law in the sense that with regard to many subject-matters it did not provide for substantive rules but confined itself to designating the competent State. This traditional "international law of co-existence" is, in the words of Friedmann, "a set of rules of abstention, of adjustment, and delimitation between different national sovereignties".[241] Modern international law, on the other hand, which he labels "international law of cooperation", is of an entirely different nature, characterized as it is by participation: "The expansion of international law from an essentially negative code of rules of abstention to positive rules of cooperation, however fragmentary and inadequate they may be in the present state of international politics, is an evolution of an immense significance for the principles and structure of international legal order.[242] In other words, international law has acquired a more "penetrating" character in that it has severely narrowed the freedom of ac-

237. See also *infra* pp. 96-97.
238. Some apply the two criteria at the same time; see for instance C. Rozakis, *The Concept of Jus Cogens in the Law of Treaties* (Amsterdam 1976), p. 55, who defines a norm of general international law as "a legal rule having a general applicability among the States of the international community", and who simultaneously upholds that the presumption is accepted "that a rule is part of general international law as long as its subject-matter deals with a question of general interest for the international community...", *ibidem*, p. 61.
239. In the same vein A. D'Amato, in discussing two kinds of custom, defines special customary law as dealing "with *non-generalizable topics* such as title or right in respect of portions of world real estate (...) or with rules expressly limited to countries of a certain region (...)" (emphasis added), *op.cit.* (note 182), p. 235. He does not, however, consistently use the scope of the rule as a criterion, but sometimes resorts again to the extent of bindingness of the rule; see for instance the phrase "General customary law applies to all States, while special custom *concerns relations between a smaller set of States*" (emphasis added), *ibidem*, p. 234, in which both criteria would seem to figure side by side.
240. See *infra* p. 71.
241. W. Friedmann, *loc.cit.* (note 231), p. 92; see also W. Levi, *op.cit.* (note 56), p. 45: "The basic change taking place is the attempt of international law to protect sovereignty through cooperation among States rather than through their separation".
242. W. Friedmann, *loc.cit.* (note 231), p. 93.

tion on the part of the States. Although it probably is an exaggeration to say that state sovereignty now consists only of "a residuum of discretionary power circumscribed by law",[243] it is undoubtedly true that today it cannot be exercised in the same absolute manner as used to be the case.

In international law this has been manifested mainly in a twofold manner. From the perspective of the State there has been an upward movement consisting of the rise and the steady growth of the phenomenon of international organizations, which have come to take their place in the international arena in both the various technical/functional and the more general political, economic, social, cultural and humanitarian fields. Even if they do not in most cases command supranational control over their member States, their functioning at the very least bears witness of the more limited room for manoeuvre left to the individual States in conducting their international relations.[244] In the downward direction the vertical expansion of international law is borne out by the continuous shrinking of areas which used to belong to the *domaine réservé* of States,[245] the most eye-catching example, at least from the perspective of traditional international law, probably being the enhanced position of the individual under international law, mainly in the form of the international protection of human rights. In short, the transformations in international law may be described as a development towards a greater "density" of that body of law: more areas are covered in a more detailed manner.

The second trend, which we referred to above as characterized by "heterogeneity", finds its roots in political developments rather than in scientific and technological developments. Nevertheless, the latter have contributed to it.[246] This second trend consists of the "population explosion" in the community of States[247] and the ensuing changes in the composition of the international society in quantitative as well as qualitative respect. Not only has the number of States more than tripled in about half a century, at the same time the world has grown from a comparatively homogeneous club of predominantly European and European-oriented States into a society where States individually or collectively have interests and views diametrically opposed to those of other States or groups of States.

As to the quantitative aspect, Röling wrote in 1960: "In the Conference of Berlin in 1885, at which Europe acted as legislator for the African world, 14 countries participated, all European with the exception of the United States. The First Peace Conference held in The Hague in 1899 united 27 countries (20 from Europe, the U.S. and Mexico from America, China, Japan, Persia and Siam from Asia); the Second Peace Conference of 1907 brought together 43 countries (21 European, 18 American and 4 Asian). The League of Nations of

---

243. W. Jenks, *Law in the World Community* (London 1973), p. 33.
244. See also *infra* pp. 210-212.
245. The much cited words, which the Permanent Court of International Justice spoke as early as 1923, have retained their significance up until today: "The question whether a certain question is or is not solely within the jurisdiction of a State is essentially a relative question; it depends upon the development of international relations", advisory opinion concerning the *Nationality Decrees in Tunis and Morocco*, Publ. PCIJ, Series B, No. 4 (1923), pp. 23-24.
246. Improved transportation and telecommunication facilities, for instance, have unquestionably fueled the political processes in many former colonies and therefore accelerated their decolonization.
247. L. Henkin, *op.cit.* (note 228), p. 99.

1919 membered between 42 and 63 members, the Pact of Paris (1928) was ratified by 63 countries. The United Nations began with 51 members (14 European, 22 American, 12 Afro-Asian and Australia, New Zealand and South-Africa) and now - October 1960 - has 98 members (27 European, 22 American, 46 Afro-Asian and Australia, New Zealand and South-Africa), while Asian and African countries are candidates for membership."[248] Today United Nations membership comprises approximately 170 States, the predominance of Afro-Asian States and of Third World countries in general being even more overwhelming.

Even more important than this numerical expansion of the international society are the qualitative changes which have occurred in the process. For, States have not only increased in number, at the same time they have grown more heterogeneous as a group. Until the First World War the world was undoubtedly eurocentric. It consisted almost exclusively of European States or at least States that had undergone a strong European influence. As a result there prevailed a comparative like-mindedness with no real challenges to the basic rules of the international game.

Since the end of the First World War this picture has drastically changed.[249] The first crack in the relative unity occurred when in 1917 the Bolshevik Revolution took place in Russia. Particularly from the point of view of international law this was more than just a change of government by force. The new regime rejected the most fundamental premises of international relations and started from an ideology diametrically opposed in almost all respects to that of the existing States. For a long time the Soviet Union has remained the only socialist State, but the socialist camp has grown after the Second World War anti-fascist alliance fell apart. For the time being the split would seem to be petrified into the now existing blocs of East and West, the main dividing line running across Europe. And although the socialist camp has modified its initial positions in various respects, East and West find themselves on opposite sides of many issues concerning international law.[250]

The afore-mentioned rise of the former colonies as new nations has initiated another qualitative change. Since the 1960's to the East-West-issue has been added the so-called North-South-issue. After the new nations had come to take their place in the international society, they, quite naturally, began to press their own interests which often differed from both those of the West and the East. Moreover, while the formal decolonization process has for all practical purposes been completed, the real emancipation of the new nations would seem to have only just started. The Third World campaign has affected almost all aspects of the international relations. In the general political field highlights have been the constitution of the so-called policy of Non-Alignment initiated by Egypt, India and Yougoslavia in 1956 and its further elaboration afterwards.[251]

248. B. Röling, *op.cit.* (note 231), p. 5.
249. J. Joll, "The Decline of Europe: 1920-1970", *IA* (special edition, November 1970), pp. 1-18.
250. A fairly complete picture of the points of disagreement (and also of those of agreement) between East and West can be gathered from the negotiations leading to the 1975 Helsinki Final Act; see in particular L. Ferraris, *op.cit.* (note 4).
251. G. Jensen, *Non-Alignment and the Afro-Asian States* (New York 1960), and T. Subba Rao, *Non-Alignment in International Law and Politics* (New Delhi 1981).

Emphasis of the Third World movement has been mainly on economic issues. The developing countries established the so-called "Group of 77", now comprising some 120 States, and held *inter alia* a number of meetings within the framework of the United Nations Conference on Trade and Development, in Geneva in 1964, in New Delhi in 1968, in Santiago in 1972, in Nairobi in 1976 and in Manilla in 1979. Since the seventies the already extensive agenda on developmental issues set by UNCTAD has been broadened in to what is called nowadays the discussion on a New International Economic Order. Through this concept of a NIEO, which is embodied in a number of important General Assembly resolutions, the developing countries in fact call for a structural reform of the international economic system.[252]

In summary, one usually discerns nowadays at least three, or even four "worlds", the fourth consisting of the poorest developing nations. This is of course an oversimplification, because States belonging to one of these "worlds" often have diverging interests and views among themselves and other divisions of the States of the world could be made along different lines. Nevertheless, the "three or four world" image has at least the merit of making perfectly clear that the relatively homogeneous international society, in which traditional international law came into being, is definitely gone. Modern international law has to operate in far more difficult circumstances. One of the consequences is that the international law-making process has become far more cumbersome. As a result of the two tendencies mentioned, we are faced now with a quite paradoxical situation. On the one hand, because of the increased and still increasing interdependence, there has never been a greater need for elaborate rules of international law in so many fields as at present. On the other hand, the heterogeneous character of the international community at the same time has made it more difficult than ever before to attain agreement between States on the content of such rules.[253]

5.5. The basis of the binding force of international law

As was explained in the introductory chapter the source in the first sense, that is the basis of the binding force of international law, does not constitute the main focus of the present study.[254] However, some observations will have to be made

252. For a general survey of the developments in international economic relations, see the Report of the Independent Commission on International Development Issues under the Chairmanship of Willy Brandt, *North-South: A Program For Survival* (Cambridge, Mass. 1980); for more details see P. VerLoren van Themaat, *The Changing Structure of International Economic Law* (The Hague 1981), and the literature discussed at pp. 293-306. On the effect with respect to the international process, see, N. Lateef, "Parliamentary Diplomacy and the North-South Dialogue", 11 *GJICL* (1981), pp. 1-44.

253. See in this respect also P. Szasz, "Improving the International Legislative Process", 9 *GJICL* (1979), pp. 519-533 (524), who stresses the same point from a somewhat different angle: "That some coordination would be valuable is suggested by several considerations. One is the desirability of creating as coherent a body of international law as possible, avoiding both gaps and overlaps between instruments relevant to the same field. Another is the need to assure at least some efficiency and rationality for the process, since the need for international law is great and increasing as the number of States grows and the world becomes more interdependent". For an enumeration of fields of international law which have become controversial as a result of the changes in international society, see G. Fitzmaurice, *loc.cit.* (note 50), p. 215.

254. See *supra* pp. 6-8.

on it in order to be able to place the sources in the second and third sense, which will be dealt with in the following sections, in a proper perspective. It is clear from what has been observed with respect to the various approaches to the sources that it is difficult to come up with one ultimate source or *Grundnorm* which is generally accepted or acceptable.[255] The divergent world outlooks that States hold do not permit the conclusion that one material basis exists from which all rules of international law could derive their binding force. At the same time, however, the distinction between material and procedural provisions of a constitution[256] makes it clear that this is not the same thing as saying that no basis for the binding force of international law could be found. Lack of agreement with regard to the material elements does not necessarily imply a similar disunity on the procedural aspects.

Mosler's observations would seem to amount to the same thing, when in dealing with the question of the binding force of law, he argues: "Eine philosophische Antwort auf diese Frage wird niemals in der Weise gegeben worden können, dass sie von allen Beteiligten akzeptiert wird. Sie wird notwendigerweise immer ein spekulatives Moment haben das von demjenigen, der von der vorgetragenen Lösung nicht überzeugt ist, als subjektive Gewissheit des anderen zur Kenntnis genommen oder abgelehnt wird. Da Religionen, Ideologien und philosphische Doktrinen über den Ursprung und das Wesen des Rechts verschieden urteilen und niemals Einigkeit über die letzte Quelle des Rechts erreicht werden wird, muss man nach meiner Meinung rationale Argumente für die Rechtsgeltung suchen, die für alle Beteiligten nachvollziehbar sind".[257] This indeed constitutes a plea for limiting the question of the basis of the binding force of international law to what was called in the foregoing its procedural aspects.

Undoubtedly, the search for the material basis or bases of international law is of the utmost importance, but up until now it has divided rather than united.[258] And indeed, from a practical point of view, the procedural constitutional elements of international law are quite pressing too. It has probably been never more urgent than in our days for the international community to have at least some degree of common ground in these vital matters of international law, since the diversity between States has dramatically increased over the past decades, while at the same time the inter-state relations require a greater degree of regulation as a result of the growing interdependence.[259]

The certainty and clarity which the law and in particular its sources are to provide imply, in the present author's view, that the source of international law in the sense of the basis of its binding force has to be rationally verifiable and cannot have a substantive content, since no single material source is capable of generating universal acceptability from the international society at this moment. It is submitted that such a source can be found in the same notion which was described as a key-element of law in general and which was listed as the third of the basic features of international society, *i.e.* the recognized necessity that international relations have to be regulated by a system of law. In order to find

255. See *supra* pp. 29-44.
256. See *supra* pp. 58-60.
257. H. Mosler, *loc.cit.* (note 196), p. 34.
258. See *supra* pp. 30-34.
259. See *supra* pp. 65-71.

the foundation for the binding force of international law, one needs not go any further than the simple and verifiable awareness on the part of the States that there is no satisfactory alternative to a set of binding rules for the regulation of their mutual relations.

To be sure, several international lawyers will not be satisfied with the recognized necessity set forth here as the basis of the binding force of international law and will insist that some further (ultimate) material source is needed on which the binding force of international law is to be based. They are rather prepared to accept some religious, ideological, philosophical, moral or political idea as an ultimate source on which the recognized necessity in its turn is based.[260] However, the moment one or more of such ideas is singled out as *the* ultimate source, one reintroduces the difficulty which the *procedural* element of the recognized necessity was designed to cope with, *i.e.* that no *material* source is either generally acceptable nor rationally verifiable.

The recognized necessity as viewed here is not linked to any material idea and precisely for that reason it can serve as the basis of the binding force of international law. It is not surprising that those who oppose necessity as the basis of the binding force of international law mostly substitute it with some material value or idea. However, even protagonists of the element of necessity usually very quickly end up in a discussion about material ideas by filling the concept of necessity with some kind of substantive content. Scelle, for instance, wrote in 1948: "L'ordre juridique est l'ensemble des normes ou règles de Droit en vigueur dans une société donnée à un moment donné. Mais cet ordre juridique n'est que l'expression partielle du 'potentiel juridique' d'une société. Ce potentiel correspond *à la nécessité sociale actuelle et future*. C'est de ce fonds commun ou source matérielle du Droit que naîtront, le moment venu, les règles et les institutions".[261] Similarly, Judge Alvarez observed in the *Anglo-Norwegian Fisheries* case that "many of the principles, particularly the great principles, have their origin in the *legal conscience of people* ... . This conscience results from social and international life; *the requirements of this social and international life naturally give rise to certain norms considered necessary to govern the conduct of States inter se.*"[262]

The view which would seem to resemble most the one advocated here, has been set forth by Fitzmaurice, although in his case too some "material flavour" is added. Writing on the ultimate source of legal obligation, he concludes: "the view that seems to be closest both to the realities of the matter and to the historical facts is the 'social' view, or in other words the idea embodied in the maxim

260. See in this respect also H. Hart, *op.cit* (note 41), p. 181, according to whom "it cannot seriously be disputed that the development of law, at all times and places, has in fact been profoundly influenced both by conventional morality and ideals of particular social groups, and also by forms of enlightened moral criticism urged by individuals, whose moral horizon has transcended the morality currently accepted. But it is possible to take this truth illicitly, as a warrant for a different proposition: namely that a legal system must exhibit some specific conformity with morality or justice, or must rest on a widely diffused conviction that there is a moral obligation to obey it. Again, though this proposition may, in some sense, be true, it does not follow from it that the criteria of legal validity of particular laws used in a legal system must include, tacitly if not explicitly, a reference to morality or justice".
261. G. Scelle, *Manuel de Droit International Public* (Paris 1948), p. 9 (emphasis added).
262. ICJ Reports (1951), pp. 148-149 (emphasis added).

'ubi societas ibi jus'. This maxim is more than a mere statement of fact. The case is not one merely of *post*, but of *propter hoc.* It is not simply that where society is found, law is found, but that it must be so found that law is a necessary condition of any systematized form of inter-relationships".[263] This passage is not entirely clear. It could be interpreted as to imply that in any kind of society law necessarily arises. On the other hand, express reference is made to "any systematized form of inter-relationships", which would seem to point to the conclusion that Fitzmaurice's view coincides with the concept of recognized necessity in the procedural sense as it was put forward above. All that is intended by the latter is simply that once the members of a given society have decided that it is necessary to regulate their relations by rules of law, this in itself constitutes a sufficient basis for the obligatory force of these rules.[264]

In reaction to the words of Fitzmaurice just quoted, Tunkin has written that the former makes law "an ahistorical category independent of the social system and peculiar to any human society".[265] According to Tunkin, Marxist-Leninist theory has shown that there was a time when human society knew no law, although there were specific rules of conduct then. He submits that such a state of affairs will recur once communist society has come to full bloom[266]: "Bourgeois science errs in accepting any rules of conduct, including rules of conduct in tribal society as norms of law. ... The rules of conduct which will exist in communist society will by their nature be different from norms of law".[267] Apart from the fact that the argument is not very convincing as long as we are left in the dark as to the difference between law and rules of conduct and no criterion is provided to distinguish between them,[268] it is misconceived as far as the concept of recognized necessity put forward here is concerned.[269] For that concept taken in the procedural sense does not "predict" that any human society will have law; it is intended to pose, as a sufficient basis for the binding force of law, the recognition (perception) that law is necessary to regulate relations in society. It, therefore, does not establish the indivisible and inevitable link between law and society which Tunkin attributes to the maxim *ubi societas, ibi jus.*[270]

---

263. G. Fitzmaurice, "The General Principles of International Law Considered from the Standpoint of the Rule of Law", 92 *RCADI* (1957-II), pp. 5-227 (38).
264. The implications of the concept of recognized necessity may be further clarified by comparing it to the views set forth in P. Fitzgerald's edition of *Salmond on Jurisprudence* (London 1966), pp. 48-59. There it is upheld that the binding force of law is ultimately to be found in "a moral principle to the effect that social life is necessary and desirable, together with a factual truth to the effect that some type of legal system ... is an essential means to this end" (p. 53). Unlike the concept of recognized necessity advocated in the present study, this view bases the binding force of law on a *moral* principle and, secondly, it would seem to entail the conclusion that any society *necessarily* has a system of law.
265. G. Tunkin, *op.cit.* (note 50), p.237.
266. *Ibidem*, p. 238.
267. *Ibidem*, p. 239.
268. To be sure, Tunkin typically upholds that the former unlike the latter "reflected the will not of all society but only of the ruling class and it was directed at maintaining and developing the social orders favourable and advantageous to this ruling class", *ibidem*, p. 238. However, whether such is indeed the character of law and, even if one accepts this, whether rules of conduct are different in this respect, is at best a matter of highly subjective appreciation.
269. See *supra* pp. 71-73.
270. Paradoxically enough, it would seem that socialist doctrine itself embraces this indivisibility and inevitability in proclaiming that "There will be formed uniform generally-recognized

74

The view expounded in the foregoing would seem to be confirmed by the attitude of States towards the fundamentals of international law. As a rule they scrupulously adhere to the requirement of *pacta sunt servanda* which can be considered as the "translation" into international law of the element of necessity. The rule of *pacta sunt servanda* is not just a general principle of international law; it indeed constitutes the very cornerstone of the whole body of international law. As such it is now widely recognized in doctrine. One of the writers who extensively dealt with it, Anzilotti, wrote: "Any legal system consists of norms whose binding force originates in a fundamental norm and to which, directly or indirectly, all norms of this system are reduced. The fundamental norm defines, therefore, what norms comprise the particular legal system and reduces them to unity. The international legal order is characterized by the fact that the principle *pacta sunt servanda* is not based, as in the case of municipal law, upon a higher norm; it is itself the higher norm".[271]

The rule of *pacta sunt servanda* has been laid down in the Vienna Convention on the Law of Treaties.[272] Its article 26 provides that "Every treaty in force is binding upon the parties to it and must be performed by them in good faith". The rationale of the rule implies that its applicability is not confined to treaties. Its scope indeed extends to every *pactum* or agreement between States, whatever its particular form. The rule of *pacta sunt servanda* is uncontested in state practice.[273] States are well aware of the fact that the *pacta sunt servanda* -rule constitutes the principle "without which no orderly international life is possible", as the representative of Turkey put it at the Conference on Security and Cooperation in Europe. He went on to explain his government's point of view by asking the rethorical question: "If we did not recognize, *a priori* the significance of this principle, what would be the practical value of our agreements on the other fundamentals which an orderly, peaceful and civilized international

rules of communist communal life, whose observance will become an internal need and habit of all people", G. Tunkin, *op.cit.* (note 50), pp. 238-239.

271. D. Anzilotti, *Corso di Diritto Internazionale*, 4th edition (Padua/Amsterdam 1955), pp. 44-45. Many others have confirmed the fundamental character of the maxim *pacta sunt servanda*, albeit from different angles; see for instance A. Verdross, *op.cit.* (note 98), p. 24; G. Fitzmaurice, *loc.cit.* (note 263), p. 41 and *loc.cit.* (note 28), p. 164; H. Kelsen, *op.cit.* (note 96), pp. 417-418; L. Henkin, *op.cit.* (note 228), pp. 19-20; and G. Tunkin, *op.cit.* (note 50), pp. 223-224.

272. 8 *ILM* (1969), pp. 679-713.

273. As with any well-established rule, in this case too, there are exceptions; see the remarkable statement by the U.S. president G. Ford, when asked with reference to the events in Chile of 1973, whether the U.S. under international law had the right to attempt to destabilize the constitutionally elected government of another country: "I'm not going to pass judgment on whether it's permitted or authorized under international law. It's a recognized fact that historically as well as presently such actions are taken in the best interests of the countries involved", quoted by R. Falk, "President Gerald Ford, CIA Covert Operations, and the Status of International Law", 69 *AJIL* (1975), pp. 354-358 (354). Compare this statement to the words of Bismarck spoken almost a century before in 1875: "Das Völkerrecht bezweckt, die Rechtliche Ordnung der einzelnen Staaten zueinander aufrecht zu erhalten; wenn aber ein grosses Reich Differenzen mit einem anderen Staate hat, dann wird es alles dem Völkerrecht entsprechend machen, vorausgesetzt, dass dies für es vorteilhaft ist; wenn dies aber nicht der Fall ist, dann will es vom Völkerrecht nichts wissen und vertritt seiner Ansprüch mit Gewalt. Das kleine Land kann aber mit Gewalt gar nichts ausrichten und muss immer nach den Bestimmungen des Völkerrechts handeln", quoted by R. Bernhardt, *loc.cit.* (note 227), pp. 56-57.

life must be based upon".[274] As McNair has rightly observed: "No Government would decline to accept the principle *pacta sunt servanda* and the very fact that Governments find it necessary to spend so much effort in explaining in a particular case that the *pactum* has ceased to exist, or that the act complained of is not a breach of it ... is the best acknowledgement of that principle."[275] Indeed, States implicitly act upon the principle *pacta sunt servanda*. When there is a dispute on international law, it is never on the validity of *pacta sunt servanda*. It rather concerns the question about the existence or exact content and interpretation of the rule or *pactum* concerned. It is this question which will be addressed next.

5.6. The constitutive element of rules of international law

As a result of the peculiar characteristics of the international society, which may be summarily described as its low degree of organization, an institutionalized law-making process as is typical for most national societies is almost non-existent at the international level. Because of the lack of organs or bodies specifically designed for that purpose, the law-making function in the international society has of necessity to be performed by the members of that society themselves. This fact has been aptly expressed by Mosler: "Fehlt eine Institution, die von den Rechtsgenossen zur Gestaltung der Rechtsordnung gebildet ist, ..., so ist es die Gesamtheit der Mitglieder, welche die Regeln des Zusammenlebens aufstellt. Das ist die Grundregel, die aus der internationalen Gesellschaft eine Rechtsgemeinschaft macht".[276] This means at the same time that the independence of States as a basic feature of international society and the ensuing lack of a hierarchically organized law-making body as described in section 5.3., results in one of the most fundamental aspects of the international law-making process, *i.e.* that the consent of States has to be regarded as the constitutive element of rules of international law. Consequently, in order to answer the question of whether a given rule is binding upon a State as a rule of international law, the point of departure must be whether or not that State has consented to the rule concerned.[277]

"Consent" is not an unequivocal term. Walden has pointed out that the word "consent" is in fact used with several meanings. He has discerned: "(1) The contractual sense: an intention to create obligations on a basis of reciprocity; (2) The intention to create obligations generally (...); (3) Willingness to be bound by rules already created; (4) Acquiescence in claims put forward by others".[278] The statement made in the preceding paragraph encompasses in fact all these meanings enumerated by Walden.[279] However, this statement should be further clarified as follows. Consent implies that there exists an intention to be bound by

---

274. Conference on Security and Cooperation in Europe, Stage I- Helsinki, *Verbatim Records*, July 3-7, 1973, CSCE/I/P.V. 6, pp. 23-25.
275. A. McNair, *The Law of Treaties* (Oxford 1961), p. 493.
276. H. Mosler, *loc.cit.* (note 196), p. 32.
277. See in this respect also L. Oppenheim, *International Law: A Treatise*, Vol. I: Peace, rev. by H. Lauterpacht, 8th edition, 3rd impression (London 1958), pp. 10-19.
278. See by R. Walden, *loc.cit.* (note 182), p. 86.
279. As to the first meaning a good example constitutes the Soviet theory on international law which usually insists on consent understood as agreement, thereby implying that the intention to create rules of law is to be based on reciprocity; see, for instance, I. Lukashuk, "Sources of

legal rules. The consent of States cannot, of course, be unintentionally. This, however, does not mean that consent has to be given expressly; it may also be given tacitly. The use, side by side, of the words "tacit" and "consent" might give rise to confusion as a number of theories on customary international law, which are labeled "tacit consent theories", have implications going beyond what is contemplated here.[280] The tenets of at least some of these theories would seem to imply that for a customary rule to become binding upon all members of society it is sufficient that a majority has expressed its consent with respect to it. It is upheld, in other words, that a minority can become bound without consenting, that is without an intention to be bound. After what has been observed in the foregoing on the basic features of the international society, it is clear that in the present author's view such a conclusion is untenable as far as international law is concerned. States cannot be bound unintentionally, even though their consent may be given tacitly.

This requirement of "intentionally, but not of necessity expressly" may best be explained by relating it to the different meanings of sources which we have discerned. In the second meaning of constitutive element consent has to be intentionally, and cannot, therefore, be "tacit" in this sense. Used in the third sense of manifestations of the constitutive element, however, consent may be both express or tacit. Tacit manifestation does not prevent the consent from being intentionally. To put it differently, States may manifest their intention to be bound through active consent as well as through more passive acceptance. Consequently, "consent" and "consensual" will be used in the following to encompass both the more active sense and the more passive sense of acceptance.

Compared to municipal legal systems the consensual basis of international law is certainly peculiar, and it is at any rate not very satisfactory. Given the basic features of international society, however, the present author knows of no convincing argument to deny that international law is a consensual system. The case against consent or acceptance as the constitutive element of rules of international law is usually made in connection with the discussion of custom as a source of international law. Customary rules of international law, it is said, do not require the consent or acceptance of all States bound by them, and the standard argument adduced is the position of new States. The argument starts from the premise that the position holding that new States are automatically bound by rules of customary international law, correctly reflects the state of international law on this issue.[281] This then is taken as conclusive evidence that

present-day international law", in: G. Tunkin (ed.), *Contemporary International Law* (Moscow 1969), pp. 164-187 (164-168), and G. Tunkin, *op.cit.* (note 50), pp. 211-216. In practice, some kind of reciprocity will most of the time be involved, but there is no objection of theory against a State creating unilateral obligations, even if at least some form of "factual acceptance" on the part of the "beneficiary" State will be required for these obligations to take effect. 377. See *infra* pp. 102-103 and 275-279.

280. For a survey of some of these theories, see R. Walden, "The Subjective Element in the Formation of Customary International Law", XII *ILR* (1977), pp. 344-364 (344-357).

281. It is true that many, and indeed very authoritative Western scholars take this position; see, *inter alia*, J. Basdevant, "Règles Général du Droit de la Paix", 58 *RCADI* (1936-IV), pp. 475-692 (515); H. Kelsen, *op.cit.* (note 96), p. 154; and J. Kunz, "The Nature of Customary International Law", 47 *AJIL* (1953), pp. 662-669 (666). Soviet theory holds the opposite view on this issue acknowledging that new States too have to consent to customary rules of interna-

international law cannot be considered a consensual system.[282]

In other words, one has to accept the premise in order to be able to agree with the conclusion. However, this line of reasoning would seem to put things upside down. If it is correct, as is very widely acknowledged, that as a result of the international society's basic features the States themselves act as the international "legislator", one cannot deny the consensual character of international law on the basis of the alleged existence of a rule of international law running counter to that point of departure. In such a case logic rather demands that one first puts into question the alleged existence of the rule concerned.

To the present author it would seem difficult to subscribe to the position that new States are automatically bound by pre-existing customary international law. Those who adhere to that view often base themselves upon some other scholarly authority without adducing any further arguments. Walden, for instance, relies on Waldock according to whom "The generally held view on the point undoubtedly is that established customary rules do automatically extend their ambit of operation to a new state", and who invokes state-practice to that effect.[283] But the attitude of States would seem hardly unequivocal in this respect; at least the position of some new States themselves points in a different direction. Algeria, for instance, declared at the United Nations that "A general distinction should be drawn between an obligation voluntarily accepted and the general imposition of a law made in other times by a small international community".[284] And at another occasion India described the whole of customary international law as "a picture of what international law had been rather than what it actually is".[285] Therefore, it would seem at least dubious whether the view, that presupposes binding force for pre-existing rules of customary international law for new States, can be upheld. It is true that in fact new States normally consent to or accept, and thus become bound by such rules. However, from this situation normally prevailing in practice it cannot be concluded that pre-existing customary rules are automatically binding on new States. Parry expresses a similar point of view when he refers to this issue as "a very puzzling problem for which various theoretical solutions, non of them particularly satisfactory, can be offered" and subsequently concludes that "If the basis of international law is consent, such [new - v.H.] states may and indeed do, consciously or unconsciously, ask why should not they be bound only by those rules to which they have expressly consented."[286]

tional law before these can be considered binding upon them; see R. Erickson, "Soviet Theory of the Legal Nature of Customary International Law", 7 *CWRJIL* (1975), pp. 148-168 (162-163); see the criticism of such views by M. Sørensen, *Les Sources du Droit International* (Copenhague 1946), p. 87.

282. See H. Thirlway, *op.cit.* (note 209), p. 56; and R. Walden, *loc.cit.* (note 280), p. 355; see also the remarkable point of view taken by M. Akehurst, "Custom as a Source of International Law", XLVII *BYIL* (1974-1975), pp. 1-53 (28): "A State can 'opt out' of a rule of customary international law by dissenting before the rule becomes well established, but not afterwards. *Unfortunately for the new States, most rules of customary law were established before the States concerned became independent; independence came too late for them to dissent effectively*" (emphasis added).

283. R. Walden, *loc.cit.* (note 280), p. 356.

284. *UN Doc.* A/Ac.125/SR.6, p. 11.

285. *UN Doc.* A/Conf.39/11, p. 3.

286. C. Parry, *op.cit.* (note 22), p. 17.

Deviating from the consensual basis of international law is at best deceiving, but may also be outright dangerous. In the best possible case it creates expectations which are irrealistic because the State, which is held to be "bound", did not really consent to or accept the rule concerned and is, therefore, unlikely to comply with it. In the worst possible case it may fuel international conflicts in that political disagreements in addition become disputes about "violations of international law". In the present author's view, detrimental effects may be involved any time a non-consensual position is taken, no matter by which "bloc" of the international society. The foregoing concerned the long-debated issue of the West holding that new States are bound by pre-existing customary international law with the latter States emphatically denying that conclusion. Paradoxically enough, today it sometimes seems as if positions have been reversed.

Illustrative in this respect is the train of thought recently put forward by an Indian scholar. After noting that "the new states in fact ... challenged the binding nature of the rules of existing customary international law to which they have not given their consent", he goes on to observe that "The problem is, however, of academic interest now to these 'new nations', as they are enjoying a substantial majority in the UN and in the General Assembly and can easily initiate new state practice, inconsistent with traditional international law".[287] He in fact has completed a full turn when it is added: "considering the obduracy of some Western states, especially like South Africa on the issue of apartheid, they [the new States - v.H.] would probably tend to agree ... that general customary international law is binding on dissenting states while special custom is not".[288] Finally, the line of reasoning is carried to the end when the author in reaction to the recalcitrance of States like South Africa concludes: "the extreme consent-oriented approach is inconsistent with the espousal of 'community norms' of law like *jus cogens* and an International Law of Crimes which obviously seek to bind the dissenting states".[289] We will get back to this issue of consensualism or non-consensualism (or constitutionalism) with respect to *jus cogens*.[290]

The example just given was meant to point out only how easy it apparently is to switch from a consensual to a non-consensual approach (and *vice versa*), depending upon the particular position one wants to advocate. Furthermore, the binding force of pre-existing customary international law which has been stubbornly upheld by the West against the new States for a long time has, in the present author's view, not been instrumental to the just and effective functioning of international law. It would be equally detrimental, if the new States were to embark on a similar course now that they have opportunities to do so.

After having put forward a consent-oriented approach in the foregoing, it is important to stress that consent or acceptance as the constitutive element for rules of international law should not be confused with any brand of voluntarism as is sometimes advocated. In its most extreme form such theories of voluntarism based on consent would seem to imply that States have the same discretionary power to free themselves from international legal obligations, once they

287. T. Rama Rao, "International Custom", 19 *IJIL* (1979), pp. 515-521 (519).
288. *Ibidem.*
289. *Ibidem,* p. 520.
290. See *infra* pp. 160-162.

have accepted them, as they have to enter into such obligations. In other words, it is claimed that a State is at liberty to contract out of binding rules of international law, for instance by simply declaring that it revokes its consent with respect to a particular rule of international law.

As pointed out above, such a position is completely incompatible with the very notion of law. Rules are to be binding in order to be considered rules of law, because only in that manner can they play their ordering and regulating role in society. Rules from which one can rid oneself at will are not binding and, therefore, no rules of law. Consequently, consent or acceptance is the constitutive element for rules of international law but cannot serve as the basis for their binding force.[291] As was explained, it was therefore thought necessary to separately deal with the latter issue in the foregoing.[292]

As will be elaborated below,[293] the view that international law is in fact a consensual system finds support also in article 38 of the Statute of the International Court of Justice enumerating the traditional sources which the Court has to apply in deciding the disputes submitted to it. According to this provision, international conventions have to be *expressly recognized* by States, international custom must be *accepted* as law, and general principles of law must be *recognized* by civilized nations. The use of the words "recognized" and "accepted" is designed to bear out the consensual basis upon which international law is to rest.[294]

Additional evidence to that effect can be found in the work of the Vienna Conference on the Law of Treaties, which was convened in two successive sessions in 1968 and 1969 with 110 States participating. On at least two occasions during the work of the Conference the participating States made it abundantly clear that they consider consent the constitutive element for rules of international law. The first one concerns the so-called subjective element in the definition of "treaty". By this one designates the intention of States to create rights and obligations under international law. The text of the Vienna Convention on the Law of Treaties as it was finally adopted does not make an explicit reference to this subjective element. Its relevant provision, article 2(1)(a), now reads: "'treaty' means an international agreement concluded between States in written form and governed by international law, ...". In a number of drafts by the International Law Commission's special rapporteurs the intention to create rights and obligations under international law was explicitly mentioned.[295] In the Commission's final draft which was submitted to the General Assembly of the United Nations, however, the phrase was omitted because, in the Commission's

291. G. Fitzmaurice has described this distinction in very clear terms: "It is agreement which brings the treaty as an instrument into force, and which creates the rule or particular obligation contained in it. But what makes those rules and obligations binding is an antecedent rule of general law outside the treaty, according to which consent to a treaty makes the treaty binding, so that once the treaty is concluded, the parties are then bound, and obliged to carry it out whether they continue to like it or not .... Put a little differently, it might be said that consent is manifested in the act of becoming a party to a treaty, but not in the act of carrying it out - that being obligatory", *loc.cit.* (note 263), p. 41.
292. See *supra* pp. 71-76.
293. See chapters VI-IX.
294. See *infra* p. 81.
295. See H. Lauterpacht's definition in *ILC Yearbook* (1954-II), p. 123, and that of G. Fitzmaurice in *ILC Yearbook* (1956-II), p. 107. Brierly, *ILC Yearbook* (1950-II), p. 226, moreover,

eyes, it would involve too many difficulties.[296] At the Vienna Conference itself a number of proposed amendments were tabled specifically designed to reintroduce the subjective element into the text of draft article 2(1)(a).[297] The reason why the Commission's draft article was not amended was that the Commission had declared, and the Drafting Committee's Chairman at the Conference confirmed, that "the element of intention is embraced in the phrase 'governed by international law' ...".[298]

The second occasion referred to above is to be found in the drafting history of what is now article 53 of the Vienna Convention, dealing with peremptory norms of general international law (*jus cogens*).[299] The draft of the International Law Commission of this article was strongly influenced by the natural law thinking of its special rapporteur, H. Lauterpacht. The States at the Conference, however, reversed this tendency and put back the concept of *jus cogens* in international law on its consensual basis. This result was achieved by inserting in the draft article the words "accepted and recognized by the international community of States as a whole".[300] Consequently, article 53 now contains the so-called "double consent" requirement: for a rule to satisfy the conditions of article 53 the consent of States must not only extend to its content as a general norm of international law, but also to its specific imperative nature, *i.e.* that it is a norm from which no derogation is permitted and which can be modified only by a subsequent norm of general international law having the same character. All this would seem to provide strong indications that the States themselves consider international law to be a consensual system.[301]

5.7. Manifestations of consent or acceptance; the impact of the changed structure of the international society

After having analyzed in the preceding sections the sources at the first and the second level, we can now proceed to the third level, *viz.* the manifestations of the constitutive element of rules of international law. It is this third level which is usually thought of when reference is made to the (formal) sources of international law. From a practical point of view the sources in the sense of manifestations are the most important. For, when confronted with practical questions, it is to these kind of sources that one has to turn in order to find out what the law is

used the phrase "agreement ... which establishes a relation under international law between the parties thereto", which can be taken to encompass the subjective element.
296. See *UN Doc.* A/4169, pp. 9-10.
297. See the Chilean proposal in *UN Doc.* A/Conf.39/c.1/L.22 and the accompanying comment in *UN Doc.* A/Conf.39/11, p. 21, and the joint Mexican/Maleysian proposal in *UN Doc* A/Conf.39/c.1/L.33 and its commentary in *UN Doc.* A/Conf.39/11, p. 23.
298. See *UN Doc.* A/Conf.39/Add.2, p. 9 and *UN Doc.* A/Conf.39/11/Add.1, p. 346.
299. The article reads: "A treaty is void if, at the time of its conclusion, it conflicts with a peremptory norm of general international law. For the purposes of the present Convention, a peremptory norm of general international law is a norm accepted and recognized by the international community of States as a whole as a norm from which no derogation is permitted and which can be modified only by a subsequent norm of general international law having the same character".
300. On this drafting history, see C. Rozakis, *op.cit.* (note 238), pp. 44-55.
301. On the basis of his elaborate and detailed study of the drafting history of article 53 Rozakis concludes: "The addition of the 'double consent' requirement was indeed a major break-

on a particular issue. As was made clear from the outset,[302] it were primarily questions arising in practice which prompted the search for the sources undertaken in the present study, and, consequently, the remaining chapters will be devoted to the sources in the sense of manifestations of consent or acceptance.

As was pointed out above,[303] it is with respect to the sources as manifestations that the second of the two requirements, which the doctrine of sources of international law has to fulfil, is particularly relevant. This second requirement implies that sufficient attention is to be paid to the link between law and relations in society. For this reason section 5.4. described the changes in the structure of international relations which have taken place during this century, particularly after the Second World War. In the following the impact of these changes on the sources of international law in the sense of manifestations will be analyzed.

In Part II the impact on the "traditional" sources will be discussed. The term "traditional" sources is meant to designate those phenomena which the International Court of Justice, according to article 38(1) of its Statute, is to apply in deciding the disputes submitted to it. In the present author's view, article 38(1) of the Statute is still a good starting point but not the final word as far as the doctrine of sources of international law is concerned. As was pointed out by Jennings, with respect to article 38 "we must ... remember that it is a 1920 draft and not always well-suited to international law of the 1980's. So we must use it, but interpreting where need be; as in a written constitution; and remembering that it is an open question whether it is now of itself a sufficient guide to the content of modern international law".[304]

In Part III it will be argued that the doctrine of sources needs to be reformulated on the basis of practice in international relations as it stands now. Nevertheless, it is obvious that Article 38 cannot be simply bypassed. The provision is generally taken as a point of departure for the discussion of the sources of international law and fairly generally considered as an authoritative enumeration in this respect.[305] Furthermore, it is precisely by analyzing the changes occurred with respect to the traditional sources first, that it is possible subsequently to determine to what extent these sources still can play the role required of them and to what extent they need reformulation and/or supplementing. This constitutes the focus of enquiry in the following. What will be looked for are the changes in the sources of international law as a result of the changed structure of international relations. Consequently, it is not intended to elaborate on all the manifold aspects involved in the sources enumerated in the Court's Statute.

through toward the exclusion from the *lex lata* of any non-consensual elements and an indication of the perseverance of States in the element of consent as the *sine qua non* prerequisite for any development wrought in international law", *ibidem*, p. 76. See in addition also the same author's "Treaties and Third States: a Study in the Reinforcement of the Consensual Standards in International Law", 35 *ZaöRV* (1975), pp. 1-40.

302. See *supra* pp. 6-8.
303. See *supra* p. 61.
304. R. Jennings, *loc.cit.* (note 1), p. 61.
305. See, for instance, M. Virally, "The Sources of International Law", in: M. Sørensen (ed.), *Manual of Public International Law* (London 1968), pp. 116-174 (121); according to R. Pathak, "The General Theory of the Sources of Contemporary International Law", 19 *IJIL* (1979), pp. 483-495 (485), "several jurists have sought to discover the sources of international law in its provisions. Some have described it as an authoritative text of the sources and evidences of international law".

PART II

THE TRADITIONAL SOURCES
OF INTERNATIONAL LAW

CHAPTER VI

CUSTOMARY INTERNATIONAL LAW

6.1. Doctrine and customary international law

Customary international law is listed at a second place in article 38(1), but it is the oldest source. At the same time, however, it is one of the most cumbersome. The confusion and divergence of opinion which were said to prevail with respect to the doctrine of sources in general,[306] reign supreme as far as customary international law is concerned. This is generally acknowledged and it has become almost customary to start off a discussion of the nature of customary international law with some kind of lamentation signaling to the reader that he is about to embark upon an extremely intricate and complex subject.[307]

Writing on customary international law is truly abundant and, in general, it cannot be said to be boring. The views represented in doctrine provide a kaleidoscòpic picture ranging from one extreme to the other.[308] On the one end of the scale there are those who stress the element of *opinio juris* while neglecting *usus*, on the other end one finds writers emphasizing the importance of *usus* while virtually doing away with the requirement of *opinio juris*.

As to the first mentioned positipn, it may be found in the *pactum tacitum* theory of customary international law, in particular in one of the most well-known versions thereof by Strupp.[309] Strupp holds that *usus* is not a necessary element of a rule of customary international law. In his view, *usus* in fact is at best relevant as evidence of the existence of customary international law. This point is more or less disguised by the complicated role usage plays in his theory. For, Strupp infers from the *present* conduct of a State that it has bound itself to a certain rule *at some time in the past*. In other words, through *usus* the truly constitu-

---

306. See *supra* pp. 13-16.
307. See, for instance, M. Akehurst, *loc.cit.* (note 282), p. 1, comparing the attitude of international lawyers towards customary international law with Saint Augustine of Hippo's remarks on time: "What then, is time? If no one asks of me, I know; if I wish to explain to him who asks, I know not"; and the words of J. Basdevant quoted by both J. Kunz, *loc.cit.* (note 281), p. 663 and H. Thirlway, *op.cit.* (note 209), p. 46 to the effect that "les idées des juristes sur le caractère de la coutume n'ont atteint ni à l'unité ni à la clarté".
308. Of the voluminous literature on the subject the following studies have in particular been used as guidance: M. Akehurst, *loc.cit.* (note 282), R. Bernhardt, *loc.cit.* (note 227), A. Bleckmann, "Zur Feststellung und Auslegung von Völkergewohnheitsrecht", 37 *ZaöRV* (1977), pp. 504-529, R. Erickson, *loc.cit.* (note 281), J. Kunz, *loc.cit.* (note 281), I. Lukashuk, *loc.cit.* (note 279), H. Meijers, *loc.cit.* (note 204), H. Thirlway, *op.cit.* (note 209), M. Virally, *loc.cit.* (note 305), R. Walden, *loc.cit.* (note 280), R. Walden, *loc.cit.* (note 182) and K. Wolfke, *Custom in Present International Law* (Wroclaw 1962).
309. See K. Strupp, "Les Règles Générales du Droit de la Paix", 47 *RCADI* (1934-I), pp. 263-595.

tive element of customary law, *i.e. opinio juris* is evidenced. The latter is pre-existing and as such unidentifiable. Therefore, Strupp's theory contains a great deal of legal fiction, which was said to be characteristic of the Positivist school[310] of which he is a member.[311]

A modern theory which plays down the material element of custom, *i.e. usus,* is that of the so-called "instant customary law". It has been introduced by Cheng. Its main theme consists of the view that "Not only is it unnecessary that the usage should be prolonged, but there need also be no usage at all in the sense of repeated practice, provided that the *opinio juris* of the states concerned can be clearly established. Consequently, international customary law has in reality only one constitutive element, the *opinio juris*".[312]

Two questions should be carefully kept apart in this context. First, whether rules of international law can come into being solely on the basis of an *opinio juris*, without there being an accompanying *usus*. Second, whether the formation of rules of *customary* international law can take place in isolation of usage. If Cheng had confined his thesis to the first mentioned question, he would, in the present author's view, have been correct. As will be argued below, one of the results of the changed structure of international relations has been the development of methods for the creation of international law besides the traditional sources. If one accepts this point of view, it becomes unnecessary to try to bring the rules thus created under the heading of custom thereby stretching the latter concept to the point where it has lost its ordinary meaning. Custom as a method of law-creation conveys the idea that the rules thus created are practice-based, *i.e.* that their content is delineated through the practice of States. Instant customary law does precisely the opposite; it suggests that such practice is irrelevant to customary international law.

In summary, therefore, customary law and instantaneousness are irreconcilable concepts. Furthermore, it is detrimental to the effective functioning of international law, as an ordering and regulating device, to water down the meaning of its sources to almost the vanishing point. For in this way the certainty and clarity, which in particular the concept of sources is to provide, is seriously reduced.

On the other end of the scale one finds theories holding that *opinio juris* is superfluous and that the existence of usage in itself suffices to establish a rule of customary international law.[313] Theories like these have one major handicap, which in the present author's view makes them difficult to uphold. They suffer from the basic flaw that abandonment of the requirement of *opinio juris* would eliminate the distinction between customary rules of law, on the one hand, and rules of international morality and conventional international rules (*courtoisie internationale*) on the other hand".[314]

---

310. See *supra* pp. 37-38.
311. For a criticism of Strupp's theory see R. Walden, *loc.cit.* (note 280), pp. 350-357.
312. .B. Cheng, "United Nations Resolutions on Outer Space: 'Instant' International Customary Law?", 5 *IJIL* (1965), pp. 23-48 (36).
313. The following authors' point of view would seem to boil down to this position: L. Kopelmanas, "Custom as a Means of the Creation of International Law", 18 *BYIL* (1937), pp. 127-151; H. Kelsen, "Théorie du droit international coutumier", 13 *RITD* (1939), pp. 253-274; and P. Guggenheim, "Les Principes de Droit International Public", 80 *RCADI* (1952-I), pp. 5-189.
314. J. Kunz, *loc.cit.* (note 281), p. 665; see also H. Thirlway, *op.cit.* (note 209), pp. 47-48.

At any rate, the "single element" theories[315] mentioned in the foregoing are exceptions and, consequently, not representative of the state of affairs in doctrine concerning custom. There is fairly widespread agreement that both *usus* and *opinio juris* are necessary elements of customary international law. However, that is as far as agreement goes, for there exists quite a variety of opinion on the precise content of these elements and on their mutual relation. Particularly the latter question concerning the relation between *opinio juris* and *usus* has posed great difficulties to the theory of custom and can be considered the main cause of the confusion surrounding it.

The problem is reflected in the wording of article 38 of the Statute of the International Court of Justice which contains the odd formula charging the Court to apply "international custom, as evidence of a general practice accepted as law". As will be pointed out below,[316] this much criticized formulation has probably contributed to the confusion surrounding custom.[317] As was observed, the main issue would seem to be the relation between *usus* and *opinio juris*. In the wake of Kelsen, who was one of the first to point to the dilemma involved, Kunz has outlined the issue in the following way: "On the one hand it is said that usage plus *opinio juris* leads to such norm [*i.e.* a norm of customary international law; v.H.], that, on the other hand, in order to lead to such a norm, the states must already practice the first cases with the *opinio juris.* Hence, the very coming into existence of such norm would presuppose that the states acted in legal error".[318] He concludes that this is "a challenging theoretical problem which, as far as the present writer can see, has not yet found a satisfactory solution".[319]

Such a solution cannot easily be found in the case-law of the International Court of Justice. As Meijers has pointed out, the Court in fact demands the impossible by posing as conditions for the creation of a rule of customary international law that it be applied and that its existence be recognized.[320]

---

315. See H. Thirlway, *op.cit.* (note 209), p. 53.
316. See *infra* pp. 95-96.
317. According to H. Meijers, *loc.cit.* (note 204), p. 12 this definition of international custom resulted from a diplomatic compromise between the historical and positivist schools of thought represented at the conference which drafted the Statute of the Court; see for more details on the genesis of article 38(1)(b) K. Wolfke, *op.cit.* (note 308), pp. 20-26.
318. J. Kunz, *loc.cit.* (note 281), p. 667; in the same vein H. Thirlway, *op.cit.* (note 209), p. 47: "The simple equation of the *opinio juris* with the intention to conform to what is recognized, at the moment of conforming, as an existing rule of law has been exposed to the objection ... that it necessarily implies a vicious circle in the logical analysis of the creation of custom"; and H. Meijers, *loc.cit.* (note 204), p. 12: "anyone who demands for the creation of such a legal rule [a norm of customary international law; v.H.] that it is applied and that its existence is recognized demands an impossibility".
319. *Ibidem.* H. Thirlway, *op.cit.* (note 209), p. 47, refers to the treatment of this issue in doctrine, as the "juridical squaring of the circle".
320. H. Meijers, *loc.cit.* (note 204), p. 12. More generally speaking the Court's case-law would not seem to be a very helpful guide in approaching theoretical questions concerning custom, for its major cases dealing with customary law are all invoked in doctrine to defend the most diverging theories on custom. (These major cases are: the *Asylum* case, ICJ Reports (1950), pp. 266-389; *Anglo-Norwegian Fisheries* case, ICJ Reports (1951), pp. 116-206; *Right of Passage* case, ICJ Reports (1960), pp. 6-144; and *North Sea Continental Shelf* cases, ICJ Reports (1969), pp. 3-257). It is of course not the Court's function to develop theories about international law, but to decide disputes between States and render advisory opinions on questions of law, which usually are quite concrete. Its pronouncements, therefore, will be tai-

Furthermore, it would seem quite natural to look to the attitude of the States themselves in order to find out the true nature of customary international law. However, this course is equally disappointing. Just as in the case of doctrine, the picture wich emerges from the various positions of the States on the subject is one of disarray. The States themselves do not express consistent, or at least consonant, views on the nature of customary international law. Rather custom often is used as a political argument. Very often one gets the impression, that both sides to a conflict or disagreement simply cite one or a number of precedents favourable to their case, add to this the magic formula of customary international law, and take this as conclusive evidence of the correctness of their point of view. The problem, of course, is that almost always one or more favourable precedents can be found and that the formula is at anyone's disposal.[321] In other words, this "competitive bidding" in the field of custom does very little, if any, good to the ordering and regulating function international law is supposed to perform.

The main reason why States can take such an unrestrained position *vis-à-vis* customary international law is to be found in the decentralized or horizontally organized character of international society, and the ensuing fact that the States are both the law-makers and the subjects of international law.[322] At the same time, this is a reason for caution when state-practice is taken into account. For, there are two forms of state-practice: on the one hand, there is the practice of States acting as the international "legislator", on the other hand, the practice of States in their role as subjects of international law. To put it a little differently, viewed from the perspective of the sources one can discern practice where States are more in the position of "producer", and practice where they act more from the position of "consumer" of international law.[323] However difficult it may be to clearly make this distinction in fact, it is of the utmost importance to keep it in mind from a theoretical point of view. For, it is obvious that States in the latter position cannot have the same impact on the creation of international law as when they act in the former. From the position of "consumer" a State may *argue* that this or that rule is a rule of international law. Such a statement cannot carry the same weight as that of a State acting as a "legislator".

The failure to make the distinction leads in some cases to an overestimation of certain types of state-practice. In the present author's view, it is this kind of defect which detracts to some extent from the usefulness of D'Amato's attempt to arrive at a complete reformulation of the theory of customary international law.[324] D'Amato's theory is revolutionary in several respects. Of the two ele-

lored to the particular facts of the case concerned. Nevertheless, it is certainly a token of the problematical nature of customary international law that, as J. Kunz, *loc.cit.* (note 281), p. 662, observes: "The fact that sometimes the pronouncements of the Court were rather to the surprise of the doctrine and of the practice of states, has not only brought into being an extensive literature, but has also directed attention once more to the problem of the nature of customary international law".

321. R. Jennings, *loc.cit.* (note 1), p. 68, would seem to go even one step further when in discussing customary international law he observes: "not surprisingly each Party is always able to give identical body of practice the stamp of its own particular thesis".

322. See *supra* pp. 61-64.

323. We will get back to this producer/consumer distinction which has been eminently elaborated by M. Bos, *loc.cit.* (note 28), pp. 11-13.

324. A. D'Amato, *op.cit.* (note 182).

ments of custom his treatment of the psychological element of *opinio juris* would, generally speaking, seem to be the most conventional one. But even on *opinio juris*, which he renames *articulation*, D'Amato's views at some points diverge quite dramatically from the more traditional ones.[325]

More interesting in the present context and more far-reaching is his treatment of the material element, which he labels *commitment*. In reading his description of the material element it is difficult to escape the impression that to D'Amato customary law is, at least partly, a matter of counting precedents. A most typical phrase reads: "There is no international 'constitution' specifying when acts become law. Rather, states resort to international law in claim-conflict situations. In such instances, counsel for either side will attempt to cite *as many acts as possible*. Thus, we may say that persuasiveness in part depends upon the number of precedents".[326] It is true, as was argued above, that there exists no international "constitution" strictly speaking, specifying when acts become law.[327] Equally, there is no denying that precedents, and for that matter the number of precedents, are relevant as far as customary international law is concerned. However, these truths should not be turned into the proposition that international law lacks all constitutional traits and that, as a result, customary international law is for all practical purposes to be equated with how States actually behave in practice. Still D'Amato's view would seem to come quite close to this proposition. What comes to the fore here is the impact of the particular view D'Amato takes on the character of international law. In setting forth his requirements of a theory of the concept of custom in international law he explicitly states that "we must view international law as a psychological bargaining mechanism involving conflicting claims among national decision-makers and their legal counsel".[328]

It can be easily conceded that international law sometimes functions as part of a bargaining process. Above it was pointed out that international law in some way may constitute a kind of instrument of communication between States.[329] It is something else, however, to maintain that this is the only or even the main feature of the character of international law. Looking at international law exclusively as a psychological bargaining mechanism distorts the picture of what that body of law actually is. In the case of D'Amato's theory it blurs the distinction between States as "producers" and States as "consumers" of international law. All state-practice is put on the same line and considered equally relevant for the formation of customary international law. For one thing this leads to the odd result that it becomes largely impossible to tell whether a given state-practice is law-creative or in violation of international law. Such a conclusion would seem possible only *after the fact*, that is in D'Amato's frame, after the claim-conflict situation has been resolved and one of two sides has prevailed. As D'Amato

---

325. In describing the element of articulation he, for instance, upholds that "There is no need for the acting state itself, through its officials, to have articulated the legal rule ... A writer on international law, a court, or an international organization may well provide the qualitative component of custom", *ibidem*, p. 85. R. Walden, *loc.cit.* (note 182), pp. 99-100, has convincingly rebutted this point of view; see also M. Akehurst, *loc.cit.* (note 282), pp. 35-36.
326. A. D'Amato, *op.cit.* (note 182), p. 91.
327. See *supra* pp. 58-59.
328. A. D'Amato, *op.cit.* (note 182), p. 18.
329. See *supra* p. 26.

himself asserts: "If we attempt to study international law as it is viewed by participants in the international arena, we will be inclined to replace absolutistic theories with the more accurate description of a process by which the better of the two conflicting claims prevails. In other words, two competing claimants may each have a case that falls short of fulfilling the requirements for a given absolutistic theory, yet the fact that one claimant has prevailed or will prevail over the other necessitates an abandonment of that 'theory' and its replacement by one which takes account of the *relative* superiority of persuasiveness".[330] What is overlooked here, and what the so-called "absolutistic theories" try to retain, is the certainty and clarity which the law is to provide *in advance* if it is to fulfil its ordering and regulating function. D'Amato virtually does away with this requirement. His claim-oriented approach to a large extent leaves customary international law with a severely reduced normative content, and as a result at least some of the rules thus designated as customary rules fall, to the present writer's mind, outside the scope of customary international law properly so-called.[331]

The foregoing survey of a number of theories on customary international law bears out two related points. First, from a theoretical point of view the precise nature of customary international law has been quite problematic for a long time already. The main issue would seem to be the relationship between the two component elements of *opinio juris* and *usus*. For an almost equally long time, on the other hand, this has not given rise to really great difficulties in the practical field. This was due to the fact that international society was composed of a rather homogeneous group of States or, maybe rather was a society in which a number of dominant States forced the others into conforming behaviour. The recent developments in international relations have changed this picture considerably. The upshot would seem to be that there is an increasing risk of customary international law losing its clarity and, therefore, its effectiveness as a source. For there is not only ever more practice, and, for that matter, more conflicting practice. It becomes also increasingly more difficult to relate this expanding state-practice adequately to customary international law as long as the latter's nature remains as troublesome as it seems to be. It follows that further analysis of its nature has to precede the effort to relate customary international law to the changed structure of the international relations.

6.2. The nature of customary international law

6.2.1. Introduction

As was observed there exists a close link between one's *Normative Concept of Law* and the view one takes of the sources.[332] There is a comparable connection between one's concept of customary international law and the role one envi-

---

330. A. D'Amato, *op.cit.* (note 182), p. 18.
331. See also *infra* pp. 99-101.
332. See *supra* pp.14-15.

sages customary international law to play in the changed conditions of present-day international society. As Thirlway has explained: "the view one takes of customary law, and particularly of the way it comes into existence, necessarily affects the view taken of the present and future part to be played by custom in developing the law".[333] It should, therefore, be made clear from the outset that in the opinion of the present writer customary international law should be narrowly defined. It was pointed out above,[334] that as a result of the changed structure of international society the latter has grown considerably more heterogeneous. Simultaneously, state-practice has become more diversified and divergent, and this is bound to affect a practice-oriented source like customary international law. It is conceivable to remedy this state of affairs by widening the concept of customary international law so as to encompass the new developments. However, in the present author's view, such an approach would likely be counter-productive. It entails the standing danger that the concept of custom will be stretched to the point where it becomes unclear or even meaningless as a source and detrimental to the effective operation of international law. In the present circumstances, therefore, it would seem far better to start from a restrictive concept of custom and try to explain methods of law-making which do not fit in by some other way.

6.2.2. *Opinio juris* and *usus*

6.2.2.1. The so-called stages-theory

On the basis of these introductory remarks, the focus can now be on the nature of customary international law. The problem, as we found it, consists mainly in the relation between the two elements of custom. Particularly, the requirement of simultaneousness or synchronism of *usus* and *opinio juris* in many theories was said to result in demanding the impossible and in an effort to square the juridical circle.[335] A very logical way out of the dilemma, therefore, would seem to be the abandonment of this requirement. A solution along this line has fairly recently been suggested by a number of writers. Thirlway[336], Walden[337] and Meijers[338] in fact all propose the chronological separation of *usus* and *opinio juris*. Apart from some terminological alterations, the following analysis will largely affiliate with their theories, because they would seem to provide a viable approach to the problem of customary international law. On that basis some connected issues, which are of special interest to the subject of the present study, will subsequently be elaborated.

The chronological separation of the two constitutive components of customary international law has in our view been advocated most lucidly by Meijers.

---

333. H. Thirlway, *op.cit.* (note 209), p. 46.
334. See *supra* pp. 69-71.
335. See *supra* pp. 87-88.
336. H. Thirlway, *op.cit.* (note 209).
337. R. Walden, *loc.cit.* (note 182), particularly pp. 53-56.
338. H. Meijers, *loc.cit.* (note 204).

The main feature of his theory consists of a distinction made between three stages which, according to Meijers, every rule of international law has to pass through before it can be said to exist. The theory applies to all methods of creating international law and is not particularly designed for rules of customary international law. Moreover, in connection with this general applicability the author upholds that the three stages discerned "contain procedural requirements and say nothing about the substantive content of the rules which are being made".[339] The three stages referred to are the following ones.

In the first stage the content of the rule is being delineated. This stage does not yet concern the (legal or non-legal) character of the rule, but simply its contents. All that happens is the prescription of a certain type of conduct without any reference to the question whether this rule will (have to) take on a binding or non-binding character. Meijers interchangeably uses a number of terms to describe this phase; he says, for instance, that the rule is being formed, formulated, delineated or created. We should like to avoid particularly the latter term in this context because it is used throughout the present study to designate the process of the birth of *legal* rules. Therefore, this first stage will be referred to as the formative stage.

The second stage is for purposes of the present study the least important of the three. It is the one in which on the part of the States concerned the will is being shaped that the rule will become law; or, to put it in Meijers' own words, "what is taking place during this stage is the development of the will to make a rule into law ...".[340] However, as this taking shape of the will of the States is an internal process, the second stage, which could be called the stage of the intent to be bound, is not directly relevant to the subject-matter discussed here.[341]

In the third stage the will developed during the second one has to become cognizable for all States for whom the rule may become law. Stage three is designed to divide up into legal rules and non-legal rules, the rules formed in stage one. Stage three may therefore be called the law-creating stage.[342]

Meijers then goes on to apply his model to the process of treaty-making and is able to show that it indeed fits the consecutive steps which States take in that process.[343] The advantage presented by treaties is that the stages one and three are clearly distinguishable, although their operation in practice sometimes overlaps. This is different with respect to customary international law. There we are not only confronted with such an overlap, but in addition "it frequently happens that the stages are not clearly differentiated".[344] This indeed would seem the heart of the problem of customary international law to which we have pointed above.[345] The distinction between the two components of customary international law, here presented as the distinction between various stages of the process of creation of customay rules of international law, is indeed vital and

---

339. *Ibidem*, p. 6; compare what has been observed above about the procedural aspects or provisions of the international "constitution" (pp. 57-60).
340. See H. Meijers, *loc.cit.* (note 204), p. 7.
341. See *supra* note 51.
342. See on the three stages in general H. Meijers, *loc.cit.* (note 204), pp. 5-7.
343. *Ibidem*, pp. 8-11.
344. *Ibidem*, p. 11.
345. See *supra* pp. 87-88.

Meijers has correctly observed that the mixing up of the operation of these elements, particularly in time, is "one of the reasons why no generally recognized, consistent theory on the creation of customary law has been realisable ...".[346]

He adds still another, although in our view closely related, reason for this state of affairs. It is to be found in the fact that "both treaty and judicial practice have repeatedly neglected to distinguish between the conditions which must be fulfilled, on the one hand for the creation of international customary law, and on the other, for its existence".[347] The result is, as was explained above,[348] demanding the impossible in that existence is made a condition for creation. Therefore, it is extremely important to keep the two elements or the two stages apart from a theoretical point of view, however difficult it may be to distinguish them clearly in practice.

It is not necessary to discuss at great length Meijers' analysis of customary international law on the basis of his model. The most important conclusion from the perspective of the present study may be summarized in the following manner: it is *usus* which is operative during the first stage and through which the content of the rule is being delineated and formulated; *opinio juris*, on the other hand, is taking shape during the second stage and expressed or made recognizable in the third one.

6.2.2.2. Advantages of the stages-theory

Not surprisingly, the theory just described, particularly in the short and abstract form in which it is presented here, still leaves a number of questions unanswered. We will get back to these later. Before that, it is useful to point to some most important advantages which this approach to customary international law entails. First and foremost, it does not assault, like some theories do,[349] the meaning of the term "custom" as a practice-based method of law-creation. On the contrary, it rather buttresses the practice-oriented character of international custom by demanding that the formulation of the content of the rule in stage one takes place through *usus*: "customary law is built upon repetition. Without the repetition of similar conduct in similar situations there can be no custom and without custom there can be no customary law".[350] It is therefore a reminder of the fact, sometimes overlooked, that although *opinio juris* turns a rule into a rule of international law, it is the *usus* which makes it a rule of *customary* law.[351]

346. H. Meijers, *loc.cit.* (note 204), p. 11.
347. *Ibidem.*
348. See *supra* p. 87.
349. See *supra* pp. 85-86.
350. H. Meijers, *loc.cit.* (note 204), p. 13.
351. See in this connection also *infra* p. 98, where a distinction will be made between the situation in which *usus* precedes *opinio juris* and *vice versa*. In the latter situation the preceding *opinio juris*, in the sense of consent or acceptance, results already in a rule of international law, and consequently it is a little odd to consider the subsequent *usus* as constitutive of a rule of (customary) international law. A similar point, it would seem, is also implied in the view of Bos according to whom the traditional definition of custom as "what one is in the habit of doing, convinced that such behaviour is legally obligatory (*opinio juris*)" needs to be supplemented by the words "*although not ordered by a written rule*", *loc.cit.* (note 28), pp. 25 jo. 74.

Secondly, the approach just outlined is compatible with, and may even help to explain, the ultimately consensual character of customary international law. This issue has already been referred to and it was noted that more than once the fact that customary international law, just like treaty-law, is in the final analysis based upon consent or acceptance, is called into question. Equally, the argument often adduced that new States are bound by customary international law without their consent or acceptance being required, was dismissed as being a reversal of argument and conclusion.[352] Here, we would like to reiterate this point, because the case against consent or acceptance as the constitutive element is often stated in the most direct manner in the context of a discussion of the concept of custom. Often it is simply asserted that a rule of customary international law, once it has duly come into existence, is binding upon all States even if a particular State has not consented to or accepted it.[353] Now, all depends of course on how the words "once it has duly come into existence" are interpreted. If one proceeds, as in the present author's view is necessitated by the basic features of international society,[354] from consent or acceptance as the constitutive element for rules of international law, it is only after all States have consented to or accepted it that a customary rule of international law is binding for all States. Otherwise, it simply is no rule binding for all States, although it may obviously be a rule of international law for a smaller number of States.

It is surprising to see that more than a few writers support the view ascribing some kind of "legislative" character to rules of customary international law, while at the same time admitting with respect to rules of international law in general that they can be created only through consent. The root of this inconsistency is difficult to trace. Often no arguments are given to support the point of view, but it is bluntly asserted. Maybe it is prompted by a desire to enrich international law with a device, like the phenomenon of legislation in municipal law, which enables the creation of legal rules against the will of a member of the society concerned. Most often the same desire also prompts the repudiation of whatever type of legal Positivism, because its emphasis on consent or acceptance is said to frustrate progress in the international society, and subsequently, the recommendation of some brand of Natural Law. We have already dealt with approaches like these.[355] Wolfke has rebutted this type of attacks on Positivism in the following way: "The charge of holding up progress is here a typical symp-

---

352. See *supra* pp. 77-78.
353. See in this respect A. D'Amato, who in the introduction to his *Concept of Custom in International Law* compares the latter with treaty-law and in connection with this question upholds that "perhaps custom is the most important, for it is generally regarded as having universal application, whether or not any given State participated in its formation or later 'consented' to it", *op.cit.* (note 182), p. 4; see also G. Arangio-Ruiz who while denying the character of legislation to rules of international law (see *supra* note 209), nevertheless is of the opinion "that customary rules bind states which had no part in their 'making' ...", *op.cit.* (note 195), p. 293; and also Thirlway's fine book on customary international law goes into the same direction when it is stated that: "It is of course fundamental that a treaty rule, as such, binds only those states which have expressly assented to its application to them, whereas a rule of customary law binds all States of the international community ...", *op.cit.* (note 209), p. 78. Thirlway softens his point of view somewhat by allowing an exception for so-called "recalcitrant states", which have manifested consistent opposition from an early enough moment. Compare also his firm statement on page 136.
354. See *supra* pp. 71-76.
355. See *supra* pp. 30-34.

tom of naiveté, common even with the most eminent scholars. It amounts to blaming effects instead of causes, and leads to the conviction that in this case it would suffice to change the effects of the conception of international customary law, to change international reality. It is obvious that it is not this or that conception which is to be blamed for unsatisfactory progress in international relations. And a change of such conception cannot by itself improve these relations. There is, on the other hand, no doubt that by accepting criteria and postulates excessively detached from actual conditions would bring about effects which would be the opposite of progress - namely complete neglect of law (and judicial organs), which would become the proverbial dead letter".[356]

At any rate, a (juridically) more tangible reason for the inconsistency just mentioned could be found in article 38(1)(b) of the Statute of the International Court of Justice. It may very well be that this enigmatic formula has contributed to causing the contradiction. It reads: "international custom, as evidence of a general practice accepted as law". Due to its peculiar drafting the formula lends itself to interpretation in a way which links the word "general" to the word "accepted". If interpreted in this way, the provision contains the burdensome requirement that one can speak of a customary rule of international law only if it is generally accepted, that is if all or at least nearly all States have expressed their *opinio juris* with respect to it. It is not difficult to see that as a result there would be hardly any rule of customary international law, if at all. Faced with such a dilemma it is of course tempting to look for a way-out in softening the requirement of the generality of the acceptance, while leaving untouched the generality of the applicability. However, such a construction is clearly incompatible with the basic features of the international society and the ensuing fundamental foundation of international law, *viz.* the consent or acceptance of the States.[357]

It is one of the merits of the stages-theory that it helps to solve this apparent dilemma in a way which is compatible with the consensual character of international law. The distinction between the first formative stage and the third creative stage makes it clear that the dilemma is not a real one. The practice of States (*usus*), which in the first stage delineates or formulates the content of the rule, needs to be general. "General" must be understood here as the requirement that the content of the rule has to take shape through similar conduct of (the generality of) the States concerned.[358]

The expression of *opinio juris* during the third stage, on the other hand, needs not to be general at all. As Meijers has pointed out, article 38 of the Statute "does not say 'a general practice generally accepted as law'".[359] This is undoubtedly correct. The present writer, therefore, can see no reason why, in a situation where not all States (concerned) are prepared to express their *opinio juris* with respect to a particular rule, a limited number of States could not do so anyway and thus create a rule of customary international law *inter se*. If States are free to withhold their consent or acceptance, other States have to be equally free to give their consent or acceptance. It follows that there can be no objection

356. K. Wolfke, *op.cit.* (note 308), p. 165.
357. *Ibidem*, p. 25.
358. To be sure, this requirement does not imply that all of the States concerned must take part in the practice. See for more details on the requirement that the practice has to be general, *infra* pp. 110-111.
359. H. Meijers, *loc.cit.* (note 204), p. 21.

of theory against the situation (and, as far as the present writer can see, neither practical impediments to it), where the number of States which through their practice contributed to the delineation of the content of the rule is larger than the circle of States for which the rule eventually becomes binding international law. Such a situation may occur of course, when some of the States which participated in the formative practice consider the rule to belong to the *comitas gentium*, international morality, or some other type of rules of conduct, but do not want it to become a rule of international law and, consequently, do not develop an *opinio juris*. Conversely, it is also theoretically possible (although not likely to occur very often in practice), that more States are eventually bound by the rule than originally contributed to the delineation of the rule. This possibility arises when the requirement of "generality" with respect to state-practice is to mean something other than universality.[360]

The foregoing raises once again the issue of "general international law". It was already pointed out that in the present study the term is used in a sense different from the one usually employed.[361] While in the present author's view it is to be preferred to relate the term to the general nature of the subject-matter which the rule in question addresses, most often it is taken to refer to the global number of States that are bound by the rule. General international law in the latter sense, therefore, connotes rules which are binding upon all or nearly all States of the international community. Interpreted in this way it becomes only a small step to equate customary international law with general international law, because, as was explained,[362] doctrine usually holds that customary rules of international law are generally binding.[363]

It is true that at the same time allowance is made for the concept of regional or local custom, which has been recognized by the International Court of Justice.[364] Regional or local custom is treated, however, as an exception to the main rule that "normal" custom is generally binding on the States of the international community.[365] Thus, the point of view would seem to be upheld that, apart from the local or regional custom, rules of customary international law are binding upon all or nearly all States of the international community.[366]

360. See *infra* pp. 110-111.
361. See *supra* pp. 67-68.
362. See *supra* pp. 94-95.
363. See, for instance, H. Thirlway, *op.cit.* (note 209), pp. 141-142: "general international customary law does not require the consent of all states to become binding on the whole international community, but only the consent of the 'generality' of states ...".
364. Most notably in its decisions in the *Asylum* case, ICJ Reports (1950), pp. 266-389 and the *Right of Passage* case, ICJ Reports (1960), pp. 6-144. See also the separate opinions of Judge Gros and of Judge Ammoun in the *Barcelona Traction* case, ICJ Reports (1970), pp. 3-357. Instead of regional or local custom it would be preferable to employ the term special or specific custom because the common characteristic of the limited number of States to which this type of custom is applicable is not necessarily to be found in geographical criteria but may also be one or more other special circumstances distinguishing them from other States, cf. M. Akehurst, *loc.cit.* (note 282), p. 29.
365. See M. Akehurst, *ibidem*: "A special custom, by definition, is one which conflicts with general custom". See on the other hand K. Wolfke's less restrictive conclusion drawn from the *Asylum* and the *Right of Passage* case: "Those precedents show beyond doubt that the Court, contrary to the provision of Subparagraph 1(b) of Article 38 of the Statute, has acknowledged customary rules binding a few or even only two states", *op.cit.* (note 308), p. 90.
366. In the same vein P. Weil, *loc.cit.* (note 216), pp. 38-39, who observes that "l'expression 'règle de droit international général' est utilisé aujourd'hui de plus en plus comme synonyme de

On the basis of what has been observed in the foregoing concerning the nature of rules of customary international law, the present author is of opinion that with respect to such rules, just as in the case of other types of international legal rules, there may exist a quite large variety in the number of States to which the various rules apply. Theoretically, the extent to which a rule is binding may range from all States down to two States. There is no reason why a limited number of States could not create *inter se* a customary rule of international law just because one or more other States are unwilling to participate in the process.[367] If this is recognized, it follows that the distinction between general and special/specific customary international law is not particularly relevant. It is therefore better to say that a customary rule of international law may encompass a greater or smaller number of States leaving the others outside its purview and to admit that such a variety in binding force is perfectly consistent with the nature of customary international law properly perceived. It meets with no objection that the number of parties to a treaty may vary from very small to very large (apart from provisions to the opposite effect in the treaty itself); the same must hold good with respect to customary international law, because like treaty-law, it is ultimately based upon consent or acceptance.[368]

All this is simply the result of the decentralized manner in which international law is created and which produces what could be called the "individualized" character of international law. By this is meant the fact that, unlike the usual state of affairs in municipal law, international law does not entail the same rights and duties for all its subjects. It may even not be too far-fetched to say that no two States are bound by exactly the same rules of international law. At the same time, however, it should not be forgotten that the increasing interdependence and the ensuing "globalization" of international law constitutes a strong countervailing force in this respect, and is likely to further push back the effects of the "individualized" character of international law.[369]

6.2.2.3 Questions concerning the change of customary international law

Some questions which were said to be left unanswered at first sight by the stages-

---

règle coutumière. Ainsi, dans l'arrêt sur le *Plateau continental de la mer du Nord*, la Cour parle indifféremment de 'droit international coutumier', de 'droit international général', de 'droit international général ou coutumier', ou encore (plus rarement) de 'règle général de droit international', de 'droit général'"; see also the Court's statement in the recent *United States Diplomatic and Consular Staff in Tehran* case, ICJ Reports (1980), pp. 3-65 (31): "In the view of the Court, the obligations of the Iranian Government here in question are not merely contractual obligations established by the Vienna Conventions of 1961 and 1963, *but also obligations under general international law*" (emphasis addes)

367. See *infra* pp. 110-111.
368. The foregoing leaves open the possibility of the existence of special custom or, more generally, special rules of international law in the sense of a rule conflicting with a more general rule. Between the parties to a special rule, the latter applies. They can, however, not encroach upon the rights of third States and in their relations with such States they consequently have to abide by the more general rule, if and to the extent that it is binding upon them. With respect to treaty law this rule has been laid down in the articles 34-38 of the Vienna Covention on the Law of Treaties.
369. See *supra* p. 66.

theory may now be taken up.[370] In the following, two problems will be discussed which in the present author's view are interrelated. They may best be set forth by first harking back to Kunz's statement on the nature of customary international law.

It was noted above that Kunz has very clearly outlined what he considers the dilemma of customary international law, *viz.* the (supposedly) required simultaneousness of *usus* and *opinio juris*.[371] He arrives at this dilemma on the basis of a distinction between two hypotheses. In the first place, "A norm of *courtoisie internationale* may become a norm of customary general international law: here the "*opinio juris* is later added to the usage and no theoretical difficulty arises".[372] Much more difficult, according to Kunz, is the second situation which could be contemplated, that is "a case of the original formation of a norm of customary general international law".[373] The latter phrase is not without ambiguity. However, what Kunz probably had in mind, when he spoke of "original custom", was the situation where *opinio juris* precedes *usus*.[374]

Now, in this second situation there is a (preceding) *opinio juris*[375] and, consequently, there exists already a rule of international law, albeit not a customary rule.[376] In such a case it would strictly speaking seem a little artificial, to the present author's mind, to consider the relevant subsequent practice as *usus* giving rise to a customary rule of international law, which would then be the same as the one resulting from the preceding *opinio juris*. Below we will return to the various forms which this relation between an existing rule and subsequent practice may take.[377]

The words "original custom" have a further implication, even if Kunz himself probably did not have it in mind, when he wrote the phrase. Particularly the word "original" (also) suggests the creation of a norm of customary international law in a situation of *tabula rasa*, that is in a situation where international law does not already contain a norm similar or contrary to (*viz.* ordering behaviour different from that ordered by) the one now to be created. As far as such a *tabula rasa*-situation is concerned, the stages-theory raises no difficulties. But what if the situation is "non-original" and a norm to the contrary already exists? In other words, Kunz' theoretical question puts us on track towards the problem of change of customary international law, which obviously is of a great practical import. It prompts the question whether the stages-theory can account for the changes in customary international law. This problem is not explicitly dealt with in Meijers' study. Indeed, the mere idea of stages leaves room for the impression that it is applicable only to "original" situations. For, as was observed, the theory seems to demand a strict order of stages: first, the formative stage in which the content of the rule is delineated through *usus*, and after that the transformation

370. See *supra* p. 93.
371. See *supra* p. 87.
372. J. Kunz, *loc.cit.* (note 281), p. 667.
373. *Ibidem.*
374. This may be deduced from the fact that the second hypothesis is set against the first one where *opinio juris* is later added to *usus*.
375. *Opinio juris* is understood here as implying an intent to be bound and therefore has the same legal effect as consent and acceptance.
376. Compare what has been observed with respect to so-called instant customary law, *supra* p. 86.
377. See *infra* pp. 102-103 and 275-279.

of the rule into one of international law by the development and subsequent expression of *opinio juris*.[378] But obviously the theory runs into problems if a new norm is to be created in contravention of an already existing one, because the first formative stage consisting of *usus* would *per definitionem* constitute a violation of the existing norm of international law. Clearly, such a contradiction could not be accepted in a theory claiming to provide an explanation of the nature of customary international law.

Nevertheless, it is true that solutions for the puzzling problems concerning change of customary international law have been proposed precisely adumbrating such a contradiction. D'Amato's position may be taken as an example. His point of view boils down to the conclusion that the smooth working of change in customary international law requires recognition of the fact that "Each deviation contains the seeds of a new rule".[379] Whatever the merit of this formula in explaining how customary international law sometimes changes in practice, it is for sure an odd point of departure for a general theory of custom. It must be quite an extraordinary system of law which incorporates as its main, if not the only, vehicle for change the violation of its own provisions. Taken to the extreme such a theory would entail a reversal of the old erroneous point of view which concluded from the absence of sanctions in international law that international law is not really law.[380] While this position has been virtually abandoned, international law now sometimes is presented, on the basis of the same fact that it lacks sanctions or even law-determining agencies, as a system of law in which violations are practically non-existent and in which every deviation of a rule has first of all to be looked at from the perspective of its contribution to the creation of new (diverging) rules of international law. This line of reasoning not only runs counter to the maxim *ex iniuria jus non oritur*, but after what has been said about the requirement of certainty in the law it needs no further explanation that in our view all this amounts to putting things upside down.[381]

In addition, it can be dangerous, particularly in present-day international relations, to conclude that States can change international law by breaking it. Ake-

---

378. Furthermore, the examples Meijers cites are equally tailored to what was called here an "original" situation. See, for instance, the observations with respect to (the state of international law concerning) the problem of hunger in the world: "In this example, the 'practice' of Article 38 of the Statute, state practice, probably consists, in the beginning, of unilateral actions, *viz.* gifts from certain rich states to certain poor states; after this there follow bilateral and probably regional aid agreements. These unilateral actions and treaty activities may at a later date exhibit a consistent pattern, which makes the subject of hunger suitable to be dealt with by states in the fora of worldwide organizations, and finally for a declaration (...) of the General Assembly of the United Nations. First by way of unilateral actions, later through the conclusion of treaties (which is also state practice), and later still through unilateral and collective actions at a world forum of the United Nations, a pattern based upon repetition will probably be discernible", H. Meijers, *loc.cit.* (note 204), pp. 14-15.
379. A. D'Amato, *op.cit.* (note 182),p. 98. In a more elaborate form his argument runs as follows: "Unquestionably customary law has changed over the years, and thus any theory must incorporate the possibility of change into its concept of custom. In particular, an 'illegal' act by a state constitutes the seeds of a new legality. When a state violates an existing rule of customary international law, it is undoubtedly 'guilty' of an illegal act, but the illegal act itself becomes a disconfirmatory instance of the underlying rule. The next state will find it somewhat easier to disobey the rule, until eventually a new line of conduct will replace the original rule by a new rule", *ibidem*, p. 97.
380. See, for instance, *supra* p. 36 on Austin's theory.
381. See *supra* pp. 24-27.

hurst, among others, appears to be fully aware of this. Although he believes that a way to change a customary rule is to break it frequently, he adds that "the process is hardly one to be recommended by anyone who wishes to strengthen the rule of law in international relations".[382]

In the present writer's view one may go even one step further: if there exists a customary rule, every deviating behaviour or practice first and foremost constitutes a violation of international law. There is no *a priori* reason to search for the seeds of a new rule in such a violation. Bernhardt has rightly put this as follows: "Mir scheint, dass dann, wenn man am Eigenwert und der normativen Kraft des Rechts und hier speziell des Völkerrechts festhält - was sowohl wissenschaftlich als auch politisch geboten ist -, weder der Faktizität allein noch dem Willen jedes einzelnen Staates normative oder normlösende Kraft zukommt und dass selbst ein Abweichen einer beträchtlichen Zahl von Staaten von bisher anerkannten Normen diese Normen nicht beseitigt".[383] This indeed should, at the very least from a theoretical point of view, be the point of departure. To hold otherwise simply constitutes a denial of one of international law's most fundamental rules: *pacta sunt servanda.*[384]

Admittedly, this theoretical point of departure cannot explain away the fact, which can be witnessed sometimes in practice, of a legal norm becoming a dead letter or even being reversed because it is more or less generally disobeyed. Lawyers in municipal legal systems are now familiar with the phenomenon of civil disobedience. In international law the disobedience of one single State may have a far-reaching impact because the approximately 170 States constitute a very "small community" compared to even the smallest of national societies. In addition, States, unlike private persons in national legal systems, are simultaneously "producers" and "consumers" of the law,[385] and even if they violate international law as "consumers", the "producer"-position is likely to have an impact too.

However, the conclusion that a rule has lost its legal character because of general disobedience takes place after the fact. It is only after the development by which a rule has become a dead letter or has been reversed that it is concluded to have lost its legal character. Therefore, admitting after the fact that such a development has taken place or, for that matter, even taking into account in advance that such a development may sometimes take place, is not at all the same thing as making it the rule in advance that changing (customary) international law requires breaking it.[386] At any rate, the present author finds it impossible to accept the extreme thesis that every violation contains the seeds of a new rule.

It is not necessary to resort to violations in order to explain changes in customary international law. Within the theoretical framework put forward in the present study, contrary practice[387] cannot strictly speaking change rules of

---

382. M. Akehurst, *loc.cit.* (note 282), p. 8.
383. R. Bernhardt, *loc.cit.* (note 227), pp. 67-68.
384. See *supra* pp. 75-76.
385. See *infra* pp. 212-214.
386. According to M. Akehurst, *loc.cit.* (note 282), p. 8, this is not the only, but one of the methods of change: "as an alternative to changing customary law by breaking it, states can change it by repeatedly declaring that the old rule no longer exists - a much more desirable way of changing the law".
387. Contrary practice is to be distinguished from a practice, previously in conformity with a legal norm, which is discontinued. This is the so-called *desuetudo* which may by itself abolish rules

100

international law. It should be recalled in this respect that *usus* (practice) makes a rule a customary rule, but it is *opinio juris* which turns it into an international rule of law. If this view is correct, then it is only through the operation of *opinio juris* that customary international law may change: what only *opinio juris* can do, only *opinio juris* can undo. In other words, it requires the crumbling away and the disappearance of *opinio juris* with respect to the old rule and, subsequently, the development and the expression of *opinio juris* with respect to the new one, to change customary international law. The fact that in actual life the two processes may somtimes coincide does not absolve theory from the need to make the distinction.

The process of change of customary international law as just described can be explained in terms of the stages-theory: the same consecutive steps which were said to lead to the building up of a rule of customary law can also tear it down, if they are taken in the reverse order. When the old norm has been abolished in this way, the process of creating a new one, through the various stages, may start again. As was implied in the observation on civil disobedience, it may be that States violate the law and that *afterwards* this turns out to have influenced the *opinio juris*, even to the extent that a new rule of customary international law has come into being. It should be stressed again that the awareness of this possibility should not be confused with an approach which looks *in advance* at violations as containing the elements for new rules. Obviously, the foregoing implies that at a certain point in time customary law on a given subject may be highly uncertain or even non-existent. It is submitted, however, that this is inherent in the rather vague and slow character of custom as a method of creating international law,[388] which in our view is precisely one of the reasons why the role of customary law is declining.[389]

The preceding analysis constitutes a theoretical explanation of the process of change of customary international law. Like almost every theoretical scheme it cannot do away with all problems arising in practice. It is submitted, however, that the stages-theory indeed provides an explanation for the bulk of instances in practice where customary international law changes. Dupuy has brilliantly clarified how all this actually takes place.[390] The core of his argument in fact is that, due to the changes in the structure of international relations, in modern (revolutionary) custom emphasis has shifted from *usus* to *opinio juris*: "The factual and consentient elements in the formation of custom assume different proportions depending on the milieu, the time and the interests concerned. As a result, there exists a continuous tension between fact and consciousness. In the case of classical custom, the multiplication of facts leads to a growth in juridical

of customary international law, as the latter are practice-based; see *supra* p. 93. However, it cannot obviously create new custom because it is in fact non-practice. In actual life, moreover, *desuetudo* is most likely to occur alongside or parallel to a declining conviction that the practice in question is to be followed in virtue of a legal obligation (*opinio juris*).

388. See in this respect M. Bos, *loc. cit.* (note 28), p. 30: "the vagueness of its beginnings are due to the nature of custom itself, and so it is with regard to its coming to an end, either through *desuetudo*, or by the creation of another, contradictory, custom. Intertemporal problems relating to custom, consequently, are among the most difficult ones to solve".

389. See *infra* pp. 113-116.

390. See in particular the first part of his essay, entitled: "Declaratory Law and Programmatory Law: From Revolutionary Custom to 'Soft Law'", in: R. Akkerman e.a. (eds.), *Liber Röling, Declarations on Principles; A Quest for Universal Peace* (Leyden 1977), pp. 247-257.

consciousness in an existential process in which existence precedes essence, termed after the fact as law. Conversely, revisionist or revolutionary custom involves the factual projection of the political will".[391] This entails the conclusion that in view of present-day international relations *opinio juris* has taken precedence over *usus*.[392] This modern *opinio juris* (or in Dupuy's terminology, the consentient elements or the political will) works first of all to signal the end of contrary (old) customary rules.[393] If Dupuy's reasoning is understood correctly, the major vehicle for the subsequent building up of new rules is again *opinio juris*. As was observed, in the present author's view, it is a little artificial to label the new rules thus created rules of customary international law. Probably, Dupuy experiences the same difficulty because he repeatedly employs terms like a revisionist, revolutionary or inchoate custom. This is buttressed by his conclusion that as a result of the changes in the international society "part of customary international law is bound to fall asunder".[394]

This leads us once again to the question of the relations between prior *opinio juris* on the one hand and posterior *usus*, which should more appropriately be labeled subsequent practice, on the other hand.[395] This relation may take different forms. The subsequent practice may be incompatible with the existing norm created by the (preceding) *opinio juris*. In this case the subsequent practice has to be considered a violation of the rule concerned. Conversely, the subsequent practice can be compatible with the existing rule. Several possibilities should be distinguished in that case. First, the practice may completely fall within the purview of the existing rule and simply constitute law-conform conduct. Secondly, the subsequent practice may be compatible with the existing rule, but still go a little further. It can then be considered an elaboration or concretization of the rule concerned. As long as the subject matter of the practice is sufficiently identical with that of the existing rule, one can indeed speak of elaboration or concretization. In such a case no separate expression of *opinio juris*, in the sense of consent or acceptance, would seem to be needed, because it may be taken to be embodied in the existing rule. Finally, the subject matter of a body of (subsequent) practice may be so "far removed" from the contents of existing rules that, although not incompatible with and related to the latter, it can no longer be considered an elaboration or concretization. Then the contents of a new (sub-)rule may have been delineated through practice which requires an additional *opinio juris* to turn it into a customary legal rule. It is only the last-mentioned situation which clearly falls within the ambit of customary international law as defined in the present study.

Admittedly, the dividing-line between the different situations just described is not seldom extremely thin.[396] Interesting in this respect is Bleckmann's view,

391. *Ibidem*, p. 249; more generally a somewhat similar idea finds expression in the words of R. Bernhardt, *loc.cit.* (note 227), p. 66: "Je klarer und eindeutiger die Zeichen gemeinsamer Rechtsanschauung sind, um so weniger wichtig ist die Umfang der einschlägigen Praxis".
392. See R. Dupuy, *loc.cit.* (note 390), p. 250: "This primacy of consciousness over fact is at the heart of revolutionary custom".
393. *Ibidem*, pp. 250-251. This does of course not apply to a *tabula rasa*-situation, but implies that a contrary norm exists.
394. *Ibidem*, p. 248.
395. See *supra* p.98.
396. See in this respect K. Wolfke, *op.cit.* (note 308), pp. 104-109 on the necessity to discern intermediate rules between conventional and customary rules. According to him "in practice,

who holds that in fact state-practice mostly develops against the background of more or less abstract norms of pre-existing law: "Abweichend von dem Eindruck, den die Literatur zum Völkergewohnheitsrecht erwecken könnte, besteht die von einer Rechtsüberzeugung getragene Praxis nicht in der Behauptung der Rechtmässigkeit oder Rechtswidrigkeit eines bestimmten tatsächlichen Verhaltens. Gegenstand der Praxis sind vielmehr meist mehr oder weniger abstrakte Rechtssätze, die über das konkrete Verhalten der Staaten weit hinausgreifen ... Die von der Rechtsüberzeugung getragene Praxis stützt sich also nicht nur auf das konkrete Verhalten, sondern gerade auf die Existenz der abstrakten Rechtsätzen".[397]

This sounds quite plausible to the extent that the greater "density" of international law, in the form mainly of its horizontal expansion, has resulted in an increase in the number of more or less abstract and vague norms.[398] Once again it should be stressed, however, that this process does not in all cases constitute the creation of customary international law, as defined in the present study, but sometimes rather the elaboration or concretization of already existing international law in general through state-practice. It can, therefore, better be dealt with within the latter framework. Furthermore, for the sake of clarity of the doctrine of sources it is important to keep the admittedly subtle distinctions made above as clear as possible. As the elaboration or concretization strictly speaking is still a derivation of an already existing rule, it is appropriate to deal with the "concretization-function" of state-practice under the heading of subsequent practice.[399] This approach entails the additional advantage of bearing out more clearly, that there exists a considerable interrelation and interaction between the various sources in the sense of manifestations, which necessitates a more integrated approach to the issue of the sources in the sense of manifestations of international law.

Finally, one more aspect of the problem of change in customary international law needs to be addressed here. It is probably the most difficult one. It was argued in the foregoing that generally speaking change must take place through the operation of *opinio juris*: its crumbling away or its revocation by States signals the end of the old rule, its subsequent development and expression with respect to a new rule delineated through practice marks the beginning of a new rule. But where does this leave the previously drawn conclusion that international law is not a voluntaristic system which leaves States the liberty to contract out of its binding rules at will?[400] If that conclusion is correct, how can States revoke their *opinio juris*? Would not such a revocation encroach upon the fundamental rule of *pacta sunt servanda*? In a more concrete form one is faced here with Friedmann's more abstract antinomy between stability and change[401]: on

---

it is found that many rules on closer examination give trouble as to their classification as between the two kinds of rules. Those are the rules which, because of the variety of elements which have contributed to their formation, lie in the no-man's land between customary and conventional rules", *ibidem*, p. 104.

397. A. Bleckmann, "Völkergewohnheitsrecht trotz widersprüchlicher Praxis?", 36 *ZaöRV* (1976), pp. 374-406 (383).
398. See *supra* p. 69.
399. See *infra* pp. 275-279.
400. See *supra* pp. 77-81.
401. See *supra* p. 28.

the one hand, the law has to provide certainty in order to be able to play its ordering role; on the other hand, it needs to change in order to keep abreast with developments in society. In this fast-moving world the matter gains particular significance with respect to international law, mainly because the latter is lacking formal law-giving and law-determining agencies.

The starting point must remain the non-voluntaristic approach. This implies of course that a State cannot rid itself of international legal obligations at will. Still, customary international law has changed and must continue to change. An answer may be found in the concept of the recognized necessity which was said above to constitute the basis of the binding force of international law as a whole.[402]. With respect to individual rules of international law the same necessity might also provide an explanation for their change. Even if States cannot simply revoke their *opinio juris* at will because of the *pacta sunt servanda* principle, there is nothing to prevent them from gaining the recognition that a certain rule of international law *has* to change. In other words, what may develop is a (negative) *opinio necessitatis* to the effect that the old rule must be abolished.

At first sight it may seem paradoxical that the same recognized necessity which is the basis of the binding force of international law at the same time constitutes the avenue through which change of individual rules of international law can be initiated. It should be recalled, however, that the recognition on the part of the States that it is necessary to abide by international law, stems from the desire for stability to keep the international society viable. That very viability, on the other hand, may prompt the conviction on the part of States that the law must change. Moreover, the expression of this conviction or *opinio non-necessitatis* does not in itself effect the abolition of an (old) rule, but only prepares the ground. If it gains sufficient support, it could arguably provide a justification for the States concerned to revoke their consent or acceptance with respect to the old rule.[403]

A vital question is, of course, what "sufficient" means in this context. Obviously, the *opinio necessitatis* or rather *opinio non-necessitatis* of one single State is not sufficient; that possibility would nullify the principle of *pacta sunt servanda*. Conversely, no problem arises if all States concerned agree on the necessity of change. For the remainder it is difficult to tell *in abstracto* what the required number is. It depends on the particular circumstances of each case, notably the number of States (originally) bound by the rule, the purpose of the rule and the interests regulated by it, and the connection of the individual States with those interests. The most that can be said is that the recognized need for change is sufficiently wide-spread,if the number and/or quality of the States supporting it make the purpose of the existing rule unattainable. Only after the "neutralization" of a rule's purpose by a sufficient number of the States involved, are individual States "justified" in revoking their *opinio juris* and can such a revocation be said to have a legal effect. Obviously, this does not (yet) in

402. See *supra* pp. 71-76.
403. A similar sequence of events can be said to take place with respect to the change of treaties. First, States gain the recognition that the old treaty has become outdated and needs to be abolished. At a certain point this negative *opinio necessitatis* may be taken to have become strong enough to "neutralize" the consent with respect to the old treaty (for instance, once the preparatory work for a new treaty gets under way); finally, the process is completed by the entry into force of the new treaty.

itself create a new rule. Particularly if some States hold on to the old rule, a shorter or longer period of time may commence in which it is impossible to tell what the law is on a given issue.[404]

In summary, the process of change of (customary) international law may schematically be presented as comprising the following stages: development and expression of an *opinio non-necessitatis* concerning the old rule; if this has become sufficiently wide-spread, the (justified) revocation of *opinio juris* by individual States which possibly initiates the complete tearing down of the old rule; if and when the latter stage has been completed, the building up of a new customary rule through *usus* or of a non-customary rule through (original) *opinio juris* may begin.

The present writer is perfectly aware of the fact that actual life does not always follow neat theorectical schemes like this one. There is no doubt that, for instance, the awareness that an old rule has to be abolished may coincide with, or even flow from, the recognition that another new rule ought to be law. For tactical reasons States may even be expected to argue that the new rule is already law. Nevertheless, it seems very helpful to approach the puzzling questions arising in practice from a consistent theoretical scheme.

It is tempting to neglect these theoretical subtleties when looking at problems in practice. It is in this respect that the views of Thirlway and Walden differ from our own. The former has addressed the problem of change of customary international law by asking whether it would not be "nearer to the likely truth of the way in which customs do in fact develop, to say that the requirement of *opinio juris* is equivalent merely to the need for the practice in question to have been accompanied by either a sense of conforming with the law, or the view that the practice was potentially law, as suited the needs of the international community, and not a mere matter of convenience or courtesy?"[405] Similarly, Walden has held that "what is involved may be, not a belief that the practice is already legally binding, but a claim that it ought to be legally binding. In other words, those who follow the practice, and treat it as a legal standard of behaviour, may be doing so with deliberate legislative intent".[406]

The main difference with the view expounded here lies in the role attributed to *usus* in the process of change. The passages just quoted show that both Thirlway and Walden, in the final analysis, hold that change is affected by *usus*, albeit accompanied by *opinio necessitatis* or *opinio juris*. In the present study, on the other hand, it was reiterated that change cannot result from the (contrary) practice itself, but that it may eventually be achieved through the operation of *opinio necessitatis* and subsequently *opinio juris*.[407] The failure to make this (admit-

404. See *supra* pp. 100-101.
405. H. Thirlway, *op.cit.* (note 209), pp. 53-54, where also a comparison is made to the views of A. Verdross and Ch. de Visscher on this point; see also pp. 55-56 where the author observes that his view constitutes the chronological reversal of the expression *opinio juris sive necessitatis.*
406. R. Walden, loc.cit. (note 182), p. 97; see in this respect also the observation by K. Wolfke, *op.cit.* (note 308), p. 66: "The motive of conduct of state organs is not the creation of international law but the desire or need to satisfy their own or common requirements resulting from political, economic, etc. situations".
407. In practice, various complicated situations may arise. It may, for instance, be that a limited number of States subsequently create a new rule of law *inter se*. See also *supra* p. 97 on the "individualized" nature of international law.

tedly subtle) distinction engenders the danger of ending up too close to the erroneous position holding that "every violation contains the seeds of a new rule".[408]

6.2.3. *Opinio juris*; remaining issues

The element of *opinio juris* taken separately can be dealt with briefly. The preceding sections bear out that the importance of *opinio juris*, understood as the intention to be legally bound, is not confined to customary international law. On the contrary, it permeates the analysis of any of the sources in the sense of manifestations. Consequently, as will be set forth below, an analysis of the sources or manifestations of international law in fact boils down to a search for the *opinio juris*, or, to put it differently, the consent or acceptance of States.[409]

With respect to *opinio juris* as an element of customary international law one point remains to be emphasized. It regards the view that a rule of custom is binding upon all States, even those that have not consented to or accepted it. We have already discussed this view in relation to the formula contained in article 38 of the ICJ's Statute.[410] Here, it may be added that this point of view is to the present author's mind, a remnant of the Natural Law approach. Walden has pointed out that classical writers on international law all agreed that a rule of customary international law bound only those States that had consented to or accepted it: "one might have expected at least some of them to adopt the view which was commonly held as regards civil and canon law, and which as we have seen, Suarez expressly adopted, that a custom practised by the majority of the members of a community would bind the minority that did not practice it. None of them did so, however, not even Suarez in his discussion of the nature of *jus gentium*".[411]

He goes on to explain that in classic international law "This approach posed no problems as long as jurists recognized the existence, side by side with positive law, of a natural law which was binding on all States irrespective of their will. ... But once natural law concepts ceased to play any significant role..., it became necessary either to concede that international law was not necessarily a universal legal order, or to recognize the possibility that customary rules accepted by the majority of States would bind even the minority which dissented".[412] If the latter path is followed, this would indeed imply an analogical application of Natural Law views to the concept of customary international law.

6.2.4. *Usus*; remaining issues

As to the element of *usus*, it is necessary to start with a preliminary observation.

---

408. See *supra* pp. 99-100.
409. See *infra* p. 205.
410. See *supra* pp. 94-97.
411. R. Walden, *loc.cit.* (note 280), p. 347; the argument underlying this point of view in classical writing is to be found in the absence of a superior authority in international law, *ibidem*, p. 348.
412. *Ibidem*, p. 348.

Above a distinction was made with respect to state-practice between the "producer" and the "consumer" approach.[413] At this place it is necessary to add another one. It consists of the difference between state-practice regarding primary or substantive rules of international law, and that concerning secondary or procedural rules (of recognition).[414] The former consists of the behaviour of States which is apt to delineate the content of a rule of customary international law and is, as will be pointed out, to be narrowly defined. The latter, on the other hand, comprises the attitudes, positions, or simply the opinions of States with respect to the question of what constitutes the (correct) way or ways of creating rules of international law. Consequently, state-practice regarding secondary rules (of recognition) is much broader and encompasses, for instance, also abstract or general declarations on the part of States.[415] In discussing *usus* as one of the constitutive components of rules of customary international law, we are obviously dealing with state-practice regarding primary rules.

There exists quite wide-ranging disagreement in doctrine on what can properly be considered *usus*. Akehurst's detailed study on custom shows that it is far from easy to indicate *in abstracto* whether a certain type of act can be taken to belong to *usus* or not.[416] Akehurst himself employs an extremely broad conception of *usus*; almost all activities of States are counted. Illustrative in this respect is his opinion on statements by states *in abstracto*: "It is impossible to study modern international law without taking account of declaratory resolutions and other statements made by states *in abstracto* concerning the content of international law".[417]

This statement as such is certainly correct. It does not follow, however, that such resolutions or declarations can be classified as *usus* giving rise to custom. They may constitute *opinio juris* which, if expressed with respect to a rule sufficiently delineated through *usus*, may create a customary rule of international law. To this extent Akehurst is correct in stating that "When states declare that something is customary law, it is artificial to classify such a declaration as about something other than customary law".[418] But if there is no preceding *usus*, such a declaration cannot give birth to a customary rule, unless, of course, the declaration itself is treated as *usus* at the same time. However, it takes too wide a stretching of the concept of *usus* to arrive at the latter conclusion. As was rightly observed: "repeated pronouncements at best develop the custom or usage of making such pronouncements".[419]

As was already reiterated in the foregoing, it is dangerous to denaturate the practice-oriented character of customary law by making it comprise methods of law-making which are not practice-based at all. This undermines the certainty and clarity which the sources of international law have to provide. The Univer-

---

413. See *supra* pp. 88-90.
414. See *supra* pp. 46-53.
415. For this reason we treated the above-mentioned declarations of States on *pacta sunt servanda* during the Conference on Security and Cooperation in Europe (see *supra* pp. 75-76) and on the nature of customary international law at the United Nations (see *supra* p. 78) as state-practice.
416. M. Akehurst, *loc.cit.* (note 282), particularly pp. 1-11.
417. *Ibidem*, p. 7.
418. *Ibidem*.
419. Judge Pal in his Dissenting Opinion to the Judgment of the International Military Tribunal for the Far-East, quoted by K. Wolfke, *op.cit.* (note 308), p. 79.

sal Declaration on Human Rights may be taken as an example in this respect.[420] It has been asserted that in the course of time its provisions have grown into rules of customary international law. This view is often being substantiated by citing abstract statements by States supporting the Declaration or references to the Declaration in subsequent resolutions or treaties. Sometimes, it is pointed out that its provisions have been incorporated in national constitutions.[421] But what if States making statements like these or drawing up their constitutions in conformity with the Universal Declaration at the same time treat their nationals in a manner which constitutes a flagrant violation of its very provisions, for instance, by not combatting large scale disappearances, by practising torture, or by imprisoning people for long periods of time without a fair trial?[422] Even if abstract statements or formal provisions in a constitution are considered as state-practice, they have at any rate to be weighed against concrete acts like the one mentioned.[423]

In the present author's view, the best position would seem to be that it is solely the material, concrete and/or specific acts of States which are relevant as *usus*. As was said, it is difficult to come up with a definition *in abstracto*, but the following description would seem to offer a useful handhold: "The substance of the practice required is that States have done or abstained from doing certain things in the international field: *e.g.* that they have exercised diplomatic protection in certain circumstances, or recognized the rights of other States to do so; that they have refrained from bringing or permitting legal proceedings against visiting diplomats; that they have claimed certain areas of submarine territory, or recognized such right claimed by other States. State-practice as the material element in the formation of custom is, it is worth emphasizing, material: it is composed of acts by States with regard to a particular person, ship, defined area of territory, each of which amounts to the assertion or repudiation of a claim

420. Examples are usually taken from, but are certainly not confined to, the field of human rights. H. Schrader, *loc.cit.* (note 21), pp. 774-781, has pointed to some important American federal court decisions which show an extreme laxity with respect to the sources of international law, *in casu* the general principles recognized by civilized nations.
421. National legislation may indeed be state-practice constitutive of rules of customary international law.
422. Particularly astonishing is one case highlighted by H. Schrader, *loc.cit.* (note 21), pp. 764-765, where an American federal court "indicated that torture could still be contrary to customary international law even if routinely practiced by the very countries that claimed to renounce it". L. Stagno, "The Application of International Human Rights Agreements in United States Courts: Customary International Law Incorporated into Domestic American Law", VIII *BJIL* (1982), pp. 207-238 (237), reviewing this and some other similar cases, welcomes them as "an exciting new trend in legal orientation for human rights proponents". No doubt, everybody who, like the present author, would like to see the effectiveness of internationally protected human rights enhanced, will be satisfied with the outcome of cases like the one just referred to. Nevertheless, from the point of the sources of international law a reasoning like the one just mentioned is certainly to be regretted.
423. The example of the Universal Declaration just mentioned wants to make clear that, according to the present author, abstract statements cannot be said to delineate the content of a rule in the face of concrete material acts to the contrary during the so-called formative stage. Once a customary rule of international law has come into being, concrete material acts to the contrary of course constitute a violation of the rule concerned. Thus, if it is established that the Universal Declaration is binding upon a State as customary international law (possibly as a result, *inter alia*, of the State's own concurring practice), its later practice to the contrary (for

relating to a particular apple of discord".[424]

For the remainder it has to be judged on a case-by-case basis whether a certain behaviour of a State constitutes *usus* capable of delineating the content of a customary rule. Consequently, we will not in this context discuss at length the various kinds of state-behaviour, but only add a few remarks with respect to some of them.

Most writers agree that treaties are to be considered state-practice which may generate customary rules of international law.[425] They may find support in the I.C.J.'s statement in the *North Sea Continental Shelf* case holding that: "There is no doubt that this process is a perfectly possible one and does from time to time occur: it constitutes indeed one of the recognized methods by which new rules of customary international law may be formed".[426] It is true that treaties may be considered *usus*, but a number of things should be kept in mind in this respect. First, the treaty concerned must be concrete or specific enough to be able to delineate the content of a customary rule. Furthermore, and this is more important here, a treaty is of course binding on the States parties to it. Consequently, the question of its being capable of generating a customary rule is relevant only with respect to States which are not parties to it. For a customary rule of international law to come into being for non-parties, the latter must express their *opinio juris* with respect to it.[427] One should be careful, however, to draw the conclusion that they indeed have done so.[428] In the example given by Meijers, for instance, of a (possible) rule concerning development assistance from rich to poor countries crystallizing out of bilateral and/or regional aid agreement[429], the *opinio juris* should not be lightly presumed, if the State concerned has in no way participated in the practice (for instance, by *ad hoc* unilateral gifts). Similarly, it would seem that in the case of a multilateral treaty which is open for ratification by all States, the *opinio juris* constituting the "accession by way of custom"[430] has to be unambiguous. The fact that a State is not prepared to ratify the treaty cannot be without significance in such a situation.[431]

instance, as a result of a change of government) is to be considered as a violation of the Declaration.

424. H. Thirlway, *op.cit.* (note 209), p. 58.
425. See for instance H. Meijers, *loc.cit.* (note 204), p. 15; H. Thirlway, *op.cit.* (note 209), pp. 58-59; M. Akehurst, *loc.cit.* (note 282), pp. 42-52; A. D'Amato, *op.cit.* (note 182), pp. 103-166.
426. ICJ Reports (1969), p. 41.
427. See also M. Akehurst, *loc.cit.* (note 282), p. 44: "treaties, like other norms of state practice, must be accompanied by *opinio juris* in order to create customary law".
428. As the International Court of Justice added to its just-quoted statement: "At the same time this result is not lightly to be regarded as having been attained", ICJ Reports (1969), p. 41.
429. H. Meijers, *loc.cit.* (note 204), pp. 14-15.
430. The expression comes from K. Wolfke, *op.cit.* (note 308), p. 78.
431. In the *North Sea Continental Shelf* cases, ICJ Reports (1969), p. 26, the International Court of Justice equally upheld: "In principle, when a number of States, including the one whose conduct is invoked, and those invoking it, have drawn up a convention specifically providing for a particular method by which the intention to become bound by the régime of the convention is to be manifested - namely by the carrying out of certain prescribed formalities (ratification, accession), it is not lightly to be presumed that a State which has not carried out these formalities, though at all times fully able and entitled to do so, has nevertheless somehow become bound in another way".

Finally, a similar *caveat* should be observed when assessing whether national legislation and national court decisions are to be considered *usus*. Both may be relevant state-practice, but no *a priori* conclusion can be drawn here. There undoubtedly is a great deal of truth in saying that "A national court decision may be good evidence, but may also, in the words of the late Professor Borchard, only be evidence of what international law is not".[432] In other words, national legislation and national court decisions may help to delineate the content of rules of customary international law, but on the other hand may also be irrelevant to, or even in violation of such rules. It should be kept in mind in this respect that national legislators and national courts in making their decisions use the national context as their frame of reference and, consequently, are often not focused primarily on the international level. What remains to be said concerning *usus* can be dealt with under the headings of the requirement of the generality of practice, of the duration of the practice, and of the consistency of practice.

As far as the generality of practice is concerned, point of departure in doctrine is usually the ICJ's requirement in the *Asylum* case "that the rule invoked ... is in accordance with a constant and uniform usage practised by the States in question ...".[433] However, in the *Asylum* case the Court was dealing with regional/local, or rather special or particular custom and consequently that judgment does not provide a very appropriate example. It would seem better to start from the *North Sea Continental Shelf* case[434] where it was said that "an indispensable requirement would be that ... State practice, including that of States whose interests are specially affected, should have been both extensive and virtually uniform in the sense of the provision invoked;".[435] From one or the other decision the conclusion is usually drawn that the requirement of generality means that the practice has to be nearly, but not completely universal. Nevertheless, the present author ventures to believe that put in this way, this conclusion is not entirely convincing. Three observations have to be made in this respect.

First of all, the ICJ's above-cited case-law does not necessitate the conclusion drawn from it. "Extensive" means wide-spread, but is not synonymous with nearly universal. Furthermore, "uniform" is not to be equated with "universal". "Uniform" relates to the practice concerned, not to the number of States involved in that practice. It may, therefore, be interpreted to mean that the practice of the States involved must be nearly identical without answering the question how many States must be involved in the practice.

Secondly, it was already extensively argued that "general practice" should not be interpreted so as to imply the requirement of the generality of *opinio*

432. J. Kunz, *loc.cit.* (note 281), p. 668.
433. ICJ Reports (1950), p. 276.
434. ICJ Reports (1969).
435. *Ibidem*, p. 43.

110

juris.[436] The wide-spread inclination to do so, it was said, stems from the conviction that customary rules of international law are (to be) generally binding, that is binding upon (nearly) all States. The Court, too, seems to follow this reasoning. Wolfke has pointed out, by means of a detailed study of a great number of relevant cases, that both World Courts have in the final analysis deduced the existence or absence of *opinio juris* from the material element of the practice concerned.[437] In particular, he has concluded that "In all cases indicated above of referring to proof of the element of acceptance, the Court took as a basis either circumstances of practice, or tacit toleration of practice, manifesting itself above all in absence of protest. The Court, then, entirely resigned from positive proof of acceptance of the practice as expression of law, at the same time taking into account all evidences to the absence of such acceptance".[438] The same holds good, in the present author's view, for the major case concerning custom after the conclusion of Wolfke's investigation, *viz.* the *North Sea Continental Shelf* case.[439]

If all this is correct, the Court's insistence upon practice being (nearly but not completely) universal can be easily explained. The reason, then, lays in the deduction of *opinio juris* from *usus* if the former has to be general, as it does in the Court's view, for a customary rule of law to come into existence, so does the latter from which *opinio juris* is inferred.

When *opinio juris* and *usus* are more clearly kept separate, as was advocated above,[440] the requirement of a general practice becomes far less stringent. For the decisive criterion then becomes that the participation in the practice should be such that the content of a rule can be deduced from it. In our view this can already be the case even if the number of States involved turns out to be relatively small. If there is no contrary practice on the part of other States, such small-scale practice may very well delineate the content of a rule which afterwards proves able to gain acceptance as law by a larger circle of States.[441] Admittedly, such a situation is not likely to occur very often in fact. Nevertheless, it is important to note that, in practice too, the possibility exists.

More directly related to the situation in practice is our third observation. On the basis of the consensual character of international law it was concluded that a rigid distinction between general custom on the one hand, and regional/local custom on the other is highly artificial, and that in fact the number of States bound by a rule of customary international law may range from two up to all States.[442] If this is acknowledged, it is clear that the requirement of generality of

---

436. See *supra* pp. 94-97.
437. K. Wolfke, *op.cit.* (note 308), pp. 122-129.
438. *Ibidem*, p. 129.
439. In considering *opinio juris* in this case the Court relied on a consideration from the *Lotus* case comprised in Wolfke's analysis and concluded that "the position is simply that in certain cases - not a great number - the States concerned agreed to draw the boundaries concerned according to the principle of equidistance. There is no evidence that they so acted because they felt legally compelled to draw them in this way by reason of a rule of customary law obliging them to do so - especially considering that they might have been motivated by other obvious factors", ICJ Reports (1969), pp. 44-45.
440. See *supra* pp. 91-93.
441. See also *supra* p. 96.
442. See *supra* pp. 96-97.

practice becomes extremely relative. For, then, the number of States needed to build up a practice becomes dependent upon the circle of the States for which the rule is designed to eventually become a rule of law. As was seen this latter circle may vary from extremely small to very large.[443]

As far as the duration of practice is concerned, it is generally recognized that this requirement is of a more or less flexible character. Despite its above-mentioned emphasis on "a constant and uniform usage"[444] the ICJ has also conceded that "even without the passage of any considerable period, a wide-spread and representative participation in the convention might suffice of itself"[445] and, subsequently, that "the passage of only a short period of time is not necessarily, or of itself a bar to the formation of a new rule of customary international law ...".[446] Generally speaking, doctrine inclines towards the same position.[447] The requirement of the duration of practice has been softened further by the changes which have taken place in international relations.[448] As the speed and the frequency of interaction of States has increased, there now is simply more state-practice in a shorter period of time than there used to be. As Wolfke has pointed out: "A much longer space of time was necessary for the establishment of a regularity of conduct as regards, for instance, the right of innocent passage and for learning the attitude to it of states in the days when one vessel passed through territorial waters every week, than is necessary nowadays, when there are hundreds and even thousands of them every day".[449]

In addition, the time requirement involved in customary international law cannot be but affected by the dramatically improved possibilities of communication in the world. While exchange of information used to take days or even weeks, at present every act of every government can be almost instantaneously known to any other government. This, too, shortens the time required to build up a practice.

Apart from these general considerations, the time needed can only be established on a case-by-case basis, because here too everything depends on the question at what point the content of a rule can be said to have been mapped out through *usus*.

Finally, the same holds good for the requirement that the practice has to be consistent, or, in the Court's words, uniform or at least virtually uniform. It is tempting to soften this requirement too now that there is so much more state-practice than in the past. The expanded body of state-practice is likely to include more conflicting behaviour, now that the international society has acquired a more heterogeneous character. Indeed, the diverging interests and views of the various States are bound to be reflected in their conduct. This divergence in its turn hampers the development of customary international law between the States taking diverging positions on a certain issue. Consequently, it is tempting

443. It is noteworthy in this respect that the International Court of Justice in the *Asylum* case when it was dealing with what it calls regional or local custom, spoke of "the practice of the states *in question*" (emphasis aded), see *supra* p. 110.
444. See *supra* p. 110.
445. *North Sea Continental Shelf* cases, ICJ Reports (1969), p. 42.
446. *Ibidem*, p. 43.
447. See for instance, M. Akehurst, *loc.cit.* (note 282), pp. 15-16.
448. See *supra* pp. 65-71.
449. K. Wolfke, *op.cit.* (note 308), p. 67.
450. See *infra* pp. 276-277.

for doctrine to "save" customary international law by softening the requirement of consistency of practice. This, however, would be putting things upside down. As will be argued in the following section, the contradictions between the positions taken by the States as manifested through their (conflicting) practice is one of the very reasons why the role of custom as a source of international law is declining.

On the other hand, the extent to which present-day state-practice is conflicting should not be exaggerated. The "proliferation" of state-practice prompts a further diversification between various kinds of practice relating to different rules or different aspects of a rule of custom as a source of international law. Consequently, as will be submitted below, practice which at first sight seems to be contrary to or conflicting with preceding practice or existing rules of international law, may after closer inspection prove compatible with the former.[450]

6.3. The declining role of custom as a source of international law

In order to be effective any system of law has to be tuned to the needs of the community in which it has to function. Undoubtedly, customary international law has in some respects adapted to the changes in international relations. In the preceding section, for instance, it was pointed out that the time needed for a custom to develop has been considerably shortened as a result of the increased speed and frequency of inter-state relations and of the improved means of communication in the world. However, the nature of customary international law, as described in the foregoing, in our view prevents this source from adapting itself adequately to the developments as they have occurred in the international society. In consequence thereof one observes, in general, a decline of custom as a source of international law, on the one hand, and a rise of the international *lex scripta*, on the other.

To be sure, there does not exist *communis opinio* on this point. Bos has pointed to what seems to be a cleavage between Civil Law orientated international lawyers and Anglo-Saxon theory in this respect.[451] The latter usually holds that custom still is the most important source, while the former as a rule maintain that treaties have taken over the first place at the expense of custom.[452]

450. See *infra* pp. 276-277.
451. M. Bos, *loc.cit.* (note 28), pp. 21-22.
452. As representatives of the two sides Bos cites A. Verdross and C. Parry. A notable exception on the Civil Law side is H. Meijers who believes that "customary law appears to be growing in importance ...", *loc.cit.* (note 204), pp. 3-4. It is submitted, however, that his arguments do not seem convincing. The first reason for the rising star of custom he describes as follows: "If a state feels that it cannot avoid submitting on a particular point, or agreeing to follow a particular policy which would be difficult to justify to a public opinion motivated by short term considerations, then it is more convenient to do what is necessary less expressly, and out of sight of the electorate", *ibidem*, p. 4. This type of "secrecy" cannot be a successful form of dealing with foreign policy issues. As a result of the increasing interdependence these issues are becoming even more within the purview of public opinion at large. Consequently, a government pursuing such an approach of "secrecy" will eventually run into conflict with its electorate or will have to change its foreign policy. Secondly, Meijers mentions as a great advantage of making law via custom that "the inactive are carried along by the active" (*ibidem*), meaning that, as far as custom is concerned, lack of open rejection is sufficient to create a new rule. As will be argued below the same holds good to a large extent for other methods of creating international law; see *infra* pp. 229-234.

The present author believes that custom is in decline.[453] If one takes into account the changes which the international society has undergone, it is difficult to escape the conclusion that the process of creation of international law through custom has become extremely cumbersome. Its major drawback would seem to consist in its relative slowness. Although the process of law-making through international custom has been considerably speeded up, it has not been able to keep up with the ever faster rhythm of international relations. As we have seen in the preceding sections, the creation of customary international law, and particularly its change, are rather painstaking. It is for this reason that in particular the developing countries are not very much inclined towards acknowledging a primary role for custom as a source of international law.[454] The increased speed and frequency of international relations make demands on the making and changing of rules of international law, which custom cannot meet, unless that concept is stretched to encompass phenomena that are irreconcilable with its nature as properly understood. Conversely, as was observed, the process of decay of some old customary rules may proceed comparatively fast as a result of rapidly arising new situations in combination with the recent entry into the international society of a larger number of new States which refuse to adhere to some of the more traditional points of view.[455]

This whole situation has, therefore, been exacerbated by what we have called the population-explosion and the ensuing increased heterogeneity in the international society. Apart from its slowness, there is still another reason why custom is not very attractive as a source of international law, in particular for developing countries. Not infrequently these countries find themselves in a comparatively weak position *vis-à-vis* other States. Consequently, in various fields of international relations, notably the economic field, they are more or less compelled to conform to what other States prefer. Their conduct or practice, therefore, must deviate from what they in fact consider desirable, or to put it differently, their *usus*, of necessity, is more "conservative" than their *opinio juris*. As custom is a practice-oriented source of international law, it is no big surprise that developing countries do not regard custom as a very suitable vehicle to initiate what in their eyes constitutes the progressive development of international law and, consequently, tend to favour methods of law-making where emphasis is more on *opinio juris*.

In short, customary law is best fit for comparatively homogeneous communities where the interests of the members do not dramatically diverge. As soon as the community grows and its members start developing different interests

---

453. See also R. Jennings, *loc.cit.* (note 1), pp. 65-66.
454. See M. Bedjaoui, *Towards A New International Economic Order* (Paris 1979), p. 136: "It is obvious that the speed necessary for the adoption of the rules of international development law squares uneasily with the need to wait for repeated acts to bestow their sanction. In fact, the developed countries are perfectly aware, that this material element can only work in their favour".
455. Compare also the observation by Judge Alvarez according to whom customs "tend to disappear as the result of the rapid changes of modern international life; and a new case strongly stated may be sufficient to render obsolete an ancient custom. Customary law, to which such frequent reference is made in the course of the arguments, should therefore be accepted only with prudence", *Anglo-Norwegian Fisheries* case, ICJ Reports (1951), p. 36.

and conflicting views, it becomes less reliable.[456] All this would seem to prevent custom from playing a leading role in those new fields into which international law was said to have horizontally expanded.[457] Customary international law simply is to slow to provide the quick regulation required in the new areas which international law now has to cover.

As a second major drawback of customary international law is usually mentioned the fact that its rules are frequently too general and vague. This characteristic Hart has termed "the open texture of precedent" which he has described as follows: "Communication by example in all its forms, though accompanied by some general verbal directions such as 'do as I do', may leave open ranges of possibilities, and hence of doubt, as to what is intended even as to matters which the person seeking to communicate has himself clearly envisaged".[458] This handicap makes custom equally not very well-suited to assist international law in the tasks resulting from its vertical expansion,[459] that is the supply of the often detailed rules required by the deeper penetration of international law into the domain formerly left to the discretion of the States.

Jennings has summarized all this in the following way: "Perhaps it is time to face squarely the fact that the orthodox tests of custom - practice and *opinio juris* -are often not only inadequate but even irrelevant for the identification of much new law today. And the reason is not far to seek: much of this law is not custom at all, and does not even resemble custom. It is recent, it is innovatory, it involves topical policy decisions, and it is often the focus of contention. Anything less like custom in the ordinary meaning of that term it would be difficult to imagine".[460] The preceding description of customary law's major drawbacks in the light of present-day international relations does not imply that we should expect the complete withering away of custom as a source of international law.

First of all, there is of course still room left for customary international law to operate in its traditional way. In particular, regional/local or rather special/particular custom may very well play quite a considerable role in certain fields of international law. Secondly, it would seem that a somewhat different role for customary law, or rather state-practice, can be envisaged. We have just observed that because of their general and vague character rules of customary international law very often are not particularly suited for fields which require more detailed regulation. This is true in cases where the content of a rule has to be deduced from the practice of States as such, without any frame of reference to relate that practice to. In such cases one of the problems is that, in consequence of the growing heterogeneity resulting in diverging views and interests, this practice too becomes more contradictory which makes it more difficult to allow the conclusion that the content of a rule has been delineated through it.

---

456. See in this respect also Ch. de Visscher, who wrote already in the fifties: "Acceleration of history, and above all diminishing homogeneity in the moral and legal ideas that have long governed the formation of law - such, in their essential elements, are the causes that today curtail the development of customary international law", *Theory and Reality in Public International Law*, translation by P. Corbett (Princeton 1957), p. 156.
457. See *supra* pp. 65-69.
458. H. Hart, *op.cit.* (note 41), p. 122.
459. See *supra* pp. 65-69; as will be pointed out below, however, treaties are also not completely free from this flaw of "open texture", *infra* pp. 124-125.
460. R. Jennings, *loc.cit.* (note 1), p. 67.

Things change, however, when practice is one of the several elements involved. If there pre-exists a (written) rule of international law laying down in only general (and maybe vague) terms the conduct required with respect to a certain subject-matter, state-practice may loose much of its contradictory character. In such a case it is not necessary to evaluate state-practice in a complete legal vacuum, but it is possible to look at it against the background of some standard, albeit a general or vague one. Viewed from this perspective, state-practice may acquire a kind of "concretization-function" in that it elaborates and specifies in more detail the pre-existing (written) general and/or vague norm.

At first glance it is often not easy to detect this "concretization-function" of state-practice; a certain practice may appear irrelevant to this norm-building process, because at first sight it does not seem to relate to the subject-matter the general rule is addressing, or even seem to be incompatible with it. The irrelevancy or contrary character of state-practice, however, should not be too readily assumed. A closer inspection of the practice concerned not infrequently reveals that it nevertheless may contribute to the elaboration and specification of a general norm.[461]

Obviously, it is perfectly possible that part of the practice concerned is indeed irrelevant to the norm-building process we have in mind here, simply because it constitutes a violation of, or is at least incompatible with the general rule. As far as the question of norm-building is concerned, however, this is bound to be only a small portion of the total amount of practice. A rule that is repeatedly violated in practice will not very likely become a rule of law, c.q. will eventually loose its legal character. Consequently, in this latter type of cases the envisaged process of elaboration and concretization of a general rule will not take place at all.

It is submitted, however, that this concretizising role of practice ancillary to written rules is gaining importance. Particularly now that international law is rapidly expanding into new areas the result is often that its written rules too are of a rather general character.[462] One of the methods to achieve the required elaboration/concretization or the crystallization of sub-rules is through practice. As was already said, the incoherence which may characterize state-practice when viewed in a legal vacuum, is here to a large extent alleviated by the fact that a general norm pre-exists as a frame of reference.

461. See also *infra* pp. 275-279.
462. See for more details on the effects of the changes in the international society on the relation between conduct, law and policy, *infra* pp. 126-128.

CHAPTER VII

TREATIES

7.1. The proliferation of treaties

Treaties in many respects present the reverse case of customary international law. They do not raise as many problems as the latter and the impact on treaties of the changes which have occurred in the international society can be more easily traced.

First and foremost, their nature as a source of international law is quite unambiguous and uncontroversial. To be sure, there are debates and differences of opinion on certain aspects of the law of treaties, but these do not go to the heart of the question, as is the case with respect to customary international law. The law of treaties has been well-developed and well-documented for quite some time.[463] Moreover, this important branch of international law has now found regulation in the 1969 Vienna Convention on the Law of Treaties.[464] All this adds up to making treaties a relatively clear and reliable source of international law.

A second advantage over customary international law is that the process of treaty-making is relatively quick. Probably because the whole process of negotiating a law-making treaty is directed exclusively towards the end of creating rules of international law, results come rather fast, if compared to law-creation through practice where other considerations than law-making usually play an important or even dominant role. Still, the drafting, negotiation, and conclusion of a treaty may take several years or even over a decade, if multilateral treaties dealing with complex and/or controversial issues are concerned.[465] Moreover,

463. Apart from the studies on sources already mentioned in the foregoing, the following works may be singled out as some of the most outstanding on the subject: H. Blix, *Treaty Making Power* (London 1960); I. Detter, *Essays on the Law of Treaties* (London 1967); J. Fawcett, "The Legal Character of International Agreements", XXX *BYIL* (1953), pp. 381-400; K. Holloway, *Modern Trends in Treaty Law* (London 1970); A. McNair, *op.cit.* (note 275); S. Rosenne, *The Law of Treaties; A Guide to the Legislative History of the Vienna Convention* (New York 1970).
464. See for an excellent survey of its most important provisions P. Menon, "The Law of Treaties with special reference to the Vienna Convention of 1969", 56 *RDISDP*, pp. 133-155 and 213-263; see also I. Sinclair, *The Vienna Convention on the Law of Treaties* (Manchester 1973). The Convention which was adopted at the Vienna Conference by an overwhelming majority (79 in favour; 1 against; 19 abstentions) has entered into force on January 27, 1980. Even for those States which have not (yet) become parties, the Convention is not without legal effect because it is considered to constitute, at least partly, a codification of already existing international law. (One of its preambular provisions refers to "the codification and progressive development of the law of treaties achieved in the present Convention".)
465. Striking examples are both UN Covenants on Economic, Social and Cultural Rights and on Civil and Political Rights. Preparatory work for these treaties started in 1948, while they were

as multilateral treaties not seldom require a minimum number of ratifications in order to take effect, very often an additional period of time lapses before they enter into force.[466] Even extreme cases like these, however, present a quite rapid process of law-making if compared to the usual pace of custom.[467]

A third advantage of treaties over custom to be mentioned here is that the instrument of language used in treaties constitutes a more clear and reliable method of conveying general standards of behaviour than the instrument of precedent or example on which custom is based. Because of the use of language treaties make it possible to avoid too general and vague standards which not seldom result from the process of custom.[468] In short, treaties may provide a more precise regulation which is likely to be more effective. This characteristic makes the treaty suited for those new tasks which international law had to take on as a result of its horizontal expansion and vertical penetration.[469] Friedmann, who was one of the first to point to this development in international law, has maintained that "in the area of the international law of cooperation, it is only by treaty or other international agreements that progress can be achieved. The objectives of international welfare organization require specific regulation, which cannot be achieved by the slow-moving and somewhat imprecise methods of custom. It is not possible to agree on fishery conservation matters, or on stabilisation of prices of commodities, or on international minimum wage standards other than by specific agreements, which formulate precise standards and obligations".[470]

Finally, also the present heterogeneous character of the international society has prompted the rise of treaties as the main source of international law, particularly in areas which belong to general international law.[471] In particular multilateral treaties have a comparatively democratic character in that all States have the opportunity to participate in their drawing up and thereby to contribute to the process of making international law. It is for this reason that the instrument of treaties is heavily favoured by at least most of the non-Western States. One

adopted by the General Assembly as late as 1966. Similarly, negotiations on the new Law of the Sea started in 1969 while the UN Convention on the Law of the Sea was concluded on December 10, 1982.

466. The UN Covenants on Human Rights entered into force in 1976, *i.e.* ten years after their adoption by the General Assembly. The 1958 Convention on Fishing and Conservation of the Living Resources of the High Seas took effect only eight years later, in 1966. The Vienna Convention on the Law of Treaties was adopted in 1969 and entered into force as late as 1980.

467. See in this respect W. Friedmann, *loc.cit.* (note 231), p. 134: "It could even be argued that at the time it was embodied in the Vienna Convention of 1958, the concept of the continental shelf had become part of customary international law. In terms of history of international law, the formation of custom within 13 years would, of course, be unprecedented. Nor is it likely that such custom could form itself with such rapidity were it not for the readiness of all states to agree on an extension of exclusive national rights and priviliges at the expense of those of the international community".

468. See H. Hart, *op.cit.* (note 41), p. 122: "In contrast with the indetermination of example, the communication of general standards by explicit forms of language ... seems clear, dependable and certain. The features to be taken as general guides to conduct are here identified in words; they are verbally extricated, not left embedded with others in a concrete example". See, however, *infra* pp. 124-125.

469. See *supra* pp. 65-69.

470. W. Friedmann, *loc.cit.* (note 231), p. 136.

471. See *supra* pp. 69-71.

118

representative to the Vienna Conference on the Law of Treaties stated that "customary law is only partly and hesitantly accepted by Communist States and the younger African and Asian members of the international community. Indeed, they refuse to be bound by rules which they did not help to create, the norms in question being, by and large, the product of a practice of the Western world. No wonder that today international law is mainly developed by bi- or multilateral treaties".[472]

The above-mentioned features taken together help to explain the proliferation of treaties which has taken place in particular after the Second World War. In quantitative and, more importantly, qualitative respect the impact of treaties on the process of making international law would seem to have grown considerably. On the one hand their number would seem to have, at least slightly, increased;[473] on the other hand, the globalization of international law to which we have referred above,[474] has largely taken place and is still taking place through the instrument of treaties.[475]

7.2. Shortcomings of treaties

7.2.1. Introduction

The preceding account of the positive features of treaties as a source of international law needs to be placed in a proper perspective. The last section consisted mainly of a comparison between treaties and custom. Treaties do present a number of important advantages over custom. However, viewed from the perspective of what present-day international relations require, it is a far from perfect source of international law. If looked at in this way treaties, too, show a number of shortcomings even though of a less serious nature than in the case of custom. The most important of these shortcomings may be dealt with under the headings of problems relating to the acceptability of treaties, to their adaptation and to their change. These types of problems will be analyzed in the subsequent sections.

---

472. Quoted by H. Neuhold, "The 1968 Session of the UN Conference on the Law of Treaties", XIX *ÖZöR* (1969), pp. 59-94 (64).
473. Some authors uphold that their number has considerably increased; see for a general indication M. Bos, *loc.cit.* (note 28), p. 22, note 52 and P. Menon, *loc.cit.* (note 464), p. 134, note 3; J. King Gamble, "Multilateral Treaties: The Significance of the Name of the Instrument", 10 *CWILJ* (1980), pp. 1-24 (13), however, denies such an increase: "Examining the overall numbers of treaties for each time interval, there has been little increase during the fifty-year period [1919-1971; v.H.]. There was a precipitous drop during World War II, but, in general, overall magnitudes are fairly constant. This refutes the assertion that there are vastly more multilateral treaties today than in the past".
474. See *supra* p. 67.
475. It suffices in this respect to point to the fact that international organizations, which in many cases symbolize this globalization of international law, are, without exception, based upon treaties.

7.2.2. Problems of acceptability

In the foregoing we pointed out that multilateral treaties, the text having been adopted, not infrequently take a considerable period of time to acquire a sufficient number of ratifications to enter into force.[476] A comparable but certainly more serious problem is that many multilateral treaties of a general character (*i.e.* dealing with subject-matters affecting the interests of all or nearly all States in the world) never seem to obtain anything close to universal acceptance on the part of the States. Non-ratification by a State does not deprive a treaty from all legal value in respect of that State, as will be argued hereafter.[477] Nevertheless, it goes without saying that from the perspective of certainty and effectiveness of international law, full-fledged acceptance in the form of ratification is clearly to be preferred to any possible less formal expressions of consent or acceptance.

The overall picture, however, is not very encouraging. In 1971 a UNITAR-study encompassing 55 multilateral treaties discovered that on the average they were ratified by only 30% of all States.[478] There are no indications that this situation has improved in the meantime. More recently, Martens has pointed out that "Kodifikationsverträge, denen mehr als zwei Drittel der Staaten angehören, sind äusserst selten; auch ein Beitrittstand von mehr als der Hälfte aller Staaten ist nicht häufig, da die meisten multilateralen Verträge weit weniger als die Hälfte der Staaten umfassen".[479] Similarly, King Gamble, distinguishing between various names of multilateral instruments, has concluded on the basis of a survey over the 1919-1971 period: "Fully half of conventions have at least one signature left 'hanging' without the required ratification. Instruments named treaty also have a fairly good record, with 70% of them having no unsubstantiated signatures. Although 80% of agreements have no signatures lacking ratification, the remaining 20% represents a large number of individual cases where agreements are signed and not ratified. Overall, there are more than 2,000 instances where a signature has been affixed to an instrument requiring ratification without the ratification materializing".[480]

Generally speaking, it would seem that there are two grounds for the slow ratification or failure to ratify multilateral treaties on the part of a large number of States, *viz.* (technical) inability and (political) unwillingness.

As far as the former is concerned, it should be kept in mind that in industrialized countries the national legal route of getting a treaty ratified is often very long and cumbersome. The national legal systems of these States usually require the involvement of various instances through elaborate procedures before a treaty can eventually be approved. In many cases, considerations derived from the national legal system simply make it impossible to speed up the process of ratification substantially. Improvement of this state of affairs would, therefore, have to be achieved mainly through changes in the national constitutional procedures. However desirable they might be, simplification of, and the intro-

476. See *supra* pp. 117-118.
477. See in particular *infra* pp. 234-235.
478. See O. Schachter, M. Nawaz and J. Fried, *Toward Wider Acceptance of UN Treaties - A UN-ITAR Study* (New York 1971), pp. 24-40.
479. E. Martens, "Problem der Entwicklung des Völkerrechts durch multilaterale internationale Verträge und Kodifikationen", 59 *FW* (1976), pp. 189-207 (195).
480. J. King Gamble, *loc.cit.* (note 473), p. 20.

duction of greater flexibility into the international legal requirements for the entry into force of treaties can at best bring partial relief. The so-called "triple-option-clause",[481] for instance, which leaves it to the discretion of the States involved to accept the treaty either by adoption of the text, by signature or by ratification, does not provide a solution for those cases where the national constitution requires ratification. More or less the same holds good for the so-called "opting out"-procedure, which could be agreed upon in certain cases. Such a procedure entails that a treaty becomes binding on adoption for all States concerned after the lapse of a certain period of time, unless they communicate within that period their rejection or reservations in a certain specified manner. Here too, certain States could be prevented from accepting such an "opting out"-procedure because of national constitutional requirements.[482] Finally, it has been suggested to discuss the feasibility of a commitment, to be accepted in a general agreement or on an *ad hoc* basis, to the provisional application of the treaty or part of it pending its entry into force.[483] The feasibility of such a commitment also depends to a large extent upon the question of whether the various municipal legal systems allow the envisaged provisional application.[484]

The case of developing countries presents special problems. The main (technical) reason why these States usually belong to the group of poor ratifiers is their lack of sufficient manpower. Developing countries often experience difficulties in staffing their missions to international organizations and other international gatherings where treaties or other forms of international agreements are to be drawn up.[485] This in itself already hampers the efforts to deal with such a treaty on the national level, once it has been concluded. In addition, both the municipal legal systems and the national bureaucracies are generally ill-equipped to cope adequately with the problems this engenders. A number of international organizations try to alleviate problems like these by offering technical assistance consisting of *inter alia* the training of technical and legal experts. Besides organizations like UNESCO and the UN through UNITAR, the ILO

481. See O. Schachter, M. Nawaz and J. Fried, *op.cit.* (note 478), p. 123.
482. See the representative of the Netherlands in the Sixth Committee of the XXXVIth General Assembly (Prof.Dr. P. van Dijk) who advocated the opting-out procedure, but added "with due consideration of the question of whether the national legal system of each individual state would allow such a procedure in a way that a real speeding-up effect could be expected", Netherlands Ministry of Foreign Affairs, *Verslag over de Hervatte Vijfendertigste Zitting, de Achtste Bijzondere Spoedzitting, de Zesendertigste Zitting en de Negende Bijzondere Spoedzitting van de Algemene Vergadering der Verenigde Naties*[Report on the resumed 35th session, the 8th special emergency session, the 36th session and the 9th special emergency session of the UN General Assembly], Publication No. 127 ('s-Gravenhage 1982), p. 571.
483. *Ibidem,* where reference is made to article 25 of the Vienna Convention on the Law of Treaties. Its paragraph (1) reads: "A treaty or a part of a treaty is applied provisionally pending its entry into force if: (a) the treaty itself so provides; or (b) the negotiating States have in some other manner so agreed."
484. See also P. Szasz, *loc.cit.* (note 253), pp. 531-532.
485. *Ibidem,* p. 525: "Governments especially the smaller ones, frequently complain that they are unable to keep up with the plethora of treaty-making activities, that is, they cannot supply sufficient representatives and experts to all the meetings and cannot properly review the many treaty proposals pending at any given time"; in the same vein R. Kearney, *loc.cit.* (note 25), p. 507.

undoubtedly has the most wide-ranging experience in this respect.[486]

If delay in, or failure of ratification are the result of unwillingness on the part of the States concerned the problem, of course, is first of all of a political nature. The political elements which influence the will of States in the period before they have formally accepted a treaty constitute a most important problem which deserves further study. Within the framework of the present study, however, this issue cannot be elaborated.[487] However, some observations will be made on the legal techniques, which are available to encourage ratification. In this field too, the ILO has done the pioneering work. The techniques it employs are well-documented and well-known. The most important ones are contained in article 19 of the ILO Constitution. The member States are under the obligation to submit the conventions (and recommendations), drawn up by the ILO, within a given period of time to the competent national authorities for the enactment of legislation or other action. This method is designed to ensure that the question of ratification is given adequate attention at the national level. Furthermore, while there is no obligation for States to ratify conventiôns, they do have to report periodically at the request of the ILO's Governing Body on how their national legislation and legal practice relates to the content of the conventions not yet ratified (and recommendations not yet implemented) by them, and on the reasons why a given convention has not yet been ratified.[488] In short, the ILO-system amounts to supervision of obligations not having (yet) a full-fledged legal character.

Obviously, mechanisms and systems of supervision proving to be effective within the framework of a given organization cannot be simply transplanted to another one and be guaranteed to offer the same results. Clearly, the ILO shows a number of peculiar characteristics not available in the more general context of the United Nations and it is, therefore, questionable whether the latter does provide a suitable environment for a comparable system of supervision. On the other hand, it has been pointed out that a system of periodic reporting on the reasons of failure to ratify, like that of the ILO, has been instituted by the League of Nations and put into practice quite successfully.[489] Given the present poor state of ratifications it would certainly be worthwhile to study the possibilities of applying this kind of techniques within the United Nations structure.[490]

---

486. For a recent survey of the ILO's efforts in this field, see N. Valticos, "The International Protection of Economic and Social Rights", in: P. van Dijk (ed.), *Rechten van de Mens in Mundiaal en Europees Perspectief* [Human Rights in a Global and European Perspective], second edition (Utrecht 1980), pp. 109-140 and the studies cited there.
487. As a general rule it may be expected that States will be more ready to accept a treaty if and to the extent that they recognize that their interests are served by doing so. The awareness of the (growing) interdependence on the part of the States may, therefore, constitute a vehicle for enhancing the States' readiness in this respect. See for more details G. van Hoof and K. de Vey Mestdagh, *loc.cit.* (note 230).
488. See N. Valticos, *loc.cit.* (note 486), pp. 120-122.
489. See E. Martens, *loc.cit.* (note 479), pp. 198-199; the same author has proposed to set up, within the framework of the United Nations, expert committees each charged with the supervision of the implementation of a number of multilateral conventions, *ibidem*, pp. 200-201.
490. For a number of suggestions to improve the UN law-making process, see E. Suy, "Innovations in International Law-making Processes", in: R. McDonald, D. Johnston and G. Morris (eds.), *The International Law and Policy of Human Welfare* (Alphen aan den Rijn 1978), pp. 187-200.

Another method designed to attract as many ratifications as possible has to do with the formulation of the norm itself. The key-word in this respect is flexibility. Various methods are available which aim at making norms acceptable to the largest possible number of States. Again the ILO has been a forerunner and, at the same time, it has largely avoided the danger of drawing up too general and too vague norms by using techniques designed to take into account the various differences existing between countries.[491] Outside the specific institutional framework of the ILO, however, the approach most commonly encountered in multilateral treaties of general international law is what could be called with some exaggeration "the lowest common denominator" approach. This term is designed to indicate that not seldom during negotiations compromises and package-deals remove difficulties which States found in a proposed text. At the same time, however, this usually results in a quite abstract and/or vague wording of the text concerned. This "lowest common denominator" approach can take different forms. The result may be, for instance, that only the fundamental principles are laid down in the text, leaving more concrete issues ambiguous or dealing with them only in passing.[492]

Obviously, this entails the standing danger that the ensuing text becomes so abstract and/or vague, or lays down such a low standard, that it becomes virtually meaningless. And even in less extreme cases one is constantly faced here with the dilemma between acceptability and effectiveness: on the one hand, interdependence requires (near) universal participation of States in many international issues; on the other hand, the problems in question cannot be tackled other than by norms which are sufficiently substantive.

From practice one gains the impression that usually more weight is attached to universality than to effectiveness and, in itself, this is not altogether incomprehensible. However, it buttresses the need for some kind of device to tailor the abstract and/or vague norms to the requirements of effectiveness. A very interesting suggestion in this respect constitutes the procedure of so-called "delegated legislation"[493] in matters which are of a comprehensive nature, but at the same time present considerable technical aspects. This suggestion envisages to begin international law-making in such fields with the conclusion of a basic treaty (*traité cadre*) containing only the most fundamental rules of a more general character - both procedural and substantive - as a programme of action, while subsequently laying down the further elaboration of the matter in annexes or additional protocols according to the rules agreed upon in the basic treaty. The advantages attached to such a procedure would be twofold. Firstly, it could speed up international law-making, as the adoption, extension and amendment of the separate annexes or protocols could be realized through simpler procedures than are required for the basic treaty. Secondly, because of the simpler

491. See J. McMahon, "The Legislative Technique of the International Labour Organization", XLI *BYIL* (1965-1966), pp. 1-102, in particular pp. 31-73; see also N. Valticos, *loc.cit.* (note 486), pp. 110-114.

492. The constitutions of international organizations very often fit into this category. As a rule their purposes are very broadly framed. They do not provide substantive solutions for all the issues involved in their field of work, but at best set up a procedural framework to arrive at such solutions.

493. See the Netherlands representative in the Sixth Committee of the XXXVIth General Assembly, Professor Dr. P. van Dijk, *loc.cit.* (note 482), p. 571.

procedures being used the possibilities for elaboration, concretization, adaptation and even change would be enhanced in comparison to the sometimes prevailing situation where the ensuing new norms are more or less equally general as a result of the "lowest common denominator" approach, while no follow-up is provided for.

7.2.3. Problems of adaptation

Adaptation should be taken here in a broad sense. It encompasses both elaboration and concretization. Furthermore, in a number of cases it proves difficult to draw the line between adaptation and change. Nevertheless, both latter issues will be discussed in separate sections. It should be kept in mind, however, that what will be said with regard to adaption may have bearing upon change, too, and *vice versa*.

The problem of open texture was already touched upon in the discussion of customary international law.[494] With respect to treaties it was added that communication of general standards of behaviour by way of language suffers far less from indeterminacies than communication through authoritative example.[495] In spite of this difference between example and language, the latter, and consequently treaties, are not completely safeguarded from the effects of open texture, which is indeed a general phenomenon.

Reference may be made to the words of Hart, who has dealt extensively with open texture: "Much of the jurisprudence of this century has consisted of the progressive realization (and sometimes the exaggeration) of the important fact that the distinction between the uncertainties of communication by authoritative example (precedent), and the certainties of communication by authoritative general language (legislation) is far less firm than this naive contrast suggests. ...In all fields of experience, not only that of rules, there is a limit, inherent in the nature of language, to the guidance which general language can provide. ...Canons of interpretation cannot eliminate, though they can diminish, these uncertainties; for these canons are themselves general rules for the use of language and make use of general terms which themselves require interpretation".[496] We are confronted here with a phenomenon which is not exclusive to international law.[497]

---

494. See *supra* pp. 114-115.
495. See *supra* p. 118.
496. H. Hart, *op.cit.* (note 41), p. 123.
497. It is interesting in this respect to point to the reasons which, according to Hart, are at the root of the phenomenon of open texture. He asserts that these are to be found in two connected human handicaps: the first one consists of our relative ignorance which prevents legislators from making provision for every possible combination of circumstances which the future may bring; this, in its turn, results in our inability to anticipate which brings with it our relative indeterminacy of aim, *ibidem*, p. 125. Because of these human handicaps Hart does not conceive of open texture in only a negative way. Ignoring this feature of language leads to formalism or conceptualism by freezing the meaning of a rule so that its general terms must have the same meaning in every case where its application is in question: "To do this is to secure a measure of certainty or predictability at the cost of blindly prejudging what is to be done in a range of future cases, about whose composition we are ignorant", *ibidem*, p. 126.

Nevertheless, its impact is undoubtedly more dramatic at the international level than it usually is in a national legal context. National legal systems have developed various techniques to cope with, or at least to neutralize as much as possible, the negative effects of open textured provisions.[498] As far as international law is concerned, such techniques can be applied to a very limited extent only. They all presuppose the existence of a hierarchical legal structure where the legal system provides for bodies which have final decision-making power and, consequently, can act as a kind of referee in cases where the rules of law do not provide readily available answers. Hart has summarized these techniques in national legal systems as follows: "The open texture of law means that there are, indeed, areas of conduct where much must be left to be developed by courts or officials striking a balance in the light of circumstances, between competing interests which vary in weight from case to case".[499]

Solutions like these cannot be provided for in international law, because in most situations the just-mentioned "courts or officials striking a balance" are not available in the international society, or even if available like in the case of international organizations, have no general power to act as the referee alluded to above. The main impediment to effectively deal with cases of open texture, is, therefore, constituted by one of the basic features of international society, *i.e.* the absence of a hierarchical/organizational structure. Consequently, the function of answering questions concerning open texture can in most situations only be performed in a decentralized manner, that is by the States themselves. The difficulties which this state of affairs taken by itself already entails are aggravated by the heterogeneous character international society has taken on in recent years.[500]

In addition to the fact that the structure of international society hampers solving the problems inherent in the use of language as a means of communicating general standards of conduct, questions of open texture would seem to have become more wide-spread in modern international law. As a result of its horizontal expansion international law has had to enter into new areas which require quick regulation. In such cases a most natural approach is to start from general principles or guidelines, which constitute the point of departure for regulating the subject-matter concerned. The ensuing rules very often are of such a nature that they require some kind of follow-up before they can be used effectively to regulate the various situations arising in practice. In other words, particularly with respect to rules addressing issues of general interest the problem of the generality and vagueness of rules of international law has grown in recent years and is still growing. It is submitted that a shift in the purpose and content of rules in certain fields of international law can be witnessed, in that the latter become more directed towards broad policy goals instead of being a reflection of actual state-conduct. This phenomenon, obviously, has a bearing upon the question concerning the sources of international law and it is, therefore, worthwhile to look at it more closely.

---

498. *Ibidem*, pp. 127-132.
499. *Ibidem*, p. 132.
500. See *supra* pp. 69-71.

7.2.4. The shift in the content of international law; the relation between conduct, law and policy

In discussing the concept of international law above the relation between law and politics was set forth on the basis of a distinction between politics in the sense of policy and politics in the sense of conduct.[501] Put in black and white, the former was said to consist of those activities on the part of the States which are aimed primarily at (long-term) community goals and objectives, while the latter refers to all the actual conduct of States which has no such specific orientation. It is important to elaborate the relation between conduct, law and policy a little further, because it may help to explain, in our view, the changed content of many modern treaties as compared to older treaty-law, consisting of a shift in the orientation of international law from conduct towards policy.

It is useful to call in the aid here of the metaphor of the three-storied building which Schachter has introduced to clarify the said relationship. He has discerned three different levels: the first one is the conduct-floor where one can find "behaviour and its associated 'subjectivities' (demands, purposes, expectations)".[502] Next, on the second floor, "we would place the obligational phenomena - the legally normative patterns - and the associated activities such as prescribing, invoking and applying. On this level, we would find the relatively well-mapped field of international legal rules and processes".[503] Finally, the third floor encompasses "the phenomena of general policy-making and articulation of major aspiration with its accompanying doctrinal formulas".[504] It is true that each of these levels of activity has its own purposes, goals, and values. Nevertheless, it can be maintained that "This 'upper-class' floor is easily distinguishable ... from the busy ground floor of conduct and from the second floor of distinctive legal phenomena. It is on this third floor that we would expect to find formulations of national interest and goals of wide generality and also such transnational principles of basic public order that we can identify".[505]

Above it was argued that law and conduct on the one hand, and law and policy on the other influence each other in various ways.[506] It is one of the advantages of Schachter's scheme that it clarifies these relationships between conduct, law and policy by presenting them as a kind of reciprocal "flows of communication". As the author himself explains: "We become more easily aware of the escalators or staircases that go in both directions, thereby avoiding analyses in which 'values' and aspirations are given one-way routes (as when legal norms are viewed as a function of behavioural goals, without reciprocal influence). An awareness that the traffic between the second and third floors can be a two-way affair enables us to avoid the pitfalls of a 'top-down' approach to policy formation".[507] More concretely, the scheme makes clear that a rule of law can be either oriented more towards conduct or towards policy; it may to a larger

---

501. See *supra* pp. 24-25.
502. O. Schachter, *loc.cit.* (note 23), p. 320.
503. *Ibidem.*
504. *Ibidem*, pp. 320-321.
505. *Ibidem*, p. 321.
506. See *supra* pp. 25-28.
507. O. Schachter, *loc.cit.* (note 23), p. 321.

extent be the "registration" of behavioural practice or the "translation" of general policy considerations.

Another important advantage of Schachter's scheme, and in particular of the image of "escalators and staircases", is that it makes visible the possibility that the emphasis in legal rules belonging to a specific field or fields may over time shift from conduct to policy or *vice versa*. It is important to be aware of this possibility, because, in the present author's view, it is precisely a shift in emphasis from conduct to policy which has been taking place in international law. Replacing Schachter's three-storied building for a moment by a scale with conduct on the one and policy on the other extreme, it might be said that a considerable number of rules of international law have moved on the scale in the direction of policy away from the area of conduct.

Obviously, this is not true for the entire body of international law. Large parts of it still embody rules which are primarily a reflection of actual state-behaviour. These rules constitute that part of international law, which is more or less taken for granted.[508] A good example is the law of diplomatic relations between States. Nevertheless, it is submitted that the change just indicated, consisting of a heavier reliance upon elements of policy and less upon conduct, can be witnessed in other, particularly the new fields of international law, which often are of a more controversial character.

The reasons for this shift in emphasis are to be found in the changes in the international society described in section 5.4. As was observed there one of the consequences of this process of change has been the horizontal expansion of international law into new fields of international relations. It is understandable that, when such new fields have to be regulated, a tendency arises to search for general principles to serve as a point of departure and a guidance for a more detailed regulation of the subject-matter concerned. Moreover, the new areas of international law often are of a more comprehensive character than the traditional fields, since they reflect the growing interdependence. Consequently, the new international law of cooperation cannot be content with prescribing rules based on a short-term or *ad hoc* approach. It needs to start from a policy framework taking into account the overall and long-term requirements of the issues involved. Therefore, general guidelines, policy considerations and even long-term objectives become embodied in the law itself. The result, of course, is that rules of international law become more abstract and general. Once again it is useful to point to the phenomenon of international organizations, which have been the main answer of the international society to the challenges posed by the changes which have taken place. Many constitutions of international organizations instituted after the Second World War on many issues in fact contain no more than the general objectives to be attained and an outline of the methods to be used.

An additional reason why rules of international law have grown more general and abstract is probably the increased heterogeneity of international society. As a result of more divergent views and interests between States, nowadays it has become significantly more difficult to reach agreement on detailed rules concerning a whole range of difficult issues. Because at the same time the increased interdependence necessitates regulation of those issues in one way or another, it

---

508. See also L. Henkin, *op.cit.* (note 228), pp. 46-49.

is not surprising that refuge is sought to more general guidelines and principles, which constitute the common denominator States can agree upon. On that basis it can subsequently be attempted to solve the more concrete problems and to work out more detailed arrangements.[509]

In conclusion, therefore, it can be said that the shift in emphasis from conduct to policy has brought about more abstract and general provisions in international law. Although such provisions should not too readily be assumed to lack normative character,[510] it cannot be denied that they sometimes do not provide clear-cut answers to every detailed question. For such rules to become fully operative additional steps of elaboration and concretization have to be taken to tailor them to the requirements of practice. As was already stressed in the preceding section, all this points to the need for some kind of follow-up to the abstract and generally-worded rules of the present international law.

7.2.5. Problems of change

What has been observed with respect to adaptation goes *mutatis mutandis* also for questions concerning the change of treaty rules. Written rules of international law present full bloom the dilemma of law in general: how to find a balance between the need to provide stability and the need to keep up with new developments in societal relations. Again it must be stressed that the dilemma is more dramatic in international society than at the national level in normal circumstances, because the former lacks a legislator, a court or other officials empowered to strike such a balance.[511] Consequently, in international law the problem is often not so much a matter of balance but rather of choice between stability and flexibility.

Law is often said to be conservative and to serve as an instrument for maintaining the *status quo*. This is true in the sense that law has to start with providing stability. Although its task of enabling change is equally important, it has to proceed from a stable situation, because it is only in this way that processes of change can be made orderly. In ideal situations the law is equipped with devices allowing change which are capable of keeping up with society. Clearly, the state of affairs in international law is far from ideal in that respect. It is, therefore, not incomprehensible that emphasis is more on stability than on change. Where, as in international law, the process of creating rules is so cumbersome and precarious, it is only natural that the rules thus duly brought about are "cherished" by not allowing them to be abolished or changed too easily. Hence, the rigidity of

---

509. Additionally, the development towards a more policy-like as opposed to conduct-oriented character of rules of international law is strengthened by the desire for change on the part of the developing countries. The latter propagate changes in international law in many respects and because of the "conservative" character of state-practice (see *supra* p. 114) they are most unlikely to rely on that practice in the formulation of new rules of international law. Rather they can be expected to introduce broad policy orientations and abstract principles which, after being generally accepted, may open up the avenues of change desired. And even if agreement on these general rules does not "trickle down", *i.e.* if agreement on more concrete and detailed provisions proves to be impossible, the broad rules, because of their often multi-interpretable nature, can be invoked to legitimize appeals for change.
510. See *infra* pp. 239-240.
511. See *supra* pp. 62-63.

the provisions on termination and suspension of treaties in the Vienna Convention on the Law of Treaties.

The emphasis on stability becomes clear, when one takes a look at the *clausula rebus sic stantibus* contained in the Convention, in relation to the *pacta sunt servanda* rule. While the latter emphasizes the element of stability, the former is designed to allow for change in that body of law, in certain circumstances. The wording of article 62 laying down the *clausula* is extremely restrictive. Its paragraph (1) reads: "A fundamental change of circumstances which has occurred with regard to those existing at the time of the conclusion of a treaty, and *which was not foreseen* by the parties, *may not be invoked* as a ground for terminating or withdrawing from the treaty *unless*:

(a) the existence of those circumstances constituted *an essential basis of the consent* of the parties to be bound by the treaty; and

(b) the effect of the change is *radically to transform* the extent of the obligations still to be performed under the treaty".[512]

The origin of the *clausula rebus sic stantibus*, of course, predates the Vienna Convention.[513] When the latter was drafted, however, the difficulties underlying it once again came clearly to the fore. The International Law Commission phrased the *raison d'être* of the *clausula* as follows: "A treaty may remain in force for a long time and its stipulations come to place an undue burden on one of the parties as a result of a fundamental change of circumstances. Then, if the other party were obdurate in opposing any change, the fact that international law recognized no legal means of terminating or modifying the treaty otherwise than through a further agreement between the same parties might impose a serious strain on the relations between the States concerned." [514] At the same time, however, the Commission, signaling the dilemma in which it found itself with respect to the doctrine of the fundamentally changed circumstances, felt obliged to "enter a strong *caveat* as to the need to confine the scope of the doctrine within narrow limits and to regulate strictly the conditions under which it may be invoked."[515] This latter consideration has turned the scale and the result, as was pointed out, is the restrictively worded article 62 of the Vienna Convention.

Narrowly defined are also the remaining provisions which the Vienna Convention makes for termination or suspension other than through the consent of all parties involved. The termination or suspension of a bilateral treaty can be invoked only after a material breach by the other party, while in the case of multilateral treaties the Convention in addition poses a number of further limiting conditions.[516] Similarly, an appeal to a supervening impossibility of performance can be successful only in carefully delimited circumstances[517], whereas termination as a result of the emergence of a new peremptory norm of general

512. Emphasis added. In addition paragraph (2) excludes the invocation of the *clausula* if the treaty concerned establishes a boundary and if the fundamental change is the result of a violation of international law by the party invoking it *vis-à-vis* any other party to the treaty.
513. See on the *clausula* in general O. Lissitzyn, "Treaties and Changed Circumstances (*Rebus Sic Stantibus*)", 61 *AJIL* (1967), pp. 895-922.
514. UN Doc. A/Conf.39/11, p. 78.
515. UN Doc. A/Conf.39/aa/Add.1, p. 118.
516. See article 60.
517. See article 61.

international law[518] is not expected to occur frequently either.[519] Finally, the Convention's article 63 provides that severance of diplomatic or consular relations between parties to a treaty does not affect the legal relations established between them by the treaty except in so far as the existence of diplomatic or consular relations is indispensable for the application of the treaty.

For the remainder, the possibilities which the Vienna Convention envisages for termination or suspension are in fact all based upon the consent of all the States involved.[520] Obviously, change through consent is the most satisfactory method, but, given the structure of present-day international society, a most difficult one. On the one hand, our times characterized by rapid changes witness a growing need for devices through which modification of rules of international law can be effected. The pattern which we said has been recently developing in reaction to problems of adaptation,[521] consisting of the increased use of some kind of follow-up mechanism, constitutes at the same time an answer to problems of change. Through such follow-up mechanisms treaty-rules are made less rigid, because the conclusion of the treaty is no longer considered the end, but rather an important step in an ongoing process. Generally speaking, international law-making diplomacy has been transformed from an *ad hoc* into a regular and sometimes even permanent affair. Obviously, international organizations very often serve as the forum to conduct this type of diplomacy[522]; and if existing ones are deemed inappropriate a new one is sometimes specifically set up. Finally, even treaties operating completely outside the framework of international organizations sometimes provide for special conferences designed to review the operation of the treaty after the lapse of a certain period of time[523], possibly resulting in adaptation or change of its provisions.

These developments are of a quite recent date and they clearly have not done away with questions of adaptation and change in international law. Nevertheless, in the present writer's view these developments in the field of follow-up have to be taken into account in analyzing the international law-making process.[524]

---

518. See article 64.
519. See *infra* pp. 165-167.
520. See the articles 54-59; the consent may be expressed in the treaty concerned or at a later date. The requirement of the consent of all States involved must be regarded applicable also to article 56(1)(b) which contains an exception to the rule that, without an express provision to that effect, treaties are not subject to denunciation or withdrawal, *i.e.* in the case that a right of denunciation or withdrawal may be implied by the nature of the treaty. If this would not be accepted, a right of unilateral denunciation or withdrawal would in fact be recognized and "the rule of *pacta sunt servanda* would have little or no meaning" (Harvard Law School, "Draft Convention on the Law of Treaties", 29 *AJIL* (1935), pp. 652-1226 (1173)); see also *supra* pp. 75-76.
521. See *supra* pp. 124-125.
522. See *infra* pp. 210-212.
523. See article IX of The Antartica Treaty (1959), 402 *UNTS* (1961), p. 71 and article VIII,3 of the Treaty on the Non-Proliferation of Nuclear Weapons (1968), 729 *UNTS* (1970), p. 161.
524. See *infra* pp. 256-275.

CHAPTER VIII

GENERAL PRINCIPLES

8.1. The continuing debate on the general principles

As a third category, which the International Court of Justice has to apply in deciding the disputes submitted to it, article 38 of the Statute enumerates "the general principles of law recognized by civilized nations". This last "full-fledged" source contained in the Court's Statute probably is the most controversial one. If one overlooks doctrine, the emerging picture is one of disarray. The state of affairs is even worse than with respect to custom. As was pointed out above, the latter's nature is subject of a quite intensive debate.[525] In the case of general principles, however, the controversy is even more far-reaching, in that their very existence as a source of international law is called into question by a number of authors.

The debate on the general principles began in 1920 within the Advisory Committee of Jurists appointed by the Council of the League of Nations for the purpose of preparing plans for the establishment of the Permanent Court of International Justice provided for in article 14 of the League Covenant. The *Procès-Verbaux* of the proceedings of the Committee show that, in dealing with what has now become article 38 of the Statute, the discussions were devoted almost entirely to the "general principles of law recognized by civilized nations".[526] The solution eventually arrived at by the Committee has not turned out to be an uncontroversial one. On the contrary, since the conclusion of the Committee's work, the debate on the exact meaning of the phrase "the general principles of law recognized by civilized nations" has rather intensified. This is not only due to the intricate character of the question of the general principles and the somewhat inconclusive discussion on the subject within the Advisory Committee. In addition, the horizontal expansion of international law together with the changes in the structure of the international society described above[527] have given rise to an increased attention for the phenomenon of the general principles.

All this, however, has not resulted in agreement on the subject. In fact, difference of opinion ranges from one extreme to the other. Some deny the character of a source of international law to the general principles, others, on the other

---

525. See *supra* pp. 85-90.
526. Permanent Court of International Justice, Advisory Committee of Jurists, *Procès Verbaux* of the Proceedings of the Committee, June 16th-July 24th 1920, with Annexes (The Hague 1920), pp. 293-351.
527. See *supra* pp. 65-71.

hand, consider them to be the most important sources of international law.[528] In the following section we will briefly discuss the school of thought holding the former point of view. Subsequently, the latter position will be analyzed while at the same time we will set forth our own view on the general principles as a source of international law.

8.2. The denial of the existence of the general principles as a source of international law

Undoubtedly, the most outspoken protagonist of the view that general principles do not exist at all, in the sense that they do not constitute a separate source to be distinguished from treaties or customary rules of international law, is Tunkin. In a study specifically devoted to the subject he concludes that "'general principles of law' are legal notions, legal postulates, rules of logic and legal technique applied in national legal systems and in international law in the process of interpretation and application of rules of law. They enter the realm of international law through treaty and custom. That means that Article 38,1,c of the Statute of the I.C.J. contemplates not a separate 'source' of international law, but a specific legal phenomena applicable in international law".[529]

This point of view is based mainly on the amendment consisting of the words "whose function it is to decide in accordance with international law such disputes as are submitted to it", which were inserted into the opening phrase of article 38 at the 1945 San Francisco Conference.[530] Soviet lawyers argue that, as a result of this amendment in combination with the phrase "general principles of law", article 38 now requires that the principles in question are common to all national legal systems and applicable to international relations.[531] In Tunkin's eyes this requirement is not fulfilled because, as he submits, "there are no normative principles or norms common to two opposing systems of law: socialist and capitalist law. Rules of these systems of law, even when they appear identical, are basically different. Rules of law are not pure rules of conduct, they are social rules, having social content. Norms of the socialist law and norms of the capitalist law are socially different: they embody different class wills, their aims are different as well as the roles they play in these two societies".[532]

528. For recent surveys of the various opinions expressed in doctrine, see J. Lammers, "General Principles of Law Recognized by Civilized Nations", in: F. Kalshoven e.a. (eds.), *Essays on the Development of the International Legal Order* (Alphen aan den Rijn 1980), pp. 53-75; and B. Vitanyi, "Les Positions Doctrinales concernant le Sense de la Notion de 'Principes Généraux de Droit Reconnus par les Nations Civilisées", 86 *RGDIP* (1982), pp. 46-116.
529. G. Tunkin, "'General Principles of Law' in International Law", in: R. Marcic e.a. (eds.), *Internationale Festschrift für Alfred Verdross* (München/Salzburg 1971), pp. 523-532 (531); similarly in G. Tunkin, *op.cit.* (note 50), p. 199, it is upheld that "The viewpoint of the majority of Soviet international lawyers ... correctly emphasizes, in counterbalance to the predominant bourgeois doctrine, that the existence of similar principles in national legal systems, even though of all States, does not signify that they therefore have effect in international law; any provision, in order to be applied in international law, must enter by treaty or customary means. But as regards equating 'general principles of law' with general principles of international law, this seems to us to be unjustified".
530. See for more details on this amendment *infra* pp. 135-136.
531. G. Tunkin, *loc.cit.* (note 529), pp. 524-526.
532. *Ibidem*, p. 527; see also G. Tunkin, *op.cit.* (note 50), pp. 199-203.

Other than Soviet authors also conclude that general principles in fact have no *raison d'être* as a source of international law. The most well-known example is Kelsen who, using more careful words than Tunkin, has, in reference to article 38, expressed doubt "whether such principles common to the legal orders of the civilized nations exist at all, especially in view of the ideological antagonism which separates the communist from the capitalist, and the autocratic from the democratic legal systems".[533] With respect to the filling of gaps in international law, which was the major reason for introducing the general principles into article 38 of the Statute,[534] he considers it arguable "that 'the general principles of law' are applicable only if they are part of international law, and that means part of the law referred to in clauses (a) and (b) of Article 38. Then, clause (c) is superfluous".[535]

Views like the ones just described suffer above all from one major handicap: implicitly or explicitly they "explain away" an entire clause from a treaty. One should not easily arrive at the conclusion that a provision of a treaty is superfluous; this holds good particularly with respect to a clause contained in such a basic provision as article 38 of the ICJ's Statute. The present article 38(1)(c) has been extensively discussed in its preparatory phase by the Advisory Committee of Jurists; it has been subsequently accepted by the States becoming parties to the Statute of the Permanent Court of International Justice; finally, it has been reaffirmed by the overwhelming majority of States which have, since 1945, become parties to the Statute of the International Court of Justice. It would take extremely convincing arguments to support the point of view that such a clause is in fact to be considered an empty shell.[536] This, therefore, justifies a closer look at the meaning of article 38(1)(c).

8.3. The meaning of the phrase "general principles of law recognized by civilized nations"

8.3.1. Introduction

To hold that article 38(1)(c) cannot be meaningless, obviously is not the same thing as saying that its meaning is clear. Although most writers reject the proposition that the provision is superfluous or meaningless, there is little agreement on the question of how the provision is to be understood. The considerable divergence of opinion in this matter was already suggested.[537]

---

533. H. Kelsen, *op.cit.* (note 96), p. 393.
534. See *infra* pp. 136-139.
535. H. Kelsen, *op.cit.* (note 96), p. 394.
536. A. Verdross has derived from the preamble of the United Nations Charter an additional argument to support the position that general principles are indeed a source of international law and not just a means for the determination of rules of law by the Court. On the basis of the provision in the preamble containing the determination "to establish conditions under which justice and respect for the obligations arising from treaties and *other sources* of international law can be maintained" (emphasis added) he concludes that "diese anderen (Mehrzahl) Quellen können nur die im Artikel 38 Abs. 1 unter b und c angeführten Normenarten sein", *op.cit.* (note 98), p. 126.
537. See *supra* pp. 131-132.

In tackling the said question some attention will first of all be paid to the proceedings of the 1920 Advisory Committee of Jurists. This is hardly avoidable, even though this part of the *travaux préparatoires* of article 38(1)(c) is extensively discussed in doctrine. For, it is in fact through the work of that Committee that the "general principles of law recognized by civilized nations" have been introduced into the realm of the sources of international law. Moreover, the analyses of the work of the Committee provided by the various authors not infrequently lead to different conclusions, and the confusion which characterized at least part of the discussions in the Committee still rings through in doctrine today.

It is submitted that the present impossibility to reach a *communis opinio* on the fundamentals of the general principles recognized by civilized nations is due, at least to some extent, to the failure to make two distinctions with respect to their nature and functioning, which in our view are vital to a correct understanding of this third source contained in article 38. The first one concerns the distinction between, on the one hand, the use or application or invocation of general principles by the International Court of Justice and in the context of proceedings before the Court respectively, and, on the other hand, the role of these principles outside the framework of the Court, that is within the inter-state relations in general. As will be argued, there is a considerable difference between these two situations as far as the functioning of general principles is concerned and, in our view, the general principles are usually looked upon too much from the perspective of the Court.

Secondly, it is important to keep in mind the above-mentioned distinction between procedural and material "constitutional" provisions of international law.[538] Applied to the general principles this distinction represents the two meanings of that phenomenon which need to be discerned: in the procedural sense general principles designate a method of creating rules of international law or, in the terminology used in the present study, a certain type of manifestation of the consent or acceptance of States; the material sense, on the other hand, refers to the intrinsic value of the substantive content of a given rule. There would seem to be a tendency in doctrine to confound these two aspects. Moreover, the analysis of the general principles of law in the material sense often leads to a comparison between the intrinsic value or substantive content of various norms and, consequently, raises the question of the hierarchy of norms of international law. Not seldom the discussion of general principles as a (procedural) source, simultaneously constitutes or results in an argument in favour of the superiority of one class of norms over others. It will be argued in the following that the two aspects mentioned represent two sides of the question of the sources of international law which should be kept apart.

It is along the lines of the two distinctions just set forth that an analysis of the meaning of "the general principles recognized by civilized nations" will now be undertaken.

538. See *supra* pp. 58-60.

8.3.2. The genesis of article 38(1)(c)

8.3.2.1. A preliminary question

Consideration of the *travaux préparatoires* concerning article 38(1)(c) is usually focused almost exclusively upon the work of the Advisory Committee of Jurists in 1920. It has been argued, however, by lawyers from socialist countries, that the materials of this Committee have become largely irrelevant for the proper interpretation of the said provision. Tunkin has submitted that as the Statute of the International Court of the United Nations is a new international agreement, "The meaning which was placed in this point by the drafters of the Statute of the Permanent Court of International Justice is only of historical importance for an understanding of the corresponding provision of the Statute of the International Court".[539] He subsequently maintains that "Evidently the drafters, representing different types of bourgeois law, had in mind expanding the possibilities for the Court in deciding cases by granting it the right to refer to principles common to the national legal systems of bourgeois States. However, this is not important in interpreting Article 38(1)(c) of the International Court, but rather that which the States represented at the San Francisco Conference, where this Statute was adopted and signed, had in mind. A sufficient reference point for this is the fact that a very important provision was inserted into Article 38 of the Statute of the International Court, that the Court 'is to decide in accordance with international law such disputes as are submitted to it'...".[540]

The point that what counts here is the intention of the parties to the Statute of the new World Court obviously is irrefutable. However, this does not justify the conclusion that the preparatory work for the old Statute has no significance anymore or is to be considered of historical importance only. On the contrary, the way in which the old Statute, including its *travaux préparatoires*, were dealt with at the 1945 San Francisco Conference, may very well contain indications as to the intentions of the parties to the new Statute. Tunkin and others taking the same position make it seem as if the insertion of the new words into the opening phrase of article 38 has radically altered the whole meaning of that provision, at least as far as its paragraph (1)(c) is concerned. However, the records of the San Francisco Conference seem to show that this is a misrepresentation of the facts.

The words "whose function is to decide in accordance with international law such disputes as are submitted to it" were inserted into article 38 as a result of a proposal made by the Chilean delegation in Committee I of Commission IV of the San Francisco Conference of 1945. It wanted to see an express mention of the application of international law by the Court, which it considered in accordance with established case-law of the Permanent Court of International Justice.[541] With respect to the addition the rapporteur of Committee IV/I explained that "The lacuna in the old Statute with reference to this point did not prevent the P.C.I.J. from regarding itself as an organ of international law; but

539. G. Tunkin, *op.cit.* (note 50), p. 197.
540. *Ibidem*, pp. 197-198; see also G. Tunkin, *loc.cit.* (note 529), pp. 524-525; a similar conclusion is reached by K. Wolfke, *op.cit.* (note 308), p. 110.
541. See *Documents of the United Nations Conference on International Organizations* (San Francisco 1945), Vol. 13, p. 493.

the addition will accentuate that character of the new Court".[542] It is difficult to see what other conclusion is to be drawn from this than that the addition was not intended to involve any substantive change.[543] Furthermore, if the States would really have wanted to change the meaning of the term "general principles" as contained in the old Statute, they could have done so in an unambiguous manner. However, as was pointed out by Kearney, they did not: "In the comments submitted by States proposing changes in the Statute of the Permanent Court as part of the preparatory work for the San Francisco Conference, Article 38 was almost invariably ignored or accepted in its original form".[544]

It follows that the work of the 1920 Advisory Committee of Jurists remains relevant also for the interpretation of the present article 38(1)(c).

8.3.2.2. The work of the 1920 Advisory Committee of Jurists

As was already observed, the *Procès-Verbaux* of the proceedings of the Advisory Committee of Jurists are widely discussed in doctrine.[545] The following will be confined to what seems to have been the focus of the Committee's attention.

The Committee seems to have been preoccupied mainly with two somewhat contradictory points. On the one hand the members of the Committee wanted to prevent a *non-liquet* on the part of the Court, while on the other hand they denied any legislative powers to the Court thereby stressing the consensual character of international law. Both points were reiterated by several members of the Committee. With respect to the question of *non-liquet*, for instance, De Lapradelle stated: "It is not possible to admit a declaration of *non-liquet* by an international court; denial of justice must be excluded from the international court just as from national courts".[546] As to the question of legislative powers Lord Phillimore stressed that "he did not wish, in any case, to give international judges legislative powers",[547] and made it clear that "legislation in matters of international law could only be carried out by the universal agreement of all States".[548]

The question arises how the Committee eventually reconciled these two objectives, which are, at least to some extent, mutually exclusive. For, if one wants to avoid a *non-liquet* in a situation where the law is supposed to show *lacunae*, a court has to be allowed at least some latitude in order to be able to fill possible gaps. The borderlines between application of the law, interpretation, concretization, elaboration, adaptation and change or (new) legislation are not always very clear. However, it is important to note that divergent perceptions on

---

542. *Ibidem*, p. 392.
543. See also R. Kearney, "Sources of Law and the International Court of Justice", in: L. Gross (ed.), *The Future of the International Court of Justice*, Vol. II (New York 1976), pp. 610-723 (653-654).
544. *Ibidem*, p. 653.
545. See for instance M. Bos, *loc.cit.* (note 28), pp. 33-37 and J. Lammers, *loc.cit.* (note 528), pp. 53-75 (59-60).
546. *Procès-Verbaux*, *loc.cit.* (note 526), p. 312.
547. *Ibidem*, p. 316.
548. *Ibidem*, p. 295.

the tasks and powers of the judge prevail in Civil Law systems as opposed to Common Law systems, because leading parts in the discussion on the general principles of law within the Committee were played by representatives of both these systems: Baron Descamps of Belgium on the one hand, and Lord Phillimore of the United Kingdom and Mr. Elihu Root of the United States, on the other hand.

Descamps, like almost all other members of the Committee, took as a point of departure that the Court should be prohibited from declaring a *non-liquet*. During one of the sessions he made this abundantly clear. In answering the question whether the judge could pronounce a *non-liquet* he stated that he "was convinced that he could not".[549] At the same time Descamps showed himself an adherent to Civil Law thinking which has for so long been influenced by Montesquieu's famous words describing the judge as an "inanimate being", which speaks the words of the law. Accordingly, Descamps envisaged to limit the Court's powers. The third item of his proposal for the rules to be applied by the Court was precisely designed to achieve this result. It read: "the rules of international law as recognized by the legal conscience of civilized nations".[550] He explained that "far from giving too much liberty to the judges' decision, his proposal would limit it. As a matter of fact it would impose on the judges a duty which would prevent them from relying too much on their own subjective opinion".[551]

It was Elihu Root who, at least in the beginning, took objection to Descamps' proposal. Coming from a Common Law country, where judges usually have a greater freedom of judgment, he was probably not particularly preoccupied by the danger of a *non-liquet*, even if the rules to be applied by the Court were to be confined to treaty and custom. At any rate, his dissent was not so much based on reasons of principle. At one point he even declared that he entirely agreed with Descamps' opinions.[552] What bothered him were the possible practical consequences. In reference to clauses 3 and 4 of Descamps' proposal[553] he remarked: "If these clauses were accepted, it would amount to saying to the States: 'You surrender your rights to say what justice should be'. Was it possible to compel nations to submit their disputes to a Court which would administer not merely law, but also what it deems to be the conscience of civilized peoples"?[554] Similarly, a little later he expressed the opinion "that the world was prepared to accept the compulsory jurisdiction of a Court which applied the universally recognized rules of international law. But he did not think it was disposed to accept the compulsory jurisdiction of a Court which would apply principles, differently understood in different countries".[555]

In the present author's view this latter point in fact became the central issue in the Committee's discussions: apart from treaty and customary rules, are any

549. *Ibidem*, p. 318.
550. *Ibidem*, p. 306.
551. *Ibidem*, p. 311; see also the speech made by Descamps where he stated that his proposal was "calculated to prevent arbitrary decisions", *ibidem*, p. 323.
552. *Ibidem*, p. 308.
553. Clause 4 read: "international jurisprudence as a means for the application and development of law".
554. *Ibidem*, p. 294.
555. *Ibidem*, p. 308.

other (type of) rules accepted (by the States) as forming part of the recognized body of international law? In the final analysis the Committee would seem to have arrived at a positive answer in the form of the proposal on the general principles elaborated by Root and Phillimore, which replaced Descamps' formula by the one now figuring in article 38(1)(c).[556] It was Lord Phillimore who explained and defended the text of the proposal, while Elihu Root hardly participated in the discussions anymore. The latter may therefore be supposed to have aligned himself with the views expressed by the former.

Early in the discussions Lord Phillimore admitted that in his view international law resembled Natural Law.[557] It was already pointed out, however, that Natural Law is not an unequivocal concept[558] and it is therefore important to see how Lord Phillimore specified his views after his proposal was tabled. In answering questions posed by De Lapradelle he pointed out that the general principles concerned "were these which were accepted by all nations *in foro domestico*"[559] and went on to explain that by the general principles of law "he had intended to mean 'maxims of law'".[560]

Descamps agreed with the Root-Phillimore formula.[561] To him it did not contain any views which were incompatible with his own. On the contrary, his opinions coincided largely with those expressed by Phillimore. At an earlier stage Descamps, in answer to Root's statement that principles of justice varied from country to country, had observed that this "might be partly true as to certain rules of secondary importance. But it is no longer true when it concerns the fundamental law of justice and injustice deeply engraved on the heart of every human being and which is given its highest and most authoritative expression in the legal conscience of civilized nations".[562] In his address explaining his proposal, moreover, he spoke of "objective justice"[563] and, in reference to the legal conscience of civilized nations, he pointed out "that there is nothing in the foregoing, *which was not already approved of by unanimous declarations of the assembly of civilized States*, both with reference to peace and war".[564]

From the proceedings of the Committee's work it is sometimes concluded that Natural Law, in the Committee's view, formed part of international law. Such a conclusion is not incomprehensible. However, it is submitted on the basis of the foregoing analysis, that the brand of Natural Law, to which both Descamps and Phillimore referred, consisted of those rules springing from the legal conscience of, or recognized by, civilized nations which had entered into the body of law through the acceptance by States. In order to understand this line of reasoning one should keep in mind the time-frame of the Committee's work. In 1920 the international society was, as far as the conceptions of international law are concerned, still relatively homogeneous and the members of the Committee

---

556. *Ibidem*, p. 344.
557. *Ibidem*, p. 318.
558. See *supra* pp. 30-34.
559. *Procès-Verbaux, loc.cit.* (note 526), p. 335.
560. *Ibidem.*
561. *Ibidem*, pp. 331-332.
562. *Ibidem*, pp. 310-311.
563. *Ibidem*, p. 322.
564. *Ibidem*, p. 323 (emphasis added).

were by and large like-minded people in this respect.[565] This situation can explain the views prevailing on the part of the members of the Committee; they were convinced that those rules (of Natural Law) which they had in mind were indeed accepted by the States through incorporation into the national legal systems.[566] At that time and given the group of States which they had in mind, they were presumably correct. The picture has changed, however, as a result of the developments in the structure of the international society.

In summary, the following conclusions may be drawn from the work of the 1920 Advisory Committee of Jurists. First, the phrase "general principles of law recognized by civilized nations" was intended to comprise those principles which were accepted by all nations *in foro domestico*. Secondly, even though members of the Committee considered the principles concerned to be part of Natural Law, they equally implied that in order for the new court to be able to apply them, these principles had to be accepted by States.[567] Thirdly, it should be kept in mind that the Committee's task was to draft a statute for a new international court. In other words, it was conducting its work from the perspective that the general principles had to function as a source within the framework of a court-situation. It is this court-situation that we will turn to next, because as was pointed out, the general principles as a source may taken on a different meaning in such a context as compared to their functioning outside the framework of a court.

8.3.3. The general principles within the framework of the International Court of Justice

8.3.3.1. Introduction

After this short discussion of the genesis of the phrase "the general principles of law recognized by civilized nations", the main question which remains to be answered is in what manner the general principles constitute a separate source of international law. In what way, different from treaty and custom, is the consent or acceptance of States manifested through the general principles of law?

565. The membership of the Committee comprised persons from the following countries: Japan, Spain, Brazil, Belgium, Norway, France, The Netherlands, The United Kingdom, Italy, and The United States, *ibidem*, pp. III and IV.
566. In the same vein B. Vitanyi, *loc.cit.* (note 528), p. 54: "Les auteurs du statut de 1920 avaient à l'esprit les nations européennes, et les nations extra-européennes issues de souche européenne, comme les nations américainnes et celles qui avaient adoptées dans leur ordre politique et juridique la civilisation européenne". With respect to article 38(1)(c) the author goes on to substantiate his contention according to which "Cette formule, controversée déjà au moment de sa création, est devenue depuis lors de plus en plus anachronique", *ibidem*, pp. 54-55.
567. It is indeed important to remember, as R. Jennings, *loc.cit.* (note 1), p. 71, has pointed out, that when article 38 "was drafted by the Committee of Jurists in 1920, it was assumed that the Statute of the Court would impose some important measure of compulsory jurisdiction. In the event this was rejected by the League of Nations; but the Articles of the Statute were not revised to take account of this fundamental change in the functions of the Court. It is clear, however, that the intention of Roots' formulation of para. (c) was to limit discretion of Judges, lest they tempted to impose subjective notions of justice".

Two methods can be discerned, *viz.* first, manifestation on the basis of reception from municipal legal systems, and second manifestation through induction from existing rules of international law. The second one can be said to be more or less inherent in the nature of the function and functioning of courts, including international courts, and will be dealt with below.[568] The first mentioned is the one which the drafters of the Statute would seem to have had primarily in mind, and will be discussed first.

8.3.3.2. General principles of the basis of reception from municipal legal systems

With respect to this method, in the present author's view, two conditions have to be fulfilled for the general principles to be considered as a source of international law. The first condition is to be found in the words of Phillimore, according to whom the general principles are those accepted by all States *in foro domestico.* If a rule or a principle is included in the national legal systems of all States, it may (potentially) also be a rule or principle of international law. To put it differently, the source of international law which is called "general principles of law" draws upon a reservoir consisting in the national legal systems of the States.

However, the fact that a certain rule or principle is indeed contained in the national legal systems of all States does not turn it automatically into a rule or principle of international law. Most writers agree that there can be no question of a kind of mechanical transplantation from national into international law.[569] Obviously not all rules or principles common to national legal systems can simply be transferred to the international level.[570] In every instance it has to be judged whether and to what extent the national rule or principle can be applied to the relations between States. As international relations diverge to a large extent from those usually prevailing in national societies, it is clear that this "applicability"-test considerably limits the number of rules or principles fit to be operative in international law.

Some go beyond this conclusion of limited applicability and argue that in practice there are no principles of international law which can be derived from the national legal systems. As was pointed out, particularly Soviet doctrine asserts that no principles common to "bourgeois" and socialist law can be found.[571]

---

568. See *infra* pp. 143-144.
569. See, for instance, H. Waldock, "General Course on Public International Law", 106 *RCADI* (1962-II), pp. 1-251 (64); see also the separate opinion by McNair appended to the advisory opinion on *International Status of South-West Africa,* ICJ Reports (1950), pp. 146-163 (148); and P. van Dijk, *Judicial Review of Governmental Action and the Requirement of an Interest to Sue* (Alphen aan den Rijn 1980), pp. 480-481.
570. Even a fundamental principle of legal procedure like *nemo judex in sua causa potest* which is generally applicable at the national level has a very limited applicability in the international sphere; see also W. Levi, *op.cit.* (note 56), p. 100, according to whom the rule "that nobody can be judged in his own case is a widely accepted general principle of law among 'civilized States'. Yet sovereignty guarantees that States can be judges in their own cases".
571. See *supra* pp. 132-133.

However, this point of view is not entirely convincing. Whatever the differences between "bourgeois" law and socialist law may be, in the present author's view they share at least some common elements. At the very least they are both systems of law and, therefore, have in common their functions of ordering and regulating relations in society. This ordering and regulating function may be directed towards diverging goals, the fact that in essence there exists an identity of purpose is bound to produce a minimum amount of similarity. Tunkin is eager to prove that this conclusion is incorrect. He maintains: "The content of a legal norm includes three elements: rule of conduct as such, aim, that always has a social character and actual influence on social relations. The last two elements of the content of norms of socialist law and norms of capitalist law are always is very often the same".[572] Even if one accepts this point of view, it has to be admitted, as Tunkin himself in fact does, that there still remains one element in common. It, therefore, seems quite artificial to subsequently deny the possibility of such systems of law containing the same provisions concerning certain issues. Because of the identity of purpose of systems of law such a similarity is indeed likely, at least as far as matters of procedure are concerned.[573]

This point apart, there is a second limitation - in addition to the one implied in the "applicability"-test just mentioned - contained in the requirement that the general principles are to be "recognized by civilized nations". Strictly speaking, in order to become part of international law a rule or a principle has to be accepted in the national legal systems of *all* States.[574] In the 1920's this was not too great an obstacle. At that time, the number of States was comparatively small and, in addition, the States were rather like-minded. Moreover, the like-minded States which considered themselves "civilized" simply excluded from the international system dissenting States as being "uncivilized".[575] The quantitative and qualitative changes in the international society have now resulted in a relatively large group of States which is very heterogeneous. The world, nowadays, consists of States which have widely diverging political, economic, social and cultural backgrounds. Consequently, it has become ever more difficult to find in their respective legal systems rules or principles which they have all in common and which are applicable to international relations. Of course, common elements may be more easily detected if not all States, but only a small group, are taken into consideration. Within a certain region or among a limited number of States sharing characteristics in some other respect common rules or principles are more likely to be found.[576] As in the case of customary international law,[577] there is no objection of theory against a limited number of States

572. G. Tunkin, *loc.cit.* (note 529), p. 527.
573. See also M. Virally, *loc.cit.* (note 305), p. 147, who adds: "In any event the existence or non-existence of common principles is a question of fact, to be resolved by examination rather than *a priori* opinion".
574. See the words of Phillimore quoted above, *supra* p. 138, who required the general principles to be accepted "by all nations *in foro domestico*".
575. See, on the other hand, R. Jennings' explanation of the term "civilized", *loc.cit.* (note 1), p. 72.
576. It may be argued, for instance, that certain principles are common to the legal systems of the member States of the European Communities and of the States parties to the European Convention for the Protection of Human Rights and Fundamental Freedoms, respectively, even apart from the rules which are binding upon these States on the basis of the treaties concerned. See P. van Dijk, *op.cit.* (note 569), pp. 482-483.
577. See *supra* pp. 96-97.

applying *inter se* a rule or principle of international law common to their respective legal systems, even though it might not be binding for other States.[578] In the area of general international law, however, it would seem far more difficult to detect common ground between the legal systems of the States.

It is here that the second condition referred to above necessary for making the general principles function as a source of international law, comes into play. It consists in the availability of a court-situation or, more broadly, of a situation of third party decision. The nature of the general principles, as just described, limits their usefulness as a source of international law mainly because of the uncertainties their application involve. In fact, these uncertainties can only be sufficiently alleviated when the general principles as a source are used in a situation of third party decision, *in casu* within the framework of the International Court of Justice.[579] Because of the particular conditions prevailing in proceedings before it, the Court is in the position to enhance the efficacy of the general principles as a source.

First of all, the scope of the requirement that the general principles must be recognized by *all* States is reduced by the construction which in fact substitutes "all municipal legal systems" for "the judges of the Court". In reference to the phrase "recognized by civilized nations", Virally has explained that "To abide strictly by this formula would necessitate a comparative study embracing all municipal systems of law in order to determine what principles are common to them. For the formula suggests a notion of common consent comparable to that requisite for the creation of customary law, but, in this context, to be found in a coincidence of municipal rules of law. In practice, however, the International Court proceeds in a more pragmatic fashion, and is satisfied with a coincidence of opinion amongst its own judges. Such a method affords sufficient safeguards, the judges having been elected so as to ensure 'the representation of the main forms of civilisation and the principal legal systems of the world' (Art. 9 of the Statute). For in view of this it may be conceded that anything which all the judges of the Court are prepared to accept as a 'general principle of law' must in fact be 'recognised by civilised nations'".[580] This, of course, considerably softens the test of general principles having to be recognized by all civilized nations. It is not difficult to imagine, that it is far easier to reach agreement among fifteen

---

578. This possibility which somewhat oddly could be termed "regional" or "specific" general principles, is also recognized by others; see, for instance, J. Lammers, *loc.cit.* (note 528), pp. 63-64 and the authors cited there.
579. It should be recalled that the general principles were introduced specifically in view of the creation of the (new) Permanent Court of International Justice in order to prevent it from having to conclude to a *non-liquet*.
580. M. Virally, *loc.cit.* (note 305), p. 146. In the passage just quoted Virally refers to "all the judges of the Court". The question arises, therefore, whether the existence of a general principle can only be established when each judge of the Court is of the opinion that it forms part of the principal legal system of the world which he represents. In other words, does the normal majority rule apply here or is unanimity required? It is imaginable that (the) members of the majority feel unable to conclude to the existence of a general principle in the face of a dissenting minority precisely because art. 38(1)(c) stipulates recognition "by civilized nations" as such. However, if they want to push through, they do not act *ultra vires*, because article 55 of the Statute stipulates that "All questions shall be decided by a majority of the judges present". If it is remembered that a quorum of nine judges is sufficient to constitute the Court (art. 25(3)), it becomes clear that, in theory at least, a decision that a general principle exists can be taken by five out of the fifteen judges.

judges considered as representatives of the principal legal systems, than to deduce common elements on the basis of a comparative analysis of all the municipal legal systems themselves.

Furthermore, it should be kept in mind that it is the Court's function to decide concrete cases involving usually two, or, at any rate, a very small number of States. This particular situation more or less invites the Court to look for general principles primarily within those legal systems to which the parties in the dispute concerned belong. While the Court cannot completely ignore the other legal systems of the world and will have to pay at least lipservice to them, it would seem only natural that the focus is on the systems of the States which seek a settlement of their dispute from the Court.

In addition to this "quantitative" advantage, there is also a "qualitative" element in the work of the Court which enables it to enhance the usefulness of the general principles as a source of international law. It is the "referee function" which is inherent in the ICJ's task, like in that of any other law-determining agency. This "referee function" somewhat disguises the fairly limited application of the general principles in general. For, it requires a certain amount of freedom of judgment to decide whether or not, and if so, to what extent, rules or principles derived from municipal law can appropriately be applied to international relations. The effective use of the general principles as a source, therefore, needs the "legislative" or "creative" powers which are implicitly entrusted to independent law-determining agencies. The International Court of Justice of course is such an agency in cases where its jurisdiction has been duly established. States submitting their dispute to the Court know that they "cede", at least in this one instance, their control over the question whether or not a rule is a rule of international law. Judicial decisions never enroll automatically from applying the relevant rules to the facts of the particular case; at the very least some element of interpretation is always involved. This holds *a fortiori* for the International Court of Justice, when it is applying such broadly framed categories as the general principles recognized by civilized nations. In other words, when we said above that the national legal systems serve as a kind of reservoir from which the general principles as a source of international law may draw, it has to be added that it is the Court which does the drawing. The decision of the Court can be considered as the final link of the process through which general principles of law in the sense of article 38(1)(c) are manifested. To put it differently, the Court "finalizes" the manifestation through which the consent or acceptance of States is shown. As will be discussed in more detail in relation to Article 38(1)(d), this process of manifestation, of which the Court's decision constitutes the final link, in fact starts with the acceptance of the jurisdiction of the Court by the States parties to the dispute concerned.[581]

8.3.3.3. General principles through induction from existing rules of international law

The above-mentioned "qualitative" element in the work of the Court or its "referee function" brings us to the second method through which the general princi-

581. See also *infra* p. 171.

ples can manifest the consent or acceptance of States.[582] This second method is reflected in the view of those who hold that article 38(1)(c) of the Statute does envisage the application of two different categories of principles, *viz.* principles of *national* law and principles of *international* law. Proponents of this view believe that besides the reception from municipal legal systems (principles of *national* law) there is still another independent source of international law implied in that provision, which they label principles of *international* law.

Most recently Lammers has taken this position thereby following a number of authoritative scholars of international law.[583] He sets forth two ways, through which the so-called principles of *international* law are said to produce rules of international law, *i.e.* principles resting on expressed general legal conviction or formless interstate consent, and through a process of induction from positive rules of international law.

The first mentioned way concerns the general principles as a source of international law outside the framework of the Court and will therefore be dealt with in the next section. The second way consisting in a process of induction by the Court from positive rules of international law would indeed seem to fit the Court quite well. Because of the same characteristics of its functioning which were described above the Court is able to perform the tasks involved in such a process of induction. Particularly, the "legislative" or "creative" aspects which are to some degree inherent in the work of all courts may play an important role in this respect. These enable the Court to generalize from existing rules of international law and thus to find "new" rules or principles, which it needs to decide the dispute submitted to it.

This brief survey shows that the Court has at its disposal tools, a-typical for the international society in general, which enable it to put into operation the source of the general principles of law.[584]

8.3.3.4. The limited use by the International Court of Justice of the general principles as a source of international law

Despite the comparatively favourable conditions the Court has not on a large scale resorted to the gap-filling device of the general principles of law. Indeed, it is fairly generally conceded in doctrine that the latter have played only a marginal role.[585] Most recently Jennings has even concluded that "The so-called 'general principles' have no very clear meaning, but the fact that the ambiguity has never had to be resolved is perhaps indicative of this provision's relative lack of

582. See *supra* p. 143.
583. J. Lammers, *loc.cit.* (note 528), pp. 57-59 jo. 66-69; the scholars cited are: Akehurst, Jaenicke, Wengler, Dahm, O'Connell, Rousseau, Verdross, Reuter, Verzijl and Siorat.
584. For more details on the functioning of the Court as far as the sources of international law are concerned, see *infra* pp. 169-176.
585. B. Cheng, *General Principles of Law as Applied by International Courts and Tribunals* (London 1953), p. 388, maintains that "The Permanent Court itself and, after it, the International Court, have on many occasions applied these principles as an integral part of international law, and individual judges, in their separate opinions, have often had recourse to them", but he cites only a handful of cases. W. Friedmann, on the other hand, has concluded: "If we were to look at the jurisprudence of the International Court itself the answer would be that the general principles have played a very minor role", *loc.cit.* (note 231), p. 148. Most other authors

144

importance in practical matters",[586] and that "One is sometimes tempted to think that Article 38(c) is truly an historical remnant of the 1920's and should be regarded today as having little more than academic interest".[587] Views like these are also expressed by proponents of the principles-of-international-law-thesis. Akehurst, for instance, holds that the general principles "are not so much a source of law as a method of using existing sources".[588] Moreover, a number of the authors concerned admit that in fact the general principles of international law often coincide with customary international law.[589] Verzijl, who is quoted as an adherent to the principles-of-international-law-thesis,[590] in the final analysis, takes a very rigid position and would seem even to reject the general principles of law as an independent source of international law.[591] Finally, Lammers has observed that "the Court has for understandable reasons made sparing use of the general principles of international law".[592]

Furthermore, a large number of the principles referred to by the Court, or mentioned in doctrine as general principles of law, are principles of a procedural nature. They relate to the administration of justice in general and the procedure before the ICJ in particular.[593] Clearly, these principles of procedure have a narrow field of application and, consequently, only a very limited impact on international law in general. As to the substantive principles which are put forward as general principles of law, at least a number of them, such as the principle of good faith and *pacta sunt servanda*, are now part of international law through treaty or custom and do, therefore, no longer have to be based on the source of the general principles.

Various reasons are adduced in doctrine to explain the minor importance of the general principles as a source of international law. In the present author's view, they can all be converted to the basic features of the international society

take a similar position: see, for instance, W. Levi, *op.cit.* (note 56), p. 99, and K. Wolfke, who asserts that "The authorization of the Court in point 1(c) of Article 38 to apply general principles of law recognized by civilized nations ... has remained a dead leter", *op.cit.* (note 308), p. 113; finally, J. Lammers, *loc.cit.* (note 528), p. 71, has inferred from a survey of both the World Courts' case law that "considered on the whole, it has to be admitted that general principles have played only a limited role in the decisions of the Court".

586. R. Jennings, *loc.cit.* (note 1), pp. 60-61.
587. *Ibidem*, p. 73.
588. M. Akehurst, *A Modern Introduction to International Law*, 3rd edition (London 1977), p. 40.
589. See J. Lammers, *loc.cit.* (note 528), pp. 68-69.
590. See *ibidem*, p. 58.
591. J. Verzijl, *International Law in Historical Perspective*, Vol. I: General Subjects (Leyden 1968), p. 62.
592. J. Lammers, *loc.cit.* (note 528), p. 73.
593. See for examples from the case-law of the Court, *ibidem* pp. 70-74; this emphasis on procedural principles in the Court's case-law is no mere coincidence. It were mainly these principles which Phillimore had in mind when he explained his statement that general principles were those accepted *in foro domestico*, by adding "such as certain principles of procedure, the principle of good faith, and the principle of *res judicata* etc.", *Procès-Verbaux, loc.cit.* (note 526), p. 335. As far as doctrine is concerned, it is illustrative to point out that B. Cheng's study on the general principles, which is one of the most comprehensive available, lists as a fourth category of principles "Certain general principles of law in Judicial Proceedings", which comprises more separate principles than the other three categories taken together. These include *inter alia: Nemo debet esse judex in propria sua causa, Audiatur et altera pars, Jura novit curia* and *Res judicata, op.cit.* (note 585), pp. 257-386. See also H. Schrader, *loc.cit.* (note 21), p. 781.

and, as far as more recent times are concerned, to the changed structure of the international society. The former force the ICJ to be prudent in using what was called in the foregoing its "legislative" or "creative" powers. More specifically, the Court's gap-filling with the aid of general principles cannot go too far beyond what is acceptable to the States. For, the "cession" of law-determining powers by States to the Court is at best partly and temporarily. In the final analysis the jurisdiction of the Court is voluntary and States can, therefore, withhold or withdraw acceptance of that jurisdiction with respect to future cases. As far as the reception from national laws is concerned, the changed structure of the international society has first of all made it much more difficult to establish the existence of a general principle of law, now that this has to be done on the basis of a multiplicity of widely diverging municipal legal systems. Furthermore, these changes have buttressed the necessity for the Court to take into account the sensitivities of States. The newly emerged States are even keener on their sovereignty than older States usually are. Therefore, the danger of alienating these new States by a liberal exercise of the judicial functions is even greater. These are probably the main reasons why the Court has been extremely careful in tapping the source of the general principles recognized by civilized nations.[594]

8.3.4. The general principles outside the framework of the International Court of Justice

As was observed in the preceding sections the general principles can be made operational as a source of international law because of the specific conditions prevailing within the framework of the procedure before the International Court of Justice. The question which now arises is, what is the case if these peculiar circumstances disappear. In other words, how can the general principles be conceived as a source of international law outside the framework of Court proceedings? This is an important question, because, as was already observed, the court-situation is very a-typical for international law. The bulk of law-determination at the international level takes place without the involvement of the ICJ and, for that matter, outside any judicial and arbitral, or other third party assessment process in general. Consequently, with respect to the question of the sources too, an investigation of the latter situation may be expected to provide a more reliable picture of the state of affairs in international law. Parry's observation on article 38 of the Statute in general holds good also for the source of the general principles: "Its content, ..., ought to be examined not so much from the point of view of the Court as from that of the State".[595] Nevertheless, there exists a strong tendency in doctrine to view the concept of sources almost solely from the perspective of the Court thereby providing a distorted picture of reality.

The question of whether the general principles as referred to in article 38(1)(c) of the Statute can be a source of international law outside the framework of the International Court of Justice, or more generally outside international judicial and arbitral or third party assessment processes, may be discussed by taking as a point of departure the view set forth by Verdross. Within the

---

594. See also W. Friedmann, *loc.cit.* (note 231), p. 149.
595. C. Parry, *loc.cit.* (note 22), p. 27.

framework of his interpretation of article 38(1)(c) of the Statute he observes: "Wie die letzten Jahre gezeigt haben, können allgemein anerkannte Rechtsgrundsätze auch ausserhalb des innerstaatlichen Rechts in der Weise entstehen, dass sich die Staaten in der GV der VN durch einseitige Erklärungen oder durch formlosen zwischenstaatlichen Consensus zu neuen Rechtsgrundsätzen bekennen, also noch bevor diese durch die Übung in das VGR eingegangen sind. Diese im Rahmen der Völkerrechtsordnung entstandenen allgemeinen Rechtsgrundsätze müssen aber von jenen unterschieden werden, die aus dem staatlichen Recht rezipiert werden. Die erste Gruppe ist im Aufstieg, während die ursprünglich dem innerstaatlichen Recht zugrundeliegenden allgemeinen Rechtsgrundsätze für den Bereich des VR als eigene Rechtsquelle immer mehr einschrumpfen, da die meisten von ihnen schon zu Normen des VGR oder zu Vertragsnormen geworden sind".[596]

This line of reasoning in fact distinguishes between two types of general principles. First, there are those general principles which are derived from municipal legal systems. This type was dealt with above, where it was argued that the general principles thus conceived as a source require the "final link" of the judgment of the International Court in order to complete the process through which the consent or acceptance of States is manifested. The other type to which Verdross refers is manifested through what may be summarily called the formless interstate consent.[597] From the outset it should be noted at this place that he confines this concept to the General Assembly of the United Nations and limits its application to the general principles of law.[598] In the present author's view, however, the creation of international law through formless interstate consent can also take place outside the framework of international organizations and, in addition, can also give rise to rules of international law other than general principles. Consequently, we will deal with it in a broader context.[599]

Another reason to do so, may be found in the following considerations. Is it really helpful to consider what Verdross labels formless interstate consent as a manifestation of general principles in the sense of a separate (procedural) source of international law? It has to be conceded that, theoretically in any case, the possibility exists. It is conceivable that the States collectively, notably through the General Assembly of the United Nations, provide the "final link" which the general principles as a source require and which within the framework of the International Court of Justice is furnished by the Court's judgment. The States could "draw upon" municipal legal systems or generalize from existing positive rules of international law (induction) and on that basis conclude, in the form of a General Assembly resolution, that this or that norm is to be recognized as a general principle of law. However, General Assembly resolutions, which are (purportedly) law-making, as a rule do not refer to, and are not based on, such reception or induction. Consequently, in the present author's view, it is rather artificial to present them as general principles in the sense of a separate (procedural) source of international law. If States wish to make rules of interna-

596. A. Verdross, *op.cit.* (note 98), pp. 128-129.
597. As was pointed out, a number of other writers too recognize this formless interstate consent as a way of creating general principles of international law; see *supra* p. 144.
598. A. Verdross, *op.cit.* (note 98), pp. 139-140.
599. See *infra* chapters XII and XIII.

tional law, other than by treaty or custom, for instance within the framework of the United Nations' General Assembly, they do not need point (c) of article 38(1). As "producers" of the law or law-givers they are not restricted to the existing sources, but may make new law also in a formless way.[600] When they do, it would seem better to deal with such formless methods on their own merits instead of trying to squeeze them into one of the traditional sources.

When reference is made, either by States or in doctrine, to general principles, what is meant very often are not the so-called "procedural constitutional provisions" but rather the "material constitutional provisions".[601] The following sections will discuss the general principles understood as "material constitutional provisions".

8.3.5. The distinction between general principles in the procedural and in the material sense

In addition to the distinction between the general principles as a source of international law within and outside the framework of the International Court of Justice, it was submitted above that two other meanings of the term "general principles" should be kept apart, *i.e.* general principles in the procedural and in the material sense. The former designates general principles as a method of creating rules of international law, while the second refers to the intrinsic value or the substantive content of a given rule. Taken in the latter sense, it was added, the analysis of the general principles often leads to a discussion of the issue of the hierarchy of norms of international law.[602] The general principles in the procedural sense were dealt with in the preceding sections. Now, the general principles in the material sense should be elaborated a little further.

In this latter sense the general principles are usually considered to take on a quite specific meaning. To lawyers the term "general principles" has a very special sound, albeit not always a very clear one. At the very least "general principles" or just "principles" connotes something different from ordinary rules of law. Fitzmaurice, for instance, distinguishes between rules and principles in the following manner: "A rule answers the question 'what', a principle in effect answers the question 'why'".[603] Similarly, Dworkin, who discerns between rules, principles and policies,[604] and indeed makes this distinction to one of the pillars of his theory, seeks the difference between rules and principles in their functioning, in the way they operate as standards: "Both sets of standards point to particular decisions about legal obligations in particular circumstances, but they differ in the character of the direction they give. Rules are applicable in an

---

600. M. Bos, *loc.cit.* (note 28), p. 11, explains with respect to the law-giver: "if a rule of law would not fit into existing 'sources', he is able to invent a new 'source' in order to accommodate that rule". See also *infra* p. 197.
601. For this distinction, see *supra* pp. 57-60.
602. See *infra* pp. 151-153.
603. G. Fitzmaurice, *loc.cit.* (note 263), p. 7.
604. A "policy" is defined as "that kind of standard that sets out a goal to be reached, generally an improvement in some economic, political or social feature of the community". A "principle" is said to be a standard "that is to be observed, not because it will advance or secure an economic, political, or social situation deemed desirable, but because it is a requirement of justice or fairness or some other dimension of morality", R. Dworkin *op.cit.* (note 87), p. 22.

all-or-nothing fashion. If the facts a rule stipulates are given, then either the rule is valid, in which case the answer it supplies must be accepted, or it is not, in which case it contributes nothing to the decision".[605] Principles are said to be different because "Even those which look most like rules do not set out legal consequences that follow automatically when the conditions provided are met".[606] Principles rather state "a reason that argues in one direction, but does not necessitate a particular decision".[607]

Views like these suggest that principles have a wider scope of application and also more far-reaching consequences than rules. The acknowledgement of such a difference in functioning, of course, comes close to acknowledging a difference in nature. Consequently, from the view just described it is only a small step to the conclusion that principles constitute more important or fundamental standards than rules. It is, therefore, not surprising that such a conclusion is often arrived at. Thus, Dworkin goes on to observe: "This first difference between rules and principles entails another. Principles have a dimension that rules do not - the dimension of weight or importance".[608] In the same vein, Cheng has concluded with respect to international law: "A consideration of the subject-matter covered by these general principles of law shows the important position they hold in the international legal order, and indeed in any juridical order. They lie at the very foundation of the legal system and are indispensable to its operation".[609]

This short explanation of the material sense of the term "general principles" suffices to resume the discussion on the distinction between the material and the procedural sense. As was submitted above, there is a tendency to mix up these two meanings of the term "general principles". Sometimes no distinction is made at all and the procedural and material sense of the term are treated simultaneously under the general heading of general principles.[610] Even when a differentiation between types of principles is made, the procedural/material distinction is not always consistently applied. Von der Heydte has discerned, in

---

605. *Ibidem*, p. 24.
606. *Ibidem*, p. 25.
607. *Ibidem*, p. 26.
608. *Ibidem*.
609. B. Cheng, *op. cit.* (note 585), p. 390; see also B. Vitanyi, *loc. cit.* (note 528), p. 52, who goes as far as to uphold that the divergences of opinion with respect to the phrase "general principles recognized by civilized nations" result mainly from the fact that "l'expression 'principes généraux de droit' est employée dans un sens impropre dans le Statut. Le terme 'principe général de droit' désigne, dans son acceptation communément admise, une norme de portée très générale qui traduit une conception fondamentale d'un système de droit et remplit, par conséquent, une fonction constitutive dans l'ordre juridique donné. Les principes de droit ne prennent pas naissance selon une mode de formation de droit reconnu dans l'ordre juridique donné, mais impliqués dans l'ensemble du système, sont déjà présent avant que les règles particulières dans lesquelles ils s'explicitent soient formées".
610. See, for instance, B. Cheng, who in the process of analyzing (the procedural source contained in) article 38(1)(c) of the I.C.J.'s Statute, simultaneously alleges the general principles to be of a fundamental character: "In the definition of the third source of international law, there is also the element of recognition on the part of the civilized peoples, but the requirement of a general practice is absent. The object of recognition is, therefore, no longer the legal character of the rule implied in an international usage, but the existence of certain principles intrinsically legal in nature. ... This part of international law does not consist, therefore, in specific rules formulated for practical purposes, but in general propositions underlying the various rules of law which express the essential qualities of juridical truth itself, in short of law", *op. cit.* (note 585), p. 24.

article 38(1)(c), between legal principles recognized by States as an essential part of any legal order, and positive rules of municipal law which, though not forming an essential part of every legal order, are recognized by States *in foro domestico*,[611] and he maintains that the former constitute *jus cogens*.[612]

This conclusion does not seem to be correct, although it is not incomprehensible. It was already pointed out that "principles" or "general principles" are usually taken to connote norms of a fundamental character or at least norms of great importance[613] and it is, therefore, not surprising to see general principles being equated with *jus cogens*. Nevertheless, in the present author's opinion this view puts at par two meanings of "general principles" which should be distinguished. Von der Heydte's second category refers to general principles as a method of creating rules of international law, *in casu* through the reception from the municipal legal systems. The first category of general principles refers to the substantive content of norms of international law. These latter norms have been created through custom or treaty or some other manifestations, but not (necessarily) through reception from municipal legal systems. Moreover, with respect to the first category it should be stressed that rules of international law do not gain *jus cogens* character, because they are labeled "general principles". As will be pointed out below, the question of whether or not a rule is *jus cogens*, is to be decided on the basis of other criteria.[614] Even apart from the merit of the distinction between "rules" and "principles" referred to above,[615] the fact that a norm is called a general principle does not necessarily entail it being *jus cogens*. In summary, without making an adequate distinction between the procedural and the material sense the treatment of the general principles carries the risk of sliding more or less imperceptibly from an analysis of a manifestation of norms of international law into a discussion concerning the hierarchy of rules of international law, while applying to the latter a criterion which holds good only with respect to the former.

The tendency just described would seem to be spreading. With respect to the general principles in the material sense Virally has observed: "Such principles, because of their generality and their firm basis in custom have understandably come to be looked upon as fundamental in the sense of having a greater validity than other rules of international law, or even as rules from which states may in no case depart (...), and have been sometimes called principles of 'international constitutional law'. ... The notion of fundamental principles of international law has gained ground since the Second World War and has invaded the sphere of conventional law".[616] As was pointed out above, this study is primarily focused

---

611. F. von der Heydte, "Glossen zu einer Theorie der allgemeinen Rechtsgrundsätze", 33 *FW* (1933), pp. 289-300 (290); see also A. Verdross, "Les Principes Généraux dans la Jurisprudence Internationale", 52 *RCADI* (1935-II), pp. 195-251 (191).

612. F. von der Heydte, *loc.cit.* (note 611), pp. 297-298.

613. See *supra* pp. 148-149.

614. See *infra* pp. 156-166.

615. See *supra*, pp. 148-149; to the present author the distinction does seem far from clear-cut and it may, therefore, be doubted whether it is workable. Characteristics which it assignes to "principles" sometimes hold good also with respect to "rules" and *vice versa*. Dworkin himself concedes that "Sometimes a rule and a principle can play much the same role, and the difference between them is almost a matter of form alone", *op.cit.* (note 87), p. 217.

616. M. Virally, *loc.cit.* (note 305), pp. 144-145; see also the conclusions by B. Vitanyi based upon his analysis of doctrinal positions regarding the general principles, *loc.cit.* (note 528), pp. 110-116.

on the sources of international law in the procedural sense.[617] However, in view of the foregoing it is necessary to pay some attention to those aspects of the issue of *jus cogens* which are most relevant in the present context.

8.3.6. Excursus: *Jus Cogens*

8.3.6.1. Introduction

In order to clarify the distinction between the so-called formal and material sources of international law, a comparison was made above with a prototype of a national constitution.[618] The latter was said to contain, broadly speaking, two types of provisions: the procedural constitutional provisions on the one hand, which outline the legal/organizational structure of the society concerned; the material constitutional provisions on the other hand, that lay down the fundamental (political) orientation in the form of basic values or ideas which society wants to uphold or attain. International *jus cogens*, of course, belongs to the "material constitutional provisions" of international law. The concept of international *jus cogens* is multi-faceted and complex and not all of its aspects can be dealt with here. The following will be confined to those questions concerning the concept of *jus cogens* which are most directly related to the problem of the sources (in the procedural sense) of international law.[619]

8.3.6.2. The hierarchy of rules of international law

In the foregoing *jus cogens* was referred to as belonging to the question of the hierarchy of rules of international law. It should be stressed from the outset, however, that the issue of hierarchy encompasses more than just the concept of

---

617. See *supra* p. 59.
618. See *supra* pp. 58-60.
619. See for more details on *jus cogens* the following studies which were used as a basis for the following analysis: M. Akehurst, "The Hierarchy of the Sources of International Law", XLVII *BYIL* (1974-1975), pp. 273-285; M. Bos, "The Hierarchy Among the Recognized Manifestations ("Sources") of International law", in: *Estudios de Derecho Internacional; Homenaje al Profesor Miaja De La Muela* (Madrid 1979), pp. 363-374; A. McNair, *op.cit.* (note 275); V. Nageswar Rao, "Jus Cogens and the Vienna Convention on the Law of Treaties", 14 *IJIL* (1974), pp. 362-385; N. Onuf and R. Birney, "Peremptory Norms of International Law: Their Source, Function and Future", 4 *DJILP* (1974), pp. 187-198; C. Rozakis, *op.cit.* (note 238); U. Scheuner, "Conflict of Treaty Provisions with a Peremptory Norm of General International Law and its Consequences", 27 *ZaöRV* (1967), pp. 520-532; I. Sinclair, *op.cit.* (note 464); M. Sørensen, *op.cit.* (note 281); E. Suy, *Papers and Proceedings of the Lagonissi Conference* (Geneva 1967); G. Schwarzenberger, "International 'Jus Cogens'?", 43 *TLR* (1965), pp. 455-478; A. Verdross, "Jus Dispositivum and Jus Cogens in International Law", 60 *AJIL* (1966), pp. 55-63; M. Virally, "Réflexions sur le 'jus cogens'", XII *AFDI* (1966), pp. 5-29; M. Whiteman, "Jus cogens in International Law, with a Projected List", 7 *GJICL* (1977), pp. 609-626; K. Wolfke, "Jus Cogens in International Law", 6 *PYIL* (1974), pp. 145-162, and M. Yasseen, "Réflexions sur la détermination du jus cogens', in: Société française pour le droit international, *L'Elaboration du Droit International Public* (Paris 1974), pp. 204-210.

151

jus cogens. As Bos has pointed out, hierarchical relationships in international law could be envisaged on the basis of three criteria, *i.e.* origin, purport, and age.[620] With respect to origin some hold, like Bos himself, that rules stemming from certain sources of international law, in the (third) sense of manifestations, take precedence over those flowing from others.[621] The criteria of purport and age are embodied in the well-known maxims: *lex specialis derogat lege generali, lex posterior derogat lege priori*, and *lex posterior generalis non derogat lege priori speciali*.[622] These three criteria are themselves subject to an hierarchical order[623] and of these three origin is often considered the most important one.

Nevertheless, the hierarchical ranking of rules of international law on the basis of their substantive content, that is on the basis of their character as *jus cogens* or as *jus dispositivum*, would seem to be even more important and far-reaching. In fact, the hierarchy of rules of international law on the basis of substantive content cuts across the ranking on the basis of other, more formal, criteria.[624] This situation has been summarized by Akehurst as follows: "In the event of a conflict between a rule of *jus cogens* and a rule of *jus dispositivum*, the rule of *jus cogens* must prevail, regardless of the sources of the conflicting rules, regardless of whether the rule of *jus dispositivum* came into existence before or after the rule of *jus cogens*, and regardless of whether the rule of *jus dispositivum* is more specific or less specific than the rule of *jus cogens*".[625] To put it differently, hierarchy on the basis of the substantive content (or *jus cogens* character) of a rule overrides hierarchy on the basis of the particular source from which a rule stems.[626]

It should be pointed out in this connection that, in the conception of sources which has been set forth in the present study, it would seem difficult to accept a hierarchical order between these sources. For the latter were all put forward as equal manifestations of the same constitutive element of rules of international law, *viz.* consent or acceptance of States. Consequently, it would seem impossible to conceive of an *a priori* hierarchical order between the sources as manifestations. Such an order could arise only as a result of consent or acceptance to that effect. Up until now, this has not been the case.[627] At any rate it would seem to

620. M. Bos, *loc.cit.* (note 619), pp. 365-366.
621. *Ibidem.*
622. *Ibidem*, p. 366.
623. *Ibidem*, p. 365, where this is called a preliminary hierarchy.
624. Cf. also M. Bos, *ibidem*.
625. M. Akehurst, *loc.cit.* (note 619), pp. 281-282.
626. Sørensen has pointed to the distinction between a hierarchy of sources and a hierarchy of rules. The latter "substantive" school of thought differentiates between rules of international law irrespective of the particular source from which they stem, *op.cit.* (note 281), pp. 238-245.
627. Article 38 of the Statute itself cannot be taken to establish an hierarchical order between the sources. On the basis of a proposal of Baron Descamps the 1920 Committee of Jurists included in its draft a provision that the items listed in paragraph (1) of article 38 should be applied *en ordre successif*. From the discussion within the Committee, however, it is not clear whether this phrase was intended to lay down a hierarchy of sources or whether it was meant to reflect the natural order in which the sources would come to the judge's mind; see *Procès Verbaux, loc.cit.* (note 526), pp. 336-338. Similarly, with respect to the subsequent deletion of the phrase by the sub-Commission of the Third Committee of the League of Nations' First Assembly it is not clear, as Akehurst observes, whether it "was inspired by a feeling that the idea contained in the words was wrong, or that the idea was so obviously right as not to need stating", *loc.cit.* (note 619), p. 274.

be generally conceded that "ever since the debate on *jus cogens* has intensified, in particular after the adoption of Articles 53 and 64 of the Vienna Convention on the Law of Treaties, the substantive school has gained ground".[628]

8.3.6.3. The basis of international *jus cogens*

As was already observed, rules of *jus cogens* belong to what we have termed "material constitutional provisions of international law" and, consequently, it is the substantive content of a rule which is the main factor in deciding whether or not it has a *jus cogens* character. This point of view is more or less generally recognized. In the words of the International Law Commission "it is not the form of a general rule of international law but the particular nature of the sub-ject-matter with which it deals that may ... give it the character of *jus cogens*".[629] The content of a *jus cogens* rule or the subject-matter which it concerns has to be of great or even fundamental importance to the international community. It is striking to see how often, in discussions concerning *jus cogens*, the words "ne-cessary" and "essential", or some synonym, are being used. During the Vienna Conference on the Law of Treaties, for instance, the Mexican representative defined rules of *jus cogens* as "those rules which derived from principles that the legal conscience of mankind deemed absolutely essential to co-existence in the international community at a given stage of its historical development".[630] Sim-ilarly, the Iraqi representative observed that "States could not by treaty override those higher norms which were essential to the life of the international commun-ity",[631] while the representative of Cyprus equated *jus cogens*, to what Wolff and Vattel had called in the middle of the eighteenth century, the "necessery law" which nations could not alter by agreement.[632] In the same vein rules of *jus cogens* are usually described in doctrine. According to McNair, for instance, these rules standing in a higher category "are rules which have been accepted either expressly by treaty or tacitly by custom, as being necessary to protect the public interests of the society of States or to maintain the standards of public morality recognized by them ...".[633]

Above, the concept of recognized necessity was put forward as an explana-tion for the binding force of international law.[634] It was said to be a sufficient basis for the binding force of international law that States are aware, that there is no satisfactory alternative to a set of binding rules for the regulation of their mutual relations. Recognized necessity, therefore, was used in the procedural sense and a *caveat* was entered not to fill the concept with a material content in the form of some basic idea or value, because this would destroy its attractive-

---

628. M. Bos, *loc.cit.* (note 619), p. 372.
629. General Assembly Official Records, Twenty-First Session, Suppl. 9/A/6309/Rev.1, pp. 76-77.
630. *UN Doc.* A/Conf.39/11, p. 294.
631. *Ibidem*, p. 296.
632. *Ibidem*, p. 305.
633. A. McNair, *op.cit.* (note 275), pp. 213-215. Very much the same would seem to be implied in Verdross' much quoted definition of rules of *jus cogens*: "The criterion for these rules consists in the fact that they do not exist to satisfy the needs of the individual states but the higher inter-est of the whole international community", *loc.cit.* (note 619), p. 58.
634. See *supra* pp. 71-76.

ness, as no such material source is generally acceptable or rationally verifiable. With regard to international *jus cogens* it is particularly tempting to read some kind of material or substantive meaning into the concept of recognized necessity. It is clear that many believe *jus cogens* ultimately to be based upon some higher value or idea.[635] For the same reason, however, as was just mentioned with respect to the question concerning the binding force of international law, the present author does not regard this as a fruitful approach in trying to reach some kind of *communis opinio* in matters of international *jus cogens*. At the same time it has to be admitted that a "procedural" approach is probably not very satisfactory either. Precisely because *jus cogens* concerns issues which people think of as fundamental to society, the "neutral" concept of recognized necessity in the procedural sense is likely to be considered by many as too limited.

Nevertheless, the present author ventures to believe that also in this respect, it might at least be of some help in providing a common denominator. It could be argued then, that the awareness of the necessity to order and regulate relations in society not only serves as the basis of the binding force of international law, but also gives rise to a number of substantive rules. Of course, all law as binding rules is in some sense necessary for the ordering and regulating of relations in society. Rules of *jus cogens*, however, may be said to be those rules which are considered more necessary or even essential in a given society. As it was put by the Iraqi representative at the Vienna Conference on the Law of Treaties: "It could be said that some rules of international law were more binding than others".[636] Generally speaking, therefore, rules of *jus cogens* may be said to be those rules which, in view of the circumstances prevailing, are so central to the very idea of ordering and regulating that they are considered "obvious" rules, even though their implications when applied in practice may be considerably less obvious. In this way the recognized necessity might serve as a theoretical explanation of the concept of *jus cogens* in international law. The present author is well aware of the limitations of the concept of recognized necessity. Recognized necessity does explain *jus cogens* so to speak only "after the fact"; it does not proclaim that this or that norm is "of necessity" a *jus cogens* norm in any society. Rules of *jus cogens* may differ from one society to the other. Neither does it lay down "eternal" *jus cogens* norms for a certain society; rules of *jus cogens* may, of course, change. Finally, it does not necessitate the conclusion that society, or rather any system of law, contains indeed *jus cogens* norms.[637] All that it does is provide a theoretical explanation for rules of international *jus cogens* which have come duly into existence.[638]

8.3.6.4. The concept of *jus cogens* in international law

635. See the statements by the various state-representatives at the Vienna Conference on the Law of Treaties quoted *supra* p. 153; see also *infra* pp. 156-166.
636. *UN Doc.* A/Conf.39/11, p. 296.
637. See in this respect the words of A. McNair: "It is difficult to imagine any society whether of individuals or of States, whose law sets no limit whatever to freedom of contract", *op.cit.* (note 275), pp. 213-214.
638. See on the *jus cogens*-making process *infra* pp. 156-166.

The lack of a generally agreed upon value or idea underlying *jus cogens* is probably the main reason for the controversial character of the latter concept in international law. The very issue whether or not there exists international *jus cogens* is subject of debate. Some deny that international law, because of its peculiar features, at present contains norms of a *jus cogens* character. Schwarzenberger, who has launched a famous attack on international *jus cogens*, is known as a most staunch proponent of this view.[639] Schwarzenberger, to be sure, is not opposed to the concept of *jus cogens* as such, but he rather upholds that the recognition of that concept in international law can at best be *de lege ferenda* and not *de lege lata*.[640]

In 1965 he wrote: "The evidence of international law on the level of unorganized international society fails to bear out any claim for the existence of *jus cogens*."[641] Subsequently, he asserts: "In organized world society, the Principles of the United Nations and corresponding forms of *jus cogens* in other international institutions present attempts at the creation of consensual rules of international public policy. As yet, these efforts are too precarious, as in the United Nations, or too limited *ratione personae* or *ratione materiae*, as in the specialized agencies of the United Nations, or the supranational European Communities, to constitute more than international quasi-orders".[642] This point of view is the result of Schwarzenberger's typical concept of (international) law, which comes to the fore in the following observation on *jus cogens*: "In fact, *jus cogens*, as distinct from *jus dispositivum*, presupposes the existence of an effective *de jure* order, which has at its disposal legislative and judicial machinery, able to formulate rules of public policy and, in the last resort, can rely on overwhelming physical force".[643] In other words, Schwarzenberger believes that the existence of *jus cogens* is conceivable only in systems of law which are equipped with organs having full-fledged legislative, executive and judicial powers. As international law is lacking these features, it cannot according to Schwarzenberger, contain rules having a *jus cogens* character.

On the basis of what has been said above on the concept of international law,[644] it is not surprising that the present author does not find Schwarzenberger's point of view entirely convincing. There would seem to be no reason to suppose that rules of *jus cogens* can arise only in hierarchically structured systems of law and not in a purely consensual system like international law. It is true that international law lacks an underlying value or idea which is generally accepted by the States and which could, on that ground, serve as the ultimate basis for its binding force. Equally, international law cannot rely on an "overwhelming physical force". Nevertheless, States reach agreement on the content of rules of international law and recognize the necessity for their binding

639. See in particular G. Schwarzenberger, *loc.cit.* (note 619).
640. See also A. Verdross, *loc.cit.* (note 619), p. 60: "Professor Schwarzenberger recognizes and has always recognized that through bilateral and multilateral consensus a rule having the character of *jus cogens* can be created *inter partes*. Its legal effect is therefore 'limited to the contracting parties'".
641. G. Schwarzenberger, *loc.cit.* (note 619), p. 476.
642. *Ibidem.*
643. G. Schwarzenberger, *A Manual of International Law*, 5th edition (London 1967), pp. 29-30.
644. See *supra* pp. 19-28.

force.[645] Consequently, it would seem difficult to come up with an objection of theory against States reaching agreement on the content of rules of *jus cogens* and assigning them a binding force of a higher character. In the final analysis the process of creating international *jus cogens* would seem in principle to be the same as the law-making process for ordinary rules of law.[646]

Although the existence of *jus cogens* is not dependent upon the presence of a hierarchical structure in a society, rules of *jus cogens* are, of course, linked to the nature of relations in society, just like other rules of law.[647] Rules of *jus cogens* are likely to arise, when societal relations acquire a certain degree of frequency and intensity and the rules of law reach a certain level of complexity. In order to be able to keep society viable, it may then be felt necessary to structure the relation between rules of law *inter se* by making one category override the other. It is submitted that, as a result of developments in international relations, international law now has reached this point. As was observed by the representative of the Federal Republic of Germany at the Vienna Conference on the Law of Treaties: "The emergence of the notion of *jus cogens* in international law was a direct consequence of social and historical evolution, which had had a far-reaching influence on the development of international law. Technical interdependence and the multiplication of links between States had produced a situation where the ordered co-existence of States became impossible not only in the absence of some sort of international public order but also for want of certain concrete rules from which derogation was not permitted".[648] Particularly after the adoption of the articles 53 and 64 of the Vienna Convention on the Law of Treaties it would indeed seem extremely difficult to deny that the concept of *jus cogens* now forms part of international law.[649] The criticism which has been expressed with regard to these articles concern mainly their wording rather than the concept they embody.[650]

8.3.6.5. Identification and validity of norms of international *jus cogens*

645. See *supra* pp. 71-76.
646. See *infra* pp. 156-166.
647. See *supra* pp. 65-71.
648. *UN Doc.* A/Conf.39/11/Add.1, pp. 95-96.
649. See also M. Yasseen, *loc.cit.* (note 619), pp. 204-205: "La Commission du droit international n'a pas hésité à reconnaître l'existence dans l'ordre juridique international des normes impératives. La Conférence de Vienne sur le droit des traités l'a suivie sur cette voie. ... Il est donc possible de dire de nos jours le principe de l'existence du *jus cogens* est incontesté". In the same vein E. Suy has conceded that "The most surprising feature of the Commission's debates is the unanimity with which members of the Commission approved the idea of *jus cogens*", *loc.cit.* (note 619), p. 50.
650. Article 53 reads: "A treaty is void if, at the time of its conclusion, it conflicts with a peremptory norm of general international law. For the purposes of the present Convention, a peremptory norm of general international law is a norm accepted and recognized by the international community of States as a whole as a norm from which no derogation is permitted and which can be modified only by a subsequent norm of general international law having the same character". Article 64 reads: "If a new peremptory norm of general international law emerges, any existing treaty which is in conflict with that norm becomes void and terminates". Article 53 was adopted by 87 votes to 8 with 12 abstentions; see *U.N. Doc.*A/Conf.39/11/Add.1, p. 107. Article 64 was approved by 84 votes to 8 with 16 abstentions, *ibidem*, p. 125. In both cases the following States were against: Australia, Belgium, France, Liechtenstein, Luxembourg, Monaco, Switzerland and Turkey.

After it has been concluded that the concept of *jus cogens* now forms part of international law, the question obviously arises as to the criteria for international *jus cogens*. How are international rules of *jus cogens* to be identified? Because of the function these rules perform, the question as to the criteria for the identification of *jus cogens* is extremely important. As far as international law is concerned, the point of departure is simple: because of the basic features of international society the process of creating *jus cogens* must be subject to the same conditions as the ordinary law-making process. This point of view has very aptly been expressed in the following words: "since nation-states can and do decide what the law shall be, the creation of peremptory norms is subject to the same rules of law-making as any valid norm. Finally, the process of acquiring legal status is identical to the process of acquiring a peremptory nature. The two processes may take place independently, as in cases where long-standing norms become peremptory at a later date, but they operate in the same way. This means simply that they operate in conformity with the requirements of one of the several modes in which the international community creates its norms. In short, peremptory norms, whether in becoming norms or in becoming peremptory or both, must be considered in terms of the sources of international law".[651]

This then leads to the conclusion that, like in the case of ordinary rules of international law, the "rule of recognition" or the constitutive element of international *jus cogens* is the consent or acceptance of States. Consent or acceptance is required not only for a rule to become a norm of international law, but also for a rule to gain the character of a peremptory norm.[652] This "double consent" requirement consisting of *opinio juris cogentis* in addition to *opinio juris* is necessary to avoid uncertainty concerning the exact character of international peremptory norms. If no additional text in the form of *opinio juris cogentis* were available, it would be impossible to tell peremptory norms apart from ordinary rules of international law.

It is sometimes suggested that the importance or the fundamental character of rules of *jus cogens* could serve as the sole criterion to discern them from ordinary rules of international law. However, importance or fundamental character on itself does not seem to provide an adequate test. Firstly, it is not clear whether "important" or "fundamental" always coincide with "peremptory". Rules may be regarded as important or fundamental without at the same time being accepted by States as peremptory norms.[653] Secondly, even in cases where important or fundamental norms at the same time constitute rules of *jus cogens*, this *jus cogens* character has to be explicitly established or determined, before such rules can begin to play their overriding function. If not, there would be too

---

651. N. Onuf and R. Birney, *loc.cit.* (note 619), p. 190; see also M. Virally, *loc.cit.* (note 619), p. 16 according to whom the sources of rules of *jus cogens* are the same as the sources of other norms of international law.

652. See on consent or acceptance as the constitutive element of ordinary rules of international law, *supra* pp. 76-81.

653. For instance, in the *United States Diplomatic and Consular Staff in Teheran* case, ICJ Reports, 1980, pp. 3-65 (42), the Court labeled the international rules on diplomatic law *inter alia* as "rules the fundamental character of which the Court must here again strongly affirm", as "of cardinal importance for the maintenance of good relations between States in the interdependent world of today", and as the most "fundamental prerequisite for the conduct of relations between States". Nevertheless, the Court nowhere qualified these rules as international *jus cogens*.

much uncertainty and it could be more or less arbitrarily put forward that norms are peremptory without this necessarily being so. Because of the structuring function of peremptory norms such a state of affairs would obviously be detrimental to the stability of the international legal order. Hence the need for an *opinio juris cogentis.*

The "double consent" test has been laid down in article 53 of the Vienna Convention on the Law of Treaties which provides that "a peremptory norm of general international law is a norm accepted and recognized by the international community of States as a whole as a norm from which no derogation is permitted and which can be modified only by a subsequent norm of general international law having the same character". As was already pointed out, the amendment inserting the words "accepted and recognized" put back the concept of international *jus cogens* on a consensual basis, after a Natural Law inclination had been prominent in some of the drafts of the ILC's special rapporteurs.[654] As Rozakis has pointed out article 53 contains "a formula which clearly and unequivocally rejected any *jus naturale* allusion that might have been suggested by the work of the International Law Commission ...".[655] Here again it should be stressed that one might very well conceive of *jus cogens* as ultimately based upon, or derived from, Natural Law.[656] One can go even one step further and uphold that Natural Law thinking to a large extent has influenced and still influences rules of *jus cogens.* However, that is not the same thing as maintaining that the test for the *jus cogens* character of rules of international law is whether or not they belong to some brand of Natural Law. What is decisive in this respect is whether or not the consent or acceptance of States has clothed the rules concerned with a peremptory character.

Despite the unequivocal intention of the States participating in the Vienna Conference on the Law of Treaties to put international *jus cogens* on a consensual basis, the formula now contained in article 53 of the Vienna Convention on the Law of Treaties is not free from difficulties. Particularly, the words "by the international community of States as a whole" lend themselves to differing interpretations. Before embarking upon an analysis of this phrase, it should be pointed out that article 53 of the Convention envisages only rules of *jus cogens* which are binding for all, or at least nearly all States of the world. This follows from the words "a peremptory norm of general international law".[657] The Con-

---

654. See *supra* p. 80; H. Waldock, however, has observed that "the International Law Commission based its approach to *jus cogens* on positive law much more than on natural law", *Yearbook ILC* (1963-I), p. 75.
655. C. Rozakis, *op.cit.* (note 238), p. 75.
656. See also *supra* pp. 153-154. See in this respect N. Onuf and R. Birney, *loc.cit.* (note 619), p. 188: "Many writers believe that peremptory norms are the concrete form taken by higher law. As a matter of definition, peremptory norms are those which cannot be changed except by norms of a comparable status. All other norms can be changed by subsequent treaty or customary practice. The difference is such as to encourage the inference that peremptory norms have their origin in a higher natural order and that our knowledge of them is received directly. The law-making procedures of the community would simply be one available means for articulating and formalizing norms whose existence is independent of and antecedent to the perception of their existence".
657. As was pointed out above, *supra* pp. 67-68, the phrase "general international law" is usually taken to designate rules which are (nearly) universally binding. At the same place it was said that the present study uses the phrase in a somewhat different meaning. Nevertheless, there can be no doubt that the drafters of article 53 had in mind "general international law" in the

vention does not seem, however, to rule out the possibility of regional, local or specific international *jus cogens*. This may be deduced from the fact that the definition of a peremptory norm of general international law in article 53 is preceded by the words "For the purposes of the present convention".[658] Moreover, just as with respect to specific custom,[659] there would seem to be no objection of theory against contemplating specific *jus cogens*.[660] Questions concerning specific international *jus cogens* will be left out of consideration in the following, because the focus of the present study is on issues of general international law.[661] Moreover, as a result of the process of "globalization" of international relations described above,[662] general *jus cogens* may be expected to grow steadily more important in relation to specific *jus cogens*.

This latter point leads to the question of the interpretation of article 53 of the Vienna Convention. How generally accepted and recognized must a peremptory norm of general international law be? Is it enough that nearly all States of the world demonstrate their *opinio juris cogentis* with respect to a rule, or is it required that the rule is universally accepted and recognized as peremptory? The words "by the international community of States as a whole" contained in article 53 would seem to imply universal acceptance and recognition. However, the *travaux préparatoires* shed a different light on this. During the Vienna Conference on the Law of Treaties the words "as a whole" were inserted into the text of the then article 50 (the present article 53) on the initiative of the Drafting Committee. Its chairman explained this amendment to the Committee of the Whole in the following way: "By inserting the words 'as a whole' in article 50 the Drafting Committee had wished to stress that there was no question of requiring a rule to be accepted and recognized as peremptory by all States. It would be enough if a very large majority did so; that would mean that, if one State in isolation refused to accept the peremptory character of a rule, or if that State was supported by a very small number of States, the acceptance and recognition of the peremptory character of the rule by the international community as a whole would not be affected".[663]

It would seem to be justified to conclude from this, as Rozakis does, "that no individual State should have the right of veto in the determination of a rule as a *jus cogens* norm".[664] In discussing customary international law it was already observed that, if one State refuses to recognize a rule as one of law, there is nothing to prevent the other States from accepting it *inter se*.[665] The same reasoning must hold good with respect to rules of *jus cogens*, although one should not lose sight of the particular function of this latter type of rules. As rules of *jus cogens* are designed to structure the entire legal system, it would be an extremely undesirable and, in the final analysis even an unworkable situation, if a large number

first sense. This is buttressed by the words "by the international community of States as a whole".

658. See also K. Wolfke, *loc.cit.* (note 619), p. 149; and M. Virally, *loc.cit.* (note 619), p. 14.
659. See *supra* pp. 95-97.
660. The possibility of such specific international *jus cogens* is also implied in the view of G. Schwarzenberger described above, see *supra* p. 155.
661. See *supra* p. 68.
662. *Supra* pp. 65-68.
663. *UN Doc.* A/Conf.39/11, p. 472.
664. C. Rozakis, *op.cit.* (note 238), p. 77.
665. See *supra* p. 97.

of rules of *jus cogens* were denied peremptory character by a minority of States, however small that minority in each case might be. Furthermore, in the present author's view it might occur that the words "as a whole" require an even stricter interpretation, in that the refusal of *opinio juris cogentis* by one single State can sometimes already be taken as conclusive evidence that a rule is not a peremptory norm of general international law. If, for instance, in the field of peace and security, the United States or the Soviet Union oppose a certain rule, it could still be, according to the official explanation of the phrase "the international community as a whole", a peremptory norm of general international law. But, it would be one of doubtful usefulness in practice. In other words, particularly in the case of *jus cogens* it would seem pointless to proclaim a rule of peremptory character against the express will of the States (or State) whose cooperation is most vital to the realization of the rule's purpose.[666]

This brings us to a related question. Sometimes the argument derived from the words "the international community of States as a whole" is carried still one step further. This phrase is not only used to solve the issue of how a peremptory norm of international law is to be created; it is also invoked to answer the question for which States such a norm is binding. Some authors do not confine themselves to the conclusion that it does not take the *opinio juris cogentis* of all States, but only that of almost all States, to create a peremptory norm of general international law; in addition it is maintained that a rule of *jus cogens* brought about by the consent or acceptance of less than all States is binding also for the State which has expressly refused its *opinio juris cogentis* to it. From the explanation of the Drafting Committee quoted above Rozakis has deduced: "What the Committee seems to imply is,..., that if a rule is one of general international law and if, furthermore, there exists substantive proof that the rule is accepted and recognized by the community of States 'as a whole' as a rule from which no derogation is permitted, that rule is a *jus cogens* norm binding upon the entire international community. In consequence, a State can no longer be dissociated from the binding peremptory character of that rule *even if it proves that no evidence exists of its acceptance and recognition of the specific function of that rule, or, moreover, that it has expressly denied it".*[667]

No doubt, there is a good deal to be said for this point of view. It would seem to flow more or less unavoidably from the nature of *jus cogens* norms as "constitutional" norms, aimed at structuring the entire legal order. And indeed, as was pointed out, at least a number of the States participating in the Vienna Conference leaned towards this position.[668] Similarly, Rozakis emphatically adds to the phrase just quoted: "the presumption on the peremptory character of a rule is not rebuttable. If it were, one would have to accept that two or more States, or a group of States, which deny the existence of a *jus cogens* norm are free to contract out of that rule thus creating a contrary legal regime. Such a situation, however, would be absurd since it would defeat the very purpose for which the *jus*

---

666. Although particularly pressing in the case of *jus cogens*, this point in fact holds good for any rule of international law, regardless of whether it belongs to *jus cogens* or to *jus dispositivum*. See also what was observed with respect to customary international law, *supra* p. 104.
667. C. Rozakis, *op.cit.* (note 238), p. 78 (emphasis added); see also U. Scheuner, *loc.cit.* (note 619), p. 531, who holds that rules of international *jus cogens* are "norms of international law creating obligations upon States independent of their agreement".
668. See *supra* p. 153.

cogens norms have been introduced in positive international law, namely, the preservation of uniformity of the international legal order in those areas where social considerations should prevail over individual interests".[669]

Despite the strong terms employed, the "constitutional" position put forward in this passage is not free from difficulties. First and foremost, it overlooks one of the basic features of international society. The alleged automatic universal validity of *jus cogens* norms runs counter to the consensual character of international law, which was, as shown above, strongly emphasized by the participants in the Vienna Conference precisely in the same article 53.[670] It indeed constitutes a strange contradiction to conclude from that very article, that a peremptory norm is binding upon a State even if it has not consented to or accepted it. The explanation by the Drafting Committee of the words "as a whole" quoted above, does not necessitate the latter conclusion. The Committee made it clear that universality is not required to establish a rule as one of *jus cogens*, but it does not follow that near-universality of recognition and acceptance would, subsequently, be turned automatically into universality of binding force; to admit the former conclusion is, of course, not the same thing as agreeing with the latter. Furthermore, although some States participating in the Vienna Conference leaned towards the "constitutional" position, others clearly rejected it.[671]

Finally, Wolfke has adduced a number of arguments, to the latter effect, by observing that automatic universal validity without at least the implied consent of all States "would be incompatible with the principle *pacta tertiis nec nocent prosunt*, recognized in the very Vienna Convention (Art. 34)".[672] He also considers the automatic universal validity out of the question, because "Article 53 has been supported without reservations by the socialist States and numerous developing countries, which consider the principles of sovereignty, equality and consent as pillars of present international relations".[673]

This survey shows that there are both arguments to support the "consensual" and to support the "constitutional" point of view. Most importantly, the issue was not settled at the Vienna Conference on the Law of Treaties, because, as was pointed out, neither the relevant provisions of the 1969 Vienna Convention nor the *travaux préparatoires* do provide a clear-cut answer to the question. A choice is therefore difficult to make. Although it fits best the present decentralized character of the international society, strict adherence to the "consensual" point of view in fact undermines the very purpose which *jus cogens* is designed to serve, that is the structuring of the (international) legal order. It is indeed difficult to see how *jus cogens* could achieve this purpose in international law, if in every case one State or a small number of States can avoid its peremptory char-

669. C. Rozakis, *op.cit.* (note 238), p. 78.
670. See *supra* p. 81.
671. See in this respect O. Deleau, "Les positions françcaises à la Conférence de Vienne sur le Droit des Traités", XV *AFDI* (1969), pp. 7-23 (19), according to whom at a certain moment during the Vienna Conference France had prepared an amendment to draft article 50 to the effect that a rule of *jus cogens* could not be held against a State which could prove that it had not expressly accepted the rule as one of *jus cogens*. The amendment was never officially tabled because not enough States did want to support it. This lack of support, it is said, was not caused by objection of principle but rather by the feeling that additional amendments would carry the danger of disturbing the precarious compromise contained in draft article 50.
672. K. Wolfke, *loc.cit.* (note 619), p. 149.
673. *Ibidem.*

acter. Moreover, because of the growing interdependence and the ensuing expansion of the body of international law, it is likely that the need for a further structuring of international law will be felt even more in the years to come. Consequently, it may be expected that the "constitutional" position will be gaining ground.

In the present author's view, opting for the "constitutional" point of view must be accompanied by the following *caveat.* As long as the international society faces deep ideological cleavages between its members, there exists a danger of the concept of international *jus cogens* being abused. In a situation of ideological rivalry, States may be tempted to abuse the concept of *jus cogens* and "proclaim" a particular norm as *jus cogens,* because they believe that this strengthens their position *vis-à-vis* certain other States. Although such a "proclamation" may not be justified in view of the *jus cogens* provisions of the Vienna Convention properly conceived, it might still, in some cases, carry some flavour of "legality", because the application of the words "as a whole" contained in article 53 of the Convention will not always be completely unambiguous. The precise number of States required by the phrase "as a whole" cannot be determined in advance, but has to be established on a case-by-case basis. Most of the time this will not give rise to insurmountable difficulties. In some cases, however, there might be doubt, at least during a certain period of time, as to the exact implications of the requirement "as a whole". In such cases there is room for the kind of abuse just mentioned. In the same vein, albeit in stronger terms, Weil has warned that "Les concepts de 'conscience juridique' et de 'communauté internationale', peuvent ainsi devenir des mots codés se prêtant à toutes sortes de manipulations et sous le couvert desquels certains Etats peuvent tenter d'instaurer un droit idéologique négateur du pluralisme inhérent de la société internationale".[674]

It needs no explaining that such an abuse of *jus cogens* would be very dangerous, because it would not enhance but rather undermine the structuring of the international legal order which peremptory norms are designed to provide. Attempts at such an abuse, if they occur, can best be warded off by maintaining a stringent interpretation of the words "as a whole" in all cases. This means that in general, as the Drafting Committee has pointed out, the peremptory character is not affected only if one State or a very small number of States refuse to accept it as such and that in some cases, depending on the issue involved, the refusal of one (particular) State may already prevent a rule from becoming international *jus cogens.*[675]

We must now return to the question of how rules of international *jus cogens* are to be identified. The point of departure, as was said, is that the *opinio juris cogentis* has to be expressed through the same manifestations of consent or acceptance in the sense of *opinio juris.*[676] Consequently, it may first of all be asked whether, and if so to what extent, the traditional sources of international law can manifest *opinio juris cogentis.* As far as the general principles of law are concerned, it was already pointed out that the issue of *jus cogens* very often

674. P. Weil, *loc.cit.* (note 216), p. 45.
675. See *supra* pp. 159-160.
676. See *supra* p. 157.

comes up within the framework of discussions about general principles as a (procedural) source of international law. In contrast, it is, therefore, quite striking to learn that those authors who focus their attention on *jus cogens* sometimes are at least hesitant to recognize the general principles of law as a possible manifestation of *opinio juris cogentis*. The reason is that these authors doubt the general principles to be an effective source of international law.[677] The tendency to deny to general principles the status of manifestation of *opinio juris cogentis* was strengthened by the rejection of a U.S. proposal at the Vienna Conference on the Law of Treaties, which wanted to define a peremptory rule of general international law as one "which is recognized in common by the national and regional legal systems of the world and from which no derogation is permitted".[678]

Above, it was submitted that the general principles of law can hardly be considered an effective source of international law outside the framework of the International Court of Justice.[679] Consequently, in the present author's view they can equally not be effective as a source of *opinio juris cogentis*. Moreover, the same conclusion must apply to the general principles within the framework of the International Court of Justice. Although it was said that general principles can constitute a source of international law in the court-situation,[680] it is difficult to see how they can strictly speaking serve as a manifestation of *opinio juris cogentis*. For, norms of *jus cogens* require general or near-universal recognition or acceptance,[681] while formally at least, the binding force of judicial or arbitral decisions extends to a few, usually even two, States only.[682]

Just like in the case of general principles, the answer to the question of whether or not customary international law can play an important role in establishing *jus cogens* also depends on what concept of this source one takes as a point of departure.[683] Those who adhere to a flexible conception of custom are most likely to consider customary international law a perfect source of *jus cogens*, because in their view it produces rules of general international law binding upon all States of the world. Universal or near-universal recognition or acceptance, it was pointed out, is one of the requirements for international *jus cogens*.

Those, in contrast, who start from a more rigid conception of custom are likely to reach the opposite conclusion; adherents to this view argue that, as a

---

677. See, for instance, also N. Onuf and R. Birney, *loc.cit.* (note 619), p. 196, who uphold that the task of defining the content of general principles of law "has proven exceedingly difficult and where successful has been undertaken, at a level of considerable generality. In as much as general principles are inefficient for identifying individual instances of deviant behaviour, we might conclude that their functioning is not specifically constraint-oriented"; similarly K. Wolfke, *loc.cit.* (note 619), p. 153.
678. United Nations Conference on the Law of Treaties, *Documents of the Conference* (New York 1971), p. 174 *UN Doc.* A/Conf.39/C.I./L.302.
679. See *supra* pp. 146-148.
680. See *supra* pp. 139-144.
681. See *supra* p. 162.
682. Article 59 of the I.C.J.'s Statute explicitly states: "The decision of the Court has no binding force except between the parties and in respect of that particular case". See on this *infra* section 9.1., where it will be argued, however, that, although the effects of the Court's judgments are formally confined to the parties to the dispute concerned, their impact may in fact go substantially further. This holds good also for the Court's role with respect to *jus cogens*.
683. See on the concept of customary international law *supra* pp. 90-91.

result of the changes in the international law-making process prompted by the structure of present international society, there are not many customary rules of international law left, which bind the entire international community of States, and, moreover, such rules cannot be expected to be very numerous in the future. From what has been observed above with respect to customary international law, it is clear that the present author counts himself among this latter school of thought.[684] Consequently, he subcribes to Wolfke's conclusion that "it is very difficult to name a purely customary peremptory norm in present international law. It seems also unlikely that many such norms will emerge".[685]

As far as the traditional sources of international law are concerned, what is left are treaties. Treaties would, indeed, seem to be quite well fit to play an important role as sources of international *jus cogens*. Their main advantage in this respect is their explicit character. Unlike custom, treaties use language as a means of communicating standards of behaviour[686] and they can, therefore, contain explicit expressions of *opinio juris cogentis*. A most clear reference to *jus cogens* would of course be, if a treaty stipulated that its provisions or some of them constitute peremptory norms in the sense of article 53 of the Vienna Convention. More generally, a treaty could provide that from (some of) its provisions no derogation is permitted. As far as general norms of international *jus cogens* are concerned, an additional requirement is, of course, that the treaty concerned is binding on all, or at least nearly all, States of the international community. It was already pointed out that it usually proves extremely difficult to ensure universal or near-universal acceptance of treaties concerning matters of general interest.[687]

Nevertheless, treaties of a (near) universal validity do exist and the one that immediately comes to mind is, of course, the Charter of the United Nations. Not only are practically all States of the world parties to the Charter, it also contains elements which are sometimes considered to indicate the *jus cogens* character of some of its provisions.[688] Very often this view is substantiated by invoking article 103 of the Charter which reads: "In the event of a conflict between the obligations of the Members of the United Nations under the present Charter and their obligations under any other international agreement, their obligations under the present Charter shall prevail".[689] It has been pointed out, however,

684. See *supra* pp. 85-116.
685. K. Wolfke, *loc.cit.* (note 619), p. 153. Apart from this point, customary international law in the "flexible" view would seem to entail a serious handicap preventing it from becoming an important *jus cogens* generating source of international law. As was pointed out, this "flexible" position allows custom to take on a quite amorphous character, in that *opinio juris* is more or less deduced from *usus*, see *supra* pp. 110-111. On the other hand, it was observed that *jus cogens* has to be unequivocal. Doubt about the *jus cogens* character of rules of law may be destabilizing because of the structuring role they are designed to play. Consequently, the *opinio juris cogentis* must be expressed and cannot merely be implied in practice. In sum conceived in a flexible fashion and expressed *opinio juris cogentis* would seem to be irreconcilable to a large extent.
686. See *supra* p. 118.
687. See *supra* pp. 119-123.
688. See also E. Suy,, *loc.cit.* (note 619), pp. 84-89, who also lists a number of other treaties which include provisions more or less explicitly derogating all agreements conflicting with their provisions.
689. See, for instance, E. Suy, *ibidem* and V. Nageswar Rao, *loc.cit.* (note 619), p. 381 and the references provided there.

164

that the drafters of this provision did not intend automatic abrogation of all obligations inconsistent with the Charter.[690] This is indeed quite plausible, for if they had, the result would have been that all the provisions of the Charter would have to be considered *jus cogens*, while it is obvious that at least some of them are not. Nevertheless, there is a general feeling that the fundamental principles of the Charter, or some of the elements contained in them, are of a peremptory nature. This may be correct, but the *opinio juris cogentis* with respect to these principles has to be proved by other means than mere reliance upon article 103.[691]

This is not the place to deal extensively with the question of which rules of international law constitute *jus cogens*. The foregoing brief reference to the United Nations Charter was designed only to show how difficult it may be to determine the *jus cogens* character of a rule of international law. The test contained in article 53 of the Vienna Convention on the Law of Treaties has reduced, but not done away with this difficulty.[692] It still is far from easy to clearly establish that a rule of international law is one of *jus cogens*. On the other hand, there is no reason to believe that it is impossible.

In trying to determine the *jus cogens* character of rules of international law it should be kept in mind that one does not have to rely on one single source only. As will be argued in more detail below, the making of international law has become a continuing and more integrated process;[693] the various sources as manifestations of rules of international law, both the more traditional and the newer ones,[694] are interrelated. Consequently, the elements necessary to build up a rule of international *jus cogens* may be found in different sources. For instance, a rule may be a general norm of international law because it is laid down in a (near) universally binding treaty; it may, subsequently, become peremptory because of a (separate) declaration by the States concerned containing their *opinio juris cogentis*. Furthermore, scepticism is sometimes based upon the abstract or vague character of principles or rules which gives rise to "doubt whether in a more precise form they would be accepted by the whole community of nations at all".[695] Such doubt may be justified, but should not be exaggerated. The fact that principles or rules are often couched in abstract or even vague words, does not necessarily deprive them of their legal or even *jus cogens* character. On closer inspection such abstract or vague principles and rules may sometimes be broken down into various aspects, on some of which there is a sufficient amount of agreement, while others still leave a number of questions. Obviously, if such a distinction can be made, it should be acknowledged that the former are of a legal character, *casu quo* of a *jus cogens* character.

690. See K. Wolfke, *loc.cit.* (note 619), p. 157.
691. See also P. Weil, *loc.cit.* (note 216), pp. 21-22.
692. Several representatives at the Vienna Conference on the Law of Treaties were very well aware of the deficiencies of article 53 leaving unanswered questions about the exact sources and nature of peremptory norms; see for instance *UN Doc.* A/Conf.39/11, p. 301 and *UN Doc.* A/Conf.39/11/Add.1, pp. 93-94, 97 and 103.
693. See *infra* pp. 206-208.
694. See *infra* pp. 208-210.
695. See K. Wolfke, *loc.cit.* (note 619), pp. 157-158.

The further development of international *jus cogens* is, of course, up to the international community of States, and in this respect, too, there seem to be no compelling reasons to be overly pessimistic. Despite deep ideological cleavages the international community has managed, in the post Second World War era, to reach at least the beginning of agreement on a number of fundamental issues.[696] In some cases these have already been laid down in legal or quasi-legal documents. If it is correct, as the present author believes, that generally speaking the awareness on the part of the States of the necessity to further structure the international legal system is growing, it may be expected that the willingness to accept and recognize rules as *jus cogens* will also increase. Increased attention for *jus cogens* should not take the form, however, of (mis)using the concept of *jus cogens* in an ideological fashion, as was described above.[697] It should be reiterated that in this way, the powerful juridical weapon of *jus cogens* carries the danger of backfiring: it breeds mutual distrust and creates uncertainty instead of structuring the international legal order.

8.3.6.6. Change of norms of international *jus cogens*

Finally, it should be observed that rules of *jus cogens* are not immutable.[698] The process of change cannot be extensively discussed within the framework of the present study.[699] However, some general observations should be made here, particularly because article 53 of the Vienna Convention is worded a little odd as far as the possibility of change of international *jus cogens* is concerned. Taken literally, the phrase "which can be *modified only* by a subsequent norm of general international law having the same character" (emphasis added) suggests that an existing *jus cogens* norm can be affected only by a subsequent peremptory norm. This, however, overlooks the possibility that States withdraw their *opinio juris cogentis* without building a new peremptory norm at the same time. In such a case the requirements for a *jus cogens* norm posed by the definition of article 53 would no longer be fulfilled and the norm would simply cease to exist as one of *jus cogens*. It cannot be assumed that the drafters of the Vienna Convention have wanted to exclude with respect to *jus cogens* this normal feature of the international law-making process. "Modified" in article 53 should, therefore, be narrowly construed as to encompass only "change" in the proper sense of that word, but not "extinguish" or "cease to exist". Nevertheless, change or

---

696. Indeed, the introduction into international law of the concept of *jus cogens* itself by way of the Vienna Convention is a remarkable achievement despite the deficiencies involved. In this light, therefore, one can subscribe to the submission by T. Rama Rao, *loc.cit.* (note 287), p. 515: "While there is some divergence of views about the content of these peremptory norms and the ultimate values of the international community, the universal acceptance of the notions of peremptory norms is a significant landmark attesting to the evolution of a community of nations in the present-day world".
697. See *supra* p. 162.
698. The Vienna Convention acknowledges this possibility in the words "and which can be modified only by a subsequent norm of general international law having the same character" contained in article 53. An indication is also contained in the opening phrase of article 64, which reads: "If a new peremptory norm of general international law emerges ...".
699. See for a more detailed discussion C. Rozakis, *op.cit.* (note 238), pp. 85-94.

extinction of *jus cogens* rules cannot lightly be assumed to have taken place. First of all, the fundamental rule of *pacta sunt servanda*, which was stressed repeatedly in the foregoing, applies *a fortiori* to *jus cogens*. Moreover, as rules of *jus cogens* lay down the most basic norms of a society, drastic reversals of existing peremptory rules cannot be expected frequently and/or rapidly.

As to the process of change or extinction, what has been observed with regard to change of customary international law[700] *mutatis mutandis* holds good with respect to *jus cogens* also. This means that a State is not at liberty to withdraw its *opinio juris cogentis* whenever it wants, thereby ridding itself from its *jus cogens* obligations. It is submitted that, like in the case of customary international law, for such a withdrawal to be admissible the ground needs to be prepared by the development of a *"opinio non-necessitatis cogentis"* on the part of a sufficient number of States. Moreover, in this case of *jus cogens* the criterion of "sufficient" would seem to require the same overwhelming majority of States as is implied in "accepted and recognized by the international community of States as a whole" which is necessary to build a *jus cogens* norm. In other words, change or extinction of *jus cogens* requires the same number of States as creating it. This would not only seem to be commensurate to the fundamental character of *jus cogens* norms, but seems to follow also from the words "which can be modified only by a subsequent norm of general international law *having the same character*" (emphasis added) in article 53 of the Vienna Convention. It is only after this condition is fulfilled that the withdrawal of *opinio juris cogentis* takes legal effect.

No doubt the schematic picture presented here leaves unanswered a number of complicated questions involved in the process of modification or extinction of *jus cogens*, but it is sufficient to show that the process is a difficult one. Nevertheless, it is important to be aware of the possibility of *jus cogens* being modified, also because it is once again a reminder of the fact that it is *opinio juris, in casu opinio juris cogentis* which makes a peremptory norm of international law, but that it is also its withdrawal which breaks a peremptory norm of international law. This awareness helps to avoid the conclusion, that a main method of changing international law is by violating it in practice. This conclusion, which would obviously be particularly dangerous with respect to *jus cogens*, was already criticized above in discussing customary international law.[701] This implies above all that the first step in the process of changing international *jus cogens* is the withdrawal of the collective *opinio juris cogentis* with respect to the old norm. Until this has occurred, contrary practice must considered to be a violation.

---

700. See *supra* pp. 97-106.
701. See *supra* pp. 99-101.

CHAPTER IX

ARTICLE 38(1)(D): SUBSIDIARY MEANS FOR THE DETERMINATION OF RULES OF LAW

9.1. Judicial decisions

In addition to the three sources dealt with in the preceding chapters, article 38 of the Statute makes reference to "judicial decisions and the teachings of the most highly qualified publicists of the various nations, as subsidiary means for the determination of rules of law". Usually these are loosely referred to as "subsidiary sources" of international law. As will be pointed out in the following, however, judicial decisions and doctrine cannot, in the present author's view, really be qualified as "sources" in the sense of that term used in the present study.

As far as judicial decisions are concerned, their inclusion in article 38 originates in the famous proposal by Descamps within the framework of the 1920 Advisory Committee of Jurists referred to above.[702] Among the rules to be considered by the Court in the solution of international disputes, item 4 of that proposal enumerated "international jurisprudence as a means for the application and development of law".[703] This phrase is not entirely free from ambiguity, because it simultaneously uses the words "application" and "development". The former entails a reference to already existing law, while the latter implies at least some element of newness and, therefore, suggests that judicial decisions create new law and in that sense are a source of international law. The subsequent draft proposed by Root and Phillimore did not alleviate this ambiguity, because it also used both words simultaneously.[704] However, the records of the debate on judicial decisions within the Advisory Committee very clearly show that its members did not consider such decisions as a source of international law in the proper sense of that term. This debate took place between the Committee-members Descamps, Phillimore and Ricci-Busatti. The silence of the other Committee-members on this issue may be taken as approval of the outcome of the debate.

In his first comment on the Root-Phillimore draft Descamps observed that "the judge must use the authority of judicial decisions, and the coinciding doc-

---

702. See *supra* p. 137.
703. *Procès-Verbaux, loc.cit.* (note 526), p. 306.
704. This draft spoke of "the authority of judicial decisions and the opinion of writers as a means for the application and development of law", *ibidem*, p. 344.

trines of jurists, as auxiliary and supplementary means only", [705] and in answer to a question by Ricci-Busatti he unequivocally upheld that "Doctrine and jurisprudence no doubt do not create law; but they assist in determining rules which exist. A judge should make use of both jurisprudence and doctrine, but they should only serve as elucidation."[706] This statement by Descamps left no room for doubt as to his opinion on the role to be assigned to judicial decisions in the draft article on the rules to be applied by the Court. However, it did not completely satisfy Ricci-Busatti who proved the most staunch opponent to the inclusion of judicial decisions in the provision on the sources. The latter maintained: "at any rate jurisprudence and doctrine may not be placed on the same level as the other sources and must not be used in the same way; although they must always be borne in mind by the judge".[707] Phillimore expressed his agreement with this point of view.[708] Faced with this continued opposition Descamps finally suggested, as a compromise, the following wording: "The Court shall take into consideration judicial decisions and the teachings of the most highly qualified publicists of the various nations as a subsidiary means for the determination of rules of law".[709] Although Ricci-Busatti still tried to have the words "determination of rules of law' substituted by the expression "juridical interpretation", Descamps' formula was eventually adopted, be it with the deletion of the first six words.[710] Later, the Council of the League of Nations inserted instead the words "subject to the provisions of Article 59".[711]

The words "subsidiary means for the determination of rules of law", therefore, would seem to reflect the intention of the drafters of article 38 that judicial decisions cannot be accorded the status of source in the formal sense of that term,[712] that is in the same sense as treaties, custom and general principles were meant to be sources of international law. It is in this way that they are understood by Schwarzenberger who has indeed made these words the basis of his interpretation of the structure of article 38. According to him, "Subparagraphs (a) to (c) are concerned with the pedigree of the rules of international law. In sub-paragraph (d) some of the means for the determination of alleged rules of law are enumerated".[713] Subsequently, he distinguishes between law-making processes and law-determining agencies, the difference being that the latter do not create (new) law, but say what the existing law is. Judicial decisions do not belong to the former category; they merely constitute subsidiary law-determining agencies.[714]

In determining the status of judicial decisions in terms of the sources of international law one must also take into account article 59 of the Court's Statute.

705. *Ibidem*, p. 322.
706. *Ibidem*, p. 336.
707. *Ibidem*, p. 338.
708. *Ibidem*.
709. *Ibidem*, p. 620.
710. *Ibidem*, p. 680.
711. See M. Bos, *loc.cit.* (note 28), p. 56.
712. For the meaning of sources in the formal sense, see *supra* pp. 57-60.
713. G. Schwarzenberger, *International Law*, Vol. 1: International Law as Applied by International Courts and Tribunals: I, 3rd edition (London 1957), pp. 26-28.
714. *Ibidem*. As primary agencies for the determination of rules of law Schwarzenberger designates the parties to the treaty in the case of treaties, the collective body of subjects of international law with respect to customary international law, and civilized nations as regards the general principles of law.

This provision stipulates: "The decision of the Court has no binding force except between the parties and in respect of that particular case". This provision prompts a distinction between States parties to a particular case and all other States.

With respect to the former, even if one acknowledges a law-developing and/or law-creating function for the Court,[715] this does not necessarily imply that the Court's decisions are full-fledged sources of international law. A decision of the Court[716] may be said to be an indirect source of international law with respect to the parties to the dispute concerned, if they are seen in relation to the latter's consent or acceptance. The decision of the Court may be viewed as a kind of delegated consent or acceptance. Through their acceptance of the jurisdiction of the Court with respect to a given case[717] the parties can in fact be said to consent or accept in advance to rules of law which might flow for them from the judgment of the Court. To put it a little differently, these States in advance consent to or accept whatever the Court will say the law is.[718] Just as with respect to the general principles, therefore, in this case, too, the Court's decision may be said to constitute the last step which "finalizes" the manifestation through which the consent or acceptance of the States concerned is shown.[719] However, such consent or acceptance is confined to the particular case concerned and does not automatically apply to other cases.

As to the second category of States referred to above, there is of course no question of consent or acceptance on the part of other States than the parties to the dispute. The decision is not binding upon other States and can, therefore, not be even an indirect source of international law for these States, as article 59 makes abundantly clear. This far-reaching limitation which article 59 of the Statute puts on decisions of the Court is generally conceded. Nevertheless, doctrine frequently presents us with instances where authors feel forced to go beyond its implications. The position of Fitzmaurice and Bos constitute examples of such a point of view. The former classifies judicial and arbitral decisions as "quasi-formal" sources or alternatively as "'formally material' - *i.e.* as sources which tribunals are bound to take into account, even if they are not bound to follow them".[720] The latter, more cogently, maintains that "judicial decisions emanat-

---

715. See *infra* p. 267.
716. In the following only decisions of the I.C.J. will be dealt with. The observations which will be made are *mutatis mutandis* applicable to decisions of other international judicial bodies, which are as a rule also subject to a provision like the one laid down in article 59 of the Statute with respect to decisions of the I.C.J.. It is not entirely clear whether the drafters of article 38 wanted to exclude reliance by the I.C.J. upon such other international judicial decisions. On the one hand, paragraph (1)(d) refers to "judicial decisions" in general, which would seem to include even decisions of national courts. On the other hand, there is the reference to article 59 of the Statute which deals with decisions of the I.C.J. only. See in this respect C. Parry, *op.cit.* (note 22), p. 94.
717. On the various forms which the acceptance of the Court's jurisdiction may take, see, P. van Dijk, *op.cit.* (note 569), pp. 366-368.
718. See also C. Parry, who in a most typical phrase observes in reference to the Court: "though in a short space of time it has most happily acquired a remarkable reputation and, by virtue of its nature as well as the sagacity of the men who have composed it, has come to lead a life and wield an influence of its own, the Court possesses and authority which is essentially a delegated authority", *op.cit.* (note 22), p. 15.
719. See *supra* p. 143.
720. G. Fitzmaurice, *loc.cit.* (note 28), pp. 172-173.

ing from authoritative judges are to be considered as recognized manifestations of international law provided they are of an innovating character or shed new light on existing law, and provided also they are capable of generalization".[721] Bos subsequently concludes in reference to the views of the 1920 Advisory Committee and of Schwarzenberger set out above that "They wrongly assumed that the Court cannot create international law".[722]

Both authors use as a main argument the Court's decision in the *Anglo Norwegian Fisheries* case. Fitzmaurice upholds with respect to this case that "it is obvious that neither the United Kingdom nor any other country could now successfully contest the general *principle* of straight base-lines, at any rate in any legal proceedings, even (in all probability) before a tribunal other than the International Court".[723] Similarly, Bos cites the *Anglo Norwegian Fisheries* case as a fine example of a decision "which any subject of law has to obey as much as all the others".[724] However, this alleged general binding force of the principle set forth by the Court in the *Fisheries* case-decision remains unexplained in the face of the unambiguous stipulations of article 59 of the Statute. Of course, it may be that decisions of the Court, like the one in the *Fisheries* case, have an impact or effect which goes far beyond the parties and the particular case. Other States may very well regard the decision, *in casu* on the principle of the straight base-lines, as a sound statement of law and come to accept it as such and, consequently, become bound by it. The point is, however, that in such instances the obligation of other States stems from some other source (in the sense of manifestation of consent or acceptance) and not strictly speaking, from the Court's decision, although it may have played a vital role in getting other States to consent to or accept the rule concerned.[725]

Be this as it may, for a number of reasons it is easy to understand the view attributing a general binding force to decisions of the International Court of Justice. Such a status comes more or less automatically with judicial institutions. The International Court of Justice as an institution is, of course, transplanted from municipal legal systems. Within the framework of these municipal systems of law court-decisions obviously exert a significant influence on the development of the law. In Common Law systems this is more or less formalized through the principle of *stare decisis* whereby a decision applies in similar cases and is binding upon lower courts. And even in systems of law where this principle does not apply, such as Civil Law systems, the courts' "legislative" impact very often goes far beyond the effect formally attributed to it. In other words, it would seem that a certain amount of authority in the field of law-making comes with a court as a matter of course, whatever its precise formal powers in this respect. To a certain extent this holds true for the International Court of Justice

---

721. M. Bos, *loc.cit.* (note 28), p. 59.
722. *Ibidem*, p. 60.
723. G. Fitzmaurice, *loc.cit.* (note 28), p. 170.
724. M. Bos, *loc.cit.* (note 28), p. 59.
725. Similarly, it is true that one has to concede to Fitzmaurice, *loc.cit.* (note 28), p. 171, "that, subject to various limitations, some kinds of decisions, once given, are almost certain, or intrinsically likely to be followed". But, in the present author's view, this is not the same thing as saying that they have to be followed *de jure*.

as well.[726]

The Court's authority derives *inter alia* from the fact that it is "the principal judicial organ of the United Nations" (article 92 of the UN Charter) and that it is composed of persons "who possess the qualifications required in their respective countries for appointment to the highest judicial offices, or are jurisconsults of recognized competence in international law" (article 2 of the Statute). Furthermore, because the Court operates on the international plane, an extra dimension would seem to be added to its authority. Compared to most national legal systems, the contents of international law may be said to be quite uncertain.[727] This state of affairs is compounded by the fact that in international law there is no institutionalized legislative procedure. As was repeatedly stressed in the foregoing, the States themselves, the (main) subjects of international law, act as the international "legislators". It is quite understandable, therefore, that in such a situation the authority of the Court extends also to the international law-making process, although it is not formally endowed with powers in this field. Because of the fact that among the formally established international organs, including those of the United Nations, the Court is the most authoritative in the field of international law, it is only natural that the Court is turned to for guidance even beyond areas of its competence strictly speaking.[728] Although it is comprehensible that decisions of the Court are viewed as a source of international law, it should not be overlooked that the explanation just provided in fact rests upon extra-legal factors. They do not, therefore, turn decisions of the Court into a *de jure* source of international law.

Moreover, the possibilities which the Court has to contribute in this "unofficial" manner to the international law-making process should not be overestimated. It was already observed that the court-situation is highly a-typical in international law.[729] Most settling of international disputes takes place outside the framework of judicial or arbitral processes. Certainly in comparison to the position of national courts, the docks of the World Courts have never been particularly crowded. As far as the International Court of Justice is concerned,

726. In the foregoing we have repeatedly cautioned against an adverse comparison between national and international law. In the same vein, the International Court of Justice should not be put completely at par with courts as they are usually operating within national legal systems despite the similarities which exist. J. Watson, *loc. cit.* (note 34), p. 621, has denounced such a comparison in particularly strong terms: "The transference of the domestic law philosophy is seen in its most elementary form in the unrelenting use of decisions of the International Court as though they were legally binding precedents. These opinions are analyzed by some writers in much the same fashion as one would analyze the opinions of a national supreme court in a common law jurisdiction, inducing from what is said in relation to various sets of facts the existence of rules or principles sufficiently broad in scope to state the law in other unrelated cases. This use of the decisions of the International Court ignores the unique socio-political context of that organ and the fact that each decision is presented in a blend of highly political factors which makes any such an analysis of the opinions entirely speculative."
727. J. Verzijl, *International Law in Historical Perspective*, Vol. VIII: Inter-State Disputes and their Settlement (Leyden 1976), p. 526, even refers to "the extreme uncertainty of the exact contents of many chapters of the present positive law of nations, not seldomly accompanied by regionally or otherwise differing legal conceptions familiar to international lawyers...".
728. For more details on the impact of the Court on international law, see M. Nawaz, "Other sources of International Law: Are Judicial Decisions of the International Court of Justice a Source of International Law?", 19 *IJIL* (1979), pp. 526-540.
729. See *supra* p. 146.

moreover, its work-load would even seem to have been declining in the last decade.[730]

Various reasons are adduced for the general reluctance on the part of States to accept judicial means for settling their disputes.[731] In the final analysis they boil down to the fact that the international society simply is not cohesive or integrated enough to have third party decisions accepted to the same extent as is usually the case in municipal legal systems.[732] Since the time the international community has been growing more heterogeneous this situation has become even worse, *inter alia* because also the younger States, developing countries as well as socialist States, generally prove quite reluctant to accept the jurisdiction of the Court.[733] It is difficult to see how this situation, where States regard so few issues justiciable, could be remedied, as long as the international society remains as it is at present. As was already observed more generally, the nature and struc-

730. One commentator in a recent book specifically devoted to the Court and the international law-making process pictures this situation with phrases like "dwindling - almost to the vanishing point - of the Court's business in recent years" and "as the contentious jurisdiction of the Court (involving one or more States directly pitted against other States, as to their vital interests) atrophies away ...", E. McWhinney, *op.cit.* (note 33), p. 164, respectively p. 168. This is not to deny, however, that during the most recent years the number of disputes submitted to the Court is increasing again. The following cases can be listed: *United States Diplomatic and Consular Staff in Tehran,* judgment of 24 May 1980, ICJ Reports (1980), p. 3; *Interpretation of the Agreement of 25 March 1951 between the WHO and Egypt,* advisory opinion of 20 December 1980, ICJ Reports (1980), p. 73; *Continental Shelf (Tunisia/Libyan Arab Jamahiriya),* judgment of 24 February 1982, ICJ Reports (1982), p. 18; and *Application for Review of Judgment No. 273 of the United Nations Administrative Tribunal,* advisory opinion of 20 July 1982, Communiqué of the ICJ, No. 82/13. Still pending at the moment of writing are: *Delimitation of the Maritime Boundary in the Gulf of Maine Area (Canada/United States of America),* Commmuniqués of the ICJ, Nos. 82/1, 82/2, 82/3 and 82/15; and *Continental Shelf (Libyan Arab Jamahiriya/Malta),* Communiqués of the ICJ, Nos. 82/14 and 83/1.
731. Q. Wright, for instance, enumerates four main reasons: (1) lack of confidence in the impartiality of international tribunals; (2) lack of confidence in the conformity of international law to what States consider the requirements of justice; (3) unwillingness to put at stake a vital interest (4) belief that the nature of international relations requires politics to be superior to law in influencing the future of international society, Q. Wright, "The Strengthening of International Law", 98 *RCADI* (1959-III), pp. 1-293; see in this respect also J. Verzijl, *op.cit.* (note 727), pp. 524-531; and M. Katz, *The Relevance of International Adjudication* (Cambridge, Mass. 1968), particularly pp. 145-161; see for detailed analyses of the various aspects of the Court's functioning L. Gross (ed.), *The Future of the International Court of Justice* (New York 1976), Vol. I and in particular also with respect to its future role Vol. II.
732. In addition, decisions of the Court are said to be unpredictable. Noteworthy in this respect is R. Jennings' observation, *loc.cit.* (note 1), pp. 59-60, holding that "It has sometimes been complained that the decisions of the World Court have been unpredictable. The problem lies deeper and is more serious than that: it is that the choice of legal principles to be applied and upon which the decision will be made is itself often unpredictable; a circumstance which must be a discouragement if not even a deterrent to governments contemplating international litigation".
733. See *supra* pp. 69-71; see also I. Sinclair, *op.cit.* (note 464), p. 134, who states four grounds for this reluctance: (1) the distrust of the international judicial process following upon the controversial 1966 judgment of the International Court of Justice in the *South-West Africa* case; (2) the expense of international judicial or arbitral proceedings and the delays involved in obtaining a decision on the merits; (3) the asserted lack of balance in the composition of the International Court which weighted in favour of the Western States; and (4) the suspicion that any judicial or arbitral tribunal would apply so-called traditional international law in contrast to so-called new international law which would be responsive to the needs of newly independent States.

ture of international society to a large extent determine the contours of international law, and this holds good in particular also with respect to (the possibilities of) international adjudication.

McWhinney, dissatisfied with the ebbing away of the International Court of Justice's contentious jurisdiction, wants to put more emphasis on its advisory opinion jurisdiction.[734] It would certainly be worthwhile to consider his suggestion as to "a widening of the range and number of United Nations organs and specialized agencies that may, in terms of Article 96(2) of the Charter, be authorized by the General Assembly to request Advisory Opinions from the Court;".[735] It is questionable, however, whether there should simultaneously occur a change of the traditional perception on the part of the Court of its proper role. McWhinney foresees, and in fact advocates, a change in this respect. There can hardly be any objection to the Court taking "a flexible approach to acceptance of new modes of international law-making, where the new norms are properly evidenced and rest upon an impeachable consensus or acceptance of the parties concerned".[736] But the present author ventures to doubt whether the world is waiting for what McWhinney calls "a new and different Court" amounting to "a species of dialectical development of International Law, with genuine philosophical debate within the Court and also testing of alternative policy constructs for the future, on a trial and error basis in the public *fora*, through their canvassing in individual judicial opinions, whether concurring or dissenting".[737]

First, even if confined to its advisory jurisdiction such a new role for the Court is not without dangers. In the present author's view, the "more consciously and avowedly law-making approach" which McWhinney suggests for the Court,[738] can be successful only in well-integrated societies. In the circumstances prevailing at the international plane it is most likely to shy off one or the other group of States, depending on the outcome of the Court's envisaged law-making activities. Moreover, the need felt for "genuine philosophical debate" and the "testing of alternative policy constructs for the future, on a trial and error basis in the public *fora*" can be provided for on the international level through means other than the Court. Secondly, the dividing-line between the effects of Court decisions in contentious cases and those of its advisory opinions is not particularly sharp, certainly not to laymen. The Court on its part has, generally speaking, not made a marked difference in approach between contentious cases and advisory opinions, even though its posture in advisory jurisdiction would seem to be a more dynamic one; in both cases it has acted as a judicial organ *stricto sensu*. This has not proved an unsatisfactory approach, if it is correct to uphold that a good deal of the Court's prestige or authority has been built up through its advisory opinions. Consequently, a shift to an approach in advisory opinions as advocated by McWhinney could also affect the Court's authority with respect to contentious cases. While these admittedly concern a fairly small number of mostly more "technical" disputes, it remains nevertheless important for the

734. McWhinney, *op.cit.* (note 33), pp. 166-169.
735. *Ibidem*, p. 168.
736. *Ibidem*.
737. *Ibidem*, p. 169.
738. *Ibidem*.

international society to have available a trusted institution for the settlement of these disputes.

9.2. Teachings of the most qualified publicists of the various nations

The second category which article 38(1)(d) lists as a subsidiary means for the determination of rules of law consists of the teachings of the most qualified publicists of the various nations. A great deal of what has been observed with respect to judicial decisions in the preceding section applies *mutatis mutandis* also to this category which is most of the time summarily described as "doctrine". However, there would seem to be virtually complete agreement as to the point that doctrine does not constitute a source of international law.

Doctrine did not figure in the proposal by Descamps which served as the point of departure for the 1920 Advisory Committee's work on the sources of international law.[739] It was for the first time mentioned in his speech elucidating his proposal. At that occasion he explained that in discovering "objective justice" he would allow the judge "to make use of the concurrent teaching of the authors whose opinions have authority".[740] To him doctrine would be placed at par with "the legal conscience of civilized nations".[741] Subsequently, the Root-Phillimore draft contained a reference to "the opinion of writers as a means for the application and development of the law".[742] Doctrine, therefore, was placed at the same level as judicial decisions and, indeed, Descamps referred to both as "auxiliary and supplementary means, only".[743] That was also the way in which both items eventually ended up in article 38(1)(d) of the Statute.

However, it may be doubted whether doctrine should indeed be assigned the same status as judicial decisions. Some of the Committee's members were of the opinion that this was not bo be the case. Ricci-Busatti "denied most emphatically that the opinions of authors could be considered as a source of law, to be applied by the Court...".[744] De Lapradelle also expressed doubt when he stated: "If it were wished to include doctrine as a source it should be at any rate limited to coinciding doctrines of qualified authors in the countries concerned in the case".[745] Phillimore, on the other hand, pointed out with respect to doctrine that "it is universally recognized as a source of international law".[746] He immediately added, however: "There is no need to say, that only the opinions of widely recognized authors were in question".[747] But this, of course, raises the question which authors are widely recognized, or, more generally, are most relevant to the issue concerned. As has been rightly pointed out by Parry, "it is as difficult to decide who 'the most highly qualified publicists' are as it is to say what is a peace-loving nation within the meaning of the Charter of the United Nations".[748]

739. *Procès-Verbaux, loc.cit.* (note 526), p. 306.
740. *Ibidem*, pp. 322-323.
741. *Ibidem.*
742. *Ibidem*, p. 344.
743. *Ibidem*, p. 332.
744. *Ibidem*, p. 332.
745. *Ibidem*, p. 336.
746. *Ibidem*, p. 333.
747. *Ibidem.*
748. C. Parry, *op.cit.* (note 22), p. 108.

Writing on international law has strongly proliferated during this century and at the same time the opinions expressed in doctrine have also grown more divergent, just like international society has become more heterogeneous. There are no hard and fast criteria to decide what part of doctrine is highly qualified and what is not, while the alternative of taken the whole body of doctrine on a given issue into account is likely to cloud rather than to clarify the issue concerned. Maybe the situation was different at the time Phillimore spoke his words just quoted, when there were indeed publicists whose authority was undisputed.[749] The authority of these publicists did probably result *inter alia* from the fact that their number was fairly limited, and, most importantly, that custom, treaties, and general principles of law did provide far less answers than today.

At any rate, the present situation is different. Today, doctrine does not even rank equal to judicial decisions. It is true, as Fitzmaurice has observed, that "the parties, their advocates and the tribunal itself, view in quite a different light such (material) sources of law, as, for instance, the opinions of jurists (however eminent) and a decision, even if the tribunal given it is composed of less eminent persons".[750] One of the main reasons for this is the higher status or authority of judicial decisions. As was pointed out in the preceding paragraph, judicial decisions constitute in fact a form of delegated consent by the States parties to the case;[751] the opinions of publicists, in contrast, have no basis in consent or acceptance whatsoever.[752] As was already pointed out above,[753] the contents of the opinions which authors advocate may at best become part of international law if and to the extent that they are adopted by one or more States and thus injected into the international law-making process.[754]

---

749. See, however, in this respect the reference by Parry to a case in which the question was how long price must be in the captor's hands for the original property in her to be divested, and in which counsel for the two parties offered opposing opinions of Grotius and Bynkershoek. According to Parry, the Court "observed that there was something ridiculous in the decisive way each lawyer, as quoted, had given his opinion. Grotius might as well have laid down, for a rule, twelve hours, as twenty-four; or forty-eight, as twelve. A pedantic man in his closet dictates the law of nations; everybody quotes, and nobody minds him. The usage is plainly as arbitrary as it is uncertain; and who shall decide, when doctors disagree? Bynkershoek, as is natural to every writer or speaker who comes after another, is delighted to contradict Grotius ...", *ibidem*, pp. 103-104.

750. G. Fitzmaurice, *loc.cit.* (note 28), pp. 171-172.

751. See *supra* p. 171.

752. G. Schwarzenberger's explanation for the greater weight of the views of international judges in their official capacity than if contained in private studies is not entirely convincing. He believes that an important reason lies "in the greater degree of responsibility and care that the average lawyer shows when he deals in a judicial capacity with real issues as compared with private comments on such issues as the discussion of hypothetical cases", *op.cit.* (note 713), pp. 31-32.

753. See *supra* p. 24.

754. G. von Glahn, *Law Among Nations; An Introduction to Public International Law*, 3rd edition (New York/London 1976), p. 21, labels doctrine an "indirect" source of international law, a term which in our view is more appropriately reserved for judicial decisions, see *supra* p. 171. According to G. von Glahn, an author "may voice his considered opinion as to how the law might be improved on a given point. To the extent that his government may adopt suggestions and utilize them in the development of a usage or by incorporating them in a law-making treaty concluded with a number of other States, the writer may be regarded as an indirect source of law". However, this description of the way in which doctrine may influence the international law-making process makes it a material source in the sense of that term as used by Parry, see *supra* p. 58, rather than a formal source which is the sense of the term source being discussed here, see *supra* pp. 57-60.

In view of the fact that doctrine cannot be considered a source of international law it is indeed remarkable to observe the phenomenon of one commentator merely invoking another in an effort to substantiate his or her point of view that a particular rule is a rule of international law. Instead of turning to those sources which can truly manifest a State's consent or acceptance one may not infrequently see writers rely on other writers in order to prove their case that this or that rule is a rule of international law. Watson in particular has castigated international legal doctrine for this basic flaw.[755] In reaction to what he labels a tendency of mutual cross-citation, he contends that "since academic sources do have a role, albeit a minor one, in the creation of rules of international law, it is crucial to the validity of one's conclusions not to confuse the snowballing acceptance of a rule by academics with snowballing acceptance by states".[756]

All this concerns the question of whether or not doctrine is to be considered as a source of international law. The negative answer to that question obviously does not detract from the fact that doctrine can have an influence on the international law-making process. It was explained above,[757] that both in a more practice-oriented as well as in a more theoretical fashion doctrine has an important role to play in improving the international law-making process.[758] The point to be stressed here, however, is that this role is one of an expert-consultant in an advisory capacity rather than that of a participant in the decision-making process itself.

755. J. Watson, *loc.cit.* (note 34), p. 636, where it is upheld that even if writers have made "immense contributions to their discipline, one must not succumb to the tendency to cite their works as authority for propositions more properly established by reference to primary sources". Watson would even go as far as accusing at least part of doctrine of bad faith, in that he puts forward the following two reasons for the wide-spread reliance on the works of (other) academic commentators: "First, the writer does not need to concern himself with a full explanation of his argument. Second, any flaws that exist in the argument cannot be easily detected by the reader, as they are contained in another article not always immediately available".
756. *Ibidem*, p. 637.
757. See *supra* pp. 17-19.
758. See also M. Bos, *loc.cit.* (note 28), p. 63; and R. Jennings, *loc.cit.* (note 1), p. 88, who con-

SOME CONCLUSIONS: THE MOVEMENT TOWARDS "OTHER SOURCES" AND THE "SOFT LAW" APPROACH

In the preceding chapters the so-called "traditional sources" of international law were analyzed particularly in the light of the changes which have occurred in the structure of international society during recent decades. A general conclusion which emerges from this analysis is that, to some extent at least, customary international law and treaties have (been) adapted to these changes while the impact on the other items listed in article 38 of the Statute has rather been that their already limited usefulness as a source has further dwindled. The overall picture thus found certainly is unsatisfactory, as the adaptation of custom and treaties has not gone far enough, or rather could not have gone any further. In fact, as was repeatedly stressed in the preceding chapters, the clarity or certainty which the law, and in particular its sources, have to provide requires these traditional sources to be strictly defined. The requirement of clarity and certainty, in other words, puts a limit to the elasticity of these sources. If the concept of each of these sources is stretched beyond a certain point, in an effort to have them encompass phenomena resulting from new developments, the results become counter-productive.[759] The sources then lose their distinctive capacity and are, consequently, prevented from playing their ordering and regulating role of distinguishing between rules of law and other types of rules of conduct. It is, therefore, absolutely essential in view of this role that they remain strictly defined.[760]

On the other hand, a rigid definition of the concept of the traditional sources, as was advocated in the preceding chapters, has its negative effects too. The most eye-catching drawback in this context is the fact that the new developments which were mentioned in the beginning of the present study[761] cannot be adequately explained in terms of the traditional sources of international law. The phenomena arising from these developments, like the "quasi-legislative" activities of the United Nations' General Assembly, the so-called "rules of the game" (tacitly) agreed upon between the Great Powers, and other agreements concluded at a high political level such as the Helsinki Final Act, cannot be satis-

cludes after highlighting some changes in the international law-making process: "One thing is certain: it is the task of professional international lawyers, especially the scholars and teachers, to systematize, interpret, explain, and adapt, these new developments".
759. R. Jennings, *loc. cit.* (note 1), p. 71 in discussing examples of the new developments referred to above very straightforwardly submits: "I am convinced it is a mistake to try to force these newer trends and techniques into one or other of the compartments of the 1920 mould".
760. See in this respect also P. Weil, *loc. cit.* (note 216), p. 9, according to whom the present weakness of the international normative system derives not only from the basic features of the international society, but also from "le manque de rigueur avec lequel on aborde trop souvent aujourd'hui la distinction entre ce qui n'est pas normatif et ce qui l'est".
761. See *supra* pp. 13-14.

factorily fitted into, or classified in terms of the traditional sources. Nevertheless, these and other phenomena are said to be of a law-making character, or at least it is fairly generally felt that they should be granted some status in the law-making process. In other words, the traditional sources of international law do not seem to cover the entire field of (alleged) law-making phenomena.

Not surprisingly, this problem has come to the fore first and foremost in relation to the legal status of resolutions of international organizations, most particularly those of the General Assembly of the United Nations.[762] Doctrine has approached the question in a comparatively early stage, because it arose rather soon after the (world-wide) international organizations were established, and the problem has been dealt with quite extensively. The other phenomena mentioned are of a more recent date, or at least came only later within the purview of doctrine as a question relating to the sources of international law.

As far as the resolutions of the General Assembly are concerned, attention has been focused on those resolutions which are not formally binding or even formally non-binding.[763] These resolutions are usually designated as "recom-

---

762. Among the abundance of writings on this question the present author has found the following studies most illuminating: O. Asamoah, *The Legal Significance of the Declarations of the General Assembly of the United Nations* (The Hague 1966); G. Arangio-Ruiz, "The Normative Role of the General Assembly of the United Nations and the Declaration of Principles of Friendly Relations", 137 *RCADI* (1972-III), pp. 419-742; *idem, op.cit.* (note 195); S. Bleicher, "The Legal Significance of Re-citation of General Assembly Resolutions", 63 *AJIL* (1969), pp. 444-478; M. Bothe, "Legal and Non-Legal Norms - A Meaningful Distinction in International Relations?", XI *NYIL* (1980), pp. 65-95; J. Castaneda, "Valeur juridique des résolutions des Nations Unies", 129 *RCADI* (1970-I), pp. 205-331; R. Falk, "On the Quasi-Legislative Competence of the General Assembly", 60 *AJIL* (1966), pp. 782-791; R. Higgins, *The Development of International Law through the Political Organs of the United Nations* (London 1963); *idem*, "United Nations and Law-making: The Political Organs", *PASIL* (1970), pp. 37-48; D. Johnson, "The Effect of Resolutions of the General Assembly of the United Nations", XXXII *BYIL* (1955-1956), pp. 97-122; N. Onuf, "Professor Falk on the Quasi-Legislative Competence of the General Assembly", 64 *AJIL* (1970), pp. 349-355; C. Schreuer, "Recommendations and the Traditional Sources of International Law", 20 *GYIL* (1977), pp. 103-118; K. Skubiszewski, "Enactment of Law by International Organizations", XIV *BYIL* (1965-1966), pp. 198-274; *idem*, "A New Source of the Law of Nations: Resolutions of International Organizations", *Receuil d'études de droit international en hommage à Paul Guggenheim* (Genève 1968), pp. 508-520; P. Sloan, "The Binding Force of a 'Recommendation' of the General Assembly of the United Nations", XXV *BYIL* (1948), pp. 1-33; A. Tammes, "Decisions of International Organs as a Source of International Law", 94 *RCADI* (1958-II), pp. 265-362; C. Tomuschat, "Die Charta der Wirtschaftlichen Rechte und Pflichten der Staaten; Zur Gestaltungskraft von Deklarationen der UN-Generalversammlung", 36 *ZaöRV* (1976), pp. 444-491; M. Virally, "La valeur juridique des récommendations des organisations internationales", II *AFDI* (1956), pp. 66-96.

763. The General Assembly has legally binding power with respect to certain internal (organizational) matters of the United Nations. The items listed in article 18(2) of the Charter, with the exception of recommendations with respect to the maintenance of international peace and security, constitute examples of such matters. On other ("external") questions, however, the General Assembly has only hortatory authority. In general, resolutions of international organizations are formally speaking not binding, at least not for States which voted against. Nevertheless, there are notable exceptions, such as the powers of the United Nations' Security Council in the field of the maintenance of international peace and security, and the decision-making process within the framework of the European Communities. This type of resolutions, which may be designated as "decisions" as opposed to "recommendations", derive their general binding force from the treaty on which the international organization concerned is based. Through their consent to that treaty States accept in advance the obligatory charac-

mendations". This latter term is generally taken to apply to resolutions which formally have no legally binding force.[764] Despite the formally non-binding character of General Assembly resolutions[765] it is fairly generally felt that an analysis of their legal nature cannot be confined to simply classifying them as non-law. Such a conclusion would result from approaching this problem on the basis of a rigid conception of the traditional sources of international law combined with a black-and-white distinction between these traditional sources and more recent phenomena.

To avoid such a conclusion efforts have been made to fit General Assembly resolutions into the concept of the traditional sources. All categories enumerated in article 38 of the ICJ's Statute have been invoked to explain at least certain General Assembly resolutions in terms of the traditional sources of international law. Thus, it has been argued that the expression of consent or acceptance through recommendations constitutes a modern extension of the law of treaties.[766] This line of reasoning has proved particularly attractive with respect to resolutions which have been adopted unanimously.[767] As will be pointed out below,[768] there can be no doubt that apart from formal ratification of a treaty international agreements may also arise from a more formless expression of consent or acceptance. Resolutions of the General Assembly may under certain conditions constitute such formless agreements, but certainly not every General Assembly resolution, even if unanimously adopted, can be considered to do so. A main argument which argues against such a conclusion is the fact that the Charter contains a strong presumption against the legally binding character of General Assembly resolutions by designating them as "recommendations", and in some cases this might be precisely the reason why States are prepared to vote in favour of them. Consequently, it takes strong countervailing indications to conclude that the States concerned nevertheless entered into a (formless) agreement which was intended to be legally binding.

More popular and, at least in certain instances, more plausible is the thesis that General Assembly resolutions are an authoritative or authentic interpretation or concretization of the provisions of the Charter.[769] It is true that in order

ter of these resolutions, even in cases where they will vote against. Just as in the case of judgments of the International Court of Justice (see *supra* pp. 170-171) these generally binding decisions can be said to constitute a case of delegated consent. See in this respect also A. Tammes, *loc.cit.* (note 762), pp. 268-269; and I. Brownlie, *op.cit.* (note 192), pp. 697-698, who refers to "Powers of legislation *delegated* to organizations" (emphasis added).

764. Deviating terminology employs article 14(3) ECSC which provides that "Recommendations shall be binding with respect to the objectives which they prescribe ...".
765. This point is usually substantiated on the basis of article 10 of the Charter which under the heading of functions and powers of the General Assembly refers to "recommendations". Moreover, during the drafting stage of the Charter a proposal put forward by the Phillipines to endow the Assembly with legislative powers was categorically rejected; see *UNCIO, Documents*, Vol. IX, p. 316 jo. 70.
766. See for instance O. Asamoah, *op.cit.* (note 762), p. 70; J. Castaneda, *loc.cit.* (note 762), pp. 214-215; and K. Skubiszewski, "Resolutions of International Organizations and Municipal Law", 2 *PYIL* (1968-1969), pp. 80-108 (83-84).
767. See in particular the references to authors from socialist countries by G. Tunkin, *op.cit.* (note 50), pp. 162-165 and K. Skubiszewski, *loc.cit.* (note 766), p. 95.
768. See *infra* pp. 199-203.
769. See O. Asamoah, *op.cit.* (note 762), p. 35; S. Bleicher, *loc.cit.* (note 762), pp. 448-449; O. Schachter, "The Relation of Law, Politics and Action in the United Nations", 109 *RCADI* (1963-II), pp. 165-256 (186); L. Sohn, "The Development of the Charter of the United

to determine the legal nature of a given rule it is important to take into account the relation of that rule with other rules of international law.[770] However, this is only one element and it does not provide an answer in all cases. Not all resolutions of the General Assembly are of the same character; they show differences in various respects.[771] Clearly, not all resolutions of the General Assembly can be regarded as an interpretation or concretization of provisions of the Charter. The interpretation/concretization-thesis therefore does not furnish an explanation for the legal nature of all resolutions.

Most often the question as to the legal nature of resolutions is linked in one way or another to the source of customary international law. It is fairly uncontested that resolutions may be the starting-point of a rule of customary international law, or that they may corroborate or evidence international custom.[772] These points of view do not raise great difficulties, because they do not as such present resolutions as constituting an element of customary international law. This is different, of course, when resolutions come to be regarded as a form of state-practice (*usus*)[773] or as an expression of *opinio juris*.[774] After what has been observed above on abstract declarations in discussing *usus* as a constitutive element of customary international law,[775] it follows that, in the present author's view, resolutions cannot normally constitute state-practice in the sense of *usus*, because they are not material acts. Just like treaties, resolutions can be considered state-practice to the extent only that they delineate the content of a rule and thereby clearly outline future conduct for States.[776]

As far as the element of *opinio juris* is concerned, General Assembly resolutions may of course contain expressions of *opinio juris* with respect to a certain rule, but it can only be judged on a case-by-case basis whether or not they in fact do. The expression of *opinio juris* should be unequivocal and should, therefore, not too lightly be assumed to be contained in resolutions of the General Assembly, as the hothouse atmosphere of that organ[777] makes it often quite difficult to judge whether States cast their votes from a "producer" or a "consumer" posi-

---

Nations: the Present State", in: M. Bos (ed.), *The Present State of International Law and other Essays* (Deventer 1973), pp. 39-59 (50); and G. Tunkin, *op.cit.* (note 50), p. 171.
770. See *infra* pp. 240-242.
771. A well-known distinction is often made between "declarations" and other resolutions. See on the different types of declarations J. Lador-Lederer, "Legal Aspects of Declarations", XII *ILR* (1977), pp. 202-231.
772. See for instance H. Thirlway, *op.cit.* (note 209), pp. 63-66; and A. Verdross, *op.cit.* (note 98), p. 116.
773. See O. Asamoah, *op.cit.* (note 762), pp. 52-55; and see also the dissenting opinion of judge Tanaka in the *South-West Africa* case, ICJ Reports (1966), pp. 250-324 (293).
774. See O. Asamoah, *op.cit.* (note 762), pp. 55-58; and S. Bleicher, *loc.cit.* (note 762), pp. 450-451.
775. See *supra* pp. 106-109.
776. See *supra* p. 109; even if successive resolutions do have the same content, it should not too quickly be concluded that they outline future state-conduct, because the majorities passing the resolutions concerned might be differently composed. To put it differently in the words of J. Watson, *loc.cit.* (note 34), p. 629: "The fact that an international organization's 'practice' may be consistent ignores the possibility that an individual state's voting record may be anything but consistent due to the fact that the majority in each vote consists of an ever fluctuating group of states who vote, not on the basis of legal principle, but on political perceptions".
777. The expression comes from S. Engel, "'Living' International Constitutions and the World Court", 16 *ICLQ* (1967), pp. 865-910 (910).

tion.[778] Moreover, even if a resolution can be taken to constitute an expression of *opinio juris*, what is required in addition is, of course, the existence of an *usus* sufficient to delineate the content of the rule concerned before one can conclude that a rule of customary international law has come into being. Some read the element of *opinio juris* in General Assembly resolutions and at the same time virtually do away with the requirement of *usus*. As was already pointed out in discussing the concept of "instant customary law",[779] views like these do not concern customary international law properly speaking. Viewed in this perspective, therefore, General Assembly resolutions should rather be equated with the formless agreements mentioned above[780] and are to be considered subject to the same conditions and criteria. These conditions and criteria for resolutions to be formless agreement are more stringent than those for resolutions as expressing *opinio juris* as an element of custom, because in the former case the additional requirement of an *usus* delineating the content of the rule concerned is lacking.[781]

Finally, efforts have been made to explain the legal nature of General Assembly resolutions on the basis of the general principles recognized by civilized nations.[782] Such efforts concern, in the terminology of the present study, the general principles as a source of international law outside the framework of a court-situation. It was admitted above that theoretically the States gathered in the General Assembly could conclude, on the basis of reception from municipal legal systems or induction from positive rules of international law, that a certain norm is to be recognized as binding international law and, subsequently, lay down this conclusion in a resolution. However, at the same time it was submitted that most of the time it is rather artificial to explain such resolutions in terms of general principles as a procedural source of international law, because in fact the States adopting the resolution were not relying on article 38(1)(c) of the ICJ's Statute.[783]

The foregoing brief outline of efforts to fit General Assembly resolutions into the concept of the traditional sources of international law obviously cannot do justice to the detailed observations and arguments of the authors concerned, each of which contains a good deal of truth in respect of the particular case being discussed by these authors. Nevertheless, it is not felt necessary to go beyond the general comments expressed in respect of them. For, over time it has become

778. See *infra* pp. 217-218.
779. See *supra* pp. 85-86.
780. See *supra* pp. 146-148.
781. The same point would seem to be implied in A. D'Amato's criticism on the concept of "instant customary law": "One cannot readily divorce the material element from the psychological element, for in specific cases where custom has been alleged both of these elements operate interdependently to qualify each other. *Opinio juris* helps to characterize practice as legal rather than a matter of comity or expediency, as international rather than domestic, or ... as obligatory non-action rather than inertia. Similarly, usage helps concretize the general asserted rule, or select it from numerous rules allegedly concurrently, or perhaps even to defeat the rule of *opinio juris* in cases where practice diverges from protestation", *loc.cit.* (note 182), pp. 111-112.
782. See O. Asamoah, *op.cit.* (note 762), pp. 61-62; and A. Verdross, "Kann die Generalversammlung der Vereinten Nationen das Völkerrecht weiterbilden?", 26 *ZaöRV* (1966), pp. 690-697.
783. See *supra* pp. 147-148.

increasingly recognized that these efforts have not proved successful in stating the main case, *i.e.* that resolutions do indeed fit into the traditional sources of international law.[784] The major drawbacks involved may be summarized as follows. Firstly, attempts to bring General Assembly resolutions within the purview of the traditional sources of international law are almost bound to result in stretching the concept of these sources beyond what would seem to be warranted in view of the clarity and certainty the sources have to provide. Secondly, even if one succeeds in explaining the binding character of a certain resolution or a certain type of resolution in terms of the traditional sources, the question as to the exact legal nature of other (types of) resolutions still remains unanswered. In other words, even if considered partly successful, the attempts discussed in the foregoing do not offer an explanation of the legal status of resolutions in general.

Another, although in some respects related line of response to the question of the legal nature of General Assembly resolutions, and one which would seem to strive for a more or less all-embracing solution, could be called the "other source" approach. Rather than seeking to link General Assembly resolutions to one or more of the traditional sources of international law, this approach sets forth a quite radical solution and in fact argues that those resolutions have become a separate, independent source.

This view has been advocated from very authoritative sides. Elias, who became a judge of the International Court of Justice and later on its President, has very straightforwardly advocated the "new source" approach and defended his thesis on the basis of the following line of reasoning: "those states that vote for a particular resolution by the requisite majority are bound on the grounds of consent and of estoppel. Those that abstain are also bound on the ground of acquiescence and tacit consent, since an abstention is not a negative vote; while those that vote against the resolution should be regarded as bound by the democratic principle that the majority view should prevail when the vote has been truly free and fair and the requisite majority has been secured. To hold otherwise would be contrary to the democratic principle that, if every state has had its say, the requisite majority must have its way".[785]

More complex and couched in more careful terms is the opinion of Sohn, advisor to the U.S. government and representative of the U.S. at several international conferences. Nevertheless, reading his studies devoted to the subject one can hardly escape the impression that in that author's view, too, (at least certain) General Assembly resolutions constitute a new independent source. After discussing the Declaration on Principles of International Law concerning Friendly Relations and Cooperation among States in accordance with the Charter of the United Nations,[786] he concludes that "This is but one important example of the legislative activity of the General Assembly, leading to the creation of new international law applicable to all States".[787] Furthermore, he adds exam-

784. See for some more detailed comments C. Schreuer, *loc.cit.* (note 762); and C. Tomuschat, *loc.cit.* (note 762).
785. T. Elias, "Modern Sources of International Law", in: W. Friedmann, L. Henkin and O. Lissitzyn (eds.), *Transnational Law in a Changing Society; Essays in Honor of Philip C. Jessup* (New York 1972), pp. 34-69 (51).
786. Resolution 2625 (XXV) of 24 October 1970.
787. L. Sohn, *loc.cit.* (note 769), p. 52.

ples of other "unanimously approved declarations" having the same character.[788] According to Sohn such declarations represent "a new method of creating customary international law".[789] And in a later study he has reiterated with respect to unanimous declarations that "having thus become a part of customary international law they are even binding on non-Member States, as some of these documents have expressly proclaimed".[790]

Despite his reference to customary international law, Sohn's treatment of the unanimous declarations leaves no doubt that he in fact drops the requirement of *usus*. Consequently, what one is faced with here is not just a new method of creating customary international law, but rather a new method of creating international law *tout court*.[791] This would seem to be confirmed by the fact that, subsequently, Sohn attributes the generally binding effect rather to consensus than to (quasi-)unanimity. According to Sohn, the upshot of the consensus-procedure is that "it becomes difficult for any minority to completely reject the final product of this prolonged negotiating process".[792]

It can be readily admitted that General Assembly resolutions may contain binding rules of international law and that those mentioned by the above-quoted authors in fact do. The point in issue, however, is whether this binding character results from the fact that these rules are contained in those resolutions, as they suggest. Given the drafting history of the UN Charter and its relevant provisions[793] the point of view which attributes generally binding force to General Assembly resolutions even if not unanimously adopted, is difficult to reconcile with the consensual basis of international law as advocated by the present author.[794]

It is not just the authority of the authors quoted which makes the "new source"thesis hard to ignore. Similar opinions have sometimes been voiced on the political plane, *i.e.* by States themselves. The president of the General Assembly, for instance, in his address at the opening of its twenty-eight session upheld that all General Assembly resolutions were binding because they are based on a binding treaty, *i.e.* the UN Charter.[795] The problem with this assertion, of course, is that the very treaty which is invoked here declares resolutions to be non-binding instruments.[796] In itself the spirit and even the provisions of the Charter as such do not present an insurmountable obstacle. For, as was already hinted at in the foregoing and as will be argued in more detail below,[797] the States acting collectively as the law-givers in international law can also

---

788. *Ibidem*, pp. 52-57.
789. *Ibidem*, p. 52.
790. L. Sohn, "The Shaping of International Law", 8 *GJICL* (1978), pp. 1-25 (22).
791. In as far as Sohn regards these "unanimous" declarations binding for States not voting in favour or even for non-member States his new method is not just a new source of law but even a new source of legislation; see also L. Sohn, "The Universal Declaration of Human Rights", 8 *JICJ* (1968), pp. 17-26 (26), where it is concluded that the Universal Declaration of Human Rights "has achieved the character of world law superior to all other international instruments and to domestic laws".
792. *Ibidem*, p. 24.
793. See *supra* pp. 180-181.
794. See *supra* pp. 76-81.
795. *UN Doc.* A/PV 2117, 18 September 1973, p. 36.
796. See *supra* pp. 180-181.
797. See *infra* pp. 195-199.

change or supplement the sources of international law. It is submitted, however, that they have not actually done so with respect to General Assembly resolutions as a separate class.[798] At the political level the drive for turning resolutions into generally binding legal instruments stems from the group of developing countries. Obviously, this group would have most to gain from such a change, because they are most eager to transform international law and they would control the means to do so through General Assembly resolutions as a result of their so-called "automatic majority" in that body. However, an important group of other States, notably the Western States but, for that matter, also the socialist countries, are not at all prepared for obvious reasons to accept a binding character for General Assembly resolutions in general. Apart from the difficulty or even impossibility to put into practice a resolution opposed by the latter groups of States, there are therefore also important theoretical objections against the conclusion that General Assembly resolutions have a generally binding effect. For resolutions to become generally binding, the consent of all member States would be required.

Furthermore, it is not entirely clear whether the developing countries as a group really want to attain the general binding force of General Assembly resolutions as a category, or whether contentions to that effect, even if put forward *in abstracto*, are in fact directed at certain (types of) resolutions only. At any rate, even at the high tide of the new-source-wave in the sixties and the seventies there has been no real consistent effort on the part of the developing countries to achieve the result of General Assembly resolutions becoming generally binding instruments. The proper way to bring about this result would have been to set into motion the procedure for amendment of the Charter.[799] They certainly command the two-thirds majority necessary for initiating that procedure, although it could be countered that the successful completion of that process is not in their hands, as the coming into force of amendments to the Charter requires the consent of all permanent members of the Security Council. Even if the lack of ultimate feasibility has withheld them from starting the amendment machinery of the Charter, it is still hard to imagine that the developing countries ever really contemplated to do so. The Third World is not a monolithic bloc in all respects and each of its members is of course perfectly aware that the clothing of General Assembly resolutions with a generally binding character might very well turn against them.[800] It is unlikely that developing countries would welcome such a far-reaching encroachment upon their sovereignty and, indeed, the positions they have taken on law-making conferences such as the Vienna Con-

---

798. See also I. Seidl-Hohenveldern, "International Economic 'Soft Law'", 163 *RCADI* (1979-II), pp. 169-238 (185), who in denying that customary international law has transplanted the majority principle into the United Nations Charter, argues: "Anyhow, the States outvoted in the General Assembly never had recognized any transformation of the latter's powers which would have authorized the introduction into the United Nations Charter of principles borrowed from the Constitutions of parliamentary democracies and, ..., these States are certainly not prepared to do so".
799. Chapter XVIII, articles 108-109 of the Charter.
800. As R. Kearney, *loc.cit.* (note 25), p. 508, has pointed out: "the developing states' monolithic position is not that much of a monolith. The developing countries' individual interests differ as all states' interest differ. Under sufficient pressure, their original unified position - which is itself a compromise - might collapse completely if pushed too hard"; similarly, S. Zamora, "Voting in International Economic Organizations", 74 *AJIL* (1980), pp. 566-608 (570).

ference on the Law of Treaties buttress this conclusion.[801] At any rate, the present author knows of no instance in which a State that voted against a certain resolution subsequently accepted its provisions as binding law because of the fact that they were contained in a resolution. In short, it would seem to be unattractive for States to attribute a law-making character to General Assembly resolutions in general.[802]

The "new source" approach in its extreme form would seem to be rather unelegant for yet another, more doctrinal reason. By proclaiming General Assembly resolutions as a category to be a new source of international law this approach not only lumps together instruments which *inter se* show a great deal of differences, at the same time it excludes the other phenomena mentioned above[803] which, although not being General Assembly resolutions, raise similar questions with respect to their precise legal nature. Some of these phenomena rank at least as high on the "legal ladder" as General Assembly resolutions. Therefore, in order to explain these other instruments in terms of the sources of international law it would be necessary to create an additional new source. To be sure, this would not present major theoretical objections, but it would be a rather haphazard way to deal with the problem if a new source would have to be created every time a new development arises which cannot be fitted into an already existing category. It is certainly to be preferred to have a more systematic effort to tackle the challenges in the field of the sources posed by the changes in international society.

This brings us to a third school of thought which has emerged in reaction to the problems concerning the sources of international law. This school of thought was to a large extent equally prompted by the questions involved in the legal nature of General Assembly resolutions, but its tenets also apply to other documents whose legal status is unclear. In this respect it constitutes, therefore, a more systematic approach. For reasons of convenience this school can be called the "soft-law" approach, a term coined by McNair.[804] The three approaches mentioned in this chapter overlap to a certain extent. Just like the other two, this third school is first of all faced with the question of classifying or explaining the new developments and phenomena in terms of the traditional sources. The term "soft law", however, bears out its main focus and distinguishing feature. For, authors belonging to this third group do not make a black-and-white distinction between law and non-law. After testing a new type of instrument on the basis of the criteria of the traditional sources, they conclude that these instruments cannot be considered as "full-fledged" rules of international law. On the other hand, they stress that these instruments fulfil at least some, if not a great number of the criteria required for rules to be considered rules of

---

801. See *supra* pp. 80-81.
802. Again it should be stressed that this is not the same thing as denying that such resolutions may contain rules of international law. Similarly, denial of a law-making character does not detract from the persuasive force which General Assembly resolutions may entail. This latter aspect is emphasized by R. Falk, *loc.cit.* (note 762).
803. See *supra* p. 14.
804. See R. Dupuy, *loc.cit.* (note 390), p. 252, according to whom the term designates a "transitional stage in the development of norms where their content is vague and their scope imprecise"; on the different meanings of the term "soft law", see P. Weil, *loc.cit.* (note 216), pp. 8-9.

international law and cannot therefore be simply put aside as non-law. In other words, they acknowledge that there exists a considerable "grey area" of "soft-law" between the white space of law and the black territory of non-law. Simultaneously, they make the salient point that the "grey area" may greatly affect the white one and explain, sometimes in considerable detail, in what ways "soft-law" can have legal effects. In doing so the "soft-law" approach more or less substantiates Friedmann's earlier perception of a development towards a "far greater variety of sources of international law" which according to him, moreover, "may vary greatly in intensity".[805]

The main focus of the "soft-law" approach, which by now has gained a considerable number of supporters, may be clarified a little further on the basis of the views of some of its most outspoken proponents.[806] A fairly early example constitutes Virally's study devoted to the United Nations' Second Development Decade.[807] Virally denounces the static kind of Positivism which rigidly defines the notion of law and, subsequently, completely ignores as irrelevant to lawyers everything that falls outside the scope of this definiton, and which Virally summarily describes as moral and political obligations. Virally himself starts from the opposite end and maintains that legal obligations and moral/political obligations have important characteristics in common. The main common feature, according to Virally, is that both types of obligations in the final analysis rest upon the concept of good faith and that as such both play an important role in ordering social relations. In emphasizing the value of moral and political obligations on the international plane, he goes as far as upholding that "On peut penser ... que, dans beaucoup de cas, les États sont fidèles à leurs obligations juridiques en raison de leurs connotations morales et politiques plus que de leur caractère juridique".[808] Now, Virally does not lose sight of the differences between legal and moral/political obligations, but his main aim is to show that the latter can have substantial legal effects, particularly in terms of their effectiveness in practice.

From a somewhat similar perspective Schachter sets out to categorize the Helsinki Final Act of 1975.[809] He ranks this document as a "non-binding international agreement" as opposed to binding (legal) international agreements, but leaves no doubt that to him the distinction is far from absolute, as the criteria which underly it are not easy to apply. He goes on to point out in some detail that (some of) these criteria are sometimes satisfied by so-called non-binding instruments and, conversely, sometimes not fulfilled by formally binding instruments. In addition, he observes that "What is meant by a political or moral commitment is rarely spelled out beyond the negative implication that it does not entail legal effects or sanctions".[810] He himself indicates two aspects which may be relevant

---

805. See the preface to O. Asamoah, *op.cit.* (note 762), p. V.
806. For examples of fields of international law where soft rules can be found see M. Bothe, *loc.cit.* (note 762), pp. 70-85.
807. M. Virally, "La deuxième décennie des Nations Unies pour le développement; Essai d'interprétation para-juridique", XVI *AFDI* (1970), pp. 9-33.
808. *Ibidem*, p. 30.
809. O. Schachter, "The Twilight Existence of Non-binding International Agreements", 71 *AJIL* (1977), pp. 296-304.
810. *Ibidem*, p. 303.

188

in this respect: "One is internal in the sense that the commitment of the State is 'internalized' as an instruction to its officials to act accordingly",[811] while the other is "external" in the sense that "The fact that the States have entered into mutual engagements confers an entitlement on each party to make represent-ations to the others on the execution of those engagements".[812]

A third example to be mentioned here is Van Dijk's study devoted to the Hel-sinki Final Act.[813] After analyzing that document on the basis of the traditional sources of international law, the author concludes that its legal nature can be described as that of a "not legally binding agreement".[814] Just like Schachter, Van Dijk is quick to point out that the binding force of the Helsinki Final Act and its precise legal implications are "carefully left vague, as is increasingly the case with international regulations falling outside the categories of treaties and binding decisions of international organizations".[815] As to these implications Van Dijk focuses on the link between existing norms and the (new) soft norms. In particular he draws attention to an "interesting interaction" existing between the two: "the rules and principles mentioned above [the existing norms; v.H.] bestow a normative value upon provisions in the Final Act, but the reaffirma-tion of these rules and principles in the Final Act ... also strengthens their own normative force, and this the more so if the participating States appear actually to conduct themselves according to these rules and principles".[816] How this pro-cess of interaction actually operates is subsequently illustrated by an indication of the various relationships between in particular the Declaration of Principles contained in the Helsinki Final Act (the so-called Decalogue) and the U.N. Charter as well as a number of instruments drawn up within the framework of the United Nations.

The "soft-law" approach is an important asset to the doctrine of international law. It has, first of all, clearly pointed at the existence of a "grey area" in interna-tional law. Apart from that, its main contribution, in the present author's view, is that it has started to map out the legal implications of legally non-binding instru-ments, in particular also their relation with full-fledged legal rules. This job per-formed by the authors mentioned above and others belonging to this school of thought[817] is extremely useful, as in international law, because of the lack of a formal organizational structure, "soft-law" rules play a more prominent role than in national legal systems and are likely to do so also in the future.[818]

However, as a result of its preoccupation with the actual operation of the "grey area" the "soft-law" approach has more or less "neglected" the reverse side of the coin: the delimitation of the "grey area" in relation to the white area of the hard law. Its proponents usually concede rather quickly that a certain

811. *Ibidem.*
812. *Ibidem*, p. 304.
813. P. van Dijk, *loc.cit.* (note 5).
814. *Ibidem*, p. 110, where this terminology is offered as more appropriate than Schachter's "non-binding agreement"; see also M. Bothe, *loc.cit.* (note 762), p. 68.
815. *Ibidem.*
816. *Ibidem*, p. 112.
817. See in particular also I. Seidl-Hohenveldern's detailed study on international economic "soft law", *loc.cit.* (note 798).
818. One reason for this is the attractiveness to States of "soft law" because of its flexible character as opposed to the rigidity of the "hard law"; see P. van Dijk, *loc.cit.* (note 5), pp. 115-118; see also M. Bothe, *loc.cit.* (note 762), pp. 88 and 90-92.

instrument is of the "soft-law" type, or at least they test the legal nature of such an instrument only on the basis of the traditional sources of international law. They do not raise, or rather do not make a real effort to answer the question of whether these sources may have been affected by the same developments which partly also have prompted the emergence of new phenomena belonging to the "soft-law" category.[819] This carries the danger of a continuous expansion of the "grey area". From a legal point of view this is an unsatisfactory state of affairs. For, however well-explored the legal implications of the "less-than-full-fledged-legal" phenomena of the "grey area" may be, it is inherent in the very concept of "soft-law" that it entails a certain amount of uncertainty, not only as to its legal implications, but also as to its scope. International lawyers, therefore, should pay equal attention to this reverse side of the coin and try, as far as possible, to "narrow down the grey area".[820] Put a little differently in the terminology employed in the foregoing, the uncertainty of the rule of recognition should be kept to a minimum.[821] A rule of recognition becomes less useful to the extent that the number of rules it is unable "to recognize" becomes larger.

Summing up the present chapter the following conclusions may be drawn. First, the situation in which the traditional sources of international law no longer cover the entire territory of allegedly legal rules should not be remedied by widening the concept of those traditional sources. In the final analysis, such a stretching to make new phenomena fit, does more harm than good. Not only does it sometimes overlook the consensual basis of international law, it also waters down the concept of the sources to the detriment of the latter's clarity and certainty. Instead, it is submitted that a rigidly formulated doctrine of the traditional sources should be supplemented in order to explain the phenomena which the traditional sources cannot account for. In the present author's view this supplementing should not take the form of the "new-source"-approach described above. In its extreme form this approach suggests to create an independent new source every time a new type of instrument would seem to have emerged. As such it provides *ad hoc* and "after the fact" solutions to problems

---

819. However, it should be noted that the "soft law" approach often bypasses this question intentionally; see explicitly P. van Dijk, *loc.cit.* (note 5), pp. 111-112, and implicitly also O. Schachter, *loc.cit.* (note 809), pp. 297-301.

820. It should be noted that efforts "to narrow down the grey area" may run parallel to or even coincide with efforts on the part of the "soft-law" approach "to discern different shades of grey"; see in this respect O. Schachter, *loc.cit.* (note 23), p. 322, who observes that "we should recognize that legal obligations - whether national or international - also may involve 'degrees'"; and P. van Dijk, *loc.cit.* (note 5), p. 120, who expresses the same idea in referring to a situation "in which there is room for 'growth norms', dependent upon the measure of consensus which comes to light in the implementation of politically binding agreements, up to the time that the consensus on goals and their achievement is sufficiently concrete and tested to allow 'petrification' in a legally binding agreement, and further institutionalisation where that is desirable". It may turn out that some of the "shades of grey" thus discerned are so light-coloured that they cannot be told apart from the white area.

821. M. Bothe, *loc.cit.* (note 762), p. 94, gives the impression that a clear-cut distinction between law and non-law can be made without having to resort to "degrees of bindingness". He concedes that "there is often doubt about the 'true' legal solution. This also applies to the definition of the dividing line between legal and non-legal norms, but it is not a problem specific to this distinction". However, in the preceding passage it is upheld that "It does not correspond to the realities of international life, in the light of state practice, to treat the distinction as being a matter of degrees. A certain rule is a legal or a non-legal one; one cannot say that one is more legal than another".

concerning the sources. Because of its *ad hoc* character it unwillingly tends to include what was intended to be excluded and *vice versa*. What is needed conversely is an explanation that is systematic and, in addition, integrated in that it sufficiently links the "supplement" to the traditional sources. Finally, international legal doctrine, while recognizing the existence of the so-called "soft-law" and acknowledging the importance of exploring the "grey area", should make every effort to "narrow down the grey area". While bearing in mind the requirements which a viable doctrine of sources has to satisfy,[822] this implies in fact an attempt at a reformulation of the doctrine of the sources of international law that "reclaims" as much as possible of territory not covered at present.

Subsequent chapters will attempt to sketch an outline of such a reformulated doctrine. Before embarking upon that attempt, two preliminary issues which were already touched upon in the foregoing must be addressed more explicitly. The first one is the question whether the sources of international law can change, while the second concerns the formless character of international law, or alternatively the dilemma between form and formlessness of international law.

822. See *supra* pp. 44-45.

PART III

TENTATIVE REFORMULATION OF THE DOCTRINE OF SOURCES

CHAPTER XI

PRELIMINARY ISSUES

11.1. Can the sources of international law change?

The question as to the possibility for the sources of international law to change is rather seldom addressed explicitly in doctrine. Still, it would seem to be an ineluctable (preliminary) question for anyone dealing with the sources in the light of the changes which have taken place in the international society. As Thirlway has put it, the question is fundamental "to any assessment of claims that a new source of law has come into existence".[823] Furthermore, phrasing the question as to possible new sources as one concerning the possibility of change of existing sources forces one to pay sufficient heed to the link between old and new sources and is, therefore, more likely to produce a systematic and integrated contribution to solving the problem.[824] Another reason for studying the question is that even if not addressed explicitly the question is given an implicit answer in any analysis of the sources of international law. Those who advocate that General Assembly resolutions, for instance, are a new source of international law apparently hold that the sources can change. Others who try to fit these resolutions into the traditional sources or test new phenomena solely on the basis of the traditional sources would seem implicitly to deny the possibility of change of the sources.

Authors expressly facing the issue generally conclude that the sources of international law may indeed change. The much-quoted words of Ross, for instance, leave no doubt that in his opinion the sources cannot be considered as a closed class. According to Ross "the doctrine of the sources can never rest on precepts contained in one among the legal sources the existence of which the doctrine itself was meant to prove. The basis of the doctrine of legal sources is in all cases actual practice and that alone. The attempt to set up authoritative precepts for the sources of law must be regarded as later doctrinal reflections of the facts, which often are incomplete or misleading in the face of reality".[825] To the present author, the heart of this statement is the ascertainment that the question of sources is in the final analysis a matter of fact. As will be pointed out below,[826] this should not be taken to imply that the practice concerning the sources is completely amorphous and that no categories can be deduced from it or, in terms of

---

823. See H. Thirlway, *op.cit.* (note 209), p. 36.
824. See *supra* pp. 190-191.
825. A. Ross, *A Textbook of International Law* (London 1947), p. 83.
826. See *infra* chapter XIII.

a phrase already referred to above,[827] that the sources cannot be stated but only discussed. Subject to this reservation the present author agrees with the observations of Ross.

At first sight, this would also seem to be Fitzmaurice's position, as he comments on the just-quoted words of Ross by saying: "There is clearly a great deal in this view".[828] On closer inspection, however, his own view turns out to be substantially different. Fitzmaurice subsequently upholds that "the sources of law are undiscoverable, as they can never be exhaustively stated - for any proposition to the effect that a, b, c, and d ... (e) ... (f) ... (etc.), are the sources, and the only sources of law, must immediately be falsified by the fact that this proposition could only be established by invoking a further and independent proposition which would give the original proposition itself its validity, but which (requiring as it must a further and separate source) would then, by its very existence, be simultaneously destructive of the original proposition".[829] This eventually leads Fitzmaurice to conclude that "there must be rules of law having an inherent and necessary validity, which are ultimate formal sources of law, but are themselves underived. These are rules of natural law".[830]

Clearly, this position is quite far removed from the one holding that the sources can be changed because they are ultimately practice-based. If Fitzmaurice's train of thought is grasped correctly, however, the divergence might be explained on the basis of the distinction between the three meanings or levels of sources which was set forth above.[831] What Fitzmaurice has in mind here would in fact seem to be the sources or source in the sense of the basis of the binding force of international law rather than the second and third meaning, *viz.* the constitutive element of rules of international law and its manifestations (together forming "the rule of recognition"), which constitute the subject-matter of the question as to the changeability or non-changeability of the sources. Such a different focus not surprisingly may lead to diverging conclusions.[832]

Parry's views on the subject were already alluded to above.[833] He leaves little doubt that to him the question of what the sources are is ultimately to be resolved on the basis of practice. In the case of international law this means the practice of the States: "States are thus not only subjects of the law but they are objects as well: their territory is themselves. Equally, while it is to them the law is given, they are the lawgivers".[834] Moreover, at the end of his analysis of the problem of the sources in general he points out, in reference to article 38 of the Statute, that "Its content ... ought to be examined not so much from the point of

---

827. See *supra* p. 13 note 22.
828. G. Fitzmaurice, *loc.cit.* (note 28), p. 161.
829. *Ibidem.*
830. *Ibidem*, p. 175.
831. See *supra* pp. 57-60.
832. See in this respect the comment on the introduction by G. Fitzmaurice of natural law elements into the concept of the basis of the binding force, *supra* pp. 73-74. See also the observations by H. Thirlway, *op.cit.* (note 209), pp. 37-39, on Fitzmaurice's contention that "the sources of international law cannot be stated, or cannot fully or certainly be stated, in terms of international law itself, and that there are and must be rules of law that have an inherent and necessary validity, in whose absence no system of law at all can exist or be originated", *loc.cit.* (note 28), p. 164.
833. See *supra* p. 63 note 221.
834. C. Parry, *op.cit.* (note 22), p. 8.

view of the Court as from that of the State".[835] Parry's emphasis on state-practice in this respect would seem to imply that he considers the sources changeable through that practice.

Something similar would seem to hold good for Bos. That author's position, too, was already referred to above.[836] It is more or less condensed in the phrase "that the 'sources' as much as the law, are the law-giver's making".[837] His point of view is more specifically explained in reference to the 'consumer' and 'producer' approach.[838] On the question "which of the two approaches should be considered to be the more realistic one" the answer is that "there is no doubt that the 'producer's' approach is the one most deserving the epithet of realism".[839]

In between the two extreme points of view of changeability and unchangeability of the sources there is a school of thought which takes a kind of middle-of-the-road position. Because of this and because of the fact that it relies heavily on certainty and stability which the sources are to provide it is bound to exert a certain attractiveness. This school concedes that the sources may change, but it argues that new sources have to be born out of already existing ones. Because of the link required between the new and the old sources, this frame can be called the "genealogical link" theory.

A clear example of this view can be found in Virally's description of the scope of article 38 of the ICJ's Statute: "If Article 38 be simply declaratory, it clearly cannot inhibit the emergence of new sources of law, brought into being by the development of the international community and its progressive organization. Where, however, new methods of law-making come into use, they are the result of the application of legal rules created by operation of sources already recognized: of treaties, that is to say, and possibly derivatively, of custom. Thus, every imaginable new source is indirectly envisaged in the list in Article 38 and is simply the product of the law emanating from the sources which are mentioned in that list".[840]

In the same vein, Thirlway, after an extensive analysis of the question has concluded that "it appears axiomatic that the class of sources should be a closed class, not in the sense of being invariable, but in the sense we have indicated, namely, of being variable only through a change brought about by the operation of one of the recognized sources, one of the members of the class".[841] Similarly, he asserts that "it is not possible for a rule to the effect that such-and-such a new source of law exists to enter the international legal order otherwise than through

835. *Ibidem.*
836. See *supra* p. 62 note 216.
837. M. Bos, *loc.cit.* (note 28), p. 11.
838. See *infra* pp. 212-214.
839. M. Bos, *loc.cit.* (note 28), p. 13. It should be noted that Parry's observation that the sources of international law cannot be stated but only be discussed, is explained by Bos on the basis of the fact, "that no single normative concept of law exists for international relations, but a plurality of such concepts leading to different theories on 'sources'", *ibidem*, p. 14. At the same time, according to Bos "it should be realized that within each normative concept of law there can be but one conviction at a time with regard to the 'sources' of law and their number. Anybody staying within the limits of his own normative concept of law, therefore, should be able exhaustively to enumerate the 'sources' as he sees it; be it only as categories, without any detailing of what they comprise ...", *ibidem.*
840. M. Virally, *loc.cit.* (note 305), p. 122.
841. H. Thirlway, *op.cit.* (note 209), p. 42.

an existing source of law recognized by the international community".[842]

The "genealogical link" theory certainly constitutes an attractive way of dealing with the question of whether or not the sources of international law can change: on the one hand it leaves room for such changes, while at the same time it provides a large degree of certainty and stability by requiring the new or changed sources to be the product of already existing ones. Nevertheless, in the present author's view the theory is not entirely correct. This may best be explained by taking a closer look at the position of Thirlway who has most extensively argued the theory.

Thirlway seems to make the certainty and stability the alpha and omega of the doctrine of the sources. He unequivocally asserts that "the purpose of a theory of sources is to ensure stability and certainty;".[843] In support of his point of view, moreover, he heavily relies on Hart's theory which was outlined above.[844] In reference to Hart's secondary rule of recognition, for instance, he upholds that "its purpose is to ensure stability and certainty in the ascertainment of law".[845] As such this point is certainly correct. As was explained above, one of the main advantages Hart seeks to gain from his concept of secondary rules is precisely such a greater certainty.[846] However, Hart does not present stability and certainty as absolute values. Indeed, Thirlway would seem to misinterpret Hart in that he overlooks another important point which is equally stressed in the latter's theory. It is the point that the binding force of the secondary rule of recognition is not a matter of validity, *i.e.* it is not derived from any other rule but results from its acceptance in practice. To repeat Hart's own words "the rule of recognition exists only as a complex, but normally concordant, practice of courts, officials, and private persons in identifying the law by reference to certain criteria. Its existence is a matter of fact".[847] Consequently, the actual practice of law-determining agencies in society may give rise to new sources without it being necessary that they are born out of existing sources. One may concede to Thirlway that a genealogical link between old and new sources is desirable or even likely, but it is no necessary requirement of theory, for in the final analysis indeed the sources are the lawgiver's making.

The foregoing may be clarified a little further by once again recalling the distinction between the three levels or meanings of sources, which were set forth above.[848] In referring to the secondary rule of recognition Thirlway is in fact dealing with what was called the second and third meaning of sources, *i.e.* the constitutive element of rules of law and the manifestations of this constitutive element.[849] The implications of the "genealogical link" theory would seem to be correct as far as the second level is concerned. As long as the international society retains the basic features which characterize it at present the constitutive element is bound to remain the consent or acceptance of States. Therefore, in the hypothetical case that another new constitutive element were to arise this

842. *Ibidem*, p. 39.
843. *Ibidem*, p. 42.
844. See *supra* pp. 44-53.
845. H. Thirlway, *op.cit.* (note 209), p. 39.
846. See *supra* p. 47.
847. See *supra* p. 48.
848. See *supra* pp. 57-60.
849. See *supra* pp. 76-82.

would of necessity have to be the result of the consent or acceptance of the States concerned. In this sense Thirlway is correct in claiming a genealogical link between the old and new source.

However, things are different at the third level. Here one finds the manifestations of the constitutive element of consent or acceptance. A number of such manifestations have been "petrified" in the form of the traditional sources of international law contained in article 38 of the Statute of the International Court of Justice. But at this level there are no strict requirements of form as long as a manifestation can be established to constitute an expression of consent or acceptance. There is no reason why States as the lawgivers of the international society could not in their practice develop new forms of expressing consent or signaling acceptance. Moreover, such new manifestations need not in any way to be related to the traditional sources in the way Thirlway has outlined,[850] precisely because old and new manifestations are in the final analysis to be ranked equally as both being (different) manifestations of consent or acceptance.[851]

In summary, the present author, subject to the reservation set out above, agrees with Ross' point of view holding that "The basis of the doctrine of legal sources is in all cases actual practice and that alone".[852] Consequently, it is concluded that the sources, understood in this context as manifestations of consent or acceptance, may be subject to change as a result of changing state-practice. Before proceeding upon the basis of this conclusion it should once again be recalled that the term "state-practice" may in fact have different meanings. In discussing customary international law a distinction was made above[853] between state-practice regarding primary or substantive rules of international law and state-practice regarding secondary or procedural rules (of recognition). The former state-practice *stricto sensu* concerns one particular source of international law, that is the material element of custom (*usus*). It, therefore, consists of the actual behaviour or conduct of States delineating the content of a rule which may eventually become customary international law through the operation of *opinio juris*. The latter state-practice *lato sensu* in fact affects all sources of international law, because it is meant to designate all the attitudes, positions or opinions of States as to what constitutes the (correct) ways of making rules of international law. State-practice *lato sensu*, consequently, includes abstract statements by States on this issue as well. This and the following sections of the present chapter use state-practice in the broad sense unless indicated otherwise.

11.2. The formless character of international law

The foregoing prompts the question as to the degree of form or formlessness in international law. If it is correct, as was concluded in the preceding section, that the sources of international law may change and that they ultimately depend upon the practice of States as the law-givers of the international society, the

---

850. See in particular Thirlway's example of "international legislation", *op.cit.* (note 209), pp. 42-45.
851. See *supra* pp. 81-82.
852. See *supra* p. 195.
853. See *supra* pp. 106-107.

question arises what forms new sources may take in practice or whether there are no requirements of form at all.

There is fairly general agreement in doctrine that the recent history of international law has been witnessing a decline of form. Under the impact of the changes in international relations, notably their increased frequency and intensity, the significance of formalities and solemnities which used to play an important part in traditional international law, is considered to be diminishing. Lachs, in a study specifically devoted to the issue of substance and form in international law, first observes: "At first sight, the international legal order gives the impression of one in which form plays an important role".[854] After pointing to some of the ceremonies accompanying early practice of concluding treaties, he goes on to submit: "However, that is history. Gradually, international practice has manifested a marked decline of form: states began to reach agreements, acquire rights, and accept obligations in the most varied ways. Documents have become workmanlike, and if they still employ stereotyped formulae, that is more for reasons of facility and interpretation than out of a search for talismans - though doubtless some would prefer to view this development as a mere shift in emphasis".[855] Subsequently, he illustrates his point of view by a description of some aspects of "deformalization" which has taken place with respect to the sources of international law, particularly in the case of treaties.

Others have put forward similar views. We have already pointed to the opinion of Verdross. According to Verdross "kann in der GV der VN durch einseitige Erklärungen oder durch formlosen zwischenstaatlichen Konsens ein neues Rechtsprinzip aufgestellt werden".[856] Tomuschat has taken the same position, although he expresses himself in a more direct fashion: "Wenn ... für den Bereich der zwischenstaatlichen Beziehungen die Staaten selbst Träger von Rechtsetzungsmacht sind, so müssen sie ihrem Rechtsgeltungswillen auch ausserhalb von Vertrag oder Gewohnheit jeden anderen sinnfälligen Ausdruck verleihen können, da eine Verfassung der Völkergemeinschaft, welche die Rechtsetzung in bestimmte Kanäle eindämmen und damit formalisieren wurde, bis heute nicht zustandegekommen ist. Einen *numerus clausus* der Rechtsquellen kann es nach alledem nicht geben".[857]

Even the position of the Soviet Union, which for a long time has been known as the most rigid with respect to the sources of international law, has been softened in recent years. Traditionally, Soviet lawyers have heavily favoured treaties as the mode of making international law. Although customary international law was never denied the status of a source, it was always very narrowly defined in the form of the tacit-agreement-theory.[858] The Soviet point of view dismissed the existence of any other sources. Under the influence of the changes in international relations and notably also as a result of the changed strategic position of the Soviet Union in the world, it has now come to recognize a somewhat wider

854. M. Lachs, "Some Reflections on Substance and Form in International Law", in: W. Friedmann, L. Henkin and O. Lissitzyn (eds.), *Transnational Law in a Changing Society; Essays in Honor of Philip C. Jessup* (New York 1972), pp. 99-112 (101).
855. *Ibidem*, pp. 101-102.
856. A. Verdross, *op.cit.* (note 98), pp. 139-140; see also *supra* pp. 000-000.
857. C. Tomuschat, *loc.cit.* (note 762), p. 485.
858. See *supra* pp. 85-86.

range of possible modes of international law-making.[859] In the wake of this changing practice Soviet doctrine, too, seems to be retreating somewhat from its traditional stringent stand and seems to become more outward-looking.[860]

Treaty-making has traditionally been the most formal mode of making international law. Apart from the simplified methods of concluding international agreements which have developed over time,[861] the decline of form in international law is most clearly manifested by the declining role that ceremonial acts play in the conclusion of treaties itself. Even one of the remnants of treaty-making in its traditional form, the act of ratification, is no longer an absolute requirement. Obviously, a treaty requires ratification in order to enter into force if it expressly provides so. However, even before the drafting of the Vienna Convention on the Law of Treaties the question of whether the requirement of ratification holds good also when an instrument is silent in this respect was often answered in the negative. As early as in the thirties, Fitzmaurice among others upheld that treaties do not require ratifiction unless they expressly say so.[862] Similarly, on the basis of a detailed investigation of state-practice in this respect, which shows a decreasing percentage of treaties requiring ratification, Blix concluded as follows: "It would appear therefore that, as the final conclusion of the present article concerning the mode of entry into force of treaties, the following rule emerges, namely that treaties enter into force in accordance with the parties' express or clearly implied intentions, or, in the case of doubt, by signature".[863]

The Vienna Convention does not expressly provide that ratification can be dispensed with if a treaty is silent on the point of entry into force, although it leaves ample room for a conclusion to that effect. The Convention mentions as means of expressing consent to be bound by a treaty signature, exchange of instruments constituting a treaty, ratification, acceptance, approval or accession, or any other means if so agreed (article 11). Subsequently, it simply lists the circumstances in which the consent to be bound by a treaty can be taken to be expressed by these different means (article 12-15). On the question of the requirement of ratification the Vienna Convention, therefore, is at least neutral. Furthermore, on the basis of a study of the *travaux préparatoires* of the Convention Bolintineanu concludes that in particular two characteristics underly the rules concerning the expression of the consent to be bound: first "the autonomy of the will of the negotiating states" and secondly "what has been called 'a decline of form' in international practice, in contradistinction to the reign of formalities and solemnities which had accompanied the conclusion of treaties from ancient times until the 19th century".[864]

---

859. See J. Hazard, "Soviet Tactics in International Law-making", 7 *DJILP* (1977), pp. 9-32.
860. See *ibidem* and for some other examples W. Butler, "Methodological Innovations in Soviet International Legal Doctrine", 32 *YWA* (1978), pp. 334-341; furthermore, a number of indications to this effect can be found in a fairly recent study by G. Tunkin, entitled: "General Theory of Sources of International Law", 19 *IJIL* (1979), pp. 474-482.
861. As was pointed out by M. Lachs, *loc.cit.* (note 854), p. 103: "Besides the treaty in its traditional form, exchanges of notes, correspondence, letters or even telegrams now constitute a considerable proportion of the body of diplomatic law;".
862. G. Fitzmaurice, "Do Treaties Need Ratification?", XV *BYIL* (1934), pp. 113-137 (129).
863. H. Blix, "The Requirement of Ratification", XXX *BYIL* (1953), pp. 352-380 (362-363).
864. A. Bolintineanu, "Expression of Consent to be Bound by a Treaty in the Light of the 1969 Vienna Convention", 68 *AJIL* (1974), pp. 672-686 (673).

To sum up, it is difficult to deny that in international law-making a shift from form towards formlessness is under way. This shift is provoked by societal changes. Particularly, the ever faster rhythm of international relations has more or less forced the international law-making process into new, alternative paths thereby opening up the more or less closed class of traditional sources of international law. The ensuing adaptations in fact result from the requirement that the law keeps up with societal developments. Because of this link between law and society[865] the international law-making process has to meet the (changed) requirements of practice in order to be able to continue to play its regulating and ordering rule. To the extent that they are necessary, adaptations should therefore be accepted and even welcomed.

On the other hand, there is, as was pointed out above,[866] another somewhat countervailing, requirement to be made with respect to the sources of international law. The regulating and ordering task of international law equally requires that the sources provide a sufficient amount of certainty and clarity. One may wonder, therefore, how far the decline of form in international law can go before the line is crossed where it becomes counter-productive. In the present author's view, the doctrine of sources should not accept or, even worse, advocate complete formlessness in the sense of amorphism. To be sure, there may be instances in practice which have to be recognized as forms of expressing consent or acceptane even if it cannot be fitted into prefixed classification or categorization of methods of making international law. But such cases should be exceptions rather than the rule. Indeed, if the doctrine of sources is not able to encompass most cases arising in practice, the regulating and ordering role of international law might be severely hampered.

This latter point is usually also stressed by those who point out that international law is witnessing a decline of form. Lachs, for instance, after signaling a continuous enrichment of instruments expressing the will of States which is frequently described as "reflecting anarchy in this field", concedes: "There is little doubt that greater uniformity could not but benefit both the practice and the theory of international agreements".[867] Equally, Tomuschat has made the observation: "Freilich darf nicht verkannt werden, dass gerade über die zur Rechtserzeugung geeigneten Verfahren Einigkeit bestehen muss".[868] However, the question of how this (greater) uniformity is to be achieved, is not really addressed.[869] Still, in the present time where the focus is on what is called the decline of form in international law, it would seem an important task for doctrine equally to pay attention to the other side of the coin, *i.e.* the question of how to retain or achieve the required degree of formalization. The importance of this task becomes clear if it is remembered that, although the law-making process encompasses a large number of participants, many areas of action, and the homogenization of many interests and values, there must be in any society, for a

865. See *supra* pp. 20-24.
866. See *supra* pp. 24-28.
867. M. Lachs, *loc.cit.* (note 854), p. 104.
868. C. Tomuschat, *loc.cit.* (note 762), p. 485.
869. According to M. Lachs: "all attempts to this end have failed", *loc.cit.* (note 854), p. 104, while C. Tomuschat concludes: "In Hinblick auf die GA-Resolutionen lässt sich aber im Augenblick noch allenfalls das eine feststellen, dass nämlich der Meinungsstand kontrovers sei", *loc.cit.* (note 762), p. 485.

rule to become a legal rule, a narrowing and formalization towards a more technical procedure.[870] To put it a little differently, the sources as the rules of recognition must be able to keep the rules "recognizable" as rules of international law. This requires at least some degree of formalization or systematization of the sources of international law. The following chapter will attempt to sketch the outlines of an approach leading to such a systematization of the "grey area" which is no longer covered by the traditional sources.

---

870. See the words of W. Levi quoted *supra* p. 27; see also P. Weil's observation, *loc. cit.* (note 216), p. 44: "Que le sociologue rende compte des nuances infinies de la réalité, c'est une chose, que le juriste, qui a besoin d'une rigueur simplificatrice, suive son example, c'est une autre".

CHAPTER XII

FIVE PROJECTED CLASSES OF MANIFESTATIONS: GENERAL OBSERVATIONS

12.1. Introduction: points of departure

Part III purports to set forth a (further) systematization of the doctrine of sources of international law with respect to that area of the international law-making process which is not (entirely) covered anymore by the traditional sources. To that end the following chapter will outline five types of manifestations of the consent or acceptance by States which, in the present author's view, may help to provide such a (further) systematization or classification and categorization of law-making as it presently takes place at the international level. These five types or classes are: (1) the general class of abstract statements; (2) the so-called *travaux préparatoires lato sensu* or the way in which the rule or the document concerned has come into being; (3) the text of a rule or document; (4) the follow-up to the rule or the document; and (5) subsequent practice relevant to the rule or document concerned. Before discussing these five classes of manifestations in some detail in the following chapter, some general observations have to be made in the present chapter on a number of considerations and circumstances concerning these various manifestations.

First of all, it should again be noted that in discussing these classes of manifestations we are in fact dealing with the third of the three levels or meanings of sources discerned above.[871] Consequently, the following does not concern the second level anymore and starts from the conclusion that the constitutive element of rules of international law is the consent or acceptance of States. Furthermore, as to the manifestations of consent or acceptance, themselves, Hart's distinction will be taken as a point of departure which discerns between two principal devices for the communication of general standards of behaviour in advance of the successive occasions on which they are to be applied. Hart calls these devices precedent and legislation.[872] Put a little differently, it may be said that basically there are two methods of manifesting consent or acceptance, that is through conduct or through language. In the final analysis the five classes of manifestations to be outlined can all be retraced to these two basic means of communicating general standards in the international society.

The following analysis will mainly concentrate on various forms of communi-

871. See *supra* pp. 57-60.
872. H. Hart, *op.cit.* (note 41), p. 121.

cation of general standards through language. For a number of reasons manifestations by way of conduct take a less prominent place. The first one is to be found in the fact that part of expressions of consent or acceptance manifested through conduct is to be related to customary international law which has already been dealt with in chapter VI. The remaining part of state-conduct relevant to the international law-making process will be discussed under the heading of subsequent practice as one of the five classes of manifestations. A second reason why manifestations through conduct will not play an important role in the following analysis is in fact the same as the one adduced to explain the declining role of customary international law as such.[873] The changes in international society have made the communication of general standards through conduct much more difficult and this has affected both the relevance of conduct as an element of custom as well as the relevance of conduct conceived as a manifestation of consent or acceptance in the form of subsequent practice.

As to the other basic method of communicating general standards, *i.e.* language, a distinction can be made between spoken and written language. Obviously, both can constitute an expression of consent. Traditionally, oral declarations on the part or on behalf of States have been considered capable of giving rise to obligations under international law.[874] However, it is clear that written language is of much greater importance to the international law-making process than spoken language, at least quantitatively. Particularly in modern times the distinction between spoken and written language has become less important as far as international law is concerned. The most important oral declarations of State-representatives are nowadays either recorded within international organizations or otherwise registered. Because of this declined relevance of the distinction between spoken and written words and because of the fact that written documents of course constitute the bulk of the raw material of the international law-making process it would seem justified to focus on the latter.

12.2. International law-making as a continuous process

It has by now become fairly generally recognized that present-day international law-making constitutes a more or less continuous process. Just like diplomatic intercourse has developed from an *ad hoc* into a continuous or at least regular and recurring affair, so has international law-making. This new insight has been pointedly set forth by Tomuschat: "Erinnert sei ferner an die Erkenntnis der neueren Rechtsquellenlehre, dass eine Norm, jedenfalls ausserhalb eines bestimmten engen Kernbereichs, niemals 'fertig' bereit liegt, sondern dass das Recht zutreffend nur als ein prozesshafter Vorgang begriffen werden kann, der niemals zu einem definitiven Abschluss kommt. Der Jurist hat es durchweg mit einer Fülle von Äusserungen über das Recht zu tun, seien diese autoritativer Art, wie im innerstaatlichen Raum ins besondere Gerichtsentscheidungen, oder seien sie lediglich durch Sachverstand legitimiert; auch ihnen wird Rechnung getragen, wenn im Einzelfall die die Auseinandersetzung entscheidende

873. See *supra* pp. 113-116.
874. One of the most well-known instances is the so-called Ihlen Declaration in the *Eastern Greenland* case, Publ. PCIJ, Series A/B, No. 53 (1933); see D. O'Connell, *International Law for Students* (London 1971), p. 85.

Regel aufgefunden werden muss".[875]

The process approach to international law-making advocated here seems to be gaining ground in doctrine.[876] As far as the relation between "codification of international law" and "progressive development of international law" is concerned for instance - being the two major tasks of the International Law Commission[877] - it has become generally conceded that in practice it is extremely difficult to make a clear-cut distinction between these two tasks. According to Jennings "the whole experience of the International Law Commission has shown that there can be no hard-and-fast distinction between codification strictly-so-called and progressive development".[878] Put in somewhat different and more general terms, it has become increasingly difficult with respect to certain rules to say with any certainty what is *lex lata* and what is *lex ferenda*.

The following chapter takes this position of the doctrine of sources of international law just described as a point of departure. Taken together, the five classes of manifestations of consent or acceptance to be outlined there are designed to encompass the entire international law-making cycle. The reason is that every step in the law-making process may contribute to the legally binding (or non-binding) character of a given rule. This means, for instance, that transferring an unwritten rule into a written text often entails some element of elaboration, adaptation or even alteration. As was explained by De Visscher: "Codification is never a mere 'declaration' (restatement) of alleged existing rules; it always aims to replace divergent practices with some unity in the interpretation and application of the law. It is therefore upon the object and purpose of the rules that governments are asked to agree, on the practices that they intend to follow and those that they are willing to amend or abandon. This is a task very different from that of the jurist exclusively concerned with formal technique".[879] Somewhat similarly Jennings has upheld that "quite apart from the creation of treaty obligations, the very writing down of existing unwritten law brings about changes in the nature of that law. It is not just a question of the difficulties of drafting and of language; though that is important. It is the availability of the considered writing that makes the effect of law in this form different, if only because the canons of interpretation are at once changes".[880]

875. C. Tomuschat, *loc.cit.* (note 762), p. 481.
876. E. McWhinney even claims that "International law on this view has never been a closed system of legal categories that jelled once and for all in some bygone era, but a dynamic, continually operating process of rejection or refinement of old rules; and the confirmation of new ones in supplement or replacement of the old", *op.cit.* (note 33, p. 1; see also p. 16).
877. The two terms are defined in article 15 of the Statute of the International Law Commission as follows: "The expression 'progressive development of international law' is used for convenience as meaning the preparation of draft conventions on subjects which have not yet been regulated by international law or in regard to which the law has not yet been sufficiently developed in the practice of States. Similarly, the expression 'codification of international law' is used for convenience as meaning the more precise formulation and systematization of rules of international law in fields where there already has been extensive State-practice, precedent and doctrine".
878. R. Jennings, *loc.cit.* (note 1), p. 62; see also F. Vallat, "The Work of the International Law Commission - The Law of Treaties", XXII *NILR* (1975), pp. 327-336 (335).
879. C. de Visscher, *op.cit.* (note 109), p. 150.
880. R. Jennings, "General Course on Principles of International Law", 121 *RCADI* (1967-II), pp. 323-606 (337); see also M. Virally, *loc.cit.* (note 305), p. 142, according to whom "any attempt at codification of a customary rule involves, inevitably, an attempt also to improve, supplement and generally reformulate the rule in the light of contemporary conditions".

The same element of "newness" contained in the very act of writing down a rule may be involved, although sometimes less dramatically, in the other consecutive steps which together make up the international law-making cycle or process. It is these consecutive steps which the proposed five classes of manifestations want to systematize thereby making them more "recognizable".[881]

12.3. The relation between the classes of manifestations of consent or acceptance and the traditional sources of international law

It should be reiterated that the classes of manifestations of consent or acceptance proposed in the following are in no way meant to replace the traditional sources of international law, but are rather designed to supplement the latter. As was made clear in Part II, it may be true that recent decades have witnessed the rise of new phenomena in the international law-making process, this does not detract from the fact that the traditional sources still have an important role to play. Traditional sources and new phenomena therefore operate side by side. In the present author's view, the new law-making phenomena have to be explained by doctrine in a way which is consistent with the traditional sources.[882] In other words, the theoretical explanation of the new phenomena has at least to be compatible with the theoretical foundation of the traditional sources. Viewed from this perspective the traditional sources can be considered as manifestations of consent or acceptance which are already "petrified" in the doctrine of sources, while the new classes of manifestations at this moment still constitute "less established" additions.

Furthermore, the traditional sources and the new law-making phenomena do not simply operate side by side, at the same time they are closely intertwined. The new insights of the doctrine of sources referred to in the preceding section imply that a (further) systematization of those phenomena through which the legally binding or non-binding character of a rule may be "recognized" is not only relevant in the case of rules belonging to the "grey area" where the legally binding or non-binding character is in doubt, but also with respect to rules of a full-fledged legal nature. Since international law-making has become a continuous process, it is clear that even such full-fledged rules do not always remain unaltered until they are formally changed or replaced, for instance by a (new) treaty or customary rule of international law. Rules like these may also be affected, that is elaborated, adapted or altered, through, for instance, the follow-up to the rule or through subsequent practice. Schreuer has formulated the same position as follows: "A closer look at the realities of international decision-making shows that an attempt to divide the law into neatly separate rules which can be allocated to official types of sources is not satisfactory. Very often it is impossible to base a decision or even a general prescription on any one type of source. The process of communication leading to legal expectations and to a conduct corresponding to them, can take place in a variety of forms which are

881. All this is not to imply that every rule must necessarily follow each of the above-mentioned steps making up the law-making cycle.
882. See *supra* p. 191.

interrelated and often not clearly distinguishable. Even a relatively clear-cut prescription like a treaty provision is in constant interaction with other types of international law, from its drafting up to its application, and can lead a decision-maker through the whole mare of sources of international law".[883]

Even in the case of full-fledged legal rules the best way to determine the precise character, scope and ultimately the content of a given rule is to take into account all its relevant features in the various stages of the law-making process. The classes of manifestations of consent or acceptance set forth in the next chapter are therefore useful also in the case of full-fledged legal rules because together they are designed to encompass the entire law-making cycle.

12.4. The relation between the various classes of manifestations of consent or acceptance inter se

Most of what has been observed in the preceding section with respect to the relation between the classes of manifestations and the traditional sources applies *mutatis mutandis* to the relation between the various classes of manifestations *inter se*. The development which has made international law-making a continuous process entails consequences particularly in respect of rules belonging to the "grey area" where the legally binding or non-binding character is most open to doubt. In order to be able to determine the precise legal nature of such rules it is necessary to take into account all the relevant elements of the law-making cycle, or to put it differently, all the points of "recognition" which may occur during the various stages of the lifetime of a rule.

A reliable picture cannot result from singling out one element at the expense of others. The fact, for instance, that a rule is contained in a resolution of the United Nations' General Assembly as such suggests that it is not a legally binding rule. However, other characteristics such as the way in which it came into existence, its text and the connection with already existing rules, and the state-practice in relation to the rule may very well point in the direction of a different conclusion. Moreover, the dividing line between binding and non-binding is often a thin one and the transition between the two is not seldom fluid. Therefore, a snapshot taken at a particular moment is not likely to present a reliable picture. Such an approach is bound to overlook the fact that earlier or later elements in the cycle may have added or will add to the binding or non-binding nature of a rule.[884] A correct picture can best be obtained from taking a process approach to the question involved. As was pointed out, this is what the five classes of manifestations are intended to do.

---

883. C. Schreuer, *loc.cit.* (note 762), pp. 112-113.
884. A good example constitutes the status of the negotiating text of the draft treaty resulting from the Third United Nations Conference on the Law of the Sea discussed by R. Jennings, *loc.cit.* (note 1), pp. 82-83: "The transference of negotiating text into treaty text will yet be another moment of truth for the whole exercise. For then there is a danger that the document may actually lose some part of its authority it already seems to possess. It is then no longer an instrument, considerable parts of which can be said to represent a consensus of the international community; but simply a draft treaty, which by definition binds only those which ratify, and will not, apart from the somewhat limited possibilities of provisional application, come into effect for any, until 60 or so ratifications have been deposited".

In addition, because they each relate to a particular stage of the law-making process, the successive classes of manifestations of consent or acceptance proposed here represent a kind of chronological order. This is particularly clear with respect to the *travaux préparatoires lato sensu*, the text, the follow-up, and the subsequent practice. On the other hand, the chronology is not very strict. In particular, abstract statements may be made by States at any stage and do not necessarily have to precede the other classes. Still, some chronological order is usually involved and it is important to stick to that order as much as possible, because this is likely to result in the best solutions possible to the questions which the five proposed classes of manifestations are designed to answer.

Finally, it has to be pointed out that the five classes of manifestations of consent or acceptance are interrelated in still another way. In order to determine the legally binding or non-binding character of a rule or document the "results" registered in one class may affect those obtained in another. A rule or document may "score" high in one class, but very low in another. In such a case the negative result may counterbalance the positive one. Obviously, the picture may be further complicated. The point is that the "results" in all classes have to be taken into account before conclusions can be drawn. All this indicates that "measuring" the legally binding or non-binding nature of a rule or document on the basis of the proposed five classes will not in all cases lead to clear-cut answers. It is therefore unlikely that the "grey area" between law and non-law can always be completely done away with. This is no problem in cases where States deliberately kept the legal or non-legal nature of a rule in doubt in order, for instance, to attain a certain degree of flexibility in the regulation concerned.[885] It is submitted, however, that in general the proposed classes of manifestations are capable of at least narrowing down the "grey area".[886]

12.5. The role of international organizations

It is probably no exaggeration to say that particularly in recent decades the continuous character of the international law-making process has been more or less "incarnated" by the phenomenon of international organizations. Generally speaking, the rise of international organizations can be considered as a response to the challenges posed by the increased and increasing speed and intensity of modern international relations. More specifically, international organizations *inter alia* constitute an answer to the requirements of modern international law-making.

It was already pointed out that the phenomenon of international organizations cannot be considered as a revolutionary deviation from traditional diplomatic intercourse. As a rule international organizations are not institutions or entities placed above States, but rather instruments of coordination and cooperation in the hands of States enabling them to look after common interests in a more structured way and on a permanent basis. In the final analysis, therefore, international organizations have not really changed the nature of international relations, but rather represent a new way of conducting them.[887] International

885. See *supra* p. 189 note 818.
886. See *supra* p. 190 and note 820.
887. See *supra* pp. 63-64.

organizations may be said to have added new dimensions to the international law-making process. It is impossible to evaluate satisfactorily the achievements of international organizations in this respect in a few lines. First, international organizations cannot all be put on the same line. The multifarious differences between the various international organizations also affect their functioning and their "effectiveness" as far as law-making is concerned. Secondly, the achievements of international organizations are difficult to measure in exact terms, because no hard and fast criteria are available; a certain degree of generalization is therefore inevitable. Nevertheless, some evaluating observations on this issue can be made.[888]

In the decentralized international society it may well be one of the most valuable contributions of international organizations to the law-making process that they provide a framework for regular contacts between the representatives of States. In this way States are offered a possibility to exchange points of view. It is very important to have a permanent device through which States can learn the views of other States on important issues of international relations. This gives States the opportunity to take into account these views of others. Beyond that, international organizations may promote a more international outlook in the foreign policy of States. Through what has been called the "influence bienfaisante du milieu"[889] of international organizations, States might be induced to give more emphasis to common interests in shaping their national and foreign policies. International organizations, therefore, can be instrumental in the forging of consensus on issues on which there was formerly disagreement.

Furthermore, a merit of international organizations is constituted by the fact that they have, to a considerable extent, institutionalized and formalized the international law-making process. This institutionalization and ensuing formalization have an important psychological effect: it is usually easier for States to avoid legal ties on an *ad hoc* basis with other States than to withdraw from the law-making process within the framework of an international organization. By such a step the State concerned would place itself more or less outside the community established by the organization. This would, in most cases, turn out to be more disadvantageous to that State than staying in the organization and subjecting itself to the pressures emanating from it. In short, international organizations can be said to exert some kind of social constraint upon member States to adapt to common interests. In this sense international organizations may sometimes give body to a more or less hidden sense of community.

The institutionalization, formalization, and in particular also the permanency which international organizations provide have had as a result that a great deal of law-making efforts at the international plane today take place within the framework of these organizations. Various stages of the law-making cycle are nowadays part of the work of international organizations. For instance, the preparation and drafting, the conclusion and acceptance of a text, as well as the follow-up are often conducted by or under the auspices of international organiz-

888. See for a detailed evaluation of the pro's and con's of international organizations I. Claude, *Swords into Plowshares, The Problems and Progress of International Organization*, 4th edition (New York 1971); in particular chapters 15, 18 and 19.
889. This expression was first used by the French diplomat Louis Renault to describe his experiences at the Second Hague Peace Conference of 1907.

ations. And even if some stages or elements take place outside the framework of international organizations, such as subsequent state-practice, evidence thereof can often be found in the records of international organizations. In this way, the activities of international organizations frequently constitute a kind of focal point of the international law-making process. Because of the institutionalization, formalization and permanency they entail, international organizations provide a fairly overall and at the same time "condensed" picture of the international law-making process. It is clear, therefore, that the search for manifestations of consent or acceptance of States must focus to a large extent on activities within the framework of international organizations.

12.6. The producer-consumer distinction

Finally, one general aspect concerning the manifestations of consent or acceptance should be discussed here. It concerns the distinction between the "producer" and the "consumer" approach to international law to which we have referred repeatedly in the foregoing. In the present author's view, the producer-consumer distinction can be very helpful as a general frame of reference, when the question has to be answered of whether and to which degree what States say and do in a particular case is relevant or not to the process of building a norm of international law. As will be pointed out, however, it does not provide a hard and fast solution to all the difficult cases which may in fact arise.

The distinction between "producers" and "consumers" of law has been elaborated by Bos.[890] According to Bos, the purpose of the quest of the sources is to know where the law may be found and ultimately to find out what the law is. These are typical "consumer" questions, not asked by the "producer" of law, the legislator, invested with all law-creating power. "In the national legal order, the principal 'consumers' of law are individuals and corporations under private law. In those national legal orders in which the State and the lower bodies corporate under public law are liable to appear in Court, they, too, in their capacity as defendants may be termed 'consumers' of the law. In this capacity, indeed, they are not empowered to create law. Called upon to justify their acts according to law, they are not allowed to invoke any other rules than those appearing in the official 'sources', exactly like their individual or corporate counterparts. This is why, before the Courts, the State and the lower bodies of necessity share the latter's interest in the 'sources' of the law. But no sooner do they act as 'producers' of law than they lose their interest: making the law themselves, how could they be interested in existing law, if not for purely informative purposes?".[891]

As to international law, Bos upholds, the situation is in fact the same, although there is a difference of degree. International adjudication, as being optional, is the exception rather than the rule and out of court States take a different attitude: "Out of Court, they are fully aware of their role as 'producers' of international law, and as a result the 'sources' of international law lose much of their meaning to them. For the sake of argument, they then may, nevertheless,

890. M. Bos, *loc. cit.* (note 28), pp. 11-13.
891. *Ibidem*, p. 11.

have recourse to the 'sources', but also may assert a 'source' which in Court would stand no chance of being accepted."[892]

As far as international law is concerned this analysis can, in the present author's view, be taken one step further. From the perspective of States as "producers" of international law it is true that, out of court, the sources lose much of their meaning. Viewed from the perspective of doctrine, however, the producer-consumer distinction may still be relevant in such a situation. Doctrine (and for that matter a State as "consumer" too) may find itself in the position where it is faced with the question of whether an asserted "source" (understood as a manifestation of consent or acceptance) stands indeed a chance of being accepted by other States as "producers" and thus whether the rule, which the asserted "source" is to accommodate, is indeed a rule of international law. Outside the framework of a court-situation it may also happen that a State asserts a "source" which stands no chance of being accepted, not in this case by a court, but by other States. Viewed from this perspective, therefore, with respect to situations out of court, too, a distinction can be made between a "producer" and a "consumer" approach to international law.

If the present author is not mistaken, a somewhat similar idea would seem to underly the distinction between law and politics which we have described above.[893] As was pointed out, doctrine sometimes equates "politics" with a State's self-interest narrowly conceived. "Politics" is thus made opposite to "law" which is held to represent the general interest. It is not difficult to understand that writers who define politics in this way sometimes reach the conclusion in analyzing a concrete case that what a particular State said or did has (had) no law-making effect, because it was "politically motivated". Schreuer's words would to seem to be a case in point, when he observes with respect to declaratory resolutions of the United Nations' General Assembly: "There is, moreover, a distinct danger that in preparing allegedly declaratory resolutions, Members will be strongly influenced by their political preferences. If so-called declaratory resolutions really become accepted as an authoritative expression of existing international law, there will be a strong temptation to establish legislative desiderata by way of declarations. A majority strongly committed to a particular policy in a legal controversy, would find it only too easy decisively to improve its position by declaring its position as a statement of existing law".[894] To the extent that this statement is to convey the idea that not everything what States say and do is equally relevant to the process of making international law, the present author agrees. The terminology employed, however, is not very fortunate as it implies the contraposition of law and politics. Obviously, the activities of States as political entities are almost always political in the sense we described above.[895] At any rate this holds good for activities related to international law-making. The distinction between "producers" and "consumers" of law would seem better suited to bear out the fact that state-practice (*lato sensu*) sometimes makes a greater, sometimes a smaller, and sometimes no contribution at all to the process of building a particular norm of international law.

---

892. *Ibidem*, p. 12.
893. See *supra* pp. 24-25.
894. C. Schreuer, *loc.cit.* (note 762), p. 111.
895. See *supra* pp. 24-25.

The producer-consumer distinction is no panacae for all puzzling questions which may arise in practice. Because of the decentralized character of decision in the international society resulting in the situation in which the States are at the same time the law-givers and the subjects of international law, elements of both the "producer" and the "consumer" approach are likely to be represented in the attitude a certain State takes at a given moment. Consequently, the distinction between a "producer" or "consumer" position is not a black-and-white one, but rather a question of more or less. It is difficult to outline *in abstracto* when the "producer" elements will outweigh the "consumer" elements and *vice versa*. Generally speaking, one cannot deny the proposition put forward by Bothe that "a certain *favor seriositatis* should be granted to states".[896] It may be conceded, therefore, that as a point of departure it will have to be presumed that States acted in a "producer" position. Nevertheless, in concrete cases States may prove to be "consumers" rather than "producers". For instance, if a State is directly involved in a controversy or dispute, it will usually lack the degree of detachment which would seem to be required of a law-giver. In short it is submitted that the producer-consumer distinction despite its imperfections may be a useful tool for analysis in concrete cases, because it keeps alive the awareness that not all state-practice *lato sensu* is equally relevant or instrumental to the international law-making process.

896. M. Bothe, *loc.cit.* (note 762), p. 85.

CHAPTER XIII

OUTLINE OF THE INDIVIDUAL CLASSES OF MANIFESTATIONS OF CONSENT OR ACCEPTANCE

13.1. Introduction

On the basis of the general observations set forth in the preceding chapter, the present chapter purports to outline five classes of manifestations of consent or acceptance by States. It thus constitutes an attempt to reformulate the doctrine of sources of international law with respect to those new (allegedly) law-making phenomena which the traditional sources do no longer cover entirely. It should by stressed once again that the various classes as presented here are not intended as a substitute, but as a supplement to the traditional sources of international law. Therefore, they are to be resorted to only in cases where the question as to whether a certain rule is rule of international law cannot by sufficiently answered on the basis of the traditional sources.

The term "reformulate" requires some explanation, as it entails a number of limitations on the analysis which is to follow. First, it was argued above that the sources of international law in the final analysis are a matter of fact, *i.e.* is the question as to what the sources are has to be answered on the basis of the practice of States *lato sensu.* This point of view implies that a doctrinal analysis of the sources, if it is to be of any practical value, cannot go beyond this state-practice; it cannot put forward (new) sources which have no basis in what States actually say and do. Doctrine, in this conception, must systematize, categorize, classify and clarify the sources of international law to be found in state-practice *lato sensu.* In this sense doctrine is to be "descriptive".

Secondly, "reformulate" implies that the points of view put forward are not completely new. Preceding chapters have shown that the literature on the sources of international law has already dealt extensively with the new (allegedly) law-making phenomena to which state-practice has given rise. Equally, it has started to map out a systematization, categorization, classification and clarification of these new phenomena.[897] The following analysis will build on the work already undertaken in doctrine. As was pointed out, it purports to enhance the "recognizability" of rules of international law by a further systematization of the criteria for the legal or non-legal character set forth in international legal doctrine.

---

897. An example constitutes Schreuer's study on the relation between recommendations and the traditional sources of international law, see C. Schreuer, *loc.cit.* (note 762).

With respect to this further systematization one final point should be kept in mind. The criteria which the various classes of manifestations provide may relate to a document or instrument as a whole or to a particular provision or rule contained in that document or instrument. These criteria, in other words, may be of a collective or of an individual character. The name of a document, for instance, has a bearing upon the status of the entire document and this bearing obviously is the same for all the provisions contained in it. The criterion of the name may, therefore, be said to have a collective character. Conversely, the precise wording of the text is relevant first and foremost with respect to the rule concerned and consequently has a more individual character. All the classes of manifestations may contain criteria of both a collective and an individual character. It is important to be aware of this distinction between collective and individual criteria, because as a result two provisions or rules contained in one and the same document do not necessarily have to be on the same line as far as their binding or non-binding character is concerned. Because of the fact that not all the criteria apply equally to such provisions, the one may be legally binding while the other is not, or, in reference to the "grey area", the one may come closer to a legally binding rule than the other.

13.2. Abstract statements

In discussing the concept of custom in international law above we subscribed to Akehurst's proposition that "It is impossible to study modern international law without taking account of declaratory resolutions and other statements made by states *in abstracto* concerning the content of international law".[898] It was argued that, although such resolutions and declarations cannot be classified as *usus*, they may constitute *opinio juris* which, if expressed with respect to a rule sufficiently delineated through *usus*, can give rise to a customary rule of international law. Abstract statements, in the form of resolutions or otherwise, may also play a role in the law-making process outside the framework of customary international law. Even if not accompanied by *usus*, abstract statements made by States may reflect their position or opinion with respect to an (alleged) rule of international law. However, for a number of reasons it may be difficult to decide whether a particular statement is relevant in this respect or not.

The category or class of abstract statements as manifestations of the consent of States is a most difficult one to outline, because it contains very few elements which lend themselves to systematization. First, it constitutes a kind of overall class which is designed to encompass elements which are not covered by any of the other classes. States can of course make statements containing indications as to their approval or non-approval of a certain rule at any time. Often such statements are made within the framework of the *travaux préparatoires* or the follow-up with respect to a certain rule and can then best be dealt with in that con-

898. See *supra* p. 107.

text.[899] On the other hand, States also make statements signaling approval or non-approval in situations which are not (directly) covered by these or one of the other classes of manifestations, that is in situations not specifically aimed at making rules. This may occur, for instance, when States are gathered at international conferences which are not specifically aimed at drawing up such rules[900] or, more generally, at (bilateral or multilateral) meetings between representatives of States.[901] This includes (other than specifically rule-making) meetings within the framework of international organizations, like the meetings during the annual sessions of the United Nations' General Assembly.[902] Because statements made at these occasions are not covered by any other class of manifestations and may still be relevant it was felt necessary to make abstract statements a separate class. The term "abstract" is meant in particular to bear out that this class concerns statements made in a context other than specific rule-making efforts.

The fact that abstract statements are not directly related to specific rule-making efforts makes the class discussed here quite amorphous. This situation is compounded by the fact that States as political entities make many statements and it is usually far from easy to exactly trace their intentions in making a particular statement. Their law-making will is often disguised and difficult to determine. As a result it is sometimes tempting to assume a law-making intention on the part of a State or States too easily. Such an assumption may have an adverse effect, if afterwards it turns out to be wrong. With respect to abstract statements, therefore, it is particularly important to keep in mind the producer-consumer distinction referred to above, because it helps to discern between situations where States do act as law-givers and those in which they find themselves more in the (consumer) position of a claimant pointing out what they would like the law to be rather than what it is.

Even with the aid of the producer-consumer distinction, however, it may still be difficult to decide whether a particular statement does indeed contain relevant indications concerning the consent of a State or States. This question can be

---

899. Within the framework of law-making processes designed to deal with a specific field States sometimes make statements which have no direct bearing upon the subject under discussion but which may be relevant to a related field or rule of international law. During the Vienna Conference on the Law of Treaties, for instance, several participants explained their position on the concept of customary international law. Within the framework of the United Nations Conference on the Law of the Sea an example would seem to be the statement of 15 September 1978 "Declaring the Position of the Group of 77 on Unilateral Legislation affecting the Resources of the Deep Seabed", referred to by R. Jennings, *loc. cit.* (note 1), p. 86. In reaction to United States' and German legislation on deep-sea mining this statement upheld that there "is no practice, much less custom in the legal sense, of actual exploitation of the seabed beyond national jurisdiction which could be deemed as a legal right or grounds for such exploitation".

900. The International Conference on Human Rights held at Teheran in 1968, for instance, adopted the so-called Proclamation of Teheran which *inter alia* solemnly proclaims that "The Universal Declaration of Human Rights ... constitutes an obligation for the members of the international community". See 63 *AJIL* (1969), pp. 674-677.

901. The statements made at such conferences or meetings may also be unilateral statements, which can also have legal effects. See in this respect J. Sicault, "Du Caractère Obligatoire des Engagements Unilatéraux en Droit International Public", 83 *RGDIP* (1979), pp. 633-688.

902. See, for instance, Resolution 2442 (XXIII) of 19 December 1968, by which the General Assembly endorsed the Proclamation of Teheran mentioned in note 900.

answered only on a case-by-case basis. It all depends on the precise content of the statement concerned and on the context in which it was made. Many abstract statements by States contain relevant indications, but in the present author's view it is probably quite exceptional that one such statement taken by itself suffices to conclude that the State or States concerned have indeed consented and are thus legally bound by the rule or rules in question. To arrive at such a conclusion both the content and the context of the statement must unequivocally point in that direction. As a rule this will not be the case and the abstract statement will have to be combined with other available evidence, such as other abstract statements,[903] the relation with existing rules of international law in the same or in related fields, and possibly the (subsequent) practice of the State(s) concerned.[904] In most cases abstract statements will not by themselves establish a new rule of international law but rather signal the beginning of the process by which an existing rule is going to be abolished and by which the creation of a new rule is set in motion.[905]

In short the present author believes that consent solely on the basis of an abstract statement cannot lightly be presumed. It would seem that the standard to be applied to abstract statements allegedly expressing consent must sometimes even be stricter than that applicable to statements concerning *opinio juris*. In discussing customary international law it was observed that *opinio juris* should be as unequivocal as possible.[906] This holds good *a fortiori* for the expression of consent through abstract statements, because in the case of *opinio juris* there always exists already an *usus* delineating the content of the rule. Consequently, the object of the *opinio juris* is comparatively clear. When it has to be decided whether abstract statements express consent, such clarifying circumstances are not seldom lacking.[907]

Finally, one other issue has to be addressed here. Throughout this section we have referred to abstract statements which express the consent of States without mentioning the possibility of acceptance by States. The reason, of course, is that a statement can only be an express manifestation of consent, while acceptance was said to refer to a tacit manifestation of consent.[908] Nevertheless, the question arises whether there are cases where the silence on the part of a State justifies the conclusion that it has the intention to be bound by a particular rule. Although this question is relevant also in relation to the class of manifestations discussed here, its ramifications, as will be pointed out, go beyond that.

903. Mere repetition of a State's position in a series of abstract statements does not necessarily enhance the legal status of that position; see also *infra* p. 241, note 991.
904. J. Watson, *loc.cit.* (note 34), p. 632, submits in this respect that "There is, of course, no direct causal relationship between a state's verbal position on a topic and its subsequent practice".
905. Examples are the 1970 Declaration of Lima, 10 *ILM* (1971), p. 207 and the 1972 Declaration of Santo Domingo, 11 *ILM* (1972), p. 892 with respect to the so-called "patrimonial sea". At the time this concept would seem to have been incompatible with the principle of freedom of the high seas. However, these declarations have turned out to be the precursors of the concept of the Exclusive Economic Zone contained in the new law of the sea.
906. See *supra* p. 182.
907. I. Seidl-Hohenveldern, *loc.cit.* (note 798), p. 189, follows a similar line of reasoning with respect to "instant customary international law": "The existence of an *opinio juris*, coupled with at least one instance of practice, thus appears sufficient to create 'instant customary international law'. As a kind of compensation, requirement as to the proof of *opinio juris* may have become stricter".
908. See *supra* p. 77.

Generally speaking, there would seem to be a tendency in doctrine to adhere to the point of view that "silence gives consent" as Jessup has pointedly summarized it.[909] Meijers, for instance, upholds that "he who does not protest consents".[910] Now, consent through silence, or in our terminology acceptance, would seem to be possible only in reaction to a manifestation of the intention to be bound on the part of another State or other States. Consent through silence or acceptance without there being an object to relate the silence to would seem to be inconceivable. In other words, there must be at least one pre-existing manifestation of the intention to be bound by one State which is clear enough to make it possible for another State to react. Meijers would seem to have the same requirement in mind, when he observes that "The manifestation of the will to create law must occur in such a manner that it is sufficiently perceptible for all potential subjects of that law".[911] If this requirement of "perceptibility" is fulfilled, it would not seem unreasonable to hold that silence may be a relevant indication with respect to a State's consent. If the State concerned does not want to become bound by the (proposed) rule, it can protest or reject it and thus avoid to become legally bound.

In addition, it should be taken into account that in deciding whether a State's silence is relevant, "perceptibility" may vary from State to State depending upon the particular situation. In abstract situations discussed here, *i.e.* outside the framework of processes or efforts specifically aimed at drawing up rules, "perceptibility" may be assumed only on the part of States whose interests are directly involved in the subject matter which the (proposed) rule is to address. In specifically rule-making situations "perceptibility" may be presumed on the part of States which participate in the law-making process. Consequently, the "silence gives consent" proposition is likely to be of greater relevance in the latter situations, which will be discussed below.

13.3. Travaux préparatoires lato sensu

13.3.1. Introduction

Unlike the class of abstract statements, the class of manifestations discussed here relates to situations which are specifically aimed at making rules. This is implied in the words *travaux préparatoires*. The question to be addressed, of course, is whether the ensuing rules are of a legal or of a non-legal character.

In the case of a treaty the process which gives rise to the birth of legal rules includes the following steps: preparation of the text, adoption of the text, authentication of the text, and the expression of consent to be bound by the text.[912] These latter steps of authentication and, in particular, of the expression

---

909. P. Jessup, "Silence Gives Consent", 3 *GJICL* (1973), pp. 46-54.
910. H. Meijers, *loc.cit.* (note 204), p. 20.
911. *Ibidem.*
912. Compare the above-mentioned application by H. Meijers of his stages-theory to the consecutive steps involved in the conclusion of a treaty, *supra* p. 92.

of consent to be bound are highly formalized in the present state of international law. The Vienna Convention on the Law of Treaties lays down procedures for authentication[913] and, more importantly, means for expressing consent to be bound.[914] Consequently, if such (formal) means of expressing consent to be bound are provided for, it is clear that the States concerned entered into the rule-making situation with the intention to create rules of international law. In these cases comparatively few problems arise.

What we purport to deal with here is the increasing number of cases where it is not immediately clear whether the States concerned intended to create rules of international law or not, because such formalized signals as specific means for expressing consent are lacking. Then it may be necessary to rely more heavily on the phases of preparation and adoption[915] in order to detect the intention of States. *The term travaux préparatoires lato sensu* encompasses the various features of the process of preparation and adoption of a text or a rule which may be relevant in determining its binding or non-binding nature. The present class of manifestations, therefore, encompasses more than the *travaux préparatoires stricto sensu* which, in the case of treaty-rules, are usually taken to designate the documents directly related to the drafting history of the treaty concerned.[916] What we have in mind here are in fact all circumstances accompanying the preparation and adoption of a text.

These circumstances obviously include the decision-making process through which the content of a text is settled or, in other words, the decision-making process of adoption. We will discuss this decision-making process as a separate subclass. It is tempting to single out the decision-making process from the *travaux préparatoires lato sensu* and put emphasis on it, because it lends itself rather well to systematization and even formalization. This is particularly so when "decision-making" is narrowly defined and confined to the actual casting of votes. Indeed, there has been a great deal of writing after the Second World War on these formal voting arrangements of international conferences and international organizations. However justified this focus has been and still is, recent years have witnessed a growing recognition of the fact that formal voting arrangements, and for that matter the sheer number of votes, do not usually tell the whole story. Because of the changes in the international society resulting in an increased heterogeneity and interdependence, it is now necessary in many instances to go beyond the formal voting arrangements. Majority decisions and even unanimously adopted texts often require recourse to the preparatory works in order to better understand their legally binding or non-binding nature. With respect to treaties article 32 of the Vienna Convention designates the preparatory works as supplementary means of interpretation. In relation to less for-

---

913. Article 10.
914. Articles 11-17.
915. In these cases adoption of a text possibly includes its authentication. The distinction between adoption and authentication is rather subtle. Adoption may be defined as the act by which the contents of a text are settled, while authentication is the act certifying the text as correct and definitive. Adoption takes place through voting, which must be taken to constitute authentication at the same time, when no separate act of authentication follows, as in the case of a text voted upon in organs of international organizations.
916. Article 32 of the Vienna Convention on the Law of Treaties lists the preparatory work as a supplementary means of interpretation.

mal texts they may be more and help to determine the legal or non-legal nature of the text concerned. These manifestations other than formal voting arrangements contained in the *travaux préparatoires lato sensu* will be discussed under the subclass of circumstances of preparation and adoption.

As a result of developments in practice the difference between circumstances of preparation and adoption on the one hand and the decision-making process on the other has become less distinct. As was pointed out, modern international law is characterized by growing formlessness. As far as decision-making is concerned this trend is reflected in the increased use of the so-called consensus-technique. As will be elaborated below, the consensus-technique constitutes in important respects the opposite of decision-making on the basis of formal voting procedures. In short, it is decision-making broadly defined. The consensus-technique encompasses not only the actual adoption of a text, but also various elements of the preparations and negotiations preceding that adoption. It should be kept in mind therefore that, as far as the consensus-technique is concerned, the sub-class of the decision-making process may (partly) overlap the sub-class of circumstances of preparation and adoption. Because this overlap is only partly and, more importantly, because it occurs to a lesser extent in the case of formal voting procedures it was thought useful to divide the *travaux préparatoires lato sensu* into two sub-classes.

13.3.2. Circumstances of preparation and adoption

The circumstances of preparation and adoption which may have a bearing upon the binding or non-binding character of a text or a rule are primarily the product of the general setting in which preparation and adoption take place. Two general types of situations can be discerned in this respect, *i.e. ad hoc* conferences on the one hand and rule-making efforts within the framework of international organizations on the other hand.

A conference may be convened specifically for the purpose of drawing up a text. In that case all kinds of procedural arrangements must be provided for which may differ from case to case entailing different consequences with respect to the binding or non-binding nature of the ensuing rules. Comparatively few problems arise when it is clear from the outset that the participating States intended the conference to result in a treaty. After the treaty has entered into force there is no uncertainty about the existence of legal obligations on the part of those States which have expressed their consent to be bound through ratification or otherwise as provided for. States that have not (yet) done so, do not in principle incur legal obligations. Nevertheless, circumstances accompanying preparation and adoption may be relevant in determining the (legal) implications of the draft-treaty before it enters into force or, after it has entered into force, in pinpointing the (legal) position of States that are not (yet) parties to the treaty.

Circumstances of preparation and adoption gain added weight when it is unclear at the beginning whether the conference was intended to result in a legally binding instrument. An illustrative example constitutes the Conference on Security and Co-operation in Europe. The so-called Final Recommendations of the Helsinki Consultations, which laid down the organizational and

other arrangements for the Conference, left vague the precise character of the documents in which the outcome of the Conference were to be contained.[917] In fact the Recommendations only stipulated that "The Conference will adopt its final documents, in formal sessions, ... " (point 12), and that "The principles to be stated shall be included in a document of appropriate form ... " (point 18). This vagueness has prompted a heavier reliance upon various (other) aspects of the *travaux préparatoires lato sensu* in order to determine the binding or non-binding character of the Helsinki Final Act, which resulted from the Conference on Security and Co-operation in Europe. Some, for instance, have concluded that the Helsinki Final Act is not a legally binding document *inter alia* on the basis of the fact that it was never contemplated that the Final Act had to be ratified.[918] In reaction, it has been pointed out that the level of State-representatives which signed the Helsinki Final Act - Heads of State and Heads of Government - was considerably higher than in the case of most treaties and conventions and that this "naturally adds very considerably to the binding force of the commitments assumed and would seem to compensate, to some extent at least, for the absence of a ratification process".[919]

Another example from the Conference on Security and Co-operation in Europe is offered by the emphasis on statements of State-representatives as indications for the status of the Helsinki Final Act. These do not primarily concern statements on (proposed) substantial provisions of that document during the second phase of the Conference (which can be considered as forming part of the consensus-procedure or technique), but rather the general addresses of the Ministers of Foreign Affairs and the Heads of State and of Government during the first and third phase of the Conference respectively. Several of these addresses implicitly or explicitly dealt with the question as to the precise legal status of the Helsinki Final Act.[920] In addition, the statements taken into account include those contained in the so-called "Communiqué Dialogue"[921] consisting of a series of declarations emanating from the Warsaw Pact and NATO respectively which date from the period preceding the Conference.[922]

The second major type of situation referred to above, that of rule-making efforts within the framework of international organizations, is slightly different.

---

917. See Publication No. 115 of the Netherlands Ministry of Foreign Affairs cited in note 4, pp. 186-209.
918. See, for instance, K. Skubiszewski, "Der Rechtskarakter der KSZE-Schlussakte", in: R. Bernhardt, I. von Münch, and W. Rudolf (eds.), *Drittes deutsch-polnisches Juristen-Kolloquium*, Band I: *KSZE-Schlussakte* (Baden-Baden 1977), pp. 13-30 (15).
919. D. Nincic, "The Nature and Significance of the Final Act of the Conference on Security and Co-operation in Europe", *RYDI* (1977), pp. 5-19 (15). Compare in this respect M. Bothe, *loc.cit.* (note 762), p. 74, who doubts the constitutional authority of the Egyptian President and the Israeli Prime Minister within the framework of the Camp David agreement to enter into a *pactum de negotiando* according to which the two countries "agree to negotiate in good faith with a goal of concluding within three months of the signing of this framework a peace treaty between them".
920. See the study of A. Klafkowski cited in note 6.
921. This term was introduced by F. Schramm e.a. (eds.), *Sicherheitskonferenz in Europa; Dokumentation 1973-1978* (Köln 1978), p. XVII.
922. See, for instance, P. van Dijk, *loc.cit.* (note 5), pp. 100-103, and T. Schweisfurth, "Zur Frage der Rechtsnatur, Verbindlichkeit und Völkerrechtlichen Relevanz der KSZE-Schlussakte", 36 *ZaöRV* (1976), pp. 681-726 (688-689).

Generally speaking, the procedural arrangements of the organization concerned will be applicable and the ensuing rules must be presumed to have the (legal or non-legal) character provided for in these arrangements. If the constitution of an international organization opens the possibility for (one of) its organs to take binding decisions, legal ties come into being after the conditions laid down have been fulfilled. If, conversely, the constitution provides for non-binding resolutions only, like in the case of the United Nations' General Assembly, all rules emanating from the organ concerned must in principle be held to be of a non-legal nature even for States voting in favour.

However, the presumption of non-binding force is refutable. As has been pointed out by Bothe: "a vote for a resolution is not equivalent to a declaration to be bound under the law of treaties. On the other hand, it is not legally impossible, depending on the circumstances, for a State, when voting on a resolution, to declare its consent to be bound by the terms thereof at the same time".[923] What may be said to take place in such a case is that the States concerned, by expressing their intention to be bound, "waive" the regular effects of a positive vote concerning a non-binding instrument.

The conclusion that this is indeed the case must be based on all the available evidence from the various manifestations. The precise wording of the text concerned constitutes a major factor in this respect. In the case, for instance, that a resolution of the General Assembly expressly states that it sets forth rules of international law, it is difficult to deny that the States which declared themselves in favour are legally bound by these rules, despite the general presumption of the legally non-binding character of General Assembly resolutions. Of course, in practice most cases are less clear-cut. Then the use of the consensus-procedure instead of, or rather next to the formal voting arrangements in itself may constitute an indication that the intention exists to become legally bound. This is not to say that rules of international law come into being every time the consensus-procedure is employed. Through the consensus-procedure States can also manifest their intention not to become legally bound. The point is, however, that the presumption of the legally non-binding character may become refutable, because the nature of the consensus-procedure is such that one can sometimes more reliably determine whether the States concerned intended legal ties or not. As will be argued in the following section, this is so because of the element of "deliberateness" of the consensus-technique - efforts are focused on producing rules - and because of the sometimes detailed and penetrating character of the process which may lead States to unveil more of their precise intentions.

As far as the present class of *travaux préparatoires* is concerned such unveiling manifestations may be deduced not only from preparatory documents themselves, but also from more *lato sensu* aspects. An example constitutes the thoroughness of the actual preparation, which according to some is made dependent upon the question of whether the preparation was conducted by legal experts. Some, for instance, tend to look more favourably upon drafts prepared by the International Law Commission than upon those drawn up by poli-

---

923. M. Bothe, *loc.cit.* (note 762), p. 69.

tical bodies. There is no doubt that the expertise of the International Law Commission may enhance the quality of the legal rules which may ensue from the law-making process. Experience shows, on the other hand, that involvement of the International Law Commission is no guarantee for a speedy and successful conclusion of the law-making process. At any rate, there is no *a priori* reason to regard drafts prepared by political bodies as inferior.

Certainly, one cannot go as far as to make the participation of lawyers in the preparatory work one of the conditions for deciding whether or not a text is binding. Russell would seem to come close to this position when he maintains that the political (as opposed to the legally binding) character of the Helsinki Final Act can be deduced *inter alia* from the fact that it was "negotiated largely by diplomats and not by lawyers".[924] However, when lawyers participate in negotiations, they often do so as diplomats and not in their capacity of (independent) legal experts.[925] Many diplomats, conversely, are not lawyers but this does not in any way affect the status of the texts or rules resulting from their negotiations. What may matter is whether these are thoroughly drafted, but it does not matter whether this is done by lawyers or by others with or without the help of lawyers.

13.3.3. The decision-making process

13.3.3.1. Introduction

The present section dealing with the decision-making process will focus on the so-called consensus-technique.[926] The reasons for this emphasis on consensus

---

924. H. Russell, "The Helsinki-Declaration: Brobdingnag or Lilliput?", 70 *AJIL* (1976), pp. 242-272 (248).
925. See in this respect L. Henkin, *op.cit.* (note 228), p. 32: "The scope and content of international law are commonly credited to (or blamed upon) lawyers. That is error. For international as for national law, law-making is a political act, the work of politicians; lawyers, *qua* lawyers, contribute to that process only peripherally and interstitially -when they advise and provide technical assistance to policy-makers engaged in law-making; when they interpret and apply the law in advising political actors, or in handling claims between their governments and others".
926. The following studies on decision-making have in particular been used for guidance: B. Buzan, *loc.cit.* (note 236); W. Jenks, "Unanimity, The Veto, Weighted Voting, Special and Simple Majorities and Consensus as Modes of Decision in International Organisations", in: *Cambridge Essays in International Law: Essays in Honour of Lord McNair* (London/New York 1965), pp. 48-63; R. Kearney, *loc.cit.* (note 25); N. Lateef, *loc.cit* (note 252); L. Sohn, "Voting Procedures in United Nations Conferences for the Codification of International Law", 69 *AJIL* (1975), pp. 310-353; E. Suy, "The Meaning of Consensus in Multilateral Diplomacy", in: R. Akkerman e.a. (eds.), *Liber Röling, Declarations on Principles; A Quest for Universal Peace* (Leyden 1977), pp. 247-257; P. Szasz, *loc. cit.* (note 253); A. Tammes, *loc. cit.* (note 762); D. Vignes, "Will the Third Conference on the Law of the Sea Work According to the Consensus Rule?", 69 *AJIL* (1975), pp. 119-129; and S. Zamora, *loc.cit.* (note 800).

was already touched upon: there seems to be an trend towards an increased use of consensus as a mode of decision-making in international practice. Buzan has cited some fifteen examples of international organizations and conferences which have employed the consensus-technique since the mid 1960's.[927] More specifically with respect to international economic organizations Zamora has observed that "The avoidance of confrontation through formal voting has become an important part of these and other economic agencies".[928] As to the United Nations Lateef upholds that "it is desirable to de-emphasize the voting process as an invariable way of making decisions. The consensus process can handily and constructively supplant formal votes for recording the sentiments of states".[929]

As far as decision-making processes based on formal voting arrangements are concerned, it was already pointed out that in cases where the constitution of an international organization or the procedural arrangements of a conference provide for binding decisions, legal obligations come into being after the required conditions have been fulfilled. If, conversely, only non-binding resolutions are provided for, the documents or rules ensuing from the decision-making process concerned must be presumed to be of a legally non-binding character. It was submitted, however, that this presumption may be refuted on the basis of evidence from the various classes of manifestations. Both in the case of unanimously adopted resolutions and of those adopted by majority-vote, States voting in favour may at the same time express their intention to be legally bound. As far as the class of the *travaux préparatoires lato sensu* is concerned, a law-making intention may be deduced from the statements of a certain State during the negotiations preceding the adoption of a text, or from an explanation of votes through which a State clarifies its position with respect to (parts of) the text at the moment of adoption.

Nowadays protracted negotiations, elaborate clarification by States of their positions, and explanation of votes often take place also before the adoption of a resolution within the framework of international organizations which are equipped with formal voting arrangements. Various resolutions of the United Nations General Assembly provide examples of this. If and to the extent that this occurs, the decision-making process in such cases comes close to, or even coincides with the consensus-technique as it will be described in the following. What in fact happens is the substitution of the formal voting procedures - the rule of unanimity or some type of majority-rule - by the consensus-procedure, even though the formal voting arrangements may still play a role in the background.[930] These cases in fact coincide with those cases where the consensus-technique is employed in a more express manner and the intention of States to be legally bound or not has therefore to be traced in the same way.

---

927. B. Buzan, *loc.cit.* (note 236), p. 326.
928. S. Zamora, *loc.cit.* (note 800), p. 568.
929. N. Lateef, *loc.cit.* (note 252), p. 41.
930. See *infra* pp. 229-230.

13.3.3.2. The increased use of the consensus-technique

Recent years have witnessed an increased use of the consensus-technique. In essence this technique is aimed at the continuation of negotiations until a compromise has been reached which makes it possible to avoid voting. The reasons for the increased use of the consensus-technique - both explicitly and more implicitly within the framework of international organizations - are to be found, in the final analysis, in the changes in the international society which has grown more heterogeneous as well as more interdependent.[931] As a result the rule of unanimity and the majority-rule have become less suitable as modes of decision-making in present-day international relations, at least at international conferences and within international organizations with a large an heterogeneous participation. There is no need to describe the developments with respect to unanimity and majority in great detail here, as others have already done so.[932] Their major drawbacks may be summarized as follows.

The problem with unanimous voting is, of course, that it is extremely difficult to bring about any decision at all. Particularly after the international society has grown more heterogeneous, States frequently hold diverging points of view. Consequently, a proposal which is simply put to the vote is unlikely to find unanimous approval. At least a number of States is likely to feel unable to give it an unqualified "yes". Thus it has become virtually impossible to rally the votes of all States behind a certain proposal without intensive and often protracted negotiations to make the proposal more or less generally acceptable. This prompts a tendency towards an increased use of the consensus-technique.

The majority-rule for its part is also hampered by a serious drawback. Although the majority rule ensures a rather smooth working of the decision-making process in itself, the ensuing decisions are often difficult to implement or to put into practice, because substantial, sometimes powerful minorities may resist them; the majority-rule suffers in the words of Buzan from a "divorce of power from the voting majorities".[933] On the other hand, given the situation of interdependence in which the international society finds itself, effective decision-making on many issues is badly needed. This effectiveness cannot be attained through "automatic" majorities on the basis of a formal majority-rule.

Theoretically, a system of weighted voting could remedy the handicap of the majority-rule and restore the link between power or responsibility and voting strength. Generally speaking, systems of weighted voting do not allot votes on the basis of formal equality, but in a way which takes into account the relative power, strength or importance of the States concerned. In practice, however, the introduction of one or another system of weighted voting would not seem to be feasible, at least not in the framework of general political organizations or conferences. First, it is probably impossible to reach agreement on any formula on the basis of which the weighting of votes would have to take place. A second obstacle would be that "as the great majority of the States at present voting in international organizations considers that it benefits from the existing rules, no

---

931. See *supra* pp. 65-71.
932. See in particular the lucid survey by S. Zamora, *loc.cit.* (note 800), pp. 571-576 and the references provided there.
933. B. Buzan, *loc.cit.* (note 236), p. 326.

voluntary change is likely and probably no involuntary one could be imposed".[934] Even in the economic field, which used to be the most susceptible to weighting of votes, Zamora has noticed a "general pressure to reverse the post-World War II tendency towards the creation of organizations with weighted voting systems, and to restore relative equality in voting procedures".[935]

Because of its nature, which will be outlined in the following sections, the consensus-technique would seem to combine a number of characteristics which make it possible to overcome the drawbacks inherent in the other modes of decision-making, while retaining at least some of their advantages. These advantages have been summarized by Charney, according to whom the consensus-technique "assures that decision-making at a multilateral negotiation ... will not be dominated by the numerical superiority of any group of nations. Rather, procedural significance will be given to the variations in the power of nations. Since it is difficult to obtain acceptance of voting systems that overtly recognize the differences in nations' importance, the consensus approach permits the maintenance of an egalitarian procedure which in practice may assure that multilateral negotiations reflect the real geopolitical power of the participating nations".[936]

13.3.3.3. The nature of the consensus-technique

The consensus-technique would still seem to be in the midst of development, but it has on the other hand been sufficiently discussed and used in practice to allow an outline of its main traits. From the outset a distinction must be made between the so-called *consensus-procedure* and what is labeled as the *consensus-compromise*. The former refers to the method used to bring a text or a rule about, the latter designates the compromise flowing from the consensus-procedure.[937] It is of course the consensus-procedure which is the most relevant in the discussion of the sub-class of decision-making. The consensus-compromise itself, which obviously constitutes an important element in determining the legally binding or non-binding character of the rule or rules contained in it, will be dealt with under the heading of the text.

As to the meaning of the consensus-procedure, Suy has defined it *in abstracto* as the adoption of a text without a vote and by no objection.[938] According to Szasz consensus "constitutes something of a reversion of the classical unanimity principle" and "may be defined briefly as taking a decision only when no participant opposes it so strongly as to insist on blocking it".[939] In reference to the United Nations Lateef observes that "Adoption of a resolution by consensus does not imply that all members present in the U.N. body fully or

---

934. See P. Szasz, *loc.cit.* (note 253), p. 528.
935. S. Zamora, *loc.cit.* (note 800), p. 599.
936. J. Charney, "United States Interests in a Convention on the Law of the Sea: The Case for Continued Efforts", 11 *VJTL* (1978), pp. 39-68 (43).
937. See E. Suy, *loc.cit.* (note 926), p. 271.
938. *Ibidem*, p. 266.
939. P. Szasz, *loc.cit.* (note 253), p. 529.

unanimously support the entire contents, but rather that no one opposes the contents strongly enough to insist upon the right to vote against the text".[940] As will be elaborated in a moment, each of these statements highlights an important characteristic of the consensus-procedure, which also seems to be emphasized in arrangements laying down the use of the consensus-technique in practice.

In practice the consensus-procedure has been taking shape through *inter alia* the following instances. A fairly early example was Resolution 1995 (XIX) on the Establishment of the United Nations Conference on Trade and Development as an organ of the General Assembly, adopted by the General Assembly on December 30, 1964. It stipulated, after laying down the two-thirds majority rule and the simple majority rule for matters of substance and of procedure respectively, that "The procedures set forth in the present paragraph are designed to provide a process of conciliation to take place before voting and to provide an adequate basis for the adoption of recommendations with regard to proposals of a specific nature for action substantially affecting the economic or financial interests of particular countries". Following the introductory texture paragraph 25 outlined in great detail the afore-said conciliatory process.[941]

Further well-known instances in which the consensus-procedure has been used are the drawing up of Resolution 2625 (XIV) of October 24, 1970 containing the Declaration on Principles of International Law concerning Friendly Relations and Cooperation among States[942] and the Third United Nations Conference on the Law of the Sea. In the latter case the term "consensus" does not appear in the Conference's rules of procedure themselves, but is mentioned in the so-called Gentleman's Agreement[943] which provides that the "Conference should make every effort to reach agreement on substantive matters by way of consensus and there should be no voting on such matters until all efforts at consensus have been exhausted". In addition Rules 37-40 inclusive lay down a number of procedures by which voting can be postponed in order to ensure that all efforts at reaching consensus have indeed been exhausted, and as a fall-back position formal voting rights and the required majority in cases consensus cannot be reached.[944]

Similarly, decision-making at the so-called "Conference on International Economic Cooperation", held at Paris in December 1975, was conducted according to the consensus-rule. In the Final Declaration of the Preparatory Meeting for that Conference of October 16, 1975 it was stated in paragraph 16

---

940. N. Lateef, *loc. cit.* (note 252), p. 41, note 94. Compare also the more general description by R. Jennings, *loc. cit.* (note 1), p. 80: "Consensus is much more flexible than an abstention mechanism; for it means that things get through when minorities do not feel minded actively and vigorously to oppose. And their torpor may be induced by more than sentiment. It may be a package deal, for instance. It may be all kinds of things. But that it has worked surprisingly effectively, nobody can deny".

941. See United Nations General Assembly Resolution 1995 (XIX) of December 30, 1964; see also M. Hardy, "Decision Making at the Law of the Sea Conference", 11 *RBDI* (1975), pp. 442-474 (445-446).

942. See *United Nations General Assembly Official Records*, 20th session, Annex III, 1965, agenda items 90 and 94, p. 81; and *United Nations General Assembly Official Records*, 25th session, 1970, supplement No. 18/A/8018, p. 1.

943. See *UN Doc.*A/CONF.62/30/Rev.2, pp. 8-9 and 17 (1976).

944. On the adoption of the rules of procedure of the Third Conference on the Law of the Sea, see L. Sohn, *loc. cit.* (note 926), pp. 333-352, and B. Buzan, *loc. cit.* (note 236), pp. 331-333.

that "The Preparatory Meeting recommends that the Conference adopt the Rules of Procedure which it has adopted itself, and which are based in particular on the principle of 'consensus', according to which decisions and recommendations are adopted when the Chair has established that no member delegation has made any objection".[945]

Another example is to be found in the Final Recommendations of the Helsinki Consultations which constituted the basis of the work of the Conference on Security and Cooperation in Europe. Paragraph (4) of Chapter 6 on the Rules of Procedure reads: "Decisions of the Conference shall be taken by consensus. Consensus shall be understood to mean the absence of any objection by a Representative and submitted by him as constituting an obstacle to the taking of the decision in question".[946]

The picture of the consensus-procedure emerging from the foregoing may be summarized by the key-words of "non-voting", "non-objection", and what may be labeled as "thoroughness". Each of these elements will be dealt with briefly in the following sections.

13.3.3.4. Non-voting

As far as the element of non-voting is concerned, Suy has pointed out that the absence of voting is not an absolute requirement and that in some instances a vote may be taken as a mere formality after the consensus-compromise has been reached.[947] Most of the time, however, a consensus-procedure ends more informally, for instance by the conclusion of the Chairman, registering the sense of the meeting, that there exists no objection to the proposal concerned.

Nevertheless, as the above-mentioned examples show, formal voting arrangements are often maintained next to the consensus-procedure. The reasons thereof are quite obvious: the formal voting arrangements constitute an incentive to reach consensus and at the same time a fall-back position in case consensus cannot be reached. In the words of Szasz "since an unqualified consensus rule still permits any participant to exercise a veto, and thus, if determined and independent enough, to exact a high price for its agreement, the now frequently used qualified rule maintains the possibility to revert to voting if the consensus process breaks down. This alternative is, however, resorted to only if the dissenters are considered to constitute a small, unreasonable and substantively overridable minority. In practice, the threat to revert to voting is one merely maintained in the background to prevent any egregious abuse of the general desire to do business by consensus".[948] In the same vein Zamora upholds that "Even where decisions are often taken informally, the resort to formal voting procedures remains a possibility and may have a profound effect on the willingness of members to arrive at a consensus, as well as on the type of con-

945. *United Nations General Assembly Documents* A/C.2/299, 27 October 1975.
946. See Publication No. 115 of the Netherlands Ministry of Foreign Affairs, *op.cit.* (note 4), p. 204.
947. E. Suy, *loc.cit.* (note 926), p. 271.
948. P. Szasz, *loc.cit.* (note 253), pp. 529-530.

sensus or compromise reached".[949] The consensus-procedure is aimed at preventing resort to voting and the role of formal voting arrangements within the framework of a consensus-technique may therefore be summarized in the words of Buzan stating that "voting rules must be there, but they must not be used".[950]

Despite the possibility of resort to voting as an incentive to reach agreement, the consensus-procedure as an informal mode of decision-making entails a number of obvious dangers. First, the process may be so slow that it runs the risk of being outran by events. Second, there is an increased risk that the outcome may be no decision at all or one which is unworkable because it represents too low a common denominator. Such a situation may be produced by the attitude of the participants in the process for whom, because of the informal nature of the consensus-procedure, it becomes "rational strategy to hold out as long as possible in the hope that the other side will concede first".[951] It should be observed from the outset that it makes sense to denounce the consensus-technique for flaws like these only if better ways of proceeding towards general agreement are available. Given the structure of the international society at this time, the present author finds himself unable to come up with a satisfactory alternative. Consequently, the most promising course would seem to consist of attempting to improve the consensus-procedure.

Practice has been witnessing developments in, or rather refinement of the consensus-procedure which would seem to obviate to some extent the disadvantages just referred to. A notable example constitutes the experience with consensus of the United Nations Conference on the Law of the Sea, which has been analyzed in considerable detail by Buzan. Buzan describes the developments at UNCLOS as a step from the *passive consensus* -procedure "which is the mere substitution of consensus for voting as a way of making decisions"[952] to the *active consensus*-procedure consisting of techniques designed "to push the process of consensus formation".[953] The heart of the techniques employed at UNCLOS lies in fact in the expansion of the powers of the Chairman. When at a certain moment UNCLOS came close to a deadlock, the proposal was accepted which mandated the Chairmen of the three main committees of the Conference to produce informal drafts (in the terminology of UNCLOS: informal single negotiating texts) covering the agendas of their respective committees.[954] Later this system was elaborated so as to give a broader set of Chairmen the same power on a narrower set of problems.[955]

The advantages to be gained from the use of these techniques are the following: first, it enhances "an outcome to the various stages of negotiation", and second it provides "incentives to the delegates themselves to initiate compromises

949. S. Zamora, *loc.cit.* (note 800), pp. 568-569.
950. B. Buzan, *loc.cit.* (note 236), p. 339.
951. *Ibidem,* p. 333.
952. *Ibidem,* p. 329.
953. *Ibidem,* p. 328.
954. *Ibidem,* p. 334.
955. *Ibidem,* p. 337.

for fear of leaving their fate in the Chairmen's hands".[956] This makes clear that the active consensus-procedure can to some extent at least alleviate the slowness and inconclusiveness which may result from the passive consensus-procedure. To be sure, this is not the same thing as saying that the use of an active consensus-procedure can guarantee that consensus on a text or a rule with sufficient substance will be reached.

The expediency of the active consensus-procedure would seem to be based to no small extent on the fact that it goes a long way towards constituting a kind of situation of third-party-decision.[957] Strictly speaking, the techniques of the active consensus-procedure do not amount to third-party-decision, but may rather be described as a situation of third-party-initiative. This "right of initiative" enables the Chairman, through the tabling of (new) proposals, to keep the process moving if a deadlock is threatening. Moreover, the participating States, consciously or unconsciously, support this initiative, because they are forced to react to the Chairman's proposals. If they keep silent, the Chairman's proposals will get through. Thus, the Chairman as a "third party" can play a pivotal role even though he lacks formal decision-making powers. Similarly, on a somewhat different level third-party-elements also surface in the form of the part played by Secretariats in the law-making process. According to Kearney "The Secretariat's contribution is a feature in the current development of international law. In nearly all United Nations activities that deal with the international law-making process, the Secretariat plays an active role".[958]

13.3.3.5. Non-objection

These just-mentioned "third-party-elements" should be no cause for forgetting that within the framework of the consensus-procedure, too, a State can disagree. This brings us to the second key-word used above to describe the nature of the consensus-procedure, i.e. non-objection. A State can at all times object and say no to a proposal. A reminder of this fact is to be found in the restriction introduced on the Chairmen's powers mentioned above at a later stage of UNCLOS. When the participating States became dissatisfied with the role of a

---

956. *Ibidem*, p. 335. Two further advantages mentioned by Buzan are related more specifically to UNCLOS: "Third, it offered prospects of progress towards an agreed convention. And fourth, it offered a mechanism whereby compromises worked out amongst interested private groups of delegates could be given some kind of working status in relation to the conference as a whole" (*ibidem*).

957. R. Kearney, *loc.cit.* (note 25), p. 506. S. Zamora, *loc.cit.* (note 800), p. 605, refers to what seems to come close to a situation of third-party-decision, *i.e.* the role of the World Bank's management and secretariat: "According to one study, most effective decisions in the World Bank are made not by the membership as a whole, but by a relatively small group of top-level management and experts from the capital-exporting countries, with staff-members making the less important decisions on the basis of agreed rules". This situation is attributed *inter alia* to high goal consensus among members, *ibidem*, p. 606. However, at another place he comments in reference *inter alia* to the World Bank: "The developing countries, more dependent on these organizations for aid in solving economic problems, submit themselves to decisions arrived at by consensus greatly influenced by the developed countries", *ibidem*, p. 592, note 104.

958. R. Kearney, *loc.cit.* (note 25), p. 506.

particular Chairman, the "right of initiative" was toned down. The rules were changed to the effect that "Any modifications or revisions to be made in the Informal Composite Negotiating Text should emerge from the negotiations themselves and should not be introduced on the initiative of any single person, whether it be the President or a Chairman of a Committee, unless presented to the Plenary and found, from widespread and substantial support prevailing in Plenary, to offer a substantially improved prospect for consensus".[959] In the same way the work of Secretariats may be counter-productive, if they play too active a role which runs counter to the positions of (part of) the participating States.[960]

On the whole the use of the consensus-technique may be said to provide for a setting which may enhance the readiness of States to accept the rule or rules proposed. In addition to the elements which may be contained in a consensus-procedure itself, the consensus-technique in general is surrounded by psychological incentives for States not to object. As has been observed by Tammes: "When something substantial has emerged from the early discussions, when amendments have been added and compromises inserted in order to meet the opposition, the final product is the work of the whole, rather than of the majority, and minorities may find it more and more difficult completely to deny or reject that product when, in the course of the successive legislative stages, it gains in weight and approval. The argument will be used that you cannot permit the result of long preparations, of laborious discussions and of happily reached compromises to be entirely lost in sight of the harbour".[961] The same psychological mechanism is operative at a later stage, *i.e.* after a rule has been accepted as binding by a (large) number of States. This is probably what Tunkin has in mind when he says that "Force of circumstances compels individual States in the majority of circumstances to consider as binding those norms which the overwhelming majority of States already have recognized ... ".[962] Such a force of circumstances or force of facts may indeed exert considerable pressure upon States, particularly within the framework of a consensus-procedure, and this may play an important role in forging agreement.[963] However, it should once again be stressed that the consensus-technique, although it compares favourably to more formal decision-making procedures in this respect, does not offer a guarantee for success.

959. See B. Buzan, *loc.cit.* (note 236), pp. 336-338.
960. For an example see N. Lateef, *loc.cit.* (note 252), p. 16.
961. A. Tammes, *loc.cit.* (note 762), p. 287.
962. G. Tunkin, *op.cit.* (note 50), p. 129.
963. See also M. Akehurst, *loc.cit.* (note 282), p. 27: "Unless dissenting States are numerous, they seldom maintain their dissent for long". He goes on to clarify this "force of facts" by the following example: "Since 1950 a new customary rule has gradually developed, allowing coastal States exclusive fishing rights for twelve miles (or possibly more) from their shores, and replacing the old rule which limited them to three miles. The United Kingdom dissented from the new rule. In theory the United Kingdom remained entitled to fish in the same area as before. In practice, however, the United Kingdom found it virtually impossible to enforce its rights (Iceland's disregard of the International Court's judgment in the *Fisheries Jurisdiction* case is a striking example). Meanwhile, the seas three miles of the British coast continued to be fished by foreign trawlers, which increased in number as they were excluded from fishing grounds of other States' coasts. The United Kingdom thus suffered all the disadvantages of upholding the three-mile limit, without enjoying any of the advantages in practice - a situation which eventually induced the United Kingdom to claim, with some exceptions, a twelve-mile exclusive fishing zone".

13.3.3.6. Thoroughness

Finally, there is the third characteristic of the consensus-procedure which was summarily called above its thoroughness. Thoroughness may also characterize decision- making processes resulting in formal voting if this is preceded by extensive negotiations. However, thoroughness is most typical for the consensus-technique. This thoroughness contributes most to the fact that the consensus-procedure enhances the possibilities for more accurately determining whether States intended to create legally binding or non-binding rules. This characteristic results from the deliberateness of the consensus-process.[964] In order to bring about rules which can effectively operate in the heterogeneous and interdependent community of States of today, negotiations must often be penetrating on many issues. This setting forces States to go into great detail in explaining their points of view and clarifying their positions. The question of whether the ensuing rules are rules of law can be more accurately answered because of the detailed character of the process. Thus, the consensus-procedure in many instances offers comparatively reliable handholds for detecting the intention of States.

The manifestations of consent or acceptance of States through the consensus-procedure can also be more subtle than through formal voting arrangements. When negotiations go into great detail, there exists of course a variety of possibilities between an outright no and a full-hearted yes to a proposal. Non-objection does not exclude the possibility that a State has a different point of view on one or more of the issues contained in the compromise. The thorough and detailed character of the consensus-procedure leaves ample room for registering such deviating points of view. A good illustration of this constitutes the discussion on the organization of the work of the Ad Hoc Committee on the Review of the Role of the United Nations in the field of disarmament.[965] During this discussion it was proposed that "delegations should ... try to achieve unanimous agreement on as many issues as possible on the understanding that the views of delegations and groups of delegations would be fully recorded in the report".[966] In response, one representative stated that the expression "unanimous agreement" implied the absence of any reservation, while "consensus" merely implied non-opposition.[967] The Chairman finally summed up the discussion in the following manner: "delegations ... wish to make every effort to achieve the broadest agreement on as many of the issues before them as possible, with the provision that delegations may have their own comments and proposals recorded in the report in addition to those findings and proposals adopted without objection by the Committee".[968]

In short, the consensus-procedure provides mechanisms for registering the intentions of States which are more refined than when the decision-making pro-

---

964. See P. Szasz, *loc.cit.* (note 253), p. 530.
965. The Committee was established by United Nations General Assembly Resolution 3404B (XXX) of 12 December 1955.
966. *UN Doc.*A/AC.181/SR.2, p. 5.
967. *UN Doc.*A/AC.181/SR.5, p. 5.
968. *UN Doc.*A/AC.181/SR.6, p. 3.

cess leads to voting without substantive negotiations. Because of this refined character of the consensus-procedure the efforts to determine the legally binding or non-binding character of the ensuing rules are often quite laborious. Moreover, the picture thus gathered may be complex. The outcome may be, for instance, that some provisions contained in the compromise have a status different from the others. Similarly, one and the same provisions may turn out to be binding for most States but not for one or a few other States. Nevertheless, despite this greater complexity, the indications as to the intention of States to be found in the consensus-procedure are usually more reliable than a mere positive vote concerning a non-binding instrument.

Finally, it should be reiterated that despite all the incentives not to object which are operative within the framework of a consensus-procedure, a State which is determined not to become bound, will not become bound. It is therefore correct to uphold that it is "impossible to overcome the resistance of a persistent objector".[969] In the final analysis, within the framework of a consensus-procedure the consent or acceptance of States is also decisive. However, when there are indications that a rule of international law is proposed and the consensus-procedure results in the non-objection of all States concerned, it cannot be said to be "a very different thing from a genuinely unanimous meeting of minds".[970] What may be different is the way in which the consent or acceptance is manifested. Within the framework of a consensus-procedure tacit consent, or rather acceptance, is sufficient and may even be the prevailing routine. This is so because the thorough and detailed character of the process results in a high degree of "perceptibility".[971] The consensus-procedure constitutes a specific rule-making effort and all participating States know when a legally binding rule is proposed. There is ample room to object and a State is expected to do so, if it does not want to become bound. If a State does not speak its mind, it may then legitimately be held to have intended to become legally bound by the proposed rule of international law. Within the framework of a consensus-procedure, therefore, it may genuinely be said that "silence gives consent".[972]

13.4. The Text

13.4.1. Introduction

The text of a rule may comprise a number of manifestations of the consent of States which may provide a comparatively reliable handhold in determining the legally binding or non-binding character of a given rule. The text of a rule often constitutes the most direct expression of the intention of the States concerned. The process of drafting of a document or a rule is itself an important step in the law-making process[973] even in cases where the document or rule is subsequently

---

969. See I. Seidl-Hohenveldern, *loc.cit. (note 798)*, p. 185.
970. *Ibidem.*
971. See *supra* p. 219.
972. See *supra* pp. 218-219.
973. See also *supra* p. 207.

formalized through, for instance, ratification. It has therefore to be taken into account regardless of whether or not such a formalization does indeed take place. In particular, however, in cases where some kind of act of formalization is not provided for, it is quite natural to look first of all to the text in order to find out whether the States concerned intended to be legally bound.[974]

The most direct expressions of the intention of States can be found in what may be called the substantive provisions in a document. By substantive provisions we mean those which lay down the purported or alleged "rights" and "obligations". This type of provisions will be dealt with in section 13.4.2.

Apart from substantive provisions international documents often contain a rather heterogeneous group of other provisions, the common characteristic of which is that they do not themselves lay down "rights" and "obligations", but rather qualify or condition the substantive provisions. For the lack of a better term these might be labeled "qualifying" provisions. These qualifying provisions, which as a rule are embodied in the preambular paragraphs and in the so-called final clauses of a document, may also furnish indications, albeit more indirectly than the substantive provisions, as to the legally binding or non-binding nature of the document concerned and/or one or more of the rules contained in it. This type of provisions will be discussed in section 13.4.3.

13.4.2. Substantive provisions

13.4.2.1. Introduction

The manifestations of consent which may be found in the so-called substantive provisions can best be discussed on the basis of three distinguishable but closely intertwined elements. These elements are: (1) the type of language or terms and formulas in which the actual content of the "rights" and "obligations" is couched; (2) the actual content itself; and (3) the relation of the content of the rule concerned with already existing rules of international law. In the following sections we will first outline these elements separately and *in abstracto*. Subsequently, it will be attempted to clarify them a little further, particularly also their interrelation, on the basis of a concrete example.

13.4.2.2. The type of language employed

As far as the first element is concerned there exists a plethora of different terms and formulas in which "rights" and "obligations" are couched in international practice. Unfortunately, a "dictionary" which precisely maps out the legal or non-legal implications of the different types of language to be found in interna-

---

974. R. Jennings, *loc. cit.* (note 1), p. 80, takes a far-reaching position in this respect, when he upholds with regard to the various so-called negotiating texts drawn up at UNCLOS: "If the Conference were to cease to function at its next session, the draft treaty would still be not only an important source of law, but probably the *most* important source of principles and rules on this very large part of international law."

tional documents does not exist. Nevertheless, a general indication can sometimes be deduced from the particular term or formula employed: some terms and formulas point in the direction of an intention to create legal rules while others, conversely, rather imply that no legal ties were intended.

Examples can be found in the various opening formulas which figure at the beginning of international documents. It is often assumed, for instance, that the use of the verb "to agree" and the use of the verb "to adopt" have different implications in this respect. Most authors would seem to take the view that the use of the verb "to adopt" constitutes an indication of the intention of States not to create legal rights and obligations. "Have adopted", so runs the argument, is no treaty language; in the case of a treaty the term "have agreed" would have been employed.[975]

It cannot be denied that "Have agreed as follows" is stronger legal language than "Have adopted the following". On the other hand, the difference between the two formulas should not be exaggerated. In a philological sense the two terms seem to be very close and are indeed sometimes used interchangeably.[976] More importantly, they are not absolute antipoles in the sense that the verb "to agree" is exclusively used in legally binding documents, while "to adopt" is reserved for legally non-binding instruments. Practice shows cases where "Have agreed as follows" is used as an opening phrase of documents which apparently are not intended to be legally binding.[977] Conversely, the use of the verb "to adopt" is not always taken as a sure sign that no legal ties are intended. This is underscored by the position taken by the United States during the Conference on Security and Co-operation in Europe. The Document on confidence-building measures and certain aspects of security and disarmament, drawn up at that Conference as part of its Final Act, provides that the participating States "have adopted the following", and subsequently enumerates a number of measures that the participating States "will" take. In the view of the United States this language was ambiguous as to the level of commitment intended and it, therefore, tabled an interpretative statement to the effect that it

---

975. The argument is made, for instance, with respect to the Helsinki Final Act in which the verb "to adopt" reoccurs several times. The final sentence of the introductory paragraph reads: "The High Representatives of the participating States have solemnly adopted the following:". Similarly, the preamble of the Declaration on Principles Guiding Relations between participating States (the so-called Decalogue of the Helsinki Final Act), the preamble of the Document on confidence-building measures and certain aspects of security and disarmament, as well as the preambles of the so-called second and third Baskets of the Helsinki Final Act all conclude with the phrase "Have adopted the following". Authors who make this argument are *inter alia*: M. Bothe, *loc. cit.* (note 762), p. 73; J. Prevost, "Observations sur la nature juridique de l'Acte Final de la Conférence sur la Sécurité et la Coopération en Europe", XXI *AFDI* (1975), pp. 129-153 (143); and K. Skubiszewski, *loc. cit.* (note 918), pp. 14-15.

976. See the definitions of the two terms in *Webster's Third New International Dictionary* 1976, pp. 29 and 43, and *Black's Law Dictionary*, Revised Fourth Edition 1968, pp. 70 and 89.

977. See M. Bothe, *loc. cit.* (note 762), pp. 72-73, who mentions *inter alia* the "Declaration of Basic Principles of Relations Between the United States of America and the Union of Soviet Socialist Republics" of 29 May 1972, which uses the formula "Have agreed as follows", and subsequently quotes Secretary of State Kissinger as stating that "These declarations of principle are not an American concession; indeed, we have been affirming them unilaterally for two decades. Nor are they legal contract;...".

did not consider the Document to lay down legally binding measures.[978]

In addition, there are various opening phrases to be found in international instruments, which on the one hand are less clear-cut than "Have agreed", but which on the other hand would seem to be stronger than "Have adopted". Again the Helsinki Final Act provides interesting examples. In part 1(b) of its First Basket entitled:" Matters related to giving effect to certain of the above Principles", and in its Fourth Basket the phrases "are resolved" and "declare their resolve" are used. Both these parts of the Final Act contain at least some provisions which can be considered as legally binding. In the first case it is *decided* to convoke a meeting of experts on the peaceful settlement of disputes, and in the second case a meeting of representatives of the Ministers of Foreign Affairs on the follow-up of the Conference is *organized*. At the same time approximate dates are set for both these meetings. This would seem to imply that "are resolved" and "declare their resolve" are considered stronger terms than "have adopted".

Another example of an "intermediate" opening formula to be mentioned here can be found in the Declaration on Principles of International Law concerning Friendly Relations and Co-operation among States in accordance with the Charter of the United Nations.[979] The operative part of the Declaration starts with the words: "[The General Assembly] *Solemnly proclaims* the following principles". Much has been written about the precise status of the Declaration.[980] The argument is often made that the Declaration, or at least parts of it, constitutes binding international law. The Declaration, in its General Part, states that "Nothing in this Declaration shall be construed as prejudicing in any manner the provisions of the Charter or the rights and duties of Member States under the Charter or the rights of peoples under the Charter, *taking into account the elaboration of these rights in this Declaration.*" (emphasis added). The General Part further declares that "The principles of the Charter which are embodied in this Declaration constitute basic principles of international law ...". Finally, the principles contained in the Declaration are, at least partly, couched in treaty type of language and the General Assembly adopted the Declaration by consensus, that is without vote.

---

978. See H. Russell, *loc.cit.* (note 924), p. 247. See in this respect also D. Nincic, "Les Implications Générales Juridiques et Historiques de la Déclaration d'Helsinki", 154 *RCADI* (1977-I), pp. 45-101(58), who has argued that the words "have adopted" in the Helsinki Final Act have a special meaning due to a number of particular circumstances prevailing: "*Cependant, la procédure selon laquelle cette 'adoption' s'est faite dans le cas de l'Acte Final de la CSCE, et notamment le 'consensus' et la signature au niveau le plus élevé, donne un sens un peu différent à ce terme, un sens plus engageant, le sens d'un consentement, qui n'est pas tellement éloigné de celui que refléteraient les termes consacrés: 'sont convenus'.*"
979. General Assembly Resolution 2625 (XXV) of 24 October 1970.
980. See on the Declaration *inter alia* G. Arangio-Ruiz, *loc.cit.* (note 762); B. Graf zu Dohna, *Die Grundprinzipien des Völkerrechts über die freundschaftlichen Beziehungen und die Zusammenarbeit zwischen den Staaten* (Berlin 1975); R. Rosenstock, "The Declaration of Principles of International Law Concerning Friendly Relations; A Survey", 65 *AJIL* (1971), pp. 713-736; and M. Sahovic, "Codification des Principes du Droit International des Relations Amicales et de la Coopération entre les Etats", 137 *RCADI* (1972-III), pp. 243-310.

It is true that a number of Western States in adopting the Declaration made a reservation as far as its normative status or significance was concerned.[981] However, shortly afterwards at the Conference on Security and Co-operation in Europe, the same Western States would seem to have changed their positions. When it had to be decided on what sources the principles to be embodied in the Helsinki Final Act had to be based, the Western States as a group repeatedly insisted that - and finally succeeded in accomplishing that - both the United Nations Charter and the Declaration on Friendly Relations should be taken into account. Indeed, they even seem to have gone a long way in putting both these documents on the same line.[982] This lends support to the view that the Declaration is to be considered as a legally binding instrument. If this is a correct characterization of the Declaration's status, its opening phrase "Solemnly proclaims" would seem to match quite well, because "to proclaim" can be regarded as rather strong language which comes close to the verb "to agree".

Admittedly, such a determination can often by made only "after the fact". Even though they may provide a general indication, the various opening formulas do not in advance spell out precise legal or non-legal implications. It is clear, therefore, that they must be read in conjunction with what follows. It may make a difference of course what precisely States have agreed to, proclaimed, resolved or adopted. In other words, the second element mentioned above, *i.e.* the actual content of "rights" and "obligations" has to be taken into account.

Apart from the opening phrases, this holds good also for other terms and formulas in which "rights" and "obligations" are couched in international documents. In this respect, too, international practice shows a wealth of variations and nuances. A familiar and fairly clear-cut distinction is that between "shall" and "should". The term "shall" usually connotes legal obligations. "Should", on the other hand, refers most of the time to situations *de lege ferenda*; something which should be done does as a rule not constitute *lex lata* (yet). Between these two extremes a great variety of different terms is employed. To mention just a few examples, it may be provided that States "will" do something, "reaffirm" something, "undertake" to do something, "commit themselves" to do something, "adhere" to something, or "pledge themselves" to do something. Generally speaking, these terms may be said to reflect varying degrees of compelling-

---

981. For the declarations of the various government representatives on this matter in the Sixth Committee, see *Doc.* A/C.6/SR.1178-1184; and in the General Assembly, GA/OR/ Plenary Meetings, 25th Session 1960, Item 85.

982. See L. Ferraris, *op.cit.* (note 4), p. 21: "The Western countries (including the neutral countries) only maintained as acceptable sources the Charter of the United Nations and the Declarations on Friendly Relations, arguing that within these documents all the essential princcipples were covered ...". See also p. 42: "The problem of the sources was resolved, ..., to the advantage of the West: reference was only made to the Charter of the United Nations and to the Declaration on Friendly Relations ...". Finally, on p. 110 it is said that "the Western and neutral countries (with the exception of Switzerland) gave particular importance to the necessity of clearly subordinating the principles of the CSCE to the Charter of the United Nations and of connecting them to the United Nations Declaration on Friendly Relations, in order to avoid any possibility of distortion by Europe of generally recognized principles". See also P. van Dijk, *loc.cit.* (note 5), p. 112. For the reason why the Declaration was not mentioned *expressis verbis* in the Helsinki Final Act, see Publication No. 115 of the Netherlands Ministry of Foreign Affairs, *op.cit.* (note 4), pp. 101-102.

ness.[983] However, in this case too it is important to take into account what the provision concerned provides further. There would seem to be a larger difference, for instance, between the terms "shall" and "should" as such than between the formulas "shall try to" on the one hand and "should make every effort to" on the other hand. Apart from these general formulas, it is of course particularly also the actual content of the provision concerned which has to be taken into consideration.

13.4.2.3. The content of a rule

This brings us to the second element of substantive provisions mentioned above, *i.e.* the actual content of a provision. It is impossible to tell *in abstracto* when the content of a provision is one which, and is laid down in a way which, reflects the intention on the part of the States concerned to be legally bound. Such a determination can only be made with respect to a concrete case. As far as the Declaration on Friendly Relations[984] is concerned, for instance, its subject matter - the principles of international law - and the way in which it is laid down - the principles dealt with are, at least partly, couched in treaty language - in the present author's view lend support to the position that the Declaration is a legally binding instrument. Below we will elaborate this element of the actual content of a provision on the basis of a concrete example taken from the field of the international economic relations.

At this place a more general issue concerning the content of substantive provisions must be briefly dealt with. It concerns the impact of the precision or the vagueness of the wording of a rule on its legally binding or non-binding nature. There would seem to prevail an inclination to assume that vaguely worded rules are not legally binding, while precise wording is often taken as a sign that legal commitments are intended. It cannot be denied that in general the function of law - *i.e.* regulating and ordering relations in society - is enhanced by precise rather than by vague terminology. Nevertheless, conclusions with respect to the legally binding or non-binding character of rules cannot *a priori* be drawn from this proposition.

Bothe has observed on this matter that "As to the content of the obligation formulated in a particular document, the certainty of expectation depends on the precision of the wording. Both non-legal and legal obligations may be put in vague or precise terms, and that influences the certainty of expectations in both cases".[985] This point of view correctly stresses the fact that a formal rule of law may be vague too without its legal character being doubted and it, consequently, implies that there is no *a priori* reason to deny the legal character of a rule merely on the basis of its vague wording.

---

983. In the present author's view the examples as listed present a declining order of compellingness.
984. See *supra* pp. 237-238.
985. M. Bothe, *loc.cit.* (note 762), p. 86.

This can be illustrated on the basis of an example taken from the field of human rights. The 1966 International Covenant on Economic, Social and Cultural Rights[986] stipulates in its article 11 *inter alia* that "The States Parties to the present covenant recognize the right of everyone to an adequate standard of living for himself and his family, including adequate ... housing ...". It is added that "The States Parties will take appropriate steps to ensure the realization of this right ...". The implications of this provision are pretty vague. It does not in any way spell out the measures which governments have to take. The fact, for instance, that there exist slums in a contracting State cannot *a priori* be said to constitute a violation. This depends on the circumstances; in the case of a developing country the government may simply lack the means to provide the entire population with housing which is considered adequate. On the other hand, article 11 of the Covenant is not an empty shell either. In the present author's view it would amount to a breach of this provision, also in the case of one of the least developed States, if the government's policy would allow the hovels of poor people to be torn down and to be replaced by luxurious housing which the original inhabitants cannot afford, without other adequate housing on reasonable conditions being offered to them.

Just as a vaguely worded rule of law should not be considered too quickly as an empty shell, rules which are not clothed with a formal legal status should not *a priori* be denied a legally binding character merely because they lack a certain degree of precision in their wording. It is true that "An indeterminate and vague wording may be just the expression of an agreement to disagree between States ...".[987] Nevertheless, even if a rule does not precisely spell out what course of action a State must take, it may on closer analysis sometimes turn out to lay down certain courses of action which a State are not allowed to take. Such a rule makes state-behaviour non-optional, albeit not completely but only partly. It thus contributes to the ordering and regulating of relations in the international society. To this extent, therefore, it qualifies as a legal rule. Whether it in fact can be considered as a legal rule then depends on other available evidence as to the intentions of the States concerned. Particularly with respect to a vaguely worded rule it is important to take into account its relation with existing rules of international law. This is the third of the elements of substantive provisions mentioned above to which we will turn now.

13.4.2.4. The relation with existing rules of international law

In the present author's view the relation with existing rules of international law constitutes an increasingly important element for the determination of whether a given provision in an international document is of a legally binding or nonbinding character. It was argued above that, because of developments in the international society, international law has expanded in both a horizontal and vertical direction; it has to cover more fields of international relations and it has to do so in a more detailed and penetrating manner.[988] We have also noticed that

986. 6 ILM (1967), p. 360.
987. See C. Schreuer, *loc.cit.* (note 762), p. 116.
988. See *supra* pp. 65-69.

the international law-making process has become a continuous one.[989] All this has resulted in what may be called with some exaggeration a "proliferation" of rules of international law. This growing body of rules, moreover, has become more interrelated. This development has even got to the point where the concept of *jus cogens* was introduced into international law because of the need felt to structure the international legal system.[990] Apart from *jus cogens*, it has become necessary in many instances to take other (related) rules of international law into account when interpreting a particular provision. On the analogy of the interdependence of States, this situation could be called the interdependence of rules of international law.

This interdependence may be operative not only between rules of international law *inter se*, but also on a slightly different level and in a somewhat different way. It is submitted that a comparable interaction may take place between full-fledged legal rules on the one hand and rules the binding or non-binding character of which is less firmly established on the other hand. A treaty-rule, for instance, may be clarified, elaborated, or given a more concrete or actual content by a provision contained in a resolution of the General Assembly or another formally non-binding instrument.[991] In such a case the legal status of the treaty-rule is enhanced, if only because it can be more effectively applied in practice. If and to the extent that this indeed happens, something is added to the status of the formally non-binding rule at the same time: it gains normative strength because of the influence exerted upon it by the treaty-rule. In other words, the interaction between a formally binding and a formally non-binding rule may result in a process of mutual reinforcement.

How this interesting process operates in practice has been demonstrated by Van Dijk in his analysis of the interrelation between the principles of the UN Charter and of the Declaration on Friendly Relations on the one hand and those of the Declaration on Guiding Principles contained in the Helsinki Final Act (the so-called Decalogue) on the other hand. He has provided several illustrations of how the former bestow a normative value upon the latter and of how 1the latter, by reaffirmation, strengthen the normative force of the former.[992] In addition, the same author points out that "It is not at all exceptional that the Final Act itself, and, above all, its implementation, should have law-creating ef-

---

989. See *supra* pp. 206-208.
990. See *supra* pp. 151-156.
991. We are not referring here to what I, Seidl-Hohenveldern, *loc.cit.* (note 798), p. 191, has described as: "The habit of the United Nations General Assembly to re-adopt again and again the same alleged general principles and to cite in the preambles of such subsequent resolutions long chains of preceding resolutions to the same effect" which according to the author "is redundant and more or less ineffective in law...". Interestingly, Seidl-Hohenveldern also upholds that "the United Nations habit of adopting or reciting again and again resolutions containing identical 'soft law' rules may lead to a certain fading into oblivion of disclaimers made, when States voted for the original resolution, while stressing nevertheless that they did not hold an *opinio juris* when accepting the rule concerned", *ibidem* p. 196. Compare the statement by R. Kearney, *loc.cit.* (note 25), p. 511, who describes the attitude of Western States towards the multiple reference to the new international economic order introduced by developing countries into resolutions of international organizations as follows: "The attitude is, therefore, to accept the resolution as mere verbiage. It is useful to inquire whether all this activity is producing international law. The answer may be that we just do not know. But if it is, we will find out too late in the day for our own good".
992. P. van Dijk, *loc.cit.* (note 5), pp. 111-115.

fect; it shares this potential with all unilateral declarations and bilateral and multilateral arrangements relating to international relations, and the State practice based thereupon".[993] In the following we will try to further clarify this point on the basis of an example taken from the field of the international economic relations. This example is designed to show *inter alia* that the determination of whether a process of mutual reinforcement has actually taken place is dependent also on the other manifestations to be taken into consideration.[994]

13.4.2.5. Excursus: a concrete example; the question of the existence of international legal obligations concerning Official Development Assistance

As was indicated above, we will now discuss a concrete example in order to clarify further the preceding analysis of the manifestations contained in the subclass of substantive provisions. The example concerns the question as to the obligatory or voluntary character of the so-called Official Development Assistance (ODA) from developed to developing countries.[995] More concretely, we will look at the question of whether there exists an obligation under international law on the part of (some of the) developed States to make available a certain amount of Official Development Assistance each year for the benefit of developing countries. This example was chosen because, in the present author's view, it clearly bears out the role of the various manifestations outlined here and particularly also their interplay.

The discussion on ODA has been taking place primarily within the framework of the United Nations. Any effort to answer the above-mentioned question must, therefore, take as a point of departure an analysis of the relevant provisions of the Charter and a number of important resolutions of the General Assembly dealing with the issue. The provisions of the Charter which immediately come to mind are the articles 1(3), 55 and 56. Article 1(3) of the Charter states as one of the main purposes of the United Nations "to achieve international cooperation in solving international problems of an economic, social, cultural, or humanitarian character". In article 55, furthermore, it is specified that the United Nations shall promote: "higher standards of living, full employment, and conditions of economic and social progress and development". To achieve the purposes of article 55, article 56 lays down the obligation for member States "to take joint and separate action in cooperation with the organization".

---

993. *Ibidem*, p. 113.
994. The same point is implied in the references to implementation and state-practice in the just-quoted words of P. van Dijk.
995. The concept of official development assistance (ODA) has mainly been elaborated within the framework of the Organization for Economic Cooperation and Development (OECD). It consists of net disbursements of loans and grants made at concessional financial terms by official agencies of the members of the Development Assistance Committee (DAC) of the OECD. A transaction is considered ODA if it meets the following tests: 1) it is administered with the promotion of the economic development and welfare of developing countries as its main objective, and 2) it is concessional in character and contains a grant element of at least 25 per cent; see OECD, *Development Cooperation 1972 Review* (Paris 1972), Annex III, para. 1, where a list is added of specific types of transactions that may not be included in official development assistance, such as military transactions.

Taken together these provisions encompass *inter alia* the duty to take joint and separate action in solving the problems of economic underdevelopment. It can hardly be doubted that the framers of the Charter had these problems in mind, even if these did not constitute the only or maybe not even the most important concern. At any rate, the real ramifications of the problems of underdevelopment became gradually to be understood during the decades after 1945. The outcome of this process is reflected in Resolution 2625(XXV) of 24 October 1970 by which the General Assembly adopted the Declaration concerning Friendly Relations and Co-operation among States in accordance with the Charter of the United Nations. The fourth principle of the Declaration is entitled: *the duty of States to cooperate with one another in accordance with the Charter.* The relevant part of this principle first reminds of the obligation contained in article 56 of the Charter: "States Members of the United Nations have the duty to take joint and separate action in cooperation with the United Nations in accordance with the relevant provisions of the United Nations Charter". In its final sentence it then goes on to specify that: "States should cooperate in the promotion of economic growth throughout the world, *especially that of the developing countries*" (emphasis added).

This provision thus puts emphasis on the need to improve the situation of the developing countries. For the remainder, principle IV adds little to the provisions of the Charter, regardless of the view one takes on the binding or non-binding character of the 1970 Declaration in general.[996] It employs the weak term "should" and, moreover, it only refers to cooperation without further specifying in what way(s) this cooperation is to take place. Consequently, even if read in conjunction with the fourth principle of the 1970 Declaration, article 56 of the Charter remains a rather vague and open-ended provision.

On the other hand, it is difficult to uphold that article 56 does not contain any obligation at all. As was already stressed in the foregoing, no treaty provision, particularly not provisions of the UN Charter, can be supposed to be devoid of any binding elements. In this respect Verwey has rightly observed that "In the case of article 56 of the UN Charter, there is a clear commitment to do something for the achievement of the purposes mentioned in article 55; there is certainly no right to do nothing ...".[997] To put it a little differently, it may be concluded that article 56 of the Charter (in conjunction with principle IV of the 1970 Declaration) entails a duty not to do nothing. However, such a commitment to do something or duty not to do nothing still is not specific enough to be able to deduce from it a particular legal obligation. For, the question remains what it exactly is that States have to do. In other words, has the obligation laid down in article 56 been further specified within the framework of the United Nations, particularly so as to include a duty to provide Official Development Assistance?

Certainly, the making available of funds by rich countries for the purpose of development to countries with an underdeveloped economy is one of the oldest

---

996. See *supra* pp. 237-238.
997. W. Verwey, *The Establishment of a New International Economic Order and the Realization of the Right to Development and Welfare; A Legal Survey*, HR/Geneva 1980/F.P., p. 22.

forms of what today is called development cooperation.[998] Since the fifties a great number of other important issues have been included in the discussion on developmental problems, which has gradually been transformed into an effort to restructure the entire international economic relations. However, this has in no way detracted from the importance assigned to financial flows from developed to developing countries, as is witnessed by several General Assembly resolutions.[999] In short, there is no doubt that Official Development Assistance constitutes one of the ways "to take joint and separate action" as provided for in article 56 of the Charter.[1000]

Even if it can be established that there exists an obligation "to take joint and separate action in the field of Official Development Assistance", this still does not constitute a hard and fast legal obligation which can be effectively implemented in practice. Obviously, put in this general fashion, the provision leaves open the amount of ODA, which the States would be obliged to provide. The developing countries have pressed hard for a more concrete obligation in this respect and it was during the sixties that the *level* of ODA was elaborated in quantitative terms.[1001] At the end of that decade a concrete target was included in the United Nations Second Development Decade. In paragraph 43 of General Assembly Resolution 2626(XXV) of 24 October 1970 it was laid down that "Each economically advanced country will progressively increase its official development assistance to the developing countries and will exert its best efforts to reach a minimum net amount of 0.7 per cent of its gross national product at market prices by the middle of the Decade". The wording of the first part of this phrase is quite unambiguous; it lays down that developed countries *will progressively increase* their ODA. The remainder of the provision, on the other hand, is rather weak. It does set a target (0.7 per cent of the gross national product) and even specifies an approximate time-limit for that purpose. However, in order to reach the target within the specified period all that is asked from the States concerned is that they *will exert their best efforts*. This is not very strong

998. As early as 1950, in its Resolution 400(V) of 20 November, the General Assembly recommended that "the Economic and Social Council ... consider practical methods, conditions and policies for achieving the adequate expansion and steadier flow of foreign capital, both private and public ...".

999. For instance, in para. 24 of Resolution 35/65 of 5 December 1980, which was adopted without vote, the General Assembly of the United Nations has laid down as a major objective of the Third United Nations Development Decade "an enhanced flow of financial resources on terms and conditions that are better attuned to the development aims and economic circumstances of developing countries". Similarly, in para. 96 it was stressed, while underlining the developing countries' own responsibility for financing their development, that "External financial resources, particularly official development assistance, constitute an indispensable element of support for the developing countries' own efforts. International financial flows, particularly public flows, should be improved and adapted consistent with the needs of developing countries as regards volume, composition, quality, forms and distribution of flows".

1000. Even the United States' government, which is, as will be pointed out below, opposed to legally binding commitments concerning the level of Official Development Assistance, stated in the Second Committee of the General Assembly that it "recognizes the need for additional flows of resources to aid the development of the developing countries. The United States plans to increase its official development assistance substantially in the future ...", *UN Doc* A/35/592/Add.1, p. 16.

1001. For a survey, see the Report of the Secretary General, *The International Dimensions of the Right to Development*, E/CN.4/1334, 2 January 1979, in particular pp. 131-133.

language and it cannot, in the present author's view, as such be construed as a legally binding obligation, now that it is contained in a formally non-binding instrument.

Ten years later the General Assembly inaugurated the United Nations Third Development Decade and adopted, through its resolution 35/65 of 5 December 1980, an International Development Strategy for that purpose. The provisions on ODA contained therein would seem, as a whole, to be more strongly worded than those pertaining to the Second Development Decade. Nevertheless, they are not wholly unambiguous or without loopholes. Paragraph 24 of the International Development Strategy provides *inter alia*: "A rapid and substantial increase will be made in official development assistance by all developed countries, with a view to reaching and where possible surpassing the international agreed target of 0.7 per cent of the gross national product of developing countries. To this end, developed countries which have not yet reached the target should make their best efforts to reach it by 1985, and in any case not later than in the second half of the Decade. The target of 1 per cent should be reached as soon as possible thereafter. The efforts of developed countries will be greater, the lower their relative performance".[1002]

The opening phrase "A rapid and substantial increase will be made ..." in itself would already seem to be stronger than that of the 1970 text. Its stronger character becomes particularly clear from the fact that this time it is linked to the words "with a view to reaching and where possible surpassing the agreed international target of 0.7 per cent". Here the target is laid down again, although this time in more obligatory terms. There is no reference here to the best efforts of States, but it is simply provided that States will increase their ODA with a view to reaching and where possible surpassing the target. The target, in addition, is referred to as *internationally agreed*. This reflects the fact that the support for the 0.7 target has indeed become wide-spread since 1970, even though it cannot be considered generally accepted.

As far as the time-limit is concerned, the 1980 text opens with approximately the same phrase as that of 1970: developed countries "should make their best efforts" to reach the target by 1985. Again, therefore, the question arises whether the developed countries fulfil the requirements of this provision as long as they *try hard* to reach the target, or whether they are required to actually reach it by 1985 or in any case by 1990. The first part of the sentence concerning the time-limit in itself would seem to necessitate the former conclusion. However, the words which follow should be taken into account. The phrase "and in any case not later than in the second half of the Decade" can be interpreted in different ways. If it is read in conjunction with the words "should make their best efforts" in the first part of the sentence, it implies the same (weak) level of commitment as was laid down in the 1970 text. Read independently, however, it goes beyond the 1970 text and takes on a much more compelling meaning. Then the result would be an obligation on the part of developed countries to actually spend 0.7 per cent of their gross national product on ODA at the latest in 1990.

1002. Paragraph 24 is contained in Part II of the International Development Strategy entitled: "Goals and Objectives". Part III entitled: "Policy Measures" comprises an identical provision in paragraph 98.

If the analysis were to be confined to the elements discussed in the foregoing, the present author would be prepared to subscribe to the latter conclusion. This conclusion would seem to be justified on the basis of the developments with respect to the ODA-target described in the foregoing, viewed against the background of the obligation contained in article 56 of the Charter. It is buttressed furthermore by the fact that the 1980 International Development Strategy was adopted by consensus. Nevertheless, the 1980 text, as was pointed out, is not without ambiguity and possible other manifestations of consent or acceptance (or non-acceptance) of the States concerned during the consensus-procedure could therefore shed more light on this matter. Indeed, various States, including a great number of developed countries, made statements clarifying and explaining their positions. These statements provide a more detailed picture and make it clear that conclusions have to be differentiated depending on the particular State in question.

A number of these statements representing the most extreme positions should be briefly mentioned. The Netherlands, Norway and Sweden unequivocally accepted the ODA-target as laid down in the 1980 International Development Strategy. The Netherlands representative declared in the General Assembly: "The Netherlands delegation regrets that a more binding formulation on the official development assistance paragraph has not been possible". He subsequently referred to a statement by the Netherlands Minister for Development Co-operation urging all developed countries to agree to the target. Finally he added: "I would also recall that my country was willing to give serious consideration to the proposal of the Group of 77 to raise the accepted target to 1 per cent at the end of the decade. I underline that my Government fully accepts the text on the 1 per cent target as formulated in the present strategy".[1003] Similarly, the Norwegian representative stated in the Second Committee: "As regards the paragraphs dealing with the targets and time-frames for official development assistance, we can go along with the text as it stands now. This being said, I should like to add that we would have preferred that those targets be more ambitious with regard to the time-frames".[1004] The Swedish representative observed that "The importance of substantially increased resources flows to the developing countries, including official development assistance, cannot be underestimated. We therefore welcome the fact that the ODA-target of 0.7 per cent is so broadly endorsed".[1005]

In contrast, the United States rejected the ODA-target in no uncertain terms. Its representative stated: "The United States recognizes the need for additional flows of external resources to aid the development of the developing countries. The United States plans to increase its development assistance substantially in the future, but, as is well known, we do not accept the 0.7 per cent ODA-target."[1006] On behalf of the States members of the United Nations belonging to the Group of 77 the Venezuelan representative reacted: "We are concerned, however, at the fact that the scope of the text ..., has been further reduced by interpretive statements and observations, *some of which are tantamount to actual*

1003. *UN Doc.* A/35/PV.83, 5 December 1980, p. 61.
1004. *UN Doc.* A/35/592/Add.1, 27 November 1980, Annex, p. 11.
1005. *Ibidem*, p. 12.
1006. *Ibidem*, p. 16; see also *UN Doc* A/C.2/35/SR.41, 21 November 1981, p. 8.

reservations."[1007]

In summary, the conclusion has to be that the question as to the existence of legal obligations concerning ODA cannot be answered in a general fashion. A differentiation must be made according to the precise position a particular State has taken. As far as the examples mentioned above are concerned, it is submitted that The Netherlands, Norway and Sweden can be held legally bound by the ODA-target contained in the 1980 International Development Strategy. The United States, on the other hand, is not so bound, given its unequivocal rejection of the target.[1008] The conclusion with respect to first-mentioned countries must be different, if it is assumed that they consented to or accepted the ODA-target on the condition of reciprocity, *i.e.* on the condition that the other Western States also consented to or accepted the target. As far as is known to the present author, there are no convincing indications that they intended to enter into such a conditional obligation.[1009]

13.4.3. Qualifying provisions

13.4.3.1. Introduction

As was already pointed out, qualifying provisions do not lay down "rights" and "obligations" like substantive provisions, but qualify the substantive provisions in one way or another. As far as these qualifying provisions are concerned, some attention will first be paid to the names of international instruments. Subsequently, we will discuss a number of preambular paragraphs and so-called final clauses, in which qualifying provisions are usually embodied.

1007. *UN Doc.* A/35/592/Add.1, 27 November 1980, Annex, p. 18 (emphasis added). The question remains how this position of the United States squares with its obligation under article 56 of the Charter. The same of course holds good with respect to other States which take a comparable position.
1008. For the positions taken by other (developed) States, see the Annex to *UN Doc* A/35/592/Add.1, 27 November 1980.
1009. In the present author's view, an intention to that effect cannot be deduced from the words which the Norwegian representative added to the above-mementioned statement (text accompanying note 1004): "we regard these targets as addressed to all developed countries." First, these words are not strong enough to be considered as implying a condition of reciprocity. Secondly, if the present author is not mistaken, the phrase is in fact meant as a rebuttal of the position taken by the Socialist States. With respect to ODA the Socialist countries usually advance their traditional argument that the problem of underdevelopment is caused by past-colonial and neo-colonial exploitation of developing countries by the West. Consequently, so runs the argument, it is not for the Socialist States to undertake obligations in order to solve this problem. This reasoning is hardly convincing, now that the international society has changed so drastically over the past decades and States have become so much more interdependent. At any rate, the argument has lost much, if not all, of its political credibility. The developing countries have made it clear that to them the Socialist point of view is unacceptable. The Socialist countries too, therefore, can be expected to come under increasing pressure to conform to demands in the field of Official Development Assistance.

13.4.3.2. The name of an instument

The Vienna Convention on the Law of Treaties provides under the heading of *Use of terms* in its article 2(1)(a): "'treaty' means an international agreement between States in written form and governed by international law, whether embodied in a single instrument or in two or more related instruments *and whatever its particular designation*;" (emphasis added). For the purpose of the Convention, therefore, an instrument can be a "treaty" whatever name it carries.[1010] In this respect the Vienna Convention keeps in line with a longstanding opinion in doctrine holding that little or no significance at all is to be attached to the designation of a particular instrument.[1011] It is fairly widely acknowledged that the very diversified names of international instruments do not have consequences under international law.

However, King Gamble has argued that scholarly international legal literature usually takes a microscopic view on this issue and that "instruments with certain names when viewed *en masse* may possess different characteristics than instruments with other names."[1012] He has subsequently conducted an empirical investigation into the differences between differently named instruments most frequently used in state-practice. He concludes that such differences indeed exist with respect to a number of attributes between multilateral treaties when classified according to their different names.[1013] For our purpose, however, his analysis is not very helpful, because it is confined to instruments which explicitly are, or were meant to be, legally binding. It does not therefore address the question whether different names of instruments may have different implications as to their legally binding or non-binding character. As far as known to the present author, such an investigation has not been conducted yet. Until this has been done, hardly any conclusion as to the legally binding or non-binding nature can be based on a particular name of a given instrument.[1014]

Nevertheless, it is sometimes argued that a certain instrument is not legally binding because of its particular name. Russell, for instance, has taken such a position with respect to the Helsinki Final Act. According to him, the designation "Final Act" was promoted by a number of participating States on the basis of the view that in international practice a "Final Act" is not normally a legal instrument and therefore created an overwhelming presumption that a legally non-binding instrument was intended.[1015] However, practice shows that instru-

---

1010. A great number of different names are employed in practice. According to J. King Gamble, *loc.cit.* (note 474), p. 5: "It should be acknowledged that at least the following names of instruments are used in multilateral treaty-making: treaty, convention, agreement, accord, code, instrument, mandate, measures, agreed minutes, optional clause, plan, *procès verbal*, provisions, recommendations, resolution, regulations, statute, and undertaking".

1011. See D. Myers, "The Names and Scope of Treaties", 51 *AJIL* (1957), pp. 574-605 (574); see also the studies discussed by J. King Gamble, *loc.cit.* (note 473), pp. 2-4.

1012. J. King Gamble, *loc.cit.* (note 473), p. 2.

1013. *Ibidem*, pp. 8-24.

1014. Maybe the only exception is the term "treaty" itself. This term carries a strong presumption that the instrument concerned was meant to be legally binding by the States concerned; see also W. Wengler, "Rechtsvertrag, Konsensus und Absichtserklärung im Völkerrecht", 31 *JZ* (1976), pp. 193-197 (194). However, this presumption may be refuted.

1015. H. Russell, *loc.cit.* (note 924), p. 246. However, D. Nincic, *loc.cit.* (note 978), p. 53, has more or less denounced this version of the *travaux préparatoires*.

ments called "Final Act" actually range from *procès verbal* type of documents which do no more than authenticate the work and the result of an international conference and contain no provisions binding under international law, through documents of a mixed character, to documents which are to be put on the same footing as treaties.[1016] Consequently, the term "Final Act" would seem to be an unreliable indication concerning the intention of States and, indeed, most authors hold that the name of the Helsinki Final Act is irrelevant in this respect.[1017]

The term "declaration" constitutes an example of a name which is often held to designate instruments of a legally binding character, although in this case too practice would seem to be inconclusive. According to McNair, for instance, a declaration "usually denotes a treaty that declares existing law, with or without modification, or creates new law."[1018] Johnson has more carefully concluded that "It is believed that the correct use of the term is to describe an instrument in which the parties have endeavoured to codify existing law, though such instruments are likely to be rare."[1019] With respect to declarations of the United Nations General Assembly Asamoah upholds that they may restate existing rules as well as create new rules of international law.[1020] Conversely, Seidl-Hohenveldern opines that "least convincing are semantic subterfuges, using more solemn sounding words such as 'Declaration', or 'Declaration of Principles', than the standard term 'Resolution' for certain decisions of the General Assembly which, nevertheless, are nothing more than 'resolutions', namely non-binding recommendations".[1021]

In summary, at this moment it would seem difficult to escape the conclusion that the name of an international instrument in itself does not furnish a reliable indication as to intention of the States concerned and that, consequently, it has to be presumed that, until empirical evidence to the contrary is provided, names have no implications as to the legally binding or non-binding character.

13.4.3.3. Preambular paragraphs

Even in the case of a treaty the preamble in itself does not lay down binding rights and obligations. Still it may contain important provisions which indirectly have a bearing upon the treaty's binding stipulations. Article 31 of the Vienna Convention on the Law of Treaties provides in its paragraph (1): "A treaty shall be interpreted in good faith in accordance with the ordinary meaning to be given to the terms of the treaty *in their context and in the light of its object and purpose.*" (emphasis added) Paragraph (2) adds *inter alia* that "The context for the

---

1016. See H. Briggs, "The Final Act of the London Conference on Germany", 49 *AJIL* (1955), pp. 148-165, and J. Prévost, *loc.cit.* (note 975), p. 130.
1017. See, for instance, H. Mahnke, "Die Prinzipienerklärung der KSZE-Schlussakte", 21 *ROW* (1977), pp. 45-56 (46); H. Schütz, "Zur Rationalität des Zielkatalogs und des Friedenssicherungsinstrumentariums der Schlussakte der Konferenz für Sicherheit und Zusammenarbeit in Europa", 18 *GYIL* (1975), pp. 146-203 (150); and T. Schweisfurth, *loc.cit.* (note 922), p. 685.
1018. A. McNair, *op.cit.* (note 275), p. 23.
1019. D. Johnson, "The Conclusion of International Conferences", 35 *BYIL* (1959), pp. 1-33 (31).
1020. O. Asamoah, *op.cit.* (note 762), pp. 20-21.
1021. I. Seidl-Hohenveldern, *loc.cit.* (note 798), p. 188.

purpose of the interpretation of a treaty shall comprise, in addition to the text, *including its preamble and annexes ...*"(emphasis added). The preamble therefore belongs to the context of a treaty and, moreover, usually embodies its object and purpose.

In the same indirect manner preambular paragraphs - and for that matter so-called post-ambular paragraphs too - may clarify the intentions of States, also in the case of not formally binding instruments. The provisions contained therein are often invoked to shed light on the parties' intentions as to the legally binding or non-binding character of the instrument concerned.

As an illustration the following examples may be briefly mentioned. We have already pointed to the provision contained in the General Part of the 1970 Declaration on Principles of International Law concerning Friendly Relations and Co-operation, where it is declared that "Nothing in this Declaration shall be construed as prejudicing in any manner the provisions of the Charter or the rights and duties of Member States under the Charter or the right of peoples under the Charter, *taking into account the elaboration of these rights in this Declaration*"[1022] (emphasis added). Particularly the italicized words would seem to imply that the States concerned intended the 1970 Declaration to contain legally binding stipulations. The remainder of the provisions, moreover, buttresses this conclusion, because it would not be necessary for an instrument, which itself is not intended to be legally binding, to provide that it does not prejudice in any manner the provisions of the UN Charter.

A comparable provision is embodied in the Declaration on Principles contained in the 1975 Helsinki Final Act, the so-called Decalogue. One of the paragraphs of its post-amble provides: "The participating States, paying due regard to the principles above and, in particular, to the first sentence of the tenth principle, 'Fulfilment in good faith of obligations under international law', note that the present Declaration does not affect their rights and obligations, nor the corresponding treaties and other agreements and arrangements." This so-called disclaimer has been the subject of arduous and intricate negotiations during the drafting of the Helsinki Final Act and has subsequently attracted much attention in scholarly writing. At this place we cannot elaborate on all the detailed aspects involved in the disclaimer and the negotiations leading to it.

For the purpose of the present study the main issue is that the inclusion of a disclaimer into a certain instrument squares uneasily with the assertion that the instrument concerned is not legally binding. Those who view the Helsinki Final Act as a political document have difficulties fitting the clause into their analysis. Recognizing the illogic of having a (legal) disclaimer in a legally non-binding instrument they tend to regard the clause as superfluous or assign it declaratory effects only. Russell, for instance, maintains that "since the Declaration was not a legal document, it could not affect such matters [*i.e.* existing rights and obligations - v.H.] and the disclaimer should be read as simply a statement of that fact."[1023] Similarly, Schweisfurth upholds: "Ergibt sich ... aus dem Gesamtzusammenhang von Text der Schlussakte und Verfahrensverhalten eindeutig, dass die Schlussakte als ganze kein Vertrag sein soll, so ist der allein auf die

1022. See *supra* p. 237.
1023. H. Russell, *loc.cit.* (note 924), p. 259.

Nichtberührungsklausel gestützten Vermutung (wenigstens) partieller Rechtsverbindlichkeit der Boden entzogen."[1024] He adds that the meaning of the disclaimer is a "zusätzlichen Klarstellung, dass die Schlussakte die Rechtspositionen der Teilnehmerstaaten nicht 'berührt'".[1025]

It is not very convincing to regard an entire clause in an international instrument as superfluous, particularly not if it resulted from long and strenuous negotiations as the one discussed here.[1026] This is not to say that one can conclude to the legally binding nature of the Decalogue solely on the basis of the disclaimer. But the inclusion of the disclaimer indicates that the States concerned did not consider the Decalogue, or at least some of its provisions, incapable of affecting existing rights and obligations.[1027] It therefore lends support to the view that the Decalogue may at least elaborate and specify existing rights and obligations in a way consistent with the rules laying down these rights and obligations.[1028]

Finally, examples of frequently invoked qualifying provisions may also be found in the general preamble and post-amble of the Helsinki Final Act. The fourth preambular paragraph stresses the *political* will of the participating States to improve and intensify their relations and to contribute to peace, security, justice and cooperation in Europe. Together with the final post-ambular paragraph according to which the participating States were "mindful of the high *political* significance which they attach to the results of the Conference ..." (emphasis added), this clause is relied on to denounce the legally binding nature of the Helsinki Final Act.[1029]

13.4.3.4. Final clauses

The so-called final clauses or final provisions deal with matters like (the requirement of) signature and ratification, official languages, designation of the depositary, registration, and possibly reservations. Legal formalities like these typically pertain to instruments which are intended to be formally binding, *i.e.* treaties. With respect to instruments the binding or non-binding character of which is open to doubt, not too much should be made out of the lack or inclusion of final

1024. T. Schweisfurth, *loc.cit.* (note 922), p. 697, note 61.
1025. *Ibidem.*
1026. Indeed, those who consider the Final Act as a legally binding document rely on the disclaimer as one of their major arguments; see, for instance, S. Bock, "Festigung der Sicherheit in Europa; Kernstück der Schlussakte von Helsinki", 20 *DA* (1975), pp. 1623-1639 (1638): "Die Aufnahme gerade dieses Passus in die Schlussakte ist auch insofern interessant, weil eine solche Aussage charakteristisch für völkerrechtlichen Verträge ist, was die Beweisführung über den völkerrechtlichen Charakter der Schlussakte einmal mehr bestätigt."
1027. D. Blumenwitz, "Die völkerrechtlichen Aspekte der KSZE-Schlussakte", in: Göttinger Arbeitskreis, *Die KSZE und die Menschenrechte* (Berlin 1977), pp. 53-71 (67).
1028. See also *supra* pp. 240-242. This interpretation of the disclaimer is compatible with the reason why it was in fact introduced into the negotiations, *i.e.* to safeguard the so-called Four-Power-rights of England, France, the Soviet Union, and the United States resulting from their victory over the Third Reich and the ensuing complex of international agreements; see H. Russell, *loc.cit.* (note 924), p. 257. The fact that these States pressed hard for the inclusion of the disclaimer in itself proves that they did not regard the Decalogue irrelevant to their existing rights and obligations.
1029. For instance, H. Russell, *loc.cit.* (note 924), p. 247.

clauses, because, as was pointed out, international law has been witnessing a decline of form.[1030] Nevertheless, final clauses may constitute indications as to the intention of the States concerned and their inclusion or non-inclusion is indeed sometimes relied upon to argue *pro* or *contra* the legally binding character of a certain instrument. In the following we will discuss a number of examples of final clauses, mainly derived from the Helsinki Final Act, because with respect to this document the pros and cons of final clauses have been most extensively dealt with in doctrine.

Above we have already pointed to the impact of the omission or inclusion of a ratification-clause upon the status of non-formally binding instruments.[1031] Here a closely related issue must be briefly analyzed. It concerns the promulgation of international instruments within the national legal context. Municipal legal systems usually lay down procedural requirements for the promulgation of treaties. If with respect to a given document this procedure is followed, this indicates, it is sometimes argued, that the State concerned intended to enter into international legal ties. If conversely, these procedural requirements are not met, it is deduced that the State in question did not want to become legally bound by the international instrument concerned.

However, it is highly questionable whether internal (constitutional) requirements on promulgation can have any bearing upon the status of an instrument under international law. The Vienna Convention on the Law of Treaties contains no conditions in this respect. Indeed, from the fact that the Convention does refer to provisions of internal law only in connection with the competence to *conclude* treaties,[1032] it seems to follow that the internal (constitutional) provisions and practices on promulgation are irrelevant with respect to the legally binding or non-binding character.[1033]

1030. See *supra* pp. 199-203.
1031. See *supra* pp. 221-222.
1032. Article 46 provides: "1. A State may not invoke the fact that its consent to be bound by a treaty has been expressed in violation of its internal law regarding competence to conclude treaties as invalidating its consent unless that violation was manifest and concerned a rule of its internal law of fundamental importance. 2. A violation is manifest if it would be objectively evident to any State conducting itself in the manner in accordance with normal practice and in good faith". Thus the Vienna Convention takes a position in between the two schools of thought which have traditionally existed on the issue. Some have argued that a State is not bound by a treaty, if its relevant constitutional requirements are not met, although the conclusion of a treaty in such a case may involve the responsibility of that State for injury to another State resulting from reasonable reliance by the latter upon the state of affairs as presented by the former. (See, for instance, Harvard Law School, "Draft Convention on the Law of Treaties", 29 *AJIL* (Supplement) (1935), pp. 657-1240 (992).) Others have upheld that international law is concerned only with the external manifestations of the expression to be bound by a treaty on the part of a State and that, consequently, internal constitutional requirements have no bearing on the validity of treaty obligations under international law. (In this sense, for instance, G. Fitzmaurice, *loc.cit.* (note 862),xpp. 129-137.)
1033. An additional argument supporting this conclusion can be found in the *travaux préparatoires* of the Convention. During the Vienna Conference on the Law of Treaties nine Latin-American countries tabled a proposal to amend what has eventually become article 12 of the Convention. According to that proposal States could express their consent to be bound by signature when a treaty so provides or when "in conformity with internal law of the State the treaty is an administrative or executive agreement", (A/Conf.39/11/Add.2, paragraph 119.) The proposal therefore wanted to consider internal (constitutional) law as relevant to the conclusion of treaties. However, it was rejected by an overwhelming majority *in-*

Nevertheless, despite their irrelevancy from the point of view of international law, steps concerning promulgation by a certain State can be relevant in that they may reflect the intention of that State as to the character of the instrument concerned. Indeed, non-promulgation has been invoked to denounce the legally binding character of the Helsinki Final Act. Schweisfurth bases this conclusion *inter alia* on the observation: "nirgendwo fand eine Promulgation der Schlussakte nach den Vorschriften über die Promulgation internationaler Verträge statt; ...".[1034] This may be true, but on the other hand in some of the participating States at least the Helsinki Final Act was treated in a way very different from formally non-binding instruments.[1035] Furthermore, that document, in the second of its final paragraphs, contains the interesting provision stipulating that "The text of this Final Act will be published in each participating State, which will disseminate it and make it known as widely as possible". On the one hand this provision does not expressly provide for promulgation required for treaties; on the other hand it goes far beyond what is usually required in the case of treaties.[1036] By requiring dissemination on the widest possible scale the provision stresses the determination on the part of the participating States to put the commitments laid down in the Helsinki Final Act into practice. Such a determination, particularly if followed by actual implementation, adds more to the legal status of a document than abiding by the formal requirement of promulgation.

Another example of a final provision usually figuring in (multilateral) treaties is the so-called language-clause, which lays down the authentic languages in which the treaty is drawn up. Article 111 of the UN Charter, for instance, reads: "The present Charter, of which the Chinese, French, Russian, English, and Spanish texts are equally authentic ...". Similarly, article 85 of the Vienna Convention provides that "The original of the present Convention, of which the Chinese, English, French, Russian and Spanish texts are equally authentic ...". Language-clauses serve as a tool for the interpretation of the treaty concerned. Usually they are not found in formally non-binding instruments. When a language-clause is contained in such an instrument, as is the case in the Helsinki Final Act the first final paragraph of which stipulates that "The original of this Final Act, drawn up in English, French, German, Italian, Russian and Spanish ...", this may indicate that the States in question regarded at least some of the

ter alia on the basis of the objection that acceptance of the proposal would have required States to study the internal law of their negotiating partners, which was deemed to be too heavy a burden. (See A. Bolintineanu, *loc.cit.* (note 864), pp. 678-679)
1034. T. Schweisfurth, *loc.cit.* (note 922), p. 691.
1035. As far as the Soviet Union and the GDR are concerned, see *ibidem*, pp. 691-692. With respect to Poland, see A. Rotfeld, "Follow-up to the Conference; Forms of Co-operation after the Conference on Security and Co-operation in Europe", in: Polish Institute of International Affairs, *Conference on Security and Co-operation; A Polish View* (Warzawa 1976), p. 221-270 (258).
1036. See in this respect S. Bastid, "The Special Significance of the Helsinki Final Act", in: T. Buergenthal (ed.), *Human Rights, International Law and the Helsinki Accord* (Montclair/New York 1977), pp. 111-19 (14): "Short of providing for its posting in every community, could any more original and significant provision have been inserted in the Final Act? Not only does it provide for publication different from that required by some constitutions for treaties - a publication which would not be required in this case - but the text speaks of 'dissemination' and of making the Final Act 'known as widely as possible'". See on this provision also A. Rotfeld, *loc.cit.* (note 1035), pp. 256-258.

provisions of that instrument as legally binding.[1037]

Article 102(1) of the UN Charter provides that "Every treaty and every international agreement entered into by any Member of the United Nations after the present Charter comes into force shall as soon as possible be registered with the Secretariat and published by it". It can therefore be argued that an instrument which is not registered in accordance with article 102 is not a "treaty" or an "international agreement" and, consequently, cannot be considered legally binding. It is this line of reasoning which underlies the third post-ambular paragraph of the Helsinki Final Act according to which "The Government of the Republic of Finland is requested to transmit to the Secretary-General of the United Nations the text of this Final Act, *which is not eligible for registration under Article 102 of the Charter of the United Nations ...*" (emphasis added). This reference to non-registration under article 102, it is argued, can only be understood as an indication that the participating States did not envisage a document of a legally binding nature because, if they had, non-registration would have implied a premeditated violation of the UN Charter to which almost all the participating States are parties.[1038]

However, it should be observed that registration with the Secretariat of the United Nations is not a constitutive element for rules of international law. In other words, an instrument does not become a "treaty" or another legally binding "international agreement" because of the fact of its registration. As the Secretariat of the United Nations has itself expressly stated "Registration of an instrument submitted by a Member State, ..., does not imply a judgment by the Secretariat on the nature of the instrument, the status of a party, or any similar question. It is the understanding of the Secretariat that its action does not confer on the instrument the status of a treaty or an international agreement if it does not already have that status and does not confer on a party a status which it would not otherwise have".[1039]

The non-constitutive character of registration is confirmed by the "sanction" provided for in case of a failure to register. Unlike article 18 of the League of Nations' Covenant, which stipulated that no treaty or international engagement was binding until it was duly registered, article 102(2) of the Charter confines the effects of non-registration to the inhibition of invoking the treaty or international agreement concerned before any organ of the United Nations. Moreover, even this modest "sanction" has not consistently been applied by the organs of the United Nations.[1040]

Nevertheless, it cannot be denied that the non-registration-clause contained in the Helsinki Final Act is an indication that the participating States did not

---

1037. T. Schweisfurth, *loc. cit.* (note 922), p. 695, note 53, has characterized the language-clause in the Helsinki Final Act as "eine normalerweise nur bei Instrumenten mit verbindlicher Wirkung zu beobachtende Sorgfalt".
1038. See, for instance, H. Mahnke, *loc.cit.* (note 1017), p. 47, and T. Schweisfurth, *loc.cit.* (note 922), pp. 689-690.
1039. See *UN Doc* ST/LEG/SER.A/105, November 1955, quoted by L. Goodrich, E. Hambro and A. Simons, *Charter of the United Nations, Commentary and Documents* (New York/London 1969), p. 612.
1040. See the examples mentioned *ibidem*, pp. 613-614.

intend to create a legally binding document. This is so, not because registration is to be regarded as constitutive for binding force, but because the participating States or at least some of them claimed it is or acted as if it is. This conclusion is buttressed by the outcome of the negotiations concerning the letter of transmittance by which the Republic of Finland was to send the text of the Final Act to the Secretary-General of the United Nations. This letter includes the phrase: "I have also been asked ... to draw your attention to the fact that the Final Act is not eligible, in whole or in part, for registration with the Secretariat under Article 102 of the Charter of the United Nations, as would be the case were it a matter of a treaty or international agreement under the aforesaid Article".[1041]

Just like in other instances, some of which were mentioned in the foregoing, in this case too the hybrid character of the Helsinki Final Act is reflected by the fact that it contains a provision which to some extent counterbalances the non-registration-clause. The first post-ambular paragraph provides that "The original of this Final Act, ..., will be transmitted to the Government of the Republic of Finland, which will retain it in its archives. Each of the participating States will receive from the Government of the Republic of Finland a true copy of this Final Act". According to Nincic this provision in fact entrusts the Finnish Gov- with the role of quasi-depository,[1042] a function typically provided for in the case of treaties.

Finally, within the framework of this survey of final clauses attention should be drawn to some questions concerning reservations. Many multilateral treaties, particular those concluded after World War II, open the possibility for States to make reservations. Even if not expressly provided for, reservations are permitted unless the treaty prohibits them or authorizes only specified reservations other than those in question, or the reservations are incompatible with the object and purpose of the treaty.[1043] Reservations are a means to limit the scope of the obligations contained in provisions which a State is unwilling to accept in order to enable that State to become a party to a treaty.[1044] Consequently, the making of reservations, or so-called interpretative statements to the same effect, is superfluous when the instrument concerned was never intended to be legally binding in the first place. Conversely, if States make reservations or interpretative statements in the case of formally non-binding instruments, this may indicate, depending on the content of the reservation or statement, that they regard the instrument concerned capable of affecting their legal position.[1045]

1041. See the Journal 80/bis of the Coordinating Committee of the Conference on Security and Co-operation in Europe, July 18, 1975; the letter is reprinted in 73 *Department of State Bulletin* (1975), p. 349.
1042. D. Nincic, *loc.cit.* (note 978), p. 57.
1043. See article 19 of the Vienna Convention on the Law of Treaties.
1044. The questions involved in the making of reservations and their validity are manifold. For a survey, see P. Menon, *loc.cit.* (note 464), pp. 146-147 and 213-217.
1045. See also I. Seidl-Hohenveldern, *loc.cit.* (note 798), p. 197, who admits in reference to the practice of recitation of disclaimers with respect to General Assembly resolutions: "In a way this practice proves that also in the eyes of these opposing or abstaining States resolutions by the General Assembly are not lacking any legal effect whatsoever. If this were the case, such disclaimers or reservations would be fully redundant".

Some examples of reservations and interpretative statements with respect to formally non-binding instruments were already mentioned in the foregoing. We have pointed to the statements by a number of States concerning the ODA-target contained the 1980 International Development Strategy adopted by the General Assembly, and the reaction of other States qualifying some of these statements as tantamount to reservations.[1046] Similarly, reference was made to the interpretative statement by the United States concerning the Document on confidence-building measures and certain aspects of security and disarmament, which forms part of the Helsinki Final Act, to the effect that it did not consider that Document to lay down legally binding measures.[1047]

Comparatively unambiguous are the positions taken by Turkey and Cyprus during the third stage of the Conference on Security and Co-operation in Europe in 1975. It is true that the statements of both these States were politically motivated and directly related to their conflict of that time, but this cannot completely do away with their significance from a legal point of view. Turkey tabled a "formal reservation relating to the decision to adopt the Final Act" in order to express its opposition to the fact that Cyprus was represented by a single representative and not by two, each representing the two communities of the island. The reservation stated "that the provisions of the Final Act of the Conference on Security and Co-operation in Europe, to which Turkey will become a party by its signature are not valid as regards the relations with the State of Cyprus, and consequently will have no effects until such time that a government legitimately representing the two national communities is established in Cyprus".[1048] In reaction Cyprus made an interpretative statement declaring that "any reservation concerning the validity of the provisions of the Final Act in the relations of each participating State with all or any other participating State is of no effect".[1049]

In the present author's view, these reservations and interpretative statement show that the States making them consider at least some of the provisions contained in the instrument concerned capable of generating legal obligations.

13.5. Follow-up

13.5.1. Introduction

The class of manifestations of consent or acceptance, which we have labeled "follow-up", comprises a number of quite wide-ranging issues. These will be discussed here only briefly, because most of them have been dealt with more extensively at another place.[1050]

1046. See *supra* p. 246.
1047. See *supra* p. 236-237.
1048. See CSCE/III/1, Helsinki, 31st July 1975. See also J. Prévost, *loc.cit.* (note 975), p. 141.
1049. See CSCE/III/2, Helsinki, 1st August 1975. See also J. Prévost, *ibidem.*
1050. See G. van Hoof and K. de Vey Mestdagh, *loc.cit.* (note 230).

At the core of the questions concerning follow-up is what used to be described as the problem of enforcement of international law or ,alternatively, the lack of sanctions in international law. Enforcement, of course, is a concept derived from municipal legal systems. These systems have developed procedures and mechanisms for enforcement which are attuned to the structure of the comparatively well-integrated societies in which they function. In international law all this is quite different due to the particular structure of the international society.

In spite of these differences, the lack of procedures and mechanisms for enforcement in international law comparable to those in most municipal legal systems has sometimes been a reason for denying the status of law to that set of rules.[1051] However, this point of view has been abandoned. Nowadays, it is generally acknowledged that in international law the main object of enforcement - *i.e.* to ensure respect for and the realization of rules of law in order to achieve the goals embodied therein - has to be attained through ways and means which are not only largely different, but also more varied and often more complex. This is reflected in the variety of terms which are used in doctrine to describe the different aspects of what we have called follow-up. Apart from enforcement and follow-up, one may for instance find terms like supervision, implementation, monitoring, and measures to ensure compliance.

For the sake of simplicity we will confine ourselves to the terms enforcement, supervision, and follow-up. These three terms taken together sufficiently bear out, in our view, the various elements contained in the present class of manifestations of consent or acceptance. Enforcement obviously is the most narrow concept. It will be taken here to connote preventing and redressing violations of rules of law. Supervision is a wider concept as it is understood to include the elaboration of rules which are not specific enough to be applied to concrete cases. Follow-up as used here is the broadest concept as it may encompass the elements of both enforcement and supervision, but may also go beyond that and in fact consists of (new) efforts to make rules even though these new rules are directly related to already existing ones. We will not try to further define enforcement, supervision, and follow-up as such. Instead the following sections will attempt to outline them on the basis of a brief description of a number of functions which are performed by States or organs of international organizations when they are engaged in enforcement, supervision or follow-up.

We will first describe these various functions with respect to enforcement, supervision and follow-up of (full-fledged) rules of international law. Subsequently, the analysis will be expanded so as to include not formally binding rules. Usually questions concerning follow-up are discussed from the perspective of what the impact of the normative status of a rule is on the form of enforcement, supervision or follow-up, *i.e.* what type of enforcement, supervision or follow-up is permissible or suited given the normative status of a particular rule. Within the framework of the present study the converse question as to the impact of enforcement, supervision, or follow-up on the normative status of a rule must also be addressed. In other words, the question must be faced in what ways enforcement, supervision and follow-up can influence the normative status of the rules concerned.

1051. See, for instance, the position of J. Austin, *supra* p. 36.

13.5.2. Enforcement, supervision, follow-up

13.5.2.1. The review-function

On the first of the various functions to be mentioned here, *i.e.* the review-function, we may be brief. Review is indeed inherent in any concept of enforcement, supervision, or follow-up, national as well as international. In general review means measuring or judging something against a standard. Within a legal context review consists of the judging of behaviour for its conformity with a rule of law. The review-function in international law can therefore be said to be exercised whenever the behaviour of States is judged against a rule of international law. The review may be performed either by one or more other States, or by an international organ or institution created by or in virtue of a treaty. The review-function results in the determination of whether or not the behaviour reviewed is/was in conformity with international law. In the case of a positive result the main object of enforcement, supervision or follow-up - to ensure respect for and the realization of rules of law - has been achieved with the completion of the review-function.

13.5.2.2. The correction-function

The second function, *i.e.* the so-called correction-function, comes into play when the behaviour reviewed has been found to be contrary to international law. The object of enforcement, supervision, or follow-up requires that infringements be corrected. Apart from cases in which the violator remedies the infringement of his own accord, compliance with legal obligations has to be ensured through outside pressure. This constitutes the correction-function which is most typical of the concept of enforcement.

In most municipal legal systems this correction-function is highly institutionalized and is usually performed by the executive branch of government or through the decisions of the judiciary which are, if necessary, implemented by the executive branch of the government. As was already indicated, in international law this is considerably different due to the fact that the international society is not, like most national societies, hierarchically organized. Third-party-elements are therefore lacking to a large extent in the "enforcement" of international law. As has been pointed out by Watson: "The 'enforcement' structure of international law is substantially different from that of domestic systems in that, instead of there being a vertical normative order based on coercion and its variants, a horizontal order has evolved. Stability and compliance are achieved by mutual accommodation, cooperation and reciprocity, the impetus coming, as in the Golden Rule, from a desire to be treated in a like manner should one find oneself in the same position at some future time. The 'sanction' for non-compliance is not administered by some superior third party but by other interested, and potentially interested, States. ... The important thing to notice for our pur-

poses is that the sanction is reciprocal, being determined and implemented by a directly interested party, almost invariably one which has been or will be affected by the violation".[1052]

Because of the horizontally structured order, which the international legal system in fact is, the judicial form of correction is rather exceptional. As a rule the jurisdiction of international judicial and arbitral tribunals is not compulsory but voluntary, and for reasons explained above States are on the whole hesitant to submit their disputes to judicial or arbitral settlement.[1053] Traditionally, therefore, the correction-function in international law has been performed through the self-help by States, the classical sanction consisting of reprisals. Reprisals may be defined as illegal acts which lose their illegal character because they are undertaken in retaliation against a State to compel it to agree to a satisfactory settlement of a dispute originating in an earlier illegal act done by it.[1054]

However, the usefulness of reprisals has become fairly limited today in that article 2(3) of the UN Charter obliges States to settle their disputes peacefully. In effect present-day international law has outlawed coercive sanctions, because article 2(4) of the Charter prohibits the use and the threat of force except in a few situations to be narrowly interpreted. Moreover, whatever the precise status of reprisals under modern international law, in today's world many violations of international law are not followed by reprisals for reasons of expediency. These reasons have been summarized by Wengler as follows: "even reprisals without 'force' are seldom regarded as a non 'peaceful' act, and are *therefore* avoided. Another reason for avoiding the use of reprisals is that a State which has violated international law, and which, therefore, may become an object of reprisals, is not forbidden by law to resort, itself, to defence measures and to 'other counter-measures', provided only that these activities are normally lawful. The arsenal of such counter-measures at the disposition of a powerful State which has violated international law is usually not only superior to all possibilities for reprisals and other counter-measures of the victim, if the victim is a small State, but the arsenal is often equal to the arsenal of reprisals and other counter-measures of all those other States which have themselves been obliged to resort to collective sanctions".[1055]

In short, resort to reprisals, and for that matter to other counter-measures with similar effects too, in many instances is likely to be counter-productive for the victim State. Moreover, it is certainly counter-productive if viewed from the perspective of international law as a whole. In the present era of interdependence in which international law has changed from a system of co-existence into a system of cooperation[1056] coercion may undermine the very basis of the system. Paradoxically therefore, the fact that international law lacks coercive sanctions to a large extent may even be regarded instrumental rather than detrimental to its effectiveness. The observance of rules of international law has to be ensured through other mechanisms.

1052. J. Watson, *loc.cit.* (note 34), p. 619.
1053. See *supra* pp. 174-175.
1054. See G. von Glahn, *op.cit.* (note 754), p. 496.
1055. W. Wengler, "Public International Law, Paradoxes of a Legal Order", 158 *RCADI* (1977-V), pp. 13-85 (23).
1056. See *supra* pp. 68-69.

Such mechanisms, which to some extent make up for the lack of formal coercive sanctions, are indeed available. They function on the basis of a combination of considerations derived from the self-interest on the part of States and the element of reciprocity in international relations. The operation of this combination of self-interest and reciprocity, which in fact is to be considered as a facet of the (recognized) necessity put forward above as the basis of the binding force of international law,[1057] has been described by Henkin as follows: "Every nation derives some benefit from international law and international agreements. Law keeps international society running, contributes to order and stability, provides a basis and a framework for common enterprise and mutual intercourse. Because it limits the actions of other governments, law enhances each nation's independence and security; in other ways, too, by general law or particular agreement, one nation gets others to behave as it desires. General law establishes common standards where they seem desirable. Both general law and particular agreement avoid the need for negotiating anew in every new instance; both create justified expectation and warrant confidence as to how others will behave. All these advantages of law and agreement have their price. Law limits freedom of action: nations are "bound" to do (or not to do) other than they might like when the time to act comes. Political arrangements legitimized by law are more difficult to undo or modify. Stability and order mean that a particular nation is not free to be disorderly or readily to promote external change. To promote its own independence and security and the inviolability of its territory, to control the behaviour of other governments, a nation may have to accept corresponding limitations on its own behaviour. For the confidence bred by law, one pays the price of not being free to frustrate the expectations of others".[1058]

In other words, as a result of the combined effect of self-interest and reciprocity there is an incentive for States to observe international law. A State derives benefits from observing international law which other States can withhold in case it breaks international law or threatens to do so. Thus States can "punish" each other for or deter each other from violating international law without having to resort to reprisals. Such "value deprivations"[1059] in fact boil down to withholding the benefits of cooperation and consist in, for instance, cutting or toning down economic and cultural contacts (where these do not constitute legal obligations), refusal to enter into or breaking off negotiations, and postponement of the ratification of a treaty. Moreover, now that efforts to ensure compliance with rules of international law are increasingly being collectivized and take place within the framework of international organizations, a number of additional corrective measures have become available. These include suspension of voting rights, suspension of representation, suspension of services of the organization concerned, and expulsion. Furthermore, less formal steps like the refusal to elect a particular State to a subsidiary organ, the withholding of a favour to a State (for instance a loan or another form of financial assistance), or attaching conditions to certain services, may under certain circumstances turn out to be important instruments to correct the behaviour of a recalcitrant party. Finally, a State may be induced to change its behaviour as a result of the pressure emanat-

---

1057. See *supra* pp. 71-76.
1058. L. Henkin, *op.cit.* (note 228), pp. 29-30.
1059. This term is employed by M. Bothe, *loc.cit.* (note 762), p. 88.

ing from political debates within the framework of international organizations in combination with the so-called "mobilization of shame" which alerts public opinion against recalcitrant States.

All this of course is quite far removed from sanctions as pertaining to the traditional (municipal) concept of enforcement. It would therefore seem better to refer to the various measures just described as instruments (of the correction-function) of supervision instead of enforcement.

13.5.2.3. The creative-function

The third function to be discussed here most typically pertains to supervision as we have described it, instead of to enforcement in the traditional sense of that term. This third function, which we will call the creative-function, is more important in the context of the present study than review and correction, because it may potentially have a more far-reaching impact on the normative status of the rules concerned.

As a result of the configuration of the international society the functions of international supervisory bodies are often not limited to supervision *stricto sensu, i.e.* review and correction. Not seldom measures of the international "legislator" are very vague and/or abstract. In many cases they contain only broad directives with regard to the subject-matter to be regulated. Such directives need to be clarified or elaborated into more specific norms before they can be applied in practice. With respect to review, too, this clarification or elaboration is necessary, because review - and consequently correction - cannot be effective if the norm which must be used as a standard is too abstract or vague.

In municipal legal systems this task of further elaborating general norms is performed partly by the legislator itself, partly by the executive branch of the State, and dependent on the powers conferred upon them in this respect, by the courts. The legislature can, of course, draw up new, more specific norms; the executive can further specify the norm concerned through its own "legislative" measures, and by interpreting general norms and by elaborating them through legal acts of an individual character. The result of these processes is that national supervisory bodies *pur sang* (judges and judicial tribunals) are usually confronted with norms of a relatively concrete character. Obviously, the work of the national supervisor is not purely mechanical. A judgment does not simply result from putting side by side the standard of review (norm) on the one hand and the behaviour to be reviewed on the other. Some degree of interpretation is almost always required. Moreover, a national supervisor, too, might find himself in a situation in which the applicable norm is abstract or vague or in which there even is no directly applicable norm at all. The decision of the judge in such a case may result in so-called judge-made-law. Thus the judicial branch also contributes to the task of elaborating general norms, even though this often is disguised as interpretation.

Generally speaking, however, it seems that the role which this aspect of clarifying and elaborating abstract and vague norms plays in the work of the national judge is a minor one compared to that of international supervisory bodies. First of all, rules of international law are often more abstract and vague than national

legislation. For, although custom has been replaced by treaties as the main source of international law, it is clear that even treaty-making cannot be put on the same level as national legislative machinery. Treaty-rules more often than rules of municipal law need elaboration or even adaptation. This is particularly so since, as was pointed out above, an increasing number of treaty-rules reflect policy rather than actual state-conduct.[1060]

In addition, the treaty-making process of the international society is less monolithic than national legislative machinery. States act collectively as the international "legislature" and international law-making is not always performed by the same group of States. The composition of the international "legislature" can obviously change depending on the subject-matter or on the international organization concerned. The cohesiveness of the international "legislature" is therefore a matter of degree, in that it may vary according to the circumstances concerned. The EEC and, to a lesser extent, the ILO, for instance, are equipped with law-making machinery (a constitutional basis and law-making procedures on a permanent and institutionalized basis with at least some democratic participation) somewhat comparable to municipal legal systems. In general, however, multilateral (law-making) treaties are concluded on an *ad hoc* basis and often constitute the lowest common denominator.[1061] Finally, international law-making bodies in most cases are not functioning permanently. Even law-making organs of international organizations usually function on a periodic basis only. Their products, consequently, are not seldom a rather *ad hoc* reaction to a current problem.

In short, it is submitted that the international law-making machinery in its present state contributes to the elaboration and adaptation of abstract and vague norms of international law to a far smaller degree than does the national legislature with respect to municipal law.

As far as the executive type of institutions are concerned, the elaboration or adaptation function is even less impressive in the international society. In national societies the executive branch of government is the most eye-catching symbol of the centralized organization of the State. In the international society comparable institutions are not available. The executive organs of international organizations resemble the executive branch of national governments in only a very marginal way at best. As a matter of fact, in many instances the executive function is hardly performed at all.

As a result of this situation the task of elaborating and adapting abstract and vague norms is in the international legal system often postponed to the supervisory phase, *casu quo* unloaded upon the supervisory organs. It is difficult to describe the content and scope of the creative-function of international supervision *in abstracto*. As was pointed out, it consists, generally speaking, of the elaboration and adaptation of already existing norms, which are not specific enough to serve as a basis of effective supervision. It therefore goes beyond normal interpretation which is inherent in the review-function. It is not always easy to draw a clear dividing line between the review-function and the creative-function: elements of the latter are sometimes interwoven within the former. However, the creative-function can go further than what can still be considered inter-

---

1060. See *supra* pp. 126-128.
1061. See *supra* p. 123.

pretation. In such cases the supervisory activity amounts to an elaboration of the purposes of the organization and/or the principles underlying the legal order concerned, and/or to the elaboration or even adaptation of the norms embodying those purposes and principles. In this sense the creative-function can be said to contribute to the realization of the legal order concerned.

13.5.2.4. Development of the law

Finally, attention must be drawn to activities which are even wider than those just described as belonging to the creative-function of international supervision, but which are still sufficiently related to existing rules to be considered part of follow-up. In some situations it is not enough to elaborate and/or adapt abstract and vague rules in order to tailor them to application in practice. What is required in such situations is to go one step further, *viz.* a further development of the rules concerned. The difference between these processes may be conceived as follows. Elaboration and adaptation constitute activities which essentially concern the original or parent-rule. Of course this parent-rule is affected precisely because it is elaborated and/or adapted, but it remains the same in the sense that the outcome of the elaboration and/or adaptation is still based on the (original) consent or *opinio juris* contained in the parent-rule. No new manifestation of consent or acceptance is required. This is different in the case of what we have called here (further) development of law or of existing rules. The result of such a development may be so far removed and different from the parent-rule that a new consent or acceptance is required. It is clear that the activities comprised in this type of development of the law verge on what simply constitute newly made rules of law. Development of the law may be distinguished from law-making in that development of existing rules is based on a system of follow-up which is provided for in the same instrument as these rules, or created specifically in view of these rules. Therefore, although development of the law as just described cannot be fitted into the concept of supervision, because of the element of "newness" contained in it can be taken to belong to follow-up because of its direct relation with existing rules.

The need for a further development of the law as part of follow-up arises, broadly speaking, in two types of situations. The first type of situation, which we have already hinted at, occurs when the parent-rule is so abstract and/or vague that elaboration or even adaptation is not enough to make the rule applicable or operative in practice. The reason for such a situation is that the consensus (here used in the material or substantive sense) underlying the rule is comparatively weak. As was repeatedly implied in the foregoing, varying degrees of consensus may exist which are expressed in different types of (stronger and weaker) rules.[1062] A completely accurate description of all the nuances in this respect is impossible, but the issue can be clarified on the basis of a very rough classification of levels of consensus.

Apart from the case where there is in fact no agreement at all, three basic

---

1062. See, for instance, the reference to the "different shades of grey" making up the so-called grey area, *supra* p. 190, note 820.

grades of consensus may be discerned. As the first level can be taken the moment when a problem is identified and a general feeling (or even agreement) exists that it should be solved. This does not imply, however, that the consensus is sufficiently strong to serve as the basis for international legal obligations on the subject-matter concerned. The second level of consensus presents itself when States agree on a common purpose to the extent that the drawing up of legal rules on the subject-matter becomes possible. However, at this stage agreement on the methods and means to realize this purpose is still lacking. On the third level there is consensus with regard to both the purpose underlying the rule and the methods and means to achieve that purpose. Within this latter category varying degrees of perfection may be found. The lower the degree of perfection of the methods and means agreed upon to achieve the purpose, the more creative aspects of supervision are likely to be needed when the rules concerned are to be put into operation.

As far as the function of further development of the law is concerned, the second of the levels of consensus just mentioned is the most relevant. Particularly in the present heterogeneous international society it happens quite frequently that States are able to agree on a set of goals and purposes, but that consensus is not sufficiently strong to make these operational. It is one thing to reach agreement on one or more abstract objectives contained in a number of general norms; it is another thing to reach genuine agreement on the ways and means through which these objectives are to be accomplished in practice. As a result there are sometimes no rules laying down ways and means for achieving the purpose agreed upon, or, if there are, they may turn out to be defective. Consequently, they need to be followed-up through further development providing for more effective instruments to put the goals set into practice. There is of course no guarantee that the originally weak consensus will grow stronger over time so as to make such effective instruments feasible. However, the fact that agreement was reached on the general objectives may in itself become an incentive for the States concerned to also take the next step.[1063] Moreover, the existence of some kind of follow-up, even if limited to the review-function, may prove capable of furthering agreement concerning the instruments required, because it lays bare the defects of the rules concerned in this respect. This is particularly so, when third-party-elements in the form of (expert) organs of international organizations are engaged in the follow-up.

The second type of situation where the need for further development of the law can arise is not caused by a weak original consensus, but by a change of circumstances. As was already observed, our times are characterized by rapid changes giving rise to a growing need for devices through which the modification of rules of international law can be effected. Sometimes the changes are so drastic that a whole new set of rules is required. Sometimes, on the other hand, minor changes can be coped with through interpretation, elaboration or adaptation of existing rules. In intermediate situations the underlying goals and purposes may remain the same, but the change of circumstances is such that existing ways and means to achieve them have become obsolete and new ones have to be devised. In such cases a solution might result from what we have called follow-

---

1063. Compare in this respect the suggestion concerning the so-called "delegated legislation" discussed *supra* p. 123.

up through development of existing rules. While the ultimate goals and purposes remain the same, modification of the instruments to achieve them can be attained by "further developing" these instruments. It is submitted that in this way a number of international organizations, for instance the United Nations in the field of the maintenance of international peace and security and the World Bank with respect to development financing, have adapted to the far-reaching changes after the Second World War without (formally) changing their respective constitutions.

It might seem artificial to bring the activities described in the foregoing as further development of law under the heading of follow-up. It has to be admitted that the difference between this further development of the law and (new) law-making is often not very sharp. Indeed both types of activities coincide in that they result in new rules. As was pointed out, the difference is that in the case of development the new rules are most directly linked to existing rules, in the sense that the former result from a system of follow-up embodied in the same instrument as the latter or created specifically in view of the latter. In addition it should be kept in mind that defects of existing rules come to the fore very often within the framework of enforcement, supervision or follow-up. It is when rules are used as a standard for reviewing behaviour that their shortcomings are most likely to surface.

Particularly now that enforcement, supervision and follow-up increasingly take place within international organizations, conditions are sometimes fulfilled for remedying such defects or shortcomings within the framework of that enforcement, supervision or follow-up. For in the bulk of cases enforcement, supervision and follow-up conducted by international organizations is non-judicial,[1064] i.e. it is performed in the final analysis by a politically representative organ of the organization concerned. In other words, in such cases the international supervisor and the international law-maker are identical, and consequently the international supervisor is in the position to make new rules if the need arises and provided the political will to do so exists. Because of this "dédoublement fonctionel" the required new rules can be drawn up within the framework of enforcement, supervision or follow-up.

If this occurs, one is faced with a special case of the phenomenon that international law has become more of a system resulting in a closer link between its various rules.[1065]

13.5.3. Follow-up with respect to formally binding rules

After the foregoing description of the various functions involved in follow-up (hereinafter used to encompass enforcement and supervision) some brief observations on the relation between follow-up and formally binding rules must suffice. As far as the main issue within the framework of the present study - *in casu* the question as to the impact of follow-up on the normative status of rules - is concerned, at first sight there would seem to be no problem at all. For, it could be argued, formally binding rules are full-fledged rules of international law and,

---

1064. On the various forms of international supervision, see *infra* pp. 266-270.
1065. See *supra* pp. 240-242.

consequently, follow-up has nothing to add to their normative status. However, presented in this general fashion this position is too simplistic.

In international law it is not uncommon that rules are not enforced or supervised. A rule of international law which is often violated without there being efforts to redress those violations is bound to lose its legal character sooner or later. In such a situation one cannot but conclude that the States concerned (both the State(s) violating the rule and the State(s) proving indifferent to such violations) have lost interest in the rule and that the rule stops functioning as a regulating and ordering device.[1066] Particularly in international law it is therefore an important indication of the intention of the States concerned with respect to a given rule, if it is indeed used as a standard for reviewing behaviour of States, and if, in case the behaviour reviewed turns out to be in contravention of the rule, efforts are made to correct that behaviour in order to bring it in conformity with the rule. In other words, without being a constitutive element for rules of international law, review and correction may more firmly establish a rule as a rule of international law.

With respect to what we have called the creative-function and development of the law things may be a little different. As was explained in the preceding sections, these do not merely provide a confirmation, but also may actually add something to existing rules of international law. How this works in practice is dependent *inter alia* on the form of supervision or follow-up which is employed within the framework of the international organization or arrangement concerned.[1067]

Three forms of supervision or follow-up may be discerned, *i.e.* judicial, quasi-judicial, and non-judicial. Generally speaking, they can be defined as follows. Judicial supervision or follow-up is exercised by independent persons or bodies competent to give, on the basis of facts determined by due process, legally binding judgments. Quasi-judicial supervision or follow-up shows characteristics which are in between those of the judicial and non-judicial form. A number of varieties are conceivable, but in this case too the organ or body concerned is usually independent from the States and applies rules of law to facts established by due process. The finding of the organ or body, however, can either be binding or non-binding. At the same time it is not subject to political reconsideration. This latter aspect is different in the case of non-judicial supervision or follow-up which is exercised, in the last resort, by a politically representative organ or body.[1068] The procedure within non-judicial supervision or

---

1066. If such a rule is not formally abolished or changed it may lose its legally binding character as a result of so-called *desuetudo*.
1067. Enforcement, supervision and follow-up may be performed individually by a State *vis-à-vis* another State. In modern international law supervision and follow-up have increasingly become a collective effort within the framework of an international organization or other type of collective arrangement. In the following the analysis will be confined to such collective effects.
1068. Within non-judicial mechanisms of supervision or follow-up often two phases can be discerned, *i.e.* a technical and a political phase. In the technical phase organs of restricted composition, mostly composed of experts, perform an investigatory function consisting for instance of fact-finding and inquiry. Generally, the findings of these organs are laid down in a report, which may or may not be supplemented by a tentative opinion. In the political phase, in which representatives of all the Member States usually participate, decisions are then taken on the basis of the outcome of the technical phase.

follow-up is generally not very well-defined, while the outcome can be a binding decision or a non-binding recommendation depending on the constitutional powers of the organ or body concerned.

Instances of judicial supervision or follow-up are quite rare in international law. Apart from the International Court of Justice, the most well-known examples are the Court of Justice of the European Communities, the European Court of Human Rights, and the Inter-American Court of Human Rights. Particularly as far as the creative-function and development of the law are concerned, the three regional Courts just mentioned find themselves in a situation which differs in important respects from that of the International Court of Justice as we have described it above.[1069] The International Court of Justice in fact has to cover the entire body of international law as becomes clear *inter alia* from article 38 of its Statute, according to which it is the Court's function "to decide in accordance with international law such disputes as are submitted to it, ...". The functions of the other three Courts on the other hand are far more restricted as their supervision is confined to the respective treaties on which they are based. Even more important in the present context is the fact that the European Courts operate as judicial organs of comparatively cohesive international organizations (the European Communities and the Council of Europe respectively). Something similar, albeit to a lesser extent, would seem to hold true with respect to the Inter-American Court of Human Rights. The International Court of Justice as the principal judicial organ of the United Nations has to serve the entire heterogeneous community of States, while the other Courts' activities concern a smaller and a greater circle respectively of comparatively like-minded States.

The result is that there exists quite a difference in the effects of the work of the International Court of Justice on the one hand, and that of the European Courts on the other hand, while the practice of the Inter-American Court is still too restricted to allow for an evaluation. As was pointed out above, the binding force of decisions of the International Court of Justice is confined to the parties to the case concerned and this puts far-reaching limits on those decisions as a source of international law.[1070] As far as the Court of Justice of the European Communities is concerned, its impact on Community Law has been and is far more substantial. Even without going into the details of the Court's multi-faceted jurisdiction and the formal effects of its judgments,[1071] it is not difficult to see why this is so. The jurisdiction of the Court of Justice is compulsory. Furthermore, complaints against member States can be lodged not only by other member States, but also by an independent international supervisor, *viz.* the European Commission.[1072] Therefore, even assuming that judgments of the Court are not binding upon Member States other than the parties to the case concerned, the Court usually has ample opportunity to bring its views to bear upon those other States. Moreover, in actual practice this is not necessary, because member States as a rule accept and abide by judgments of the Court even if not formally involved in the case concerned.

1069. See *supra* pp. 169-176.
1070. See *supra* pp. 170-172.
1071. For more details, see P. Kapteyn and P. VerLoren van Themaat, *Introduction to the Law of the European Communities* (London, etc. 1973), pp. 157-191.
1072. For more details, see H. Audretsch, *Supervision in European Community Law* (Amsterdam 1978).

Because of its strong position the role that the Court of Justice has played comes close to that of national courts. Through the use of what we have called the creative-function it has contributed considerably to the elaboration and adaptation of Community Law. In short, the Court of Justice has been able "to function as a catalyst of the integration between the Member States".[1073]

To a lesser extent something similar holds good for the European Court of Human Rights which is to ensure the observance of the engagements undertaken by the States parties to the European Convention for the Protection of Human Rights and Fundamental Freedoms.[1074] The Court's jurisdiction is optional, but in fact all but two of the twenty-one parties to the Convention have accepted it.[1075] In addition, seventeen States have also recognized the right of individual complaint under article 25 of the Convention, so that private persons and organizations are entitled to file complaints with the European Commission of Human Rights. After the Commission has declared such an individual complaint admissible and has conducted an investigation on the merits, it is empowered to refer the case to the Court.[1076] Therefore, under the European Convention too complaints can be lodged by others than States and referral of cases to the Court is not (solely) dependent upon States. In this case too, the judgments of the Court are taken into account by the States concerned even if they were not a party to the particular case. Thus the Court has been able in several respects to give substance to the often vague and abstract provisions of the Convention to an extent which goes beyond the formal effects of its judgments.

In summary, the greater impact of the European Courts as compared to the International Court of Justice is to be attributed to the fact that the former function within comparatively well-integrated groups of States. Particularly Community Law, but also the European Convention for the Protection of Human Rights and Fundamental Freedoms cannot be understood without taking into account the elaborations, adaptations and even additions contained in the case-law of the Court of Justice and the European Court of Human Rights respectively.

As was already observed, judicial supervision, and for that matter quasi-judicial supervision too, is quite rare. As a rule the form of international enforcement, supervision or follow-up is non-judicial, the most important aspect of which in this respect is the fact that it is performed in the last resort by a politically representative organ. This situation may enhance the possibilities for the creative-function and for further development of the law, because the international supervisor then is identical to the international law-maker.[1077] Whether such better possibilities in fact materialize depends on the circumstances of each

1073. See P. van Dijk, op.cit. (note 569), p. 242, and the studies cited there.
1074. For details on the Convention, see P. van Dijk and G. van Hoof, De Europese Conventie in Theorie en Praktijk, 2nd edition (Nijmegen 1982); an English edition of this book will be published in the fall of 1983 by Kluwer (Deventer) entitled: Theory and Practice of the European Convention on Human Rights.
1075. These two States are: Malta and Turkey.
1076. If a case is for one reason or another not referred to the Court, the final decision is taken by the Committee of Ministers of the Council of Europe.
1077. See supra pp. 261-265.

case, in particular on the (political) cohesiveness of the international organization or arrangement concerned.

The reporting system of the ILO is generally considered an effective supervisory mechanism also with respect to its creative aspects.[1078] Under article 22 of the ILO Constitution every member State has to report periodically on the measures which it has taken to give effect to the ILO conventions ratified by it. The Director-General of the ILO submits abstracts of these reports to the plenary organ of the ILO, *i.e.* the Conference. These are accompanied by a report from a Committee of Independent Experts. These documents are subsequently discussed during the annual sessions of the Conference in a committee specifically set up for this purpose, consisting of representatives of the governments, the employers and the workers, which in its turn reports to the Conference. The results of this supervisory mechanism have been summarized as follows: "While there is still a certain proportion of cases where no improvement has yet taken place, the general situation shows progress every year. In the last 17 years, there have been over 1300 cases concerning more than 150 countries ... where governments have taken the measures recommended by the supervisory bodies."[1079]

Finally, the World Bank can be mentioned as an example of an international organization equipped with a system of supervision or follow-up in which the creative-function and further development of the law play a considerable role. The World Bank exercises a very tight type of supervision over the projects it (co-)finances in its member States. It is performed, in the last resort, by the Board of Directors which is the executive (political) organ of the World Bank. The Board, however, has to a large extent delegated its supervisory powers to the World Bank staff. World Bank supervision, therefore, resembles the two-phased structure consisting of a technical and a political phase which is typical for the non-judicial form of supervision or follow-up.[1080]

The creative-function is exercised by the World Bank staff in that the experience gathered through the supervision of a project in a given country is used with respect to following projects. Defects can be remedied by entering new (adapted) provisions into the so-called Loan Documents (various types of legal instruments between the World Bank and its borrowers) pertaining to a new project. Furthermore, on a broader scale supervision of all projects is evaluated by a special department of the World Bank on a more or less permanent basis.

1078. On the ILO supervisory system, see E. Landy, *The Effectiveness of International Supervision; Thirty Years of ILO Experience* (London/New York 1966); N. Valticos, "Un Système de Contrôle International: La Mise en Oeuvre des Conventions Internationales du Travail au Bureau International du Travail", 123 *RCADI* (1968-I), pp. 311-407; see also the studies cited *supra* note 491.

1079. See N. Valticos, *loc.cit.* (note 486), p. 127. A special case constitutes the ILO machinery in the field of freedom of association under which complaints can be made even against States which have not ratified the ILO conventions on freedom of associaton. The justification for this is found in the fact that the ILO constitution lays down the principle of freedom of association and that member States, because of their acceptance of the constitution, are bound to observe it. The Freedom of Associaton Committee, which has been set up for this purpose, has dealt with a great number of cases and in many instances the governments concerned have given effect to its recommendations; see *ibidem*, pp. 128-130, and the studies cited there.

1080. See *supra* note 1068.

The experience resulting from this evaluation is channeled *inter alia* to the Board of Directors. It may then be used to effect (minor) changes in (new) projects in more or even all borrowing States, but also more generally as an instrument in support of the policy-making of the Board of Directors. Thus, modifications in the World Bank's policy with regard to projects have, at least partly, been the result of, and effected within its system of supervision or follow-up.[1081]

Cases like these show that non-judicial supervision or follow-up, if exercised in cohesive international organizations, can have considerable effects on the law of the organization concerned. The elaborations, adaptations, additions or even modifications flowing from it cannot be ignored when the precise content of that law is to be determined.

13.5.4. Follow-up with respect to formally non-binding rules

In the preceding section the question was addressed when and in what ways enforcement, supervision or follow-up can elaborate, adapt, or further develop formally binding rules, *i.e.* full-fledged rules of international law. In the present section the question must be faced whether, and if so in what ways, comparable devices can affect the normative status of formally non-binding rules.

It is clear that the term "enforcement" squares uneasily with the idea of formally non-binding rules. Such rules can obviously not be enforced in the legal sense of that term.[1082] The terms "supervision" and, in particular, "follow-up" have a more neutral meaning and can therefore be retained with respect to formally non-binding rules. These terminological differences, however, do not detract from the fact that devices of supervision or follow-up, comparable to those applying to full-fledged legal rules, do also exist in the case of formally non-binding rules. Bothe pictures the general situation in this field as follows: "implementation procedures, essentially monitoring devices, are used without significant distinction for observing compliance with both legal and non-legal obligations".[1083] In the following we will attempt to clarify the impact of supervision and follow-up on the normative status of formally non-binding rules along the lines of the various functions of supervision and follow-up described in the preceding sections.

As far as the first of these functions, *i.e.* review, is concerned, there is no significant difference between formally binding and formally non-binding rules. The question of whether a rule can be used as a standard for reviewing the behaviour of States is not dependent upon its precise legal nature. What counts is whether the norm contained in the rule is sufficiently clear to "judge" the behaviour of States. As far as clarity is concerned, there is no inherent difference between legal and other types of rules.

It is therefore not surprising that practice shows an - in recent years increasing - number of international instruments which, although not of a full-fledged

1081. For more details, see G. van Hoof, "World Bank Supervision", in: P. van Dijk, *op.cit.* (note
1082. See also I. Seidl-Hohenveldern, *loc.cit.* (note 798), p. 205, who, in reference to international economic soft law, observes: "Enforcing, of course, often will almost be too strong a word for the following-up of State attitudes concerning 'soft law' commitments".
1083. M. Bothe, *loc.cit.* (note 762), p. 87.

legal character, provide for some kind of review on the basis of the rules they contain. We have already referred to the system contained in the so-called Basket IV of the Helsinki Final Act, which provides for follow-up in the form of meetings of representatives of the participating States at intervals of approximately two years. The Final Act stipulates that these meetings aim *inter alia* at "proceeding to a thorough exchange of views ... on the implementation of the provisions of the Final Act ...".[1084] Similarly, the International Development Strategy for the Third United Nations Development Decade, which we have discussed above [1085], includes an elaborate Part IV entitled: "Review and Appraisal of the Implementation of the New International Development Strategy". Its paragraph 169 designates the process of review and appraisal as an integral part of the Strategy and provides *inter alia* that "Its aim will be to ensure the effective implementation of the International Development Strategy ...".

Because review can be conducted on the basis of both formally binding and formally non-binding rules, the mere fact that a system of review is provided for cannot justify the conclusion that the instruments or rules concerned are therefore rules of international law. Nevertheless, even with respect to formally non-binding rules review may prove important in the following respects. The setting up of a system of review may be a reflection of the genuine determination or resolve of the States in question to effectively implement or put into operation the rules concerned. If and to the extent that such efforts prove successful, these rules resemble rules of law in at least one important respect: just like rules of law, they perform the function of ordering and regulating relations between States, albeit in a different, *i.e.* formally non-binding, way. Whether or not, and if so to what extent, such rules can be effectively implemented, depends at least partly upon the possibilities to induce States to behave in conformity with the rule concerned. This then brings us to the second function, *viz.* correction.

It was already pointed out that the correction-function is most typical for enforcement in the legal sense of that term and, consequently, is difficult to reconcile with the idea of formally non-binding rules. It is obvious that formal legal sanctions or enforcement in the form of reprisals or judicial supervision cannot be applied to formally non-binding rules.[1086] However, the other available instruments, which we have described above as "counter-measures", "value deprivations", and the "other than formal steps" within the framework of international organizations,[1087] are compatible with formally non-binding rules, precisely because they are themselves of a non-legal nature. Indeed, such instruments are in fact applied with respect to formally non-binding rules. When these instruments are used for the purpose of ensuring compliance with formally non-binding rules, their effectiveness depends mainly on the interplay between the self-interest of the States concerned and the mechanism of reci-

---

1084. See *supra* p. 4.
1085. See *supra* pp. 245-247.
1086. See *supra* pp. 258-260, where it was simultaneously pointed out that reprisals often are counter-productive or, at least, are not very frequently used in modern international law, and that the judicial form of enforcement or supervision is quite rare.
1087. See *supra* pp. 259-261. The instruments mentioned here include the analogous application of the rule of *non adimplendi non est adimplendum* as laid down in article 60 of the Vienna Convention on the Law of Treaties.

procity in international relations.[1088]

Practice shows examples of cases in which formally non-binding rules are quite effectively implemented as a result *inter alia* of supervision and follow-up. Well-known is the work of the so-called Committee of Twenty-Four set up by the General Assembly of the United Nations in 1961.[1089] The official name of the Committee indicates the task which was entrusted to it: Special Committee on the Situation with Regard to the Implementation of the Declaration on the Granting of Independence to Colonial Countries and Peoples. This Declaration had been adopted by the General Assembly one year before.[1090] It proclaims the necessity of bringing colonialism to a speedy and unconditional end. Furthermore, the Declaration states that the subjection of peoples to alien subjugation, domination and exploitation constitutes a denial of human rights, is contrary to the Charter and an impediment to the promotion of world peace and cooperation. The Committee of Twenty-Four was charged with examining the application of the Declaration and with making suggestions and recommendations on the progress and extent of its application.

The Committee of Twenty-Four has produced a large number of suggestions, recommendations and reports. In this way it has contributed to the specification and elaboration of the 1960 Declaration. Moreover, the Committee has also engaged in supervisory activities *stricto sensu* in that it has dispatched visiting missions in order to obtain information or to observe the conduct of elections or popular consultations in a number of non-self-governing territories.[1091] The goals which were set by the 1960 Declaration have been achieved to a very large extent. The speed with which colonies have been transformed in self-governing States during the sixties and the seventies has been due mainly to the prevailing political circumstances. Nevertheless, it is believed that on the basis of these circumstances the pressure emanating from the United Nations, in particular the Committee of Twenty-Four, has contributed considerably to that process.

A most eye-catching example of supervision or follow-up with respect to formally non-binding rules constitute the steps taken by the Organization for Economic Cooperation and Development (OECD) to ensure the implementation of the Guidelines for Multinational Enterprises, which were issued in 1976[1092] and revised and reapproved in 1979.[1093] The Guidelines themselves provide that "observance of the guidelines is voluntary and not legally enforceable".[1094] In contrast, the supervisory system is based upon decisions of the OECD Council which are binding upon member States.[1095] The system has

1088. Compare *supra* pp. 259-261.
1089. General Assembly Resolution 1654 (XVI), 27 November, 1961.
1090. General Assembly Resolution 1514 (XV), 14 December, 1960.
1091. For more details on the work of the Committee of Twenty-Four, see L. Goodrich, *The United Nations in a Changing World* (New York 1975), pp. 191-201; and Department of Public Information of the United Nations, *Everyone's United Nations*, 9th edition (New York 1979), pp. 282-290.
1092. 15 *ILM* (1976), pp. 969-977.
1093. 18 *ILM* (1979), pp. 986-989.
1094. See Introductory Understanding, no. 6.
1095. Decision C(76)117 of the OECD Council on Intergovernmental Consultation Procedures on Guidelines for Multinational Enterprises, 15 *ILM* (1976), pp. 977-978, and its revised 1979 version Decision C(79)143, 18 *ILM* (1979), pp. 1171-1173. See also M. Bothe,

been quite extensively dealt with in international legal writing.[1096] A brief enumeration of its main features and effects suffices for our purposes.

The OECD has set up a Committee on International Investment and Multinational Enterprises (CIME) composed of the representatives of the OECD member States. The CIME is charged with conducting, periodically or at the request of a member State, an exchange of views on matters related to the Guidelines and the experience gained in their application. To that end, the CIME must periodically invite the Business and Industry Advisory Committee to the OECD and the Trade Union Advisory Committee to the OECD to express their views on matters related to the Guidelines. Furthermore, the CIME may decide on the proposal of a Member State whether individual enterprises should be given the opportunity to express their views concerning the application of the Guidelines. It is specifically provided that the CIME "shall not reach conclusions on the conduct of individual enterprises".

The CIME has stuck to the letter of its mandate rather than to its (original) spirit. In fact, its procedures have gained, according to Seidl-Hohenveldern, a "quasi-judicial character".[1097] The CIME has not discussed "cases", but "issues", and it has not "interpreted", but "clarified" the Guidelines. The result is that "By thus clarifying the content of the guidelines the Committee can do hardly otherwise than reach conclusions which will establish, at least indirectly, whether or not the conduct of the enterprise concerned was in conformity with the context of the guidelines as clarified".[1098]

Of the first fifteen cases brought before CIME twelve were abandoned or withdrawn and three have been pursued further. All three were settled after a clarification. As a conclusion Seidl-Hohenveldern has observed with respect to this OECD procedure that "its merits may extend beyond having permitted a settlement of these cases. Could or should the solutions found not serve as a precedent for other cases? As the solutions in these cases, found in compromises outside this Committee, were welcomed by the State representatives forming the Committee one might consider the solutions arrived at as admission by the States concerned of the existence of an *opinio juris* to this effect."[1099]

The preceding examples show that formally non-binding rules can, as a result of effective supervision or follow-up the outcome of which is accepted by the States concerned, operate in practice with similar effects as formally binding rules: they can order and regulate relations between States. The question is whether an effective system of supervision or follow-up can also "harden" such "soft law" rules into full-fledged rules of law. It should not be too easily assumed that this process has taken place, particularly not when, as in the case of the OECD Guidelines, the instrument concerned expressly provides that it is "voluntary and not legally enforceable".[1100] Nevertheless, it is submitted that the growth of formally non-binding rules into legal rules is feasible.

loc.cit. (note 762), p. 82, who refers to the OECD set up as "a somewhat surprising mixture of a substantive regulation which is not legally binding and a binding implementation procedure".
1096. See in particular I. Seidl-Hohenveldern, *loc.cit.* (note 798), pp. 207-213, and the studies cited there.
1097. *Ibidem*, p. 208.
1098. *Ibidem.*
1099. *Ibidem*, p. 211.
1100. See *supra* p. 272.

It is possible that an originally weak consensus resulting in formally non-binding rules strengthens over time precisely because the successful operation of supervision or follow-up makes the rules concerned more acceptable to the States in question. It should be kept in mind that the reason for the existence of formally non-binding rules is often their flexibility at the stage of adoption: it is sometimes easier to induce States to commit themselves to formally non-binding rules than to have them enter into legal obligations. States might feel unable to accept the latter because of their rigidity combined with the impossibility to foresee all the consequences of the rules concerned at the stage of adoption. This feeling may change as a result of the actual operation of the rules which may make them more acceptable to the States concerned. In other words, after a certain lapse of time the flexibility of formally non-binding rules might have served the purpose of "getting the rules concerned accepted", thus preparing the ground for full-fledged legal rules.

It is often asserted that the flexibility of formally non-binding rules is relevant not only in view of adoption, but also with respect to the subsequent operation of the rules concerned. It is argued that the "soft" character of the rules coupled with the "soft" character of supervision of follow-up can bring about results which could not be attained by legal rules applied by a court of law.[1101] This may be true, but it should be remembered that the judicial form of supervision is not a necessary sequel of rules of international law. As was pointed out, most of the time efforts to implement rules of international law are made through (some type of) non-judicial form of supervision or follow-up.[1102] This combination may provide the same amount of flexibility while entailing at the same time the advantage of the greater degree of certainty inherent in full-fledged legal rules. Flexibility of operation, therefore, is not necessarily a reason for prefering formally non-binding rules to full-fledged legal rules.

In the present author's view, the foregoing makes clear that, depending on the particular case under discussion, supervision *stricto sensu, i.e.* review and correction, may indeed add to the normative status of a given instrument or rule. It must, therefore, be taken into account when one tries to determine the legally binding or non-binding character of an instrument or rule.

Finally, some observations must be made concerning the creative- and development-function of supervision or follow-up with respect to formally non-binding rules. It is clear that supervision or follow-up, in cases where it takes on the "quasi-judicial" character as described above, involves interpretation. Furthermore, particularly formally non-binding rules, because they often result from a relatively weak consensus, may require elaboration and adaptation in order to become operative. Therefore, the so-called creative-function of supervision or follow-up will, if possible, have to be performed with respect to such rules. The possibility to perform the creative-function would, for instance, seem to be provided for in the power of the CIME to "clarify" the OECD Guidelines. A very striking example presents the so-called *Hertz Rent a Car* case. In that case the Guidelines proved to contain no provisions on the issue at stake. The CIME however, proceeded to base its finding in this case on the so-called Tripartite Declaration drawn up within the framework of the International Labour

1101. See, for instance, I. Seidl-Hohenveldern, *loc.cit.* (note 798), pp. 209-210.
1102. See *supra* pp. 267-270.

Organization. It justified this approach by pointing out that the parties to the case had in fact accepted the Tripartite Declaration.[1103]

The development-function with respect to formally non-binding rules obviously cannot consist of development of the law. It may, however, constitute development of formally non-binding rules *towards* rules of law. An increasing number of international instruments contain provisions providing for the holding of some kind of follow-up conference or meeting in the future. The task of such conferences or meetings is often twofold: review of implementation and, on that basis, further development of the rules concerned. Thus the follow-up system outlined in the Helsinki Final Act provides for a thorough exchange of views between the participating States "on the deepening of their mutual relations, the improvement of security and the development of cooperation in Europe, and the development of the process of détente in the future;".[1104] Similarly, the review and appraisal system of the 1980 International Development Strategy referred to above[1105] is designed to ensure effective implementation of the Strategy and "to strengthen it as an instrument of policy".[1106] The review, which is to be carried out by the General Assembly for the first time in 1984,[1107] is described as an occasion "to see how the implementation of the Strategy can be strengthened and the necessary political impulses given and to carry out, if necessary, the adjustment, intensification or reformulation of the policy measures in the light of evolving needs and developments".[1108]

Nothing guarantees, of course, that occasions for follow-up like these will be successful, let alone that the rules concerned will be developed into legal rules. The point is, however, that such a process may take place and that the results of such a follow-up have to be taken into consideration as far as the normative status of the rules in question is concerned.

13.6. Subsequent practice.

The final class of manifestations of consent or acceptance by States to be dealt with here consists of subsequent practice. Various aspects of the manifestations contained in this class were already referred to in the foregoing. Subsequent practice has been discussed expressly within the framework of the analysis of customary international law.[1109] Implicitly, a number of aspects have been covered in the preceding sections on follow-up. As will become clear, subsequent practice can have an impact on the normative status and the content of rules in ways, which are in some respects comparable to the ways in which the various functions of supervision of follow-up may affect the normative status or the content of rules. In the following we will summarize the aspects already referred to and also discuss a number of additional issues.

State-practice in the present heterogeneous international society is highly

1103. I. Seidl-Hohenveldern, *loc.cit.* (note 798), p. 000.
1104. See *supra* p. 4.
1105. See *supra* p. 271.
1106. Paragraph 169.
1107. Paragraph 180.
1108. Paragraph 171.
1109. See *supra* pp. 102-103 and 115-116.

amorphous and, at first glance, often contradictory. It is therefore important to distinguish, if possible, between different types of practice. We have already attempted to delimit customary international law on the one hand, and subsequent practice on the other.[1110] Put summarily, customary international law was defined as *usus* delineating the content of a rule through the practice of States, followed by *opinio juris* which turns the custom concerned into a rule of international law. Because the essence of customary law consists in the fact that it is practice-based, the reverse case, where *opinio juris* precedes the practice, cannot strictly speaking be considered as customary law. For, in that case the content of the rule does not primarily take shape through the (later) practice of States, but has in essence already been formed at the time the *opinio juris* was expressed. Consequently, it was suggested to refer to such later practice not as *usus* (being one of the constitutive elements of customary international law), but as *subsequent* practice.

The relation between subsequent practice and a pre-existing rule may take different forms. First we will start from the position that the pre-existing rule is already a rule of international law. As a first possibility, the subsequent practice may be in line with the existing rule. No problems arise in such a case of law-conform conduct. The practice strenghtens the normative status of the rule concerned by confirming it. Subsequent practice in the form of law-conform conduct includes what has been called practice or custom *secundum legem, i.e.* practice or custom applied by virtue of the written law itself.[1111] However, examples of practice or custom *secundum legem* are likely to be rare.[1112]

The opposite of the case of *secundum legem* constitutes practice or custom *contra legem*, which is practice or custom in oppostition of the law.[1113] If a subsequent practice is contrary to an existing rule of international law, it obviously constitues a violation. However, it should not be taken for granted too quickly that practice is of such a contrary character. Practice, which at first glance seems to be contrary to existing rules, may on closer inspection prove not, or not entirely, to be so. Bleckmann has pointed out, that there exist a number of ways in which the contrary character of practice may be reduced,[1114] and has provided several examples thereof.[1115] It may turn out, for instance, that a practice is contrary to the general rule, but compatible with one or more parts or sub-

---

1110. See *supra* p. 102.
1111. This terminology is derived from H. Thirlway, *op.cit.* (note 209), p. 95. Thirlway's book deals with the relation between codification and customary international law. In the present context particularly chapter VII entitled: Custom as Law Ancillary to Codified Law, and chapter IX entitled: Codification and After: The Subsequent Development of the Law, are of interest. Thirlway recognizes the possibility that customary international law comes into being in cases when *opinio juris* precedes *usus*. In this respect his definition of customary international law differs from that put forward in the present study. Nevertheless, bearing this difference in mind, Thirlway's observations in the above-mentioned chapters are *mutatis mutandis* relevant with respect to the relation between pre-existing law and what we have called subsequent practice.
1112. *Ibidem*, pp. 96-97.
1113. *Ibidem*.
1114. A. Bleckmann, *loc.cit.* (note 397), p. 376: "Die Völkerrechtspraxis hat eine Anzahl von Methoden entwickelt, mit deren Hilfe Widersprüche der Praxis reduziert werden können, so dass man trotz Festhaltnens an der Notwendigkeit einer einheitlichen Praxis zu Völkergewohnheitsrecht gelangt."
1115. *Ibidem*, pp. 376-383.

rules of the general rule, so that a uniform practice can be established with respect to the latter. Sometimes a distinction can be made between the principal rule and exceptions to the principal rule. Practice then may lose its contrary character if it is related to the former instead of to the latter or *vice versa*. A similar conclusion may result from the distinction between universal and regional, or rather general and specific,[1116] international law. Clearly, it will not be possible to whitewash all practice in this manner and obviously practice which turns out to be *contra legem* constitutes a violation of international law. However, if the contrary character of practice is reduced in one way or another, its impact on existing rules of law may take the same form as in the case of practice or custom *praeter legem* to which we will turn now.

Between the two extreme cases of *secundum legem* and *contra legem* one may find pratice or custom *praeter legem*, which is practice or custom operating alongside the law in order to remedy its insufficiencies and fill its logical *lacunae*.[1117] In the case of practice *praeter legem* the practice is not incompatible with the existing rule concerned, but does not completely fit that rule either; it goes beyond the rule in question in the sense that it constitutes a concretization or elaboration. The case of practice *praeter legem* therefore may contribute to the normative status or the content of rules of law in a way which is comparable to the creative-function of supervision or follow-up as described above.[1118] Thirlway has summarized the operation of practice or custom *praeter legem* as "filling in the inevitable gaps which, if they were not realised and intended at the time when the treaty was concluded, are bound to emerge in the course of the application of the treaty to the manifold circumstances of international relations".[1119]

This "concretization-function" of practice or custom *praeter legem* is likely to be of great practical importance in present-day international law.[1120] As was pointed out, the horizontal expansion of international law has resulted in an increased number of abstract and vague norms which need concretization and elaboration before they can be effectively used to order and regulate international relations.[1121] This concretization and elaboration can be, at least partly, achieved trough subsequent practice.[1122]

Next, the question arises of whether practice or custom *praeter legem* can also provide for adaptation or even further development of the law like international supervision or follow-up. In the present author's view, the capabilities of practice or custom *praeter legem* are more limited than those of supervision or follow-up in this respect. The reason is that practice at best constitutes a tacit manifestation of the intent to be bound. Consequently, when the precise intention of States has to be determined, practice cannot be relied on to the same extent as supervision or follow-up, which can provide more express manifestations

---

1116. On this distinction, see *supra* p. 96.
1117. H. Thirlway, *op.cit.* (note 209), p. 95.
1118. See *supra* pp. 261-263.
1119. H. Thirlway, *op.cit.* (note 209), p. 98.
1120. See also *ibidem*, p. 97.
1121. See *supra* pp. 126-128.
1122. See in this respect also A. Bleckmann, *loc.cit.* (note 397), p. 8383: "Die Konkretisierung dieser abstrakten Rechtssätze erfolgt zwar auch, aber nicht immer und nicht einmal überwiegend wiederum durch von Rechtsüberzeugung getragene Praxis."

of consent.

Thirlway takes a more far-reaching position in this respect. In fact, he would seem to give an affirmative answer to the question: "can an accumulation of acts contrary to existing law abrogate that law and give rise to a new rule of customary law?"[1123] Thirlway quotes Thomas Aquinas to substantiate his position: "Human laws prove inadequate in particualr cases; it is therefore sometimes possible to act alongside the law (*praeter legem*), that is to say, in those cases in which the law is found wanting, and yet so to act will nog be wrongful. When such cases become frequent, as a result of some change in human affairs, it becomes manifest through custom that the law is no longer appropriate (*utilis*), just as it would become manifest that this was the case if a specific new law to the contrary were promulgated".[1124] On the basis of this reasoning Thirlway concludes: "Thus when custom *praeter legem* begins, as a result of social development, so to encroach on the existing law's domain as to verge on the *contra legem*, it can nonetheless be regarded, in the light of social development, as still only *praeter legem*, and as tacit law-making so as to effect a repeal.[11][1125]

It may be true, as is implied in the passage just quoted, that in some cases a precise distinction between situations *praeter legem* and *contra legem* is difficult to make and that the transition can be fluid. Nevertheless, in the present author's view, the conclusion that contrary (subsequent) practice has changed existing rules of international law can be arrived at only in exceptional cases. A repeal of existing law will almost always require an express manifestation of the intention to that effect. For such a repeal to result from a tacit manifestation through subsequent practice, that manifestation must be extremely unequivocal. This means that the practice concerned must be completely uniform and of considerable duration, while countervailing manifestation must be lacking. As was said, a repeal of an existing rule of law merely through subsequent practice is bound to happen rarely; if the process of development through practice (initially) *praeter legem* and (subsequently) *contra legem* leads to the formation of a new contrary rule in the face of an existing rule of law, this process is likely to be accompanied or followed by an express manifestation of consent (*opinio juris*) with respect to the new rule, which then may abolish or repeal the old one. If this happens, one is confronted with the repeal of a rule through contrary customary international law (and not merely subsequent practice). This latter process can also not be assumed to occur very frequently in practice.[1126]

The preceding analysis of the relation between existing rules and subsequent practice started from the proposition that the existing rules constitute full-fledged rules of international law. On the basis of the foregoing the possible impact of subsequent practice on the normative status of formally non-binding rules can be summarized as follows. Rule-conform conduct may enhance the normative status of formally non-binding rules. On the analogy of the operation of mechanisms of supervision and follow-up, practice confirming the rule may strengthen an originally weak consensus because the rule proves to effectively order and regulate the relations between the States concerned. Similarly, concretization and elaboration through practice may get abstract and vague rules

1123. H. Thirlway, *op.cit.* (note 209), p. 131.
1124. *Ibidem.*
1125. *Ibidem.*
1126. See *supra* pp. 97-106 on the problems of change of customary international law.

accepted because they turn out to have taken a shape acceptable to States.[1127] However, further development of formally non-binding rules towards rules of law, which may indeed result from supervision or follow-up, is not likely to be effectuated through subsequent practice. As was pointed out, such further development requires an additional manifestation of the intent to be bound which has to be more unequivocal than a tacit one through practice. It should be kept in mind, however, that because of the fact that the existing rule is formally non-binding, the subsequent practice can more easily be regarded as *usus* delineating the content of a rule which may develop into a new rule of customary international law, if followed by *opinio juris*.

13.7. Summary

The preceding sections constitute an attempt to provide some degree of systematizing with respect to the increasing number of multifarious manifestations of consent or acceptance of States which are no longer covered by the traditional sources of international law. The various classes of manifestations of consent or acceptance outlined in the foregoing are meant to be a supplement to the traditional sources. They may be used as a kind of scheme for analysis or checklist, when the legally binding or non-binding nature of (new) phenomena belonging to the so-called "grey" area has to be determined.

The following classes, here presented in a declining order of importance, were outlined in the preceding sections: The most reliable handhold as to the intention of States can usually be found in the (sub-classes of the) precise content of a rule and particularly also its relation with existing rules of the system, belonging to the class of the text. Furthermore, it was pointed out that the decision-making process (*travaux préparatoires lato sensu*), the follow-up to the rule, and the subsequent practice may in various ways clarify and sometimes even add to the (precise) normative status of a given rule. With respect to a number of other (sub-)classes it was argued that they should be used with care, because they at best provide more indirect indications as to the precise intention of the States concerned. These are the circumstances of preparation and adoption (*travaux préparatoires lato sensu*), and the so-called qualifying provisions contained in preambular paragraphs and final clauses (text). With respect to names of instruments it was concluded that, until empirical evidence to the contrary is provided, they must be presumed to have no implications as to the legally binding or non-binding nature of the instrument concerned. Finally, the relevance of absract statements on the part of States was said to depend entirely upon the content and context of the statement concerned.

It should be stressed again that the systematization attempted here is tentative. The various classes of manifestations were outlined *in abstracto*. They need to be tested with respect to concrete cases and on that basis to be elaborated and improved. Furthermore, the order of the various (sub-)classes just set forth is tentative. In a concrete case a particular manifestation belonging to one of the classes may be so unequivocal that it overrides those contained in the others.

1127. See *supra* p. 274.

CHAPTER XIV

CONCLUDING REMARKS

The history of recent decades has undoubtedly been one of far-reaching changes in various respects, both on the national and the international level. Although such a judgment is difficult to make for contemporaries, it would not seem too far-fetched to uphold that, particularly on the international level, never before developments of the same scope and magnitude took place in such a short period of time. Obviously, all this has not failed to make its impact felt on international law. The present study purports to determine the effects of the changes in the international society upon the sources of international law. Its first and main theme is to pinpoint the influence of these changes on the so-called traditional sources of international law. On the basis of the outcome of this analysis, the book aims in addition at providing an outline of an approach as to how the doctrine of the sources of international law might cope with these new developments in international relations. The results of the preceding chapters may be summed up as follows.

It proved clear from the outset that a sound approach to the questions involved in the theory of the sources of international law required a perspective which would encompass more than just the issue of the sources. No doubt, the recent developments in international relations have added to the number and ramifications of the problems surrounding the sources of international law. However, compared to other fields of international law the doctrine of sources has always been characterized by a fairly large amount of confusion and controversy. This may, at least partly, be explained by the fact that questions concerning the sources of international law are very closely related to other fundamental theoretical questions of international law. Even a cursory look at scholarly writing in the field of the sources suffices to show that on these fundamental matters, which may be summarily described as pertaining to the normative concept of international law, authors take radically divergent points of view. These implied or express disagreements on the normative concept subsequently result in differences of opinion on the sources of international law. It was therefore considered impossible to completely by-pass the most relevant questions concerning the concept of international law.

Consequently, in Part I those aspects of the normative concept of international law were first dealt with, which bear most directly upon the doctrine of sources. The analysis focused on the function and functioning of international law. As far as the sources of international law are concerned, two main conclusions flowed from this analysis. The law's function of ordering and regulating relations in society requires it to reflect or even mirror the underlying structure of society. Without a sufficient link between law and relations in society the for-

mer cannot successfully play its ordering and regulating role. Because of this ordering and regulating role there has to be some minimum amount of certainty and clarity as to where the law can be found and what the law is. By categorizing and classifying various types of behaviour law has to distil a more or less clearly arranged picture from the chaotic reality which practice in society presents, thereby making relations in society more viable. Law, therefore, cannot reflect or mirror relations in society in a complete way because this would deprive it from its normative character and thus from its ordering and regulating capabilities. In short, the doctrine of the sources has to avoid both the Scylla of exaggerated formalism which loses sight of the link between law and society and the Charibdys of complete amorphism which lacks the necessary certainty and clarity.

These two requirements for a viable doctrine of sources, *i.e.* sufficient attention for the link between law and society as well as for the certainty and clarity which the law is to furnish, were subsequently taken as points of departure for analyzing a number of so-called basic approaches to international law. Conducting this latter analysis was prompted by reasons of both efficiency and simplicity. It aimed at identifying those elements of existing approaches to, or theories of international law which could be instrumental in clarifying questions concerning the sources. By doing so, we could simultaneously build upon an already existing basis and avoid having to map out ourselves in great detail a theoretical framework for approaching the sources of international law.

Three basic approaches to, or major theoretical frameworks for international law were taken into consideration. These three approaches were termed legal idealism, the analytical approach and the sociological approach, because these names indicate best the most fundamental feature of each of these approaches. While this classification, as a result of its very general and broad character, is undoubtedly inadequate in a number of respects, it was considered workable for the purpose of the present study, because it sets forth and distinguishes three main methods which are usually employed to deal with questions concerning the sources of international law.

The first category, that of legal idealism, or more specifically the Natural Law frame, was said to comprise, generally speaking, the theories which search for and/or try to formulate ideals and values constituting the basis of, or underlying a legal system. It was found that, as far as the sources of international law are concerned, the legal idealistic approach suffers from a number of drawbacks which may be summarized as follows: either the allegedly universal ideals and values put forward by Natural Law theories are too few and too abstract to really give substance to rules of international law, or the ideals and values advocated by adherents to the Natural Law frame are neither universally accepted nor rationally verifiable. Particularly the latter characteristic greatly affects the usefulness of Natural Law thinking with respect to the sources of international law. Unlike most national societies the international society is characterized by a low degree of integration and lacks an organizational/hierarchical structure. Consequently, for ideals or values to be considered as the basis of international law, they have to be generally accepted as such or rationally and scientifically so cogent that their acceptance becomes unavoidable (irresistible). Neither would seem to be the case with respect to Natural Law theories. Different sections of the international society hold and advocate different basic values and ideals.

Moreover, ideals and values adhered to by the one side are not plausible to the other, but are considered rather a kind of "faith" or ideology and *vice versa*.

It is difficult to see how an approach which is so prone to controversy could effectively serve as a point of departure for dealing with the sources of international law. Obviously, all this does not imply, as was reiterated, a negative judgment on legal idealism in general. On the contrary, it cannot be denied that ideal blueprints of how the world ought to be organized on the basis of international law may sharpen the awareness of present shortcomings and even stimulate States into meeting those shortcomings to a certain extent. More specifically, the elaboration of basic values and ideals may further the interpretation of the law in certain fields in a(nother) more preferable direction and provide guidance when it comes to creating new law or changing existing law. All this, however, is not the same thing as saying that a particular brand of legal idealism constitutes the sole basis of the sources of international law in the sense that it can adequately answer the question of where the law may be found or what it is.

As to the other two basic approaches, each of them turned out to (over)emphasize only one of the two requirements which were found to be fundamental to the doctrine of sources. On the one hand, the analytical approach, generally labeled Positivism, was said to be essentially concerned with the legal technique and primarily aimed at clarifying and ordering (of) the legal system. Because of their extreme concern with order, stability and certainty Positivists are often tempted to overlook what is happening in actual practice and are, consequently, liable to lose sight of the link between law and society. For the sake of order, stability and certainty their models start from *a priori* assumptions and postulates and run the risk of coming up with fictitious answers.

The sociological approach, on the other hand, was found to focus almost entirely upon the link between law and society. Particularly the so-called Policy Oriented school of thought belonging to the sociological approach was characterized as a kind of "panta-rhei-view", because it concentrates on a great many, sometimes very detailed, aspects encompassing almost the entire international process, and views these as in more or less constant motion. There can be no objection against the view that the international process, including the international law-making process, comprises many participants, interests and values and that all of these are worthwhile studying in order to better understand the law. However, the sociological approach tends to forget that for a rule to become a legal rule, there is in all societies a narrowing and formalization of this process towards a more technical procedure and that, as far as the sources of international law are concerned, this procedure and its outcome must be the focus of study.

On the basis of the analysis of these three basic approaches it was concluded that a theory is to be preferred which takes a kind of middle-of-the-road position between the extreme formalism of traditional Positivism and the almost complete amorphism of the sociological approach. Hart's theory, which was labeled Structural Positivism, was found to satisfy this requirement to a very large extent, in the sense that it provides a model consisting of the union of so-called primary and secondary rules. On the one hand, an outline of this model showed that it pays sufficient attention to the certainty and clarity which the sources are to provide. This is ensured, as was pointed out, by the so-called "rule of recognition" which is accorded a central place in Hart's theory. A "rule of

recognition" is defined as a secondary rule specifying some feature or features, possession of which by a suggested primary rule is taken as a conclusive affirmative indication that it is a rule of law. Primary rules may be summarily defined as rules laying down (material) rights and obligations. On the other hand, the theory takes duly into account the link between law and society in that, in the final analysis, it seeks the basis of the "rule of recognition" in the practice of the law-determining agencies in a given society. Because of these features of Hart's theory, it was decided to try to apply the model of Structural Positivism to international law. As was shown, Hart himself in fact fails to do so, although he devotes an entire chapter of his book to international law.

Before embarking thereupon it was found necessary to take a closer look at the concept of the sources itself. For, although the connotation of the term "source" or "sources" would seem to be clear at first glance, closer inspection reveals that it is not unequivocal. Three meanings of the term "sources", or three levels on which the sources are to be analyzed, were discerned. At the first level the term "sources" designates the basis of the binding force of international law. At the second level "source" indicates the constitutive element for rules of international law being the criterion by which one can decide whether or not a suggested rule is indeed a rule of international law. Finally, at the third level the sources represent the relevant manifestations on the basis of which the presence or absence of the constitutive element can be established.

All three levels or meanings of sources are subject to the requirements flowing from the necessary certainty or clarity and from the link between law and society. As was explained, however, particularly as far as the link between law and society is concerned, there is a difference between the first two meanings and the third one. In the first and the second sense the sources are dependent mainly on the so-called basic features of international society, while the sources in the third sense are influenced in particular by what is called the structure of international relations. It was pointed out that in essence the international society has remained unchanged during long periods of time. Since a long time the most characteristic feature of the international society has been and still is that of the sovereign independence of States. Put summarily, this sovereign independence entails that from the perspective of international law the States are not subjected to any higher entity or agency, and that, as far as the relations of States *inter se* are concerned, no State is placed above another.

This double aspect of the independence of States has far-reaching consequences with respect to the sources of international law. At the first level it entails the conclusion that no single ideal or value with a material or substantive content can be considered as the basis of the binding force of international law, as long as no such ideal or value has gained general acceptance by the community of States. As long as this situation prevails, the search for a common denominator as the basis of the binding force of international law has to be confined to what is called the recognized necessity as a "procedural" source. By this we mean that in order to find the foundation for the binding force of international law one needs to go no further than the simple and verifiable awareness on the part of the States that there is no satisfactory alternative to a set of binding rules for ordering and regulating their mutual relations. Moreover, it was pointed out that the fundamental rule of *pacta sunt servanda* can be taken as the "translation" into international law of this "procedural" source of the recognized

necessity.

With regard to the second meaning of the term "sources" the conclusion flowing from the independence of States is the following: because of this independence and the ensuing decentralized process of decision-making there does not exist an international "legislature" and the subjects of international law, *i.e.* the States, have to act as lawgivers themselves. Consequently, the consent of States, in the sense of the intention to be bound, is to be regarded as the constitutive element of rules of international law. Or, to put it differently, in order to answer the question of whether a given rule is binding upon a State as a rule of international law the point of departure has to be whether or not that State has consented to or accepted the rule concerned, acceptance being understood as tacit consent.

Unlike the basic features of the international society the structure of international relations, which particularly affects the sources in the third sense of manifestations of consent or acceptance, has undergone quite dramatic changes in recent decades. The two main trends or developments which have taken place can be characterized by the keywords "interdependence" and "heterogeneity". These two trends are more or less countervailing. On the one hand, scientific and technological changes have fueled an increasing interdependence in the sense that States have become steadily more dependent upon each other in an ever greater number of fields. In its turn, this growing interdependence has prompted a greater "density" of international law, *i.e.* international law has to cover more areas and the areas to be covered have to be penetrated in a more detailed manner. On the other hand, the relatively homogeneous international society of the nineteenth century has by now turned into a quite heterogeneous group of States. The twentieth century has not only witnessed a split between East and West, but also, more recently, between North and South. Although this image of the two splits is undoubtedly a simplification of reality, it suffices to show that the time when the international society consisted of a comparatively like-minded club of States is definitely gone. Put together the two trends mentioned have resulted in quite a paradoxical situation: while there probably has never been a greater need for elaborate rules of international law in so many fields as at present, it is at the same time more difficult than ever before to attain agreement between States on such rules.

On the basis of the theoretical framework set forth in Part I, Part II tries to make an inventory of how the recent changes in the structure of international relations have affected the so-called traditional sources of international law. Successive chapters, therefore, deal with customary international law, treaties, general principles of international law as well as judicial decisions and doctrine, the latter being listed in article 38 of the Statute of the International Court of Justice as subsidiary means for the determination of rules of law.

With respect to customary international law scholarly writing proved to be quite contradictory and in some respects also confusing. Before dealing with the impact of societal changes it was, therefore, necessary to try to pinpoint the exact nature of customary rules of international law. This required an extensive analysis of both the constitutive elements of custom, *i.e. usus* and *opinio juris*, and particularly also the relation between these two elements. It proved possible to clarify the troublesome character of custom with the aid of the so-called stages-theory, which was briefly outlined. In a nutshell this theory boils down to

the conclusion that while it is *opinio juris* which clothes a rule with the status of rule of international law, it is the *usus* which turns it into a rule of customary international law. Moreover, it was submitted that in view of the certainty and clarity which the sources are to provide, the concept of customary international law as a practice-based source of international law has to be narrowly defined, particularly in the present circumstances. At the same time this practice-oriented character of custom entails the conclusion that the role of custom as a source of international law is relatively declining. The changes in the international society, particularly the faster rhythm and more complex character of international relations and the present heterogeneous character of the community of States, have decreased the usefulness of custom as a source of international law. All this does not imply that one is to expect the complete whithering away of customary international law. Apart from the fact that custom will continue to play its traditional role in a certain number of fields, a kind of new role may be envisaged for custom in the form of subsequent practice, that is in the form of an elaboration or concretization of already existing (written) rules of international law.

Treaties in many respects present the opposite case of rules of customary international law. The nature of treaties as a source of international law is unambiguous and largely uncontroversial. Compared to custom, moreover, the treaty-making process is relatively quick and produces more unequivocal results. Not surprisingly, therefore, treaties have become the most important source of international law. Nevertheless, even traties have not been left unaffected by the recent changes in the international society, but show a number of shortcomings in view of the requirements of today's international law-making. These shortcomings were discussed under the headings of problems of acceptability, problems of adaptation, and problems of change. The first-mentioned category refers to the fact that in practice multilateral treaties often acquire a relatively small amount of ratifications. The second and third catergory together point to the difficulties resulting from the formalism and rigidity which are more or less inherent in treaties as a source of international law. Because of these characteristics treaties cannot always keep pace with developments in practice. In other words, treaty-law sometimes very quickly lags behind because of changed situations. Treaty-law therefore often needs devices of flexibility which can ensure the required adaptation or even change. This holds good in particular now that the content of many rules of international law would seem to be shifting. As a result of the changes in international relations international law in many cases cannot provide *ad hoc* regulations and solutions anymore, but needs to start from a policy framework taking into account the overall and long-term requirements of the issues involved. The upshot is that, unlike traditional international law, modern international law very often consists of rules of an abstract, general and sometimes even vague character. Such "program"-like provisions can only succesfully be applied to concrete situations after elaboration and adaptation. This is to be ensured, as was pointed out, through follow-up mechanisms provided for in a growing number of treaties, particularly within the framework of international organizations, and through the moulding of such rules in the subsequent practice of the States concerned.

With respect to the third source enumerated in article 38 of the Statute of the International Court of Justice, the general principles of law recognized by civi-

lized nations, the situation turned out to be more or less the same as in the case of customary international law. The nature of the general principles, too, is hotly debated in doctrine. After tracing the genesis and the history of the general principles an effort was made to explain their nature as a source of international law on the basis of a twofold distinction. Is was concluded that the general principles constitute a source of international law within the framework of proceeding before the International Court of Justice, or, more generally, within judicial and arbitral processes. It was argued that the existence of general principles needs to be established or determined by an independent third instance, provided for in judicial or arbitral processes. Although the theoretical possibility exists, the general principles do not in fact constitute an independent source outside the framework of judicial or arbitral processes. Outside judicial and arbitral processes general principles are often taken in a material sense, which refers to the substantive content of the rules concerned. Because of the connotation of the term "general principles", this frequently results in a discussion of the hierarchical order of rules of international law. Strictly speaking, the general principles in this material sense fall outside the scope of the present study. Nevertheless, because the procedural and material sense are often dealt with simultaneously in doctrine, it was decided to pay some attention to the issue of the hierarchical order of rules of international law in the form of an outline of the concept of international *jus cogens.*

Finally, judicial decisions and doctrine as subsidiary means for the determination of rules of law were dealt with. The conclusion drawn from an analysis of both these phenomena was that judicial decisions can be considered as a source in the sense of a manifestation of consent or acceptance only with respect to the States parties to the case concerned. For other States judicial decisions are at best an indirect source in that they may influence the consent or acceptance of States, but not directly manifest it. The latter conclusion *mutatis mutandis* holds good also with respect to doctrine.

The overall conclusion emerging from Part II is that the traditional sources of international law have definitely been losing ground. The traditional sources, in other words, do not entirely cover the territory of new phenomena and new types of instruments which suggestedly or allegedly constitute binding international law. The changes in the international society have given rise to new elements in the international law-making process which cannot be identified as either binding or non-binding rules on the basis of the criteria provided by the traditional sources of international law.

This state of affairs has provoked various responses in the doctrine of the sources. One line of reasoning has tried to widen the concept of the traditional sources in an effort to have the new phenomena fitted in. Not infrequently this entails the risk of stretching the concept of these sources to the point where the latter become virtually meaningless, and, consequently, cannot provide the required certainty and clarity anymore. Another school of thougt takes what was called the "other source" approach. Put bluntly, it proclaims a new type of source every time a new type of intrument arises in practice, the best known example being declarations, or more generally, resolutions of the United Nations General Assembly. The disadvantages contained in this approach are twofold. First, the proclaimed new sources are not always consistent with the consensual basis of international law which underlies the traditional sources.

Secondly, it has a strong *ad hoc* character and does not provide a solution for additional developments which might take place in practice. What is needed, in short, would seem to be a more integrated approach consistent with the traditional sources and at the same time capable of explaining new developments in a more structural way.

Finally, a so-called "soft-law" approach has come into being. Its main theme is that there exists a "grey area" between the white area of law and the black territory of non-law. This "soft-law" approach has played an important role in the doctrine of sources of international law, particularly also because it has set itself to elaborating the relation between the "grey" and the white areas just mentioned. Most of the proponents of the "soft-law" approach, however, do not directly address the problem which is the focus of the present study, *i.e.* the delimitation between the white and the grey area.

In the present author's view, the effective functioning of international law requires a narrowing down of the grey area to the largest possible extent. The final Part, therefore, attempted to sketch a tentative outline of an approach aimed at that result. Two preliminary issues had to be dealt with first. The question of whether or not the sources of international law can change was answered in the affirmative on the basis mainly of the argument derived from the theory of Structural Positivism that, in the final analysis, the sources or the "rule of recognition" of a given system of law are based upon the practice of the law-determining agencies. In the international society the States in the final analysis are the law-determining agencies and, consequently, the sources of international law may change through state-practice *lato sensu*. Secondly, it was pointed out that there exists a dilemma in international law between form and formlessness. On the one hand it was noted that there is a tendency in doctrine to picture international law as a largely formless system. While this point of view is not incorrect, is has simultaneously to be stressed that law, in view of its ordering and regulating task, cannot do without some minimum amount of form in order to keep its rules "recognizable".

In essence Part III of the present study presents an effort to attain, as a supplement to the traditional sources, some further systematization and "recognizability" of the highly amorphous elements which at present characterize the international law-making process. For that purpose, it was attempted to categorize the (new) manifestations of the consent or acceptence of States into five different classes. Each of these classes were outlined under the headings of (1) abstract statements, (2) *travaux préparatoires lato sensu*, (3) text, (4) follow-up, and (5) subsequent practice. Together these five classes purport to encompass the entire law-making cycle which nowadays has become a more or less continuous process. Each of the classes is designed to help identify the manifestations of the consent of acceptance of States at the various stages of the law-making cycle in order to get a better overall picture of the binding or non-binding character of the instrument or rule concerned. Obviously, the classes of manifestations as set forth in the present study are rudimentary. They need to be further tested to concrete cases for their practability and, on that basis, elaborated. Nevertheless, it is submitted that taken together they provide an outline of an approach which might prove helpful in solving at least some of the questions involved in the doctrine of sources of international law, at least with respect to the new allegedly

law-making phenomena contained in the so-called grey area.

The present author is perfectly aware of the fact that the contribution of this study to the doctrine of sources of international law is only a modest one. Moreover, the results flowing from and the positions taken on the basis of the preceding analysis may be regarded by some as disappointing and discomforting.

As far as the sources in the sense of the basis of the binding force of international law is concerned, disappointment may be caused by the conclusion drawn in the present study that no idea or value with a substantive content is available at this moment to serve as the basis of the binding force of international law. If such a material idea or value underlies a set of rules, it can play a guiding role and thus provide the unity which some regard necessary in order to turn a set of rules into a system of law. To those who take this position it is therefore problably small comfort, if it is reiterated here, that from the point of view of effectiveness the procedural source of recognized neccessity, which was put forward in the present study as the basis of the binding force of international law, does not have to yield to a material source. If and to the extent that States accept the binding character of international law on the basis of the recognized necessity that there is no satisfactory alternative to a set of binding rules for the regulation of their mutual relations, there is no difference as far as effectiveness is concerned with a situation in which this binding haracter would be founded on some material idea or value.

Furthermore, the recognized necessity as put forward was said to constitute a common denominator which leaves open the possibility for different people to regard different ideas or values as the ultimate sources underlying this recognized recessity. It might be more desirable to have one such idea or value generally accepted, but that is unlikely to be attained as long as the present heterogeneous character of the international society continues. In this situation it may be helpful to have a common basis even if it is confined to the procedural source of recognized necessity.

Secondly, the point of view that consent is the constitutive element of rules of international law, which has been quite rigidly adhered to in the present study, is bound to meet with discontent and objection. More than a few international lawyers vehemently denounce the conclusion that international law is a consensual system. However, the arduous opposition voiced against the consent approach from various quarters, including some of the most eminent international lawyers, has not convinced the present author. One may concede that international law as a consensual system is in many respects unsatisfactory and still feel unable, given the basic features of the present international society, to reach any other conclusion than that it is the consent or acceptance of States which gives rise to rules of international law.

It is a kind of paradox that those who adhere to the consent approach or, as it was put above,[1128] who take the "is" approach to international law, are blamed for the fact that the results required by the "ought" approach do not actually materialize. The requirement of consent or acceptance, it is often argued, results in too few international legal rules embodying the idea of justice and holds back progress in the international society. This may be true. However, even if justice

1128. See *supra* pp. 24-25.

is not hallmark of international law and if progress in the international society is slow, it still constitues a confusion of causes and effects to blame this on the consensual character of international law. The cause of the present situation is to be found in the nature of the international society and one cannot remedy this cause by trying to take away - or rather to reason away - the effects in the form of the consensual character of international law.

In the present author's view, it is a more promising course of action to accept - for the time being - the specific structure of the international law-making process and to try to enhance the quality of the rules of international law on the basis of that factual situation. Although prospects are far from ideal, the present author believes that there is no reason to be overly pessimistic in this respect either. It is true that the international law-making process often resembles a tug-of-war with no solution in sight. However, closer inspection of its often intricate and complex elements not infrequently reveals a greater degree of agreement between the States concerned than there seemed to be at first sight. It may be difficult to collate such an agreement through the various manifestations of consent or acceptace by States, but it is the task of the doctrine of the sources of international law to facilitate this process.

The rigidity with which the consent approach is put forward in the present study should be no cause for denying that consent as the constitutive element for rules of international law has been, and likely will be, under increasing pressure. This pressure is generated by a tendency in international relations which somewhat counterwails the heterogeneity of the present international society, *i.e.* the increasing interdependence which has made the need for elaborate rules of international law more pertinent than ever before. This tendency may become so strong that future historians of international law will look at our era as a stage of transition which has witnessed, at least to some extent, the abandonment of the consent requirement.

Jennings, with whose thoughts we have largely affiliated ourselves throughout this book, gives the impression that he foresees a development away from the consensual basis of international law. He concludes his analysis of the traditional sources of international law as follows: "So the main burden of this part of my discourse has been, that the 'subsidiary means for the ascertainment of the law' - judicial decisions and commentators - are today probably of greater importance than ever before; and that it is these two sources which are most likely to bring certainty and clarity in the places where the mass of material evidences is so large and confused as to obscure the basic distinction between law and proposal."[1129]

It would certainly be desirable if States made greater use of judicial and arbitral processes so as to enable international judicial and arbitral tribunals to contribute to the elaboration of international law to a greater extent. For reasons set forth in section 9.1., however, the present author ventures to doubt whether this will occur on a scale commensurate to the need for law-making in the interna-

1129. R. Jennings, *loc.cit.* (note 1), pp. 78-79; see also p. 77, where the author states: "It may cause surprise that I have spent so long on merely one [judicial decisions - v.H.] of the sources which is described in Article 38 as a 'subsidiary means for the ascertainment of the law'. This is because it is precisely here - the analysis, refinement, clarification and systematising of a mass of existing law, or near-law, that our contemporary problem arises. Paradoxically, the subsidiary means are now, at least for a season, of the first importance...".

tional society. As far as commentators are concerned, it is true that an important task for doctrine consists in the analysis, refinement, clarification and systematising of existing law and near-law or alleged-law. However, as was argued in section 9.2., the results of these activities by commentators do not themselves constitute rules of international law. In order to become international law these results need to be "finalized" through manifestations of consent or acceptance by States.

It is submitted here that modifications within the international law-making process are unlikely to be very drastic in the sense that dramatic deviations from the consent requirement can be expected. The above-mentioned pressure on the consent requirement will problably result in rather unspectacular changes which may nevertheless be of considerable importance. The beginnings of a number of such changes may be found in what we have summarily described as the introduction of "third-party-elements" in the international law-making process.

One example constitutes the so-called active consensus procedure in which the powers of the chairman enable him to keep the decision-making process moving. Although this does not guarantee a successful outcome, States are kept under pressure by a "third party" to bring the process to an end. This procedure provides at least some certainty and clarity, which would be lacking if the process would drag on or result in a deadlock. More far-reaching may be the impact of what we have called the creation-function of supervision of follow-up. The elaboration and adaptation which are involved in this function may contribute considerably to the international law-making process. As was argued in section 13.5.2., once States have subjected to some form of supervision or follow-up, this may generate its own dynamics in that the mechanisms of supervision or follow-up may eventually lead to the acceptance of certain results which (some) States initially opposed. A final example concerns the borderline between the creative-function of supervision or follow-up and what was called further development of the law or existing rules. The difference between these two functions was said to consist in the fact that further development requires a new manifestation of consent or acceptance, while in the case of the creative-function the original consent or acceptance is considered an adequete basis for elaboration and adoptation. If we are not mistaken, a shift from further development to the-function may be expected in the sense that within the framework of supervision or follow-up it will be more readily assumed that the original consent or acceptance is sufficient and that no new manifestation thereof is required.

Even if the tendencies just hinted at will indeed evolve, it will still be difficult in many instances, at least for a considerable time to come, to exactly answer the question whether or not a given rule is a rule of international law. This then brings us to the sources in the third sense of manifestations of consent or acceptance. Under the influence of the changes in the international society the traditional sources of international law can no longer play their ordering and regulating role to the same extent as in the past. The criteria they provide for determining the binding or non-binding character of a rule leave a large "grey" area of new phenomena arising in practice. The various classes of manifestations of consent or acceptance outlined in the preceding chapter are designed to provide additional criteria for that area and thus to facilitate an answer to the question of whether or not a given rule is binding under international law. Nevertheless,

they cannot do away with the fact that today an answer to that question in many instances requires a painstaking analysis of the various elements involved. The discomfort which this entails for the doctrine of sources has been pointedly set forth as follows: "das allegemeine Völkerrecht ist bekanntlich einem Puzzle-Spiel nicht unähnlich, bei dem mühsam Stück für Stück zusammenggesetzt werden muss. Und während das Puzzle aus Teilen von einheitlicher Konsistenz zusammengefügt wird, hat es der Rechtsanwender im Völkerrecht mit Bestand-teilen aus unterschiedlichen Zeitepochen zu tun, der Präjudizwert höchst zwei-felhaft sein kann".[1130]

However discomforting this may be, the present author knows of no more satisfactory supplement to the traditional doctrine of sources of international law than to try to take into account all these multifarious elements, to arrange them into a more or less orderly picture, and eventually build them into a con-sistent and workable theory.

1130. C. Tomushat, *loc.cit.* (note 762), p. 480.

BIBLIOGRAPHY

Ago, R., "Positive Law and International Law", 51 *American Journal of International Law* (1957), pp. 691-733.

Akehurst, M., "Custom as a Source of International Law", XLVII *British Yearbook of International Law* (1974-1975), pp. 1-53.

Akehurst, M., "The Hierarchy of the Sources of International Law", XLVII *British Yearbook of International Law* (1974-1975), pp. 273- 285.

Akehurst, M., *A Modern Introduction to International Law*, 3rd edition (London 1977).

Anzilotti, D., *Corso di Diritto Internazionale*, 4th edition (Padua/Amsterdam 1955).

Aquinas, Th., *Summa Theologiae*, Latin text and English translation, T. Gilby general editor (London/New York 1964-1981), Volume XXVIII (1966).

Arangio-Ruiz, G., "The Normative Rôle of the General Assembly of the United Nations and the Declaration of Principles of Friendly Relations", 137 *Recueil des Cours de l'Académie de Droit International de La Haye* (1972-III), pp. 419-742.

Arangio-Ruiz, G., *The UN Declaration on Friendly Relations and the System of Sources of International Law* (Alphen aan den Rijn 1979).

Asamoah, O., *The Legal Significance of the Declarations of the General Assembly of the United Nations* (The Hague 1966).

Audretsch, H., *Supervision in European Community Law* (Amsterdam 1978).

Austin, J., *Lectures on Jurisprudence or the Philosophy of Positive Law*, Vol. I, reprint of the 5th edition, revised and edited by R. Campbell, London 1885 (Glashütten im Taunus 1972).

Basdevant, J., "Règles Général du Droit de la Paix", 58 *Recueil des Cours de l'Académie de Droit International de La Haye* (1936- IV), pp. 475-692.

Bastid, S., "The Special Significance of the Helsinki Final Act", in: T. Buergenthal (ed.), *Human Rights, International Law and the Helsinki Accord* (Montclair/New York 1977), pp. 11-19.

Bedjaoui, M., *Towards A New International Economic Order* (Paris 1979).

Bernhardt, R., "Ungeschriebenes Völkerrecht", 30 *Zeitschrift für ausländisches öffentliches Recht und Völkerrecht* (1976), pp. 50-76.

Bleckmann, A., "Völkergewohnheitsrecht trotz widersprüchlicher Praxis?", 36 *Zeitschrift für ausländisches öffentliches Recht und Völkerrecht* (1976), pp. 374-406.

Bleckmann, A., "Zur Feststellung und Auslegung von Völkergewohnheitsrecht", 37 *Zeitschrift für ausländisches öffentliches Recht und Völkerrecht* (1977), pp. 504-529.

Bleicher, S., "The Legal Significance of Re-citation of General Assembly Resolutions", 63 *American Journal of International Law* (1969), pp. 444-478.

Blix, H., "The Requirement of Ratification", XXX *British Yearbook of International Law* (1953), pp. 352-380.

Blix, H., *Treaty Making Power* (London 1960).

Blumenwitz, D., "Die völkerrechtlichen Aspekte der KSZE-Schlussakte", in: Göttinger Arbeitskreis, *Die KSZE und die Menschenrechte* (Berlin 1977), pp. 53-71.

Bock, S., "Festigung der Sicherheit in Europa; Kernstück der Schlussakte von Helsinki", 20 *Deutsche Aussenpolitik* (1975), pp. 1623-1639.

Bolintineanu, A., "Expression of Consent to be Bound by a Treaty in the Light of the 1969 Vienna Convention", 68 *American Journal of International Law* (1974), pp. 672-686.

Bos, M., "Legal Archetypes and the Normative Concept of Law as Main Factors in the Defining and Development of International Law", XXIII-1 *Netherlands International Law Review* (1976), pp. 71-87.

Bos, M., "The Recognized Manifestations of International Law; A New Theory of 'Sources'", 20 *German Yearbook of International Law* (1977), pp. 9-76.

Bos, M., "Old Germanic Law Analogies in International Law, or the State as Homo Liber", XV-1 *Netherlands International Law Review* (1978), pp. 51-62.

Bos, M., "The Hierarchy Among the Recognized Manifestations ('Sources') of International Law", in: *Estudios de Derecho Internacional; Homenaje al Profesor Miaja De La Muela* (Madrid 1979), pp. 363-374.

Bos, M., "Will and Order in the Nation-State System, Observations on Positivism and Positive International Law", XXIX-1 *Netherlands International Law Review* (1982), pp. 3-31.

Bothe, M., "Legal and Non-Legal Norms - A Meaningful Distinction in International Relations?", XI *Netherlands Yearbook of International Law* (1980), pp. 65-95.

Brandt, W. (chairman of the Independent Commission on International Development Issues), *North-South: A Program For Survival* (Cambridge, Mass 1980).

Briggs, H., "The Final Act of the London Conference on Germany", 49 *American Journal of International Law* (1955), pp. 148-165.

Brownlie, I., *Principles of Public International Law*, 3rd edition (Oxford 1979)

Butler, W., "Methodological Innovations in Soviet International Legal Doctrine", 32 *Yearbook of World Affairs* (1978), pp. 334-341.

Buzan, B., "Negotiating by Consensus: Developments in Technique at the United Nations Conference on the Law of the Sea", 75 *American Journal of International Law* (1981), pp. 324-348.

Castaneda, J., "Valeur juridique des résolutions des Nations Unies", 129 *Receuil des Cours de l'Académie de Droit International de La Haye* (1970-I), pp. 205-331.

Charney, J., "United States Interests in a Convention on the Law of the Sea: The Case for Continued Efforts", 11 *Vanderbilt Journal of Transnational Law* (1978), pp. 39-68.

Cheng, B., *General Principles of Law as Applied by International Courts and Tribunals* (London 1953).

Cheng, B., "United Nations Resolutions on Outer Space: 'Instant' Internation-

al Customary Law?", 5 *Indian Journal of International Law* (1965), pp. 23-48.

Chroust, A., "On the Nature of Natural Law", in: P. Sayre (ed.), *Interpretations of Modern Legal Philosophies; Essays in Honor of Roscoe Pound* (New York 1947), pp. 70-84.

Claude, I., *Swords into Plowshares: The Problems and Progress of International Organization,* 4th edition (New York 1971).

Cohen, B., *The Question of Imperialism: The Political Economy of Dominance and Dependence* (London 1974).

Corbett, P., "The Consent of States and the Sources of the Law of Nations", VI *British Yearbook of International Law* (1925), pp. 20-30.

D'Amato, A., "The Neo-Positivist Concept of International Law", 59 *American Journal of International Law* (1965), pp. 321-325.

D'Amato, A., "On Consensus", VII *Canadian Yearbook of International Law* (1970), pp. 104-122.

D'Amato, A., *The Concept of Custom in International Law* (Ithaca/London 1971).

Deleau, O., "Les positions françaises à la Conférence de Vienne sur le Droit des Traités", XV *Annuaire Français de Droit International* (1969), pp. 7-23.

Detter, I., *Essays on the Law of Treaties* (London 1967).

Dohna, B. Graf zu, *Die Grundprinzipien des Völkerrechts über die freundschaftlichen Beziehungen und die Zusammenarbeit zwischen den Staaten* (Berlin 1973).

Dupuy, R., "Declaratory Law and Programmatory Law: From Revolutionary Custom to 'Soft Law'", in: R. Akkerman e.a. (eds.), *Liber Röling, Declarations on Principles; A Quest for Universal Peace* (Leyden 1977), pp. 247-257.

Durkheim, E., *De la Division du Travail Social,* 5th edition (Paris 1926).

Dworkin, R., *Taking Rights Seriously,* 6th print (Cambridge, Mass. 1979).

Dijk, P. van, *Judicial Review of Governmental Action and the Requirement of an Interest to Sue* (Alphen aan den Rijn 1980).

Dijk, P. van, "The Final Act of Helsinki - Basis for a Pan-European System?", XI *Netherlands Yearbook of International Law* (1980), pp. 97-124.

Dijk, P. van (ed.), *Supervision within International Economic Organizations: The NIEO Perspective* (Deventer 1983).

Dijk, P. van, and Hoof, G. van, *De Europese Conventie in Theorie en Praktijk* [Theory and Practice of the European Convention on Human Rights], 2nd edition (Nijmegen 1982).

Ehrlich, E., *Grundlegung der Soziologie des Rechts* (München/Leipzig 1929).

Elias, T., "Modern Sources of International Law", in: W. Friedmann, L. Henkin and O. Lissitzyn (eds.), *Transnational Law in a Changing Society; Essays in Honor of Philip C. Jessup* (New York 1972), pp. 34-69.

Engel, S., "'Living' International Constitutions and the World Court", 16 *International and Comparative Law Quarterly* (1967), pp. 865-910.

Erickson, R., "Soviet Theory of the Legal Nature of Customary International Law", 7 *Case Western Reserve Journal of International Law* (1975), pp 148-168.

Falk, R., "International Legal Order: Alwyn V. Freeman vs. Myres S. McDougal", 59 *American Journal of International Law* (1965), pp. 66-71.

Falk, R., "On the Quasi-Legislative Competence of the General Assembly", 60 *American Journal of International Law* (1966), pp. 782-791.

Falk, R., *The Status of Law in International Society* (Princeton 1970).

Falk, R., "President Gerald Ford, CIA Covert Operations, and the Status of International Law", 69 *American Journal of International Law* (1975), pp. 354-358.

Fawcett, J., "The Legal Character of International Agreements", XXX *British Yearbook of International Law* (1953), pp. 381-400.

Ferraris, L. (ed.), *Report on a Negotiation, Helsinki-Geneva-Helsinki 1972-1975*, Institut Universitaire de Hautes Etudes Internationales (Alphen aan den Rijn/Genève 1979).

Finnis, J., *Natural Law and Natural Rights* (Oxford 1980).

Fitzgerald, P. (ed.), *Salmond on Jurisprudence* (London 1966). Fitzmaurice, G., "Do Treaties Need Ratification?", XV *British Yearbook of International Law* (1934), pp. 113-137.

Fitzmaurice, G., "The General Principles of International Law, Considered from the Standpoint of the Rule of Law", 92 *Recueil des Cours de l'Académie de Droit International de La Haye* (1957-II), pp. 5-227.

Fitzmaurice, G., "Some Problems Regarding the Formal Sources of International Law", in: *Symbolae Verzijl* (The Hague 1958), pp. 153-176.

Fitzmaurice, G., "The Future of Public International Law and of the International Legal System in the Circumstances of Today", in: *Livre du Centenaire de l'Institut de Droit International 1873-1973: Evolution et perspectives du droit international* (Bâle 1973), pp. 196-363.

Friedmann, W., *Legal Theory*, 4th edition (London 1960).

Friedmann, W., *Legal Theory*, 5th edition (London 1967).

Friedmann, W., *The Changing Structure of International Law* (London 1964).

Friedmann, W., "Law and Politics in the Vietnamese War: A Comment", 61 *American Journal of International Law* (1967), pp. 776-785.

Friedmann, W., "General Course in Public International Law", 127 *Recueil des Cours de l'Académie de Droit International de La Haye* (1969-II), pp. 41-246.

Geiger, Th., *Vorstudiën zu einer Soziologie des Rechts* (København 1947).

Glahn, G. von, *Law Among Nations; An Introduction to Public International Law*, 3rd edition (New York/London 1976).

Goodrich, L., *The United Nations in a Changing World* (New York 1975).

Goodrich, L., Hambro, E., and Simons, A., *Charter of the United Nations, Commentary and Documents* (New York/London 1969).

Gosovic, B., *UNCTAD, Conflict and Cooperation* (Leyden 1972).

Gross, L. (ed.), *The Future of the International Court of Justice*, Vols. I and II (New York 1976).

Grotius, H., *De Jure Belli ac Pacis Libri Tres*, translation in: J. Brown Scott (ed.), *The Classics of International Law*, Volume II (New York/London 1964).

Guggenheim, P., "Les Principes de Droit International Public", 80 *Recueil des Cours de l'Académie de Droit International de La Haye* (1952-I), pp.

5-189.

Hardy, M., "Decision Making at the Law of the Sea Conference", 11 *Revue Belge de Droit International* (1975), pp. 442-474.
Hart, H., "Positivism and the Separation of Law and Morals", in: R. Dworkin (ed.), *The Philosophy of Law* (Oxford 1979), pp. 17-37.
Hart, H., *The Concept of Law*, 10th impression (Oxford 1979).
Hart Ely, J., *Democracy and Distrust; A Theory of Judicial Review* (Cambridge, Mass. 1980).
Hazard, J., "Soviet Tactics in International Law-making", 7 *Denver Journal of International Law and Policy* (1977), pp. 9-32.
Henkin, L., *How Nations Behave; Law and Foreign Policy*, 2nd edition (New York 1979).
Heydte, F. von der, "Glossen zu einer Theorie der allgemeinen Rechtsgrundsätze", 33 *Die Friedens-Warte* (1933), pp. 289-300.
Higgins, R., *The Development of International Law through the Political Organs of the United Nations* (London 1963).
Higgins, R., "United Nations and Law-making: The Political Organs", *Proceedings of the American Society of International Law* (1970), pp. 37-48.
Holloway, K., *Modern Trends in Treaty Law* (London 1970).
Hoof, G. van, "World Bank Supervision", in: P. van Dijk (ed.), *Supervision within International Economic Organizations: The NIEO Perspective* (Deventer 1983).
Hoof, G. van, and Vey Mestdagh, K. de, "Mechanisms of International Supervision", in: P. van Dijk (ed.), *Supervision within International Economic Organizations: The NIEO Perspective* (Deventer 1983).
Huber, M., "Beiträge zur Kenntnis der Soziologischen Grundlagen des Völkerrechts und der Staatengesellschaft", IV *Jahrbuch des öffentlichen Rechts der Gegenwart* (1910), pp. 56-134.
Huber, M., *Die Soziologischen Grundlagen des Völkerrechts* (Berlin 1928).

Jacobsen, H., e.a. (eds.), *Sicherheit und Zusammenarbeit in Europa; Analyse und Dokumentation 1973-1978* (Köln 1978).
Jenks, W., *The Common Law of Mankind* (London 1958).
Jenks, W., "Unanimity, The Veto, Weighted Voting, Special and Simple Majorities and Consensus as Modes of Decision in International Organisations", in: *Cambridge Essays in International Law: Essays in Honour of Lord McNair* (London/New York 1965), pp. 48-63.
Jenks, W., "The New Science and the Law of Nations", 17 *International and Comparative Law Quarterly* (1968), pp. 321-345.
Jenks, W., *A New World of Law* (London 1969).
Jenks, W., *Law in the World Community* (London 1973).
Jennings, R., "General Course on Principles of International Law", 121 *Recueil des Cours de l'Académie de Droit International de La Haye* (1967-II), pp. 323-606.
Jennings, R., "What Is International Law And How Do We Tell It When We See It?", XXXVII *Annuaire Suisse de Droit International* (1981), pp. 59-88.
Jensen, G., *Non-Alignment and the Afro-Asian States* (New York 1960).

Jessup, P., "Silence Gives Consent", 3 *Georgia Journal of International and Comparative Law* (1973), pp. 46-54.

Johnson, D., "The Effect of Resolutions of the General Assembly of the United Nations", XXXII *British Yearbook of International Law* (1955-1956), pp. 97-122.

Johnson, D., "The Conclusion of International Conferences", XXXV *British Yearbook of International Law* (1959), pp. 1-33.

Joll, J., "The Decline of Europe: 1920-1970", *International Affairs* (special edition, November 1970), pp. 1-18.

Kapteyn, P., and VerLoren van Themaat, P., *Introduction to the Law of the European Communities* (London, etc. 1973).

Katz, M., *The Relevance of International Adjudication* (Cambridge, Mass. 1968).

Katzenstein, P., "International interdependence: some long-term trends and recent changes", 29 *International Organization* (1975), pp. 1021-1034.

Katzenstein, P., "International relations and domestic structures: foreign economic policies of advanced industrial states", 30 *International Organization* (1976), pp. 1-45.

Kearney, R., "Sources of Law and the International Court of Justice", in: L. Gross (ed.), *The Future of the International Court of Justice*, Vol. II (New York 1976), pp. 610-723.

Kearney, R., "International Legislation: The Negotiating Process", 9 *California Western International Law Journal* (1979), pp. 504-513.

Kelsen, H., "Théorie du droit international coutumier", 13 *Revue Internationale de la Théorie du Droit* (1939), pp. 253-274.

Kelsen, H., *General Theory of Law and State*, translated by A. Wedberg (Cambridge, Mass. 1949).

Kelsen, H., *Principles of International Law*, 2nd printing (New York 1956).

Kelsen, H., *The Pure Theory of Law*, translation by M. Knight (Berkeley 1970).

Khol, A., *Zwischen Staat und Weltstaat* (Wien 1969).

Kimminich, O., "Konferenz über Sicherheit und Zusammenarbeit in Europa und Menschenrechte", 17 *Archiv des Völkerrechts* (1977/1978), pp. 274-294.

King Gamble, J., "Multilateral Treaties: The Significance of the Name of the Instrument", 10 *California Western International Law Journal* (1980), pp. 1-24.

Klafkowski, A., "CSCE Final Act - The Bases for Legal Interpretation", 8 *Studies on International Relations* (Warsaw 1977), pp. 76-87.

Kopelmanas, L., "Custom as a Means of the Creation of International Law", XVIII *British Yearbook of International Law* (1937), pp. 127-151.

Kunz, J., "The Nature of Customary International Law", 47 *American Journal of International Law* (1953), pp. 662-669.

Lachs, M., "Some Reflections on Substance and Form in International Law", in: W. Friedmann, L. Henkin and O. Lissitzyn (eds.), *Transnational Law in a Changing Society; Essays in Honor of Philip C. Jessup* (New York 1972), pp. 99-112.

Lador-Lederer, J., "Legal Aspects of Declarations", XII *Israel Law Review*

(1977), pp. 202-231.

Lammers, J., "General Principles of Law Recognized by Civilized Nations", in: F. Kalshoven e.a. (eds.), *Essays on the Development of the International Legal Order* (Alphen aan den Rijn 1980), pp. 53-75.

Landy, E., *The Effectiveness of International Supervision; Thirty Years of ILO Experience* (London/New York 1966).

Lateef, N., "Parliamentary Diplomacy and the North-South Dialogue", 11 *Georgia Journal of International and Comparative Law* (1981), pp. 1-44.

Lauterpacht, H., *International Law; Collected Papers*, Vol.I: The General Works, edited by E. Lauterpacht (Cambridge 1970).

Levi, W., *Law and Politics in the International Society* (Beverley Hills/London 1976).

Lissitzyn, O., "Treaties and Changed Circumstances (Rebus Sic Stantibus)", 61 *American Journal of International Law* (1967), pp. 895-922.

Lukashuk, I., "Sources of present-day international law", in: G. Tunkin (ed.), *Contemporary International Law* (Moscow 1969).

Mahnke, H., "Die Prinzipienerklärung der KSZE-Schlussakte", 21 *Recht in Ost und West* (1977), pp. 45-56.

Martens, E., "Problem der Entwicklung des Völkerrechts durch multilaterale internationale Verträge und Kodifikationen", 59 *Die Friedens-Warte* (1976), pp. 189-207.

McDougal, M., "International Law, Power and Policy; A Contemporary Conception", 82 *Recueil des Cours de l'Académie de Droit International de La Haye* (1953-I), pp. 137-258.

McDougal, M. and Associates, *Studies in World Public Order* (New Haven 1960).

McDougal, M., and Feliciano, F., *Law and Minimum World Public Order: The Legal Regulations of International Coercion* (New Haven/London 1961).

McDougal, M., Lasswell, H., and Miller, J., *The Interpretation of Agreements and World Public Order, Principles of Content and Procedure* (New Haven 1967).

McDougal, M., Lasswell, H., and Reisman, W., "Theories about International Law: Prologue to a Configurative Jurisprudence", 8 *Virginia Journal of International Law* (1967), pp. 188-299.

McMahon, J., "The Legislative Technique of the International Labour Organization", XLI *British Yearbook of International Law* (1965-1966), pp. 1-102.

McNair, A., *The Law of Treaties* (Oxford 1961).

McWhinney, E., *The World Court and the Contemporary International Law-Making Process* (Alphen aan den Rijn 1979).

Menon, P., "The Law of Treaties with special reference to the Vienna Convention of 1969", 56 *Revue de Droit International de Sciences Diplomatiques et Politiques* (1978), pp. 133-155 and 213-263.

Meijers, H., "How is international law made? - The stages of growth of international law and the use of its customary rules", IX *Netherlands Yearbook of International Law* (1978), pp. 3-26.

Moore, J., "The Lawfulness of Military Assistance to the Republic of Vietnam", 61 *American Journal of International Law* (1967), pp. 1-34.

301

Mosler, H., "Völkerrecht als Rechtsordnung", 36 *Zeitschrift für ausländisches öffentliches Recht und Völkerrecht* (1976), pp. 6-49.

Myers, D., "The Names and Scope of Treaties", 51 *American Journal of International Law* (1957), pp. 574-605.

Nageswar Rao, V., "Jus Cogens and the Vienna Convention on the Law of Treaties", 14 *Indian Journal of International Law* (1974), pp. 362-385.

Nawaz, M., "Other Sources of International Law: Are Judicial Decisions of the International Court of Justice a Source of International Law?", 19 *Indian Journal of International Law* (1979), pp. 526-540.

Netherlands Ministry of Foreign Affairs, *Conferentie over Veiligheid en Samenwerking in Europa, Helsinki-Genève-Helsinki 1973-1975* [Conference on Security and Cooperation in Europe, Helsinki-Geneva-Helsinki 1972-1975], Publication No. 115 ('s-Gravenhage 1976).

Netherlands Ministry of Foreign Affairs, *Verslag over de Hervatte Vijfendertigste Zitting, de Achtste Bijzondere Spoedzitting, de Zesendertigste Zitting en de Negende Bijzondere Spoedzitting van de Algemene Vergadering der Verenigde Naties* [Report on the Resumed 35th Session, the 8th Special Emergency Session, the 36th Session and the 9th Special Emergency Session of the UN General Assembly], Publication No. 127 ('s-Gravenhage 1982).

Neuhold, H., "The 1968 Session of the UN Conference on the Law of Treaties", XIX *Österreichische Zeitschrift für öffentliches Recht* (1969), pp. 59-94.

Nincic, D., "Les Implications Générales Juridiques et Historiques de la Déclaration d'Helsinki", 154 *Recueil des Cours de l'Académie de Droit International de La Haye* (1977-I), pp. 45-101.

Nincic, D., "The Nature and Significance of the Final Act of the Conference on Security and Co-operation in Europe", 1-2 *Revue Yougoslave de Droit International* (1977), pp. 5-19.

O'Brien, W., "Natural Law and International Law in the American Tradition", 141 *World Affairs* (1978), pp. 104-117.

O'Connell, D., *International Law for Students* (London 1971).

Onuf, N., "Professor Falk on the Quasi-Legislative Competence of the General Assembly", 64 *American Journal of International Law* (1970), pp. 349-355.

Onuf, N., and Birney, R., "Peremptory Norms of International Law: Their Source, Function and Future", 4 *Denver Journal of International Law and Policy* (1974), pp. 187-198.

Oppenheim, L., *International Law: A Treatise*, Vol. I: Peace, rev. by H. Lauterpacht, 8th edition, 3rd impression (London 1958).

Parry, C., *The Sources and Evidences of International Law* (Manchester 1965).

Pathak, R., "The General Theory of the Sources of Contemporary International Law", 19 *Indian Journal of International Law* (1979), pp. 483-495.

Prévost, J., "Observations sur la nature juridique de l'Acte Final de la Conférence sur la Sécurité et la Coopération en Europe", XXI *Annuaire Français de Droit International* (1975), pp. 129-153.

Rama Rao, T., "International Custom", 19 *Indian Journal of International Law* (1979), pp. 515-521.

Röling, B., *International Law in an Expanded World* (Amsterdam 1960).

Rogoff, M., "International Law in Legal Theory: The New Positivism", 1 *University of Toledo Law Review* (1970), pp. 1-30.

Rosenne, S., *The Law of Treaties; A Guide to the Legislative History of the Vienna Convention* (New York 1970).

Rosenstock, R., "The Declaration of Principles of International Law Concerning Friendly Relations; A Survey", 65 *American Journal of International Law* (1971), pp. 713-736.

Ross. A., *A Textbook of International Law* (London 1947).

Rotfeld, A., "Follow-up to the Conference; Forms of Co-operation after the Conference on Security and Co-operation in Europe", in: Polish Institute of International Affairs, *Conference on Security and Co-operation; A Polish View* (Warzawa 1976), pp. 221-270.

Rozakis, C., "Treaties and Third States: a Study in the Reinforcement of the Consensual Standards in International Law", 35 *Zeitschrift für ausländisches öffentliches Recht und Völkerrecht* (1975), pp. 1-40.

Rozakis, C., *The Concept of Jus Cogens in the Law of Treaties* (Amsterdam 1976).

Russell, H., "The Helsinki-Declaration: Brobdingnag or Lilliput?", 70 *American Journal of International Law* (1976), pp. 242-272.

Sahovic, M., "Codification des Principes de Droit International des Rélations Amicales et de la Coopération entre les Etats", 137 *Recueil des Cours de l'Académie de Droit International de La Haye* (1972-III), pp. 243-310.

Savigny, F. von, *On the Vocation of Our Age for Legislation and Jurisprudence*, translation by A. Hayward (London 1831).

Scelle, G., *Manuel de Droit International Public*, (Paris 1948).

Scelle, G., "Le phénomène juridique du dédoublement fonctionnel", in: W. Schätzel and H. Schlochauer (eds.), *Rechtsfragen der Internationalen Organisation (Festschrift für Hans Wehberg)*(Frankfurt am Main 1956), pp. 324-342.

Schachter, O., "The Relation of Law, Politics and Action in the United Nations", 109 *Recueil des Cours de l'Académie de Droit International de La Haye* (1963-II), pp. 165-256.

Schachter, O., "Towards a Theory of International Obligation", 8 *Virginia Journal of International Law* (1967), pp. 300-322.

Schachter, O., "The Twilight Existence of Non-binding International Agreements", 71 *American Journal of International Law* (1977), pp. 296-304.

Schachter, O., Nawaz, M., and Fried, J., *Towards Wider Acceptance of UN Treaties - A UNITAR Study* (New York 1971).

Scheuner, U., "Conflict of Treaty Provisions with a Peremptory Norm of General International Law and its Consequences", 27 *Zeitschrift für ausländisches öffentliches Recht und Völkerrecht* (1967), pp. 520-532.

Schrader, H., "Custom and General Principles as Sources of International Law in American Federal Courts", 82 *Columbia Law Review* (1982), pp. 751-783.

Schramm, F., e.a. (eds.), *Sicherheitskonferenz in Europa; Dokumentation*

1973-1978 (Köln 1978).

Schreuer, C., "Recommendations and the Traditional Sources of International Law", 20 *German Yearbook of International Law* (1977), pp. 103-118.

Schütz, H., "Zur Rationalität des Zielkatalogs und des Friedenssicherungsinstrumentariums der Schlussakte der Konferenz für Sicherheit und Zusammenarbeit in Europa", 18 *German Yearbook of International Law* (1975), pp. 146-203.

Schwarzenberger, G., *International Law*, Vol. 1: International law as applied by international courts and tribunals, 3rd edition (London 1957).

Schwarzenberger, G., *The Frontiers of International Law* (London 1962) Schwarzenberger, G., "International 'Jus Cogens'?", 43 *Texas Law Review* (1965), pp. 455-478.

Schwarzenberger, G., *A Manual of International Law*, 5th edition (London 1967).

Schweisfurth, T., "Zur Frage der Rechtsnatur, Verbindlichkeit und Völkerrechtlichen Relevanz der KSZE-Schlussakte", 36 *Zeitschrift für ausländisches öffentliches Recht und Völkerrecht* (1976), pp. 681-726.

Schweitzer, M., "Synopsis des Völkerrechtlers", in: B. Simma and E. Blenk-Knocke (eds.), *Zwischen Intervention und Zusammenarbeit* (Berlin 1979).

Seidl-Hohenveldern, I., "International Economic 'Soft Law'", 163 *Recueil des Cours de l'Académie de Droit International de La Haye* (1979-II), pp. 169-238.

Sicault, J., "Du Caractère Obligatoire des Engagements Unilatéraux en Droit International Public", 83 *Revue Générale de Droit International Public* (1979), pp. 633-688.

Sinclair, I., *The Vienna Convention on the Law of Treaties* (Manchester 1973).

Skubiszewski, K., "Enactment of Law by International Organizations", XVI *British Yearbook of International Law* (1965-1966), pp. 198-274.

Skubiszewski, K., "A New Source of the Law of Nations: Resolutions of International Organizations", *Recueil d'études de droit international en hommage à Paul Guggenheim* (Genève 1968), pp. 508-520.

Skubiszewski, K., "Resolutions of International Organizations and Municipal Law", 2 *Polish Yearbook of International Law* (1968-1969), pp. 80-108.

Skubiszewski, K., "Der Rechtskarakter der KSZE-Schlussakte", in: R. Bernhardt, I. von Münch and W. Rudolf (eds.), *Drittes deutsch-polnisches Juristen-Kolloquium*, Band I: *KSZE-Schlussakte* (Baden-Baden 1977), pp. 13-30.

Sloan, P., "The Binding Force of a 'Recommendation' of the General Assembly of the United Nations", XXV *British Yearbook of International Law* (1948), pp. 1-33.

Sørensen, M., *Les Sources du Droit International* (Copenhague 1946).

Sohn, L., "The Universal Declaration of Human Rights", 8 *Journal of the International Commission of Jurists* (1968), pp. 17-26.

Sohn, L., "The Development of the Charter of the United Nations: the Present State", in: M. Bos (ed.), *The Present State of International Law and other Essays* (Deventer 1973), pp. 39-59.

Sohn, L., "Voting Procedures in United Nations Conferences for the Codification of International Law", 69 *American Journal of International Law* (1975), pp. 310-353.

Sohn, L., "The Shaping of International Law", 8 *Georgia Journal of International and Comparative Law* (1978), pp. 1-25.

Stagno, L., "The Application of International Human Rights Agreements in United States Courts: Customary International Law Incorporated into Domestic American Law", VIII *Brooklyn Journal of International Law* (1982-I), pp. 207-238.

Steinert, M., and Kapur, H., "New Configurations of Power in International Relations", in: Institut universitaire de hautes études internationales, *Les rélations internationales dans un monde en mutation* (Genève/Leiden 1977), pp. 123-161.

Strebel, H., "Quellen des Völkerrechts als Rechtsordnung", 36 *Zeitschrift für ausländisches öffentliches Recht und Völkerrecht* (1976), pp. 301-346.

Strupp, K., "Les Règles Générales du Droit de la Paix", 47 *Recueil des Cours de l'Académie de Droit International de La Haye* (1934-I), pp. 263-595.

Subba Rao, T., *Non-Alignment in International Law and Politics* (New Delhi 1981).

Suy, E., *Papers and Proceedings of the Lagonissi Conference* (Geneva 1967).

Suy, E., "The Meaning of Consensus in Multilateral Diplomacy", in: R. Akkerman e.a. (eds.), *Liber Röling, Declarations on Principles; A Quest for Universal Peace* (Leyden 1977), pp. 247-257.

Suy, E., "Innovations in International Law-making Processes", in: R. McDonald, D. Johnston and G. Morris (eds.), *The International Law and Policy of Human Welfare* (Alphen aan den Rijn 1978), pp. 187-200.

Szasz, P., "Improving the International Legislative Process", 9 *Georgia Journal of International and Comparative Law* (1979), pp. 519-533.

Tammes, A., "Decisions of International Organs as a Source of International Law", 94 *Recueil des Cours de l'Académie de Droit International de La Haye* (1958-II), pp. 265-362.

Thirlway, H., *International Customary Law and Codification* (Leyden 1972).

Tomuschat, C., "Die Charta der Wirtschaftlichen Rechte und Pflichten der Staaten; Zur Gestaltungskraft von Deklarationen der UN-Generalversammlung", 36 *Zeitschrift für ausländisches öffentliches Recht und Völkerrecht* (1976), pp. 444-491.

Tunkin, G., "'General Principles of Law' in International Law", in: R. Marcic e.a. (eds.), *Internationale Festschrift für Alfred Verdross* (München/Salzburg 1971), pp. 523-532.

Tunkin, G., *Theory of International Law*, translation by W. Butler (Cambridge, Mass. 1974).

Tunkin, G., "General Theory of Sources of International Law", 19 *Indian Journal of International Law* (1979), pp. 474-482.

Unger, R., *Knowledge and Politics* (New York/London 1975).

United Nations Department of Public Information, *Everyone's United Nations*, 9th edition (New York 1979).

Vallat, F., "The Work of the International Law Commission - The Law of Treaties", XXII *Netherlands International Law Review* (1975), pp. 327-336.

Valticos, N., "Un Système de Contrôle International: La Mise en Oeuvre des Conventions Internationales du Travail au Bureau International du Travail", 123 *Recueil des Cours de l'Académie de Droit International de La Haye* (1968-I), pp. 311-407.

Valticos, N., "The International Protection of Economic and Social Rights", in: P. van Dijk (ed.), *Rechten van de Mens in Mundiaal en Europees Perspectief* [Human Rights in a Global and European Perspective], 2nd edition (Utrecht 1980), pp. 109-140.

Verdross, A., *Die Einheit des rechtlichen Weltbildes auf der Grundlage der Völkerrechtsverfassung* (Tübingen 1923).

Verdross, A., *Die Verfassung der Völkerrechtsgemeinschaft* (Wien/Berlin 1926).

Verdross, A., "Les Principes Généraux dans la Jurisprudence Internationale", 52 *Recueil des Cours de l'Académie de Droit International de La Haye* (1935-II), pp. 195-251.

Verdross, A., "Jus Dispositivum and Jus Cogens in International Law", 60 *American Journal of International Law* (1966), pp. 55-63.

Verdross, A., "Kann die Generalversammlung der Vereinten Nationen das Völkerrecht weiterbilden?", 26 *Zeitschrift für ausländisches öffentliches Recht und Völkerrecht* (1966), pp. 690-697.

Verdross, A., *Die Quellen des universellen Völkerrechts* (Freiburg 1973).

VerLoren van Themaat, P., *The Changing Structure of International Economic Law* (The Hague 1981).

Verwey, W., *The Establishment of a New International Economic Order and the Realization of the Right to Development and Welfare; A Legal Survey* (HR/Geneva 1980/F.P.3).

Verzijl, J., *International Law in Historical Perspective*, Vol. I: General Subjects (Leyden 1968).

Verzijl, J., *International Law in Historical Perspective*, Vol. VIII: Inter-State Disputes and their Settlement (Leyden 1976).

Vignes, D., "Will the Third Conference on the Law of the Sea Work According to the Consensus Rule?", 69 *American Journal of International Law* (1975), pp. 119-129.

Virally, M., "La valeur juridique des récommendations des organisations internationales", II *Annuaire Français de Droit International* (1956), pp. 66-96.

Virally, M., "Réflexions sur le 'jus cogens'", XII *Annuaire Françcais de Droit International* (1966), pp. 5-29.

Virally, M., "The Sources of International Law", in: M. Sørensen (ed.), *Manual of Public International Law* (London 1968), pp. 116-174.

Virally, M., "La deuxième décennie des Nations Unies pour le développement; Essai d'interprétation para-juridique", XVI *Annuaire Français de Droit International* (1970), pp. 9-33.

Visscher, Ch. de, *Theory and Reality in Public International Law*, translation by P. Corbett (Princeton 1957).

Visscher, Ch. de, *Theory and Reality in Public International Law*, revised edition, translated by P. Corbett (Princeton 1968).

Vitanyi, B., "Les Positions Doctrinales concernant le Sens de la Notion de 'Principes Généraux de Droit Reconnus par les Nations Civilisées'", 86 *Revue Générale de Droit International Public* (1982), pp. 46-116.

Vree, J. de, "On the Origins and Growth of Law and Morals", 23 *Philosophica* (1979), pp. 129-176.

Walden, R., "The Subjective Element in the Formation of Customary International Law", XII *Israel Law Review* (1977), pp. 344-364.

Walden, R., "Customary International Law: A Jurisprudential Analysis", XIII *Israel Law Review* (1978), pp. 86-102.

Waldock, H., "General Course on Public International Law", 106 *Recueil des Cours de l'Académie de Droit International de La Haye* (1962-II), pp. 1-251.

Watson, J., "Legal Theory, Efficacy and Validity in the Development of Human Rights Norms in International Law", 3 *University of Illinois Law Forum* (1979), pp. 609-641.

Weber, M., *Law in Economy and Society*, edited with introduction and annotations by M. Rheinstein, translation by E. Shills and M. Rheinstein, 2nd print (New York 1954).

Weil, P., "Vers une normativité relative en droit international", 86 *Revue Générale de Droit International Public* (1982), pp. 5-47.

Wengler, W., "Rechtsvertrag, Konsensus und Absichtserklärung im Völkerrecht", 31 *Juristenzeitung* (1976), pp. 193-197.

Wengler, W., "Public International Law, Paradoxes of a Legal Order", 158 *Recueil des Cours de l'Académie de Droit International de La Haye* (1977-V), pp. 13-85.

Whiteman, M., "Jus Cogens in International Law, with a Projected List", 7 *Georgia Journal of International and Comparative Law* (1977), pp. 609-626.

Wolfke, K., *Custom in Present International Law* (Wroclaw 1962).

Wolfke, K., "Jus Cogens in International Law", 6 *Polish Yearbook of International Law* (1974), pp. 145-162.

Wright, Q., "The Strengthening of International Law", 98 *Recueil des Cours de l'Académie de Droit International de La Haye* (1959-III), pp. 1-293.

Yasseen, M., "Réflexions sur la détermination du jus cogens", in: Société française pour le droit international, *L'Elaboration du Droit International Public* (Paris 1974), pp. 204-210.

Zamora, S., "Voting in International Economic Organizations", 74 *American Journal of International Law* (1980), pp. 566-608.

INDEX

SAMENVATTING

De periode van na de Tweede Wereldoorlog wordt zowel op nationaal als op internationaal niveau gekenmerkt door ingrijpende veranderingen op velerlei terreinen. Hoewel definitieve conclusies beter getrokken kunnen worden, wanneer deze ontwikkelingen volledig zijn uitgekristalliseerd, kan nu al wel gesteld worden, dat waarschijnlijk nooit tevoren veranderingen van dezelfde omvang en diepgang in zo'n kort tijdsbestek hebben plaatsgevonden. Vanzelfsprekend heeft dit zijn uitwerking op het internationale recht niet gemist. Met de onderhavige studie wordt beoogd de effecten van de veranderingen in de internationale samenleving op het internationale recht te onderzoeken. De nadruk ligt daarbij op de vraag, welke de invloed van deze veranderingen is (geweest) op de zogenaamde traditionele bronnen van het internationale recht. In aansluiting daarop wordt in het laatste deel van het boek bovendien getracht de grote lijnen aan te geven van een methode via welke de bedoelde veranderingen in de bronnenleer van het internationale recht verwerkt zouden kunnen worden. De resultaten van dit onderzoek kunnen als volgt worden samengevat.

Het is van meet af aan duidelijk geweest, dat een zinvolle behandeling van de vragen betreffende de bronnen van het internationale recht een benadering vereist die meer moet omvatten dan alleen de bronnen als zodanig. De recente ontwikkelingen in de internationale betrekkingen hebben ongetwijfeld het aantal en de omvang van de problemen inzake de bronnen van het internationale recht doen toenemen. De bronnenleer van het internationale recht is echter altijd al gekenmerkt geweest door een vrij grote mate van verwarring en meningsverschillen. Dit laat zich, althans ten dele, verklaren uit het feit, dat vragen betreffende de bronnen ten nauwste samenhangen met andere fundamentele theoretische kwesties van internationaal recht. Een vluchtige blik op de literatuur maakt duidelijk, dat er ten aanzien van deze fundamentele zaken, die samenvattend aangeduid kunnen worden als behorend tot het zogenaamde "normative concept" van het internationale recht, vaak zeer uiteenlopende opvattingen bestaan. Dergelijke expliciete of impliciete meningsverschillen over het "normative concept" van het internationale recht liggen ten grondslag aan de uiteenlopende standpunten aangaande de bronnen. Derhalve kon aan een aantal vragen betreffende het "normative concept" niet volledig worden voorbijgegaan.

In Deel I vinden dan ook die aspecten van het "normative concept" behandeling die rechtstreeks van belang zijn voor de bronnenleer. Deze analyse is vooral toegespitst op de functie en het functioneren van het internationale recht. Voor wat de bronnen betreft leverde dit met name twee conclusies op. Globaal genomen bestaat de functie van het recht uit het ordenen en reguleren van verhoudingen in de samenleving. Voor de vervulling van deze functie is vereist, dat het recht een afspiegeling vormt van de onderliggende maatschappelijke structuur. Zonder een voldoende band met het maatschappelijk gebeuren kan het recht zijn

ordenende en regulerende rol niet met succes spelen. Deze ordenende en regulerende rol eist echter tegelijkertijd, dat er een zeker minimum aan zekerheid en duidelijkheid bestaat over de vraag, waar het recht gevonden kan worden en wat het inhoudt. Het recht moet, door het classificeren van verschillende soorten van gedrag, als het ware een duidelijk en overzichtelijk beeld distilleren uit de vaak chaotische werkelijkheid zoals die in de praktijk bestaat. Op die wijze levert het recht een bijdrage aan het functioneren van de samenleving. Hieruit blijkt tevens dat het recht niet een volledige afspiegeling van de maatschappelijke verhoudingen kan vormen, omdat dan zijn normatieve karakter en daarmee zijn ordenend en regulerend vermogen verloren zou gaan. Met andere woorden, de bronnenleer moet aan de ene kant een overdreven formalisme vermijden, waarmee de band tussen recht en samenleving uit het oog verloren zou worden, en aan de andere kant waken tegen volledige vormloosheid, waardoor de noodzakelijke zekerheid en duidelijkheid zouden komen te ontbreken.

Deze beide voorwaarden, waaraan een werkbare bronnenleer naar ons inzicht dient te voldoen (te weten de band tussen recht en samenleving en de noodzakelijke zekerheid en duidelijkheid), zijn vervolgens tot uitgangspunt genomen bij het analyseren van een aantal zogenaamde standaard-theorieën inzake het internationale recht. Deze analyse is ondernomen om redenen van zowel efficiency als eenvoud. Daarmee konden namelijk die elementen van een aantal bestaande theorieën worden geïdentificeerd, met behulp waarvan vragen betreffende de bronnen van het internationale recht dichter bij een oplossing gebracht kunnen worden. Op deze manier kon worden voortgebouwd op een reeds bestaande basis, terwijl daarmee tegelijkertijd de noodzaak kwam te vervallen die basis eerst zelf uitvoerig te schetsen.

Drie standaard-theorieën zijn in de beschouwingen betrokken. Deze drie theorieën zijn achtereenvolgens genoemd: het "legal idealism", de "analytical approach", en de "sociological approach". Deze namen zijn gebruikt, omdat zij ieder een zo goed mogelijke indicatie geven van het meest fundamentele kenmerk van elk van deze theorieën. Deze indeling is zeer algemeen en breed en daarom in een aantal opzichten ontoereikend. Voor de onderhavige studie voldeed de genoemde indeling niettemin goed, omdat daarmee een onderscheid kan worden gemaakt tussen drie belangrijke methoden met behulp waarvan vragen betreffende de bronnen van het internationale recht gewoonlijk benaderd worden.

In de eerste categorie, het "legal idealism", meer specifiek ook wel de natuurrechtelijke benadering genoemd, zijn hier al die theorieën ondergebracht, die zoeken en/of streven naar de formulering van idealen en waarden waarop een rechtsstelsel is gebaseerd. Wat de bronnen van het internationale recht betreft is het standpunt ingenomen, dat "legal idealism" behebt is met een aantal tekortkomingen, die als volgt kunnen worden samengevat: ofwel de beweerdelijk universele idealen en waarden, die door natuurrechtstheorieën worden gepropageerd, zijn te weinig in getal en te abstract om werkelijk de basis van het internationale recht te kunnen vormen, ofwel de idealen en waarden, die door natuurrecht-aanhangers worden voorgestaan zijn niet algemeen aanvaard noch wetenschappelijk controleerbaar. Vooral dit laatste aspect beperkt de bruikbaarheid van de natuurrechtelijke benadering met betrekking tot de bronnen van het internationale recht in aanzienlijke mate. Anders dan de meeste nationale samenlevingen wordt de internationale samenleving namelijk vooral geken-

314

merkt door een lage integratiegraad en het ontbreken van een hierarchische/organisatorische structuur. Willen idealen en waarden beschouwd kunnen worden als basis van het internationale recht, dan moeten zij daarom ofwel algemeen aanvaard zijn, ofwel wetenschappelijk zo overtuigend beargumenteerd kunnen worden, dat aan hun aanvaarding niet te ontkomen valt. Geen van beide lijkt het geval te zijn met natuurrechtstheorieën. De verschillende Staten en groepen van Staten binnen de internationale samenleving houden er uiteenlopende idealen en waarden op na. De idealen en waarden die worden voorgestaan door de ene Staat of groep zijn voor de andere niet aanvaardbaar en worden beschouwd als een soort "religie" of althans ideologie.

Het valt moeilijk in te zien hoe een benadering, die aanleiding geeft tot zulke verschillen van opvatting, het uitgangspunt kan vormen voor een behandeling van de bronnen van het internationale recht. Zoals verscheidene malen is benadrukt, impliceert dit niet een negatief oordeel over "legal idealism" als zodanig. Integendeel, uitgewerkte voorstellen voor een betere wereld op basis van het internationale recht kunnen de bewustwording bevorderen van de huidige tekortkomingen en Staten er wellicht toe brengen die tekortkomingen tot op zekere hoogte weg te nemen. Meer in het bijzonder kan het ontwikkelen en nader uitwerken van fundamentele waarden en idealen bijdragen tot een gewijzigde interpretatie van het recht en daardoor tot richtsnoer dienen bij het opstellen van nieuwe of het veranderen van bestaande regels. Een en ander betekent echter nog niet, dat (een bepaalde stroming in) het "legal idealism" nu ook de algehele basis kan vormen voor de bronnen van het internationale recht in die zin, dat aan de hand daarvan de vraag afdoende beantwoord kan worden waar het recht gevonden kan worden of wat het precies inhoudt.

De andere twee zogenaamde standaard-theorieën blijken elk slechts aan één van de beide genoemde voorwaarden te voldoen, die naar onze mening aan de bronnenleer gesteld dienen te worden. De "analytical approach", gewoonlijk Positivisme genoemd, houdt zich voornamelijk bezig met de juridische techniek en is op de eerste plaats gericht op de doorzichtigheid en de structurering van een rechtsstelsel. Vanwege het extreme belang dat de Positivisten hechten aan orde, stabiliteit en zekerheid, zijn zij geneigd de praktijk, en daarmee de band tussen recht en samenleving, uit het oog te verliezen. Als gevolg van deze nadruk op orde, stabiliteit en zekerheid gaan hun modellen vaak uit van *a priori*-veronderstellingen en vereisten met als gevaar dat zij fictieve antwoorden opleveren.

De "sociological approach" daarentegen richt zich nagenoeg volledig op de band tussen recht en samenleving. Dat geldt in bijzonder voor de zogenaamde "Policy Oriented Approach". Deze kan worden gekarakteriseerd als een "panta-rhei" benadering, omdat deze stroming een groot aantal, soms zeer gedetailleerde, aspecten, die te zamen nagenoeg het geheel der internationale betrekkingen omvatten, in haar beschouwingen betrekt. Deze aspecten worden bovendien geacht aan voortdurende verandering onderhevig te zijn. Er valt niets af te dingen op de stelling, dat de internationale betrekkingen, waaronder begrepen het proces van internationale rechtsvorming, vele deelnemers, belangen en waarden omvat, die alle het bestuderen waard zijn wil men tot een beter begrip van het recht geraken. Dat neemt echter niet weg, en de "sociological approach" lijkt dit over het hoofd te zien, dat in elke samenleving dit proces tot op zekere hoogte gecomprimeerd en geformaliseerd is in de vorm van een meer

technische procedure en dat, waar het gaat om de bronnen van het internationale recht, deze procedure en de daaruit voortvloeiende resultaten het belangrijkste object van studie vormen.

De analyse van de drie zogenaamde standaard-theorieën heeft tot de conclusie geleid, dat de voorkeur gegeven dient te worden aan een benadering die het midden houdt tussen het extreme formalisme van het traditionele Positivisme en de bijna volledige vormeloosheid van de beschreven sociologische stroming. De theorie van Hart, die we hebben aangeduid met de term "Structural Positivism", blijkt in belangrijke mate aan dit vereiste te voldoen. Deze theorie bestaat in feite uit een model, dat wordt gevormd door een combinatie van zogenaamde primaire en secundaire regels. Een korte schets van Hart's model leert dat daarin voldoende rekening gehouden wordt met het vereiste van zekerheid en duidelijkheid, die de bronnen van het recht moeten verschaffen. Dit resultaat wordt bereikt door middel van de zogenaamde "rule of recognition", waaraan Hart een centrale plaats toekent in zijn theorie. Een "rule of recognition" wordt gedefinieerd als een regel, die een bepaalde eigenschap of bepaalde eigenschappen aangeeft welke een gegeven primaire regel moet bezitten wil de conclusie kunnen worden gerechtvaardigd, dat die regel een rechtsregel is. Primaire regels kunnen kortweg worden omschreven als regels, die (materiële) rechten en plichten vastleggen. Tegelijkertijd verliest de theorie van Hart de band tussen recht en samenleving niet uit het oog. De uiteindelijke basis van de "rule of recognition" wordt namelijk gezocht in de praktijk van de zogenaamde "law-determining agencies" van een bepaalde samenleving. Deze kenmerken van Hart's theorie zijn de aanleiding geweest om te trachten het model van het "Structural Positivism" toe te passen op het internationale recht. Hart zelf doet dat in feite niet, ofschoon een heel hoofdstuk van zijn boek aan het internationale recht gewijd is.

Tevoren diende echter nader ingegaan te worden op het begrip "bronnen" zelf. Immers, hoewel de betekenis van "bron" of "bronnen" op het eerste gezicht duidelijk lijkt, leert nadere bestudering dat deze termen niet ondubbelzinnig zijn. Drie verschillende betekenissen van de term "bronnen", of beter gezegd drie verschillende niveaus waarop de bronnen geanalyseerd dienen te worden, kunnen worden onderscheiden. Op het eerste niveau duidt de term "bron" op de grondslag van de bindende kracht van het internationale recht. Op het tweede niveau geeft de term "bron" het constitutive element aan voor regels van internationaal recht. Daaronder wordt verstaan het criterium op grond waarvan men kan uitmaken, of een bepaalde regel al dan niet een regel van internationaal recht is. Op het derde niveau, ten slotte, worden met de term "bron" de relevante manifestaties bedoeld op grond waarvan het al dan niet voldaan zijn aan het constitutieve element kan worden vastgesteld.

Alle drie de niveaus of betekenissen van de bronnen moeten voldoen aan het vereiste van zowel voldoende duidelijkheid en zekerheid als van voldoende aandacht voor de band tussen recht en samenleving. Niettemin, zo is gesteld, bestaat er in dit opzicht een verschil tussen de beide eerste niveaus en het derde, in het bijzonder voor wat de band tussen recht en samenleving betreft. In de beide eerstgenoemde betekenissen worden de bronnen vooral bepaald door de fundamentele kenmerken van de internationale samenleving. In de als derde genoemde betekenis worden zij met name beïnvloed door wat is omschreven als de structuur van de internationale betrekkingen.

De meest karakteristieke eigenschap van de internationale samenleving is sinds lange tijd nog steeds de souvereine onafhankelijkheid van de Staten. Samenvattend houdt deze souvereine onafhankelijkheid in, dat, althans bezien vanuit het internationale recht, de Staten niet aan enige hogere authoriteit onderworpen zijn en dat, voor wat de onderlinge betrekkingen tussen de Staten aangaat, geen enkele Staat geplaatst is boven een andere Staat. Dit tweezijdige aspect van de onafhankelijkheid van de Staten heeft vergaande consequenties met betrekking tot de bronnen van het internationale recht. Ten aanzien van de term "bron" in de eerstgenoemde zin betekent het, dat geen enkele (materiële) waarde of ideaal kan dienen als de enige grondslag voor de bindende kracht van het internationale recht, zolang geen enkele zodanige waarde of ideaal in de statengemeenschap algemeen is aanvaard. Zolang deze situatie blijft bestaan, kan een grootste gemene deler als grondslag voor de bindende kracht van het internationale recht naar onze mening slechts gevonden worden in wat is genoemd de erkende noodzaak (recognized necessity) als procedurele bron. Daarmee wordt bedoeld, dat de grondslag voor de bindende kracht van het internationale recht vooralsnog gezocht moet worden in het vaststelbare bewustzijn aan de kant van de Staten, dat er geen bevredigend alternatief bestaat voor een stelsel van bindende regels om hun onderlinge betrekkingen te ordenen en te regelen. Betoogd is bovendien, dat de fundamentele regel *pacta sunt servanda* beschouwd kan worden als de "vertaling" in het internationale recht van deze "procedurele" bron van de erkende noodzaak.

Met betrekking tot de tweede betekenis van de term "bron" heeft de genoemde onafhankelijkheid van Staten de consequenties dat het proces van besluitvorming gedecentraliseerd is en er geen echte internationale "wetgevende macht" bestaat. De subjecten van het internationale recht, dat wil zeggen de Staten zelf, treden op als "wetgever". Dientengevolge vormt de instemming van de Staten, in de zin van de intentie aan hun kant om gebonden te worden, het constitutieve element voor regels van het internationale recht. Met andere woorden, voor de beantwoording van de vraag, of een bepaalde regel al dan niet bindend is voor een Staat als een regel van internationaal recht, dient als uitgangspunt te worden genomen de vraag, of de desbetreffende Staat met die regel heeft ingestemd of deze heeft aanvaard, waarbij aanvaarding wordt verstaan als stilzwijgende instemming.

Anders dan dit hierboven genoemde fundamentele kenmerk van de internationale samenleving, heeft de structuur van de internationale betrekkingen, die in het bijzonder van invloed is op de bronnen in de derde betekenis van manifestaties van instemming of aanvaarding, recentelijk aanzienlijke veranderingen ondergaan. Twee belangrijke ontwikkelingen die zich met name hebben voorgedaan, kunnen worden gekarakteriseerd met de trefwoorden "interdependentie" en "heterogeniteit". Deze beide ontwikkelingen werken min of meer tegen elkaar in. Aan de ene kant hebben wetenschappelijke en technologische veranderingen een proces van toenemende interdependentie in gang gezet in die zin, dat Staten steeds afhankelijker van elkaar worden op een steeds groter wordend aantal terreinen. Deze groeiende interdependentie heeft op haar beurt geleid tot een grotere "dichtheid" van het internationale recht, dat wil zeggen dat het internationale recht steeds meer aspecten van de internationale betrekkingen moet bestrijken op een steeds gedetailleerdere wijze. Aan de andere kant is de relatief homogene internationale samenleving van de negentiende eeuw veran-

derd in de huidige heterogene groep van Staten. De twintigste eeuw heeft niet alleen een verdeling te zien gegeven tussen Oost en West, maar, meer recent, ook tussen Noord en Zuid. Dit beeld van een wereld verdeeld in kampen is ongetwijfeld een oversimplificatie van de werkelijkheid, maar het maakt wel overduidelijk, dat de tijd waarin de wereld bestond uit een betrekkelijk gelijk-gezinde club van Staten definitief tot het verleden behoort. De twee genoemde ontwikkelingen samen hebben geleid tot een nogal paradoxale situatie: terwijl de behoefte aan gedetailleerde regels op velerlei terreinen waarschijnlijk nooit zo groot geweest is als tegenwoordig, is het tegelijkertijd moeilijker dan ooit tevoren om overeenstemming over dergelijke regels tussen de Staten te bereiken.

Op basis van het in Deel I geschetste theoretische kader, wordt in Deel II getracht te inventariseren op welke wijze de recente veranderingen in de structuur van de internationale betrekkingen de zogenaamde traditionele bronnen van het internationale recht hebben beïnvloed. Daartoe worden achtereenvolgens behandeld: het internationaal gewoonterecht, de verdragen, de algemene rechtsbeginselen, alsmede jurisprudentie en doctrine, welke beide laatste in artikel 38 van het Statuut van het Internationaal Gerechtshof worden aangeduid als subsidiaire methoden voor de vaststelling van rechtsregels.

Met betrekking tot het internationaal gewoonterecht bleek de literatuur nogal tegenstrijdig en in een aantal opzichten ook verwarrend te zijn. Alvorens de invloed van maatschappelijke veranderingen op deze bron te kunnen analyseren, was het daarom nodig het karakter van het internationaal gewoonterecht zo nauwkeurig mogelijk aan te geven. Dit vroeg om een uitvoerige analyse van de beide samenstellende delen van gewoonterecht, te weten *usus* and *opinio iuris*, en met name ook van de relatie tussen beide. Het is mogelijk gebleken het ingewikkelde karakter van het internationaal gewoonterecht te ontrafelen met behulp van de zogenaamde fasen-theorie. Deze theorie komt in feite neer op de conclusie, dat terwijl *opinio iuris* een regel de status verleent van rechtsregel, het de *usus* is die de regel maakt tot een regel van internationaal gewoonterecht. Bovendien is de stelling verdedigd, dat, met het oog op de zekerheid en duidelijkheid die de bronnen moeten verschaffen, internationaal gewoonterecht als een op de praktijk gebaseerde bron van internationaal recht eng gedefinieerd moet worden.

Tegelijkertijd heeft het feit dat gewoonterecht op de praktijk is gebaseerd, tot gevolg, dat de rol van gewoonte als bron van het internationale recht verhoudingsgewijze aan belang inboet. De veranderingen in de internationale samenleving, met name het snellere ritme en het meer complexe karakter van de internationale betrekkingen, alsmede de heterogeniteit die de statengemeenschap tegenwoordig kenmerkt, hebben de rol van gewoonte als bron van het internationale recht doen afnemen. Dit betekent uiteraard niet, dat internationaal gewoonterecht geheel zal verdwijnen. Afgezien van het feit, dat gewoonte zijn traditionele rol zal blijven spelen op een aantal terreinen, kan een nieuwe rol voor de gewoonte tegemoet gezien worden in de vorm van latere praktijk (subsequent practice), dat wil zeggen in de vorm van uitwerking en concretizering van reeds bestaande (geschreven) regels van internationaal recht.

Verdragen bieden in vele opzichten het tegenovergestelde beeld van internationaal gewoonterecht. Het karakter van verdragen als bron van internationaal recht is ondubbelzinnig en in feite onomstreden. In vergelijking met gewoonte-

rechtsvorming voltrekt het sluiten van verdragen zich bovendien relatief snel en leidt het tot duidelijkere resultaten. Het behoeft dan ook geen verbazing te wekken, dat verdragen de belangrijkste bron van het internationale recht zijn geworden. Niettemin is ook deze bron niet onberoerd gelaten door de recente veranderingen in de internationale samenleving, maar vertoont ook deze wel degelijk een aantal tekortkomingen gelet op de eisen waaraan het proces van rechtsvorming tegenwoordig zou moeten voldoen. Deze tekortkomingen zijn besproken onder de volgende rubrieken: problemen betreffende aanvaarding van verdragen, problemen betreffende aanpassing van verdragen, en problemen inzake wijziging van verdragen. De eerstgenoemde categorie van problemen ziet op de situatie, dat vele multilaterale verdragen in de praktijk slechts door een relatief klein aantal Staten geratificeerd worden. De tweede en de derde categorie duiden op de moeilijkheden, die het gevolg zijn van het formele en weinig soepele karakter van verdragen als bron van het internationale recht. Daardoor kunnen de verdragen niet altijd gelijke tred houden met ontwikkelingen in de praktijk, waardoor het gevaar bestaat dat zij snel achter raken bij een gewijzigde situatie. Teneinde de nodige flexibiliteit te verkrijgen moeten verdragen daarom vaak voorzien worden van speciale procedures om een snelle aanpassing en wijziging mogelijk te maken. Dit geldt in het bijzonder nu de inhoud van veel verdragsregels aan het verschuiven is. Ten gevolge van de veranderingen in de internationale samenleving kan het internationale recht tegenwoordig niet meer volstaan met *ad hoc* regelingen en oplossingen, maar dient het een kader tot uitgangspunt te nemen waarin met de algemene en lange-termijn-aspecten van beleid rekening is gehouden. Anders dan het traditionele internationale recht, bestaat het moderne internationale recht daarom niet zelden uit abstracte, algemene en vaak zelfs vage regels. Dergelijke "programmatische" regels kunnen doorgaans slechts op concrete situaties worden toegepast, nadat ze zijn uitgewerkt en aangepast. Dit wordt bereikt door middel van follow-up procedures waarin een groeiend aantal verdragen is voorzien, vooral in het kader van internationale organisaties, en door middel van latere statenpraktijk.

De situatie met betrekking tot de derde bron die in artikel 38 van het Statuut van het Internationaal Gerechtshof wordt genoemd, de algemene rechtsbeginselen, blijkt min of meer vergelijkbaar te zijn met die van het gewoonterecht. Ook het karakter van de algemene rechtsbeginselen is sterk omstreden in de doctrine. Na een korte schets van het ontstaan en de geschiedenis van de algemene rechtsbeginselen is een poging ondernomen hun karakter als bron van het internationale recht te verduidelijken aan de hand van een tweeledig onderscheid. Op basis daarvan is het standpunt ingenomen, dat de algemene rechtsbeginselen een bron van internationaal recht vormen in het kader van de procedure voor het Internationaal Gerechtshof of, meer in het algemeen, in het kader van rechterlijke en arbitrale procedures. Als argument daarvoor is aangevoerd, dat het bestaan van algemene rechtsbeginselen vastgesteld dient te worden door onafhankelijke derde instanties, zoals die in rechterlijke en arbitrale procedures zijn voorzien. Hoewel dat in theorie wel mogelijk is, vormen de algemene rechtsbeginselen in feite geen zelfstandige bron van internationaal recht buiten rechterlijke en arbitrale procedures. In die situatie worden de algemene rechtsbeginselen vaak opgevat in een betekenis, die betrekking heeft op de materiële inhoud van de desbetreffende regels. Deze betekenis van de term "algemene rechtsbeginselen" leidt dan vaak tot een discussie over de hierarchie van regels

van internationaal recht. Strikt genomen vallen de algemene rechtsbeginselen in deze materiële zin buiten het bestek van de onderhavige studie. Omdat echter de procedurele en de materiële betekenis in de literatuur vaak gelijktijdig behandeld worden, is ook in deze studie enige aandacht besteed aan de hiërarchie van regels van internationaal recht in de vorm van een analyse van het begrip *jus cogens*.

Ten slotte zijn de rechterlijke beslissingen en de doctrine besproken als subsidiaire methoden voor het vaststellen van rechtsregels. Rechterlijke beslissingen, zo is betoogd, kunnen alleen als bron in de zin van een manifestatie van instemming of aanvaarding worden beschouwd met betrekking tot die Staten, die partij waren bij de desbetreffende zaak. Met betrekking tot andere Staten zijn rechterlijke beslissingen ten hoogste een indirecte bron in die zin, dat zij de instemming of aanvaarding door die Staten kunnen beïnvloeden, maar daarvan niet een directe manifestatie kunnen vormen. *Mutatis mutandis* gaat deze laatste conclusie ook op voor de doctrine.

De eindconclusie van Deel II luidt, dat de traditionele bronnen van het internationale recht zonder twijfel terrein hebben verloren. De traditionele bronnen zijn niet toereikend om als basis te dienen ook voor het gehele terrein van nieuwe instrumenten en andere phenomenen, die beweerdelijk bindend internationaal recht vormen. De veranderingen in de internationale samenleving hebben nieuwe elementen geïntroduceerd in het proces van rechtsvorming, die niet als bindend of niet-bindend geïdentificeerd kunnen worden op basis van de criteria welke de traditionele bronnen van het internationale recht daarvoor bieden.

Deze situatie heeft uiteenlopende reacties uitgelokt in de literatuur over de bronnen. Sommigen proberen de inhoud van de traditionele bronnen te verbreden teneinde de nieuwe phenomenen daarin te kunnen passen. Dit bergt het gevaar in zich, dat de traditionele bronnen zodanig worden "uitgerekt", dat zij nagenoeg inhoudsloos worden en bijgevolg niet meer de vereiste zekerheid en duidelijkheid kunnen verschaffen. Anderen kiezen voor wat genoemd kan worden de "andere bron"-benadering. Deze komt er zwart-wit gesteld op neer, dat een nieuwe bron wordt afgekondigd telkens, wanneer een nieuw soort instrument in de praktijk ontstaat. Het meest bekende voorbeeld van een dergelijke nieuwe bron vormen de declaraties of, meer algemeen, de resoluties van de Algemene Vergadering van de Verenigde Naties. Aan een dergelijke benadering zijn twee grote nadelen verbonden. In de eerste plaats vallen de afgekondigde nieuwe bronnen soms niet te rijmen met het consensuele karakter van het internationale recht dat ten grondslag ligt aan de traditionele bronnen. In de tweede plaats heeft deze benadering een sterk *ad hoc* karakter en biedt zij geen oplossing voor verdere ontwikkelingen die zich in de praktijk kunnen voordoen. Er is kortom behoefte aan een meer geïntegreerde benadering, die enerzijds consistent is met de traditionele bronnen, maar tegelijk ook nieuwe ontwikkelingen op een meer structurele manier kan verklaren. Ten slotte is er een zogenaamde "soft law"-benadering tot stand gekomen. Deze heeft vooral duidelijk gemaakt, dat er een grijze zone bestaat tussen het witte gebied van het recht en het zwarte van niet-recht. De "soft law"-benadering speelt een belangrijke rol in de huidige bronnenleer van het internationale recht, met name omdat zij zich ten doel stelt de wisselwerking tussen de zojuist genoemde grijze en witte zones nader uit te werken. De meeste aanhangers van de "soft law"-benadering houden zich ech-

ter slechts zijdeling bezig met het onderwerp van dit boek, te weten de afbakening tussen de witte en de grijze zone.

Naar onze mening vereist een effectief functioneren van het internationale recht een zo eng mogelijke omlijning van de grijze zone. Het laatste deel van dit boek bevat een voorlopige schets van een op dat resultaat gerichte benadering. Daartoe moesten allereerst twee preliminaire kwesties aan de orde worden gesteld. De vraag of de bronnen van het internationale recht kunnen veranderen, is bevestigend beantwoord met name op basis van de stelling, ontleend aan de theorie van het "Structural Positivism", dat de bronnen of de "rule of recognition" uiteindelijk gebaseerd zijn op de praktijk van de "law-determining agencies" in een bepaald rechtsstelsel. In de internationale samenleving vormen de Staten de "law-determining agencies", en de bronnen van het internationale recht kunnen daarom veranderen via de staten-praktijk *lato sensu*. In de tweede plaats is het in het internationale recht bestaande dilemma tussen vorm en vormvrijheid besproken. Er bestaat een tendens in de literatuur het internationale recht af te schilderen als een in hoge mate vormvrij systeem. Ook al is deze karakterisering op zichzelf niet onjuist, tegelijkertijd moet worden benadrukt, dat het recht, met het oog op zijn ordenende en regelende taak, het niet buiten een zeker minimum aan vorm kan stellen teneinde zijn regels "herkenbaar" te houden.

Deel III van dit boek vormt in feite een poging om, als aanvulling op de traditionele bronnen, een grotere mate van systematisering en "herkenbaarheid" aan te brengen in de vaak in hoge mate vormeloze elementen, waardoor het huidige internationale proces voor rechtsvorming wordt gekenmerkt. Daartoe is getracht de (nieuwe) manifestaties van instemming en aanvaarding van de kant van Staten te classificeren in vijf categorieën. Deze categorieën zijn: (1) abstracte verklaringen, (2) *travaux préparatoires lato sensu*, (3) tekst, (4) follow-up, en (5) latere praktijk. Te zamen beogen deze categorieën de gehele kringloop van de rechtsvorming, welke tegenwoordig een continu-proces is geworden, te omvatten. Elk van de categorieën is erop gericht de manifestaties van instemming en aanvaarding van Staten te helpen identificeren in de verschillende stadia van het proces van rechtsvorming, met als uiteindelijk doel een beter totaalbeeld te verkrijgen van het bindende of niet-bindende karakter van een bepaalde regel of instrument. Vanzelfsprekend hebben de behandelde categorieën nog een rudimentair karakter. Zij dienen op hun bruikbaarheid te worden getoetst aan de hand van concrete gevallen en op basis daarvan verder te worden uitgewerkt. Naar onze mening kan een benadering als deze niettemin van nut zijn bij de beantwoording van een aantal vragen betreffende de bronnenleer van het internationale recht, althans voor wat betreft de beweerdelijk rechtsvormende phenomenen in de zogenaamde grijze zone.

CURRICULUM VITAE

Godefridus J.H. van Hoof werd geboren te Eindhoven op 7 maart 1949. Na het L.O. volgde hij aldaar het V.W.O. aan het Gymnasium Augustianum (eindexamen gymnasium alpha in 1968). Hij begon zijn rechtenstudie aan de Rijksuniversiteit te Utrecht in 1968. In 1974 behaalde hij het einddoctoraalexamen in de Internationale Richting der Staatkundige Studierichtingen, en in 1976 het einddoctoraalexamen Nederlands Recht in de Staatsrechtelijke Richting. Sinds 1975 is hij werkzaam bij de Rijksuniversiteit te Utrecht, vanaf 1982 in de rang van wetenschappelijk hoofdmedewerker (Faculteit der Rechtsgeleerdheid, Vakgroep Internationale, Sociale en Economische Vakken, sectie Recht der Internationale Organisaties).